CRIMINAL JUSTICE: LAW AND POLITICS

FIFTH EDITION

CRIMINAL JUSTICE: LAW AND POLITICS

FIFTH EDITION

EDITED BY GEORGE F. COLE
University of Connecticut

Brooks/Cole Publishing Company
Pacific Grove, California

Brooks/Cole Publishing Company
A Division of Wadsworth, Inc.

Printed in the United States of America

10 9 8 7 6 5 4 3 2

Library of Congress Cataloging in Publication Data

Criminal justice.

1. Criminal justice, Administration of—United States. I. Cole, George F. [date].
KF9223.A75C753 1987 345.73'05 87-21806
ISBN 0-534-08382-X 347.3055

Sponsoring Editor: *Claire Verduin*
Marketing Representative: *Richard Giggey*
Editorial Assistant: *Linda Ruth Wright*
Production Editor: *Penelope Sky*
Manuscript Editor: *Peggy Hoover*
Permissions Editor: *Carline Haga*
Interior and Cover Design: *Roy R. Neuhaus*
Art Coordinator: *Sue C. Howard*
Typesetting: *Graphic Typesetting Service, Los Angeles, California*
Printing and Binding: *The Maple-Vail Book Manufacturing Group, Manchester, Pennsylvania*

PREFACE

While preparing this fifth edition of *Criminal Justice: Law and Politics* I had an opportunity to reflect on the changes in criminal justice research during the past two decades. The contents of the first edition, published in 1972, reflected the fact that the field was characterized by articles advocating reform and by case studies of individual agencies of criminal justice. The heavy federal funding of criminal justice research since that time has enabled scholars to describe ongoing practices systematically, to use the tools of empirical methodologies, and thus to improve law enforcement, adjudication, and correctional strategies. As a result, much of the conventional wisdom has been challenged. Research has also led to new theoretical perspectives, to interdisciplinary studies, and to an expanded research community, so that in addition to academic studies there are investigations by members of quasi-governmental agencies, nonprofit organizations, and private research companies.

As the editor of this book, I am pleased that it has received such wide and continuing use in political science, criminal justice, law, and sociology courses. Because I am also aware of the responsibility of maintaining a collection that is current, academically sound, and readable, I have included articles that reflect the developments noted above. To do this, I have had to drop several favorite but dated pieces. I have rewritten the introductory sections so that they are up-to-date and serve to integrate the individual articles; as a result, the book is more than a mere assemblage of readings. The changes in this edition are consistent with the original theme: Criminal justice can be understood as a relationship between law and politics that operates within the context of an administrative system.

Special thanks are extended to the following reviewers: Marc G. Gertz, Florida State University; James L. Gibson, University of Houston; William E. Hemple, American University; Milton Loewenthal, John Jay College; Michael E. Meyer, University of North Dakota; and Susette M. Talarico, University of Georgia. Each made helpful suggestions. Claire Verduin, criminal justice editor at Brooks/Cole, was an important source of encouragement. Christopher E. Smith helped with the literature survey. The invaluable editorial assistance of Betty Seaver is once again acknowledged. Working with these people made my tasks most pleasant.

George F. Cole

CONTENTS

PART ONE

POLITICS AND THE ADMINISTRATION OF JUSTICE

The close relationship between law and politics has been recognized since ancient times. Yet it has taken the social conflicts of the past two and a half decades to make us aware that the way criminal justice is allocated reflects the values of the individuals and groups that hold the power in the political system. Consider the changes over the past ten years. Public policies toward crime and justice, formulated in another political era, have changed along with our attitudes. Consequently, the ways that government tries to deal with the problem of crime and justice have also changed.

In the mid-1960s "crime and lawlessness" became a concern for most Americans. Statistics such as those in the Federal Bureau of Investigation (FBI) *Uniform Crime Reports* showed that crimes of violence rose 156 percent from 1960 to 1970. Opinion surveys demonstrated that the public was more concerned about crime than about any other local problem. Always quick to sense certain types of public unease, politicians found that voters were easily aroused by the phrase "law and order." Lyndon Johnson created the President's Commission on Law Enforcement and Administration of Justice, which presented its report in 1967. It concluded that crime was caused essentially by disorganization in U.S. society; that agencies of law enforcement, adjudication, and corrections lacked resources; and that rehabilitation had not been used enough as a means of treating offenders. The overriding theme of the report was that efforts must be made to eliminate the social conditions that bring about crime. There must be an end to social and racial injustices so that the ideals of the American ethic could be achieved and so that persons convicted of crimes could be reintegrated into their communities. Congress responded to these recommendations in 1968 by establishing the Law Enforcement Assistance Administration (LEAA) to experiment with new approaches in dealing with crime and to help the states with crime-prevention and crime-control efforts. Yearly appropriations for the LEAA exceeded $850 million by 1974; before its demise in 1982, it had spent more than $5 billion.

Although crime remained high on the national political agenda through the 1970s, there was criticism of the way the LEAA was spending public funds. Critics challenged the assumptions undergirding the report of the 1967 presidential commission and the accepted wisdom of the leading approaches to crime and to offender rehabilitation. As the findings of studies funded by the LEAA and its research arm, the National Institute of Justice, began to accumulate, it became clear to many social scientists that little was known about the causes of crime, that many standard police tactics had little impact on crime prevention, that the courts had problems more complicated than mere case overload, and that most efforts to rehabilitate offenders had been unsuccessful.

It is not clear why there was a major shift in policies toward crime and justice by 1980, but it is certain that such a shift took place. During the Carter administration, funding for the LEAA started to decline. State legislatures began to enact laws mandating stiff sentences for certain offenders; aspects of the correctional treatment model, such as parole and therapeutic programs, came under attack; and "deserved punishment" replaced rehabilitation as the primary justification for the criminal sanction. Some argue that this shift in policies was a reflection of conservative trends throughout the society, whereas others believe that these changes were the logical extensions of research findings. It is even claimed that on civil-libertarian grounds it is better to have forthright crime-control policies in the administration of justice than to allow psychologists, social planners, and criminal justice officials the wide discretion they held under a system of well-meaning governmental intervention.

The Comprehensive Crime Control Act, passed by Congress in 1984, contains provisions that reflect the shift in public policies toward crime and the administration of justice. The legislation provides for tightening of the insanity defense, abolition of parole release, harsher sentences, and preventive detention of dangerous persons awaiting trial. It should be emphasized that the act affects only the federal justice system and not the state systems, where 95 percent of all crimes are prosecuted. During the previous decade, however, many of the states had already enacted laws similar to the new federal legislation. Other policies at both levels of government have aimed at mandatory sentences, programs for career criminals, shifts in police strategies, and increased use of the death penalty.

Dramatic events and major shifts in public policies illumine the most obvious connections between criminal justice and the political system, yet even the most mundane criminal justice decisions, such as the allocation of police resources, have political ramifications because influential people in the community work to ensure that the law will be applied in ways that are consistent with their perception of local values. Because laws are often ambiguous, full enforcement may be both impossible and undesirable, and many laws no longer have public support. In addition, the actors in the legal system, who have a wide range of discretionary powers, determine who will be arrested, on what charges they will be prosecuted, and how their cases will be decided. Should police be instructed to keep vagrants on skid row and away from the "better" hotels? Should gambling be allowed to flourish? Do defendants with counsel get more lenient treatment from the prosecutor's office than indigents? Are suburban juveniles who steal cars sent home for parental discipline while juveniles from the ghetto are sent to reformatories? Such questions make it clear that crminal justice is not a neatly structured, impartial decision-making process in which the rule of law always prevails and each individual is treated equally.

Like all legal institutions, the criminal justice system is "political"; it is engaged in the formulation and administration of public policies, where choices must be made among such competing values as the rights of defendants, protection of persons and property, justice, and freedom. Various groups in society interpret these values differently. The effect of community norms on the criminal justice machinery can be seen by comparing the disposition of criminal cases in different cities, or sentences handed out by judges in small towns, and in metropolitan areas. What a rural judge may perceive as a crime wave is often viewed as routine by that judge's urban counterpart. Definitions of what is criminal are applied by members of society who have the power to shape the enforcement and administration of criminal law. Thus, judicial personnel are engaged in the "authoritative allocation of values" just as are other governmental decision makers whose positions are generally perceived as political.

Besides the pervasiveness of politics in the administration of justice, political influences permeate the legal system. Political parties have a great influence on recruitment of judges, prosecutors, and other legal personnel. In many cities the road to a judgeship is paved with deeds performed for a political party. Prosecuting attorneys are recognized as political actors of consequence. Because of their discretionary powers, because they are usually elected with party support, and because of the patronage they have at their disposal, prosecutors are key figures that have ties both to the internal politics of the justice system and to local political organizations. Likewise, appointment of the police administrator is a political decision that determines the style of law enforcement a community can expect.

It is difficult to speak of a single criminal justice system in the United States, for there are many systems. Every village, town, county, city, and state has its own criminal justice system, and there is a federal one as well. All operate somewhat alike, but never precisely alike. Community influences, as well as the historical evolution of the federal system, which gives the states freedom to create and direct their own basic institutions, lead to differences in criminal justice systems.

The FBI and the Justice Department are much in the news, but the executive branch of the federal government plays a minor role in the broad perspective of criminal justice. Most crimes are violations of state laws, but enforcement is left to a multitude of local agencies that have wide powers of discretion. Few states have a unit to coordinate activities among law-enforcement officials. Likewise, the independent election or appointment of judges means that the state appellate courts have little formal authority over the lower courts headed by local judges.

It is at the local level that the individual has contact with the legal process. Most citizens are not destined to appear in court or at the police station, but their perception of the quality of justice meted out there to others greatly affects their willingness to abide by the laws. Robert Kennedy noted that the "poor man looks upon the law as an enemy, not as a friend. For him the law is always taking something away." Thus, if it is widely assumed that the police can be bribed, that certain groups are singled out for harsh treatment, or that lawbreaking will not result in the punishment of offenders, the political system loses much of its dominion over the behavior of the affected populace. As Roscoe Pound once said, criminal law "must safeguard the general security and the individual life against abuse of criminal procedure while at the same time making that procedure as effective as possible for the securing of the whole scheme of social interests."

Although there is a tendency to divide administration of criminal justice into enforcement, adjudication, and corrections, this distinction neglects the very close interrelationship and overlapping among the various actors. Within the justice system, the outputs of one decision-making section, such as the police, become the inputs of another, such as the prosecutor. Likewise, the court, coroner, grand jury, bondsman, and defense counsel have continuing relationships concerning a wide variety of actions that have an impact on the allocation of justice. Similarly, the work of correctional officials is influenced by the sentencing behavior of the judges and the decisions of parole agencies. As a result, the internal politics of the criminal justice bureaucracy immerses officials in a network of interpersonal contacts that emphasize their dependence upon one another. Each actor in the judicial system has goals and values related to his or her own job situation. To achieve these goals, each needs the cooperation of others. Bargaining among judicial officials over the conditions governing the disposition of each case appears to be typical of decision making. To view the justice process as a machine in which decisions are made solely on the basis of "rational" criteria, such as evidence, is to overlook the very personal ways in which justice is individualized.

The confluence of law, administration, and politics results in a system in which officials who are sensitive to the political process make decisions at various points concerning the arrest, charges, conviction, and sentences of defendants. The local legal subsystem is very much involved in the allocation of costs and benefits of the political system. Thus the judicial process induces conditions that are important to the political needs of actors in the legal system. Criminal prosecutions provide opportunities for the political system to affect judicial decisions and for the judicial process to provide favors that nourish political organizations.

THE CRISIS OF CRIMINAL JUSTICE

No one can seriously question that crime is prevalent in the United States. What is in question is the amount of crime, the types of crime, the causes of crime, and the policies that will or will not be effective in dealing with the problem of crime. Law-enforcement officials and much of the public have a picture of a nation under siege by criminals being pampered by the civil-libertarian bias of recent court decisions, by sentences that are merely a slap on the wrist, and by correctional practices that do not work. But critics of this assessment say that the amount of crime is actually decreasing, that the criminal justice system discriminates against the poor, that due process rights are being neglected, and that correctional facilities often turn minor offenders into criminals.

Although references are made to the increase of crime, it should be emphasized that it is primarily "visible" crime rather than "upperworld" or "organized" crime that makes the headlines, arouses the community, and attracts the major thrust of law-enforcement resources. *Upperworld crimes* are violations committed in the business world—tax evasion, price fixing, consumer fraud, health and safety infractions—activities that are often thought of as shrewd business practices rather than crimes. Such offenses are highly profitable but rarely come to the attention of the public. Much of society does not perceive upperworld crime the way that it views purse snatching. The term *organized crime* describes a social framework for committing criminal acts, rather than specific types of offenses. Organized criminal groups participate in illegal activities that offer maximum profit at minimum risk of interference from law enforcers. These groups offer goods and services that millions of Americans desire even though they have been declared illegal. With minor exceptions, organized crime seldom provides input to the criminal justice process. *Visible crimes* are committed primarily by the lower classes and run the gamut from shoplifting to homicide. They are the least remunerative violations and, because they are visible, the least protected. These are the crimes that are used for the statistics in the *Uniform Crime Reports*; they are the acts that most of the public considers criminal. To a great extent, society has oriented law-enforcement, judicial, and correctional resources toward violators of laws that have to do with visible crimes.

Much crime goes unreported. On the basis of data collected by the U.S. Census Bureau as part of its 1975 crime victimization survey, Wesley Skogan has estimated that 72 percent of serious crimes went unreported. The reason most often given for failure to report a crime was "Nothing could be done." In addition, some victims did not report crimes because they regarded the offense as a private matter or did not want to hurt the perpetrator, especially if he or she was a family member or acquaintance. These facts show that there is an additional ingredient in the criminal justice picture, reflecting the potential caseload and the influence of detection criteria on the crime rate.

The number of court officials and the size of facilities have been based on the premise that up to 90 percent of defendants will plead guilty. Attorneys have learned that court congestion can be used to their clients' advantage so that their cases will be dropped or they will receive lighter sentences. When the defense adopts an adversarial stance, invoking due process criteria and requesting a jury trial or continuances, the fine balance that keeps the justice system in equilibrium may be upset. Demands that formal procedures be followed slow down the process, often creating turmoil in courts that must dispose of cases as quickly as possible to prevent a backlog. Delaying cases usually weakens prosecution efforts because evidence becomes "stale," witnesses are lost, and public interest lapses.

To cope with the pressures of a higher crime rate and a lack of resources, the criminal justice system has placed greater emphasis on administrative decision-making in the pretrial period, when the primary objective of law officials is to screen out cases that do not contain the elements necessary for a speedy prosecution and conviction. Such practices require that society choose between the need for order and the individual's civil liberties. This precarious balance is subject to political influences because various groups have different conceptions of the rights and duties of those who are part of the judicial system. The defendant is often caught between demands for order and the inadequacies of the criminal justice machinery.

DEFINING CRIMINAL BEHAVIOR

Since the beginning of Western law, forcible rape has been defined as criminal behavior and is almost universally condemned. In the United States, the women's movement has focused attention on the treatment of rape victims by the police and courts, so that these incidents often take on the aura of political symbolism. However, it can be shown that the precise definition of the act, the defenses that may be used by the accused, and the sanctions prescribed allow for considerable latitude in applying the law. In most states, for example, intercourse accompanied by the woman's consent, even if consent has been forced, is not defined as rape. In England, the woman's consent is no defense if consent has been obtained by force. Some state legislatures have changed their penal codes to allow wives to accuse their husbands of rape. Until declared unconstitutional by the Supreme Court, the death penalty was the penalty for rape in some states. In some areas of the world, rape is not charged if certain classes of women are involved; among the Gusii tribe of Kenya, forcible rape is an accepted form of sexual relations for unmarried males. What must be emphasized is that even though this behavior has been declared wrong almost everywhere in the world since ancient times, there is considerable variation in the way the criminal act has been defined and in the sanctions prescribed by law.

As with the range of definitions and sanctions applied to rape, one might ask why the consumption of alcohol in the United States during the 1920s was considered a criminal act when it is not so considered now. Why are the penalties for possession of marijuana severe in some states, while little attention is paid to the act in Oregon, Alaska, and Maine? What was it about Puritan Massachusetts that caused certain ways of behaving to be called witchcraft, the penalty for which was death? It appears that in different locations and times certain behaviors have been defined as criminal and other behaviors have not. What are the social and political forces that determine the law? It is important to remember that laws are written by legislators and emerge from human experience. There are usually disagreements in society about the exact nature of the laws defining behavior as criminal.

As the common law of crimes emerged in England during the twelfth century, one of the primary distinctions made was between offenses considered *mala in se*—"ordinary crimes," acts bad in themselves (murder, rape, arson, theft)—and offenses considered *mala prohibita*—acts that were crimes because they were prohibited by the positive law (rioting, poaching, vagrancy, drunkenness). "Ordinary crimes" were considered felonies that could be prosecuted in the central criminal courts; acts that were *mala prohibita* were proclaimed by legislation, considered misdemeanors, and enforced by justices of the peace. By and large the types of crimes classified as *mala in se* have remained static and those known as *mala prohibita* have greatly expanded. Modern legislatures have added three major groups to the traditional offenses: crimes without victims, political crimes, and regulatory offenses. Today there are many more arrests and prosecutions for the total number of offenses belonging to these latter categories than for the traditional violations of the criminal law.

The distinction between ordinary crimes and those that are prohibited serves the useful purpose of pointing to the sources of the criminal law. Scholars of the sociology of law have developed two major theories to explain the focus and functions of criminal laws and the processes by which they evolve: a "consensus model," wherein a group or society expresses its will or values through the criminal law, and a "conflict model," which emphasizes the role of political interests in the formulation of the law.

The consensus position asserts that the criminal law reflects societal values that transcend the immediate interests of particular groups and individuals; it is an expression of the social consciousness of the whole society. From this perspective, legal norms emerge through the dynamics of cultural processes to meet certain functional needs and requirements that are essential for maintaining the social fabric. It assumes that the society has achieved a well-integrated and relatively stable agreement on basic values.

In contrast to the view of the criminal code as a product of the consensus of values in society, a relatively new approach emphasizes that it is through the conflict of political power that interest groups affect the content of the code. Power, force, and constraint, rather than common values, are the fundamental organizing principles of society. Because political influence is unequally distributed, some groups have greater access to decision makers and use their influence to ensure the enactment of legislation that protects their interests. According to this approach, wrongful acts are characteristic of all classes in society, and the powerful not only shape the law to their own advantage but also are able to dictate the use of enforcement resources in such a way that certain groups are labeled and processed by the criminal justice system.

At this point in the development of a sociology of law, it is impossible to reach a conclusion about the theoretical value of the consensus and conflict models. In the case of some laws, especially those prohibiting crimes that are *mala in se,* there is a consensus in most Western societies as to the values espoused. It is also easy to show how the laws prohibiting cattle-rustling, the consumption of alcohol, vagrancy, and the sale of pornography—crimes *mala prohibita*—have their source in the political power of special interests. Because the great bulk of criminal violations now are those of the latter type, attention logically focuses on the conflict model.

THE SUPREME COURT AND CRIMINAL JUSTICE

The Warren Court will be remembered for its insistence that constitutional guarantees be extended throughout the administration of criminal justice. Long concerned with individuals' rights in the courtroom, the justices directed their attention during the 1960s to *pretrial* rights, in a series of decisions that had the intention of bolstering adversary elements during the crucial period between commission of a crime and the defendant's appearance in court. To ensure defendants' rights, provisions were made, beginning with *Gideon v. Wainwright* (1963), for indigents to have the assistance of counsel throughout the process. In this connection, the justices addressed themselves to questions concerning citizens' rights in the areas of search and seizure, interrogation, confessions, and jury trial.

These decisions have been called the "due process revolution," a term that says much about conditions before the 1960s and the speed with which the Warren Court shattered accepted legal theory. Since the 1833 decision in *Barron v. Baltimore,* citizens had not enjoyed the protections guaranteed in the Bill of Rights when it came to state action. The actions of state governments in the field of criminal justice had been free from Supreme Court scrutiny. Even with the addition of the Fourteenth Amendment and its "due process" clause, incorporation of the basic criminal procedural guarantees of the Bill of Rights protections against state action was long in coming.

Until 1961, when it ruled that states could not use evidence obtained in violation of the Fourth Amendment's restrictions on unreasonable searches and seizures, the Supreme Court had insisted essentially that states maintain standards of "fundamental fairness" in the criminal justice process. This meant that only the most blatant examples of injustice in criminal administration were outlawed by the Court. Thus the 1923 murder convictions of five black men sentenced to death after a forty-five-minute trial dominated by a mob were overturned. The Court also disallowed a confession beaten out of two Mississippi defendants by deputies using metal-studded belts. As Justice Cardozo noted, the test for determining the legitimacy of state action was to ask if due process of law had been denied to a citizen by practices that violated those "fundamental principles of justice which lie at the base of our civil and political institutions." From the 1920s until the 1960s the Court adhered to this dictum, only gradually giving citizens Bill of Rights protection against state actions.

The leading critic of the fairness doctrine was Justice Black, who believed that it was unconstitutional because it did not provide for absolute protection of civil liberties and meant that the Supreme Court had to apply uncertain standards to each case. Black argued that the Fourteenth Amendment made the entire Bill of Rights binding on the states and that the courts had a duty to enforce these rights. Although First Amendment rights and the right to counsel in capital cases were incorporated by earlier Courts, the Warren Court began the piecemeal incorporation of most of the remaining basic rights in the first ten amendments. These new decisions focused primarily on the pretrial actions of the police and the prosecutor. By 1969 the safeguards had been applied to all the civil-liberties provisions, with the exception of questions concerning capital punishment, excessive bail, and grand jury indictments.

The decision that has caused the greatest public interest is that of *Miranda v. Arizona* (1966), in which the Chief Justice outlined a code of conduct for police interrogation. The decision requires that accused persons be told that they have the right to remain silent, that statements they make may be used as evidence against them, and that they have a right to the presence of an attorney, either appointed or retained. In effect, the Warren Court said that it is not enough for the states to follow procedures that allow for "fundamental fairness" in criminal proceedings; there must also be absolute compliance by state and local officials with the provisions of the Bill of Rights.

The political reaction to the Warren Court decisions was immediate and vociferous, especially to those that concerned restrictions on police activities. Law-enforcement groups such as the International Association of Chiefs of Police and the National District Attorneys Association claimed that the presence of counsel during all phases of the interrogation process would burden the system and reduce the number of convictions. This view was supported by most of the representatives of police and prosecutors on the President's Crime Commission. In a supplement to the final report, these members wondered whether "the scales have tilted in favor of the accused and against law enforcement and the public further than the best interest of the country permits."

Many observers believed that the 1969 appointment of Warren Burger as Chief Justice and the reconstitution of the Court by Richard Nixon would bring an end to the due process revolution, but this was not to be the case, particularly with regard to provision of counsel. In *Argersinger v. Hamlin* (1972) the right to counsel was extended to persons charged with misdemeanors where imprisonment might result. After ruling the death penalty as then administered to be unconstitutional (*Furman v. Georgia,* 1972), the Court approved revised statutes under which the sentencing judge or jury could take into account specific aggravating or mitigating circumstances in deciding whether a convicted murderer should be put to death (*Gregg v. Georgia,* 1976). Also, since the Burger Court, the importance and legitimacy of plea bargaining has been recognized (*North Carolina v. Alford,* 1970), and rules have been drawn up to ensure that the promises made to defendants are fulfilled (*Santobello v. New York,* 1971).

Cases arising out of the exclusionary rule and the protections against unreasonable search caused libertarians the most concern about the Burger Court. *Mapp v. Ohio* (1961) applied provisions of the Fourth Amendement to the states, but the facts in that case were more straightforward than in most law-enforcement situations. The U.S. Constitution does not prohibit searches, but only "unreasonable searches and seizures." It is the ambiguity of this phrase and the complexity of some arrest and investigation incidents that have created problems for the Court. It is clear that a search based on a warrant issued by a magistrate is reasonable. The more difficult cases involve searches without a warrant that are made "incident to a lawful arrest." What is a lawful arrest, and how much can be seized? The police justify their need for this type of search as a protection for an officer—to remove weapons from the suspect and to gain evidence before it can be destroyed. What if the officer mistakenly thought he or she was following consitutional procedures? Should a "good faith exception" be granted to evidence illegally seized under these conditions? By the end of the Burger era the Court was inching toward answers to such questions.

High on the agenda of the Rehnquist Court are issues concerning the exclusionary rule, the insanity defense, prisoners' rights, and the death penalty. Although obervers believe that the new conservative majority will shift the direction of defendants' rights on some of these questions, the general thrust of the Warren and Burger decisions will probably remain. It now seems accepted that the states must uphold the rights declared by the Constitution.

ADMINISTRATIVE POLITICS

Social scientists have recognized that discussing an organization solely in terms of its structure does not tell us much about its dynamic processes. Although the term *organization* suggests a certain bareness—a lean, no-nonsense construct of consciously coordinated activities—all organizations are molded by forces tangential to their rationally ordered structures and stated ends. The formal rules do not completely account for the behavior of the actors, because there is also an informal structure resulting from the social environment and the interaction of these actors. Organizations have formal decision-making processes, but these may serve mostly to legitimize organizational goals and may act to enhance the symbolic needs of authority. Emphasis on the prescribed structure may overlook the way the achievement of goals depends upon the behavior of actors who have their own agendas, which may run counter to the professed aims of the organization. In addition, the organization itself has needs that have to be fulfilled in order for it to survive. Thus, realization of system aims is only one of the several important purposes of an organization. The system adapts its responses to meet its needs, because informal arrangements arise to meet the goals of both the organization and the people in it.

The administration of criminal justice is characterized by certain essential features. First, it is an open system; new cases, changes in personnel, and different conditions in the political arena mean that it must deal with constant variations in its milieu. Second, there is a condition of scarcity within the system; shortages of such resources as time, information, and personnel are characteristic. The system's inability to process every case according to the formally prescribed criteria affects the subunits of law enforcement—police, prosecutor, courts—so that each competes with the others for the available resources. Central to this analysis is the politics of administration—the variety of interactions between an agency and its environment that augment, retain, or diminish the basic resources needed to attain organizational goals.

The President's Crime Commission referred to the legal process as a continuum—an orderly progression of events. As in all legally constituted structures, there are formally designated points in the process where decisions concerning the disposition of cases are made. To speak of the system as a continuum, however, may underplay the complexity and the flux of relationships within it; although the administration of criminal justice is composed of a set of subsystems, there are no formal provisions for subordination of one unit to another. Each unit has its own clientele, goals, and norms, yet the outputs of one unit constitute the inputs of another.

Conflicts always exist among the various actors in the criminal justice process. Each actor sees the problem of crime and the administration of justice from a different perspective. The daily experiences, social background, and professional norms of the police, prosecutor, defense attorney, and judge influence the way each makes decisions. The police officer who has seen the agony of crime victims and risked his or her life to protect society may be unable to understand why defendants are released on bail or why prosecutors willingly reduce charges to gain guilty pleas. At the same time, the prosecutor may be concerned about the police officer's lack of attention to detail in collecting evidence, while the judge may be upset by a failure to maintain a defendant's civil rights. One characteristic of the criminal justice process is that all participants are dependent on others to assist them in their work. At every stage from arrest to sentencing, a variety of actors with different viewpoints and goals are involved in making decisions about the disposition of each case.

Given the fragmentation of the system, we may ask how decisions are made. As interdependent subunits of a system, each organization and its clientele are engaged in a set of exchange relationships across their boundaries. The need for participants to interact leads to the making of bargains that determine the conditions under which a defendant's case will be handled. The police, charged with making decisions concerning the apprehension of suspects, interact with the prosecutor's office when presenting evidence and recommending charges. The defendant, through counsel, may make a guilty plea in exchange for a reduction of the charges by the prosecutor. Likewise, the courts and prosecutor are linked by the decision to bring charges, by the activities in the courtroom, and by the disposition of the case.

Although the formal structures of the judicial process stress antagonistic and competitive subunits, interaction may strengthen cooperation within the system, thereby deflecting it from its manifest goals. For example, the roles of prosecutor and defense counsel are antagonistic, but continued interaction on the job, in professional associations, and in political or social groups may produce a friendship that influences how they play their roles. Combat in the courtroom, as ordained by the formal structure, may not only endanger a personal relationship but also expose weaknesses to their own clientele. Instead of promoting the unpredictability and professional insecurity stressed by the system, decisions on cases may be arranged to be mutually beneficial to the actors in the exchange.

The most distinctive feature of the administration of criminal justice is the high degree of discretion. As in few other social organizations, the amount of discretion in law-enforcement and judicial agencies increases as one moves *down* the administrative hierarchy. In most organizations, the observer usually finds the lowest-ranking members performing the most routine tasks under supervision, with various mechanisms of quality control employed to check their work. With the police, prosecutor, and lower-court judges, discretion is exercised more frequently by those who are newest to the organization, who maintain the primary contact with the public, and whose work is usually shielded from the view of supervisors and outside observers. Thus, patrol officers have wide discretion in determining whom they should arrest and on what charges; the deputy prosecutor makes vital decisions concerning who shall be put up for indictment; and lower-court judges operate without the dominating influence of higher courts.

A final characteristic of the administration of justice is that the process resembles a filter through which cases are screened. Some cases are advanced to the next level of decision making; others are either rejected or the conditions under which they are processed are changed. As the President's Crime Commission noted, "Approximately one-half of those arrested are dismissed by the police, prosecutor, or magistrate at an early stage of the case." Other evidence is equally impressive. Sobel found that 62 percent of the adult felony arrests in Kings County, New York, resulted in either dismissal or reduction to a misdemeanor before the case went to the grand jury for indictment. In Detroit's Recorders Court, prosecution was instituted in only 60 percent of 46,800 cases. A study by the Rand Institute showed that of 330,000 cases in the New York City Criminal Court, 90,000 never went beyond the preliminary examination because they were dismissed or transferred to other jurisdictions or because the defendants could not be located. Only 7 percent of the 200,000 persons found guilty received a trial; sentences were imposed on the rest following a plea of guilty.

Criminal justice is greatly affected by the values of each decision maker, whose career, influence, and position may be more important to him or her than consideration for the formal requirements of the law. Accommodation will be sought with those in the exchange system so that decisions that are consistent with the values of the participants and the organization are reached. A wide variety of departures from the formal rules of the due process ideology are accepted by judicial actors but never publicly acknowledged. Because of the strain of an overwhelming caseload and the adversary nature of the formal structure, members of the bureaucracy can reduce stress while maximizing rewards by filtering out cases that are disruptive or potentially threatening to the established norms. Because defendants pass through the system and the judicial actors remain, the accused may become secondary figures in the bureaucratic setting. The administrative norms are so well established that judges may agree that defendants who survive the scrutiny of the police and prosecutor must be guilty.

The administration of criminal justice may be viewed as having goals that are antagonistic to the due process model. Decisions concerning the disposition of cases are influenced by the selective nature of a filtering process in which administrative discretion and interpersonal exchange relationships are extremely important. At each decision-making level, actors in the judicial system are able to determine which types of crime will come to official notice, which kinds of offenders will be processed, and how enthusiastically a conviction will be sought. It is in these day-to-day practices and policies of the criminal justice agencies that the law is put into effect, and it is out of this activity that organizations and individuals shape the law.

SUGGESTIONS FOR FURTHER READING

ALLEN, FRANCIS A. *The Borderland of Criminal Justice.* Chicago: University of Chicago Press, 1964. An examination of the hazy areas of criminal justice, where the use of discretion is most prominent.

CURRIE, ELLIOTT. *Confronting Crime.* New York: Pantheon Books, 1985. Why is criminal violence so much worse in the United States than in other affluent industrial societies? Currie critiques both conservative and liberal prescriptions for reducing crime and offers new directions.

DAVIS, KENNETH CULP. *Discretionary Justice.* Baton Rouge: Louisiana State University Press, 1969. A seminal work exploring the nature of discretion. Davis suggests that opportunities for discretionay decisions be formalized to prevent abuse.

ENCYCLOPEDIA OF CRIME AND JUSTICE. Edited by Sanford H. Kadish et al. 4 vols. New York: Free Press, 1983. An excellent source for students of criminal justice, containing articles by major scholars in the field.

ERIKSON, KAI T. *Wayward Puritans.* New York: John Wiley, 1966. Analysis of three "crime waves" in Puritan Massachusetts. The findings indicate that persons are labeled deviant when the community is undergoing periods of stress.

HALL, JEROME. *General Principles of Criminal Law.* 2nd ed. Indianapolis: Bobbs-Merrill, 1947. One of the clearest texts outlining the foundations of the criminal law and the defenses that may be used.

MUSTO, DAVID. *The American Disease.* New Haven: Yale University Press. 1973. A history of policies for dealing with the use of addictive drugs. Shows the political role of interest groups in the formulation of these policies and the various reasons drugs have been declared illegal.

SILBERMAN, CHARLES E. *Criminal Violence, Criminal Justice.* New York: Random House, 1978. A widely praised examination of criminal justice in the United States, with a special emphasis on the relationship of poverty to violence.

WILSON, JAMES Q., and RICHARD J. HERRNSTEIN. *Crime and Human Nature.* New York: Simon & Schuster, 1985. A major work summarizing research that addresses the causes of criminal behavior. The authors focus on the importance of such factors as gender, age, family, and schooling.

ARTICLE ONE

Two Models of the Criminal Process

HERBERT L. PACKER

In one of the most important contributions to systematic thought about the administration of criminal justice, Herbert Packer articulates the values supporting two models of the justice process. He notes the gulf existing between the "Due Process Model" of criminal administration, with its emphasis on the rights of the individual, and the "Crime Control Model," which sees the regulation of criminal conduct as the most important function of the judicial system.

Two models of the criminal process will let us perceive the normative antinomy at the heart of the criminal law. These models are not labeled Is and Ought, nor are they to be taken in that sense. Rather, they represent an attempt to abstract two separate value systems that compete for priority in the operation of the criminal process. Neither is presented as either corresponding to reality or representing the ideal to the exclusion of the other. The two models merely afford a convenient way to talk about the operation of a process whose day-to-day functioning involves a constant series of minute adjustments between the competing demands of two value systems and whose normative future likewise involves a series of resolutions of the tensions between competing claims.

I call these two models the Due Process Model and the Crime Control Model. . . . As we examine the way the models operate in each successive stage, we will raise two further inquiries: first, where on a spectrum between the extremes represented by the two models do our present practices seem approximately to fall; second, what appears to be the direction and thrust of current and foreseeable trends along each such spectrum?

There is a risk in an enterprise of this sort that is latent in any attempt to polarize. It is, simply, that values are too various to be pinned down to yes-or-no answers. The models are distortions of reality. And, since they are normative in character, there is a danger of seeing one or the other as Good or Bad. The reader will have his preferences, as I do, but we should not be so rigid as to demand consistently polarized answers to the range of questions posed in the criminal process. The weighty questions of public policy that inhere in any attempt to discern where on the spectrum of normative choice the "right" answer lies are beyond the scope of the present inquiry. The attempt here is primarily to clarify the terms of discussion by isolating the assumptions that underlie competing policy claims and examining the conclusions that those claims, if fully accepted, would lead to.

VALUES UNDERLYING THE MODELS

Each of the two models we are about to examine is an attempt to give operational content to a complex of values underlying the criminal law. As I have suggested earlier, it is possible to identify two competing systems of values, the tension between which accounts for the intense activity now observable in the development of the criminal process. The actors in this development—lawmakers, judges, police, prosecutors, defense lawyers—do not often pause to articulate the values that underlie the positions that they take on any given issue. Indeed, it would be a gross oversimplification to ascribe a coherent and consistent set of values to any of these actors. Each of the two competing schemes of values we will be developing in this section contains components that are demonstrably present some of the time in some of the actors' preferences regarding the criminal process. No one person has ever identified himself as holding all of the values that underlie these two models. The models are polarities, and so are the schemes of values that underlie them. A person who subscribed to all of the values underlying the other would be rightly viewed as a fanatic. The values are presented here as an aid to analysis, not as a program for action.

Some Common Ground

However, the polarity of the two models is not absolute. Although it would be possible to construct models that exist in an institutional vacuum, it would not serve our purposes to do so. We are postulating, not a criminal process that operates in any kind of society at all, but rather that operates within the framework of contemporary American society. This leaves plenty of room for polarization, but it does require the observance of some limits. A model of the criminal process that left out of account relatively stable and enduring features of the American legal system would not have much relevance to our central inquiry. For convenience, these elements of stability and continuity can be roughly equated with minimal agreed limits expressed in the Constitution of the United States and, more importantly, with unarticulated assumptions that can be perceived to underlie those limits. Of course, it is true that the Constitution is constantly appealed to by proponents and opponents of many measures that affect the criminal process. And only the naive would deny that there are few conclusive positions that can be reached by appeal to the Constitution. Yet there are assumptions about the criminal process that are widely shared and that may be viewed as common ground for the operation of any model of the criminal process. Our first task is to clarify these assumptions.

First, there is the assumption, implicit in the ex post facto clause of the Constitution, that the function of defining conduct that may be treated as criminal is separate from and prior to the process of identifying and dealing with persons as criminals. How wide or narrow the definition of criminal conduct must be is an important question of policy that yields highly variable results depending on the values held by those making the relevant decisions. But that there must be a means of definition that is in some sense separate from and prior to the operation of the process is clear. If this were not so, our efforts to deal with the phenomenon of organized crime would appear ludicrous indeed (which is not to say that we have by any means exhausted the possibilities for dealing with that problem within the limits of this basic assumption).

A related assumption that limits the area of controversy is that the criminal process ordinarily ought to be invoked by those charged with the responsibility for doing so when it appears that a crime has been committed and that there is a reasonable prospect of apprehending and convicting its perpetrator. Although police and prosecutors are allowed broad discretion for deciding not to invoke the criminal process, it is commonly agreed that these officials have no general dispensing power. If the legislature has decided that certain conduct is to be treated as criminal, the decision makers at every level of the criminal process are expected to accept that basic decision as a premise for action. The controversial nature of the occasional case in which the relevant decision makers appear not to have played their appointed role only serves to highlight the strength with which the premise holds. This assumption may be viewed as the other side of the ex post facto coin. Just as conduct that is not proscribed as criminal may not be dealt with in the criminal process, so conduct that has been denominated as criminal must be treated as such by the participants in the criminal process acting within their respective competences.

Next, there is the assumption that there are limits to the powers of government to investigate and apprehend persons suspected of committing crimes. I do not refer to the controversy (settled recently, at least in broad outline) as to whether the Fourth Amendment's prohibition against unreasonable searches and seizures applies to the states with the same force with which it applies to the federal government. Rather, I am talking about the general assumption that a degree of scrutiny and control must be exercised with respect to the activities of law-enforcement officers, that the security and privacy of the individual may not be invaded at will. It is possible to imagine a society in which even lip service is not paid to this assumption. Nazi Germany approached but never quite reached this position. But no one in our society would maintain that any individual may be taken into custody at any time and held without any limitation of time during the process of investigating his possible commission of crimes, or would argue that there should be no form of redress for violation of at least some standards for official investigative conduct. Although this assumption may not appear to have much in the way of positive content, its absence would render moot some of our most hotly controverted problems. If there were not general agreement that there must be some limits on police power to detain and investigate, the highly controversial provisions of the Uniform Arrest Act, permitting the police to detain a person for questioning for a short period even though they do not have grounds for making an arrest, would be a magnanimous concession by the all-powerful state rather than, as it is now perceived, a substantial expansion of police power.

Finally, there is a complex of assumptions embraced by terms such as "the adversary system," "procedural due process," "notice and an opportunity to be heard," and "day in court." Common to them all is the notion that the alleged criminal is not merely an object to be acted upon but an independent entity in the process who may, if he so desires, force the operators of the process to demonstrate to an independent authority (judge and jury) that he is guilty of the charges against him. It is a minimal assumption. It speaks in terms of "may" rather than "must." It permits but does not require the accused, acting by himself or through his own agent, to play an active role in the process. By virtue of that fact the process becomes or has the capacity to become a contest between, if not equals, at least independent actors. As we shall see, much of the space between the two models is occupied by stronger or weaker notions of how this contest is to be arranged, in what cases it is to be played, and by what rules. The Crime Control Model tends to de-emphasize this adversary aspect of the process; the Due Process Model tends to make it central. The common ground, and it is important, is the agreement that the process has, for everyone subjected to it, at least the potentiality of becoming to some extent an adversary struggle.

So much for common ground. There is a good deal of it, even in the narrowest view. Its existence should not be overlooked, because it is, by definition, what permits partial resolutions of the tension between the two models to take place. The rhetoric of the criminal process consists largely of claims that disputed territory is "really" common ground: that, for example, the premise of an adversary system "necessarily" embraces the appointment of counsel for everyone accused of crime, or conversely, that the obligation to pursue persons suspected of committing crimes "necessarily" embraces interrogation of suspects without the intervention of counsel. We may smile indulgently at such claims; they are rhetoric, and no more. But the form in which they are made suggests an important truth: that there *is* a common ground of value assumption about the criminal process that makes continued discourse about its problems possible.

Crime Control Values

The value system that underlies the Crime Control Model is based on the proposition that the repression of criminal conduct is by far the most important function to be performed by the criminal process. The failure of law enforcement to bring criminal conduct under tight control is viewed as leading to the breakdown of public order and thence to the disappearance of an important condition of human freedom. If the laws go unenforced—which is to say, if it is perceived that there is a high percentage of failure to apprehend and convict in the criminal process—a general disregard for legal controls tends to develop. The law-abiding citizen then becomes the victim of all sorts of unjustifiable invasions of his interests. His security of person and property is sharply diminished, and, therefore, so is his liberty to function as a member of society. The claim ultimately is that the criminal process is a positive guarantor of social freedom. In order to achieve this high purpose, the Crime Control Model requires that primary attention be paid to the efficiency with which the criminal process operates to screen suspects, determine guilt, and secure appropriate dispositions of persons convicted of crime.

Efficiency of operation is not, of course, a criterion that can be applied in a vacuum. By "efficiency" we mean the system's capacity to apprehend, try, convict, and dispose of a high proportion of criminal offenders whose offenses become known. In a society in which only the grossest forms of antisocial behavior were made criminal and in which the crime rate was exceedingly low, the criminal process might require the devotion of many more man-hours of police, prosecutorial, and judicial time per case than ours does, and still operate with tolerable efficiency. A society that was prepared to increase even further the resources devoted to the suppression of crime might cope with a rising crime rate without sacrifice of efficiency while continuing to maintain an elaborate and time-consuming set of criminal processes. However, neither of these possible characteristics corresponds with social reality in this country. We use the criminal sanction to cover an increasingly wide spectrum of behavior thought to be antisocial, and the amount of crime is very high indeed, although both level and trend are hard to assess. At the same time, although precise measures are not available, it does not appear that we are disposed in the public sector of the economy to increase very drastically the quantity, much less the quality, of the resources devoted to the suppression of criminal activity through the operation of the criminal process. These factors have an important bearing on the criteria of efficiency, and therefore on the nature of the Crime Control Model.

The model, in order to operate successfully, must produce a high rate of apprehension and conviction, and must do so in a context where the magnitudes being dealt with are very large and the resources for dealing with them are very limited. There must then be a premium on speed and finality. Speed, in turn, depends on informality and on uniformity; finality depends on minimizing the occasions for challenge. The process must not be cluttered up with ceremonious rituals that do not advance the progress of a case. Facts can be established more quickly through interrogation in a police station than through the formal process of examination and cross-examination in a court. It follows that extrajudicial processes should be preferred to judicial processes, informal operations to formal ones. But informality is not enough; there must also be uniformity. Routine, stereotyped procedures are essential if large numbers are being handled. The model that will operate successfully on these presuppositions must be an administrative, almost a managerial, model. The image that comes to mind is an assembly-line conveyor belt down which moves an endless stream of cases, never stopping, carrying the cases to workers who stand at fixed stations and who perform on each case as it comes by the same small but essential operation that brings it one step closer to being a finished product, or, to exchange the metaphor for the reality, a closed file. The criminal process, in this model, is seen as a screening process in which each successive state—prearrest investigation, arrest, postarrest investigation, preparation for trial, trial or entry of plea, conviction, disposition—involves a series of routinized operations whose success is gauged primarily by their tendency to pass the case along to a successful conclusion.

What is a successful conclusion? One that throws off at an early stage those cases in which it appears unlikely that the person apprehended is an offender and then secures, as expeditiously as possible, the conviction of the rest, with a minimum of occasions for challenge, let alone post-audit. By the application of administrative expertness, primarily that of the police and prosecutors, an early determination of the probability of innocence or guilt emerges. Those who are probably innocent are screened out. Those who are probably guilty are passed quickly through the remaining stages of the process. The key to the operation of the model regarding those who are not screened out is what I shall call a presumption of guilt. The concept requires some explanation, since it may appear startling to assert that what appears to be the precise converse of our generally accepted ideology of a presumption of innocence can be an essential element of a model that does correspond in some respects to the actual operation of the criminal process.

The presumption of guilt is what makes it possible for the system to deal efficiently with large numbers, as the Crime Control Model demands. The supposition is that the screening processes operated by police and prosecutors are reliable indicators of probable guilt. Once a man has been arrested and investigated without being found to be probably innocent, or, to put it differently, once a determination has been made that there is enough evidence of guilt to permit holding him for further action, then all subsequent activity directed toward him is based on the view that he is probably guilty. The precise point at which this occurs will vary from case to case; in many cases it will occur as soon as the suspect is arrested, or even before, if the evidence of probable guilt that has come to the attention of the authorities is sufficiently strong. But in any case the presumption of guilt will begin to operate well before the "suspect" becomes a "defendant."

The presumption of guilt is not, of course, a thing. Nor is it even a rule of law in the usual sense. It simply is the consequence of a complex of attitudes, a mood. If there is confidence in the reliability of informal administrative fact-finding activities that take place in the early stages of the criminal process, the remaining stages of the process can be relatively perfunctory without any loss in operating efficiency. The presumption of guilt, as it operates in the Crime Control Model, is the operational expression of that confidence.

It would be a mistake to think of the presumption of guilt as the opposite of the presumption of innocence that we are so used to thinking of as the polestar of the criminal process and that, as we shall see, occupies an important position in the Due Process Model. The presumption of innocence is not its opposite, it is irrelevant to the presumption of guilt; the two concepts are different rather than opposite ideas. The difference can perhaps be epitomized by an example. A murderer, for reasons best known to himself, chooses to shoot his victim in plain view of a large number of people. When the police arrive, he hands them his gun and says, "I did it and I'm glad." His account of what happened is corroborated by several eyewitnesses. He is placed under arrest and led off to jail. Under these circumstances, which may seem extreme but which in fact characterize with rough accuracy the evidentiary situation in a large proportion of criminal cases, it would be plainly absurd to maintain that more probably than not the suspect did not commit the killing. But that is not what the presumption of innocence means. It means that until there has been an adjudication of guilt by an authority legally competent to make such an adjudication, the suspect is to be treated, for reasons that have nothing whatever to do with the probable outcome of the case, as if his guilt is an open question.

The presumption of innocence is a direction to officials about how they are to proceed, not a prediction of outcome. The presumption of guilt, however, is purely and simply a prediction of outcome. The presumption of innocence is, then, a direction to the authorities to ignore the presumption of guilt in their treatment of the suspect. It tells them, in effect, to close their eyes to what will frequently seem to be factual probabilities. The reasons why it tells them this are among the animating presuppositions of the Due Process Model, and we will come to them shortly. It is enough to note at this point that the presumption of guilt is descriptive and factual; the presumption of innocence is normative and legal. The pure Crime Control Model has no truck with the presumption of innocence, although its real-life emanations are, as we shall see, brought into uneasy compromise with the dictates of this dominant ideological position. In the presumption of guilt this model finds a factual predicate for the position that the dominant goal of repressing crime can be achieved through highly summary processes without any great loss of efficiency (as previously defined), because of the probability that, in the run of cases, the preliminary screening process operated by the police and the prosecuting officials contains adequate guarantees of reliable fact-finding. Indeed, the model takes an even stronger position. It is that subsequent processes, particularly those of a formal adjudicatory nature, are unlikely to produce as reliable fact-finding as the expert administrative process that precedes them is capable of. The criminal process thus must put special weight on the quality of administrative fact-finding. It becomes important, then, to place as few restrictions as possible on the character of the administrative fact-finding processes and to limit restrictions to such as enhance reliability, excluding those designed for other purposes. As we shall see, this view of restrictions on administrative fact-finding is a consistent theme in the development of the Crime Control Model.

In this model, as I have suggested, the center of gravity of the process lies in the early, administrative fact-finding stages. The complementary proposition is that the subsequent stages are relatively unimportant and should be truncated as much as possible. This, too, produces tensions with presently dominant ideology. The pure Crime Control Model has very little use for many conspicuous features of the adjudicative process, and in real life works out a number of ingenious compromises with them. Even in the pure model, however, there have to be devices for dealing with the suspect after the preliminary screening process has resulted in a determination of probable guilt. The focal device, as we shall see, is the plea of guilty; through its use, adjudicative fact-finding is reduced to a minimum. It might be said of the Crime Control Model that, when reduced to its barest essentials and operating at its most successful pitch, it offers two possibilities: an administrative fact-finding process leading (1) to exoneration of the suspect, or (2) to the entry of a plea of guilty.

Due Process Values

If the Crime Control Model resembles an assembly line, the Due Process Model looks very much like an obstacle course. Each of its successive stages is designed to present formidable impediments to carrying the accused any further along in the process. Its ideology is not the converse of that underlying the Crime Control Model. It does not rest on the idea that it is not socially desirable to repress crime, although critics of its application have been known to claim so. Its ideology is composed of a complex of ideas, some of them based on judgments about the efficacy of crime control devices, others having to do with quite different considerations. The ideology of due process is far more deeply impressed on the formal structure of the law than is the ideology of crime control; yet an accurate tracing of the strands that make it up is strangely difficult. What follows is only an attempt at an approximation.

The Due Process Model encounters its rival on the Crime Control Model's own ground in respect to the reliability of fact-finding processes. The Crime Control Model, as we have suggested, places heavy reliance on the ability of investigative and prosecutorial officers, acting in an informal setting in which their distinctive skills are given full sway, to elicit and reconstruct a tolerably accurate account of what actually took place in an alleged criminal event. The Due Process Model rejects this premise and substitutes for it a view of informal, nonadjudicative fact-finding that stresses the possibility of error. People are notoriously poor observers of disturbing events—the more emotion-arousing the context, the greater the possibility that recollection will be incorrect; confessions and admissions by persons in police custody may be induced by physical or psychological coercion so that the police end up hearing what the suspect thinks they want to hear rather than the truth; witnesses may be animated by bias or interest that no one would trouble to discover except one specially charged with protecting the interests of the accused (as the police are not). Considerations of this kind all lead to a rejection of informal fact-finding processes as definitive of factual guilt and to an insistence on formal, adjudicative, adversary fact-finding processes in which the factual case against the accused is publicly heard by an impartial tribunal and is evaluated only after the accused has had a full opportunity to discredit the case against him. Even then, the distrust of fact-finding processes that animates the Due Process Model is not dissipated. The possibilities of human error being what they are, further scrutiny is necessary, or at least must be available, in case facts have been overlooked or suppressed in the heat of battle. How far this subsequent scrutiny must be available is a hotly controverted issue today. In the pure Due Process Model the answer would be: at least as long as there is an allegation of factual error that has not received an adjudicative hearing in a fact-finding context. The demand for finality is thus very low in the Due Process Model.

This strand of due process ideology is not enough to sustain the model. If all that were at issue between the two models was a series of questions about the reliability of fact-finding processes, we would have but one model of the criminal process, the nature of whose constituent elements would pose questions of fact not of value. Even if the discussion is confined, for the moment, to the question of reliability, it is apparent that more is at stake than simply an evaluation of what kinds of fact-finding processes, alone or in combination, are likely to produce the most nearly reliable results. The stumbling block is this: how much reliability is compatible with efficiency? Granted that informal fact-finding will make some mistakes that can be remedied if backed up by adjudicative fact-finding, the desirability of providing this backup is not affirmed or negated by factual demonstrations or predictions that the increase in reliability will be *x* percent or *x* plus *n* percent. It still remains to ask how much weight is to be given to the competing demands of reliability (a high degree of probability in each case that factual guilt has been accurately determined) and efficiency (expeditious handling of the large numbers of cases that the process ingests). The Crime Control Model is more optimistic about the improbability of error in a significant number of cases; but it is also, though only in part therefore, more tolerant about the amount of error that it will put up with. The Due Process Model insists on the prevention and elimination of mistakes to the extent possible; the Crime Control Model accepts the probability of mistakes up to the level at which they interfere with the goal of repressing crime, either because too many guilty people are escaping or, more subtly, because general awareness of the unreliability of the process leads to a decrease in the deterrent efficacy of the criminal law. In this view, reliability and efficiency are not polar opposites but rather complementary characteristics. The system is reliable *because* efficient; reliability becomes a matter of independent concern only when it becomes so attenuated as to impair efficiency. All of this the Due Process Model rejects. If efficiency demands shortcuts around reliability, then absolute efficiency must be rejected. The aim of the process is at least as much to protect the factually innocent as it is to convict the factually guilty. It is a little like quality control in industrial technology; tolerable deviation from standard varies with the importance of conformity to standard in the destined uses of the product. The Due Process Model resembles a factory that has to devote a substantial part of its input to quality control. This necessarily cuts down on quantitative output.

All of this is only the beginning of the ideological difference between the two models. The Due Process Model could disclaim any attempt to provide enhanced reliability for the fact-finding process and still produce a set of institutions and processes that would differ sharply from those demanded by the Crime Control Model. Indeed, it may not be too great an oversimplification to assert that in point of historical development the doctrinal pressures emanating from the demands of the Due Process Model have tended to evolve from an original matrix of concern for the maximization of reliability into values quite different and more far-reaching. These values can be expressed in, although not adequately described by, the concept of the primacy of the individual and the complementary concept of limitation on official power.

The combination of stigma and loss of liberty that is embodied in the end result of the criminal process is viewed as being the heaviest deprivation that government can inflict on the individual. Furthermore, the processes that culminate in these highly afflictive sanctions are seen as in themselves coercive, restricting, and demeaning. Power is always subject to abuse—sometimes subtle, other times, as in the criminal process, open and ugly. Precisely because of its potency in subjecting the individual to the coercive power of the state, the criminal process must, in this model, be subjected to controls that prevent it from operating with maximal efficiency. According to this ideology, maximal efficiency means maximal tyranny. And, although no one would assert that minimal efficiency means minimal tyranny, the proponents of the Due Process Model would accept with considerable equanimity a substantial diminution in the efficiency with which the criminal process operates in the interest of preventing official oppression of the individual.

The most modest-seeming but potentially far-reaching mechanism by which the Due Process Model implements these antiauthoritarian values is the doctrine of legal guilt. According to this doctrine, a person is not to be held guilty of a crime merely on a showing that in all probability, based upon reliable evidence, he did factually what he is said to have done. Instead, he is to be held guilty if and only if these factual determinations are made in procedurally regular fashion and by authorities acting within competences duly allocated to them. Furthermore, he is not to be held guilty, even though the factual determination is or might be adverse to him, if various rules designed to protect him and to safeguard the integrity of the process are not given effect: the tribunal that convicts him must have the power to deal with his kind of case ("jurisdiction") and must be geographically appropriate ("venue"); too long a time must not have elapsed since the offense was committed ("statute of limitations"); he must not have been previously convicted or acquitted of the same or a substantially similar offense ("double jeopardy"); he must not fall within a category of persons, such as children or the insane, who are legally immune to conviction ("criminal responsibility"); and so on. None of these requirements has anything to do with the factual question of whether the person did or did not engage in the conduct that is charged as the offense against him; yet favorable answers to any of them will mean that he is legally innocent. Wherever the competence to make adequate factual determination lies, it is apparent that only a tribunal that is aware of these guilt-defeating doctrines and is willing to apply them can be viewed as competent to make determinations of legal guilt. The police and the prosecutors are ruled out by lack of competence, in the first instance, and by lack of assurance of willingness, in the second. Only an impartial tribunal can be trusted to make determinations of legal as opposed to factual guilt.

In this concept of legal guilt lies the explanation for the apparently quixotic presumption of innocence of which we spoke earlier. A man who, after police investigation, is charged with having committed a crime can hardly be said to be presumptively innocent, if what we mean is factual innocence. But if what we mean is that it has yet to be determined if any of the myriad legal doctrines that serve in one way or another the end of limiting official power through the observance of certain substantive and procedural regularities may be appropriately invoked to exculpate the accused man, it is apparent that as a matter of prediction it cannot be said with confidence that more probably than not he will be found guilty.

Beyond the question of predictability this model posits a functional reason for observing the presumption of innocence: by forcing the state to prove its case against the accused in an adjudicative context, the presumption of innocence serves to force into play all the qualifying and disabling doctrines that limit the use of the criminal sanction against the individual, thereby enhancing his opportunity to secure a favorable outcome. In this sense, the presumption of innocence may be seen to operate as a kind of self-fulfilling prophecy. By opening up a procedural situation that permits the successful assertion of defenses having nothing to do with factual guilt, it vindicates the proposition that the factually guilty may nonetheless be legally innocent and should therefore be given a chance to qualify for that kind of treatment.

The possibility of legal innocence is expanded enormously when the criminal process is viewed as the appropriate forum for correcting its own abuses. This notion may well account for a greater amount of the distance between the two models than any other. In theory the Crime Control Model can tolerate rules that forbid illegal arrests, unreasonable searches, coercive interrogations, and the like. What it cannot tolerate is the vindication of those rules in the criminal process itself through the exclusion of evidence illegally obtained or through the reversal of convictions in cases where the criminal process has breached the rules laid down for its observance. And the Due Process Model, although it may in the first instance be addressed to the maintenance of reliable fact-finding techniques, comes eventually to incorporate prophylactic and deterrent rules that result in the release of the factually guilty even in cases in which blotting out the illegality would still leave an adjudicative fact-finder convinced of the accused person's guilt. Only by penalizing errant police and prosecutors within the criminal process itself can adequate pressure be maintained, so the argument runs, to induce conformity with the Due Process Model.

Another strand in the complex of attitudes underlying the Due Process Model is the idea—itself a shorthand statement for a complex of attitudes—of equality. This notion has only recently emerged as an explicit basis for pressing the demands of the Due Process Model, but it appears to represent, at least in its potential, a most powerful norm for influencing official conduct. Stated most starkly, the ideal of equality holds that "there can be no equal justice where the kind of trial a man gets depends on the amount of money he has." The factual predicate underlying this assertion is that there are gross inequalities in the financial means of criminal defendants as a class, that in an adversary system of criminal justice an effective defense is largely a function of the resources that can be mustered on behalf of the accused, and that the very large proportion of criminal defendants who are, operationally speaking, "indigent" will thus be denied an effective defense. This factual premise has been strongly reinforced by recent studies that in turn have been both a cause and an effect of an increasing emphasis upon norms for the criminal process based on the premise.

The norms derived from the premise do not take the form of an insistence upon governmental responsibility to provide literally equal opportunities for all criminal defendants to challenge the process. Rather, they take as their point of departure the notion that the criminal process, initiated as it is by the government and containing as it does the likelihood of severe deprivations at the hands of government, imposes some kind of public obligation to ensure that financial inability does not destroy the capacity of an accused to assert what may be meritorious challenges to the processes being invoked against him. At its most gross, the norm of equality would act to prevent situations in which financial inability forms an absolute barrier to the assertion of a right that is in theory generally available, as where there is a right to appeal that is, however, effectively conditional upon the filing of a trial transcript obtained at the defendant's expense. Beyond this, it may provide the basis for a claim whenever the system theoretically makes some kind of challenge available to an accused who has the means to press it. If, for example, a defendant who is adequately represented has the opportunity to prevent the case against him from coming to the trial stage by forcing the state to its proof in a preliminary hearing, the norm of equality may be invoked to assert that the same kind of opportunity must be available to others as well. In a sense the system, as it functions for the small minority whose resources permit them to exploit all its defensive possibilities, provides a benchmark by which its functioning in all other cases is to be tested: not, perhaps, to guarantee literal identity but rather to provide a measure of whether the process as a whole is recognizably of the same general order. The demands made by a norm of this kind are likely by their very nature to be quite sweeping. Although the norm's imperatives may be initially limited to determining whether in a particular case the accused was injured or prejudiced by his relative inability to make an appropriate challenge, the norm of equality very quickly moves to another level on which the demand is that the process in general be adapted to minimize discriminations rather than that a mere series of post hoc determinations of discriminations be made or makeable.

It should be observed that the impact of the equality norm will vary greatly depending upon the point in time at which it is introduced into a model of the criminal process. If one were starting from scratch to decide how the process ought to work, the norm of equality would have nothing very important to say on such questions as, for example, whether an accused should have the effective assistance of counsel in deciding whether to enter a plea of guilty. One could decide, on quite independent considerations, that it is or is not a good thing to afford that facility to the generality of persons accused of crime. But the impact of the equality norm becomes far greater when it is brought to bear on a process whose contours have already been shaped. If our model of the criminal process affords defendants who are in a financial position to do so the right to consult a lawyer before entering a plea, then the equality norm exerts powerful pressure to provide such an opportunity to all defendants and to regard the failure to do so as a malfunctioning of the process of whose consequences the accused is entitled to be relieved. In a sense, this has been the role of the equality norm in affecting the real-world criminal process. It has made its appearance on the scene comparatively late, and has therefore encountered a system in which the relative financial inability of most persons accused of crime results in treatment very different from that accorded the small minority of the financially capable. For this reason, its impact has already been substantial and may be expected to be even more so in the future.

There is a final strand of thought in the Due Process Model that is often ignored but that needs to be candidly faced if thought on the subject is not to be obscured. This is a mood of skepticism about the morality and utility of the criminal sanction, taken either as a whole or in some of its applications. The subject is a large and complicated one, comprehending as it does much of the intellectual history of our times. It is properly the subject of another essay altogether. To put the matter briefly, one cannot improve upon the statement by Professor Paul Bator:

> In summary we are told that the criminal law's notion of just condemnation and punishment is a cruel hypocrisy visited by a smug society on the psychologically and economically crippled; that its premise of a morally autonomous will with at least some measure of choice whether to comply with the values expressed in a penal code is unscientific and outmoded; that its reliance on punishment as an educational and deterrent agent is misplaced, particularly in the case of the very members of society most likely to engage in criminal conduct; and that its failure to provide for individualized and humane rehabilitation of offenders is inhuman and wasteful.[1]

This skepticism, which may be fairly said to be widespread among the most influential and articulate contemporary leaders of informed opinion, leads to an attitude toward the processes of the criminal law that, to quote Mr. Bator again, engenders "a peculiar receptivity toward claims of injustice which arise within the traditional structure of the system itself; fundamental disagreement and unease about the very bases of the criminal law has, inevitably, created acute pressure at least to expand and liberalize those of its processes and doctrines which serve to make more tentative its judgments or limit its power." In short, doubts about the ends for which power is being exercised create pressure to limit the discretion with which that power is exercised.

The point need not be pressed to the extreme of doubts about or rejection of the premises upon which the criminal sanction in general rests. Unease may be stirred simply by reflection on the variety of uses to which the criminal sanction is put and by a judgment that an increasingly large proportion of those uses may represent an unwise invocation of so extreme a sanction. It would be an interesting irony if doubts about the propriety of certain uses of the criminal sanction prove to contribute to a restrictive trend in the criminal process that in the end requires a choice among uses and finally an abandonment of some of the very uses that stirred the original doubts, but for a reason quite unrelated to those doubts.

There are two kinds of problems that need to be dealt with in any model of the criminal process. One is what the rules shall be. The other is how the rules shall be implemented. The second is at least as important as the first, as we shall see time and again in our detailed development of the models. The distinctive difference between the two models is not only in the rules of conduct that they lay down but also in the sanctions that are to be invoked when a claim is presented that the rules have been breached and, no less importantly, in the timing that is permitted or required for the invocation of those sanctions.

As I have already suggested, the Due Process Model locates at least some of the sanctions for breach of the operative rules in the criminal process itself. The relation between these two aspects of the process—the rules and the sanctions for their breach—is a purely formal one unless there is some mechanism for bringing them into play with each other. The hinge between them in the Due Process Model is the availability of legal counsel. This has a double aspect. Many of the rules that the model requires are couched in terms of the availability of counsel to do various things at various stages of the process—this is the conventionally recognized aspect; beyond it, there is a pervasive assumption that counsel is necessary in order to invoke sanctions for breach of any of the rules. The more freely available these sanctions are, the more important is the role of counsel in seeing to it that the sanctions are appropriately invoked. If the process is seen as a series of occasions for checking its own operation, the role of counsel is a much more nearly central one than is the case in a process that is seen as primarily concerned with expeditious determination of factual guilt. And if equality of operation is a governing norm, the availability of counsel is seen as requiring it for all. Of all the controverted aspects of the criminal process, the right to counsel, including the role of government in its provision, is the most dependent on what one's model of the process looks like, and the least susceptible of resolution unless one has confronted the antinomies of the two models.

I do not mean to suggest that questions about the right to counsel disappear if one adopts a model of the process that conforms more or less closely to the Crime Control Model, but only that such questions become absolutely central if one's model moves very far down the spectrum of possibilities toward the pure Due Process Model. The reason for this centrality is to be found in the assumption underlying both models that the process is an adversary one in which the initiative in invoking relevant rules rests primarily on the parties concerned, the state, and the accused. One could construct models that placed central responsibility on adjudicative agents such as committing magistrates and trial judges. And there are, as we shall see, marginal but nonetheless important adjustments in the role of the adjudicative agents that enter into the models with which we are concerned. For present purposes it is enough to say that these adjustments are marginal, that the animating presuppositions that underlie both models in the context of the American criminal system relegate the adjudicative agents to a relatively passive role, and therefore place central importance on the role of counsel.

One last introductory note: . . . What assumptions do we make about the sources of authority to shape the real-world operations of the criminal process? Recognizing that our models are only models, what agencies of government have the power to pick and choose between their competing demands? Once again, the limiting features of the American context come into play. Ours is not a system of legislative supremacy. The distinctively American institution of judicial review exercises a limiting and ultimately a shaping influence on the criminal process. Because the Crime Control Model is basically an affirmative model, emphasizing at every turn the existence and exercise of official power, its validating authority is ultimately legislative (although proximately administrative). Because the Due Process Model is basically a negative model, asserting limits on the nature of official power and on the modes of its exercise, its validating authority is judicial and requires an appeal to supralegislative law, to the law of the Constitution. To the extent that tensions between the two models are resolved by deference to the Due Process Model, the authoritative force at work is the judicial power, working in the distinctively judicial mode of invoking the sanction of nullity. That is at once the strength and the weakness of the Due Process Model: its strength because in our system the appeal to the Constitution provides the last and overriding word; its weakness because saying no in specific cases is an exercise in futility unless there is a general willingness on the part of the officials who operate the process to apply negative prescriptions across the board. It is no accident that statements reinforcing the Due Process Model come from the courts, while at the same time facts denying it are established by the police and prosecutors.

NOTES

1. Paul Bator, "Finality in Criminal Law and Federal Habeas Corpus for State Prisoners," *Harvard Law Review* 76 (1963): 441–442.

ARTICLE TWO

Vice, Corruption, Bureaucracy, and Power

WILLIAM J. CHAMBLISS

Although attention is usually focused on the criminal, many social scientists believe that the spotlight should also be on the conditions that encourage and permit illegal behavior. Among these factors is the link between crime and legal-political corruption. Often described as "American as apple pie," these links among criminals, the police, and political leaders in one city are discussed in this article by William J. Chambliss. One must ask whether these conditions are typical, and to what extent the example of Rainfall West applies throughout the nation.

At the turn of the century Lincoln Steffens made a career and helped elect a President by exposing corruption in American cities.[1] In more recent years the task of exposure has fallen into the generally less daring hands of social scientists who, unlike their journalistic predecessors, have gathered their information from police departments, attorney generals' offices, and grand jury records.[2] Unfortunately, this difference in source of information has probably distorted the descriptions of organized crime and may well have led to premature acceptance of the Justice Department's long-espoused view regarding the existence of a national criminal organization.[3] It almost certainly has led to an overemphasis on the criminal in organized crime and a corresponding deemphasis on corruption as an institutionalized component of America's legal-political system.[4] Concomitantly, it has obscured perception of the degree to which the structure

Source: From *Wisconsin Law Review* 4 (1971):1150–1173. Reprinted by permission.

of America's law and politics creates and perpetuates syndicates that supply the vices in our major cities.

Getting into the bowels of the city, rather than just the records and IBM cards of the bureaucracies, brings the role of corruption into sharp relief. Organized crime becomes not something that exists outside law and government but is instead a creation of them, or perhaps more accurately, a hidden but nonetheless integral part of the governmental structure. The people most likely to be exposed by public inquiries (whether conducted by the FBI, a grand jury, or the Internal Revenue Service) may officially be outside of government, but the cabal of which they are a part is organized around, run by, and created in the interests of economic, legal, and political elites.

Study of Rainfall West (a pseudonym), the focus of this analysis of the relationship between vice and the political and economic system, dramatically illustrates the interdependency. The cabal that manages the vices is composed of important businessmen, law-enforcement officers, political leaders, and a member of a major trade union. Working for, and with, this cabal of respectable community members is a staff which coordinates the daily activities of prostitution, gambling, bookmaking, the sale and distribution of drugs, and other vices. Representatives from each of these groups, comprising the political and economic power centers of the community, meet regularly to distribute profits, discuss problems, and make the necessary organizational and policy decisions essential to the maintenance of a profitable, trouble-free business.

DATA COLLECTION

The data reported in this paper were gathered over a period of seven years, from 1962 to 1969. Most came from interviews with persons who were members of either the vice syndicate, law-enforcement agencies, or both. The interviews ranged in intensity from casual conversations to extended interviewing, complete with tape recording, at frequent intervals over the full seven years of the study. In addition, I participated in many, though not all, of the vices that comprise the cornerstone upon which corruption of the law-enforcement agencies is laid.

There is, of course, considerable latitude for discretion on my part as to what I believe ultimately characterizes the situation. Obviously not everyone told the same story, nor did I give equal credibility to all information acquired. The story that does emerge, however, most closely coincides with my own observations and with otherwise inexplicable facts. I am confident that the data are accurate, valid, and reliable; but this cannot be demonstrated by pointing to unbiased sampling, objective measures, and the like for, alas, in this type of research such procedures are impossible.

THE SETTING: RAINFALL WEST

Rainfall West is practically indistinguishable from any other city of a million population. The conspicuous bulk of the population—the middle class—shares with its contemporaries everywhere a smug complacency and a firm belief in the intrinsic worth of the area and the city. Their particular smugness may be exaggerated due to relative freedom from the urban blight that is so often the fate of larger cities and to the fact that Rainfall West's natural surroundings attract tourists, thereby providing the citizenry with confirmation of their faith that this is, indeed, a "chosen land."[5]

However, an invisible, although fairly large minority of the population, does not believe it lives in the promised land. These are the inhabitants of the slums and ghettos that make up the center of the city. Camouflaging the discontent of the center are urban renewal programs which ring the slums with brick buildings and skyscrapers. But satisfaction is illusory; it requires only a slight effort to get past this brick and mortar and into the not-so-enthusiastic city center—a marked contrast to the wildly bubbling civic center located less than a mile away. Despite the ease of access, few of those living in the suburbs and working in the area surrounding the slums take the time to go where the action is. Those who do go for specific reasons: to bet on a football game, to find a prostitute, to see a dirty movie, or to obtain a personal loan that would be unavailable from conventional financial institutions.

BUREAUCRATIC CORRUPTION AND ORGANIZED CRIME: A STUDY IN SYMBIOSIS

Laws prohibiting gambling, prostitution, pornography, drug use, and high interest rates on personal loans are laws about which there is a conspicuous lack of consensus. Even persons who agree that such behavior is improper and should be controlled by law disagree on the proper legal response. Should persons found guilty of committing such acts be imprisoned or counseled? Reflecting this dissension, large groups of people, some with considerable political power, insist on their right to enjoy the pleasures of vice without interference from the law.

In Rainfall West, those involved in providing gambling and other vices enjoy pointing out that their services are profitable because of the demand for them by members of the respectable community. Prostitutes work in apartments which are on the fringes of the lower-class area of the city, rather than in the heart of the slums, precisely because they must maintain an appearance of ecological respectability so that their clients will not feel contaminated by poverty. While professional pride may stimulate exaggeration on the part of the prostitutes, their verbal reports are always to the effect that "all" of their clients are "very important people." My own observations of the comings and goings in several apartment houses where prostitutes work generally verified the girls' claims. Of some fifty persons seen going to prostitutes' rooms in apartment houses, only one was dressed in anything less casual than a business suit.

Observations of panorama—pornographic films shown in the back rooms of restaurants and game rooms—also confirmed the impression that the principal users of vice are middle- and upper-class clientele. During several weeks of observations, over 70 percent of the consumers of these pornographic vignettes were well dressed, single-minded visitors to the slums, who came for fifteen or twenty minutes of viewing and left as inconspicuously as possible. The remaining 30 percent were poorly dressed, older men who lived in the area.

Information on gambling and bookmaking in the permanently established or floating games is less readily available. Bookmakers report that the bulk of their "real business" comes from "doctors, lawyers, and dentists" in the city:

> It's the big boys—your professionals—who do the betting down here. Of course, they don't come down themselves; they either send someone or they call up. Most of them call up, 'cause I know them or they know Mr. ____ [one of the key figures in the gambling operation].
>
> Q. How 'bout the guys who walk off the street and bet?
>
> A. Yeh; well, they're important. They do place bets and they sit around here and wait for the results. But that's mostly small stuff. I'd be out of business if I had to depend on them guys.

The poker and card games held throughout the city are of two types: (1) the small, daily game that caters almost exclusively to local residents of the area or working-class men who drop in for a hand or two while they are driving their delivery route or on their lunch hour; and (2) the action game which takes place twenty-four hours a day, and is located in more obscure places such as a suite in a downtown hotel. Like the prostitutes, these games are located on the edges of the lower-class areas. The action games are the playground of well-dressed men who were by manner, finances, and dress clearly well-to-do businessmen.

Then, of course, there are the games, movies, and gambling nights at private clubs—country clubs, Elks, Lions, and Masons clubs—where gambling is a mainstay. Gambling nights at the different clubs vary in frequency. The largest and most exclusive country club in Rainfall West has a funtime once a month at which one can find every conceivable variety of gambling and a limited, but fairly sophisticated, selection of pornography. Although admission is presumably limited to members of the club, it is relatively easy to gain entrance simply by joining with a temporary membership, paying a $2 fee at the door. Other clubs, such as the local fraternal organizations, have pinball machines present at all times; some also provide slot machines. Many of these clubs have ongoing poker and other gambling card games, run by people who work for the crime cabal. In all of these cases, the vices cater exclusively to middle- and upper-class clients.

Not all the business and professional men in Rainfall West partake of the vices. Indeed, some of the leading citizens sincerely oppose the presence of vice in their city. Even larger numbers of the middle and working classes are adamant in their opposition to vice of all kinds. On occasion, they make their views forcefully known to the politicians and law-enforcement officers, thus requiring these public officials to express their own opposition and appear to be snuffing out vice by enforcing the law.

The law-enforcement system is thus placed squarely in the middle of two essentially conflicting demands. On the one hand, the job obligates officers to enforce the law, albeit with discretion; at the same time, considerable disagreement rages over whether or not some acts should be subject to legal sanction. This conflict is heightened by the fact that some influential persons in the community insist that all laws be rigorously enforced while others demand that some laws not be enforced, at least not against themselves.

Faced with such a dilemma and such an ambivalent situation, the law enforcers do what any well-managed bureaucracy would do under similar circumstances—they follow the line of least resistance. Using the discretion inherent in their positions, they resolve the problem by establishing procedures which minimize organizational strains and which provide the greatest promise of rewards for the organization and the individuals involved. Typically, this means that law enforcers adopt a tolerance policy toward the vices, selectively enforcing these laws only when it is to their advantage to do so. Since the persons demanding enforcement are generally middle-class persons who rarely venture into the less prosperous sections of the city, the enforcers can control visibility and minimize complaints by merely regulating the ecological location of the vices. Limiting the visibility of such activity as sexual deviance, gambling, and prostitution appeases those persons who demand the enforcement of applicable laws. At the same time, since controlling visibility does not eliminate access for persons sufficiently interested to ferret out the tolerated vice areas, those demanding such services are also satisfied.

This policy is also advantageous because it renders the legal system capable of exercising considerable control over potential sources of real trouble. For example, since gambling and prostitution are profitable, competition among persons desiring to provide these services is likely. Understandably, this competition is prone to become violent. If the legal system cannot control those running these vices, competing groups may well go to war to obtain dominance over the rackets. If, however, the legal system cooperates with one group, there will be a sufficient concentration of power to avoid these uprisings. Similarly, prostitution can be kept clean if the law enforcers cooperate with the prostitutes; the law can thus minimize the chance, for instance, that a prostitute will steal money from a customer. In this and many other ways, the law-enforcement system maximizes its visible effectiveness by creating and supporting a shadow government that manages the vices.

Initially this may require bringing in people from other cities to help set up the necessary organizational structure. Or it may mean recruiting and training local talent or simply co-opting, coercing, or purchasing the knowledge and skills of entrepreneurs who are at the moment engaged in vice operations. When made, this move often involves considerable strain, since some of those brought in may be uncooperative. Whatever the particulars, the ultimate result is the same: a syndicate emerges—composed of politicians, law enforcers, and citizens—capable of supplying and controlling the vices in the city. The most efficient cabal is invariably one that contains representatives of all the leading centers of power. Businessmen must be involved because of their political influence and their ability to control the mass media. This prerequisite is illustrated by the case of a fledgling magazine which published an article intimating that several leading politicians were corrupt. Immediately major advertisers canceled their advertisements in the magazine. One large chain store refused to sell that issue of the magazine in any of its stores. And when one of the leading cabal members was accused of accepting bribes, a number of the community's most prominent businessmen sponsored a large advertisement declaring their unfailing support for and confidence in the integrity of this "outstanding public servant."

The cabal must also have the cooperation of businessmen in procuring the loans which enable them individually and collectively to purchase legitimate businesses, as well as to expand the vice enterprises. A member of the banking community is therefore a considerable asset. In Rainfall West the vice-president of one of the local banks (who was an investigator for a federal law-enforcement agency before he entered banking) is a willing and knowledgeable participant in business relations with cabal members. He not only serves on the board of directors of a loan agency controlled by the cabal, but also advises cabal members on how to keep their earnings a secret. Further, he sometimes serves as a go-between, passing investment tips from the cabal onto other businessmen in the community. In this way the cabal serves the economic interests of businessmen indirectly as well as directly.

The political influence of the cabal is more directly obtained. Huge, tax-free profits make it possible for the cabal to generously support political candidates of its choice. Often the cabal assists both candidates in an election, thus assuring itself of influence regardless of who wins. While usually there is a favorite, ultracooperative candidate who receives the greater proportion of the contributions, everyone is likely to receive something.

The Bureaucracy

Contrary to the prevailing myth that universal rules govern bureaucracies, the fact is that in day-to-day operations rules can—and must—be selectively applied. As a consequence, some degree of corruption is not merely a possibility, but rather is a virtual certainty which is built into the very structure of bureaucratic organizations.

The starting point for understanding this structural invitation to corruption is the observation that application of all the rules and procedures comprising the foundation of an organization inevitably admits of a high degree of discretion. Rules can only specify what would be done when the actions being considered fall clearly into unambiguously specifiable categories, about which there can be no reasonable grounds of disagreement or conflicting interpretation. But such categories are a virtual impossibility, given the inherently ambiguous nature of language. Instead, most events fall within the penumbra of the bureaucratic rules where the discretion of officeholders must hold sway.

Since discretionary decision making is recognized as inevitable in effect, all bureaucratic decisions become subject to the discretionary will of the officeholder. Moreover, if one has a reason to look, vagueness and ambiguity can be found in any rule, no matter how carefully stipulated. And if ambiguity and vagueness are not sufficient to justify particularistic criteria being applied, contradictory rules or implications of rules can be readily located which have the same effect of justifying the decisions which, for whatever reason the officeholder wishes, can be used to enforce his position. Finally, since organizations characteristically develop their own set of common practices which take on the status of rules (whether written or unwritten), the entire process of applying rules becomes totally dependent on the discretion of the officeholder. The bureaucracy thus has its own set of precedents which can be invoked in cases where the articulated rules do not provide precisely the decision desired by the officeholder.

Ultimately, the officeholder has license to apply rules derived from a practically bottomless set of choices. Individual self-interest then depends on one's ability to ingratiate himself to officeholders at all levels in order to ensure that the rules most useful to him are applied. The bureaucracy therefore is not a rational institution with universal standards, but is instead irrational and particularistic. It is a type of organization in which the organization's reason for being is displaced by a set of goals that often conflict with the organization's presumed purposes. This is precisely the consequence of the organizational response to the dilemma created by laws prohibiting the vices. Hence, the bureaucratic nature of law enforcement and political organization makes possible the corruption of the legal-political bureaucracy.

In the case of Rainfall West the goal of maintaining a smooth-functioning organization takes precedence over all other institutional goals. Where conflict arises between the long-range goals of the law and the short-range goal of sustaining the organization, the former lose out, even at the expense of undermining the socially agreed-upon purposes for which the organization presumably exists.

Yet, the law-enforcement agency's tendency to follow the line of least resistance of maintaining organizational goals in the face of conflicting demands necessarily embodies a choice as to whose demands will be followed. For bureaucracies are not equally susceptible to all interests in the society. They do not fear the castigation, interference, and disruptive potential of the alcoholics on skid row or the café owners in the slums. In fact, some residents of the black ghetto in Rainfall West and of other lower-class areas of the city have been campaigning for years to rid their communities of the gambling casinos, whorehouses, pornography stalls, and bookmaking operations. But these pleas fall on deaf ears. The letters they write and the committees they form receive no publicity and create no stir in the smoothly functioning organizations that occupy the political and legal offices of the city. On the other hand, when the president of a large corporation in the city objected to the "slanderous lies" being spread about one of the leading members of the crime cabal in Rainfall West, the magazine carrying the "lies" was removed from newsstand sale, and the editors lost many of their most profitable advertisers. Similarly, when any question of the honesty or integrity of policemen, prosecuting attorneys, or judges involved in the cabal is raised publicly, it is either squelched before being aired (the editor of the leading daily newspaper in Rainfall West is a longtime friend of one of the cabal's leading members) or it arouses the denial of influential members of the banking community (especially those bankers whose institutions loan money to cabal members), as well as leading politicians, law-enforcement officers, and the like.

In short, bureaucracies are susceptible to differential influence, according to the economic and political power of the groups attempting to exert influence. Since every facet of politics and the mass media is subject to reprisals by cabal members and friends, exposition of the ongoing relationship between the cabal and the most powerful economic groups in the city is practically impossible.

The fact that the bureaucrats must listen to the economic elites of the city and not the have-nots is then one important element that stimulates the growth and maintenance of a crime cabal. But the links between the elites and the cabal are more than merely spiritual. The economic elite of the city does not simply play golf with the political and legal elite. There are in fact significant economic ties between the two groups.

The most obvious nexus is manifested by the campaign contributions from the economic elite to the political and legal elites. We need not dwell on this observation here; it has been well documented in innumerable other studies.[6] However, what is not well recognized is that the crime cabal is itself an important source of economic revenue for the economic elite. In at least one instance, the leading bankers and industrialists of the city were part of a multimillion-dollar stock swindle engineered and manipulated by the crime cabal with the assistance of confidence men from another state. This entire case was shrouded in such secrecy that Eastern newspapers were calling people at the University of Rainfall West to find out why news about the scandal was not forthcoming from local wire services. When the scandal was finally exposed, the fact that industrialists and cabal members heavily financed the operation (and correspondingly reaped the profits) was conveniently ignored in the newspapers and the courts; the evildoers were limited to the outsiders, who were in reality the front men for the entire confidence operation.

In a broader sense, key members of the economic elite in the community are also members of the cabal. While the day-to-day, week-to-week operations of the cabal are determined by the criminal-political-legal elite, the economic elite benefits mightily from the cabal. Not surprisingly, any threat to the cabal is quickly squelched by the economic elite under the name of "concerned citizens," which indeed they are.

The crime cabal is thus an inevitable outgrowth of the political economy of American cities. The ruling elites from every sphere benefit economically and socially from the presence of a smoothly running cabal. Law-enforcement and government bureaucracies function best when a cabal is part of the governmental structure. And the general public is satisfied when control of the vices gives an appearance of respectability, but a reality of availability.

Vice in Rainfall West

The vices available in Rainfall West are varied and tantalizing. Gambling ranges from bookmaking (at practically every streetcorner in the center of the city) to open poker games, bingo parlors, off-track betting, casinos, roulette and dice games (concentrated in a few locations and also floating out into the suburban country clubs and fraternal organizations), and innumerable $2 and $5 stud-poker games scattered liberally throughout the city.

The most conspicuous card games take place from about ten in the morning—varying slightly from one fun house to the next—until midnight. A number of other twenty-four-hour-a-day games run constantly. In the more public games, the limit ranges from $1 to $5 for each bet; in the more select twenty-four-hour-a-day games, there is a pot limit or no limit rule. These games are reported to have betting as high as $20,000 and $30,000. I saw a bet made and called for $1,000 in one of these games. During this game, the highest-stakes game I witnessed in the six years of the study, the police lieutenant in charge of the vice squad was called in to supervise the game—not, need I add, to break up the game or make any arrests, but only to ensure against violence.

Prostitution covers the usual range of ethnic group, age, shape, and size of female. It is found in houses with madams à la New Orleans stereotype, on the street through pimps, or in suburban apartment buildings and hotels. Prices range from $5 for a short time with a streetwalker to $200 for a night with a lady who has her own apartment (which she usually shares with her boyfriend who is discreetly gone during business operations).

High-interest loans are easy to arrange through stores that advertise "your signature is worth $5,000." It is really worth considerably more; it may in fact be worth your life. The interest rates vary from a low of 20 percent for three months to as high as 100 percent for varying periods. Repayment is demanded not through the courts, but through the help of "The Gaspipe Gang," who call on recalcitrant debtors and use physical force to bring about payment. "Interest only" repayment is the most popular alternative practiced by borrowers and is preferred by the loan sharks as well. The longer repayment can be prolonged, the more advantageous the loan is to the agent.

Pinball machines are readily available throughout the city, most of them paying off in cash.

The gambling, prostitution, drug distribution, pornography, and usury which flourish in the lower-class center of the city do so with the compliance, encouragement, and cooperation of the major political and law-enforcement officials in the city. There is in fact a symbiotic relationship between the law-enforcement–political organizations of the city and a group of *local*, as distinct from national, men who control the distribution of vices.

Corruption in Rainfall West

In the spring of 19— a businessman whom I shall call Mr. Van Meter sold his restaurant and began looking for a new investment when he noticed an advertisement in the paper which read:

> Excellent investment opportunity for someone with $30,000 cash to purchase the good will and equipment of a long established restaurant in downtown area. . . .

After making the necessary inquiries, inspecting the business, and evaluating its potential, Mr. Van Meter purchased it. In addition to the restaurant, the business consisted of a card room which was legally licensed by the city, operating under a publicly acknowledged tolerance policy which allowed card games, including poker, to be played. These games were limited by the tolerance policy to a maximum $1 limit for each bet.

Thus, Mr. Van Meter had purchased a restaurant with a built-in criminal enterprise. It was never clear whether he was, at the time of purchasing the business, fully aware of the criminal nature of the card room. Certainly the official tolerance policy was bound to create confusion over the illegality of gambling in the licensed card rooms. The full extent of which this purchase involved Mr. Van Meter in illegal activities crystallized immediately upon purchase of the property.[7]

> [W]e had just completed taking the inventory of [the restaurant]. I was then handed the $60,000 keys of the premises by Mr. Bataglia, and he approached me and said, "Up until now, I have never discussed with you the fact that we run a bookmaking operation here, and that we did not sell this to you; however if you wish to have this operation continue here, you must place another $5,000 to us, and we will count you in. Now, if you do not buy it, we will put out this bookmaking operation, and you will go broke." "In other words," Mr. Bataglia continued, "we will use you, and you need us." I told Mr. Bataglia that I did not come to this town to bookmake or to operate any form of rackets, and I assumed that I had purchased a legitimate business. Mr. Bataglia said, "You have purchased a legitimate business; however, you must have the bookmaking operation in order to survive." I promptly kicked him out of the place.

The question of how "legitimate" the business Mr. Van Meter had purchased was not so simple as he thought. It was, to be sure, a licensed operation; there was a license to operate the restaurant, a license to operate the card room attached to the restaurant, and a license to operate the cigar stand (where much of the bookmaking operation had taken place before Mr. Van Meter purchased the place). These licenses, although providing a "legitimate business," also had the effect of making the owner of the business constantly in violation of the law, for the laws were so constructed that no one could possibly operate a "legitimate" business "legally." Thus, anyone operating the business was vulnerable to constant harassment and even closure by the authorities if he failed to cooperate with law-enforcement personnel.

The card room attached to the business was the most flagrant example of a legitimate enterprise that was necessarily run illegally. The city of Rainfall West had adopted by ordinance a tolerance policy toward gambling. This tolerance policy consisted of permitting card rooms, which were then licensed by the city, pinball machines that paid off money to winners, and panorama shows. The city ordinance allowed a maximum $1 bet at the card table in rooms such as those in Mr. Van Meter's restaurant.

This ordinance was in clear and open violation of state law. The state attorney general had publicly stated that the tolerance policy of the city was illegal and that the only policy for the state was that all gambling was illegal. Despite these rulings from higher state officials, the tolerance policy continued and flourished in the city, although it did so illegally.

This general illegality of the card room was not, however, easily enforceable against any one person running a card room without enforcement against all persons running card rooms. There were, however, wrinkles in the tolerance-policy ordinance which made it possible discriminately to close down one card room without being forced to take action against all of them. This was accomplished in part by the limit of $1 on a bet. The card room was allowed to take a certain percentage of the pot from each game, but the number of people playing and the amount of percentage permitted did not allow one to make a profit if the table limit remained at $1. Furthermore, since most people gambling wanted to bet more, they would not patronize a card room that insisted on the $1 limit. Mr. Van Meter, like all other card-room operators, allowed a $2 to $5 limit. The ordinance was written in such a way that, in reality, everyone would be in violation of it. It was therefore possible for the police to harass or close down whatever card rooms they chose at their own discretion.

The health and fire regulations of the city were also written in such a way that no one could comply with all the ordinances. It was impossible to serve meals and still avoid violation of health standards required. Thus, when the health or fire department chose to enforce the rules, they could do so selectively against whatever business they chose.

The same set of circumstances governed the cabaret licenses in the city. The city ordinances required that every cabaret have a restaurant attached; the restaurant, the ordinance stated, had to comprise at least 75 percent of the total floor space of the cabaret and restaurant combined. Since there was a much higher demand for cabarets than restaurants in the central section of the city, this meant that cabaret owners were bound by law to have restaurants attached, some of which would necessarily lose money. Moreover, these restaurants had to be extremely large in order to constitute 75 percent of the total floor space. For a 100-square-foot cabaret, an attached 300-square-foot restaurant was required. The cabaret owner's burden was further increased by an ordinance governing the use of entertainers in the cabaret, requiring that any entertainer be at least twenty-five feet from the nearest customer during her act. Plainly, the cabaret had to be absolutely gigantic to accommodate any customers after a twenty-five-foot buffer zone encircled the entertainer. Combined with the requirement that this now very large cabaret had to have attached to it a restaurant three times as large, the regulatory scheme simply made it impossible to run a cabaret legally.

The effect of such ordinances was to give the police and the prosecuting attorney complete discretion in choosing who should operate gambling rooms, cabarets, and restaurants. This discretion was used to force payoffs to the police and cooperation with the criminal syndicate.

Mr. Van Meter discovered the payoff system fairly early in his venture:

> I found shortages that were occurring in the bar, and asked an employee to explain them, which he did, in this manner: "The money is saved to pay the 'juice' of the place." I asked him what was the "juice." He said in this city you must "pay to stay." Mr. Davis said, "You pay for the beat-man [from the police department] $250.00 per month. That takes care of the various shifts, and you must pay the upper brass, also $200.00 each month. A beat-man collects around the first of each month, and another man collects for

> the upper brass. You get the privilege to stay in business." That is true; however, you must remember that it is not what they will do for you, but what they will do *to* you, if you don't make these payoffs as are ordered. "If I refuse, what then?" I asked. "The *least* that could happen to you is you will lose your business."

During the next three months, Mr. Van Meter made the payoffs required. He refused, however, to allow the bookmaking operation back into the building or to hire persons to run the card room and bar whom members of the organized crime syndicate and the police recommended to him for the job. He also fired one employee whom he found was taking bets while tending bar.

In August of the same year, a man whom Mr. Van Meter had known prior to buying the restaurant met him in his office:

> Mr. Danielski met with me in my office and he came prepared to offer me $500 per month—in cash deductions—of my remaining balance of the contract owing against [the restaurant] if I would give him the bookmaking operations, and he would guarantee me another $800 a month more business. He warned that if he wanted to give my establishment trouble, he would go to a certain faction of the police department; if he wanted me open, he would go to another faction. "So do some thinking on the subject, and I will be in on Monday for your answer." Monday, I gave Mr. Danielski his answer. The answer was no.
>
> In June of 19—, a man by the name of Joe Link, who I found later was a second-string gang member of Mr. Bataglia's, made application to me to operate my card room. I did give him the opportunity to operate the card room because I had known him some 20 years ago when he was attending the same high school that I was. After I had refused the offer of Mr. Danielski, Mr. Joe Link had received orders from Mr. Danielski and Mr. Bataglia to run my customers out and, in any way he could, cripple my operation to bring me to terms. I terminated Mr. Link on November 6, 19—, and shortly after, after I had removed Mr. Link, Police Officer Herb C. conferred with me in my office, and Officer Herb C. said that I had better reappoint Mr. Link in my card room, that his superiors were not happy with me. If I did not return Mr. Link to his former position, then it would be necessary to clear anyone that I wanted to replace Mr. Link with. Officer C. felt that no one else would be acceptable. He further stated I had better make a decision soon, because he would not allow the card room to run without an approved boss. I informed Officer C. that I would employ anyone I chose in my card room or in any other department. Officer C. said, "Mr. Van Meter, you, I think, do not realize how powerful a force you will be fighting or how deep in City Hall this reaches. Even I do not yet know all the bosses or where the money goes." I did not return Mr. Link, as I was ordered by Officer C., and I did select my own card room bosses.
>
> On November 7, 19—, I received a phone call stating that I soon would have a visitor who was going to shoot me between the eyes if I did not comply with the demands to return Mr. Link to his former position.

The crime cabal in Rainfall West (including police officers, politicians, and members of the organized criminal syndicate), like the criminal law which underpins it, relies on the threat of coercion to maintain order. That threat, however, is not an empty one. Although Mr. Van Meter was not "shot between the eyes" as threatened, others who defied the cabal were less fortunate. Although it has never been established that any of the suspicious deaths that have taken place involving members of crime cabal were murder, the evidence, nonetheless, points rather strongly in that direction. Eric Tandlin, former county auditor for Rainfall West, is but one of thirteen similar cases which occurred from 1955 to 1969.

Tandlin had been county auditor for seventeen years. He kept his nose clean, did the bidding of the right politicians, and received a special gift every Christmas for his cooperation. In the course of doing business with the politicians and criminals, he also developed extensive knowledge of the operations. Suddenly, without warning or expectation on his part, Eric was not supported by his party for reelection as auditor, losing the nomination to the brother-in-law of the chief of police. It was a shock from which Eric did not soon recover. He began drinking heavily and frequenting the gambling houses; he also began talking a great deal. One Friday evening, he made friends with a reporter who promised to put him in touch with someone from the attorney general's office. Saturday night at 6:30, just as the card rooms were being prepared for the evening, word spread through the grapevine along First Street that Eric had been done in: "Danielski took Eric for a walk down by the bay."

The Sunday morning paper carried a small front-page story:

> Eric Tandlin, aged forty-seven, was found drowned in Back Bay yesterday at around 5:00 P.M. The coroner's office listed the cause of death as possible suicide. Friends said Mr. Tandlin, who had been county auditor for many years until his defeat in the primaries last fall, had been despondent over his failure to be reelected.

The coroner, who was the brother-in-law of the chief of police, described the probable cause of death as "suicide." The people of Miriam Street knew better. They also knew that this was a warning not to talk to reporters, sociologists, or anyone else "nosing around." In the last few years the cabal has been responsible for the deaths of several of its members. Drowning is a favorite method of eliminating troublemakers, because it is difficult to ascertain whether or not the person fell from a boat by accident, was held under water by someone else, or committed suicide.[8] L.S., who was in charge of a portion of the pinball operations, but who came into disfavor with the cabal, was found drowned at the edge of a lake near his home. J.B., an assistant police chief who had been a minor member of the cabal for years, drowned while on a fishing trip aboard one of the yachts owned by a leading member of the cabal. In both instances the coroner, who was the brother-in-law of one of the leading cabal members, diagnosed the deaths as "accidental drownings." Over the years, he has often made that diagnosis when cabal members or workers in the organization have met with misfortune.

Other deaths have been arranged in more traditional ways. At least one man, for example, was shot in an argument in a bar. The offender was tried before a judge who has consistently shown great compassion for any crimes committed by members of the cabal (although he has compensated for this leniency with cabal members by being unusually harsh in cases against blacks who appear before him), and the case was dismissed for lack of evidence.

However, murder is not the preferred method of handling uncooperative people. Far better, in the strategy of the crime cabal, is the time-honored technique of blackmail and co-optation. The easiest and safest tactic is to purchase the individual for a reasonable amount, as was attempted with Mr. Van Meter. If this fails, then some form of blackmail or relatively minor coercion may be in order.

For instance, Sheriff McCallister was strongly supported by the cabal in his bid for office. Campaign contributions were generously provided since McCallister was running against a local lawyer who was familiar with the goings-on of the cabal and had vowed to attack its operations. McCallister won the election—cabal candidates almost never lose local elections—but underwent a dramatic change of heart shortly thereafter. He announced in no uncertain terms that he would not permit the operation of gambling houses in the county, although he did not intend to do anything about the operations within the city limits since that was not his jurisdiction. Nevertheless the county, he insisted, would be kept clean.

The cabal was as annoyed as it was surprised. The county operations were only a small portion of the total enterprise, but they were nonetheless important, and no one wanted to give up the territory. Further, the prospect of closing down the layoff center operating in the county was no small matter. The center is crucial to the entire enterprise, because it is here that the results of horse races and other sports events come directly to the bookmakers. The center also enables the cabal to protect itself against potential bankruptcy. When the betting is particularly heavy in one direction, bets are laid off by wiring Las Vegas, where the national betting pattern always takes care of local variations. Clearly, something had to be done about McCallister.

No man is entirely pure, and McCallister was less pure than many. He had two major weaknesses: gambling and young girls. One weekend shortly after he took office a good friend of his asked if he would like to go to Las Vegas for the weekend. He jumped at the opportunity. While the weekend went well in some respects, McCallister was unlucky at cards. When he flew back to Rainfall West Sunday night, he left $14,000 worth of IOUs in Las Vegas.

Monday morning one of the cabal chiefs visited McCallister in his office. The conversation went like this:

> Say, Mac, I understand you was down in Vegas over the weekend.
> Yeah.
> Hear you lost a little bit at the tables, Mac.
> Uuh-huh.
> Well the boys wanted me to tell you not to worry about those pieces of paper you left. We got them back for you.
> I don't. . . .
> Also, Mac, we thought you might like to have a memento of your trip; so we brought you these pictures. . . .

The "mementos" were pictures of McCallister in a hotel room with several young girls. Thereafter things in the county returned to normal.

Lest one think the cabal exploitative, it should be noted that McCallister was not kept in line by the threat of exposure alone. He was, in fact, subsequently placed on the payroll in the amount of $1,000 a month. When his term as sheriff was over, an appointment was arranged for him to the state parole board. He was thus able to continue serving the cabal in a variety of ways for the rest of his life. Cooperation paid off much better than would have exposure.

Threats from outside the organization are more rare than are threats from within. Nevertheless, they occur and must be dealt with in the best possible way. Since no set strategy exists, each incident is handled in its own way. During Robert Kennedy's days as Attorney General, the federal attorney for the state began a campaign to rid the state of the members of the cabal. People who held political office were generally immune, but some of the higherups in the operational section of the cabal were indicted. Ultimately five members of the cabal, including a high-ranking member of the local Teamsters Union, were sentenced to prison. The entire affair was scandalous; politicians whose lives depended on the cabal fought the nasty business with all their power. They were able to protect the major leaders of the cabal and to avert exposure of the cabal politicians. However, some blood ran, and it was a sad day for the five sentenced to prison terms. Yet the organization remained intact and, indeed, the five men who went to prison continued to receive their full share of profits from the cabal enterprises. Corruption continued unabated, and the net effect on organized crime in the state was nil.

One reason that Mr. Van Meter was not "shot between the eyes" was that, although not fully cooperative, he was nonetheless paying into the cabal $450 a month in "juice." Eventually he cut down on these payments. When this happened Mr. Van Meter became a serious problem for the cabal, and something more than mere threats was necessary:

> No extortion was paid by me directly to them, but it involved a third party. Some time shortly after the first of each month, the sum of $250.00

> was paid to [the above-mentioned] Officer C., which he presumably divided up with other patrolmen on the beat. Two hundred dollars each month was given to [another bagman] for what the boys termed as "It was going to the upper braid." The $200.00 per month was paid each month from June 19— with payment of $200.00 being made in January 19—. After that I refused to make further payments. . . . After some wrangling back and forth, I just told them that I would not pay any more. They said, "Well, we will take $100.00 per month on a temporary basis." I paid $100.00 per month for the next twelve months. Early the next year I had planned to cut off all payments to the patrolmen. . . . About the 8th of July the explosion occurred. Police officers Merrill and Lynch conducted a scare program; jerked patrons off stools, ran others out of my establishment; Patrolman Lynch ordered my card room floorman into the rest room; and ordered my card room closed. When my floorman came out of the rest room, he left white and shaking and never to be seen in the city again.

Following this incident, Mr. Van Meter met with his attorney, the chief of police, and a former mayor. Although the meeting was cordial, he was told they could do nothing unless he could produce affidavits substantiating his claims. He did so, but quickly became enmeshed in requests and demands for more affidavits, while the prosecuting attorney's office resisted cooperating.

The refusal of cooperation from the prosecuting attorney was not surprising. What Mr. Van Meter did not realize was that the prosecuting attorney was the key political figure behind the corruption of the legal and political machinery. He was also the political boss of the county and had great influence on state politics, coming as he did from the most populous area of the state. Over the years his influence had been used to place men in key positions throughout the various government bureaucracies, including the police department, the judiciary, the city council, and relevant governmental agencies such as the tax office and the licensing bureau.

There was, however, a shift in emphasis for a short time in the cabal's dealings with Mr. Van Meter. They offered to buy his business at the price he had paid for it. But when he refused, the pace of harassment increased. Longshoremen came into his restaurant and started fights. Police stood around the card room day and night observing. City health officials would come to inspect the cooking area during mealtimes, thereby delaying the food being served to customers; the fire department made frequent visits to inspect fire precautions. On several occasions, Mr. Van Meter was cited for violating health and safety standards.

Finally, he was called to the city council to answer an adverse police report stating that he allowed drunks and brawling in his establishment. At the hearing, he was warned that he would lose all of his licenses if a drunk were ever again found in his restaurant.

During the next six months, the pressure on Mr. Van Meter continued at an ever-increasing rate. Longshoremen came into the restaurant and card room and picked fights with customers, employees, and Mr. Van Meter himself. The health department chose 5:00 in the evening several days running to inspect the health facilities of the establishment. The fire inspector came at the lunch hour to inspect the fire equipment, writing up every minor defect detectable. Toward the end of Mr. Van Meter's attempt to fight the combine of the government, the police force, and the criminal syndicate, he received innumerable threats to his life. Bricks and stones were thrown through the windows of his building. Ultimately, he sold his business back to the man from whom he had purchased it at a loss of $30,000 and left the city.

The affair caused considerable consternation among the legal-political-criminal cabal which controlled and profited from the rackets in Rainfall West. In the "good old days" the problem would have been quickly solved, one informant remarked, "by a bullet through the fat slob's head." But ready resort to murder as a solution to problems was clearly frowned upon by the powers that operated organized crime in Rainfall West. Although the syndicate had been responsible for many murders over the past ten years, these murders were limited to troublesome persons within the syndicate. As nearly as could be determined, no outsider had been murdered for a number of years.

Overall the gambling, bookmaking, pinball, and usury operations grossed at least $25 million dollars a year in the city alone. It was literally the case that drunks were arrested on the street for public intoxication while gamblers made thousands of dollars and policemen accepted bribes five feet away.

Payoffs, bribes, and associated corruption were not limited solely to illegal activities. To obtain a license for towtruck operations one had to pay $10,000 dollars to the licensing bureau; a license for a taxi franchise cost $15,000 dollars. In addition, taxi drivers who sold bootleg liquor (standard brand liquors sold after hours or on Sunday) or who would steer customers to prostitutes or gambling places paid the beat policeman and the sergeant of the vice squad. Towtruck operators also paid the policeman who called the company when an accident occurred.

As one informant commented:

> When I would go out on a call from a policeman I would always carry matchbooks with three dollars tucked behind the covers. I would hand this to the cops when I came to the scene of the accident.
>
> Q. Did every policeman accept these bribes?
>
> A. No. Once in a while you would run into a cop who would say he wasn't interested. But that was rare. Almost all of them would take it.

Most of the cabarets, topless bars, and taverns were owned either directly or indirectly by members of the organized crime syndicate. Thus, the syndicate not only controlled the gambling enterprises, but also "legitimate" businesses associated with nightlife as well. In addition, several of the hotels and restaurants were also owned by the syndicate. Ownership of these establishments was disguised in several ways, such as placing them formally in the name of a corporation with a board of directors who were really front men for the syndicate or placing them in the names of relatives of syndicate members. It should further be underlined that the official ownership by the syndicate must be interpreted to mean by all of the members who were in the political and legal bureaucracies and simultaneously members of the syndicate, as well as those who were solely involved in the day-to-day operations of the vice syndicate.

The governing board of the syndicate consisted of seven men, four of whom held high positions in the government and three of whom were responsible for the operation of the various enterprises. The profits were split among these seven men. We are not then talking about a syndicate that paid off officials, but about a syndicate that is part and parcel of the government, although not subject to election.

CONCLUSION

There is abundant data indicating that what is true in Rainfall West is true in virtually every city in the United States and has been true since at least the early 1900s. Writing at the turn of the century, Lincoln Steffens observed that "the spirit of graft and of lawlessness is the American spirit." He went on to describe the results of his inquiries:

> In the very first study—St. Louis—the startling truth lay bare that corruption was not merely political: it was financial, commercial, social; the ramifications of boodle were so complex, various and far-reaching, that our mind could hardly grasp them. . . . St. Louis exemplified boodle; Minneapolis police graft; Pittsburgh a political and industrial machine; Philadelphia general civil corruption. . . .[9]

In 1931, after completing an inquiry into the police, the National Commission on Law Observance and Enforcement concluded:

> Nearly all of the large cities suffer from an alliance between politicians and criminals. For example, Los Angeles was controlled by a few gamblers for a number of years. San Francisco suffered similarly some years ago and at one period in its history was so completely dominated by the gamblers that three prominent gamblers who were in control of the politics of the city and who quarrelled about the appointment of the police chief settled their quarrel by shaking dice to determine who would name the chief for the first two years, who for the second two years, and who for the third.
>
> Recently the gamblers were driven out of Detroit by the commissioner. These gamblers were strong enough politically to oust this commissioner from office despite the fact that he was recognized by police chiefs as one of the strongest and ablest police executives in America. For a number of years Kansas City, Missouri, was controlled by a vice ring and no interference

> with their enterprises was tolerated. Chicago, despite its unenviable reputation, is but one of numerous cities where the people have frequently been betrayed by their elected officials.[10]

Frank Tannenbaum once noted:

> It is clear from the evidence at hand that a considerable measure of the crime in the community is made possible and perhaps inevitable by the peculiar connection that exists between the political organizations of our large cities and the criminal activities of various gangs that are permitted and even encouraged to operate.[11]

Similarly, the Kefauver Commission summarized the results of its extensive investigation into organized crime in 1951:

1. There is a nationwide crime syndicate known as the Mafia, whose tentacles are found in many large cities. It has international ramifications which appear most clearly in connection with the narcotics traffic.
2. Its leaders are usually found in control of the most lucrative rackets in their cities.
3. There are indications of centralized direction and control of these rackets, but leadership appears to be in a group rather than in a single individual.[12]

And in 1969, Donald R. Cressey, using data gathered from the Attorney General of the United States and local crime commissions, capsulized the state of organized crime in the United States:

> In the United States, criminals have managed to put together an organization which is at once a nationwide illicit cartel and a nationwide confederation. This organization is dedicated to amassing millions of dollars by means of extortion, and from usury, the illicit sale of lottery tickets, chances on the outcome of horse races and athletic events, narcotics and untaxed liquor.[13]

The frequency of major scandals linking organized criminals with leading political and legal figures suggests the same general conclusion. Detroit; Chicago; Denver; Reading, Pennsylvania; Columbus and Cleveland, Ohio; Miami; New York; Boston; and a hoard of other cities have been scandalized and cleansed innumerable times.[14] Yet organized crime persists and, in fact, thrives. Despite periodic forays, exposures, and reform movements prompted by journalists, sociologists, and politicians, organized crime has become an institution in the United States and in many other parts of the world as well.[15]

Once established, the effect of a syndicate on the entire legal and political system is profound. Maintenance of order in such an organization requires the use of extralegal procedures since, obviously, the law cannot always be relied on to serve the interests of the crime cabal. The law can harass uncooperative people; it can even be used to send persons to prison on real or faked charges. But to make discipline and obedience certain, it is often necessary to enforce the rules of the syndicate in extralegal ways.

To avoid detection of these procedures, the police, prosecuting attorney's office, and judiciary must be organized in ways that make them incapable of discovering events that the cabal does not want disclosed. In actual practice, policemen, prosecutors, and judges who are *not* members of the cabal must not be in a position to investigate those things that the syndicate does not want investigated. The military chain of command of the police is, of course, well suited to such a purpose. So, in fact, is the availability of such subtle but nonetheless important sanctions as relegating uncooperative policemen to undesirable positions in the department. Conversely, cooperative policemen are rewarded with promotions, prestigious positions on the force, and of course a piece of the action.

Another consequence is widespread acceptance of petty graft. The matchbox fee for accident officers is but one illustration. Free meals and cigarettes, bottles of whiskey at Christmas, and the like are practically universal in the police department. Television sets, cases of expensive whiskey, and on occasion new automobiles or inside information on investments are commonplace in the prosecuting attorney's office.

Significantly, the symbiotic relationship between organized crime and the legal system not only negates the law-enforcement function of the law vis-à-vis these types of crimes but actually increases crime in a number of ways. Perhaps most important, gradual commitment to maintaining the secrecy of the relationship in turn necessitates the commission of crimes other than those involved in the vices per se. At times, it becomes necessary to intimidate through physical punishment and even to murder recalcitrant members of the syndicate. Calculating the extent of such activities is risky business. From 1955 to 1969 in Rainfall West, a conservative estimate of the number of persons killed by the syndicate is fifteen. However, estimates range as high as "hundreds." Although such information is impossible to verify in a manner that creates confidence, it is virtually certain that some murders have been perpetrated by the syndicate in order to protect the secrecy of their operations. It is also certain that the local law-enforcement officials, politicians, and businessmen involved with the syndicate have cooperated in these murders.

The location of the vices in the ghettos and slums of the city may well contribute to a host of other types of criminality as well. The disdain which ghetto residents have for the law and law enforcers is likely derived from more than simply their own experiences with injustice and police harassment. Their day-to-day observations that criminal syndicates operate openly and freely in their areas with complete immunity from punishment, while persons standing on a corner or playing cards in an apartment are subject to arrest, cannot help but affect their perception of the legal system. We do not know that such observations undermine respect for and willingness to comply with the law, but that conclusion would not seem unreasonable.

It is no accident that whenever the presence of vice and organizations that provide the vices is exposed to public view by politicians, exposure is always couched in terms of organized crime. The question of corruption is conveniently left in the shadows. Similarly, it is no accident that organized crime is inevitably seen as consisting of an organization of criminals with names like Valachi, Genovese, and Joe Bonana. Yet the data from the study of Rainfall West, as well as those from earlier studies of vice, make it abundantly clear that this analysis is fundamentally misleading.

I have argued, and I think the data demonstrate quite convincingly, that the people who run the organizations which supply the vices in American cities are members of the business, political, and law-enforcement communities—not simply members of a criminal society. Furthermore, it is also clear from this study that corruption of political-legal organizations is a critical part of the lifeblood of the crime cabal. The study of organized crime is thus a misnomer; the study should consider corruption, bureaucracy, and power. By relying on governmental agencies for their information on vice and the rackets, social scientists and lawyers have inadvertently contributed to the miscasting of the issue in terms that are descriptively biased and theoretically sterile. Further, they have been diverted from sociologically interesting and important issues raised by the persistence of crime cabals. As a consequence, the real significance of the existence of syndicates has been overlooked; for instead of seeing these social entities as intimately tied to, and in symbiosis with, the legal and political bureaucracies of the state, they have emphasized the criminality of only a portion of those involved. Such a view contributes little to our knowledge of crime and even less to attempts at crime control.

NOTES

1. J. Steffens, *The Shame of the Cities* (New York: McClure, Philipe & Co., 1904). See *The Autobiography of Lincoln Steffens* (Chautauqua, N.Y.: Chautauqua Press, 1931).

2. D. Cressey, *Theft of the Nation* (New York: Harper & Row, 1969); Gardiner, *Wincanton: The Politics of Corruption* (New York: Russell Sage Foundation); Appendix B, *The President's Commission on Law Enforcement and Administration of Justice, Task Force Report: Organized Crime* (1967), in W. Chambliss, *Crime and the Legal Process* (New York: McGraw-Hill, 1969), p. 103.

3. The view of organized crime as controlled by a national syndicate appears in Cressey, *Theft of the Nation.* For a criticism of this view, see N. Morris and G. Hawkins, *The Honest Politician's Guide to Crime Control* (Chicago: University of Chicago Press, 1970).

4. Most recent examples of this are Cressey, *Theft of the Nation;* N. Morris and G. Hawkins, *The Honest Politician* (1970); King, "Wild Shots in the War on Crime," *Journal of Public Law* 20 (1971): 85; Lynch and Phillips, "Organized Crime, Violence, and Corruption," *Journal of Public Law* 20 (1971): 59; McKeon, "The Incursion by Organized Crime into Legitimate Business," *Journal of Public Law* 20 (1971): 117; Schelling, "What Is the Business of Organized Crime?" *Journal of Public Law* 20 (1971): 71; Thrower, "Symposium: Organized Crime, Introduction," *Journal of Public Law* 20 (1971): 33; Tyler, "Sociodynamics of Organized Crime," *Journal of Public Law* 20 (1971): 41. For a discussion of the importance of studying corruption, see Chambliss, *Crime and the Legal Process,* p. 89; W. Chambliss and Seidman, *Law, Order, and Power* (Reading, Mass.: Addison-Wesley Publishing Co., 1971); McKitvick, "The Study of Corruption," *Political Science Quarterly* 72 (1957): 502.

5. Thinking of one's own residence as a "chosen land" need not of course be connected with any objectively verifiable evidence. A small Indian farm town where the standard of

living is scarcely ever above the poverty level has painted signs on sidewalks which read "Isn't God good to Indians?" Any outside observer knowing something of the hardships and disadvantages that derive from living in this town might well answer an unequivocal "no." Most members of this community nevertheless answer affirmatively.

6. See Domhoff, *Who Rules America?* (Englewood Cliffs, N.J.: Prentice-Hall, 1969); Overa, *Presidential Campaign Funds* (Boston: Boston University Press, 1946); J. Shannon, *Money and Politics* (New York: Random House, 1959); Overa, *Money in Elections* (Boston: Boston University Press, 1932); Bernstein, "Private Wealth and Public Office: The High Cost of Campaigning," *The Nation* 22 (1960): 77.

7. All quotations are from taped interviews. The names of persons and places are fictitious.

8. According to one informant: "Murder is the easiest crime of all to get away with. There are 101 ways to commit murder that are guaranteed to let you get away with it." He might have added that this was especially true when the coroner, the prosecuting attorney, and key policy officials were cooperating with the murders.

9. See Steffens, *The Shame of the Cities,* p. 151.

10. Garrett and Monroe, "Police Conditions in the United States," *National Commission on Law Observance and Enforcement Report on Police* 14 (1931): 45.

11. F. Tannenbaum, *Crime and the Community* (1938), p. 128.

12. From *The Challenge of Crime in a Free Society* (Boston: Ginn, 1967), p. 7. *President's Commission on Law Enforcement and Administration of Justice.*

13. Cressey, *Theft of the Nation.* For a discussion of similar phenomena in Great Britain, see Lucas, *Britain's Gangland* (New York: Free Press, 1969). See also D. Bell, *End of Ideology* (1960).

14. Wilson, "The Police and Their Problems: A Theory," *Public Policy* 12 (1963): 189.

15. See McMullen, "A Theory of Corruption," *Social Review* 9 (1961): 181.

ARTICLE THREE

Toward a Theory of Street-Level Bureaucracy

MICHAEL LIPSKY

Most people employed by criminal justice organizations can be described as street-level bureaucrats. They are public employees who interact constantly with nonvoluntary clients and have a considerable amount of discretion about how to deal with them. Michael Lipsky argues that street-level bureaucrats must do their jobs in spite of inadequate resources and in an environment where their authority is regularly challenged and where expectations about how they should be doing their job are contradictory and/or ambiguous.

I. STREET-LEVEL BUREAUCRACY AND THE STRUCTURE OF WORK

This essay is an attempt to develop a theory of the political behavior of street-level bureaucrats and their interactions with clients. Street-level bureaucrats, defined below, are those men and women who, in their face-to-face encounters with citizens, "represent" government to the people. The essay is also an effort to inquire into aspects of organizational life common to various urban bureaucracies, so that we may begin to develop generalizations about urban bureaucratic behavior that transcend discussions of individual bureaucratic contexts. We seek answers to the general

Source: Reprinted from Michael Lipsky, "Street-Level Bureaucracy and the Analysis of Urban Reform," *Urban Affairs Quarterly*, Vol. 6 (June, 1971), pp. 391–409.

question What behavioral and psychological factors are common to such bureaucratic roles as teacher, policeman, welfare worker, lower-court judge? To identify such common elements would be to make a start toward theory in the study of urban bureaucracy.

Concentrating on the reactions of some urban bureaucrats to conditions of stress, this essay also draws attention to various structural factors that may contribute to the inherent inability of some urban bureaucracies to provide objective, nondiscriminatory service, to recognize the existence of biased behavior, and to respond to pressures from some client groups. These assertions are matters of public urgency at a time when police departments, school systems, welfare offices, and urban legal systems increasingly have come under severe criticism.

The discussion is focused upon two types of urban public service employees currently experiencing considerable pressure from many groups: policemen and teachers. The example provided by lower-court judges is also utilized considerably, and other urban bureaucracies are referred to when relevant.

While we concentrate on the relationship of some urban bureaucrats to conditions of stress, the term street-level bureaucrat is used throughout to draw attention to individuals in organizational roles requiring frequent and significant contacts with citizens. Specifically, a "street-level bureaucrat" is defined as a public employee whose work is characterized by the following three conditions:

1. He is called upon to interact constantly with citizens in the regular course of his job.
2. Although he works within a bureaucratic stucture, his independence on the job is fairly extensive. One component of this independence is discretion in making decisions; but independence is not limited to discretion. The attitude and general approach of the street-level bureaucrat toward the citizen may affect the individual significantly. These considerations are broader than the term discretion suggests.
3. The potential impact on citizens with whom he deals is fairly extensive.

This paper will concentrate on the interaction of street-level bureaucrats and the nonvoluntary clients with whom they deal in the course of their jobs.

In American cities today, their work environments frequently require street-level bureaucrats to confront problems stemming from lack of organizational and personal resources, physical and psychological threat, and conflicting and/or ambiguous role expectations. People in these bureaucratic roles both deliberately and unconsciously develop mechanisms to cope with these problems. Street-level bureaucrats are also receptive to and supportive of organizational structural mechanisms that simplify and reduce the burdens of office. We will attempt to describe and assess the impact of selected bureaucratic resolutions of these problems on job performance and community relations.

A few other job conditions common to street-level bureaucrats should be mentioned here. They perform their jobs with nonvoluntary clients, and, no doubt related, these clienteles for the most part do not serve as primary bureaucratic reference groups. These points may be illustrated by considering the nature of police interactions with offenders and suspects, teachers' interactions with pupils, and lower-court judges' interactions with individuals charged with criminal or deviant behavior.

Another condition commonly characterizing street-level bureaucrats is that they have limited control—although extensive influence—over clientele performance, accompanied in part by high expectations and demands concerning that performance. Police and lower-court judges are charged with controlling behavior that has profound social roots. Teachers are asked to compensate for aspects of children's upbringing for which they are not responsible.

Still another condition characterizing street-level bureaucracies is the difficulty in measuring job performance in terms of ultimate bureaucratic objectives. Work standards may be established and attempts made to determine if those standards are being achieved. For example, when policemen are asked to make a certain number of arrests per month, or social workers are asked to maintain a certain size caseload, they are being asked to measure up to work standards. But these measures are only problematically related to public safety or clients' ability to cope with problems, which are the ultimate objectives in police–citizen or social worker–client interactions. The practical impossibility of accurately measuring job performance, in combination with wide discretion, contributes to substantial problems in controlling or shaping these organizations from above.

Although the theoretical aspects of this essay to some degree are generally applicable to interactions between street-level bureaucrats and citizens, they are most applicable to interactions with low-income and minority-group clients. Poor people and minority-group members tend to command fewer personal resources than more favored individuals and thus are more dependent upon governmental bureaucratic structures for fair treatment or provision of basic services.

In this brief essay I will not be able to provide a comprehensive analysis of street-level bureaucratic groups. Nor can the jobs or professions be described in monolithic fashion; they encompass a wide range of variation. In attempting to develop a parsimonious theory of governmental organizational behavior and client interaction, I am interested rather in making more understandable certain problems of these bureaucratic structures and in initiating critical analysis of certain aspects of governmental organizational behavior at the point of consumption.

The discussion will apply to aspects of street-level bureaucracy when the following conditions are relatively salient in the job environment:

1. Available resources are inadequate.
2. Work proceeds in circumstances where there exists clear physical and/or psychological threat and/or the bureaucrat's authority is regularly challenged.
3. Expectations about job performance are ambiguous and/or contradictory and include unattainable idealized dimensions.

Although to some extent these conditions prevail in most bureaucratic contexts, they are *relatively salient* in street-level bureaucracies in the contemporary American urban setting. They are the result of (and I will suggest they are in some ways the causes of) what is known as the urban "crisis." Evidence of the existence of these conditions may be found in contemporary discussions of these professions and to some degree in general analyses of organizational behavior. The conditions do not invariably obtain, and they are less salient in some bureaucratic contexts than in others. In some settings street-level bureaucrats are relatively free from these conditions. This fact does not invalidate the argument. It only suggests that at times the inferences drawn here are not applicable and that it would be useful to specify those conditions under which they *are* applicable. Although the analysis is concentrated to some extent on police, teachers, and lower-court judges, it is intended to be relevant in other bureaucratic contexts when the characteristics and qualifications discussed above obtain.

The remainder of this section extends and amplifies the discussion of conditions of stress under which street-level bureaucrats often must work.

Inadequate Resources

Almost all bureaucratic decision-making contexts are characterized by limited time and information. Street-level bureaucrats, however, work in a relatively high degree of uncertainty relative to the complexity of individuals about whom they must make decisions, although they are required to act as if certainty were achievable and were regularly achieved.

Resources necessary to function adequately as street-level bureaucrats may be classified as organizational resources and personal resources. Organizationally, street-level bureaucrats must be provided with adequate technical assistance and tools and with settings conducive to client compliance. Perhaps most important, the manpower/client ratio must be such that service may be provided with a relatively low degree of stress consistent with expectations of service provision.

Typical personal resources necessary for adequate job performance are sufficient time to make decisions (and act upon them), access to information, and information itself. For the policeman in many encounters with citizens, scarce personal resources frequently make it difficult to collect relevant information or process information adequately. When breaking up a fight in a bar, a policeman may not have time to determine the initiating party and so must make a double arrest. The need to mobilize information quickly in an uncertain bureaucratic environment may account for police practices of collecting or hoarding as much information as possible on individuals and situations in which policemen may be called to intervene, even if this information is inadmissible in court. It is not only that guidelines governing police behavior are inadequate but that inadequacy of personal and organizational resources contributes to the "improvisational" ways in which law enforcement is carried out.

In big cities, lower-court judges who process tens of thousands of cases each year and have great difficulty bringing cases to trial in timely fashion hardly have time to obtain a comprehensive picture of every case on which they sit. One might attribute this pressure to lack of manpower, since more judges would permit each case to be heard more fully. But whether one attributes it to lack of time or to inadequate staffing, lower-court judges lack the resources to do their job adequately. Many big-city teachers must perform in overcrowded classrooms with inadequate materials and with clients requiring intense personal attention.

Threats and Challenges to Authority

The conditions under which street-level bureaucrats are asked to do their jobs often include distinct physical and psychological threats. This component is most clearly relevant to the police role. Police constantly work under the threat of violence that may come from any direction at any time. Threat may exist independent of the actual incidence of threat materialization. The fact that policemen spend most of their time in nonthreatening tasks does not reduce the threat affecting their job orientations.

Teachers in inner-city schools under some circumstances also appear to work under threat of physical harm. But more common may be the threat that chaos poses for a teacher attempting to perform his job. The potential for chaos, or a chaotic classroom, implies the elimination of the conditions under which teaching can take place. The threat of chaos is present whether or not teachers commonly experience chaos and regardless of whether chaotic classroom conduct is caused by students or inspired by the teacher.

Although the institutional setting in which lower-court judges conduct cases reduces the potential for threat, judges are harried by the enormous case backlogs that confront them and by the knowledge that individuals who cannot make bail spend long periods in jail without trial. They are under constant pressure from administrative judicial superiors to reduce this backlog. The imperative to "keep the calendar moving," reinforced by the (often unrealized) judicial goal of a minimum wait from arrest to trial, is distinctly dissonant with the component of the ideal judicial image, which stresses hearing each case on its merits.

Threat and authority seem reciprocally related for street-level bureaucrats. The greater the degree of personal or role authority, the less the threat. One might also hypothesize that the greater the threat, the less bureaucrats feel that authority is respected, and the more they feel the need to invoke it. These hypotheses are supported by invocations to teachers to establish classroom control as a precondition to teaching. They also tend to be confirmed by studies of police behavior. Danger and authority have been identified as the two principal variables of the police role. The authority vested in the role of policeman is seen by police as an instrument of control, without which they are endangered. Hence comes the often reported tendency to be lenient with offenders whose attitude and demeanor are penitent, but harsh and punitive to those offenders who show signs of disrespect. Indeed, policemen often appear to "test" the extent to which an offender is respectful in order to determine whether he is a "wise guy" and thus has an improper attitude.

Expectations about Job Performance

Street-level bureaucrats often must perform their jobs in response to ambiguous and contradictory expectations. These expectations in part may be unattainable. Some goal orientations may be unrealistic, mutually exclusive, or unrealized because of lack of control over the client's background and performance, as discussed above.

Role theorists generally have attempted to locate the origin of role expectations in three "places": in peers and others who occupy complementary role positions; in reference groups, in terms of whom expectations are defined, although they are not literally present; and in public expectations generally, where consensus about role expectations can sometimes be found. While we cannot specify here how role expectations are generated for various street-level bureaucrats, we can make a few points concerning conflict in urban areas over these bureaucracies.

Conflicting and ambiguous role expectations stemming from divided community sentiments are the source of considerable bureaucratic strain. As public officials, street-level bureaucrats are subject to expectations that they will treat individuals fairly and impartially. To some degree they are also subject, as public officials, to expectations that individuals and individual cases will be treated on their unique merits. Provision of services in terms of the ideal is constantly challenged by "realists," who stress the legitimacy of adjustments to working conditions and the unavailability of resources.

Apparently in direct conflict with expectations concerning equal treatment are expectations from more parochial community interests, to which street-level bureaucrats are also subject as public officials. In a real sense, street-level bureaucrats are expected by some reference groups to recognize the desirability of providing *unequal* treatment. Invocations to "clean up" certain sections of town, to harass undesirables through heavy surveillance (prostitutes, motorcycle or juvenile gangs, civil rights workers, hippies), to prosecute vigorously community "parasites" (junkies, slumlords), and even to practice reverse discrimination (for minority groups)—all such instances represent calls for unequal bureaucratic treatment. They illustrate the efforts of some community segments to use street-level bureaucracies to gain relative advantages.

Conflicts stemming from divisive, parochial community expectations will be exacerbated in circumstances of attitudinal polarization. As relative consensus or indifference concerning role expectations diminishes, street-level bureaucrats may respond by choosing among conflicting expectations rather than attempting to satisfy more than one of them. In discussing police administrative discretion, James Q. Wilson suggests that there is a "zone of indifference" in the prevailing political culture within which administrators are free to act. When values are polarized the zone may become wider. But indifference and, as a result, discretion, may be diminished as bureaucratic performance is increasingly scrutinized and practices formerly ignored assume new meaning for aroused publics.

The police role is significantly affected by conflicting role expectations. In part stemming from public ambivalence about the police, policemen must perform their duties somewhere between the demands for strict law enforcement, the necessity of discretion in enforcement, and various community mores. They must accommodate the constraints of constitutional protection and demands for efficiency in maintenance of order and crime control. They must enforce laws they did not make in communities where demands for law enforcement vary with the laws and with the various strata of the population, and where police may perceive the public as hostile yet dependent. Police role behavior may conflict significantly with their own value preferences as individuals and with the behavior and outlook of judges. They are expected to be scrupulously objective and impartial, protective of all segments of society. Speaking generally, we may expect lack of clarity in role expectations in these cases to be no less dysfunctional than in other circumstances where lack of role clarity has been observed.

In discussing the generation of role expectations in street-level bureaucracies, we should note the relative unimportance of nonvoluntary clients. This is not to say that children are unimportant to teachers, or that litigants and defendants are unimportant to judges. But they do not primarily, or even secondarily, determine bureaucratic role expectations. Some contemporary political movements that appear to be particularly upsetting to some street-level bureaucrats, such as demands for community control and community health planning, may be understood as demands for inclusion in the constellation of bureaucratic reference groups by nonvoluntary clients. It may not be that street-level bureaucracies are *generally* unresponsive, as is sometimes claimed. Rather, they have been responsive in the past to constellations of reference groups that have excluded a significant portion of the population with whom they regularly deal.

Public bureaucracies are somewhat vulnerable to the articulated demands of any organized segment of society because they partially share the ethos of public responsiveness and fairness. But street-level bureaucracies seem particularly incapable of responding positively to the new groups because of the ways in which their role expectations are currently framed. Demands for bureaucratic changes are most likely to be responded to when they are articulated by primary reference groups. When they are articulated by client groups outside the regular reference group arena, probabilities of responsiveness in ways consistent with client demands are likely to be significantly lower.

II. ADAPTATIONS TO THE WORK SITUATION

In order to make decisions when confronted with a complex problem and an uncertain environment, individuals who play organizational roles will develop bureaucratic mechanisms to make the tasks easier. To the extent that street-level bureaucrats are threatened by the three kinds of problems described in the first section, they will develop coping mechanisms specifically related to these concerns. In this discussion we will focus on the ways in which simplifications, routines, and various coping mechanisms or strategies for dealing with the bureaucratic problems described earlier are integrated into the behavior of street-level bureaucrats and their organizational lives.

By simplifications, we refer to those symbolic constructs in terms of which individuals order their preceptions so as to make the perceived environment easier to manage. They may do this for reasons of instrumental efficiency and/or reasons of anxiety reduction. By routines, we mean the establishment of habitual or regularized patterns in terms of which tasks are performed. For this essay we will concentrate on routines for the purpose of, or with the effect of, alleviating bureaucratic difficulties arising from resource inadequacy, threat perception, and unclear role expectations. This essay may be said to focus on the trade-offs incurred in, and the unintended consequences of, developing such mechanisms.

Having discussed three conditions under which street-level bureaucrats frequently must work, we now examine some of the ways in which they attempt to accommodate these conditions and some of the implications of the mechanisms developed in the coping process.

Accommodations to Inadequate Resources

The development of simplifications and routines permits street-level bureaucrats to make quick decisions and thereby accomplish their jobs with less difficulty (perhaps freeing scarce resources through time saving), while at the same time partly reducing tensions with clients or personal anxiety over the adequacy of decisions made. "Shortcuts" developed by these bureaucracies are often made because of inadequate resources. Police limit enforcement because of inability to enforce constantly all laws (even if the community wanted total enforcement). Routinization of judicial activities in the lower courts is pervasive. Decisions on bail and sentencing are made without knowledge of the defendant's background or an adequate hearing of the individual cases, as judges "become preoccupied simply with moving the cases. Clearing the dockets becomes a primary objective of all concerned, and cases are dimissed, guilty pleas are entered, and bargains are struck with that end as the dominant consideration."

Not only does performance on a case basis suffer with routinization but critical decisions may effectively be made by bureaucrats not ultimately responsible for the decisions. Thus, for example, judges in juvenile courts have effectively transferred decision making to the police or probationary officers whose undigested reports form the basis of judicial action. Both in schools and in the streets, the record of an individual is likely to mark him for special notice by teachers and policemen who, to avoid trouble or find guilty parties, look first among the pool of known "troublemakers." Certain types of crimes, and certain types of individuals, receive special attention from street-level bureaucrats who develop categorical attitudes toward offenses and offenders.

Additionally, routines may become ends in themselves. Special wrath is often reserved for clients who fail to appreciate the bureaucratic necessity of routine. Clients are denied rights as individuals because to encourage exercise of individual rights would jeopardize processing of caseloads on a mass basis.

Accommodations to Threat

Routines and simplifications are developed by street-level bureaucrats who must confront physical and psychological threat. Inner-city school teachers, for example, consider maintaining discipline one of their primary problems. It is a particularly critical problem in "slum" schools, where "keeping them in line" and avoiding physical confrontations consume a major portion of teachers' time, detracting from available educational opportunities. Even under threatening circumstances, elementary school teachers are urged to "routinize as much as possible" in order to succeed.

"You gotta be tough, kid, or you'll never last" appears to be typical of the greeting most frequently exchanged by veteran officers in socializing rookies into the force. Because a policeman's job continually exposes him to potential for violence, he develops simplifications to identify people who might pose danger. Skolnick has called individuals so identified "potential assailants." Police may find clues to the identity of a potential assailant in the way he walks, his clothing, his race, previous experiences with police, or other "nonnormal" qualities. The moral worthiness of clients also appears to have an impact on judicial judgment. In this regard, the police experience may be summed as the development of faculties for suspicion.

Mechanisms may be developed to reduce threat potential by minimizing bureacratic involvement. Thus policemen are tutored in how to distinguish cases that should be settled on the spot with minimal police intervention. Ploys are developed to disclaim personal involvement or to disclaim discretion within the situation. "It's the law," or "Those are the rules" may be empirically accurate assertions, but they are without substance when weighed with the relationship between discretion and law enforcement. Street-level bureaucrats may totally evade involvement through avoidance strategies. Thus, according to one account, failure to report incidents in ghetto neighborhoods are "rationalize[d] . . . with theories that the victim would refuse to prosecute because violence has become the accepted way of life for his community, and that any other course would result in a great loss of time in court, which would reduce the efficiency of other police functions."

Routines also serve to provide more information about potential difficulties and to protect an image of authority. "Potential assailants"are frequently approached by police in a brusque, imperious manner in order to determine if they respect police authority. Early teacher identification of "troublemakers," and the sensitivity of policemen to sudden movements on the part of a suspect (anticipating the reaching for a weapon), further illustrate the development of simplifications for the purposes of reducing the possibility of physical threat.

Threats to the systems of which street-level bureaucrats are a part also contribute to the sense of threat personally perceived. Thus street-level bureaucrats attempt to provide an atmosphere in which their authority will be unquestioned and conformity to their system of operation will be enhanced. The courtroom setting of bench, bar, and robes, as well as courtroom ritual, all function to establish such an environment. Uniforms also support the authoritative image, as do institutional rules governing conduct and dress. Imposition of symbols of authority function to permit street-level bureaucrats to test the general compliance of the client to the system. Thus the salute to the uniform, not the man; thus a policeman's concern that disrespect for him is disrespect for the law.

We suggest the following hypotheses about these mechanisms for threat reduction. The mechanisms will be employed more frequently than objective conditions might seem to warrant because for them to be effective they must be employed in all instances of possible threat. The consequences of failure to guard against physical threat are so severe that the tendency will develop to employ safety mechanisms as often, rather than as little, as possible. This pattern contrasts significantly with routines invoked for efficiency. Traffic law enforcement, for example, may be ensured by sporadic enforcement; occasional intervention serves as a sufficient deterrent for the police department. But in threatening circumstances, the risks are too great for *individual* bureaucrats to depend upon sporadic invocation.

Threat-reduction mechanisms also are more likely to be invoked in circumstances where the penalties for employing them are nonexistent, rarely imposed, or not severe. Penalties for using threat-reducing mechanisms are least likely to be invoked in street-level bureaucracies where employees are most exposed to threat, because for these bureaucracies ability to reduce threat and thus reduce personnel anxiety are organizational maintenance requisites.

Additionally, street-level bureaucrats may have a stake in exaggerating the potential for danger or job-oriented difficulties. The reasoning is similar. If the threat is exaggerated, then the threat-reduction mechanisms will be employed more often, presumably decreasing the likelihood of actual physical danger. However, as suggested below, increased invocation of threat-reducing routines may evoke the very actions that are feared.

Exaggerating the threat publicly will also reduce the likelihood of imposition of official sanctions, since bureaucrats' superiors will have greater confidence that knowledge of the dangers accompanying job performance will be widely disseminated. Thus street-level bureaucrats paradoxically have a stake in continuing to promote information about the difficulties of their jobs at the same time that they seek to publicize their professional competence. This is analogous to the paradox of police administrators who thrive simultaneously on public anxiety over crime waves and public recognition of victories over crime.

One function of professional associations of policemen and teachers has been to publicize information about the lack of adequate resources with which they must work. This public relations effort permits the street-level bureaucrat to say (to himself and publicly) with greater confidence that his position will be appreciated by others: "Any failures attributed to me can be understood as failures to give me the tools to do the job."

The psychological reality of the threat may bear little relationship to the statistical probabilities. One teacher knifed in a hallway will evoke concern among teachers for order, even though statistically the incident might be insignificant. Policemen may imagine an incipient assault and shoot to kill, not because of the probabilities that the putative assailant will have a knife, but perhaps because once, some years ago, a policeman failed to draw a gun on an assailant and was stabbed to death. Such incidents may also be affected by tendencies to perceive some sets of people as hostile and potentially dangerous. In such circumstances the threat would be heightened by the conjunction of both threatening event and actor.

Accommodations to Role Expectations

Role expectations that are ambiguous, contradictory, and in some ways unrealizable represent additional job difficulties with which street-level bureaucrats must cope. Here we will discuss two coping processes with which street-level bureaucrats may effectively reduce the pressures generated by lack of clarity and unattainability of role expectations.

Changing role expectations Street-level bureaucrats may attempt to alter expectations about job performance. They may try to influence the expectations of people who help give their role definition. They may try to create a definition of their roles that includes a heroic component recognizing the quality of job performance as a function of the difficulties encountered. Teachers may see themselves and try to get others to see them as the unsung heroes of the city. They may seek an image of themselves as people who work without public recognition or reward, under terrific tension, and who, whatever their shortcomings, are making the greatest contribution to the education of minority groups. Similarly, policemen appear interested in projecting an image of themselves as soldiers of pacification, keeping the streets safe despite community hostility and general lack of recognition. Judges, too, rationalize their job performance by stressing the physical strain under which they work and the extraordinary caseloads they must process.

One of the implications of role redefining may be the disclaiming of responsibility over the results of work. It is surely difficult to demand improvement in job performance if workers are not responsible for the product. Furthermore, the claim of lack of responsibility is often not falsifiable unless illustrations are available of significantly more successful performances under similar constraints.

Another facet of role redefinition may be efforts to perform jobs *in some way* in accordance with perceived role expectations. Such efforts are manifested in greater teacher interest in some children who are considered bright ("If I can't teach them all, I can at least try to teach the few who have something on the ball"); in the extraordinary time some judges will take with a few cases while many people wait for their turn for a hearing; and in the time policemen spend investigating certain crimes. In these cases, street-level bureaucrats may be responding to role expectations that emphasize individual attention and personal concern for community welfare. The judge who takes the time to hear a case fully is hardly blameworthy. But these tendencies, which partially fulfill role expectations, deflect pressures for adequate routine treatment of clienteles. They also marginally divert resources from the large bulk of cases and clients, although not so many resources as to make a perceptible dent in public impressions of agency performance. Like the public agency that creates a staff to ensure a quick response to "crisis" cases, these developments may be described as routines to deal with public expectations on a selective case basis, reducing pressures to develop routines conforming to idealized role expectations on a *general* basis.

Changing definition of the clientele A second set of strategies by which street-bureaucrats can attempt to alter expectations about job performance is to alter assumptions about the clientele to be served. This approach may take the form either of attributing responsibility for all actions to the client or of perceiving the client as so victimized by social forces that he cannot really be helped by service. Goffman explains well the function of the first mode of perception:

> Although there is a psychiatric view of mental disorder and an environmental view of crime and counterrevolutionary activity, both freeing the offender from moral responsibility for his offense, total institutions can little afford this particular kind of determinism. Inmates must be caused to *self-direct* themselves in a manageable way, and, for this to be promoted, both desired and undesired conduct must be defined as springing from the personal will and character of the individual inmate himself, and defined as something he himself can do something about.

Police tendencies to attribute riots to the riffraff of the ghettos (criminals, transients, and agitators) may also be explained in this way. Instances of teachers beating children who clearly display signs of mental disturbance provide particularly brutal illustrations of the apparent need of at least some street-level bureaucrats to attribute self-direction to noncompliant clients.

The second perceptual mode also functions to absolve street-level bureaucrats from responsibility by attributing clients' performance difficulties to cultural or societal factors. If children are perceived to be primitive, racially inferior, or "culturally deprived," a teacher can hardly fault himself if his charges fail to progress. Just as policemen respond to calls in different ways depending on the victim's "legitimacy," teachers often respond to children in terms of their "moral acceptability." According to Howard Becker, children may be morally unacceptable to teachers in terms of values centered around health and cleanliness, sex and aggression, ambition and work, and age-group relations. These considerations are particularly related to class discrepancies between teacher and pupil.

Undeniably there are cultural and social factors that affect client performance. Similarly, there is a sense in which people are responsible for their actions and activities. What is important to note, however, is that these explanations function as cognitive shields between the client and street-level bureaucrat, reducing what responsibility and accountability may exist in the role expectations of street-level bureaucrats. These explanations may also contribue to hostility between clients and bureaucrats.

The street-level bureaucrat can conform to role expectations by redefining the clientele in terms of which expectations are framed. This may be called "segmenting the population to be served." In police work the tendency to segment the population may be manifested in justifications for differential rates of law enforcement between white and black communities. It is also noticeable in police harassment of "hippies," motorcycle gangs, and college students where long hair has come to symbolize the not-quite-human quality that a black skin has long played in some aspects of law enforcement. The police riots during the Democratic National Convention of 1968, and since then in various university communities, may be more explicable if one recognizes that long-haired white college students are considered by police in some respects to be "outside" of the community that can expect to be protected by norms of due process. Segmenting the population to be served reinforces police and judicial practices that condone failure to investigate crimes involving black against black or encourage particular vigilance in attempting to control black crime against whites. In New York City, the landlord orientations of public officials and judges concerned with landlord-tenant disputes are reinforced by diffuse but widely accepted assumptions that low-income blacks and Puerto Ricans are insensitive to property and property damage.

As coping behavior these strategies are similar to defense mechanisms, in that they involve reappraisal and distortion of the conditions of threat and work-related stresses. For street-level bureaucrats segmentation functions psychologically to permit bureaucrats to make some of their clienteles even more remote in their hierarchies of reference groups. At the same time, it allows bureaucrats to perform without the need to confront their manifest failure. They can think of themselves as having performed adequately in situations where raw materials were weak or the resources necessary to deploy their technical skills were insufficient.

We conclude this section by noting some of the institutional mechanisms developed in street-level bureaucracies that are conducive to greater bureaucratic control over the work environment and thus responsive to the needs of street-level bureaucrats. These relationships obtain regardless of the reasons for introducing the structural arrangements discussed here. The tracking system, whereby early in a pupil's career schools institutionally structure teacher expectations about him, represents one such institutional mechanism. Thus the educational "system" becomes responsible for pupils' progress and direction, and teachers are free to make only marginal decisions about their students (to decide in rare cases whether a student should leave a given track). In addition to reducing the decision-making burden, the tracking system, as many have argued, largely determines its own predicted stability.

Another institutional mechanism that results in reducing client-related difficulties in street-level bureaucracies is the development of procedures for effectively limiting clientele demands by making systems financially or psychologically costly or irritating to use. For lower courts this kind of development results in inducing people to plead guilty in exchange for lighter sentences. Welfare procedures and eligibility requirements have been credited with limiting the number of actual recipients. Inability to solve burglary cases results in peremptory investigations by police departments, resulting further in reduced citizen burglary reports. The Gothic quality of civilian review board procedures effectively limits complaints. The unfathomable procedures for filing housing violation complaints in New York City provides yet another illustration of effective limitation of demand.

Still another institutional mechanism resulting in reduced pressures on the general system is the "special unit" designed to respond to particularly intense client complaints. Illustrations may be found in the establishment of police review boards, human relations units of public agencies, and public agency emergency services. The establishment of such units, whether or not they perform their manifest functions, also works to take bureaucracies off the hook by making it appear that something is being done about problems. However, usually in these cases the problems about which clients want something done (police brutality, equitable treatment for minority groups, housing inspections and repairs) are related to *general* street-level bureaucratic behavior. Thus they can only be ameliorated through *general* attacks on bureaucratic performance. These units permit street-level bureaucrats to allege that problems are being handled and provide a "place" in the bureaucracy where particularly vociferous and persistent complainants can be referred. At the same time, the existence of the units deflects pressures for general reorientations.

III. THE ROLE OF STEREOTYPES

Routines, simplifications, and other mechanisms utilized by street-level bureaucrats in interactions with their nonvoluntary clients are not made in a social vacuum. The ways in which these mechanisms are structured will be highly significant. Some simplifications will have a greater impact on people's lives than others, and the ways they are structured will affect some groups more than others. The simplifications by which park department employees choose which trees to trim will have much less impact on people's lives than the simplifications in terms of which policemen make judgments about potential suspects.

In urban bureaucracies, stereotyping and other forms of racial and class biases significantly inform the ways in which simplifications and routines are structured. This simple conclusion is inescapable for anyone familiar with studies of police, teachers, and judges.

Stereotypes affect simplifications and routines, but they are not equivalent. In the absence of stereotypes, simplifying and routinizing would go on anyhow. Categorization is a necessary part of the bureaucratic process. But in American urban life, easily available stereotypes affect bureaucratic decision making in ways which independently exacerbate urban conflict.

First, in a society that already stigmatizes certain racial and income groups the bureaucratic needs to simplify and routinize become colored by the available stereotypes, resulting in *institutionalization* of the stereotyping tendencies.

Second, as will be discussed below, street-level bureaucratic behavior is perceived as bigoted and discriminatory, probably to a greater degree than the sum of individual discriminatory actions.

Third, and perhaps most interesting, the results of the interaction between simplifications, routines, and biases are masked from both bureaucrats and clients. Clients primarily perceive bias, while street-level bureaucrats primarily perceive their own responses to bureaucratic necessities as neutral, fair, and rational (that is, based upon empirical probabilities). The bureaucratic mode becomes a defense against allegations of unfairness or lack of service. By stressing the need for simplifying and routinizing, street-level bureaucrats can effectively deflect confrontations concerning inadequate client servicing by the mechanisms mentioned earlier. And when confrontations do occur, street-level bureaucrats may effectively diminish the claims of organized client groups by insisting that clients are unappreciative of service, ignorant of bureaucratic necessity, and unfair in attributing racial motives to ordinary bureaucratic behavior.

The conflict over the tracking systems in Washington, D.C., and other cities illustrates this point. The school bureaucracy defended tracking as an inherently neutral mechanism for segregating students into ability groupings for more effective teaching. Rigidities in the system were denied; reports that tracking decisions were made on racial bases were ignored; and evidence of abuse of the tracking system was attributed to correctable malfunctioning of an otherwise useful instrument. Missing from the school bureaucracy's side of the debate was recognition that in the District school system, tracking would inevitably be permeated by stereotypic and biased decision making.

In addition to the interaction between stereotyping and simplifications, three developments may be mentioned briefly that tend to reinforce bureaucratic biases: (1) playing out of self-fulfilling prophecies; (2) street-level bureaucrats' acceptance of partial empirical validation; and (3) their acceptance of illustrative validation.

In categorizing students as low or high achievers, in a sense predicting their capacity to achieve, teachers appear to create validity for the very simplifications in which they engage. Evidence has been presented that suggests that on the whole students will perform better in class if teachers think pupils are bright, regardless of whether or not they are. Policemen ensure the validity of their suspicions in many ways. They provoke "symbolic assailants" through baiting them or through oversurveillance tactics. They also concentrate patrol among certain segments of the population, thereby ensuring that there will be more police confrontations with that group. In this context there is triple danger in being young, black, and noticed by the law. Not only may arrests be more frequent, but employers' concerns for clean arrest records and the ways in which American penal institutions function as schools for criminals rather than rehabilitative institutions increase the probabilities that the arrested alleged petty offender will become the hardened criminal that he was assumed to be turning into. Hospital staffs, to illustrate from somewhat different sets of bureaucrats, appear to "teach" people how to be mentally and physically ill by subtly rewarding conforming behavior. Value judgments may intrude into supposedly neutral contexts to ensure that the antipathies of some bureaucrats will be carried over in subsequent encounters, for instance, in the creating of client "records" that follow them throughout their dealings with bureaucracies.

Partial empirical validation of the legitimacy of simplifications informed by stereotypes may occur through selective attention to information. Statistics can be marshaled to demonstrate that black crime has increased. A policeman may screen out information that places the statistical increase in perspective, never recognizing that his own perceptions of the world have contributed to the very increases he deplores. He also "thinks" he knows that black crime is worse than it was, although some studies have suggested that he overestimates its extent. Similarly, it is unquestionable that children from minority groups with language difficulties have greater problems in school than those without difficulties. Obviously there is something about lack of facility in English in an English-speaking school system that will affect achievement, although it may not be related to potential.

Illustrative validation may confirm simplifications by illustration. The common practice of "proving" the legitimacy of stereotypes, and thus the legitimacy of biased simplifications, by example may be a logical horror but it is also a significant social fact that influences the behavior of street-level bureaucracies. Illustrative validity not only confirms the legitimacy of simplifications but also affects the extent to which simplifications are invoked. The policeman killed in the course of duty because he neglected to shoot his assailant provides the basis for illustrative validity not only about the group of which the assailant is a part but also about the importance of invoking simplifications in the first place.

IV. STREET-LEVEL BUREAUCRACY AND URBAN CONFLICT

To better understand the interaction between government and citizens at the "place" where government meets people, I have attempted to demonstrate common factors in the behavior of street-level bureaucrats. I have suggested that there are patterns to this interaction, that continuities may be observed which transcend individual bureaucracies, and that certain conditions in the work environment of these bureaucracies appear to be relatively salient in structuring the bureaucrat-citizen interaction.

This analysis may help to explain some aspects of citizen antagonism to contemporary urban bureaucracies. Clients may conclude that service is prejudiced, dehumanizing, and discriminatory in greater degree than is warranted by the incidence of such behavior. Just as it may take only one example of a policeman killed by an assailant to reinforce police tendencies to overreact to potential assailants, so it only takes a few examples of bigoted teachers or prejudiced policemen to reinforce widespread conviction on the part of clients that the system is prejudiced. As Herman Goldstein has put it in discussing police-client relations:

> A person who is unnecessarily aggrieved is not only critical of the procedure which was particularly offensive to him. He tends to broaden his interest and attack the whole range of police procedures which suddenly appear to him to be unusually oppressive.

To refer again to propositions concerning threat, citizen stereotyping of bureaucracies may be greater in direct relation to the extent of control and impact that these bureaucracies have on their lives. Thus these tendencies will be relatively salient in institutional settings with considerable impact on citizens, such as schools, in courts, and in police relations. And they will be relatively salient to low-income clients, whose resource alternatives are minimal. Furthermore, such clients may recognize the sense in which the bureaucracies "create" them and the circumstances in which they live.

Just as street-level bureaucrats develop conceptions of nonvoluntary clients that deflect responsibility away from themselves, so citizens may also respond to bureaucracies by attributing to bureaucracies qualities that deflect attention away from their own shortcomings. This may result in citizens' developing conceptions of bureaucrats and bureaucracies as more potent than they actually are. On the other hand, because of predicted neglect or negative experiences in the past, citizens may withdraw from bureaucratic interaction or act with hostility toward street-level bureaucrats, evoking the very reactions *they* have "predicted." Minority groups particularly may have negative experiences with these bureaucracies, since they may be the citizens most likely to be challenged by street-level bureaucrats and most likely to be unable to accept gracefully challenges to self-respect.

Citizens will also share to some extent the role expectations of street-level bureaucrats, although they may have had little influence in shaping them. This may be another source of tension, since citizens may expect personal, individualized consideration or may demand it in spite of bureaucratic needs to provide impersonal treatment in a routinized fashion.

This analysis may help place in perspective the apparent paradox that some community groups insist that street-level bureaucracies are biased and discriminatory, while at the same time members of these bureaucracies insist in good faith that their members do not engage in discriminatory and biased practices. Regardless of whatever dissemblance may be involved here, we can partially explain the paradox by noting: (1) the ways in which relatively little discriminatory behavior can result in client ascription of a great deal of bureaucratic behavior to discriminatory attitudes; (2) the ways in which mechanisms developed by street-level bureaucrats to cope with problems in job performance are informed and colored by discriminatory stereotypes; and (3) the ways in which street-level bureaucrats institutionalize bias without necessarily recognizing the implications of their actions.

If this analysis has been at all persuasive, it suggests that in significant respects street-level bureaucracies as currently structured may be inherently incapable of responding favorably to contemporary demands for improved and more sympathetic service to some clients. Street-level bureaucrats respond to work-related pressures in ways that, however understandable or well-intentioned, may have invidious effects on citizen impressions of governmental responsiveness and equity in performance. If, indeed, government may be most salient to citizens where there is frequent interaction with its "representatives" and where the interactions may have important consequences for their lives, then these conclusions should evoke sympathy for current proposals for urban decentralization of authority. Whatever their other merits or difficulties, these proposals commend themselves at least for their concentration on fundamental alterations of the work environment of street-level bureaucrats.

PART TWO

POLICE

From philosophical, historical, and administrative perspectives, the concept of "law and order" is not a simple one. It has wide implications for the preservation of civil rights and the rule of law. A key question in a democratic society is, "For what social purpose do police exist?" History gives us little help in providing an answer, because law-enforcement agencies have often played many different and contradictory roles. Are the police to be concerned primarily with peacekeeping or with crime fighting? Should they be social workers with guns, or guntoters in social work? Should they be instruments of social change or defenders of the faith?

Law and order is not a new problem, but it has been a focus for discussion since the first police force was formed in metropolitan London in 1829. If society gives arrest and incarceration powers to the police, it must control the power it has delegated so that the civil liberties of citizens are not infringed. The potential for misuse of power by law-enforcement agencies led many thoughtful nineteenth-century Americans to contend that an organized police force is alien to democracy and would lead to an end of freedom. Looking even further back in history, to the Magna Carta, we can see that limits were placed upon the constables and bailiffs of thirteenth-century England. Reading between the lines of this ancient document, we can see that abuses by police, maintenance of order, and the rule of law were problems then, as they are today. What is surprising is that the same remedies—recruitment of better police officers, stiffening the penalties for official malfeasance, creation of a civilian board of control—were suggested in that earlier time to ensure that order was kept according to the rule of law.

The 20,000 law-enforcement agencies that are today dispersed throughout the counties, cities, and towns of the United States have their origins in the second quarter of nineteenth-century England, during the early stages of the Industrial Revolution. Arguing for establishment of a police force in metropolitan London, Sir Robert Peel cited the need for public order, using statistics indicating that crime was increasing faster than the population and pointing out that slum residents were rioting and destroying property and life in the "respectable" sections. Yet even under these conditions, there was so much fear of centralizing power in a quasi-military body that it took Peel seven years to persuade Parliament to establish the Metropolitan Constabulary for London. Organized along military lines, this 1,000-man force was responsible to the home secretary. Because the home secretary was accountable to Parliament, the first regular police force was actually controlled by the democratically elected legislature. Opposition to the new force came mostly from people of goodwill of all classes who genuinely believed that police of any kind were destructive of liberty.

As with so many other public institutions, the English example was quickly copied in the United States. Between 1830 and 1870 there was unprecedented civil disorder, caused by the social upheavals of massive immigration, hostility toward nonslave blacks and abolitionists, and mob actions against banks. The major cities of the United States created daytime police forces to supplement the night watchmen. Boston and Philadelphia became the first cities to augment their forces, and in 1844 the New York legislature authorized creation of city uniformed police forces under the command of a chief appointed by the mayor and the council. By the middle of the century, most principal U.S. cities had followed this pattern.

Throughout much of the nineteenth century, law enforcement in the United States was plagued by corruption, political patronage, and struggles for control. In too many cities the police were identified in the public mind with the political machine. It was not until the early twentieth century that civic reform with the goal of truly professional police forces was attempted. Selection of police personnel on the basis of merit rather than appointment helped insulate officers from the demands of political parties. New law-enforcement techniques were inaugurated by such administrators as August Vollmer, police chief of Berkeley, California, and later by O. W. Wilson, who gained national attention as a result of innovations he made in Wichita, Kansas. Building on this basis and the progressive tradition of civic reform, the professional model of police work became dominant. This ethos stressed that the police should stay out of politics, that members should be well trained and disciplined, that technological developments should be used, and that the crime-fighter role should be primary.

With the rise of urban crime in the 1960s and demands from minority communities that public services be delivered in a manner consistent with local values, questions about the exercise of discretion within the professional model began to arise. There was no consensus on whether the police officer's main role should be that of crime fighter, maintainer of order, or public service worker. Many argued that the professional model was too impersonal to be responsive to differences in the community and that crime fighting played a minor role in police work. These questions remain unresolved.

POLICE FUNCTIONS

Police decisions and practices are greatly shaped by the local community. Although statutes insist that all laws be fully implemented, they usually do not provide specific instructions for carrying out this policy. Even if the police were given the necessary resources, a policy of "enforcement" would make life intolerable and almost surely preclude the protection of civil rights. In reality, although laws are written as if full enforcement were expected, the police determine the outer limits of "actual enforcement." A number of factors lead them to enforce some laws but not others: the difficulty of making arrests, the resources needed to obtain evidence, disagreement in the community about whether certain acts should be unlawful, and pressure from influential people. These low-visibility choices by police administrators are among the political ingredients of the criminal justice system. Enforcement agencies must fulfill their obligations under the law, but they must do so in ways that will ensure community and organizational support.

The work of the police is more complex than most of us assume. Police officers are charged with maintaining order, enforcing the law, providing a variety of social services, and carrying out policies that specify the persons and offenses to be labeled deviant. If we agree with French sociologist Emile Durkheim that no society is free of crime, the determination of policies allocating resources and setting criteria for law-enforcement goals becomes an important variable. This consideration was well stated by the President's Crime Commission: "The police must make important judgments about what conduct is in fact criminal; about the allocation of scarce resources; and about the gravity of each individual incident and the proper steps that should be taken."

In a heterogeneous society such as the United States, there are bound to be varying interpretations of deviance. Should emphasis be on "white-collar" crimes such as embezzlement, on "organized crime," or on "low-level" violations such as public drunkenness, shoplifting, and crimes without victims? Each of these categories involves different social classes, different perceptions of deviance, and different modes of enforcement. Each type of deviation embodies different threats and rewards for criminal justice agencies.

To help in conceptually organizing the functions of the police, three primary categories have been developed: order maintenance, law enforcement, and service. The order maintenance function is a broad mandate to prevent behavior that disturbs or threatens to disturb the public peace. Domestic quarrels, a noisy "drunk," a tavern brawl, a panhandler soliciting on the streets—these are examples of behavior that may require peacekeeping efforts of the police. Whereas most criminal laws specify acts that are illegal, laws regarding disorderly conduct define conditions that are ambiguous and that depend on the social environment and on the perceptions and norms of the actors. Law enforcement involves violations of the law in which only guilt must be assessed (murder, rape, burglary), whereas order maintenance involves violations of the law when interpretation of right conduct and assignment of blame may be in dispute. In modern society the police are increasingly called upon to perform a number of services for the populace. This service function—providing first aid, rescuing animals, finding missing persons, and helping the disabled—has become the dominant source of police activities. Although the public may depend on the order maintenance and service functions of the police, it acts as if law enforcement—catching lawbreakers—were the most important function.

In a democracy, efforts of police to carry out their functions are mainly reactive (citizen invoked) rather than proactive (police invoked). Only in the vice, narcotics, and traffic divisions of the modern police department does one find law officers activated by information gathered internally by the organization. Most criminal acts occur at times that are unpredictable and in a private rather than public place. The police respond to calls from persons who telephone, who signal a patrol car or an officer on foot, or who appear at the station to register a need or complaint. All these factors influence the way the police do their job. In addition, because the police usually arrive at the scene only after the crime has been committed and the perpetrator has fled, the job of finding the guilty party is hampered by the time lapse and the reliability of the information supplied by the victim. To a large extent, reports by victims define the boundaries of law enforcement.

Recent research has challenged the effectiveness of many police practices. The Kansas City Preventive Patrol Experiment showed that the level of police services did not make any significant change in the amount of crime reported, the crime known to citizens, or the extent to which citizens feared criminal attack. Other studies showed that the belief that a speedy response by police to crime scenes was not essential proved to be unfounded in research carried out in a number of cities. The use of foot patrol, long considered of little value compared to motorized patrol, has reemerged as an important strategy for maintaining order and reducing the fear of crime. The value of criminal investigations and the role played by detectives in apprehending offenders has also been scrutinized. A Rand Corporation study of 153 large police departments found that it was information identifying the perpetrator supplied by the victim or witnesses, not detective work, that determined whether a crime could be successfully solved.

The role of the police in U.S. society is indeed undergoing a critical rethinking. After many years of focusing on the law-enforcement/crime-fighter role, we are now emphasizing the value of order maintenance and service as a primary focus of police resources. Parallel to this reorientation is an emphasis upon greater community response by the police and the importance of police accountability for police actions. If these trends become widespread, a restructuring of police organizations will probably follow.

In the justice system, the police stand as the gateway for the entrance of the raw materials to be processed. The cases sent to the prosecutor for charging, and thence to the courts of adjudication, begin with the decision of an individual police officer that probable cause exists to make an arrest. In the criminal justice system the ultimate fate of one group of clients rests with another group of clients. Decisions made by the police concerning offenders may be reversed by the prosecutor or the judge. Although the police may introduce clients into the system through their power of arrest, the outcome of each case is in the hands of others. The police have final power only in those cases filtered out of the system at the intake point.

POLICE CULTURE

The position of "police officer" is more than a cluster of formally prescribed duties and role expectations held jointly by criminal justice officials and members of the political community. In addition to the formal administrative language that specifies duties and responsibilities, there is a cultural dimension to the position that has a profound influence on the operational code of the police, both as a unit and as individuals behaving within a bureaucratic framework.

Social scientists have demonstrated that there is a definite relationship between one's occupational environment and the way one interprets events; an occupation may be seen as a major badge of identity that an individual acts to protect as a facet of his or her self-esteem and person. Thus, entry requirements, training, and professional socialization produce a homogeneity of attitudes that guides the police in their daily work.

National studies of occupational status have shown that the public ascribes more prestige to the police now than in prior decades, even though police officers do not believe the public regards their calling as honorable. Publications of police organizations repeatedly take up the theme that the public does not appreciate law-enforcement agents. In a Denver survey, 98 percent of police officers reported that they had experienced verbal or physical abuse and that these incidents tended to occur in neighborhoods of minority and underprivileged groups. Part of the burden of the police is that they have doubts about their professional status. Yet opinion polls consistently indicate that the overwhelming majority of citizens, even those in the ghetto, see the police as protectors of persons and property.

Discretion is a characteristic of bureaucracy. Unlike most organizations, however, the discretion the police have increases as one moves down the hierarchy. Thus the patrol officer, the most numerous and lowest-ranking of officers, has the greatest amount of discretion. He or she deals with clients alone and is almost solely in charge of enforcing the most ambiguous laws—conflicts among citizens where the definition of offensive behavior is most often open to dispute. The police officer's perception of the situation, as shaped by his or her personal values and norms, is crucial in determining what action the officer will take and what charges will be filed.

The police officer's world is circumscribed by the all-encompassing demands of the job. Not only are the police socialized to norms that accentuate loyalty to fellow officers, a professional esprit de corps, and the symbolism of authority, but the situational context of their position limits their freedom to isolate their vocational role from other aspects of their lives. From the time they are first given their badges and guns, they must always carry these reminders of their position—the tools of the trade—and be prepared to use them. Thus, the requirements that the police maintain vigilance against crime even when off duty and that they work at "odd hours," along with the limited opportunities for social contact with persons other than fellow officers, reinforce the values of the police subculture.

THE "IMPOSSIBLE" MANDATE

In a thoughtful essay Peter Manning wrote that the police agree with their audiences, their professional interpreters—the American family, criminals, and politicians—in at least one respect: they have an "impossible" mandate. In society, various occupational groups are given license to carry out certain activities that others are not. Indeed, groups achieving professional status have formal rules and codes of ethics that not only set their own standards but also define their occupational mandate. Medical doctors, for example, have the right to prescribe drugs and perform operations, but they are also able to set the boundaries of their mandate. Because over time the practice of medicine has become a secure profession, there is little disagreement in society about the tasks, attitudes, and values that set its practitioners apart.

The police in contemporary society are in trouble largely because they have been unable to define their mandate; it has been defined for them by those they serve. As a result, citizens have a distorted notion of police work. People are aware of the excitement of a small portion of police work, but then mistakenly broaden this notion to include all police activities. For much of the public, the police are viewed as always ready to respond to citizen demands—as highly organized crime fighters able to keep society from falling apart.

Sociopolitical changes in the United States have added to the tensions between the mandate of the police and their ability to fulfill it. In the past hundred years there have been massive shifts of population from rural areas to the cities. Criminal law has been called upon to serve a variety of purposes that are only tangentially related to law enforcement and order maintenance. Affluence has brought the criminal justice system new problems—such as the ease of communication and the abundance of property. Police have been assigned the tasks of crime prevention, crime detection, and the apprehension of criminals. Because they have a monopoly on legal violence, they have a mandate that claims to include efficient, apolitical, and professional enforcement of the law. All this is to be accomplished within the bounds dictated by a democratic society that values due process of law.

The mandate given the police is indeed "impossible." This will be true so long as there are misunderstandings, on the part of the police and the public, about the nature of law-enforcement work, the potential for success in controlling crime, and the role of law in a democratic society.

SUGGESTIONS FOR FURTHER READING

BAKER, MARK. *Cops.* New York: Simon & Schuster, 1985. A picture of police work based on interviews of officers in both rural and urban police departments throughout the United States.

BAYLEY, DAVID, and JEROME SKOLNICK. *The New Blue Line: Police Innovation in Six American Cities.* New York: Free Press, 1986.

GELLER, WILLIAM A., ed. *Police Leadership in America.* New York: Praeger, 1985. Forty-one essays by leaders of police organizations and scholars concerned with law enforcement and order maintenance in the United States. The focus is on the questions "Who runs the police?" and "Who should?"

MAAS, PETER. *Serpico.* New York: Bantam Books, 1973. The experience of a New York City police officer's fight against corruption in his department.

MANNING, PETER K. *Police Work.* Cambridge, Mass.: M.I.T. Press, 1977. An analysis of police work and the dilemma of the police mandate. The author discusses the political means and strategies that police use in an attempt to live up to the ideal imposed by the public's expectations.

McCLURE, JAMES. *Cop World.* New York: Pantheon Books, 1984. A case study of the San Diego Police Department giving an in-depth account of police work.

MUIR, WILLIAM K., JR. *Police: Streetcorner Politicians.* Chicago: University of Chicago Press, 1977. A study of the attitudes and values of police officers.

REISS, ALBERT J. *The Public and the Police.* New Haven: Yale University Press, 1971. Police-citizen relationships as observed by a team of investigators for the President's Commission on Law Enforcement and Administration of Justice.

RUBINSTEIN, JONATHAN. *City Police.* New York: Farrar, Straus & Giroux, 1972. A description of the work of big-city police officers and the way they regard their profession, based on observations gathered during a year spent riding in Philadelphia police squad cars.

WESTLEY, WILLIAM. *Violence and the Police.* Cambridge, Mass.: M.I.T. Press, 1971. Although somewhat dated, this is a seminal work on the sociological context that promotes secrecy among the police.

WILSON, JAMES Q. *Varieties of Police Behavior.* Cambridge, Mass.: Harvard University Press, 1968. An examination of the police function and the styles of policing in a variety of communities. Shows the links between culture, politics, and law-enforcement policies.

ARTICLE FOUR

Police Discretion Not to Invoke the Criminal Process: Low-Visibility Decisions in the Administration of Justice

JOSEPH GOLDSTEIN

Legislatures write the criminal laws as if they were commands to be enforced by the police, but officers have wide latitude in determining how the laws will be enforced. Professor Joseph Goldstein of the Yale Law School notes that decisions not to invoke the law are shielded from the public's view. Of particular interest is his development of the concepts of "total," "full," and "actual" enforcement. The extent to which the police pursue a policy approaching "full" enforcement for all offenses depends upon the values of the community.

Police decisions not to invoke the criminal process largely determine the outer limits of law enforcement. By such decisions, the police define the ambit of discretion throughout the process of other decision makers—prosecutor, grand and petit jury, judge, probation officer, correction authority, and parole and pardon boards. These police decisions, unlike their decisions to invoke the law, are generally of extremely low visibility and consequently are seldom the subject of review. Yet an opportunity for review and appraisal of nonenforcement decisions is essential to the functioning of the rule of law in our system of criminal justice. This article will therefore be an attempt to determine how the visibility of such police decisions may be increased and what procedures should be established to evaluate them on a continuing basis, in the light of the complex of objec-

Source: Reprinted by permission of the Yale Law Journal Company and Fred B. Rothman & Company from *The Yale Law Journal,* Vol. 69, pp. 543 – 594. Footnotes omitted.

tives of the criminal law and of the paradoxes toward which the administration of criminal justice inclines.

I. The criminal law is one of many intertwined mechanisms for the social control of human behavior. It defines behavior which is deemed intolerably disturbing to or destructive of community values and prescribes sanctions which the state is authorized to impose upon persons convicted or suspected of engaging in prohibited conduct. Following a plea or verdict of guilty, the state deprives offenders of life, liberty, dignity, or property through convictions, fines, imprisonments, killings, and supervised releases, and thus seeks to punish, restrain, and rehabilitate them, as well as to deter others from engaging in proscribed activity. Before a verdict, and despite the presumption of innocence which halos every person, the state deprives the suspect of life, liberty, dignity, or property through the imposition of deadly force, search and seizure of persons and possessions, accusation, imprisonment, and bail, and thus seeks to facilitate the enforcement of the criminal law.

These authorized sanctions reflect the multiple and often conflicting purposes which now surround and confuse criminal law administration at and between key decision points in the process. The stigma which accompanies conviction, for example, while serving a deterrent, and possibly retributive function, becomes operative upon the offender's release and thus impedes the rehabilitation objective of probation and parole. Similarly, the restraint function of imprisonment involves the application of rules and procedures which, while minimizing escape opportunities, contributes to the deterioration of offenders confined for reformation. Since police decisions not to invoke the criminal process may likewise further some objectives while hindering others, or, indeed, run counter to all, any meaningful appraisal of these decisions should include an evaluation of their impact throughout the process on the various objectives reflected in authorized sanctions and in the decisions of other administrators of criminal justice.

Under the rule of law, the criminal law has both a fair-warning function for the public and a power-restricting function for officials. Both post- and preverdict sanctions, therefore, may be imposed only in accord with authorized procedures. No sanctions are to be inflicted other than those which have been prospectively prescribed by the Constitution, legislation, or judicial decision for a particular crime or a particular kind of offender. These concepts, of course, do not preclude differential disposition, within the authorized limits, of persons suspected or convicted of the same or similar offenses. In an ideal system differential handling, individualized justice, would result, but only from an equal application of officially approved criteria designed to implement officially approved objectives. And finally a system which presumes innocence requires that preconviction sanctions be kept at a minimum consistent with assuring an opportunity for the process to run its course.

A regularized system of review is a requisite for ensuring substantial compliance by the administrators of criminal justice with these rule-of-law principles. Implicit in the word "review" and obviously essential to the operation of any review procedure is the visibility of the decisions and conduct to be scrutinized. Pretrial hearings on motions, the trial, appeal, and the writ of habeas corpus constitute a formal system for evaluating the actions of officials invoking the criminal process. The public hearing, the record of proceedings, and the publication of court opinions—all features of the formal system—preserve and increase the visibility of official enforcement activity and facilitate and encourage the development of an informal system of appraisal. These proceedings and documents are widely reported and subjected to analysis and comment by legislative, professional, and other interested groups and individuals.

But police decisions not to invoke the criminal process, except when reflected in gross failures of service, are not visible to the community. Nor are they likely to be visible to official state reviewing agencies, even those within the police department. Failure to tag illegally parked cars is an example of gross failure of service, open to public view and recognized for what it is. An officer's decision, however, not to investigate or report adequately a disturbing event which he has reason to believe constitutes a violation of the criminal law does not ordinarily carry with it consequences sufficiently visible to make the community, the legislature, the prosecutor, or the courts aware of a possible failure of service. The police officer, the suspect, the police department, and frequently even the victim, when directly concerned with a decision not to invoke, unlike the same parties when responsible for or subject to a decision to invoke, generally have neither the incentive nor the opportunity to obtain review of that decision or the police conduct associated with it. Furthermore, official police records are usually too incomplete to permit evaluations of nonenforcement decisions in the light of the purposes of the criminal law. Consequently, such decisions, unlike decisions to enforce, are generally not subject to the control which would follow from administrative, judicial, legislative, or community review and appraisal.

Confidential reports detailing the day-to-day decisions and activities of a large municipal police force have been made available to the author by the American Bar Foundation. These reports give limited visibility to a wide variety of police decisions not to invoke the criminal process. Three groups of such decisions will be described and analyzed. Each constitutes a police "program" of nonenforcement either based on affirmative departmental policy or condoned by default. All of the decisions, to the extent that the officers concerned thought about them at all, represent well-intentioned, honest judgments, which seem to reflect the police officer's conception of his job. None of the decisions involve bribery or corruption, nor do they concern "obsolete," though unrepealed, criminal laws. Specifically, these programs involve police decisions (1) not to enforce the narcotics laws against certain violators, who inform against other "more serious" violators; (2) not to enforce the felonious assault laws against an assailant whose victim does not sign a complaint; and (3) not to enforce gambling laws against persons engaged in the numbers racket, but instead to harass them. Each of these decisions is made even though the police "know" a crime has been committed and even though they may "know" who the offender is and may, in fact, have apprehended him. But before describing and evaluating these nonenforcement programs, as an agency of review might do, it is necessary to determine what discretion, if any, the police, as invoking agents, have, and conceptually to locate the police in relation to other principal decision makers in the criminal law process.

II. The police have a duty not to enforce the substantive law of crimes unless invocation of the process can be achieved within bounds set by constitution, statute, court decision, and possibly official pronouncements of the prosecutor. *Total enforcement,* were it possible, is thus precluded, by generally applicable due process restrictions on such police procedures as arrest, search, seizure, and interrogation. *Total enforcement* is further precluded by such specific procedural restrictions as prohibitions on invoking an adultery statute unless the spouse of one of the parties complains, or an unlawful-possession-of-firearms statute if the offender surrenders his dangerous weapons during a statutory period of amnesty. Such restrictions of general and specific application mark the bounds, often ambiguously, of an area of *full enforcement* in which the police are not only authorized but expected to enforce fully the law of crimes. An area of *no enforcement* lies, therefore, between the perimeter of *total enforcement* and the outer limits of *full enforcement.* In this *no enforcement* area, the police have no authority to invoke the criminal process.

Within the area of *full enforcement,* the police have not been delegated discretion not to invoke the criminal process. On the contrary, those state statutes providing for municipal police departments which define the responsibility of police provide:

> It shall be the duty of the police . . . under the direction of the mayor and chief of police and in conformity with the ordinances of the city, and the laws of the state, . . . to pursue and arrest any persons fleeing from justice . . . to apprehend any and all persons in the act of committing any offense against the laws of the state . . . and to take the offender forthwith before the proper court or magistrate, to be dealt with for the offense; to make complaints to the proper officers and magistrates of any person known or believed by them to be guilty of the violation of the ordinances of the city or the penal laws of the state; and at all times diligently and faithfully to enforce all such laws. . . .

Even in jurisdictions without such a specific statutory definition, declarations of the *full enforcement* mandate generally appear in municipal charters, ordinances, or police manuals. Police manuals, for example, commonly provide, in sections detailing the duties at each level of the police hierarchy, that the captain, superintendent, lieutenant, or patrolman shall be responsible, so far as is in his power, for the prevention and detection of crime and the enforcement of all criminal laws and ordinances. Illustrative of the spirit and policy of *full enforcement* is this protestation from the introduction to the Rules and Regulations of the Atlanta, Georgia, Police Department:

> Enforcement of all Criminal Laws and City Ordinances, is my obligation. There are no specialties under the Law. My eyes must be open to traffic problems and disorders, though I move on other assignments, to slinking vice in back streets and dives though I have been directed elsewhere, to the suspicious appearance of evil wherever it is encountered. . . . I must be impartial because the Law surrounds, protects, and applies to all alike, rich and poor, low and high, black and white. . . .

Minimally, then, *full enforcement,* so far as the police are concerned, means (1) the investigation of every disturbing event which is reported to or observed by them and which they have reason to suspect may be a violation of the criminal law; (2) following a determination that some crime has been committed, an effort to discover its perpetrators; and (3) the presentation of all information collected by them to the prosecutor for his determination of the appropriateness of further invoking the criminal process.

Full enforcement, however, is not a realistic expectation. In addition to ambiguities in the definitions of both substantive offenses and due process boundaries, countless limitations and pressures preclude the possibility of the police seeking or achieving *full enforcement.* Limitations of time, personnel, and investigative devices—all in part but not entirely functions of budget—force the development, by plan or default, of priorities of enforcement. Even if there were "enough police" adequately equipped and trained, pressures from within and without the department, which is after all a human institution, may force the police to invoke the criminal process selectively. By decisions not to invoke within the area of *full enforcement,* the police largely determine the outer limits of *actual enforcement* throughout the criminal process. This relationship of the police to the total administration of criminal justice can be seen in the diagram [Figure 1]. They may reinforce, or they may undermine, the legislature's objectives in designating certain conduct "criminal" and in authorizing the imposition of certain sanctions following conviction. A police decision to ignore a felonious assault "because the victim will not sign a complaint," usually precludes the prosecutor or grand jury from deciding whether to accuse, judge or jury from determining guilt or innocence, judge from imposing the most "appropriate" sentence, probation or correctional authorities from instituting the most "appropriate" restraint and rehabilitation programs, and finally parole or pardon authorities from determining the offender's readiness for release to the community. This

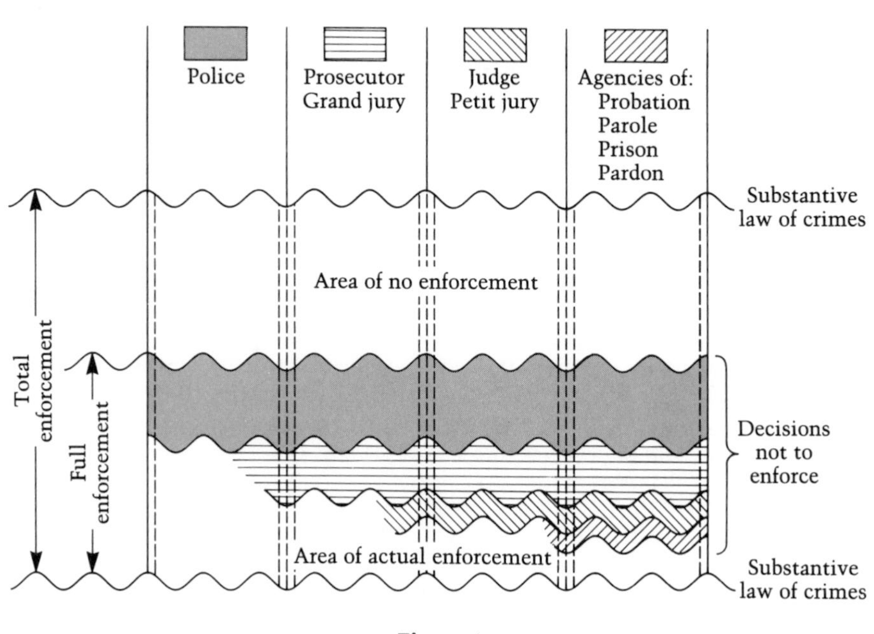

Figure 1

example is drawn from one of the three programs of nonenforcement about to be discussed.

III. Trading enforcement against a narcotics suspect for information about another narcotics offense or offender may involve two types of police decisions not to invoke fully the criminal process. First, there may be a decision to ask for the dismissal or reduction of the charge for which the informant is held; second, there may be a decision to overlook future violations while the suspect serves as an informer. The second type is an example of a relatively pure police decision not to invoke the criminal process while the first requires, at a minimum, tacit approval by prosecutor or judge. But examination of only the pure types of decisions would oversimplify the problem. They fail to illustrate the extent to which police nonenforcement decisions may permeate the process as well as influence, and be influenced by, prosecutor and court action in settings which fail to prompt appraisal of such decisions in light of the purposes of the criminal law. Both types of decision, pure and conglomerate, are nonetheless primarily police decisions. They are distinguishable from a prosecutor's or court's decision to trade information for enforcement under an immunity statute, and from such parliamentary decisions as the now-repealed seventeenth- and eighteenth-century English statutes which gave a convicted offender who secured the conviction of his accomplice an absolute right to pardon. Such prosecutor and parliamentary decisions to trade information for enforcement, unlike the police decisions to be described, have not only been authorized by a legislative body, but have also been made sufficiently visible to permit review.

In the municipality studied, regular uniformed officers, with general law enforcement duties on precinct assignments, and a special narcotics squad of detectives, with citywide jurisdiction, are responsible for enforcement of the state narcotics laws. The existence of the special squad acts as a pressure on the uniformed officer to be the first to discover any sale, possession, or use of narcotics in his precinct. Careful preparation of a case for prosecution may thus become secondary to this objective. Indeed, approximately 80 percent of those apprehended for narcotics violations during one year were discharged. In the opinion of the special squad, which processes each arrested narcotics suspect, either the search was illegal or the evidence obtained inadequate. The precinct officer's lack of interest in carefully developing a narcotics case for prosecution often amounts in effect to a police decision not to enforce but rather to harass.

But we are concerned here primarily with the decisions of the narcotics squad, which, like the Federal Narcotics Bureau, has established a policy of concentrating enforcement efforts against the "big supplier." The chief of the squad claimed that informers must be utilized to implement that policy, and that in order to get informants it is necessary to trade "little ones for big ones." Informers are used to arrange and make purchases of narcotics, to elicit information from suspects, including persons in custody, and to recruit additional informants.

Following arrest, a suspect will generally offer to serve as an informer to "do himself some good." If an arrestee fails to initiate such negotiations, the interrogating officer will suggest that something may be gained by disclosing sources of supply and by serving as an informer. A high mandatory minimum sentence for selling, a high maximum sentence for possession, and, where users are involved, a strong desire on their part to avoid the agonies of withdrawal, combine to place the police in an excellent bargaining position to recruit informers. To assure performance, each informer is charged with a narcotics violation, and final disposition is postponed until the defendant has fulfilled his part of the bargain. To protect the informer, the special squad seeks to camouflage him in the large body of releasees by not disclosing his identity even to the arresting precinct officer, who is given no explanation for release. Thus persons encountered on the street by a uniformed patrolman the day after their arrest may have been discharged, or they may have been officially charged and then released on bail or personal recognizance to await trial or to serve as informers.

While serving as informers, suspects are allowed to engage in illegal activity. Continued use of narcotics is condoned; the narcotics detective generally is not concerned with the problem of informants who make buys and use some of the evidence themselves. Though informers are usually warned that their status does not give them a "license to peddle," possession of a substantial amount of narcotics may be excused. In one case, a defendant found guilty of possession of marijuana argued that she was entitled to be placed on probation since she had cooperated with the police by testifying against three persons charged with the sale of narcotics. The sentencing judge denied her request because he discovered that her cooperation was related to the possession of a substantial amount of heroin, an offense for which she was arrested (but never charged) while on bail for the marijuana violation. A narcotics squad inspector, in response to an inquiry from the judge, revealed that the defendant had not been charged with possession of heroin because she had been cooperative with the police on that offense.

In addition to granting such outright immunity for some violations, the police will recommend to the prosecutor either that an informer's case be *nolle prossed* or, more frequently, that the charge be reduced to a lesser offense. And, if the latter course is followed, the police usually recommend to the judge, either in response to his request for information or in the presentence report, that informers be placed on probation or given relatively light sentences. Both the prosecutor and judge willingly respond to police requests for reducing a charge of sale to a lesser offense because they consider the mandatory minimum too severe. As a result, during a four-year period in this jurisdiction, less than 2.5 percent of all persons charged with the sale of narcotics were convicted of that offense.

The narcotics squad's policy of trading *full enforcement* for information is justified on the grounds that apprehension and prosecution of the "big supplier" is facilitated. The absence of any such individual is attributed to this policy. As one member of the squad said, "[The city] is too hot. There are too many informants." A basic, though untested, assumption of the policy is that ridding the city of the "big supplier" is the key to solving its narcotics problem. Even if this assumption were empirically validated, the desirability of continuing such a policy cannot be established without taking into account its total impact on the administration of criminal justice in the city, the state, and the nation. Yet no procedure has been designed to enable the police and other key administrators of criminal justice to obtain such an appraisal. The extent and nature of the need for such a procedure can be illustrated, despite the limitations of available data, by presenting in the form of a mock report some of the questions, some of the answers, and some of the proposals a Policy Appraisal and Review Board might consider.

Following a description of the informer program, a report might ask: *To what extent, if at all, has the legislature delegated to the police the authority to grant, or obtain a grant of, complete or partial immunity from prosecution, in exchange for information about narcotics suppliers?* No provisions of the general immunity or narcotics statutes authorize the police to exercise such discretion. The general immunity statute requires a high degree of visibility by providing that immunity be allowed only on a written motion by the prosecuting attorney to the court and that the information given be reduced to writing under the direction of the judge to preclude future prosecution for the traded offense or offenses. The narcotics statutes, unlike comparable legislation concerning other specific crimes, make no provision for obtaining information by awarding immunity from prosecution. Nor is there any indication, other than possibly in the maximum sentences authorized, that the legislature intended that certain narcotics offenses be given high priority or be enforced at the expense of other offenses. What evidence there is of legislative intent suggests the contrary; this fact is recognized by the local police manual. And nothing in the statute providing for the establishment of local police departments can be construed to authorize the policy of trading enforcement for information. That statute makes *full enforcement* a duty of the police. The narcotics squad has ignored this mandate and adopted an informer policy which appears to constitute a usurpation of legislative function. It does not follow that the police must discontinue employing informers, but they ought to discontinue trading enforcement for information until the legislature, the court, or the prosecutor explicitly initiates such a program. Whether the police policy of trading enforcement for information should be proposed for legislative consideration would depend upon the answers to some of the questions which follow.

Does trading enforcement for information fulfill the retributive, restraining, and reformative functions of the state's narcotics laws? By in effect licensing the user-informer to satisfy his addiction and assuring the peddler-informer, who may also be a user, that he will obtain dismissal or reduction of the pending charge to a lesser offense, the police undermine, if not negate, the retributive and restraining functions of the narcotics laws. In addition, the community is deprived of an opportunity to subject these offenders, particularly the addicts, to treatment aimed at reformation. In fact, the police ironically acknowledge the inconsistency of their program with the goal of treatment: "cured" addicts are not used as informers for fear that exposure to narcotics might cause their relapse. A comparison of the addict-release policies of the police, sentencing judge, and probation and parole authorities demonstrates the extent to which the administration of criminal justice can be set awry by a police nonenforcement program. At one point on the continuum, the police release the addict to informer status so that he can maintain his association with peddlers and users. The addict accepts such status on the tacit condition that continued use will be condoned. At other points on the continuum, the judge and probation and parole authorities make treatment a condition of an addict's release and continued use or even association with narcotics users the basis for revoking probation or parole. Thus the inherent conflict between basic purposes of the criminal law is compounded by conflicts among key decision-points in the process.

Does trading enforcement for information implement the deterrent function of criminal law administration? If deterrence depends—and little if anything is really known about the deterrent impact of the criminal law—in part at least, upon the potential offender's perception of law enforcement, the informer policy can have only a negative effect. In addition to the chance of nondetection which accompanies the commission of all crimes in varying degrees, the narcotics suspect has four-to-one odds that he will not be charged following detection and arrest. And he has a high expectation, even if charged, of obtaining a reduction or dismissal of an accurate charge. These figures reflect and reinforce the offender's view of the administration of criminal justice as a bargaining process initiated either by offering information "to do himself some good" or by a member of the narcotics squad advising the uninformed suspect, the "new offender," of the advantages of disclosing his narcotics "connections." Such law enforcement can have little, if any, deterrent impact.

That the "big supplier," an undefined entity, has been discouraged from using the city as a headquarters was confirmed by a local federal agent and a U.S. attorney in testimony before a Senate committee investigating illicit narcotics traffic. They attributed the result, however, to the state's high mandatory minimum sentence for selling, not to the informer policy. In fact, that municipal police policy was not made visible at the hearings. It was mentioned neither in their testimony nor in the testimony of the chief of police and the head of the narcotics squad. These local authorities may have reasoned that since the mandatory sentence facilitates the recruitment of informers who, in turn, are essential to keeping the "big supplier" outside city limits, the legislature's sentencing policy could be credited with the "achievement."

Whether the police informer program, the legislature's sentencing policy, both, or neither, caused the "big supplier" to locate elsewhere is not too significant; the traffic and use of narcotics in the city remain major problems. Since user-demand is maintained, if not increased, by trading enforcement for information, potential and actual peddlers are encouraged to supply the city's addicts. Testimony before the Senate committee indicates that although the "big suppliers" have moved their headquarters to other cities, there are now in the city a large number of small peddlers serving a minimum of 1,500 and in all probability a total of 2,500 users, and that the annual expenditure for illicit narcotics in the city is estimated at not lower than $10 million and probably as high as $18 million. Evaluated in terms of deterrent effect, the program of trading enforcement for information to reach the "big supplier" has failed to implement locally the ultimate objective of the narcotics laws—reducing addiction. Furthermore, the business of the "big supplier" has not been effectively deterred. At best suppliers have been discouraged from basing their operations in the city, which continues to be a lucrative market. Thus by maintaining the market, local policy, although a copy of national policy, may very well hinder the efforts of the Federal Narcotics Bureau.

A report of a Policy Appraisal and Review Board might find: "Trading little ones for big ones" is outside the ambit of municipal police discretion and should continue to remain so because it conflicts with the basic objectives of the criminal law. Retribution, restraint, and reformation are subverted by a policy which condones the use and possession of narcotics. And deterrence cannot be enhanced by a police program which provides potential and actual suppliers and users with more illustrations of nonenforcement than enforcement.

A report might conclude by exploring and suggesting alternative programs for coping with the narcotics problem. No attempt will be made here to exhaust or detail all possible alternatives. An obvious one would be a rigorous program of *full enforcement* designed to dry up, or at least drastically reduce, local consumer and peddler demand for illicit narcotics. If information currently obtained from suspects is essential and worth a price, compensation might be given to informers, with payments deferred until a suspect's final release. Such a program would neither undermine the retributive and restraining objectives of the criminal law nor deprive the community of an opportunity to impose rehabilitation regimes on the offender. Funds provided by deferred payments might enhance an offender's chances of getting off to a good start upon release. Moreover, changing the picture presently perceived by potential violators from nonenforcement to enforcement would at least not preclude the possibility of deterrence. Such a program might even facilitate the apprehension of "big suppliers" who, faced with decreasing demand, might either be forced to discontinue serving the city because sales would no longer be profitable or to adopt bolder sales methods which would expose them to easier detection.

Full enforcement will place the legislature in a position to evaluate its narcotics laws by providing a basis for answering such questions as: Will *full enforcement* increase the price of narcotics to the user? Will such inflation increase the frequency of crimes committed to finance narcotics purchases? Or will *full enforcement* reduce the number of users and the frequency of connected crimes? Will too great or too costly an administrative burden be placed on the prosecutor's office and the courts by *full enforcement?* Will correctional institutions be filled beyond "effective" capacity? The answers to these questions are now buried or obscured by decisions not to invoke the criminal process.

Failure of a *full enforcement* program might prompt a board recommendation to increase treatment or correctional personnel and facilities. Or a board, recognizing that *full enforcement* would be either too costly or inherently ineffective, might propose the repeal of statutes prohibiting the use and sale of narcotics and/or the enactment, as part of a treatment program, of legislation authorizing sales to users at a low price. Such legislative action would be designed to reduce use and connected offenses to a minimum. By taking profits out of sales it would lessen peddler incentive to create new addicts and eliminate the need to support the habit by the commission of crimes.

These then are the kinds of questions, answers, and proposals a Policy Appraisal and Review Board might explore in its report examining this particular type of police decision not to invoke the criminal process.

IV. Another low-visibility situation which an Appraisal and Review Board might uncover in this municipality stems from police decisions not to invoke the felonious assault laws unless the victim signs a complaint. Like the addict-informer, the potential complainant in an assault case is both the victim of an offense and a key source of information. But unlike him, the complainant, who is not a suspect, and whose initial contact with the police is generally self-imposed, is not placed under pressure to bargain. And in contrast with the informer program, the police assault program was clearly not designed, if designed at all, to effectuate an identifiable policy.

During one month under the nonenforcement program of a single precinct, thirty-eight out of forty-three felonious assault cases, the great majority involving stabbings and cuttings, were cleared "because the victim refused to prosecute." This program, which is coupled with a practice of not encouraging victims to sign complaints, reduces the pressure of work by eliminating such tasks as apprehending and detaining suspects, writing detailed reports, applying for warrants to prefer charges, and appearing in court at inconvenient times for long periods without adequate compensation. As one officer explained, "run-of-the-mill" felonious assaults are so common in his precinct that prosecution of each case would force patrolmen to spend too much time in court and leave too little time for investigating other offenses. This rationalization exposes the private value system of individual officers as another policy-shaping factor. Some policemen feel, for example, that assault is an acceptable means of settling disputes among Negroes, and that when both assailant and victim are Negro, there is no immediate discernible harm to the public which justifies a decision to invoke the criminal process. Anticipation of dismissal by judge and district attorney of cases in which the victim is an uncooperative witness, the police claim, has been another operative factor in the development of the assault policy. A Policy Appraisal and Review Board, whose investigators had been specifically directed to examine the assault policy, should be able to identify these or other policy-shaping factors more precisely. Yet on the basis of the data available, a board could tentatively conclude that court and prosecutor responses do not explain why the police have failed to adopt a policy of encouraging assault victims to sign complaints, and, therefore, that the private value system of department members, as reflected in their attitude toward workload and in a stereotypical view of the Negro, is of primary significance.

Once some of the major policy-shaping factors have been identified, an Appraisal and Review Board might formulate and attempt to answer the following or similar questions: Would it be consistent with any of the purposes of the criminal law to authorize police discretion in cases of felonious assaults as well as other specified offenses? Assuming that it would be consistent or at least more realistic to authorize police discretion in some cases, what limitations and guides, if any, should the legislature provide? Should legislation provide that factors such as workload, willingness of victims or certain victims to sign a complaint, the degree of violence, and attitude of prosecutor and judge be taken into account in the exercise of police discretion? If workload is to be recognized, should the legislature establish priorities of enforcement designed to assist the police in deciding which offenses among equally pressing ones are to be ignored or enforced? If assaults are made criminal in order to reduce threats to community peace and individual security, should a victim's willingness to prosecute, if he happens to live, be relevant to the exercise of police discretion? Does resting prosecution in the hands of the victim encourage him to "get even" with the assailant through retaliatory lawlessness? Or does such a policy place the decision in the hands of the assailant whose use of force has already demonstrated an ability and willingness to fulfill a threat?

Can the individual police officer, despite his own value system, sufficiently respond to officially articulated community values to be delegated broad powers of discretion? If not, can or should procedures be designed to enable the police department to translate these values into rules and regulations for individual policemen? Can police officers or the department be trained to evaluate the extent to which current practice undermines a major criminal law objective of imposing upon all persons officially recognized minimum standards of human behavior? For example, can the individual officer of the department be trained to evaluate the effect of decisions in cases of felonious assault among Negroes on local programs for implementing national or state policies of integration in school, employment, and housing, and to determine the extent to which current policy weakens or reinforces stereotypes which are used to justify not only police policy, but more importantly, opposition to desegregation programs? Or should legislation provide that the police invoke the process in all felonious assault cases unless the prosecutor or court publicly provides them in recorded documents with authority and guides for exercising discretion, and thus make visible both the policy of nonenforcement and the agency or agencies responsible for it?

Some of these issues were considered and resolved by the Oakland, California, Police Department in 1957 when, after consultation with prosecutors and judges, it decided to abandon a similar assault policy and seek *full enforcement.* Chief of Police W. W. Vernon, describing Oakland's new program, wrote:

> In our assault cases for years we had followed this policy of releasing the defendant if the complainant did not feel aggrieved to the point of being willing to testify. . . . [Since] World War II . . . our assault cases increased tremendously to the point where we decided to do something about the increase.

Training materials prepared by the Oakland Police Academy disclose that between 1952 and 1956, while the decision to prosecute was vested in the victim, the rate of reported felonious assaults rose from 93 to 161 per 100,000 population and the annual number of misdemeanor assaults rose from 618 to 2,630. The materials emphasize that these statistics mean a workload of "nearly ten assault reports a day every day of the year." But they stress:

> The important point about these figures is not so much that they represent a substantial police workload, which they do, but more important, that they indicate an increasing lack of respect for the laws of society by a measurable segment of our population, and a corresponding threat to the rest of the citizens of our city. The police have a clear responsibility to develop respect for the law among those who disregard it in order to ensure the physical safety and well-being of those who do. . . .
>
> We recognize that the problem exists mainly because the injured person has refused to sign a complaint against the perpetrator. The injured person has usually refused to sign for two reasons: first, because of threats of future bodily harm or other action by the perpetrator and, secondly, because it has been a way of life among some people to adjust grievances by physical assaults and not by the recognized laws of society which are available to them.
>
> We, the police, have condoned these practices to some extent by not taking advantage of the means at our disposal; that is, by not gathering sufficient evidence and signing complaints on information and belief in those cases where the complainant refuses to prosecute. The policy and procedure of gathering sufficient evidence and signing complaints on information and belief should instill in these groups the realization that the laws of society must be resorted to in settling disputes. When it is realized by many of these people that we will sign complaints ourselves and will not condone fighting and cuttings, many of them will stop such practices.

Following conferences with the police, the local prosecutors and judges pledged their support for the new assault program. The district attorney's office will deny a complainant's request that a case be dropped and suggest that it be addressed to the judge in open court. The judge, in turn, will advise the complainant that the case cannot be dismissed, and that a perjury, contempt, or false-report complaint will be issued in "appropriate cases" against the victim who denies facts originally alleged. The police have been advised that the court and prosecutor will actively cooperate in the implementation of the new program, but that every case will not result in a complaint since it is the "job [of the police] to turn in the evidence and it's the prosecuting attorney's job to determine when a complaint will be issued." Thus the role of each of the key decision-making agencies with preconviction invoking authority is clearly delineated and integrated.

With the inauguration of a new assault policy, an Appraisal and Review Board might establish procedures for determining how effectively the objectives of the policy are fulfilled in practice. A board might design intelligence-retrieving devices which would provide more complete data than the following termed by Chief Vernon "the best evidence that our program is accomplishing the purpose for which it was developed." Prior to the adoption of the new policy, 80 percent of the felonious assault cases "cleared" were cleared because "complainant refuses to prosecute," while only 32.2 percent of the clearances made during the first three months in 1958 were for that reason, even though the overall clearance rate rose during that period. And "during the first quarter of this year Felony Assaults dropped 11.1 percent below the same period last year, and in March they were 35.6 percent below March of last year. Battery cases were down 19.0 percent for the first three months of 1958." An Appraisal and Review Board might attempt to determine the extent to which the police in cases formerly dropped because "complainant refused to testify" have consciously or otherwise substituted another reason for "case cleared." And it might estimate the extent to which the decrease in assaults *reported* reflects, if it does, a decrease in the *actual* number of assaults or only a decrease in the number of victims willing to report assaults. Such follow-up investigations and what actually took place in Oakland on an informal basis between police, prosecutor, and judge illustrate some of the functions an Appraisal and Review Board might regularly perform.

V. Police decisions to harass, though generally perceived as overzealous enforcement, constitute another body of nonenforcement activities meriting investigation by an Appraisal and Review Board. Harassment is the imposition by the police, acting under color of law, of sanctions prior to conviction as a means of ultimate punishment, rather than as a device for the invocation of criminal proceedings. Characteristic of harassment are efforts to annoy certain "offenders" both by temporarily detaining or arresting them without intention to seek prosecution and by destroying or illegally seizing their property without any intention to use it as evidence. Like other police decisions not to invoke the criminal process, harassment is generally of extremely low visibility, probably because the police ordinarily restrict such activity to persons who are unable to afford the costs of litigation, who would, or think they would, command little respect even if they were to complain, or who wish to keep themselves out of public view in order to continue their illicit activities. Like the informer program, harassment is conducted by the police in an atmosphere of cooperation with other administrators of criminal justice. Since harassment, by definition, is outside the rule of law, any benefits attributed to such police activity cannot justify its continuation. An Appraisal and Review Board, however, would not limit its investigations to making such a finding. It would be expected to identify and analyze factors underlying harassment and to formulate proposals for replacing harassment—lawless nonenforcement—with enforcement of the criminal law.

Investigators for an Appraisal and Review Board in this jurisdiction would discover, for example, a mixture of enforcement and harassment in a police program designed to regulate the gambling operations of mutual-numbers syndicates. The enforcement phase is conducted by a highly trained unit of less than a dozen men who diligently gather evidence in order to prosecute and convict syndicate operators of conspiracy to violate the gambling laws. This specialized unit, which operates independently of and without the knowledge of other officers, conducts all its work within the due process boundaries of *full enforcement.* Consequently, the conviction rate is high for charges based upon its investigations. The harassment phase is conducted by approximately sixty officers who tour the city and search on sight, because of prior information, or such telltale actions as carrying a paper bag, a symbol of the trade, persons who they suspect are collecting bets. They question the "suspect" and proceed to search him, his car, or home without first making a valid arrest to legalize the search. If gambling paraphernalia are found, the police, fully aware that the exclusionary rule prohibits its use as evidence in this jurisdiction, confiscate the "contraband" and arrest the individual without any intention of seeking application of the criminal law.

Gambling operators treat the harassment program as a cost of doing business, "a risk of the trade." Each syndicate retains a bonding firm and an attorney to service members who are arrested. When a "runner" or "bagman" is absent from his scheduled rounds, routine release procedures are initiated. The bondsman, sometimes prematurely, checks with the police to determine if a syndicate man has been detained. If the missing man is in custody, the syndicate's attorney files an application for a writ of habeas corpus and appears before a magistrate who usually sets bail at a nominal amount and adjourns hearing the writ, at the request of the police, until the following day. Prior to the scheduled hearing, the police usually advise the court that they have no intention of proceeding, and the case is closed. Despite the harassee's release, the police retain the money and gambling paraphernalia. If the items seized are found in a car, the car is confiscated, with the cooperation of the prosecutor, under a nuisance abatement statute. Cars are returned, however, after the harassee signs a "consent decree" and pursuant to it, pays "court costs"—a fee which is based on the car's value and which the prosecutor calls "the real meat of the harassment program." The "decree," entered under a procedure devised by the court and prosecutor's office, enjoins the defendant from engaging in illegal activity and, on paper, frees the police from any tort liability by an acknowledgment that seizure of the vehicle was lawful and justified—even though one prosecutor has estimated that approximately 80 percent of the searches and seizures were illegal. A prosecuting attorney responsible for car confiscation initially felt that such procedures "in the ordinary practice of law would be unethical, revolting, and shameful," but explained that he now understands why he acted as he did:

> To begin with . . . the laws in . . . [this state] with respect to gambling are most inadequate. This is equally true of the punishment feature of the law. To illustrate . . . a well-organized and productive gambling house or numbers racket would take in one-quarter of a million dollars each week. If, after a long and vigorous period of investigation and observation, the defendant was charged with violating the gambling laws and convicted therefor, the resulting punishment is so obviously weak and unprohibitive that the defendants are willing to shell out a relatively small fine or serve a relatively short time in prison. The . . . [city's] gamblers and numbers men confidently feel that the odds are in their favor. If they operate for six months or a year, and accumulate untold thousands of dollars from the illegal activity, then the meager punishment imposed upon them if they are caught is well worth it. Then, too, because of the search and seizure laws in . . . [this state], especially in regard to gambling and the numbers rackets, the hands of the police are tied. Unless a search can be made prior to an arrest so that the defendant can be caught in the act of violating the gambling laws, or a search warrant issued, there is no other earthly way of apprehending such people along with evidence sufficient to convict them that is admissible in court.
>
> Because of these two inadequacies of the law (slight punishment and conservative search and seizure laws with regard to gambling) the prosecutor's office and the police department are forced to find other means of punishing, harassing, and generally making life uneasy for gamblers.

This position, fantastic as it is to be that of a law-trained official, a guardian of the rule of law, illustrates how extensively only one of many police harassment programs in this jurisdiction can permeate the process and be tolerated by other decision makers in a system of criminal administration where decisions not to enforce are of extremely low visibility.

Having uncovered such a gambling-control program, an Appraisal and Review Board should recommend that the police abandon such harassment activities because they are antagonistic to the rule of law. In addition, the board might advance secondary reasons for eliminating harassment by exposing the inconsistencies between this program and departmental justifications for its narcotics and assault policies. While unnecessary to the condemnation of what is fundamentally lawless nonenforcement, such exposure might cause the police to question the wisdom of actions based on a personal or departmental belief that the legislature has authorized excessively lenient sanctions and restrictive enforcement procedures. The comparison might emphasize the inconsistencies of police policy toward organized crime by exposing the clash between an informer program designed to rid the city of the "big supplier" and a harassment program which tends to consolidate control of the numbers racket in a few syndicates "big" enough to sustain the legal, bonding, and other "business" costs of continued interruptions and the confiscation of property. More importantly, it should cause a reexamination and redefinition of "workload" which was so significant in the rationalization of the assault policy. A cost accounting would no doubt reveal that a significant part of "workload," as presently defined by the police, includes expenditures of public funds for personnel and equipment employed in unlawful activities. Once harassment is perceived by municipal officials concerned with budgets as an unauthorized expenditure of public funds, consideration for increased awards to the police department might be conditioned upon a showing that existing resources are now deployed for authorized purposes. Such action should stimulate police cooperation in implementing the board's proposal for curtailing harassment.

Further, to effectuate its recommendation, the board might attempt to clarify and redefine the duties of the police by a reclassification of crimes which would emphasize the mandate that no more than *full enforcement* of the existing criminal law as defined by the legislature is expected. For many crimes, this may mean little or no *actual enforcement* because the values protected by procedural limitations are more important than the values which may be infringed by a particular offense. A board might propose, for example, that crimes be classified not only as felonies and misdemeanors, but in terms of active and passive police enforcement. An *active enforcement* designation for an offense would mean that individual police officers or specialized squads are to be assigned the task of ferreting out and even triggering violations. *Passive enforcement* would mean that the police are to assume a sit-back-and-wait posture, i.e., that they invoke the criminal process only when the disturbing event is brought to their attention by personal observation during a routine tour of duty or by someone outside the police force registering a complaint. Designation of gambling, for example, as a *passive enforcement* offense would officially apprise the police that substantial expenditures of personnel and equipment for enforcement are not contemplated unless the local community expresses a low tolerance for such disturbing events by constantly bringing them to police attention. The adoption of this or a similar classification scheme might not only aid in training the police to understand that harassment is unlawful, but it may also provide the legislature with a device for officially allowing local differences in attitude toward certain offenses to be reflected in police practice and for testing the desirability of removing criminal sanctions from certain kinds of currently proscribed behavior.

VI. The mandate of *full enforcement,* under circumstances which compel selective enforcement, has placed the municipal police in an intolerable position. As a result, nonenforcement programs have developed undercover, in a hit-or-miss fashion, and without regard to impact on the overall administration of justice or the basic objectives of the criminal law. Legislatures, therefore, ought to reconsider what discretion, if any, the police must or should have in invoking the criminal process, and what devices, if any, should be designed to increase visibility and hence reviewability of these police decisions.

The ultimate answer is that the police should not be delegated discretion not to invoke the criminal law. It is recognized, of course, that the exercise of discretion cannot be completely eliminated where human beings are involved. The frailties of human language and human perception will always admit of borderline cases (although none of the situations analyzed in this article are "borderline"). But nonetheless, outside this margin of ambiguity, the police should operate in an atmosphere which exhorts and commands them to invoke impartially all criminal laws within the bounds of *full enforcement*. If a criminal law is ill-advised, poorly defined, or too costly to enforce, efforts by the police to achieve *full enforcement* should generate pressures for legislative action. Responsibility for the enactment, amendment, and repeal of the criminal laws will not, then, be abandoned to the whim of each police officer or department, but retained where it belongs in a democracy—with elected representatives.

Equating *actual enforcement* with *full enforcement*, however, would be neither workable nor humane nor humanly possible under present conditions in most, if not all, jurisdictions. Even if there were "enough police" (and there are not) to enforce all of the criminal laws, too many people have come to rely on the nonenforcement of too many "obsolete" laws to justify the embarrassment, discomfort, and misery which would follow implementation of *full enforcement* programs for every crime. *Full enforcement* is a program for the future, a program which could be initiated with the least hardship when the states, perhaps stimulated by the work of the American Law Institute, enact new criminal codes clearing the books of obsolete offenses.

In the interim, legislatures should establish Policy Appraisal and Review Boards not only to facilitate coordination of municipal police policies with those of other key criminal law administrators, but also to assist commissions drafting new codes in reappraising basic objectives of the criminal law and in identifying laws which have become obsolete. To ensure that board appraisals and recommendations facilitate the integration of police policies with overall state policies and to ensure the cooperation of local authorities, board membership might include the state's attorney general, the chief justice of the supreme court, the chairman of the department of correction, the chairman of the board of parole and the chief of parole supervision, the chairman of the department of probation, the chairman of the judiciary committees of the legislature, the chief of the state police, the local chief of police, the local prosecutor, and the chief judge of each of the local trial courts. In order regularly and systematically to cull and retrieve information, the board should be assisted by a full-time director who has a staff of investigators well trained in social science research techniques. It should be given power to subpoena persons and records and to assign investigators to observe all phases of police activity including routine patrols, bookings, raids, and contacts with both the courts and the prosecutor's office. To clarify its functions, develop procedures, determine personnel requirements, and test the idea itself, the board's jurisdiction should initially be restricted to one or two major municipalities in the state. The board would review, appraise, and make recommendations concerning municipal police nonenforcement policies as well as follow up and review the consequences of implemented proposals. In order to make its job both manageable and less subject to attack by those who cherish local autonomy and who may see the establishment of a board as a step toward centralization, it would have solely an advisory function and limit its investigations to the enforcement of state laws, not municipal ordinances. And to ensure that board activity will not compromise current enforcement campaigns or place offenders on notice of new techniques of detection or sources of information, boards should be authorized, with court approval, to withhold specified reports from general publication for a limited and fixed time.

Like other administrative agencies, a Policy Appraisal and Review Board will in time no doubt suffer from marasmus and outlive its usefulness. But while viable, such a board has an enormous potential for uncovering in a very dramatic fashion basic inadequacies in the administration of criminal justice and for prompting a thorough community reexamination of the why of a law of crimes.

ARTICLE FIVE

Broken Windows: The Police and Neighborhood Safety

JAMES Q. WILSON and GEORGE L. KELLING

The role of the police in the United States today is being reexamined. After almost a half-century of emphasis on professionalism, crime control, and efficiency, James Q. Wilson and George L. Kelling argue that there should be a shift in patrol strategy toward a focus on order maintenance and community accountability.

In the mid-1970s, the state of New Jersey announced a "Safe and Clean Neighborhoods Program," designed to improve the quality of community life in twenty-eight cities. As part of that program, the state provided money to help cities take police officers out of their patrol cars and assign them to walking beats. The governor and other state officials were enthusiastic about using foot patrol as a way of cutting crime, but many police chiefs were skeptical. Foot patrol, in their eyes, had been pretty much discredited. It reduced the mobility of the police, who thus had difficulty responding to citizen calls for service, and it weakened headquarters control over patrol officers.

Many police officers also disliked foot patrol, but for different reasons: it was hard work, it kept them outside on cold, rainy nights, and it reduced their chances for making a "good pinch." In some departments, assigning officers to foot patrol had been used as a form of punishment. And academic experts on policing doubted that foot patrol would have any impact on crime rates; it was, in the opinion of most, little more than a sop to

Source: Atlantic Monthly 249 (March 1982): 29–38. By permission of the publisher.

public opinion. But since the state was paying for it, the local authorities were willing to go along.

Five years after the program started, the Police Foundation, in Washington, D.C., published an evaluation of the foot-patrol project. Based on its analysis of a carefully controlled experiment carried out chiefly in Newark, the foundation concluded, to the surprise of hardly anyone, that foot patrol had not reduced crime rates. But residents of the foot-patrolled neighborhoods seemed to feel more secure than persons in other areas, tended to believe that crime had been reduced, and seemed to take fewer steps to protect themselves from crime (staying at home with the doors locked, for example). Moreover, citizens in the foot-patrol areas had a more favorable opinion of the police than did those living elsewhere. And officers walking beats had higher morale, greater job satisfaction, and a more favorable attitude toward citizens in their neighborhoods than did officers assigned to patrol cars.

These findings may be taken as evidence that the skeptics were right—foot patrol has no effect on crime; it merely fools the citizens into thinking that they are safer. But in our view, and in the view of the authors of the Police Foundation study (of whom Kelling was one), the citizens of Newark were not fooled at all. They knew what the foot-patrol officers were doing, they knew it was different from what motorized officers do, and they knew that having officers walk beats did in fact make their neighborhoods safer.

But how can a neighborhood be "safer" when the crime rate has not gone down—in fact, may have gone up? Finding the answer requires first that we understand what most often frightens people in public places. Many citizens, of course, are primarily frightened by crime, especially crime involving a sudden, violent attack by a stranger. This risk is very real, in Newark as in many large cities. But we tend to overlook or forget another source of fear: the fear of being bothered by disorderly people—not violent people, nor, necessarily, criminals, but disreputable or obstreperous or unpredictable people: panhandlers, drunks, addicts, rowdy teenagers, prostitutes, loiters, the mentally disturbed.

What foot-patrol officers did was to elevate, to the extent they could, the level of public order in these neighborhoods. Though the neighborhoods were predominantly black and the foot patrolmen were mostly white, this "order-maintenance" function of the police was performed to the general satisfaction of both parties.

One of us (Kelling) spent many hours walking with Newark foot-patrol officers to see how they defined "order" and what they did to maintain it. One beat was typical: a busy but dilapidated area in the heart of Newark, with many abandoned buildings, marginal shops (several of which prominently displayed knives and straight-edged razors in their windows), one large department store, and, most important, a train station and several major bus stops. Though the area was run-down, its streets were filled with people, because it was a major transportation center. The good order of this area was important not only to those who lived and worked there but also to many others who had to move through it on their way home, to supermarkets, or to factories.

The people on the street were primarily black; the officer who walked the street were white. The people were made up of "regulars" and "strangers." Regulars included both "decent folk" and some drunks and derelicts who were always there but who "knew their place." Strangers were, well, strangers, and viewed suspiciously, sometimes apprehensively. The officer—call him Kelly—knew who the regulars were, and they knew him. As he saw his job, he was to keep an eye on strangers, and make certain that the disreputable regulars observed some informal but widely understood rules. Drunks and addicts could sit on the stoops, but could not lie down. People could drink on the side streets, but not on the main intersection. Bottles had to be in paper bags. Talking to, bothering, or begging from people waiting at the bus stop was strictly forbidden. If a dispute erupted between a businessman and a customer, the businessman was assumed to be right, especially if the customer was a stranger. If a stranger loitered, Kelly would ask him if he had any means of support and what his business was; if he gave unsatisfactory answers, he was sent on his way. Persons who broke the informal rules, especially those who bothered people waiting at bus stops, were arrested for vagrancy. Noisy teenagers were told to keep quiet.

These rules were defined and enforced in collaboration with the "regulars" on the street. Another neighborhood might have different rules, but these, everybody understood, were the rules for *this* neighborhood. If someone violated them, the regulars not only turned to Kelly for help but also ridiculed the violator. Sometimes what Kelly did could be described as "enforcing the law," but just as often it involved taking informal or extralegal steps to help protect what the neighborhood had decided was the appropriate level of public order. Some of the things he did probably would not withstand a legal challenge.

A determined skeptic might acknowledge that a skilled foot-patrol officer can maintain order but still insist that this sort of "order" has little to do with the real sources of community fear—that is, with violent crime. To a degree, that is true. But two things must be borne in mind. First, outside observers should not assume that they know how much of the anxiety now endemic in many big-city neighborhoods stems from a fear of "real" crime and how much from a sense that the street is disorderly, a source of distasteful, worrisome encounters. The people of Newark, to judge from their behavior and their remarks to interviewers, apparently assign a high value to public order, and feel relieved and reassured when the police help them maintain that order.

Second, at the community level, disorder and crime are usually inextricably linked, in a kind of developmental sequence. Social psychologists and police officers tend to agree that if a window in a building is broken *and is left unrepaired,* all the rest of the windows will soon be broken. This is as true in nice neighborhoods as in run-down ones. Window breaking does not necessarily occur on a large scale because some areas are inhabited by determined window breakers whereas others are populated by window lovers; rather, one unrepaired broken window is a signal that no one cares, and so breaking more windows costs nothing. (It has always been fun.)

Philip Zimbardo, a Stanford psychologist, reported in 1969 on some experiments testing the broken-window theory. He arranged to have an automobile without license plates parked with its hood up on a street in the Bronx and a comparable automobile on a street in Palo Alto, California. The car in the Bronx was attacked by "vandals" within ten minutes of its "abandonment." The first to arrive were a family—father, mother, and young son—who removed the radiator and battery. Within twenty-four hours, virtually everything of value had been removed. Then random destruction began—windows were smashed, parts torn off, upholstery ripped. Children began to use the car as a playground. Most of the adult "vandals" were well-dressed, apparently clean-cut whites. The car in Palo Alto sat untouched for more than a week. Then Zimbardo smashed part of it with a sledgehammer. Soon, passersby were joining in. Within a few hours, the car had been turned upside down and utterly destroyed. Again, the "vandals" appeared to be primarily respectable whites.

Untended property becomes fair game for people out for fun or plunder, and even for people who ordinarily would not dream of doing such things and who probably consider themselves law-abiding. Because of the nature of community life in the Bronx—its anonymity, the frequency with which cars are abandoned and things are stolen or broken, the past experience of "no one caring"—vandalism begins much more quickly than it does in staid Palo Alto, where people have come to believe that private possessions are cared for, and that mischievous behavior is costly. But vandalism can occur anywhere once communal barriers—the sense of mutual regard and the obligations of civility—are lowered by actions that seem to signal that "no one cares."

We suggest that "untended" behavior also leads to the breakdown of community controls. A stable neighborhood of families who care for their homes, mind each other's children, and confidently frown on unwanted intruders can change, in a few years or even a few months, to an inhospitable and frightening jungle. A piece of property is abandoned, weeds grow up, a window is smashed. Adults stop scolding rowdy children; the children, emboldened, become more rowdy. Families move out, unattached adults move in. Teenagers gather in front of the corner store. The merchants asks them to move; they refuse. Fights occur. Litter accumulates. People start drinking in front of the grocery; in time, an inebriate slumps to the sidewalk and is allowed to sleep it off. Pedestrians are approached by panhandlers.

At this point it is not inevitable that serious crime will flourish or violent attacks on strangers will occur. But many residents will think that crime, especially violent crime is on the rise, and they will modify their behavior accordingly. They will use the streets less often, and when on the streets will stay apart from their fellows, moving with averted eyes, silent lips, and hurried steps. "Don't get involved." For some residents, this growing atomization will matter little, because the neighborhood is not their "home" but "the place where they live." Their interests are elsewhere; they are cosmopolitans. But it will matter greatly to other people, whose lives derive meaning and satisfaction from local attachments rather than worldly involvement; for them, the neighborhood will cease to exist except for a few reliable friends whom they arrange to meet.

Such an area is vulnerable to criminal invasion. Though it is not inevitable, it is more likely that here, rather than in places where people are confident they can regulate public behavior by informal controls, drugs will change hands, prostitutes will solicit, and cars will be stripped. That the drunks will be robbed by boys who do it as a lark, and the prostitutes' customers will be robbed by men who do it purposefully and perhaps violently. That muggings will occur.

Among those who often find it difficult to move away from this are the elderly. Surveys of citizens suggest that the elderly are much less likely to be the victims of crime than younger persons, and some have inferred from this that the well-known fear of crime voiced by the elderly is an exaggeration: perhaps we ought not to design special programs to protect older persons; perhaps we should even try to talk them out of their mistaken fears. This argument misses the point. The prospect of a confrontation with an obstreperous teenager or a drunken panhandler can be as fear-inducing for defenseless persons as the prospect of meeting an actual robber; indeed, to a defenseless person, the two kinds of confrontation are often indistinguishable. Moreover, the lower rate at which the elderly are victimized is a measure of the steps they have already taken—chiefly, staying behind locked doors—to minimize the risks they face. Young men are more frequently attacked than older women, not because they are easier or more lucrative targets but because they are on the streets more.

Nor is the connection between disorderliness and fear made only by the elderly. Susan Estrich, of the Harvard Law School, has recently gathered together a number of surveys on the sources of public fear. One, done in Portland, Oregon, indicated that three-fourths of the adults interviewed cross to the other side of a street when they see a gang of teenagers; another survey, in Baltimore, discovered that nearly half would cross the street to avoid even a single strange youth. When an interviewer asked people in a housing project where the most dangerous spot was, they mentioned a place where young persons gathered to drink and play music, despite the fact that not a single crime had occurred there. In Boston public housing projects, the greatest fear was expressed by persons living in the buildings where disorderliness and incivility, not crime, were the greatest. Knowing this helps one understand the significance of such otherwise harmless displays as subway graffiti. As Nathan Glazer has written, the proliferation of graffiti, even when not obscene, confronts the subway rider with the "inescapable knowledge that the environment he must endure for an hour or more a day is uncontrolled and uncontrollable, and that anyone can invade it to do whatever damage and mischief the mind suggests."

In response to fear, people avoid one another, weakening controls. Sometimes they call the police. Patrol cars arrive, an occasional arrest occurs, but crime continues and disorder is not abated. Citizens complain to the police chief, but he explains that his department is low on personnel and that the courts do not punish petty or first-time offenders. To the residents, the police who arrive in squad cars are either ineffective or uncaring; to the police, the residents are animals who deserve each other. The citizens may soon stop calling the police, because "they can't do anything."

The process we call urban decay has occurred for centuries in every city. But what is happening today is different in at least two important respects. First, in the period before, say, World War II, city dwellers—because of money costs, transportation difficulties, familial and church connections—could rarely move away from neighborhood problems. When movement did occur, it tended to be along public-transit routes. Now mobility has become exceptionally easy for all but the poorest or those who are blocked by racial prejudice. Earlier crime waves had a kind of built-in self-correcting mechanism: the determination of a neighborhood or community to reassert control over its turf. Areas in Chicago, New York, and Boston would experience crime and gang wars, and then normalcy would return, as the families for whom no alternative residences were possible reclaimed their authority over the streets.

Second, the police in this earlier period assisted in that reassertion of authority by acting, sometimes violently, on behalf of the community. Young toughs were roughed up, people were arrested "on suspicion" or for vagrancy, and prostitutes and petty thieves were routed. "Rights" were something enjoyed by decent folk, and perhaps also by the serious professional criminal, who avoided violence and could afford a lawyer.

This pattern of policing was not an aberration or the result of occasional excess. From the earliest days of the nation, the police function was seen primarily as that of a night watchman: to maintain order against the chief threats to order—fire, wild animals, and disreputable behavior. Solving crimes was viewed not as a police responsibility but as a private one. In the March 1969 *Atlantic,* one of us (Wilson) wrote a brief account of how the police role had slowly changed from maintaining order to fighting crimes. The change began with the creation of private detectives (often ex-criminals), who worked on a contingency-fee basis for individuals who had suffered losses. In time, the detectives were absorbed into municipal police agencies and paid a regular salary; simultaneously, the responsibility for prosecuting thieves was shifted from the aggrieved private citizen to the professional prosecutor. The process was not complete in most places until the twentieth century.

In the 1960s, when urban riots were a major problem, social scientists began to explore carefully the order-maintenance function of the police, and to suggest ways of improving it—not to make streets safer (its original function) but to reduce the incidence of mass violence. Order maintenance became, to a degree, co-terminous with "community relations." But, as the crime wave that began in the early 1960s continued without abatement throughout the decade and into the 1970s, attention shifted to the role of the police as crime fighters. Studies of police behavior ceased, by and large, to be accounts of the order-maintenance function and became, instead, efforts to propose and test ways whereby the police could solve more crimes, make more arrests, and gather better evidence. If these things could be done, social scientists assumed, citizens would be less fearful.

A great deal was accomplished during this transition, as both police chiefs and outside experts emphasized the crime-fighting function in their plans, in the allocation of resources, and in deployment of personnel. The police may well have become better crime fighters as a result. And doubtless they remained aware of their responsibility for order. But the link between order maintenance and crime prevention, so obvious to earlier generations, was forgotten.

That link is similar to the process whereby one broken window becomes many. The citizen who fears the ill-smelling drunk, the rowdy teenager, or the importuning beggar is not merely expressing his distaste for unseemly behavior, he is also giving voice to a bit of folk wisdom that happens to be a correct generalization—namely, that serious street crime flourishes in areas in which disorderly behavior goes unchecked. The unchecked panhandler is, in effect, the first broken window. Muggers and robbers, whether opportunistic or professional, believe they reduce their chances of being caught or even identified if they operate on streets where potential victims are already intimidated by prevailing conditions. If the neighborhood cannot keep a bothersome panhandler from annoying passersby, the thief may reason, it is even less likely to call the police to identify a potential mugger or to interfere if the mugging actually takes place.

Some police administrators concede that this process occurs, but argue that motorized patrol officers can deal with it as effectively as foot patrol officers. We are not so sure. In theory, an officer in a squad car can observe as much as an officer on foot; in theory, the former can talk to as many people as the latter. But the reality of police-citizen encounters is powerfully altered by the automobile. An officer on foot cannot separate himself from the street people; if he is approached, only his uniform and his personality can help him manage whatever is about to happen. And he can never be certain what that will be—a request for directions, a plea for help, an angry denunciation, a teasing remark, a confused babble, a threatening gesture.

In a car, an officer is more likely to deal with street people by rolling down the window and looking at them. The door and the window exclude the approaching citizen; they are a barrier. Some officers take advantage of this barrier, perhaps unconsciously, by acting differently if in the car than they would on foot. We have seen this countless times. The police car pulls up to a corner where teenagers are gathered. The window is rolled down. The officer stares at the youths. They stare back. The officer says to one, "C'mere." He saunters over, conveying to his friends by his elaborate casual style the idea that he is not intimidated by authority. "What's your name?" "Chuck." "Chuck who?" "Chuck Jones." "What'ya doing, Chuck?" "Nothin'." "Got a P.O. [parole officer]?" "Nah." "Sure?" "Yeah." "Stay out of trouble, Chuckie." Meanwhile, the other boys laugh and exchange comments among themselves, probably at the officer's expense. The officer stares harder. He cannot be certain what is being said, nor can he join in and, by displaying his own skill at street banter, prove that he cannot be "put down." In the process, the officer has learned almost nothing, and the boys have decided the officer is an alien force who can safely be disregarded, even mocked.

Our experience is that most citizens like to talk to a police officer. Such exchanges give them a sense of importance, provide them with the basis for gossip, and allow them to explain to the authorities what is worrying them (whereby they gain a modest but significant sense of having "done something" about the problem). You approach a person on foot more easily, and talk to him more readily, than you do a person in a car. Moreover, you can more easily retain some anonymity if you draw an officer aside for a private chat. Suppose you want to pass on a tip about who is stealing handbags, or who offered to sell you a stolen TV. In the inner city, the culprit, in all likelihood, lives nearby. To walk up to a marked patrol car and lean in the window is to convey a visible signal that you are a "fink."

The essence of the police role in maintaining order is to reinforce the informal control mechanisms of the community itself. The police cannot, without committing extraordinary resources, provide a substitute for that informal control. On the other hand, to reinforce those natural forces the police must accommodate them. And therein lies the problem.

Should police activity on the street be shaped, in important ways, by the standards of the neighborhood rather than by the rules of the state? Over the past two decades, the shift of police from order maintenance to law enforcement has brought them increasingly under the influence of legal restrictions, provoked by media complaints and enforced by court decisions and departmental orders. As a consequence, the order-maintenance functions of the police are now governed by rules developed to control police relations with suspected criminals. This is, we think, an entirely new development. For centuries, the role of the police as watchmen was judged primarily not in terms of its compliance with appropriate procedures but rather in terms of its attaining a desired objective. The objective was order, an inherently ambiguous term but a condition that people in a given community recognized when they saw it. The means were the same as those the community itself would employ, if its members were sufficiently determined, courageous, and authoritative. Detecting and apprehending criminals, by contrast, was a means to an end, not an end in itself; a judicial determination of guilt or innocence was the hoped-for result of the law-enforcement mode. From the first, the police were expected to follow rules defining that process, though states differed in how stringent the rules should be. The criminal-apprehension process was always understood to involve individual rights, the violation of which was unacceptable because it meant that the violating officer would be acting as a judge and jury—and that was not his job. Guilt or innocence was to be determined by universal standards under special procedures.

Ordinarily, no judge or jury ever sees the persons caught up in a dispute over the appropriate level of neighborhood order. That is true not only because most cases are handled informally on the street but also because no universal standards are available to settle arguments over disorder, and thus a judge may not be any wiser or more effective than a police officer. Until quite recently in many states, and even today in some places, the police makes arrests on such charges as "suspicious person" or "vagrancy" or "public drunkenness"—charges with scarcely any legal meaning. These charges exist not because society wants judges to punish vagrants or drunks but because it wants an officer to have the legal tools to remove undesirable persons from a neighborhood when informal efforts to preserve order in the streets have failed.

Once we begin to think of all aspects of police work as involving the application of universal rules under special procedures, we inevitably ask what constitutes an "undesirable person" and why we should "criminalize" vagrancy or drunkenness. A strong and commendable desire to see that people are treated fairly makes us worry about allowing the police to rout persons who are undesirable by some vague or parochial standard. A growing and not-so-commendable utilitarianism leads us to doubt that any behavior that does not "hurt" another person should be made illegal. And thus many of us who watch over the police are reluctant to allow them to perform, in the only way they can, a function that every neighborhood desperately wants them to perform.

This wish to "decriminalize" disreputable behavior that "harms no one"—and thus remove the ultimate sanction the police can employ to maintain neighborhood order—is, we think, a mistake. Arresting a single drunk or a single vagrant who has harmed no identifiable person seems unjust, and in a sense it is. But failing to do anything about a score of drunks or a hundred vagrants may destroy an entire community. A particular rule that seems to make sense in the individual case makes no sense when it is made a universal rule and applied to all cases. It makes no sense because it fails to take into account the connection between one broken window left untended and a thousand broken windows. Of course, agencies other than the police could attend to the problems posed by drunks or the mentally ill, but in most communities—especially where the "deinstitutionalization" movement has been strong—they do not.

The concern about equity is more serious. We might agree that certain behavior makes one person more undesirable than another, but how do we ensure that age or skin color or natural origin or harmless mannerisms will not also become the basis for distinguishing the undesirable from the desirable? How do we ensure, in short, that the police do not become the agents of neighborhood bigotry?

We can offer no wholly satisfactory answer to this important quesion. We are not confident that there *is* a satisfactory answer, except to hope that by their selection, training, and supervision the police will be inculcated with a clear sense of the outer limit of their discretionary authority. That limit, roughly, is this—the police exist to help regulate behavior, not to maintain the racial or ethnic purity of a neighborhood.

Consider the case of the Robert Taylor Homes in Chicago, one of the largest public housing projects in the country. It is home for nearly 20,000 people, all black, and extends over ninety-two acres along South State Street. It was named after a distinguished black who had been, during the 1940s, chairman of the Chicago Housing Authority. Not long after it opened, in 1962, relations between project residents and the police deteriorated badly. The citizens felt that the police were insensitive or brutal; the police, in turn, complained of unprovoked attacks on them. Some Chicago officers tell of times when they were afraid to enter the Homes. Crime rates soared.

Today, the atmosphere has changed. Police-citizen relations have improved—apparently, both sides learned something from the earlier experience. Recently, a boy stole a purse and ran off. Several young persons who saw the theft voluntarily passed along to the police information on the identity and residence of the thief, and they did this publicly, with friends and neighbors looking on. But problems persist, chief among them the presence of youth gangs that terrorize residents and recruit members in the project. The people expect the police to "do something" about this, and the police are determined to do just that.

But do what? Though the police can obviously make arrests whenever a gang member breaks the law, a gang can form, recruit, and congregate without breaking the law. And only a tiny fraction of gang-related crimes can be solved by an arrest; thus, if an arrest is the only recourse for the police, the residents' fears will go unassuaged. The police will soon feel helpless, and the residents will again believe that the police "do nothing." What the police in fact do is to chase known gang members out of the project. In the words of one officer, "We kick ass." Project residents both know and approve of this. The tacit police-citizen alliance in the project is reinforced by the police view that the cops and the gangs are the two rival sources of power in the area, and that the gangs are not going to win.

None of this is easily reconciled with any conception of due process or fair treatment. Since both residents and gang members are black, race is not a factor. But it could be. Suppose a white project gang confronted a black gang, or vice versa. We would be apprehensive about the police taking sides. But the substantive problem remains the same: How can the police strengthen the informal social-control mechanisms of natural communities in order to minimize fear in public places? Law enforcement, per se, is no answer. A gang can weaken or destroy a community by standing about in a menacing fashion and speaking rudely to passersby without breaking the law.

We have difficulty thinking about such matters, not simply because the ethical and legal issues are so complex but because we have become accustomed to thinking of the law in essentially individualistic terms. The law defines *my* rights, punishes *his* behavior, and is applied by *that* officer because of *this* harm. We assume, in thinking this way, that what is good for the individual will be good for the community, and what doesn't matter when it happens to one person won't matter when it happens to many. Ordinarily, those are plausible assumptions. But in cases where behavior that is tolerable to one person is intolerable to many others, the reactions of the others—fear, withdrawal, flight—may ultimately make matters worse for everyone, including the individual who first professed his indifference.

It may be their greater sensitivity to communal as opposed to individual needs that helps explain why the residents of small communities are more satisfied with their police than are the residents of similar neighborhoods in big cities. Elinor Ostrom and her co-workers at Indiana University compared the perception of police services in two poor, all-black Illinois towns—Phoenix and East Chicago Heights—with those of three comparable all-black neighborhoods in Chicago. The level of criminal victimization and the quality of police-community relations appeared to be about the same in the towns and the Chicago neighborhoods. But the citizens living in their own villages were much more likely than those living in the Chicago neighborhoods to say that they do not stay at home for fear of crime, to agree that the local police have "the right to take any action necessary" to deal with problems, and to agree that the police "look out for the needs of the average citizen." It is possible that the residents and the police of the small towns saw themselves as engaged in a collaborative effort to maintain a certain standard of communal life, whereas those of the big city felt themselves to be simply requesting and supplying particular services on an individual basis.

If this is true, how should a wise police chief deploy his meager forces? The first answer is that nobody knows for certain, and the most prudent course of action would be to try further variations on the Newark experiment, to see more precisely what works in what kinds of neighborhoods. The second answer is also a hedge—many aspects of order maintenance in neighborhoods can probably best be handled in ways that involve the police minimally, if at all. A busy, bustling shopping center and a quiet, well-tended suburb may need almost no visible police presence. In both cases, the ratio of respectable to disreputable people is ordinarily so high as to make informal social control effective.

Even in areas that are in jeopardy from disorderly elements, citizen action without substantial police involvement may be sufficient. Meetings between teenagers who like to hang out on a particular corner and adults who want to use that corner might well lead to an amicable agreement on a set of rules about how many people can be allowed to congregate, where, and when.

Where no understanding is possible—or, if possible, not observed—citizen patrols may be a sufficient response. There are two traditions of communal involvement in maintaining order. One, that of the "community watchmen," is as old as the first settlement of the New World. Until well into the nineteenth century, volunteer watchmen, not policemen, patrolled their communities to keep order. They did so, by and large, without taking the law into their own hands—without, that is, punishing persons or using force. Their presence deterred disorder or alerted the community to disorder that could not be deterred. There are hundreds of such efforts today in communities all across the nation. Perhaps the best known is that of the Guardian Angels, a group of unarmed young persons in distinctive berets and T-shirts, who first came to public attention when they began patrolling the New York City subways but who claim now to have chapters in more than thirty American cities. Unfortunately, we have little information about the effect of these groups on crime. It is possible, however, that whatever their effect on crime, citizens find their presence reassuring, and that they thus contribute to maintaining a sense of order and civility.

The second tradition is that of the "vigilante." Rarely a feature of the settled communities of the East, it was primarily to be found in those frontier towns that grew up in advance of the reach of government. More than 350 vigilante groups are known to have existed; their distinctive feature was that their members did take the law into their own hands, by acting as judge, jury, and often executioner as well as policeman. Today, the vigilante movement is conspicuous by its rarity, despite the great fear expressed by citizens that the older cities are becoming "urban frontiers." But some community watchmen groups have skirted the line, and others may cross it in the future. An ambiguous case, reported in the *Wall Street Journal,* involved a citizens' patrol in the Silver Lake area of Belleville, New Jersey. A leader told the reporter, "We look for outsiders." If a few teenagers from outside the neighborhood enter it, "we ask them their business," he said. "If they say they're going down the street to see Mrs. Jones, fine, we let them pass. But then we follow them down the block to make sure they're really going to see Mrs. Jones."

Though citizens can do a great deal, the police are plainly the key to order maintenance. For one thing, many communities, such as the Robert Taylor Homes, cannot do the job by themselves. For another, no citizen in a neighborhood, even an organized one, is likely to feel the sense of responsibility that wearing a badge confers. Psychologists have done many studies on why people fail to go to the aid of persons being attacked or seeking help, and they have learned that the cause is not "apathy" or "selfishness" but the absence of some plausible grounds for feeling that one must personally accept responsibility. Ironically, avoiding responsibility is easier when a lot of people are standing about. On streets and in public places, where order is so important, many people are likely to be "around," a fact that reduces the chance of any one person acting as the agent of the community. The police officer's uniform singles him out as a person who must accept responsibility if asked. In addition, officers, more easily than their fellow citizens, can be expected to distinguish between what is necessary to protect the safety of the street and what merely protects its ethnic purity.

But the police forces of America are losing, not gaining, members. Some cities have suffered substantial cuts in the number of officers available for duty. These cuts are not likely to be reversed in the near future. Therefore, each department must assign its existing officers with great care. Some neighborhoods are so demoralized and crime-ridden as to make foot patrol useless; the best the police can do with limited resources is respond to the enormous number of calls for service. Other neighborhoods are so stable and serene as to make foot patrol unnecessary. The key is to identify neighborhoods at the tipping point—where the public order is deteriorating but not unreclaimable, where the streets are used frequently but by apprehensive people, where a window is likely to be broken at any time, and must quickly be fixed if all are not to be shattered.

Most police departments do not have ways of systematically identifying such areas and assigning officers to them. Officers are assigned on the basis of crime rates (meaning that marginally threatened areas are often stripped so that police can investigate crimes in areas where the situation is hopeless) or on the basis of calls for service (despite the fact that most citizens do not call the police when they are merely frightened or annoyed). To allocate patrol wisely, the department must look at the neighborhoods and decide, from firsthand evidence, where an additional officer will make the greatest difference in promoting a sense of safety.

One way to stretch limited police resources is being tried in some public housing projects. Tenant organizations hire off-duty police officers for patrol work in their buildings. The costs are not high (at least not per resident), the officer likes the additional income, and the residents feel safer. Such arrangements are probably more successful than hiring private watchmen, and the Newark experiment helps us understand why. A private security guard may deter crime or misconduct by his presence, and he may go to the aid of persons needing help, but he may well not intervene—that is, control or drive away—someone challenging community standards. Being a sworn officer—a "real cop"—seems to give one the confidence, the sense of duty, and the aura of authority necessary to perform this difficult task.

Patrol officers might be encouraged to go to and from duty stations on public transportation and, while on the bus or subway car, enforce rules about smoking, drinking, disorderly conduct, and the like. The enforcement need involve nothing more than ejecting the offender (the offense, after all, is not one with which a booking officer or a judge wishes to be bothered). Perhaps the random but relentless maintenance of standards on buses would lead to conditions on buses that approximate the level of civility we now take for granted on airplanes.

But the most important requirement is to think that to maintain order in precarious situations is a vital job. The police know this is one of their functions, and they also believe, correctly, that it cannot be done to the exclusion of criminal investigation and responding to calls. We may have encouraged them to suppose, however, on the basis of our oft-repeated concerns about serious, violent crime, that they will be judged exclusively on their capacity as crime fighters. To the extent that this is the case, police administrators will continue to concentrate police personnel in the highest-crime areas (though not necessarily in the areas most vulnerable to criminal invasion), emphasize their training in the law and criminal apprehension (and not their training in managing street life), and join too quickly in campaigns to decriminalize "harmless" behavior (though public drunkenness, street prostitution, and pornographic displays can destroy a community more quickly than any team of professional burglars).

Above all, we must return to our long-abandoned view that the police ought to protect communities as well as individuals. Our crime statistics and victimization surveys measure individual losses, but they do not measure communal losses. Just as physicians now recognize the importance of fostering health rather than simply treating illness, so the police—and the rest of us—ought to recognize the importance of maintaining, intact, communities without broken windows.

ARTICLE SIX

A Sketch of the Policeman's "Working Personality"

JEROME H. SKOLNICK

Each of us views the real world through cognitive lenses that influence our perception and interpretation of events. Because their role contains the two important variables of danger and authority, police officers develop a distinctive view of the world. Sociologist Jerome Skolnick explores this view and shows how the "working personality" affects the actions of the police.

A recurrent theme of the sociology of occupations is the effect of a man's work on his outlook on the world.[1] Doctors, janitors, lawyers, and industrial workers develop distinctive ways of perceiving and responding to their environment. Here we shall concentrate on analyzing certain outstanding elements in the police milieu, danger, authority, and efficiency, as they combine to generate distinctive cognitive and behavioral responses in police: a "working personality." Such an analysis does not suggest that all police are alike in "working personality," but that there are distinctive cognitive tendencies in police as an occupational grouping. Some of these may be found in other occupations sharing similar problems. So far as exposure to danger is concerned, the policeman may be likened to the soldier. His problems as an authority bear a certain similarity to those of the schoolteacher, and the pressures he feels to prove himself efficient are not unlike those felt by the industrial worker. The combination of these

Source: From *Justice Without Trial: Law Enforcement in a Democratic Society* by Jerome H. Skolnick (New York: John Wiley & Sons, 1966), pp. 42–62. Reprinted by permission of the author and publisher.

elements, however, is unique to the policeman. Thus, the police, as a result of combined features of their social situation, tend to develop ways of looking at the world distinctive to themselves, cognitive lenses through which to see situations and events. The strength of the lenses may be weaker or stronger depending on certain conditions, but they are ground on a similar axis.

Analysis of the policeman's cognitive propensities is necessary to understand the practical dilemma faced by police required to maintain order under a democratic rule of law. . . . A conception of order is [essential] to the resolution of this dilemma. [We suggest] that the paramilitary character of police organization naturally leads to a high evaluation of similarity, routine, and predictability. Our intention is to emphasize features of the policeman's environment interacting with the paramilitary police organization to generate a "working personality." Such an intervening concept should aid in explaining how the social environment of police affects their capacity to respond to the rule of law.

[Emphasis] will be placed on the division of labor in the police department . . . ; "operational law enforcement" [cannot] be understood outside these special work assignments. It is therefore important to explain how the hypothesis emphasizing the generalizability of the policeman's "working personality" is compatible with the idea that police division of labor is an important analytic dimension for understanding "operational law enforcement." Compatibility is evident when one considers the different levels of analysis at which the hypotheses are being developed. Janowitz states, for example, that the military profession is more than an occupation; it is a "style of life" because the occupational claims over one's daily existence extend well beyond official duties. He is quick to point out that any profession performing a crucial "life and death" task, such as medicine, the ministry, or the police, develops such claims.[2] A conception like "working personality" of police should be understood to suggest an analytic breadth similar to that of "style of life." That is, just as the professional behavior of military officers with similar "styles of life" may differ drastically depending upon whether they command an infantry battalion or participate in the work of an intelligence unit, so too does the professional behavior of police officers with similar "working personalities" vary with their assignments.

The policeman's "working personality" is most highly developed in his constabulary role of the man on the beat. For analytical purposes that role is sometimes regarded as an enforcement specialty, but in this general discussion of policemen as they comport themselves while working, the uniformed "cop" is seen as the foundation for the policeman's "working personality." There is a sound organizational basis for making this assumption. The police, unlike the military, draw no caste distinction in socialization, even though their order of ranked titles approximates the military's. Thus, one cannot join a local police department as, for instance, a lieutenant, as a West Point graduate joins the army. Every officer of rank must serve an apprenticeship as a patrolman. This feature of police organization means that the constabulary role is the primary one for all police officers, and that whatever the special requirements of roles in enforcement specialties, they are carried out with a common background of constabulary experience.

The process by which this "personality" is developed may be summarized: the policeman's role contains two principal variables, danger and authority, which should be interpreted in the light of a "constant" pressure to appear efficient.[3] The element of danger seems to make the policeman especially attentive to signs indicating a potential for violence and lawbreaking. As a result, the policeman is generally a "suspicious" person. Furthermore, the character of the policeman's work makes him less desirable as a friend, since norms of friendship implicate others in his work. Accordingly, the element of danger isolates the policeman socially from that segment of the citizenry which he regards as symbolically dangerous and also from the conventional citizenry with whom he identifies.

The element of authority reinforces the element of danger in isolating the policeman. Typically, the policeman is required to enforce laws representing puritanical morality, such as those prohibiting drunkenness, and also laws regulating the flow of public activity, such as traffic laws. In these situations the policeman directs the citizenry, whose typical response denies recognition of his authority, and stresses his obligation to respond to danger. The kind of man who responds well to danger, however, does not normally subscribe to codes of puritanical morality. As a result, the policeman is unusually liable to the charge of hypocrisy. That the whole civilian world is an audience for the policeman further promotes police isolation and, in consequence, solidarity. Finally, danger undermines the judicious use of authority. Where danger, as in Britain, is relatively less, the judicious application of authority is facilitated. Hence, British police may appear to be somewhat more attached to the rule of law, when, in fact, they may appear so because they face less danger, and they are as a rule better skilled than American police in creating the appearance of conformity to procedural regulations.

THE SYMBOLIC ASSAILANT AND POLICE CULTURE

In attempting to understand the policeman's view of the world, it is useful to raise a more general question: What are the conditions under which police, as authorities, may be threatened?[4] To answer this, we must look to the situation of the policeman in the community. One attribute of many characterizing the policeman's role stands out: the policeman is required to respond to assaults against persons and property. When a radio call reports an armed robbery and gives a description of the man involved, every policeman, regardless of assignment, is responsible for the criminal's apprehension. The raison d'être of the policeman and the criminal law, the underlying collectively held moral sentiments which justify penal sanctions, arises ultimately and most clearly from the threat of violence and the possibility of danger to the community. Police who "lobby" for severe narcotics laws, for instance, justify their position on grounds that the addict is a harbinger of danger since, it is maintained, he requires one hundred dollars a day to support his habit, and he must steal to get it. Even though the addict is not typically a violent criminal, criminal penalties for addiction are supported on grounds that he may become one.

The policeman, because his work requires him to be occupied continually with potential violence, develops a perceptual shorthand to identify certain kinds of people as symbolic assailants, that is, as persons who use gesture, language, and attire that the policeman has come to recognize as a prelude to violence. This does not mean that violence by the symbolic assailant is necessarily predictable. On the contrary, the policeman responds to the vague indication of danger suggested by appearance.[5] Like the animals of the experimental psychologist, the policeman finds the threat of random damage more compelling than a predetermined and inevitable punishment.

Nor, to qualify for the status of symbolic assailant, need an individual ever have used violence. A man backing out of a jewelry store with a gun in one hand and jewelry in the other would qualify even if the gun were a toy and he had never in his life fired a real pistol. To the policeman in the situation, the man's personal history is momentarily immaterial. There is only one relevant sign: a gun signifying danger. Similarly, a young man may suggest the threat of violence to the policeman by his manner of walking or "strutting," the insolence in the demeanor being registered by the policeman as a possible preamble to later attack.[6] Signs vary from area to area, but a youth dressed in a black leather jacket and motorcycle boots is sure to draw at least a suspicious glance from a policeman.

Policemen themselves do not necessarily emphasize the peril associated with their work when questioned directly, and may even have well-developed strategies of denial. The element of danger is so integral to the policeman's work that explicit recognition might induce emotional barriers to work performance. Thus, one patrol officer observed that more police have been killed and injured in automobile accidents in the past ten years than from gunfire. Although his assertion is true, he neglected to mention that the police are the only peacetime occupational group with a systematic record of death and injury from gunfire and other weaponry. Along these lines, it is interesting that of the two hundred and twenty-four working Westville policemen (not including the sixteen juvenile policemen) responding to a question about which assignment they would like most to have in the police department,[7] 50 percent selected the job of detective, an assignment combining elements of apparent danger and initiative. The next category was adult street work, that is, patrol and traffic (37 percent). Eight percent selected the juvenile squad,[8] and only 4 percent selected administrative work. Not a single policeman chose the job of jail guard. Although these findings do not control for such factors as prestige, they suggest that confining and routine jobs are rated low on the hierarchy of police preferences, even though such jobs are least dangerous. Thus, the policeman may well, as a personality, enjoy the possibility of danger, especially its associated excitement, even though he may at the same time be fearful of it. Such "inconsistency" is easily understood. Freud has by now made it an axiom of personality theory that logical and emotional consistency are by no means the same phenomenon.

However complex the motives aroused by the element of danger, its consequences for sustaining police culture are unambiguous. This element requires him, like the combat soldier, the European Jew, the South African (white or black), to live in a world straining toward duality, and suggesting danger when "they" are perceived. Consequently, it is in the nature of the policeman's situation that his conception of order emphasize regularity and predictability. It is, therefore, a conception shaped by persistent *suspicion.* The English "copper," often portrayed as a courteous, easygoing, rather jolly sort of chap, on the one hand, or as a devil-may-care adventurer, on the other, is differently described by Colin MacInnes:

> The true copper's dominant characteristic, if the truth be known, is neither those daring nor vicious qualities that are sometimes attributed to him by friend or enemy, but an ingrained conservatism, and almost desperate love of the conventional. It is untidiness, disorder, the unusual, that a copper disapproves of most of all: far more, even than of crime which is merely a professional matter. Hence his profound dislike of people loitering in streets, dressing extravagantly, speaking with exotic accents, being strange, weak, eccentric, or simply any rare minority—of their doing, in fact, anything that cannot be safely predicted.[9]

Policemen are indeed specifically *trained* to be suspicious, to perceive events or changes in the physical surroundings that indicate the occurrence or probability of disorder. A former student who worked as a patrolman in a suburban New York police department describes this aspect of the policeman's assessment of the unusual:

> The time spent cruising one's sector or walking one's beat is not wasted time, though it can become quite routine. During this time, the most important thing for the officer to do is notice the *normal.* He must come to know the people in his area, their habits, their automobiles and their friends. He must learn what time the various shops close, how much money is kept on hand on different nights, what lights are usually left on, which houses are vacant . . . only then can he decide what persons or cars under what circumstances warrant the appellation "suspicious."[10]

The individual policeman's "suspiciousness" does not hang on whether he has personally undergone an experience that could objectively be described as hazardous. Personal experience of this sort is not the key to the psychological importance of exceptionality. Each, as he routinely carries out his work, will experience situations that threaten to become dangerous. Like the American Jew who contributes to the "defense" organizations such as the Anti-Defamation League in response to Nazi brutalities he has never experienced personally, the policeman identifies with his fellow cop who has been beaten, perhaps fatally, by a gang of young thugs.

SOCIAL ISOLATION

The patrolman in Westville, and probably in most communities, has come to identify the black man with danger. James Baldwin vividly expresses the isolation of the ghetto policeman:

> The only way to police a ghetto is to be oppressive. None of the police commissioner's men, even with the best will in the world, have any way of understanding the lives led by the people they swagger about in twos and threes controlling. Their very presence is an insult, and it would be, even if they spent their entire day feeding gumdrops to children. They represent the force of the white world, and that world's criminal profit and ease, to keep the black man corralled up here, in his place. The badge, the gun in the holster, and the swinging club make vivid what will happen should his rebellion become overt. . . .
>
> It is hard, on the other hand, to blame the policeman, blank, good-natured, thoughtless, and insuperably innocent, for being such a perfect representative of the people he serves. He, too, believes in good intentions and is astounded and offended when they are not taken for the deed. He has never, himself, done anything for which to be hated—which of us has?—and yet he is facing, daily and nightly, people who would gladly see him dead, and he knows it. There is no way for him not to know it; there are few things under heaven more unnerving than the silent, accumulating contempt and hatred of a people. He moves through Harlem, therefore, like an occupying soldier in a bitterly hostile country; which is precisely what, and where he is, and is the reason he walks in twos and threes.[11]

While Baldwin's observations on police-black relations cannot be disputed seriously, there is greater social distance between police and "civilians" in general regardless of their color than Baldwin considers. Thus, Colin MacInnes has his English hero, Mr. Justice, explaining:

> The story is all coppers are just civilians like anyone else, living among them not in barracks like on the Continent, but you and I know that's just a legend for mugs. We *are* cut off: we're *not* like everyone else. Some civilians fear us and play up to us, some dislike us and keep out of our way but no one—well, very few indeed—accepts us as just ordinary like them. In one sense, dear, we're just like hostile troops occupying an enemy country. And say what you like, at times that makes us lonely.[12]

MacInnes' observation suggests that by not introducing a white control group, Baldwin has failed to see that the policeman may not get on well with anybody regardless (to use the hackneyed phrase) of race, creed, or national origin. Policemen whom one knows well often express their sense of isolation from the public as a whole, not just from those who fail to share their color. Westville police were asked, for example, to rank the most serious problems police have. The category most frequently selected was not racial problems, but some form of public relations: lack of respect for the police, lack of cooperation in enforcement of law, lack of understanding of the requirements of police work.[13] One respondent answered:

> As a policeman my most serious problem is impressing on the general public just how difficult and necessary police service is to all. There seems to be an attitude of "law is important, but it applies to my neighbor—not to me."

Of the two hundred and eighty-two Westville policemen who rated the prestige police work receives from others, 70 percent ranked it as only fair or poor, while less than 2 percent ranked it as "excellent" and another 29 percent as "good." Similarly, in Britain, two-thirds of a sample of policemen interviewed by a Royal Commission stated difficulties in making friends outside the force; of those interviewed 58 percent thought members of the public to be reserved, suspicious, and constrained in conversation; and 12 percent attributed such difficulties to the requirements that policemen be selective in associations and behave circumspectly.[14]

A Westville policeman related the following incident:

> Several months after I joined the force, my wife and I used to be socially active with a crowd of young people, mostly married, who gave a lot of parties where there was drinking and dancing, and we enjoyed it. I've never forgotten, though, an incident that happened on one Fourth of July party. Everybody had been drinking, there was a lot of talking, people were feeling boisterous, and some kid there—he must have been twenty or twenty-two—threw a firecracker that hit my wife in the leg and burned her. I didn't know exactly what to do—punch the guy in the nose, bawl him out, just forget it. Anyway, I couldn't let it pass, so I walked over to him and told him he ought to be careful. He began to rise up at me, and when he did, somebody yelled, "Better watch out, he's a cop." I saw everybody standing there, and I could feel they were all against me and for the kid, even though he had thrown the firecracker at my wife. I went over to the host and said it was probably better if my wife and I left because a fight would put a damper on the party. Actually, I'd hoped he would ask the kid to leave, since the kid had thrown the firecracker. But he didn't, so we left. After that incident, my wife and I stopped going around with that crowd, and decided that if we were going to parties where there was to be drinking and boisterousness, we weren't going to be the only police people there.

Another reported that he seeks to overcome his feelings of isolation by concealing his police identity:

> I try not to bring my work home with me, and that includes my social life. I like the men I work with, but I think it's better that my family doesn't become a police family. I try to put my police work into the background,

> and try not to let people know I'm a policeman. Once you do, you can't have normal relations with them.[15]

Although the policeman serves a people who are, as Baldwin says, the established society, the white society, these people do not make him feel accepted. As a result, he develops resources within his own world to combat social rejection.

POLICE SOLIDARITY

All occupational groups share a measure of inclusiveness and identification. People are brought together simply by doing the same work and having similar career and salary problems. As several writers have noted, however, police show an unusually high degree of occupational solidarity.[16] It is true that the police have a common employer and wear a uniform at work, but so do doctors, milkmen, and bus drivers. Yet it is doubtful that these workers have so close knit an occupation or so similar an outlook on the world as do police. Set apart from the conventional world, the policeman experiences an exceptionally strong tendency to find his social identity within his occupational milieu.

Compare the police with another skilled craft. In a study of the International Typographical Union, the authors asked printers the first names and jobs of their three closest friends. Of the 1,236 friends named by the 412 men in their sample, 35 percent were printers.[17] Similarly, among the Westville police, of seven hundred friends listed by 250 respondents, 35 percent were policemen. The policemen, however, were far more active than printers in occupational social activities. Of the printers, more than half (54 percent) had never participated in any union clubs, benefit societies, teams, or organizations composed mostly of printers, or attended any printers' social affairs in the past five years. Of the Westville police, only 16 percent had failed to attend a single police banquet or dinner in the past *year* (as contrasted with the printers' *five years*); and of the 234 men answering this question, 54 percent had attended three or more such affairs *during the past year.*

These findings are striking in light of the interpretation made of the data on printers. Lipset, Trow, and Coleman do not, as a result of their findings, see printers as an unintegrated occupational group. On the contrary, they ascribe the democratic character of the union in good part to the active social and political participation of the membership. The point is not to question their interpretation, since it is doubtless correct when printers are held up against other manual workers. However, when seen in comparison to police, printers appear a minimally participating group; put positively, police emerge as an exceptionally socially active occupational group.

POLICE SOLIDARITY AND DANGER

There is still a question, however, as to the process through which danger and authority influence police solidarity. The effect of danger on police solidarity is revealed when we examine a chief complaint of police: lack of public support and public apathy. The complaint may have several referents including police pay, police prestige, and support from the legislature. But the repeatedly voiced broader meaning of the complaint is resentment at being taken for granted. The policeman does not believe that his status as civil servant should relieve the public of responsibility for law enforcement. He feels, however, that payment out of public coffers somehow obscures his humanity and, therefore, his need for help.[18] As one put it:

> Jerry, a cop, can get into a fight with three or four tough kids, and there will be citizens passing by, and maybe they'll look, but they'll never lend a hand. It's their country too, but you'd never know it the way some of them act. They forget that we're made of flesh and blood too. They don't care what happens to the cop so long as they don't get a little dirty.

Although the policeman sees himself as a specialist in dealing with violence, he does not want to fight alone. He does not believe that his specialization relieves the general public of citizenship duties. Indeed, if possible, he would prefer to be the foreman rather than the workingman in the battle against criminals.

The general public, of course, does withdraw from the workday world of the policeman. The policeman's responsibility for controlling dangerous and sometimes violent persons alienates the average citizen perhaps as much as does his authority over the average citizen. If the policeman's job is to ensure that public order is maintained, the citizen's inclination is to shrink from the dangers of maintaining it. The citizen prefers to see the policeman as an automaton, because once the policeman's humanity is recognized, the citizen necessarily becomes implicated in the policeman's work, which is, after all, sometimes dirty and dangerous. What the policeman typically fails to realize is the extent he becomes tainted by the character of the work he performs. The dangers of their work not only draw policemen together as a group but separate them from the rest of the population. Banton, for instance, comments:

> Patrolmen may support their fellows over what they regard as minor infractions in order to demonstrate to them that they will be loyal in situations that make the greatest demands upon their fidelity. . . .
>
> In the American departments I visited it seemed as if the supervisors shared many of the patrolmen's sentiments about solidarity. They too wanted their colleagues to back them up in an emergency, and they shared similar frustrations with the public.[19]

Thus, the element of danger contains seeds of isolation which may grow in two directions. In one, a stereotyping perceptual shorthand is formed through which the police come to see certain signs as symbols of potential violence. The police probably differ in this respect from the general middle-class white population only in degree. This difference, however, may take on enormous significance in practice. Thus, the policeman works at identifying and possibly apprehending the symbolic assailant; the ordinary citizen does not. As a result, the ordinary citizen does not assume the responsibility to implicate himself in the policeman's required response to danger. The element of danger in the policeman's role alienates him not only from populations with a potential for crime but also from the conventionally respectable (white) citizenry, in short, from that segment of the population from which friends would ordinarily be drawn. As Janowitz has noted in a paragraph suggesting similarities between the police and the military, ". . . any profession which is continually preoccupied with the threat of danger requires a strong sense of solidarity if it is to operate effectively. Detailed regulation of the military style of life is expected to enhance group cohesion, professional loyalty, and maintain the martial spirit."[20]

SOCIAL ISOLATION AND AUTHORITY

The element of authority also helps to account for the policeman's social isolation. Policemen themselves are aware of their isolation from the community, and are apt to weight authority heavily as a causal factor. When considering how authority influences rejection, the policeman typically singles out his responsibility for enforcement of traffic violations.[21] Resentment, even hostility, is generated in those receiving citations, in part because such contact is often the only one citizens have with police, and in part because municipal administrations and courts have been known to utilize police authority primarily to meet budgetary requirements, rather than those of public order. Thus, when a municipality engages in "speed trapping" by changing limits so quickly that drivers cannot realistically slow down to the prescribed speed or, while keeping the limits reasonable, charging high fines primarily to generate revenue, the policeman carries the brunt of public resentment.

That the policeman dislikes writing traffic tickets is suggested by the quota system police departments typically employ. In Westville, each traffic policeman has what is euphemistically described as a working "norm." A motorcyclist is supposed to write two tickets an hour for moving violations. It is doubtful that "norms" are needed because policemen are lazy. Rather, employment of quotas most likely springs from the reluctance of policemen to expose themselves to what they know to be public hostility. As a result, as one traffic policeman said:

> You learn to sniff out the places where you can catch violators when you're running behind. Of course, the department gets to know that you hang around one place, and they sometimes try to repair the situation there. But a lot of the time it would be too expensive to fix up the engineering fault, so we keep making our norm.

When meeting "production" pressures, the policeman inadvertently gives a false impression of patrolling ability to the average citizen. The traffic cyclist waits in hiding for moving violators near a tricky intersection, and is reasonably sure that such violations will occur with regularity. The violator believes he has observed a policeman displaying exceptional detection capacities and may have two thoughts, each apt to generate hostility toward the policeman: "I have been trapped," or "They can catch me; why can't they catch crooks as easily?" The answer, of course, lies in the different behavior patterns of motorists and "crooks." The latter do not act with either the frequency or predictability of motorists at poorly engineered intersections.

While traffic patrol plays a major role in separating the policeman from the respectable community, other of his tasks also have this consequence. Traffic patrol is only the most obvious illustration of the policeman's general responsibility for maintaining public order, which also includes keeping order at public accidents, sporting events, and political rallies. These activities share one feature: the policeman is called upon to *direct* ordinary citizens, and therefore to restrain their freedom of action. Resenting the restraint, the average citizen in such a situation typically thinks something along the lines of "He is supposed to catch crooks; why is he bothering me?" Thus, the citizen stresses the "dangerous" portion of the policeman's role while belittling his authority.

Closely related to the policeman's authority-based problems as *director* of the citizenry are difficulties associated with his injunction to *regulate public morality*. For instance, the policeman is obliged to investigate "lovers' lanes," and to enforce laws pertaining to gambling, prostitution, and drunkenness. His responsibility in these matters allows him much administrative discretion since he may not actually enforce the law by making an arrest, but instead merely interfere with continuation of the objectionable activity.[22] Thus, he may put the drunk in a taxi, tell the lovers to remove themselves from the back seat, and advise a man soliciting a prostitute to leave the area.

Such admonitions are in the interest of maintaining the proprieties of public order. At the same time, the policeman invites the hostility of the citizen so directed in two respects: he is likely to encourage the sort of response mentioned earlier (that is, an antagonistic reformulation of the policeman's role) and the policeman is apt to cause resentment because of the suspicion that policemen do not themselves strictly conform to the moral norms they are enforcing. Thus, the policeman, faced with enforcing a law against fornication, drunkenness, or gambling, is easily liable to a charge of hypocrisy. Even when the policeman is called on to enforce the laws relating to overt homosexuality, a form of sexual activity for which police are not especially noted, he may encounter the charge of hypocrisy on grounds that he does not adhere strictly to prescribed heterosexual codes. The policeman's difficulty in this respect is shared by all authorities responsible for maintenance of disciplined activity, including industrial foremen, political leaders, elementary schoolteachers, and college professors. All are expected to conform rigidly to the entire range of norms they espouse.[23] The policeman, however, as a result of the unique combination of the elements of danger and authority, experiences a special predicament. It is difficult to develop qualities enabling him to stand up to danger, and to conform to standards of puritanical morality. The element of danger demands that the policeman be able to carry out efforts that are in their nature overtly masculine. Police work, like soldiering, requires an exceptional caliber of physical fitness, agility, toughness, and the like. The man who ranks high on these masculine characteristics is, again like the soldier, not usually disposed to be puritanical about sex, drinking, and gambling.

On the basis of observations, policemen do not subscribe to moralistic standards for conduct. For example, the morals squad of the police department, when questioned, was unanimously against the statutory rape age limit, on grounds that as late teenagers they themselves might not have refused an attractive offer from a seventeen-year-old girl.[24] Neither, from observations, are policemen by any means total abstainers from the use of alcoholic beverages. The policeman who is arresting a drunk has probably been drunk himself; he knows it and the drunk knows it.

More than that, a portion of the social isolation of the policeman can be attributed to the discrepancy between moral regulation and the norms and behavior of policemen in these areas. We have presented data indicating that police engage in a comparatively active occupational social life. One interpretation might attribute this attendance to a basic interest in such affairs; another might explain the policeman's occupational social activity as a measure of restraint in publicly violating norms he enforces. The interest in attending police affairs may grow as much out of security in "letting oneself go" in the presence of police, and a corresponding feeling of insecurity with civilians, as an authentic preference for police social affairs. Much alcohol is usually consumed at police banquets with all the melancholy and boisterousness accompanying such occasions. As Horace Cayton reports on his experience as a policeman:

> Deputy sheriffs and policemen don't know much about organized recreation; all they usually do when celebrating is get drunk and pound each other on the back, exchanging loud insults which under ordinary circumstances would result in a fight.[25]

To some degree the reason for the behavior exhibited on these occasions is the company, since the policeman would feel uncomfortable exhibiting insobriety before civilians. The policeman may be likened to other authorities who prefer to violate moralistic norms away from onlookers for whom they are routinely supposed to appear as normative models. College professors, for instance, also get drunk on occasion, but prefer to do so where students are not present. Unfortunately for the policeman, such settings are harder for him to come by than they are for the college professor. The whole civilian world watches the policeman. As a result, he tends to be limited to the company of other policemen for whom his police identity is not a stimulus to carping normative criticism.

CORRELATES OF SOCIAL ISOLATION

The element of authority, like the element of danger, is thus seen to contribute to the solidarity of policemen. To the extent that policemen share the experience of receiving hostility from the public, they are also drawn together and become dependent upon one another. Trends in the degree to which police may exercise authority are also important considerations in understanding the dynamics of the relation between authority and solidarity. It is not simply a question of how much absolute authority police are given, but how much authority they have relative to what they had, or think they had, before. If, as Westley concludes, police violence is frequently a response to a challenge to the policeman's authority, so too may a perceived reduction in authority result in greater solidarity. Whitaker comments on the British police as follows:

> As they feel their authority decline, internal solidarity has become increasingly important to the police. Despite the individual responsibility of each police officer to pursue justice, there is sometimes a tendency to close ranks and to form a square when they themselves are concerned.[26]

These inclinations may have positive consequences for the effectiveness of police work, since notions of professional courtesy or colleagueship seem unusually high among police.[27] When the nature of the policing enterprise requires much joint activity, as in robbery and narcotics enforcement, the impression is received that cooperation is high and genuine. Policemen do not appear to cooperate with one another merely because such is the policy of the chief, but because they sincerely attach a high value to teamwork. For instance, there is a norm among detectives that two who work together will protect each other when a dangerous situation arises. During one investigation, a detective stepped out of a car to question a suspect who became belligerent. The second detective, who had remained overly long in the back seat of the police car, apologized indirectly to his partner by explaining how wrong it had been of him to permit his partner to encounter a suspect alone on the street. He later repeated this explanation privately, in genuine consternation at having committed the breach (and possibly at having been culpable in the presence of an observer). Strong feelings of empathy and cooperation, indeed almost of "clannishness," a term several policemen themselves used to describe the attitude of police toward one another, may be seen in the daily activities of police. Analytically, these feelings can be traced to the elements of danger and shared experiences of hostility in the policeman's role.

Finally, to round out the sketch, policemen are notably conservative, emotionally and politically. If the element of danger in the policeman's role tends to make the policeman suspicious, and therefore emotionally attached to the status quo, a similar consequence may be attributed to the element of authority. The fact that a man is engaged in enforcing a set of rules implies that he also becomes implicated in *affirming* them. Labor disputes provide the commonest example of conditions inclining the policeman to support the status quo. In these situations, the police are necessarily pushed on the side of the defense of property. Their responsibilities thus lead them to see the striking and sometimes angry workers as their enemy and, therefore, to be cool, if not antagonistic, toward the whole conception of labor militancy.[28] If a policeman did not believe in the system of laws he was responsible for enforcing, he would have to go on living in a state of conflicting cognitions, a condition which a number of social psychologists agree is painful.[29]

This hypothetical issue of not believing in the laws they are enforcing simply does not arise for most policemen. In the course of the research, however, there was one example. A Negro civil rights advocate (member of CORE) became a policeman with the conviction that by so doing he would be aiding the cause of impartial administration of laws for Negroes. For him, however, this outside rationale was not enough to sustain him in administering a system of laws that depends for its impartiality upon a reasonable measure of social and economic equality among the citizenry. Because this recruit identified so much with the Negro community as to be unable to meet the enforcement requirements of the Westville Police Department, his efficiency was impaired, and he resigned in his rookie year.

Police are understandably reluctant to appear to be anything but impartial politically. The police are forbidden from publicly campaigning for political candidates. The London police are similarly prohibited, and before 1887 were not allowed to vote in parliamentary elections or in local ones until 1893.[30] It was not surprising that the Westville chief of police forbade questions on the questionnaire that would have measured political attitudes.[31] One policeman, however, explained the chief's refusal on grounds that "A couple of jerks here would probably cut up, and come out looking like Commies."

During the course of administering the questionnaire over a three-day period, I talked with approximately fifteen officers and sergeants in the Westville department, discussing political attitudes of police. In addition, during the course of the research itself, approximately fifty were interviewed for varying periods of time. Of these, at least twenty were interviewed more than once, some over time periods of several weeks. Furthermore, twenty police were interviewed in Eastville, several for periods ranging from several hours to several days. Most of the time was *not* spent on investigating political attitudes, but I made a point of raising the question, if possible, making it part of a discussion centered around the contents of a right-wing newsletter to which one of the detectives subscribed. One discussion included a group of eight detectives. From these observations, interviews, and discussions, it was clear that a Goldwater type of conservatism was the dominant political and emotional persuasion of police. I encountered only three policemen who claimed to be politically "liberal," at the same time asserting that they were decidedly exceptional.

Whether or not the policeman is an "authoritarian personality" is a related issue, beyond the scope of this discussion partly because of the many questions raised about this concept. Thus, in the course of discussing the concept of "normality" in mental health, two psychologists make the point that many conventional people were high scorers on the California F scale and similar tests. The great mass of the people, according to these authors, is not much further along the scale of ego development than the typical adolescent who, as they describe him, is "rigid, prone to think in stereotypes, intolerant of deviations, punitive and anti-psychological—in short, what has been called an authoritarian personality."[32] Therefore it is preferable to call the policeman's a conventional personality.

Writing about the New York police force, Thomas R. Brooks suggests a similar interpretation. He writes:

> Cops are conventional people. . . . All a cop can swing in a milieu of marijuana smokers, interracial dates, and homosexuals is the night stick. A policeman who passed a Lower East Side art gallery filled with paintings of what appeared to be female genitalia could think of doing only one thing—step in and make an arrest.[33]

Despite his fundamental identification with conservative conventionality, however, the policeman may be familiar, unlike most conventional people, with the argot of the hipster and the underworld. (The policeman tends to resent the quietly respectable liberal who comes to the defense of such people on principle but who has rarely met them in practice.) Indeed, the policeman will use his knowledge of the argot to advantage in talking to a suspect. In this manner, the policeman *puts on* the suspect by pretending to share his moral conception of the world through the use of "hip" expressions. The suspect may put on a parallel show for the policeman by using only conventional language to indicate his respectability. (In my opinion, neither fools the other.)

NOTES

1. For previous contributions in this area, see the following: Ely Chinoy, *Automobile Workers and the American Dream* (Garden City: Doubleday and Company, Inc., 1955); Charles R. Walker and Robert H. Guest, *The Man on the Assembly Line* (Cambridge: Harvard University Press, 1952); Everett C. Hughes, "Work and the Self," in his *Men and Their Work* (Glencoe, Illinois: The Free Press, 1958), pp. 42–55; Harold L. Wilensky, *Intellectuals in Labor Unions: Organizational Pressures on Professional Roles* (Glencoe, Illinois: The Free Press, 1956); Wilensky, "Varieties of Work Experience," in Henry Borow, ed., *Man in a World at Work* (Boston: Houghton Mifflin Company, 1964), pp. 125–154; Louis Kriesberg, "The Retail Furrier: Concepts of Security and Success," *American Journal of Sociology* 57 (March 1952): 478–485; Waldo Burchard, "Role Conflicts of Military Chaplains," *American Sociological Review* 19 (October 1954): 528–535; Howard S. Becker and Blanche Geer, "The Fate of Idealism in Medical School," *American Sociological Review* 23 (1958): 50–56; and Howard S. Becker and Anselm L. Strauss, "Careers, Personality, and Adult Socialization," *American Journal of Sociology* 62 (November 1956): 253–363.

2. Morris Janowitz, *The Professional Soldier: A Social and Political Portrait* (New York: The Free Press of Glencoe, 1964), p. 175.

3. By no means does such an analysis suggest there are no individual or group differences among police. On the contrary, most of this study emphasizes differences, endeavoring to relate these to occupational specialties in police departments. This chapter, however, explores similarities rather than differences, attempting to account for the policeman's general disposition to perceive and to behave in certain ways.

4. William Westley was the first to raise such questions about the police, when he inquired into the conditions under which police are violent. Whatever merit this analysis has, it owes much to his prior insights, as all subsequent sociological studies of the police must. See his "Violence and the Police," *American Journal of Sociology* 59 (July 1953): 34–41; also his unpublished Ph.D. dissertation "The Police: A Sociological Study of Law, Custom, and Morality," University of Chicago, Department of Sociology, 1951.

5. Something of the flavor of the policeman's attitude toward the symbolic assailant comes across in a recent article by a police expert. In discussing the problem of selecting subjects for field interrogation, the author writes:

A. Be suspicious. This is a healthy police attitude, but it should be controlled and not too obvious.

B. Look for the unusual.
   1. Persons who do not "belong" where they are observed.
   2. Automobiles which do not "look right."
   3. Businesses opened at odd hours, or not according to routine or custom.

C. Subjects who should be subjected to field interrogations.
   1. Suspicious persons known to the officer from previous arrests, field interrogations, and observations.
   2. Emaciated appearing alcoholics and narcotics users who invariably turn to crime to pay for cost of habit.
   3. Person who fits description of wanted suspect as described by radio, teletype, daily bulletins.
   4. Any person observed in the immediate vicinity of a crime very recently committed or reported as "in progress."
   5. Known troublemakers near large gatherings.
   6. Persons who attempt to avoid or evade the officer.
   7. Exaggerated unconcern over contact with the officer.
   8. Visibly "rattled" when near the policeman.
   9. Unescorted women or young girls in public places, particularly at night in such places as cafés, bars, bus and train depots, or streetcorners.
   10. "Lovers" in an industrial area (make good lookouts).
   11. Persons who loiter about places where children play.
   12. Solicitors or peddlers in a residential neighborhood.

13. Loiterers around public rest rooms.
14. Lone male sitting in car adjacent to schoolground with newspaper or book in his lap.
15. Lone male sitting in car near shopping center who pays unusual amount of attention to women, sometimes continuously manipulating rearview mirror to avoid direct eye contact.
16. Hitchhikers.
17. Person wearing coat on hot days.
18. Car with mismatched hub caps, or dirty car with clean license plate (or vice versa).
19. Uniformed "deliverymen" with no merchandise or truck.
20. Many others. How about your own personal experiences?

From Thomas F. Adams, "Field Interrogation," *Police* (March–April 1963): 28.

6. See Irving Piliavin and Scott Briar, "Police Encounters with Juveniles," *American Journal of Sociology* 70 (September 1964): 206–214.

7. A questionnaire was given to all policemen in operating divisions of the police force: patrol, traffic, vice control, and all detectives. The questionnaire was administered at police lineups over a period of three days, mainly by the author but also by some of the police personnel themselves. Before the questionnaire was administered, it was circulated to and approved by the policemen's welfare association.

8. Indeed, the journalist Paul Jacobs, who has ridden with the Westville juvenile police as part of his own work in poverty, observed in a personal communication that juvenile police appear curiously drawn to seek out dangerous situations, as if juvenile work without danger is degrading.

9. Colin MacInnes, *Mister Love and Justice* (London: New English Library, 1962), p. 74.

10. Peter J. Connell, "Handling of Complaints by Police," unpublished paper for course in criminal procedure, Yale Law School, Fall, 1961.

11. James Baldwin, *Nobody Knows My Name* (New York: Dell Publishing Company, 1962), pp. 65–67.

12. MacInnes, op. cit., p. 20.

13. Respondents were asked, "Anybody who knows anything about police work knows that police face a number of problems. Would you please state—in order—what you consider to be the most serious problems police have." On the basis of a number of answers, the writer and J. Richard Woodworth devised a set of categories. Then Woodworth classified each response into one of the categories (see table below). When a response did not seem clear, he consulted with the writer. No attempt was made to independently check Woodworth's classifications because the results are used impressionistically, and do not test a hypothesis. It may be, for instance, that "relations with public" is sometimes used to indicate racial problems, and vice versa. "Racial problems" include only those answers having specific reference to race. The categories and results were as follows:

Westville police ranking of number-one problem faced by police

	Number	*Percent*
Relations with public	74	26
Racial problems and demonstrations	66	23
Juvenile delinquents and delinquency	23	8
Unpleasant police tasks	23	8
Lack of cooperation from authorities (DA, legislature, courts)	20	7
Internal departmental problems	17	6
Irregular life of policeman	5	2
No answer or other answer	56	20
	284	100

14. Royal Commission on the Police, 1962, Appendix IV to *Minutes of Evidence,* cited in Michael Banton, *The Policeman in the Community* (London: Tavistock Publications, 1964), p. 198

15. Similarly, Banton found Scottish police officers attempting to conceal their occupation when on holiday. He quotes one as saying: "If someone asks my wife 'What does your husband do?', I've told her to say, 'He's a clerk,' and that's the way it went because she found that being a policeman's wife—well, it wasn't quite a stigma, she didn't feel cut off, but that sort of invisible wall was up for conversation purposes when a policeman was there" (p. 198).

16. In addition to Banton, William Westley and James Q. Wilson have noted this characteristic of police. See Westley, op. cit., p. 294; Wilson, "The Police and Their Problems: A Theory," *Public Policy* 12 (1963): 189–216.

17. S. M. Lipset, Martin H. Trow, and James S. Coleman, *Union Democracy* (New York: Anchor Books, 1962), p. 123. A complete comparison is as follows:

Closest friends of printers and police, by occupation

	Printers N=1236 (%)	*Police N=700*
Same occupation	35	35
Professionals, business executives, and independent business owners	21	30
White-collar or sales employees	20	12
Manual workers	25	22

18. On this issue there was no variation. The statement "the policeman feels" means that there was no instance of a negative opinion expressed by the police studies.

19. Banton, op. cit., p. 114.

20. Janowitz, op. cit.

21. O. W. Wilson, for example, mentions this factor as a primary source of antagonism toward police. See his "Police Authority in a Free Society," *Journal of Criminal Law, Criminology, and Police Science* 54 (June 1964): 175–177. In the current study, in addition to the police themselves, other people interviewed, such as attorneys in the system, also attribute the isolation of police to their authority. Similarly, Arthur L. Stinchcorabe, in "The Control of Citizen Resentment in Police Work," provides a stimulating analysis, to which I am indebted, of the ways police authority generates resentment.

22. See Wayne R. La Fave, "The Police and Nonenforcement of the Law," *Wisconsin Law Review* (1962): 104–137, 179–239.

23. For a theoretical discussion of the problems of leadership, see George Homans, *The Human Group* (New York: Harcourt, Brace and Company, 1950), especially the chapter on "The Job of the Leader," pp. 415–440.

24. The work of the Westville morals squad is analyzed in detail in an unpublished master's thesis by J. Richard Woodworth, "The Administration of Statutory Rape Complaints: A Sociological Study" (University of California, 1964).

25. Horace R. Cayton, *Long Old Road* (New York: Trident Press, 1965), p. 154.

26. Ben Whitaker, *The Police* (Middlesex, England: Penguin Books, 1964), p. 137.

27. It would be difficult to compare this factor across occupations, since the indicators could hardly be controlled. Nevertheless, I felt that the sense of responsibility to policemen in other departments was on the whole quite strong.

28. In light of this, the most carefully drawn lesson plan in the "professionalized" Westville police department, according to the officer in charge of training, is the one dealing with the policeman's demeanor in labor disputes. A comparable concern is now being evidenced in teaching policemen appropriate demeanor in civil rights demonstrations. See, e.g., Juby E. Towler, *The Police Role in Racial Conflicts* (Springfield: Charles C. Thomas, 1964).

29. Indeed, one school of social psychology asserts that there is a basic "drive," a fundamental tendency of human nature, to reduce the degree of discrepancy between conflicting cognitions. For the policeman, this tenet implies that he would have to do something to reduce the discrepancy between his beliefs and his behavior. He would have to modify his behavior, his beliefs, or introduce some outside factor to justify the discrepancy. If he were to modify his behavior, so as not to enforce the law in which he disbelieves, he would not hold his position for long. Practically, then, his alternatives are to introduce some outside factor, or to modify his beliefs. However, the outside factor would have to be compelling in order to reduce the pain resulting from the dissonance between his cognitions. For example, he would have to be able to convince himself that the only way he could possibly make a living was by being a policeman. Or he would have to modify his beliefs. See Leon Festinger, *A Theory of Cognitive Dissonance* (Evanston, Ill.: Row-Peterson, 1957). A brief explanation of Festinger's theory is reprinted in Edward E. Sampson, ed., *Approaches, Contexts, and Problems of Social Psychology* (Englewood Cliffs, N.J.: Prentice-Hall, 1964), pp. 9–15.

30. Whitaker, op. cit., p. 26.

31. The questions submitted to the chief of police were directly analogous to those asked of printers in the study of the I.T.U. See Lipset et al., op. cit., "Appendix II–Interview Schedule," pp. 493–503.

32. Jane Loevinger and Abel Ossorio, "Evaluations of Therapy by Self-Report: A Paradox," *Journal of Abnormal and Social Psychology* 58 (May 1959): 392; see also Edward A. Shils, "Authoritarianism: 'Right' and 'Left'," in R. Christie and M. Jahoda, eds., *Studies in Scope and Method of "The Authoritarian Personality"* (Glencoe, Ill.: The Free Press, 1954), pp. 24–49.

33. Thomas R. Brooks, "New York's Finest," *Commentary* 40 (August 1965): 29–30.

ARTICLE SEVEN

The Functional Nature of Police Reform: The "Myth" of Controlling the Police

GARY W. SYKES

Major movements to reform the police through professionalization, policy making, and administrative decentralization have been launched during the past half-century. A major goal has been to subordinate patrol-officer discretion to bureaucratic due process. In this article Gary Sykes argues that these reforms primarily produced merely the appearance of change and did not alter the status quo.

For at least five decades, major reform efforts focused on American police (Brown 1981; Sherman 1974; Walker 1976a; 1976b) and almost universally supported a primary goal—changing street practices to conform with classical liberal democratic values (see Berkeley 1969; Johnson 1981). Patterns of corruption, inefficiency, abuse of force, misconduct, and racial, social, and sex discrimination all seem to provide evidence that police were largely beyond accountability to the liberal institutions designed to check, balance, or structure their powers. The so-called police problem can be summarized into three broad categories: conduct, corruption, and productivity.

Although the federal and state courts initiated, maintained, and in some ways continued the due process "revolution" by standardizing local criminal justice administration, most landmark decisions were aimed at defining access to the courts and administrative procedures rather than police accountability (Bittner 1971). Reformers advocated programs in education

Source: Justice Quarterly 2 (March 1985): 52–65. Reprinted by permission of Princeton University Press.

and training that expanded the idea of police *professionalism* (Goldstein 1977; Kelling and Kliesmet 1972; Walker 1976b; Plumer 1979), while other groups encouraged police administrators to increase organizational efficiency and productivity (see Guyot 1979). In sum, reform movements on a variety of fronts made an extensive effort to alter traditional police street policies and practices.

After decades of sustained activities and enormous public expenditures, some recent studies now contend that the impact of these reforms was less than anticipated (Bordner 1983; Brown 1981; Johnson 1981). In fact, one writer judges the long-standing professional reform movement to be at a standstill (Fogelson 1977). Another maintains that the success of extensive organizational and personnel reforms can be characterized by the metaphor "bending granite" (Guyot 1979). Other researchers question whether the resources invested in police education brought the presumed payoff, especially when studies designed to measure its impact failed to provide substantial evidence of change (Sherman 1982; Plumer 1979).

Indirect evidence of the shifting emphasis in reform may be that current research efforts seem narrower in scope, focusing primarily on more efficient strategies to enhance the crime control function (see Sherman 1982). Most studies currently sponsored by the National Institute of Justice target administrative attempts to structure police patrol activities based on findings regarding the efficacy of random preventive patrol, or examine career criminal apprehension programs and prosecutorial administrative problems. Such concerns are remarkably different from previous research on the use of force, racism and minorities, police compliance with constitutional guarantees, and massive federal educational programs in the humanities and social sciences designed to nurture democratic values among police (see Berkeley 1969).

For a variety of reasons, the momentum of police reform seems either to have stalled or paused in a period of assessment. Given such allegations regarding the limited impact of reform, it is likely that its proponents have exaggerated both the depth and scope of change; and evidence suggests that a significant number of urban police organizations resisted efforts directed at fundamental reorganization (Brown 1981). For example, the most intensive and expansive movement, labeled "professional," was allegedly co-opted, redefined, or selectively adopted during the conflict over unionization in the last few decades (Fogelson 1977).

REFORM MOVEMENTS: A TYPOLOGY

Michael Brown defined four dimensions (models) of police reform. The idea of *profession,* widely supported among practitioners, represented a conventional wisdom among in-house progressives. Articulated orginally by August Vollmer and his disciple O. W. Wilson, it sought the inculcation of an internalized code of ethics and defined professionalism generally as a careerist orientation complemented by technical efficiency. In other words, its aim was what Egon Bittner (1971) called an "informed, deliberating and technically efficient *professional* who knows that he must operate within the limits set by a moral and legal trust."

The initial view of professionalism by Vollmer and his followers reflects the classical idea of profession by emphasizing preprofessional classical education in the liberal arts and social sciences, scientific theory, and crime prevention, as well as professional training. However, the prevailing use of the term focuses primarily on training (not preprofessional education) and technical proficiency within the parameters of a code of ethics, thereby losing some of the central concerns of Vollmer's proposal (Douthit 1975).

In addition, this selective idea of policing as a profession also lacks several important elements included in the classical meaning of the term, such as a body of specialized, internationally recognized knowledge, certified preprofessional education followed by accredited professional training, legal autonomy to exercise discretionary judgment, lateral movement among personnel from one geographic and political jurisdiction to another, and authorized self-regulation based on a universally defined and maintained code of ethics.

At best, this modern professional movement among police remains incomplete, in part because of some unique factors. It is highly unlikely that legalized autonomy (in the sense of authorized professional discretion) and self-regulation would be permitted politically. On the contrary, major reform activities in recent decades, though offered under the label of "professional," have aimed at restricting police discretion and enhancing external regulation. There is provocative evidence that the movement toward professional status is generally "stalled" at this point in time, or that the definition has been so extensively modified that it bears little resemblance to the socially accepted meaning of that term (Fogelson 1977).

The decade of the 1960s, with its social and political turmoil, produced an additional complementary reform movement—structuring police discretion through administrative policy making. Landmark Supreme Court decisions exemplified only a small part of this movement, which attempted to develop explicit rules and policies to clarify the ambiguities of the police task and to enhance accountability (see Goldstein 1977). Such policy-making reforms included specified objectives (MBO was one variant), proposed and funded detailed policy and procedure manuals, and the adoption of performance evaluation systems.

Broadly speaking, a primary goal of such changes was to strengthen administrative and political supervision of line officers (Van Maanen 1978; Brown 1981). This policy-making movement represented reform via rule reification through which control over police discretion and administrative centralization reflected many of the classical aspects of bureaucratization (Brown 1981). In other words, policy-making reforms complemented the Vollmer/Wilson movement by attempting to professionalize police administration (Van Maanen 1973; Harris 1973). Understood functionally, it encouraged a new kind of leadership with the skills to manage bureaucratic organizations and it employed due process procedures, productivity, and managerial efficiency as the primary rationales for standardization and centralization—that is, bureaucratic control.

Another major reform effort, administrative decentralization (e.g., team policing) reached its zenith in the early 1970s and primarily focused on the lack of career incentives for line officers in the organization. This motivational problem allegedly contributed to management difficulties defined in terms of bureaucratic efficiency—for example, encouraging unionism.

Dorothy Guyot (1979) characterized team policing, as well as many similar experiments, as an attempt to overcome organizational problems inherent in the military rank structure of policing. She listed organizational difficulties such as the lack of management flexibility in personnel decisions, the lack of material and organizational incentives within the police officer rank, excessive formality related to militarism, communication blockages and distortions caused by "tall" organizations, and organizational and professional insularity. Guyot evaluated various measures designed to ameliorate these problems, including the elimination of ranks, positions or levels, agency reorganization proposals and experiments, assessment center screening programs, task force or matrix-type project experiments, expanded pay scale systems, career development reorganizations, demilitarized titles and symbols, lateral entry mechanisms, team policing trials, civilianization efforts focused on the higher levels in management. Taken together, these combined reforms reflected a broadly conceived challenge to many widely recognized problems within the traditional pyramid in police organizations.

Brown's typology of professional, policy making, and administrative decentralization can be synthesized. These efforts incorporated three complementary dimensions rather than distinct reform models and resulted in a multifaceted movement to confront the alleged police problem (conduct, corruption, and productivity). These efforts were designed to professionalize the line officer (selective Vollmer/Wilson elements), develop sophisticated administrative leadership (policy-making approaches), and encourage the ideology of participatory management to provide for job enrichment and enlargement as solutions to motivational problems of line officers (administrative decentralization).

Brown also highlighted one additional reform movement, political decentralization, which supported increased community involvement in police policy making—for example, citizen participation groups such as civilian review boards, police commissions, and citizen advisory boards.

This movement never enjoyed extensive support among police administrators, perhaps due in part to the fact that pressure for change was external to the agency, was political in nature, and was initiated principally by community groups critical to the police.

To some degree, political decentralization ideas were ideologically incompatible with some major tenets of the professional movement. A significant accomplishment of the latter reform effort was a decline in political patronage and its replacement with civil service reforms. Consequently, community control proponents were open to the allegation that they were encouraging a return to the past, when overt political interference was widespread (Fogelson 1977).

One suggested interpretation of these issues was that some of the changes initiated by the professional movement provided the basis for arguments against increased community control and were functional to the status quo in the face of demands for greater political accountability. The movement for community involvement was not complementary to increased bureaucratization and received an unsympathetic reception in police circles (Fogelson 1977). At least one generalization seems warranted—a widespread answer to the call for police reform during recent decades was increased bureaucratization, including experiments in participatory management, rather than citizen participation or political control of police policy making (Johnson 1981; Brown 1981).

THE LIMITS OF REFORM

Fogelson (1977) alleged that the professional reforms initiated by Vollmer and his disciples resulted in the following anomalies: promotional procedures based on civil service criteria did not necessarily create more capable leadership or eliminate discrimination; the idea of professionalism was defined selectively and never actually penetrated deeply into agency culture; the line officers' role did not appear to change substantially; and there were continued questions about whether postsecondary education ought to be required or whether it was relevant at all (Sherman 1974; 1978).

In addition, police corruption in major cities seemed relatively resistant to reform efforts in the name of the professional movement, while at the same time serious questions surfaced about police effectiveness in dealing with crime (Sherman 1983). The 1970s provided some support for the contention that what the police did, or did not do, had little measurable influence on the level of crime. Fogelson concluded that such anomalies nurtured a "dwindling confidence" in the police as crime fighters and in police agencies as capable of fulfilling their societal mandate to control crime.

Other evidence recently emerged to challenge the efficacy of the managerial reforms of organizational problems related to the rank structure.

Guyot (1979) found (1) many of these changes were co-opted (e.g., the Jacob's Plan in Los Angeles); (2) other changes represented only symbolic rather than substantive changes and sometimes were abandoned (e.g., the Lakewood "experiment"); and (3) with the exceptions of team policing (the evidence was tentative) and civilianization, virtually all of the major types of organizational and personnel reforms were limited in their impact on the problems associated with police rank structure. The metaphor used to illustrate the resistance to these efforts was "bending granite."

Guyot listed the following possible factors as explaining police resistance: impenetrable opposition of line officers and sergeants, generalized agency opposition because some of the changes limited upward mobility by reducing the number of potential positions, and limited time horizons in police circles based on immediate rather than long-run perspectives. She found that the only developments that could potentially bring change were an erosion of the rank structure by civilianization, team policing (tentatively), and expanded pay scales. The goal of an open system for police agencies—that is, flexible and responsive to change—remained elusive. In short, Guyot presented strong evidence that reforms tended to have a superficial impact on agency practices and policies, echoing Johnson's (1981) conclusion that police administrators expressed a fundamental unwillingness to confront and to implement changes necessary to deal with the problems of conduct, corruption, and/or productivity.

Such findings and conclusions reflect a virtually universal conclusion among prominent police researchers that the limited success of change can be blamed largely on police intransigence. Johnson (1981) and Walker (1976b) concluded in their histories of law enforcement that, compared to other local government institutions, police continue to be unique in their resistance to change and are an anachronism in the modern world of public administration.

Sherman (1978) provided a clear example of the limits of reform in his assessment of the impact of education. He found that many, and possibly most, local police agencies succeeded in using educational institutions to support the status quo, giving only the image and not the substance of preprofessional and professional programs. Others also alleged that the police demonstrated a remarkable ability to give the appearance without the substance of change (for a discussion of police image building, see Manning 1971). However, such conclusions may be premature and overlook several important considerations, which will be explored below.

Given the variety of reforms in the name of professionalization, what seems unexplored and puzzling is the persistence of the rank structure and other "anachronistic" practices in the face of enormous criticism and extensive experimentation. In other words, what requires more extensive explanation is why the police continue to cling to an allegedly outmoded, inefficient, and discredited organizational form despite overwhelming contrary evidence and intense criticism. Other possible reasons for resistance to change are not mentioned by critics.

Intransigence to fundamental police reform in fact may result from such things as shortsightedness in defense of the status quo, but an alternative hypothesis is also worth consideration. Specifically, the relative inertia of police agencies could be related to the nature of the police role and the cultural context in which it operates. The alleged resistance to reform might have an institutional basis which reflects values other than liberal due process.

BUREAUCRATIZATION VERSUS THE MILITARY PYRAMID

The professional movement incorporating both the policy-making and administrative decentralization ideologies remains the prevailing answer to the "police problem" among many academic and "progressive" reformers concerned with policing (Brown 1981). Widely supported goals include ensuring that police discretion is exercised ethically and responsively within explicit liberal democratic norms; developing accountability through both personnel and agency evaluation; and encouraging efficiency in police management practices, borrowed largely from business administration. In other words, the bureaucratization of the street-officer role, with the standardization, routinization, and centralization inherent in that process, remains the implicit means of reformers to confront the problems of police misconduct, corruption, and lack of productivity in crime control.

The judgment that reforms falter because of intransigent leadership in police agencies perhaps underestimates the functional significance of traditional policing in American culture. Any attempt to rationalize the police role must recognize its idiosyncratic nature, or, as Bittner called it, the "intuitive" dimension of police discretion. The police function includes inherently discretionary powers in order maintenance activities and the use of force. Aside from a few qualifications involving jurisdiction, personal interest, and frivolous use, there are no guidelines or range of objectives instructing a police officer on what he must do in a given situation. The officer decides what is necessary and proper under the circumstances and "it is exceedingly rare that police actions involving the use of force are actually reviewed and judged by anyone at all" (Bittner 1971).

James Q. Wilson (1968b) described policing as a "craft" partly because it was based on skills acquired only through experiential learning, which defied the rational, systematic, and rule-governed processes associated with classroom pedagogy and formal education. In whatever way this dimension was defined (idiosyncratic, experiential, or intuitive), it remained a significant challenge to those attempting to rationalize this role through liberal bureaucratic reform measures.

Paradoxically, "structuring police discretion," as Goldstein (1977) proposed, may be a contradiction in terms. Street policing as a community-based institution, with its idiosyncratic nature, resists attempts at administrative rationalization—the standard liberal method for achieving a degree of accountability. Bureaucratization as a process partially involves increasing control over discretionary action in conformity with collective goals "to routinize and make more predictable the cooperative efforts of individuals" (Wilson 1980). In policing, however, the conflict between the bureaucracy and the "street" represents a problematic difference that distinguishes it from other public occupations, because the role requires that use of "non-negotiable coercive force" be employed *intuitively* (Bittner 1971).

Another significant implication relates to this dimension of the police function—its military trappings project an image of controlled officers and of an organization designed to "fight" the "enemies" of society. In other words, the military symbols nurture the public view of strict organizational supervision while the perceived target of such awesome discretionary power is implicitly external to the community—that is, criminals, as the "out-group." A "war on crime" fought by an "army" diminishes anxiety about police power being directed against decent, law-abiding citizens (Bittner 1971). Militarization constitutes one answer to the anomaly of policing in a "free" society. As such, the military image plays a functional role by requiring the police to be part of an extraordinary institution controlled by an explicit hierarchy or chain of command.

If an essential function of the military structure is to promote an image of police accountability and limited discretion, the efforts to demilitarize in the name of management efficiency are likely to be perceived as problematic by both the police and the public. In fact, one of the dangers of police reform pointed out by Van Maanen (1978) is that buraucratic professionalism may result in less control over street officers than is currently the case in the military pyramid.

Militarization is not an organizational form designed for efficiency, but rather aims to achieve compliance to centralized rules, plans, or strategies. If the "craft" of street policing is essentially informal community peacekeeping and order maintenance, as opposed to an emphasis on law enforcement and crime control, then reform efforts based on professional criteria are likely to be limited until there is a change in the nature of the police role (Van Maanen 1973). If carried to its logical conclusion, the nature of the police task makes it an anomaly in liberal society and perhaps unique in terms of conventional liberal reform (Goldstein 1977). It is by nature a situationally based decision-making role resistant to bureaucratic rationalization and an evolved community-based institution relatively independent of state and federal controls in American society.

The possibility must be considered that police organizations were not designed for efficiency in crime control, but instead were constructed along military lines to reassure a liberal society that it is not in danger of unrestrained power—that is, military symbols function as myth in much the same way that the idea of the "rule of law" underscores the legitimacy of the legal order. In addition, as a community-based institution, the primary function of the police traditionally involved order and community peacekeeping functions, which included discretionary actions in problem solving and little practical institutional surveillance.

If the military symbols surrounding the police function were mandated culturally to provide support for the myth that police were subject to both internal rules and organizational leadership, it is possible that many of the reform efforts, especially policy-making and managerial proposals, would represent an attempt to rationalize a functional role in society that by its nature resisted reduction to the framework of bureaucratic due process. It was the fear of uncontrolled police discretion that fueled reform movements.

This fear of discretionary power requires that the police be visible (dressed in soldier uniforms and riding around in specially marked vehicles visible from several blocks away), subject to explicit legal rules and procedures, and subordinate to a clear chain of command. To demilitarize the police or dilute the rank structure through managerial reform perhaps violates accepted understandings about the exercise, control, and organization of police power.

In fact, reflecting this mythical understanding, many Americans seem to believe that police powers are more restricted than they actually are, contributing to numerous confrontations in which citizens often say to police officers, "You can't do that!" The police response is often a knowing smile as the officer realizes he or she is dealing with a "know-nothing" or a "taxpayer," terms sometimes used to distinguish the average citizen from "assholes" and "suspicious persons" (Van Maanen 1978).

This alternative hypothesis of the police function presents a formidable challenge to reforms. By its very nature, street policing resists professionalization, bureaucratization, and managerial efforts to change it. These efforts seem to fall short in the context of the idiosyncratic reality of the police role. To attribute the stuttering reform movement to intransigent leadership or police myopia is perhaps to overlook that the military rank structure is the institutional solution to the problem of police discretion in a society based on a commitment to due process.

CONCLUSION: REFORM AS MYTH

Traditional policing in America was often stereotyped as corrupt, repressive, and inefficient (Fogelson 1977; Walker 1984). The "watchman" style of policing and its informal "street justice" practices represented a target few reformers could resist. The presumption was that informal community-based constraints on police were inadequate and must be replaced by political-legal-managerial measures to assure predictability, accountability, and effectiveness against crime.

At least it seems clear that many reformers implicitly recognized the mythical nature of the police organization—that is, the military pyramid did not provide adequate protection from arbitrary and capricious use of power by the police. Their primary solution was to "liberalize" the police—impose administrative and legal due process. What they largely failed to take into account were both the costs involved and how those costs might provide the basis for resistance to reform by police and the public. In other words, reformers did not take into account the ironic value of the paramilitary structure: it creates an image of police accountability, while leaving them relatively free to use their discretion to perform community peacekeeping tasks.

The most significant factors, which ultimately influence and define the conduct of the police function, may not be the formal institutional context, but rather the extent to which police officers reflect and mirror the values, expectations, and demands of their community. Van Maanen (1978) and Skolnick (1966) portrayed the street officer as sensitive to a "moral mandate" which flowed from the community and required informal "street justice" to control neighborhood "terrorism" or the "assholes" who violate norms of decency and cooperation.

Community peacekeeping actions by street officers often do not require the use of formal institutions; "justice without trial" involves relatively minor offenses recognized not to be serious by prosecutors and judges—for example, verbal harassment, threatening behavior, assaults (especially among acquaintances), and minor property damage incidents. Such misdemeanors are generally not crimes, but are forfeiture offenses under the law. However, these offenses are not perceived to be minor by the victims in the community; they are regarded as terrorist threats to lives and property, contributing to a generalized fear that alters the social fabric of a neighborhood (Wilson and Kelling 1982; see pp. 55–73 of this reader).

Reform measures which rationalize the police role, both legally and administratively, and promote crime control or enforcement at the expense of peacekeeping and order maintenance functions, may result in unintended consequences. If street police officers are under continuous scrutiny and formal surveillance by administrative and procedural due process institutions, their reaction might be a tendency to reduce "street justice" as an expected community service.

James Q. Wilson and George Kelling (1982) provided a provocative hypothesis in a study in which professional policing and enforcement policies reduced the informal peacekeeping function. Neighborhood terrorism increased (the fear of crime), the potential for serious crime grew, and implicitly police officers spent less time responding to the "community mandate" for peacekeeping.

When confronted with those who threaten a neighborhood's peace and security, there is an implicit community mandate for "somebody to do something" and to reinforce the image that "someone is in control." To deny street officers the informal powers to act intuitively and spontaneously in the face of these problems cuts at the very heart of the police function as it has evolved in the neighborhood context.

One possible consequence of professionalized police might well be both communal and moral decay (see Wilson and Kelling 1982). Reform measures to bureaucratize, professionalize, and/or structure police discretionary power ultimately may threaten the very fabric of the social order if they result in undermining the "street justice" function. Further research examining this hypothesis is needed.

In other words, there is widespread recognition that the military organization of the police function does not provide for strict accountability, nor does it seem to provide an adequate formal institutional check on the discretionary power of the police. Despite these concerns, it continues to enjoy widespread support in liberal society (Van Maanen 1978).

Some reformers, concerned that efforts so far have failed to foster the anticipated changes in police behavior and practices, implicitly recognize definite limits to the impact of reform (see Sherman 1978). Other writers, including "progressive" police administrators, argue that reform movements have resulted in substantial change and have ushered in a new era (see Staufenberger 1980). Both recent assessments question whether the reform movement actually achieved many of its goals (Fogelson 1977). The extent to which reforms were successful is problematic and cannot be answered with finality.

One possibility must be recognized, but it is only speculative at this point: the selective incorporation of professionalism, the policy-making attempts to standardize and to routinize officer responses, and the organizational reforms designed to alter the rank structure may give the appearance of reform that is functional to the status quo in policing. Such reforms provide an image of change without substance, especially regarding the peacekeeping role.

Perhaps the limited impact of these reforms is strong evidence that policing is unique and involves expansive autonomy to provide effective community services. The risk may be that if reform efforts are successful in inducing police behavior to confine itself to liberal-bureaucratic constraints, neighborhood terrorism might not only increase but in the long run contribute to a decaying environment in which serious crime breeds.

To put the matter differently, the reform movements may have succeeded to some extent in creating the appearance without the substance of fundamental reform. The adoption of professional values and symbols, the development of policy and procedure manuals, the publicizing of landmark court decisions, the proliferation of educational programs, and the emphasis on participatory management all contribute to the image of change. Recent assessments question the efficacy of these changes given the continuation of some traditional practices and institutions targeted by the reformers.

Whatever the functional role of the myths surrounding American policing, reformers cannot afford to ignore their complexity or the cultural expectations which surround them. The current "standstill" in reform may be less the result of police resistance to change than of the limits imposed by the nature of the police function itself. The possibility must at least be considered—the limits of reform are defined by the public's expectations that the police will do more than control crime; they also will control informally those in the community who violate standards of decency and conduct. Failure in peacekeeping may be a cost demanded by successful reforms, but one that many police and citizens are unwilling to pay.

REFERENCES

BITTNER, E. (1971) *The Functions of the Police in Modern Society*. Washington, D.C.: U.S. Government Printing Office.

BERKELEY, G. F. (1969) *The Democratic Policeman*. Boston: Beacon Press.

BORDNER, D. C. (1983) "Routine Policing, Discretion, and the Definition of Law, Order, and Justice in Society." *Criminology* 21:2.

BROWN, M. K. (1981) *Working the Street: Police Discretion and the Dilemmas of Reform* New York: Russell Sage Foundation.

DOUTHIT, N. (1975) "August Vollmer, Berkeley's First Chief of Police, and the Emergence of Police Professionalism." *California Historical Quarterly* Spring: 101-124.

FOGELSON, R. M. (1977) *Big City Police*. Cambridge, Mass.: Harvard University Press.

GOLDSTEIN, H. (1963) "Police Discretion: The Ideal Versus the Real." *Public Administration Review* 23:140-148.

——— (1977) *Policing a Free Society*. Cambridge, Mass.: Ballinger.

GUYOT, D. (1979) "Bending Granite: Attempts to Change the Rank Structure of American Police Departments." *Journal of Police Science and Administration* 7:3.

HARRIS, R. N. (1973) *The Policy Academy: An Inside View*. New York: John Wiley & Sons.

JOHNSON, D. R. (1981) *American Law Enforcement: A History*. St. Louis: Forum Press.

KELLING, G. L., and R. B. KLIESMET (1972) "Resistance to the Professionalization of the Police." *The Law Officer* 5:16-22.

LIPSKY, M. (1980) *Street-Level Bureaucracy: Dilemmas of the Individual in Public Service*. New York: Russell Sage Foundation.

LUNDMAN, R. J. (1980) *Police Behavior: A Sociological Perspective*. New York: Oxford University Press.

MANNING, P. K. (1971) "The Police: Mandate, Strategies and Appearances." In J. D. Douglas, ed., *Crime and Justice in American Society*. Indianapolis: Bobbs-Merrill.

MUIR, W. K., JR. (1977) *Police: Streetcorner Politicians*. Chicago: University of Chicago Press.

——— (1977) *Police Work*. Cambridge, Mass.: M.I.T. Press.

PLUMER, D. (1979) "Higher Education for Police: Catch-22 by Any Other Name." Paper presented at the Annual Meeting of the Academy of Criminal Justice Sciences, Cincinnati, Ohio.

RUBINSTEIN, J. (1973) *City Police*. New York: Ballantine.

SHERMAN, L. W. (1974) "The Sociology and the Social Reform of the American Police: 1950-1973." *Journal of Police Science and Administration* 2(2):255-262.

——— (1978) *The Quality of Police Education*. Washington, D.C.: Jossey-Bass Publishers.

——— (1983) *Patrol Strategies for Police. Crime and Public Policy*. San Francisco: ICS Press.

SKOLNICK, J. H. (1966) *Justice Without Trial: Law Enforcement in Democratic Society*. New York: John Wiley.

STAUFENBERGER, R. A., ed. (1980) *Progress in Policing: Essays on Change*. Cambridge, Mass.: Ballinger.

TERRITO, L., and R. L. SMITH (1976) "The Internal Affairs Unit: Friend or Foe." *The Police Chief* 43 (July).

VAN MAANEN, J. (1973) "Observations on the Making of Policemen." *Human Organization* 32.

——— (1974) "Working the Street: A Developmental View of Police Behavior." In H. Jacob, *The Potential for Reform of Criminal Justice*. Beverly Hills, Calif.: Sage Publications, pp. 83-130.

——— (1978) "The Asshole." In P. Manning and J. Van Maanen, eds., *Policing a View from the Street*. Santa Monica, Calif.: Goodyear.

VOLLMER, A. (1936) *The Police in Modern Society*. Berkeley: University of California Press.

WALKER, S. (1976a) "The Urban Police in American History: A Review of the Literature," *Journal of Police Science and Administration* 4:252-260.

——— (1976b) "Police Professionalism: Another Look at the Issues." *Journal of Sociology and Social Welfare* 3 (July): 701-710.

——— (1977) *A Critical History of Police Reform*. Lexington: Lexington Books.

——— (1984). "Broken Windows and Fractured History: The Use and Misuse of History in Recent Police Patrol Analysis." *Justice Quarterly* 1:1.

WAMBAUGH, J. (1973) *The Blue Knight*. Boston: Little, Brown.

WILSON, J. Q. (1968) "Dilemmas of Police Administration." *Public Administration Review* 28(5).

——— (1968b) *Varieties of Police Behavior: The Management of Law and Order in Eight Communities*. Cambridge, Mass.: Harvard University Press.

——— (1980) "Police Research and Experimentation." In R. A. Staufenberger, ed., *Progress in Policing: Essays on Change*. Cambridge, Mass.: Ballinger.

——— and B. BOLAND (1978) "The Effects of the Police on Crime," *Law and Society Review* 12:367-390.

WILSON, J. Q., and G. L. KELLING (1982) "Broken Windows: The Police and Neighborhood Safety." *Atlantic Monthly* 249 (March): 29–38.

WILSON, ORLANDO W. (1963) *Police Administration*. New York: McGraw-Hill.

PART THREE

PROSECUTION

For many years the radio serial "Mr. District Attorney" held audiences spellbound as its namesake sought "not only to prosecute to the limit of the law all persons accused of crime within this county, but to defend with equal vigor the rights and privileges of all its citizens." In real life, there are counterparts to the crusading fictional prosecutors. Over the years a number of political leaders at the national and state levels have come to prominence as fighting prosecutors, and many have based campaigns for higher political office on reputations gained from widely publicized investigations or trials. The influence prosecutors have flows directly from their legal duties, but must be understood within the context of the administrative and political environment of the system.

It seems natural that the prosecutor's office should serve as a stepping stone to advancement. Because they deal with dramatic and sensational situations, prosecutors can use the communications media to create a favorable climate of opinion. They can also use discretionary powers to impress voters with their prosecuting ability. To avoid difficult cases, prosecutors can just drop charges. They can also initiate investigations at politically opportune times, and disclose suspected wrongdoing by members of the opposition. Because they have a staff that they can use for campaign work, and hold offices that make it easy to gather political contributions, prosecutors may be formidable opponents in politics.

Although the partisan advantages of the prosecutor's office are great, they tend to overshadow the real political importance of daily decisions the office makes. These decisions exert a tremendous influence on the values in the community. Of the many positions within the legal process, the position of prosecuting attorney is distinctive because it is concerned with all aspects of the criminal justice system. Not only do prosecutors have the formal power to determine which cases will be prosecuted, what charges will be made, and what bargains there will be with defendants, but what prosecutors do also influences the operations of the police, the coroner, the grand jury, and the judge. Accordingly, if we were to place prosecutors' activities on a scale, we would see that at one end they perform many tasks concurrently and in cooperation with the police. They may, for instance, investigate areas of suspected wrongdoing, directing the police in the actual apprehension of law violators. At the other end of the scale, we would recognize prosecutors as officers of the court, concerned in the role of adjudicator that justice be accorded defendants. In the United States, where public prosecution is the only means by which defendants are brought to trial, the prosecuting attorney is the vital link between the police and the courts. In each role, prosecutors are able to make decisions that vitally affect the administration of justice without strictly adhering to legal rules, relying rather on their personal judgment. This faculty is often influenced by their exchange relationships with other actors in the judicial and political system.

The powers of prosecutors are enhanced by the circumstances under which they may make decisions. Prosecutors are usually elected on a partisan basis for a four-year term; there are few other public checks on their actions. In most states, the prosecutor is responsible either to no one other than the voters, or to the governor—and then only for aggravated nonfeasance or misfeasance. In addition, the prosecutor generally makes decisions out of the glare of publicity. For example, a deputy prosecutor and a defense attorney may reach a verbal agreement over a cup of coffee or in the hall outside the courtroom. This agreement may result in a reduced charge in exchange for a guilty plea, or dismissal of the charge if the defendant is willing to seek psychiatric help.

As the nexus of the adjudicative and enforcement functions, the prosecutor has been called the most powerful single individual in local government. If the prosecutor does not act, the judge and the jury are helpless and the police officer's word is meaningless. In this position, the prosecutor plays many roles: crusader, administrator, counselor to other government officials, advocate. Each person occupying the position interprets the roles differently, depending on the others in the relationship, the environment within which he or she operates, and his or her own personality. The power of the prosecuting attorney was well stated by the Wickersham Commission in 1931.

> The prosecutor [is] the real arbiter of what laws shall be enforced and against whom, while the attention of the public is drawn rather to the small percentage of offenders who go through the courts.

DECISION MAKING

At each stage of prosecution there are a number of ways to deal with each case. The closer a case is to coming to trial, the less latitude is available to decision makers. A sieve effect operates, so that a case is handled in an increasingly finite manner as it goes from the police to a preliminary hearing and trial. At each succeeding step the number of judicial personnel associated with the case increases and the formal requirements of the system become more intricate. As a case moves toward the courtroom, the visibility of decision making increases and the exchange relationships of participants become more complex. Under these circumstances, the prosecutor, the accused, and the court have less freedom in their attempts to find a solution beneficial to all.

To the layperson it might appear that there is little discretion in determining what charge should be made against a lawbreaker. But because of the nature of the charging process, prosecutors actually have a great deal of discretion as they define cases and file information or indictments.

Suppose that Smith—carrying a gun—breaks into a grocery store, assaults the proprietor, and robs the cash drawer. What charges can the prosecutor file? The accused can be charged with at least four violations: breaking and entering, assault, armed robbery, and carrying a dangerous weapon. Other charges might be added, depending on the circumstances—whether it was day or night, for instance.

David Sudnow has distinguished between "necessarily included offenses" and "situationally included offenses." He asks, "Could Smith have committed crime A and not crime B?" If the answer is yes, B is not a necessarily included offense. In the example of the grocery store, Smith has committed the necessarily included crime of carrying a dangerous weapon in the course of the armed robbery. The prosecutor may either charge Smith solely with the armed robbery, or include any number of other charges or combination of charges in the information. With multiple charges, the prosecutor increases his bargaining power in plea negotiations.

It is difficult to determine the exact motives of decision makers in selecting one alternative over another. As the exchange model emphasizes, decision making is a product of the needs and goals of the system as affected by the environment in which it exists. The factors that influence the decision to prosecute seem to fall into three categories: evidential, humanitarian, and organizational.

Evidential

"Is there a case?" "Does the evidence warrant the arrest of an individual and the expense of a trial?" These are two major questions prosecutors ask when deciding whether to prosecute. The prosecutor must determine whether a violation of the criminal law, as seen within the context of the local political system, has been committed. There are many borderline offenses, particularly those concerned with morality, that will not result in prosecution. The nature of the case may require presentation of evidence that can prove such broadly defined terms as *neglect* or *intent.* The prosecutor must be certain that the evidence will coincide with the court's interpretation of these terms. In many cases, the facts may be clear but the ambiguity of the law makes application of these facts difficult.

Evidence is considered weak when it is difficult to use in proving the charges, when the value of a stolen article is questionable, when the case results from a brawl, or when there is lack of corroboration. Prosecution of cases involving victimless crimes is especially difficult for these reasons. In prostitution and narcotics cases, evidence is usually produced by plainclothesmen or stool pigeons, whose effectiveness is lost once they appear in court. Judicial strictures against "entrapment" may make the evidence inadmissible. Community standards may not support prosecution efforts in all cases.

The prosecutor's position in the judicial process requires that the evidence be considered before a decision to file is made. At the initial stage, the amount and type of evidence reflected by the police report appears to be a dominant factor. As one deputy prosecutor told the author, "If you have the evidence, you file, then bring the other considerations in during the bargaining phase."

Humanitarian

The prosecutor can individualize justice in ways that will benefit the accused, the victim, and society. Especially when the offense involves conduct arising from mental illness, the prosecutor may believe that some form of psychiatric treatment is needed, rather than imprisonment. Protection of the victim can also be a reason for deciding against prosecution. In cases involving sexual molestation of a child, prosecution may not be sought if conviction hinges on the testimony of the victim and there is a possibility that the courtroom experience would hurt the child. The character of the accused, his or her status in the community, and the impact of prosecution on the family may be factors influencing the charge filed.

Prosecutors seem to believe that punishments stipulated in criminal laws affect the guilty in different ways, depending upon their socioeconomic background and status. Often one hears the remark that a year in jail will hurt an upper-status person much more than it will hurt someone from the ghetto. Charges are often filed with this in mind. Perhaps a felony charge will be changed to a misdemeanor if the defendant is a lawyer, because conviction on a felony would mean disbarment. Such actions are rationalized on humanitarian grounds—the desire to use the law to see justice accomplished.

Organizational

The exchange relationships among units of the judicial system, the political environment of the community, and the resource demands placed upon the system figure in the decision to prosecute. In this context, public reaction is often important. The nature of the crime, the pressure of publicity, and the influence of complaining victims circumscribe the prosecutor's discretion. Another consideration affecting the prosecutor's actions is the cost of expending organization resources when the matter is trivial, when extradition from another state is required, or when caseload pressures on the system are great. In these contexts, the attitudes and potential actions of the police, defense attorneys, and judges—actors whose cooperation makes the prosecutor's job easier—may influence the decision.

PLEA BARGAINING

As a case moves toward trial, it is often assumed that the court acquires the power to determine the fate of the defendant because the prosecutor takes on the role of advocate. However, the prosecuting attorney and defense counsel may negotiate a reduction of the charges in exchange for a guilty plea, thus limiting the sentencing decision of the judge. Plea bargaining has the obvious advantage of helping with processing a large number of cases, but it also assures conviction of the guilty, all for a minimal expenditure of resources. From the perspective of the organization, the guilty plea performs the latent function of helping to maintain the equilibrium and viability of the system. Not only does it help achieve the efficient use of the organization's resources, it also allows the system to operate in a more predictable environment. Because actors do not have to expose themselves to the unpredictable results of a jury trial, the cooperative (some might say "symbiotic") relationships necessary for operation of the system are maintained.

This emphasis on the role of negotiation within the criminal justice process seems to be at variance with our theory and customs, which have emphasized the adversary nature of the system. According to the traditional concept, criminal cases are not "settled" as in civil law; the outcome is determined through the symbolic combat of the state against the accused. Yet it has been estimated that up to 90 percent of all defendants charged with crimes before the state and federal courts plead guilty rather than exercise their right to trial. When a case does go to trial, it is usually won by the prosecutor. Prosecutors seek to avoid trials through compromise; there are incentives for them to take to court only those cases that seem winnable.

The prosecutor and defense attorney both bring certain objectives to a bargaining session. Each has attempted to structure the situation to personal advantage and comes armed with tactics designed to improve his or her position. It is common for prosecutors to draw up multiple-offense indictments; defense counsel may threaten to ask for a jury trial if concessions are not made. Another tactic is to seek pretrial continuances in hopes that witnesses will become unavailable, that public interest will die, and that memories of the incident will fade. Neither partner in the exchange is a free agent. Each depends on the cooperation of the defendant and the judge. In addition, the partners recognize that they will probably face their adversaries again in the future. Concessions extracted at a high cost may prove to be a disadvantage in the long run.

Plea bargaining is often criticized on the ground that it is hidden from judicial scrutiny. Because the bargain is generally made at an early stage of the proceedings, the judge has little information about the crime or the defendant and is not able to review prosecutorial judgment. As a result, there is no judicial review of the propriety of the bargain—no check on the amount of pressure applied to the defendant to plead guilty. Unconstitutional behavior may contribute to successful prosecution. The police may engage in illegal searches, neglect the procedural rights of the defendant, and carry out station-house punishment because they know the case will never come to trial.

Until public attention became focused on crime and the administration of justice in the 1970s, plea bargaining was one of the secrets of the legal profession. It was rarely mentioned, and the scholarly literature took little note of it until the 1960s. Journalists' exposés of the extent of plea bargaining increased public awareness of the practice, and decisions by the U.S. Supreme Court granted it legitimacy. In the case *North Carolina v. Alford* (1970), the Court ruled that a trial court could accept a guilty plea even though the defendant maintained innocence, providing there was evidence of guilt and no indication of coercion in securing the plea. In *Santobello v. New York* (1971) the justices indirectly approved the practice by holding that the parties were required to keep the agreed-upon bargain. The prosecutor in *Blackledge v. Allison* (1976) clearly acknowledged the legitimacy of plea bargaining, saying, "Whatever might be the situation in an ideal world, the fact is that the guilty plea and the often concomitant plea bargain are important components of this country's criminal justice system. Properly administered, they can benefit all concerned."

INTERCITY VARIATIONS

The criminal justice system clearly responds to the values of the local community. The prosecutor's office in a major metropolitan area such as Los Angeles, which has more than 400 deputies, operates quite differently from the one- or two-person offices found in most counties in the United States. One might also assume that cities where political parties are weak and the civil service ethos is strong would have prosecution offices that function quite differently from those where traditional political considerations such as patronage hold sway. More important, the crucial functions of filtering, charging, and plea bargaining are made at different points in the real criminal justice continuum and by different actors.

Recent research has documented the many variations in the felony disposition process. Although the formal organization of decision making from arrest to conviction is similar throughout the United States, informal practices may shift the point of filtering from one part of the process to another. Therefore, to focus, for example, on the conviction rate of an individual prosecutor's office may obscure what is actually the situation: the police in that jurisdiction forward only the cases that they believe are "solid." In some cities, case screening is accomplished primarily by the police; in others, this is done by the prosecutor's office; in still others, by judges. Comparisons of felony dispositions in a number of cities show that great numbers of cases are dropped at some juncture but that local customs and policies have a lot to do with which agency is the major filter.

Feeney, Dill, and Weir describe the procedural and policy differences in the prosecutors' offices in two cities. Prosecutors in both offices eliminate weak cases through rigorous early screening, but in Jacksonville cases are organized vertically (the attorney who files a case is responsible for its disposition), while in San Diego they are organized horizontally (cases are assigned to specialists for charging and to a separate group of attorneys for trial). Even though there are many procedural differences between the systems, the outcomes for robbery, burglary, and felony assault cases appear to be about the same. The study found that arrest and prosecutorial screening policies determine the attrition rate. In both systems, many cases are weeded out (in San Diego the police do most of this, in Jacksonville the district attorney does it), plea bargaining is used extensively, and convictions at trial are proportionately the same.

Variations in the role of the prosecutor in the cities examined seem to reflect divergent responses by the various parts of the criminal justice system. These responses are shaped by the power of the exchange relations, the influence of particular actors, and the political environment of the community. More important, *somewhere* in the system cases are screened or removed, or the charges are altered. Under pressures caused by limited resources, political and social forces, and the desire to remove uncertainty, administrative decision making replaces adjudication of offenses through the adversarial process.

SUGGESTIONS FOR FURTHER READING

ALSCHULER, ALBERT. "The Prosecutor's Role in Plea Bargaining." *University of Chicago Law Review* 36 (1968): 50. One of the few examinations of this subject based on comparative data.

CARTER, LIEF. *The Limits of Order.* Lexington, Mass.: D. C. Heath, Lexington Books, 1974. A case study of a prosecuting attorney's office in California, with an important theoretical discussion of the role of prosecution.

FEENEY, FLOYD, FORREST DILL, and ADRIANNE WEIR. *Arrests Without Convictions: How Often They Occur and Why.* Washington, D.C.: National Institute of Justice, 1983. A study of felony case processing in two cities, showing how arrest and prosecutorial screening policies determine the attrition rate.

JACOBY, JOAN. *The American Prosecutor: Search for Identity.* Lexington, Mass.: Lexington Books, 1980. An overview of the development and role of the prosecutor in the U.S. criminal justice system.

MC DONALD, WILLIAM F., ed. *The Prosecutor.* Beverly Hills, Calif.: Sage Publications, 1979. Ten essays discussing various aspects of the prosecutor's role

MOLEY, RAYMOND. *Politics and Criminal Prosecution.* New York: Minton, Balch & Company, 1929. Written by one of the major participants in the crime commission studies of the 1920s, this book shows the direct relationship of politics to the prosecutor's office in urban areas in the United States.

NEUBAUER, DAVID W. *Criminal Justice in Middle America.* Morristown, N.J.: General Learning Press, 1974. Much of the criminal justice literature focuses on big-city crime, but Neubauer examines the criminal justice system of Prairie City, a medium-sized industrial city in Illinois.

NEWMAN, DONALD J. *Conviction: The Determination of Guilt or Innocence Without Trial.* Boston: Little, Brown, 1966. An analysis of plea bargaining based on data gathered in three states. The first major study of plea bargaining.

VERA FOUNDATION. *Felony Arrests: Their Prosecution and Disposition in New York City's Courts.* New York: Vera Institute of Justice, 1977. A study of the charging process and the "deterioration" of cases as they make their way toward final disposition.

ARTICLE EIGHT

The Decision to Prosecute

GEORGE F. COLE

The prosecuting attorney works within the context of an exchange system of clientele relationships that influence decision making. In this case study I explore the nature of these relationships and link politics to the allocation of justice.

This paper is based on an exploratory study of the Office of Prosecuting Attorney, King County (Seattle), Washington. The lack of social-scientific knowledge about the prosecutor dictated the choice of this approach. An open-ended interview was administered to one-third of the former deputy prosecutors who had worked in the office during the ten-year period 1955–1965. In addition, interviews were conducted with court employees, members of the bench, law-enforcement officials, and others having reputations for participation in legal decision making. Over fifty respondents were contacted during this phase. A final portion of the research placed the author in the role of observer in the prosecutor's office. This experience allowed for direct observation of all phases of the decision to prosecute so that the informal processes of the office could be noted. Discussions with the prosecutor's staff, judges, defendants' attorneys, and the police were held so that the interview data could be placed within an organizational context.

Source: From *Law and Society Review* 4 (February 1970): 313–343. By permission of the author and publisher.

The primary goal of this investigation was to examine the role of the prosecuting attorney as an officer of the legal process within the context of the local political system. The analysis is therefore based on two assumptions. First, that the legal process is best understood as a subsystem of the larger political system. Because of this choice, emphasis is placed upon the interaction and goals of the individuals involved in decision making. Second, and closely related to the first point, it is assumed that broadly conceived political considerations explained to a large extent "who gets or does not get—in what amount—and how, the good (justice) that is hopefully produced by the legal system."[1] By focusing upon the political and social linkages between these systems, it is expected that decision making in the prosecutor's office will be viewed as a principal ingredient in the authoritative allocation of values.

THE PROSECUTOR'S OFFICE IN AN EXCHANGE SYSTEM

While observing the interrelated activities of the organizations in the legal process, one might ask, "Why do these agencies cooperate?" If the police refuse to transfer information to the prosecutor concerning the commission of a crime, what are the rewards or sanctions that might be brought against them? Is it possible that organizations maintain a form of "bureaucratic accounting" that, in a sense, keeps track of the resources allocated to an agency and the support returned? How are cues transmitted from one agency to another to influence decision making? These are some of the questions that must be asked when decisions are viewed as an output of an exchange system.

The major findings of this study are placed within the context of an exchange system.[2] This serves the heuristic purpose of focusing attention upon the linkages found between actors in the decision-making process. In place of the traditional assumptions that the agency is supported solely by statutory authority, this view recognizes that an organization has many clients with which it interacts and upon whom it is dependent for certain resources. As interdependent subunits of a system, then, the organization and its clients are engaged in a set of exchanges across their boundaries. These will involve a transfer of resources between the organizations that will affect the mutual achievement of goals.

The legal system may be viewed as a set of interorganizational exchange relationships analogous to what Long has called a community game.[3] The participants in the legal system (game) share a common territorial field and collaborate for different and particular ends. They interact on a continuing basis as their responsibilities demand contact with other participants in the process. Thus, the need for cooperation of other participants can have a bearing on the decision to prosecute. A decision not to prosecute a narcotics offender may be a move to pressure the U.S. Attorney's Office to cooperate on another case. It is obvious that bargaining occurs not only between the major actors in a case—the prosecutor and the defense attorney—but also between the clientele groups that are influential in structuring the actions of the prosecuting attorney.

Exchanges do not simply "sail" from one system to another, but take place in an institutionalized setting that may be compared to a market. In the market, decisions are made between individuals who occupy boundary-spanning roles, and who set the conditions under which the exchange will occur. In the legal system, this may merely mean that a representative of the parole board agrees to forward a recommendation to the prosecutor, or it could mean that there is extended bargaining between a deputy prosecutor and a defense attorney. In the study of the King County prosecutor's office, it was found that most decisions resulted from some type of exchange relationship. The deputies interacted almost constantly with the police and criminal lawyers; the prosecutor was more closely linked to exchange relations with the courts, community leaders, and the county commissioners.

THE PROSECUTOR'S CLIENTELE

In an exchange system, power is largely dependent upon the ability of an organization to create clientele relationships that will support and enhance the needs of the agency. For, although interdependence is characteristic of the legal system, competition with other public agencies for support also exists. Because organizations operate in an economy of scarcity, the organization must exist in a favorable power position in relation to its clientele. Reciprocal and unique claims are made by the organization and its clients. Thus, rather than being oriented toward only one public, an organization is beholden to several publics, some visible and others seen clearly only from the pinnacle of leadership. As Gore notes when these claims are "firmly anchored inside the organization and the lines drawn taut, the tensions between conflicting claims form a net serving as the institutional base for the organization."[4]

An indication of the stresses within the judicial system may be obtained by analyzing its outputs. It has been suggested that the administration of justice is a selective process in which only those cases that do not create strains in the organization will ultimately reach the courtroom.[5] As noted in Figure 1, the system operates so that only a small number of cases arrive for trial, the rest being disposed of through reduced charges, *nolle prosequi,* and guilty pleas.[6] Not indicated are those cases removed by the police and prosecutor prior to the filing of charges. As the focal organization in an exchange system, the office of the prosecuting attorney makes decisions that reflect the influence of its clientele. Because of the scarcity

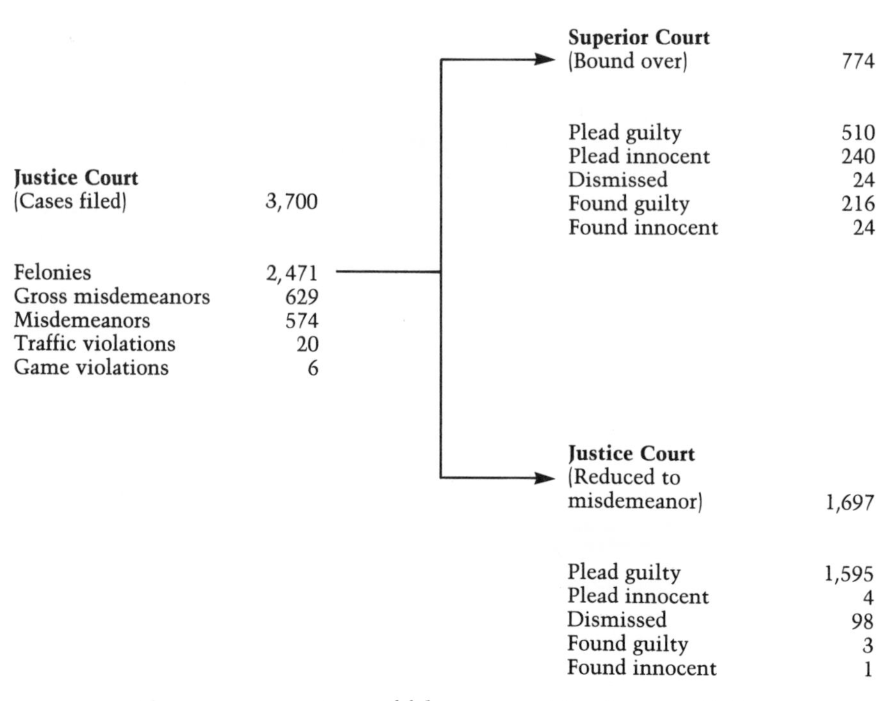

Figure 1 Disposition of felony cases, King County, 1964

of resources, marketlike relationships, and the organizational needs of the system, prosecutorial decision making emphasizes the accommodations made to the needs of participants in the process.

Police

Although the prosecuting attorney has discretionary power to determine the disposition of cases, this power is limited by the fact that usually he is dependent upon the police for inputs to the system of cases and evidence. The prosecutor does not have the investigative resources necessary to exercise the kind of affirmative control over the types of cases that are brought to him. In this relationship, the prosecutor is not without countervailing power. His main check on the police is his ability to return cases to them for further investigation and to refuse to approve arrest warrants. By maintaining cordial relations with the press, a prosecutor is often able to focus attention on the police when the public becomes aroused by incidents of crime. As the King County prosecutor emphasized, "That [investigation] is the job for the sheriff and police. It's their job to bring me the charges." As noted by many respondents, the police, in turn, are dependent upon the prosecutor to accept the output of their system; rejection of too many cases can have serious repercussions affecting the morale, discipline, and workload of the force.

A request for prosecution may be rejected for a number of reasons relating to questions of evidence. Not only must the prosecutor believe that the evidence will secure a conviction, but he must also be aware of community norms relating to the type of acts that should be prosecuted. King County deputy prosecutors noted that charges were never filed when a case involved attempted suicide or fornication. In other actions, the heinous nature of the crime, together with the expected public reaction, may force both the police and prosecutor to press for conviction when evidence is less than satisfactory. As one deputy noted, "In that case [murder and molestation of a six-year-old girl] there was nothing that we could do. As you know the press was on our back and every parent was concerned. Politically, the prosecutor had to seek information."

Factors other than those relating to evidence may require that the prosecutor refuse to accept a case from the police. First, the prosecuting attorney serves as a regulator of caseloads not only for his own office, but for the rest of the legal system. Constitutional and statutory time limits prevent him and the courts from building a backlog of untried cases. In King County, when the system reached the "overload point," there was a tendency to be more selective in choosing the cases to be accepted. A second reason for rejecting prosecution requests may stem from the fact that the prosecutor is thinking of his public exposure in the courtroom. He does not want to take forward cases that will place him in an embarrassing position. Finally, the prosecutor may return cases to check the quality of police work. As a former chief criminal deputy said, "You have to keep them on their toes, otherwise they get lazy. If they aren't doing their job, send the case back and then leak the situation to the newspapers." Rather than spend the resources necessary to find additional evidence, the police may dispose of a case by sending it back to the prosecutor on a lesser charge, implement the "copping out" machinery leading to a guilty plea, drop the case, or in some instances send it to the city prosecutor for action in municipal court.

In most instances, a deputy prosecutor and the police officer assigned to the case occupy the boundary-spanning roles in this exchange relationship. Prosecutors reported that after repeated contacts they got to know the policemen whom they could trust. As one female deputy commented, "There are some you can trust, others you have to watch because they are trying to get rid of cases on you." Deputies may be influenced by the police officer's attitude on a case. One officer noted to a prosecutor that he knew he had a weak case, but mumbled, "I didn't want to bring it up here, but that's what they [his superiors] wanted." As might be expected, the deputy turned down prosecution.

Sometimes the police perform the ritual of "shopping around," seeking to find a deputy prosecutor who, on the basis of past experience, is liable to be sympathetic to their view on a case. At one time, deputies were given complete authority to make the crucial decisions without coordinating their activities with other staff members. In this way the arresting officer would search the prosecutor's office to find a deputy he thought would be sympathetic to the police attitude. As a former deputy noted, "This meant that there were no departmental policies concerning the treatment to be accorded various types of cases. It pretty much depended upon the police and their luck in finding the deputy they wanted." Prosecutors are now instructed to ascertain from the police officer if he has seen another deputy on the case. Even under this more centralized system, it is still possible for the police to request a specific deputy or delay presentation of the case until the "correct" prosecutor is available. Often a prosecutor will gain a reputation for specializing in one type of case. This may mean that the police will assume he will get the case anyway, so they skirt the formal procedure and bring it to him directly.

An exchange relationship between a deputy prosecutor and a police officer may be influenced by the type of crime committed by the defendant. The prototype of a criminal is one who violates person and property. However, a large number of cases involve "crimes without victims." This term refers to those crimes generally involving violations of moral codes, where the general public is theoretically the complainant. In violations of laws against bookmaking, prostitution, and narcotics, neither actor in the transaction is interested in having an arrest made. Hence, vice control men must drum up their own business. Without a civilian complainant, victimless crimes give the police and prosecutor greater leeway in determining the charges to be filed.

One area of exchange involving a victimless crime is that of narcotics control. As Skolnick notes, "The major organizational requirement of narcotics policing is the presence of an informational system."[7] Without a network of informers, it is impossible to capture addicts and peddlers with evidence that can bring about convictions. One source of informers is among those arrested for narcotics violations. Through promises to reduce charges or even to *nolle pros.*, arrangements can be made so that the accused will return to the narcotics community and gather information for the police. Bargaining observed between the head of the narcotics squad of the Seattle police and the deputy prosecutor who specialized in drug cases involved the question of charges, promises, and the release of an arrested narcotics pusher.

In the course of postarrest questioning by the police, a well-known drug peddler intimated that he could provide evidence against a pharmacist suspected by the police of illegally selling narcotics. Not only did the police representative want to transfer the case to the friendlier hands of this deputy, but he also wanted to arrange for a reduction of charges and bail. The police officer believed that it was important that the accused be let out in such a way that the narcotics community would not realize that he had become an informer. He also wanted to be sure that the reduced charges would be processed so that the informer could be kept on the string, thus allowing the narcotics squad to maintain control over him. The deputy prosecutor, on the other hand, said that he wanted to make sure that procedures were followed so that the action would not bring discredit on his office. He also suggested that the narcotics squad "work a little harder" on a pending case as a means of returning the favor.

Courts

The ways used by the court to dispose of cases is a vital influence in the system. The court's actions affect pressures upon the prison, the conviction rate of the prosecutor, and the work of probation agencies. The judge's decisions act as clues to other parts of the system, indicating the type of action likely to be taken in future cases. As noted by a King County judge, "When the number of prisoners gets to the 'riot point,' the warden puts pressure on us to slow down the flow. This often means that men are let out on parole and the number of people given probation and suspended sentences increases." Under such conditions, it would be expected that the prosecutor would respond to the judge's actions by reducing the inputs to the court either by not preferring charges or by increasing the pressure for guilty pleas through bargaining. The adjustments of other parts of the system could be expected to follow. For instance, the police might sense the lack of interest of the prosecutor in accepting charges, hence they will send only airtight cases to him for indictment.

The influence of the court on the decision to prosecute is very real. The sentencing history of each judge gives the prosecutor, as well as other law-enforcement officials, an indication of the treatment a case may receive in a courtroom. The prosecutor's expectation as to whether the court will convict may limit his discretion over the decisions on whether to prosecute. "There is great concern as to whose court a case will be assigned. After Judge ——— threw out three cases in a row in which entrapment was involved, the police did not want us to take any cases to him." Since the prosecutor depends upon the plea-bargaining machinery to maintain the flow of cases from his office, the sentencing actions of judges must be predictable. If the defendant and his lawyer are to be influenced to accept a lesser charge or the promise of a lighter sentence in exchange for a plea of guilty, there must be some basis for belief that the judge will fulfill his part of the arrangement. Because judges are unable formally to announce their agreement with the details of the bargain, their past performance acts as a guide.

Within the limits imposed by law and the demands of the system, the prosecutor is able to regulate the flow of cases to the court. He may control the length of time between accusation and trial; hence he may hold cases until he has the evidence that will convict. Alternatively, he may seek repeated adjournment and continuances until the public's interest dies; problems such as witnesses becoming unavailable and similar difficulties make his request for dismissal of prosecution more justifiable. Further, he may determine the type of court to receive the case and the judge who will hear it. Many misdemeanors covered by state law are also violations of a city ordinance. It is a common practice for the prosecutor to send a misdemeanor case to the city prosecutor for processing in the municipal court when it is believed that a conviction may not be secured in justice court. As a deputy said, "If there is no case—send it over to the city court. Things are speedier, less formal, over there."

In the state of Washington, a person arrested on a felony charge must be given a preliminary hearing in a justice court within ten days. For the prosecutor, the preliminary hearing is an opportunity to evaluate the testimony of witnesses, assess the strength of the evidence, and try to predict the outcome of the case if it is sent to trial. On the basis of this evaluation, the prosecutor has several options: he may bind over the case for trial in superior court; he may reduce the charges to those of a misdemeanor for trial in justice court; or he may conclude that he has no case and drop the charges. The presiding Judge of the Justice Courts of King County estimated that about 70 percent of the felonies are reduced to misdemeanors after the preliminary hearing.

Besides having some leeway in determining the type of court in which to file a case, the prosecutor also has some flexibility in selecting the judge to receive the case. Until recently the prosecutor could file a case with a specific judge. "The trouble was that Judge ——— was erratic and independent, [so] no one would file with him. The other judges objected that they were handling the entire workload, so a central filing system was devised." Under this procedure cases are assigned to the judges in rotation. However, as the chief criminal deputy noted, "The prosecutor can hold a case until the 'correct' judge comes up."

Defense Attorneys

With the increased specialization and institutionalization of the bar, it would seem that those individuals engaged in the practice of criminal law have been relegated, both by their profession and by the community, to a low status. The urban bar appears to be divided into three parts. First there is an inner circle, which handles the work of banks, utilities, and commercial concerns; second, another circle includes plaintiffs' lawyers representing interests opposed to those of the inner circle; and finally, an outer group scrapes out an existence by "haunting the courts in hope of picking up crumbs from the judicial table."[8] With the exception of a few highly proficient lawyers who have made a reputation by winning acquittal for their clients in difficult, highly publicized cases, most of the lawyers dealing with the King County prosecutor's office belong to this outer ring.

In this study, respondents were asked to identify those attorneys considered to be specialists in criminal law. Of the nearly 1,600 lawyers practicing in King County, only 8 can be placed in this category. Of this group, 6 were reported to enjoy the respect of the legal community, while the others were accused by many respondents of being involved in shady deals. A larger group of King County attorneys will accept criminal cases, but these lawyers do not consider themselves specialists. Several respondents noted that many lawyers, because of inexperience or age, were required to hang around the courthouse searching for clients. One Seattle attorney described the quality of legal talent available for criminal cases as "a few good criminal lawyers and a lot of young kids and old men. The good lawyers I can count on my fingers."

In a legal system where bargaining is a primary method of decision making, it is not surprising that criminal lawyers find it essential to maintain close personal ties with the prosecutor and his staff. Respondents were quite open in revealing their dependence upon this close relationship to pursue their careers successfully. The nature of the criminal lawyer's work is such that his saleable product or service appears to be influence rather than technical proficiency in the law. Respondents hold the belief that clients are attracted partially on the basis of the attorney's reputation as a fixer, or as a shrewd bargainer.

There is a tendency for ex-deputy prosecutors in King County to enter the practice of criminal law. Because of his inside knowledge of the prosecutor's office and friendships made with court officials, the former deputy feels that he has an advantage over other criminal law practitioners. All of the former deputies interviewed said that they took criminal cases. Of the eight criminal law specialists, seven previously served as deputy prosecutors in King County and the other was once prosecuting attorney in a rural county.

Because of the financial problems of the criminal lawyer's practice, it is necessary that he handle cases on an assembly-line basis, hoping to make a living from a large number of small fees. Referring to a fellow lawyer, one attorney said, "You should see ———. He goes up there to Carroll's office with a whole fistful of cases. He trades on some, bargains on others, and never goes to court. It's amazing but it's the way he makes his living." There are incentives, therefore, to bargaining with the prosecutor and other decision makers. The primary aim of the attorney in such circumstances is to reach an accommodation so that the time-consuming formal proceedings need not be implemented. As a Seattle attorney noted, "I can't make money if I spend my time in a courtroom. I make mine on the telephone or in the prosecutor's office." One of the disturbing results of this arrangement is that instances were reported in which a bargain was reached between the attorney and deputy prosecutor on a "package deal." In this situation, an attorney's clients are treated as a group; the outcome of the bargaining is often an agreement whereby reduced charges will be achieved for some, in exchange for the unspoken assent by the lawyer that the prosecutor may proceed as he desires with the other cases. One member of the King County bar had developed this practice to such a fine art that a deputy prosecutor said, "When you saw him coming into the office, you knew that he would be pleading guilty." At one time this situation was so widespread that the "prisoners up in the jail had a rating list which graded the attorneys as either 'good guys' or 'sell-outs.' "

The exchange relationship between the defense attorney and the prosecutor is based on their need for cooperation in the discharge of their responsibilities. Most criminal lawyers are interested primarily in the speedy solution of cases because of their precarious financial situation. Because they must protect their professional reputations with their colleagues, judicial personnel, and potential clientele, however, they are not completely free to bargain solely with this objective. As one attorney noted, "You can't afford to let it get out that you are selling out your cases."

The prosecutor is also interested in the speedy processing of cases. This can only be achieved if the formal processes are not implemented. Not only does the pressure of his caseload influence bargaining, but also the legal process, with its potential for delay and appeal, creates a degree of uncertainty that is not present in an exchange relationship with an attorney with whom you have dealt for a number of years. As the presiding judge of the Seattle District Court said, "Lawyers are helpful to the system. They are able to pull things together, work out a deal, keep the system moving."

Community Influentials

As part of the political system, the judicial process responds to the community environment. The King County study indicated that there are different levels of influence within the community and that some people had a greater interest in the politics of prosecution than others. First, the general public is able to have its values translated into policies followed by law-enforcement officers. The public's influence is particularly acute in those gray areas of the law where full enforcement is not expected. Statutes may be enacted by legislatures defining the outer limits of criminal conduct, but they do not necessarily mean that laws are to be fully enforced to these limits. There are some laws defining behavior that the community no longer considers criminal. It can be expected that a prosecutor's charging policies will reflect this attitude. He may not prosecute violations of laws regulating some forms of gambling, certain sexual practices, or violations of Sunday Blue Laws.

Because the general public is a potential threat to the prosecutor, staff members take measures to protect him from criticism. Respondents agreed that decision making occurs with the public in mind—"Will a course of action arouse antipathy toward the prosecutor rather than the accused?"

Several deputies mentioned what they called the "aggravation level" of a crime. This is a recognition that the commission of certain crimes, within a specific context, will bring about a vocal public reaction. "If a little girl, walking home from the grocery store, is pulled into the bushes and indecent liberties taken, this is more disturbing to the public's conscience than a case where the father of the girl takes indecent liberties with her at home." The office of the King County prosecuting attorney has a policy requiring that deputies file all cases involving sexual molestation in which the police believe the girl's story is credible. The office also prefers charges in all negligent homicide cases where there is the least possibility of guilt. In such types of cases the public may respond to the emotional context of the case and demand prosecution. To cover the prosecutor from criticism, it is believed that the safest measure is to prosecute.

The bail system is also used to protect the prosecutor from criticism. Thus it is the policy to set bail at a high level with the expectation that the court will reduce the amount. "This looks good for Prosecutor Carroll. Takes the heat off of him, especially in morals cases. If the accused doesn't appear in court the prosecutor can't be blamed. The public gets upset when they know these types are out free." This is an example of exchange where one actor is shifting the responsibility and potential onus onto another. In turn, the court is under pressure from county jail officials to keep the prison population down.

A second community group having contact with the prosecutor is composed of those leaders who have a continuing or potential interest in the politics of prosecution. This group, analogous to the players in one of Long's community games, is linked to the prosecutor because his actions affect their success in playing another game. Hence community boosters want either a crackdown or a hands-off policy toward gambling, political leaders want the prosecutor to remember the interests of the party, and business leaders want policies that will not interfere with their own game.

Community leaders may receive special treatment by the prosecutor if they run afoul of the law. A policy of the King County office requires that cases involving prominent members of the community be referred immediately to the chief criminal deputy and the prosecutor for their disposition. As one deputy noted, "These cases can be pretty touchy. It's important that the boss knows immediately about this type of case so that he is not caught 'flat-footed' when asked about it by the press."

Pressure by an interest group was evidenced during a strike by drugstore employees in 1964. The striking unions urged Prosecutor Carroll to invoke a state law which requires the presence of a licensed pharmacist if the drugstore is open. Not only did union representatives meet with Carroll, but picket lines were set up outside the courthouse protesting his refusal to act. The prosecutor resisted the union's pressure tactics.

In recent years, the prosecutor's tolerance policy toward minor forms of gambling led to a number of conflicts with Seattle's mayor, the sheriff, and church organizations. After a decision was made to prohibit all forms of public gaming, the prosecutor was criticized by groups representing the tourist industry and such affected groups as the bartenders' union which thought the decision would have an adverse economic effect. As Prosecutor Carroll said, "I am always getting pressures from different interests—business, the Chamber of Commerce, and labor. I have to try and maintain a balance between them." In exchange for these considerations, the prosecutor may gain prestige, political support, and admission into the leadership groups of the community.

SUMMARY

By viewing the King County Office of Prosecuting Attorney as the focal organization in an exchange system, data from this exploratory study suggests the market-like relationships that exist between actors in the system. Because prosecution operates in an environment of scarce resources and because the decisions have potential political ramifications, a variety of officials influence the allocation of justice. The decision to prosecute is not made at one point, but rather the prosecuting attorney has a number of options he may employ during various stages of the proceedings. But the prosecutor is able to exercise his discretionary powers only within the network of exchange relationships. The police, court congestion, organizational strains, and community pressures are among the factors that influence prosecutorial behavior.

NOTES

1. James R. Klonoski and Robert I. Medelsohn, "The Allocation of Justice: A Political Analysis," *Journal of Public Law* 14 (May 1965): 323–342.
2. William M. Evan, "Towards a Theory of Inter-Organizational Relations," *Management Science* 11 (August 1965): 218–230.
3. Norton Long, *The Polity* (Chicago: Rand McNally, 1962), p. 142.
4. William J. Gore, *Administrative Decision-Making* (New York: John Wiley, 1964), p. 23.
5. William J. Chambliss, *Crime and the Legal Process* (New York: McGraw-Hill, 1969), p. 84.
6. The lack of reliable criminal statistics is well known. These data were gathered from a number of sources, including King County, "Annual Report of the Prosecuting Attorney," State of Washington, 1964.
7. Jerome L. Skolnick, *Justice Without Trial* (New York: John Wiley, 1966), p. 120.
8. Jack Ladinsky, "The Impact of Social Backgrounds of Lawyers on Law Practice and the Law," *Journal of Legal Education* 16 (1963): 128.

ARTICLE NINE

The Impact of Victim Assessment on Prosecutors' Screening Decisions: The Case of the New York County District Attorney's Office

ELIZABETH ANNE STANKO

What factors influence a prosecutor's decisions? Elizabeth Stanko focuses on the impact that victim characteristics have on this prosecutorial process. She found that charges were not preferred against all those arrested and that the law was not applied impartially. When victims were judged not to be credible complainants, charges were apt to be dropped.

Prosecutors, armed with the power to charge a suspect with a criminal offense, allocate their limited resources to those cases, which, they believe, constitute the most "trouble" for society. Not surprisingly, what is defined as trouble corresponds with the organizational goal of achieving a high conviction record.

Earlier studies have examined prosecutors' use of legal and social criteria for handling serious criminal offenses. The seriousness of a crime and its evidentiary strength influence the prosecutability of particular cases. Defendant characteristics, such as the existence of a prior criminal record, are also important components of prosecutorial strategy. Some attention has also been given to the victim and the impact of victim characteristics on prosecutorial decision making.

Myers and Hagan (1979: 448), in finding that "the troubles of older, white, male, and employed victims" are considered more worthy of public

Source: Law and Society Review 16 (1981–1982): 225–238. Copyright by the Law and Society Association. Reprinted by permission. Notes and some references omitted.

processing, suggest that certain *types* of victims affect the allocation of prosecutorial resources. Stereotypes about victims assist them in the sorting of serious cases (those deserving full prosecution) from less serious ones.

This paper explores prosecutors' use of victim stereotypes during the screening and charging stage of serious felony prosecutions. It concludes that the character and credibility of the victim is a key factor in determining prosecutorial strategies, one at least as important as "objective" evidence about the crime or characteristics of the defendant.

Prosecutorial focus on victim character is particularly evident in the early stages of the criminal justice process. As a gatekeeping function to limit prosecutors' workloads, the sorting of serious felony cases is a necessary and routine function of a prosecutor's office. With an eye to assuring a high conviction rate, screening prosecutors are likely to devote limited resources to those felony cases with "good" victim/witnesses; "stand-up" witnesses' overall credibility lends strength and legitimacy to the sure case. Throughout my thirteen months of observation, it was frequently the victim—not the facts of the case, the seriousness of the crime, or the dangerousness of the defendant—upon whom the prosecutor focused for the *prediction* of an assured conviction.

THE RESEARCH SETTING AND ITS ORGANIZATIONAL CONTEXT

The setting of this study is a bureau within the New York County (Manhattan) prosecutor's office that is devoted solely to the screening of felony arrests. This particular office screens a high volume of cases 365 days a year. Focusing only upon serious offenses, assistant prosecutors assigned to this bureau review all the arrest circumstances, assess the evidence against the arrested individual, interview the complainant, and draw an affidavit summarizing the case against the defendant.

For approximately thirteen months (March 1975 through March 1976), I observed this felony arrest screening process, recording descriptive accounts of the interactions among the assistant prosecutor, arresting police officer, and complaining witness(es). During the last six months of observation, I was able to transcribe the dialogue among these actors. Of the roughly 1,000 felony screenings I witnessed, I transcribed over 100 conversational exchanges regarding felony case assessment for assault, rape, and robbery offenses.

Prior to 1975, assistant prosecutors assigned to the complaint room reviewed the arrest charges and prepared an affidavit that served as the charging instrument in arraignment proceedings. Determinations about the merits and eventual outcome of a case were rarely made at this time. In 1975, a newly elected district attorney (following Frank Hogan, who controlled the D.A.'s office for over three decades) began restructuring the process of prosecution. One of his priorities was to establish the Early Case Assessment Bureau (ECAB), whose primary purpose was to review all incoming felony arrests, to weed out those cases that would not lead to convictions, and to forward only solid, convictable cases to the supreme court bureau.

The new D.A. believed that establishment of early case screening would enable his office to predict the probability of successful prosecution. Screening prosecutors now prepare incoming felony arrests for prosecution along selected routes. They scrutinize each arrest for its evidentiary strength, seriousness, and witness credibility. At this point in the process, prosecutors determine whether a particular case warrants supreme court prosecution; all the remaining cases are disposed of in the lower court.

During the period of my observations, the ECAB was staffed by nine assistant prosecutors: a bureau chief, four senior prosecutors, and four junior prosecutors. The senior prosecutors came to the ECAB from the trial bureau. Their experience, the bureau chief felt, enabled them to assess how a felony case would be received in supreme court. As described by one ECAB prosecutor, this alleged predictive capacity was the result of "acquired experience in how the case is processed throughout the whole system. Then we can use this [information] to determine what is a legally prosecutable case." Not only did the senior prosecutors possess the organizationally acquired skill suitable for identifying solid cases, but they had an awareness of what Dill (1980) refers to as a "laundry list" of other institutional considerations: knowledge about resource limitations, competence of other bureaus within the prosecutor's office, judge and jury reactions to different types of cases and witnesses, likely sentences, and so forth.

Through a process of organizational socialization, junior prosecutors learned this predictive skill from the senior prosecutors. "After all," commented one senior prosecutor, "he's been to law school and he's got common sense." With these basic skills, junior prosecutors then become members of the prosecutor's subculture. Developed within a bureaucratic setting geared only to selecting convictable cases, knowledge shared among this subculture includes a tacit understanding of how victims and their credibility are a key to predicting solid cases.

THE VICTIM AS AN ORGANIZATIONAL CONSIDERATION FOR SOLID CASES

How do prosecutors actually make screening decisions? As noted earlier, New York County prosecutors utilize a convictability standard against which each felony case is assessed. Similar to what Mather (1979) describes as a "dead bang" serious case, screening prosecutors refer to their sure cases as solid cases.

After lengthy discussions, ECAB prosecutors could not agree on formal criteria to define a solid case. They turned instead to a series of questions they asked of each case. As told by one senior ECAB prosecutor, they were:

1. Is the matter of law sufficient?
2. If sufficient, does it establish a felony offense in the eyes of society?
3. Am I (the prosecutor) personally assured of the defendant's guilt?
4. Can the case be persuasive to a jury?

(Note how these criteria blend both legal and organizational requirements: legal sufficiency and socially recognized "trouble" are important aspects of solid cases.)

Prosecutors were particularly concerned with evidentiary matters, with the defendant's guilt, and with predicting the organizational success of the case—its persuasiveness to a jury. This latter concern is pivotal. If a case has strong evidence and an apparently guilty defendant, but is nonetheless not persuasive to a jury, then the outcome is not likely to be successful. In crimes against persons, especially, the victim is both witness to and object of the offense. In these types of crimes, then, the case's persuasiveness to a jury is integrally linked to the victim's credibility. In short, the credibility of the victim becomes an *organizational* problem for screening prosecutors: whether the victim's story is sufficiently believable to assure a "solid" case.

Victim credibility is less important in cases slated for disposition in the lower courts, since most of these cases will be resolved through plea bargaining. But if those cases forwarded to the supreme court go to trial, then the victim or complaining witness is likely to be subjected to severe cross-examination ("impeaching the witness") by defense attorneys. Prosecutors must predict how a judge and jury will react to the victim under these circumstances. And they often base these predictions on commonsense evaluation of how judge and jury will assess a victim's lifestyle and moral character, and derivatively their honesty and trustworthiness as witnesses. Moreover, prosecutors are prone to attribute credibility to certain *types* of individuals, those who fit society's stereotypes of who is credible: older, white, male, employed victims. In Goffman's (1963) sense, this is what constitutes *stereotypical credibility.* Indeed, prosecutors are no exception to the generalization that organizations are particularly prone to the use of stereotypical thinking. Bureaucracies routinely structure the interaction of participants and, as Goffman notes, this structuring is often without "special attention or thought" (1963:2).

The process of selecting "solid" cases, therefore, focuses on identifying problems that reduce the chance of a successful prosecution. Such problems are likely to be perceived in a victim's appearance or character, or in the defects or weaknesses of a *category* of individuals of which the victim is a part. Gender, race, and occupation have important social meanings;

power and status are often accorded on these grounds. A pleasant appearance, residence in a good neighborhood, a respectable job or occupation, lack of nervous mannerisms, and an ability to articulate clearly are decided advantages. Inferences that a victim might be a prostitute or pimp, a homosexual, or an alcoholic, on the other hand, may seriously damage a victim's credibility. All of these factors must be carefully weighed.

The seven case studies which follow illustrate how prosecutors explore the"problems" of victims in otherwise solid cases. In each case, the screening prosecutor (D.A.) discusses the case with the arresting officer (A.O), another D.A., or the victim (C.W.). These cases are not a random sample of prosecutorial screening activity, but they do illustrate the process of victim assessment in the selection of solid cases.

EXAMPLE 1: ROBBERY IN THE FIRST DEGREE

Three individuals were arrested and charged with robbery in the first degree. The two complainants in the case had not yet arrived at the D.A.'s office. The D.A. began questioning the arresting officer about the case before the complainants arrived. Here, a prior relationship did not seem to be a problem.

D.A.: Does the complainant know the defendant?
A.O.: No, never seen him before.

However, the address of the complainant was not in the neighborhood the D.A. considered an "upstanding" one. Finally, the question was asked:

D.A.: What do we know about the complaining witness?
A.O.: He's a Columbia University student.

The D.A. told the arresting officer to bring in the complainants as soon as they arrived. Later, the complainants walked in: two white, articulate graduate students. The D.A. remarked to me after he briefly interviewed them: "Stand-up complainants—I knew they were stand-up—I marked it [to be forwarded to the grand jury] before I saw them."

The use of the term "stand-up victim" appears frequently in prosecutor's talk. It describes the ideal victim for the solid case: one who can *stand up* before any jury or judge and present him-herself as a credible witness. As noted by Myers and Hagan (1979) and others, when evidentiary strength is held constant, higher-status victims are likely to increase the prosecutability of a case.

Note the stereotypical imagery. The prosecutor assesses this victim on the basis of what is "known" about the typical Columbia University student. It is assumed that these students are, as a category, "law-abiding" citizens with no noticeable character flaws that undermine their credibility. Indeed, if the victim seems categorically credible, the prosecutor may view the criminal incident more seriously than the arresting officer did. For instance, in the following example, prosecutorial attention focuses primarily on the victim, altering the arresting officer's definition of the criminal offense.

EXAMPLE 2: ROBBERY IN THE THIRD DEGREE

The complainant is an elderly woman. The incident involved a purse snatching by a sixteen-year-old male. The complainant chased the defendant through a park after the purse was taken. The prosecutor admired the complainant as an individual least deserving of harassment. After the complainant reported the incident, she was excused from the ECAB; the prosecutor became excited about the potential case: "I'm going to write it up as a robbery one [first degree] with a tree branch [as the dangerous weapon]. I only wrote up one rob[bery] before with a tree branch [as a weapon] and that was because the victim was John F. Kennedy, Jr. These are the cases that try themselves. Any case that has a stand-up complainant should be indicted. You put her on the stand—the judge loves her, the jury loves her—dynamite complainant!

Although the arrest charge was robbery in the third degree, the prosecutor changed the affidavit charge to read robbery in the first degree by defining a tree branch as a "dangerous" weapon." In such instances (rare but not unheard of), sympathy for the victim and the prosecutor's positive assessment of the victim's credibility will result in upgrading to a more severe charge. Presumably, if that same tree branch had been wielded against another teenage male, it would have been viewed as less threatening and thus less likely to sustain a first-degree robbery charge.

In the next example, the vulnerability of a victim's lifestyle is explored for its possible detrimental effects on the seriousness (and thus prosecutability) of an offense.

EXAMPLE 3: ROBBERY IN THE FIRST DEGREE

The complainant is a professional man who works for the Better Business Bureau. He entered the Early Case Assessment Bureau with his Sunday *New York Times* tucked under his arm. His recall of the incident was clear, and he presented his story articulately. After the complainant had received instructions to appear before the grand jury the next morning and had then left the room, the D.A. remarked to the arresting officer:

D.A.: Do you think the defendants know the complainant is a homosexual?

A.O.: No.

D.A.: Would have been a great alibi [for the defendants]. They could claim that they had met and the complainant invited them up for a drink.

Essentially, the prosecutor indicates that, on second thought, he might have accorded this case nonfelony status (and thus deny it a supreme court hearing) because the victim's homosexuality raised questions about his credibility. Being labeled a homosexual, prosecutors recognize, casts doubt upon the victim's credibility; stereotypes about homosexuals, and the kinds of encounters they are alleged to have, can jeopardize the chances of winning the case. Yet in this particular instance, other factors such as the clarity of the victim's recall and his professional status compensated for this vulnerability. The charge was not altered.

As Goffman (1963) notes in his study of social stigma, characterizations such as those associated with homosexuality inherently carry with them suspicion of deviousness or dishonesty, which in turn invites disbelief of accounts reported by such people. Applying some character labels to victims implies a participation in other activities that are not "law-abiding." Similarly, during the screening of another robbery complaint, the prosecutor specifically addressed the problem with victims who were prostitutes. Reducing the charges, the prosecutor stated: "I have to deal with two complainants who will get up on the stand and say they work the streets." One prosecutor described this practice as turning "complainants into defendants."

Anticipating problems with a victim's character is an organizational strategy where prosecutors predict that a witness will be successfully impeached; they must commit their resources accordingly.

EXAMPLE 4: ROBBERY IN THE SECOND DEGREE

A young black complainant was accosted by two males. The defendants stopped the complainant and told him they wanted money. One put his hand on the complainant's chest and told him if he didn't produce "they would 'cap' him." The prosecutor asked the complainant what "cap" meant. The complainant replied that he didn't know; all he knew was that he didn't want to be hurt and he assumed that whatever capping was, he didn't want to find out. He gave the defendants his money—included was one $10 bill torn in half, which was found in the possession of the defendant. The complainant was not harmed. The prosecutor reduced the charges from robbery in the second degree to grand larceny in the third degree, stating that if the grand jury asked what "cap" meant he couldn't answer and therefore wouldn't be able to prove the threat of force in the robbery charge.

Rather than concern himself initially with the circumstances of the actions of the defendants, here the prosecutor questions the victim's actions and explanations. The prosecutor reduced the seriousness of the original arrest charge by anticipating the reactions of the grand jury. But how is it possible for the prosecutor not to accept the victim's definition of the encounter as threatening, involving sufficient force to compel him to cooperate with his assailants' demands? Perhaps, as Swigert and Farrell (1976: 18) note, "institutionalized conceptions of crime and criminality" influenced the prosecutor's view of the victim's actions. He may suspect, for example, that the victim was in the area for other illegal activities such as the purchase of illegal drugs. Whatever the rationale, the prosecutor relying upon stereotypes about the probable actions of victims in this situation concludes that this particular victim cannot be one who is *clearly* classified among those who have been threatened during a robbery (certainly the victim would not have given up his momey without a threat of force!).

In another similar incident, the prosecutor's first question to the victim was "What caused you to be in the area when you were robbed?" As in Example 4, the victim is being asked to justify his presence in a location, including his possible motives for being there and his actions throughout the criminal incident. The prosecutor's mandate to forward only solid cases requires selection of cases with victims whose reactions to a criminal offense somehow fit the assumed reactions of victims in "real" criminal encounters. The prosecutor must anticipate similar reactions from the judge or jury and therefore prepares the case for what "will happen," not according to what happened.

In the next example, the prosecutor questions the case's seriousness because of the assumed relationship between the complainant and the defendant.

EXAMPLE 5: ROBBERY IN THE FIRST DEGREE

D.A.: How long have you known the defendant?

C.W.: I was a counselor in a drug program—Neighborhood Thing—in 1971–72, and I met her there. I've seen her around since then. She was a Muslim and had a boyfriend and I didn't see her much then. But since she split I've seen her around. [D.A. then asks the complainant to go out to the waiting room while he draws up the affidavit in the presence of the A.O.]

A.O.: He's the best complainant I've had in two years.

D.A.: The people in supreme court don't like prior relationship cases. I think he was going out with her. The jury wouldn't like this. It's just a feel for the case. I don't like it.

This unknown but assumed prior relationship between the victim and the defendant somehow "normalizes" this encounter, relegating it to the range of typical everyday interactions that might occur between the victim and the defendant. The victim, in order to be seen as a "real" victim, must at least convince the prosecutor of the irregular character of the event. (Other studies, too, indicate that the relationship between the victim and the defendant is an important element in the presumed prosecutability of a felony case.)

Even the slightest hint of implausibility in the victim's story imperils conviction by a jury which must be convinced of the defendant's guilt "beyond a reasonable doubt." What could be only a criminal act between strangers looms as possibly less so betwen persons who have experienced a prior relationship. The law does not distinguish between the two, of course, but juries often do.

EXAMPLE 6: ATTEMPTED MURDER; RECKLESS ENDANGERMENT

During the day, people had talked about a Chinese gang case that one ECAB D.A. had marked for further investigation while another ECAB D.A. had changed its status to a nonfelony case. A district attorney from the arraignment court entered the ECAB and could not believe that the case was not to be sent to the grand jury.

The case is as follows. A major Chinese gang had split into two factions. One faction had attacked members of the other faction as they were walking down one of the busiest streets in Chinatown. Several shots were fired. No one was injured, and the defendant was arrested for attempted murder.

During the police investigation, two different bullet fragments were found in an ice-cream shop. An account of one witness, who had identified the defendant as being at the scene of the incident, revealed that someone said, "Get ready, here they come"; but that witness did not observe the firing of shots. Another witness, one from the ambushed faction, identified the defendant as the individual who fired the shots and was willing to cooperate with the prosecution.

The ECAB D.A. who assessed the case as a nonfelony cited the witness' credibility as the major problem in this case. The witness from the rival faction, the one who could identify the defendant as the person who fired the gun, had a prior record of several assaults. Yet the D.A. handling the case in arraignment could not believe that the incident itself did not warrant more serious treatment by the prosecutor's office. "After all, they the police] found fragments [of bullets]." But the ECAB D.A.s began to raise issues that would weaken the strength of the case. "How do you know they [the bullets] came from the gun? You can't prove it. It's not a grand jury case. You'll be lucky to get an A mis[demeanor] on the thing [in the lower court]."

The arraignment D.A. would not give up, and he continued to question the ECAB D.A.s. "But the witness [who could identify the defendant]," repeated the arraignment D.A. "What witness," replied the ECAB D.A., "You've got one guy who hears someone say 'here they come' and a complainant who's got a rap sheet all over the place. Go ahead, put him on the stand. They'll tear him to pieces. If you want to send it to the grand jury, go ahead. That is, if you want [the indictment bureau head] to send a pack of wolves after you." But the arraignment D.A. continued to argue with the ECAB D.A.s, particularly about the fact that someone could have been injured. "What do we do about this? They'll wind up killing each other," stated the arraignment D.A. "Good," retorted the ECAB D.A. "So what," replied the other ECAB D.A. "But what about innocent people; they could have shot someone innocent," continued the arraignment D.A. "Not them, they're too good a shot," retorted the ECAB D.A. [forgetting, of course, that even when firing at close range, the defendant shot into a store and missed the complainant]. "They'll kill each other," stated the ECAB D.A., hoping to end the discussion.

This case had many problems. How strong was the evidence (were the bullet fragments from the gun used in the shooting)? Would the victim's prior record affect his credibility? Would the court regard this as a criminal encounter, or "merely" a violent encounter between warring gang factions? A recurring encounter between gangs is often assumed to be unworthy of full prosecutorial effort, particularly where no serious injuries were reported, and no "innocent" people were involved.

Does the prosecutor's assessment of a particular witness actually become pivotal in determinations of seriousness? In the last example, we see the prosecutor's screening activity as a fluid one—one that may alter definitions of seriousness in light of additional information about the victim.

EXAMPLE 7: ROBBERY IN THE FIRST DEGREE

The complainants were a young, white couple. The male was the primary storyteller. He stated that he was delivering furniture in the area. His girlfriend accompanied him occasionally on his deliveries and was with him the night of the robbery. As they parked on the street, three individuals approached them, displayed knives, took them inside a building, and robbed them of $80. He had never seen these individuals before. The police arrived on the scene as the defendants were fleeing the building. The young woman was not able to report many of the details of the robbery. She could not estimate the amount of time they were held in the building or the amount of money that was taken from her. However, she was visibly shaken, attractive, and concerned about the case. The D.A. attended to the woman, focusing his attention upon her. He determined that they were an innocent young couple; the case was slated for the grand jury. About two minutes after the case was sent to the typist, the male complainant returned to the D.A. and stated that he was in the area to buy heroin. He did not want his girlfriend to know about the buy. The D.A. recalled the papers and reduced the charge to a misdemeanor.

The above example illustrates the flexibility of the prosecutor's definition of a serious crime. The robbery offense was determined to be legally sufficient and the witness credible. However, after the male complainant described his motives for being in the area, a felony prosecution was no longer tenable. An individual seeking to purchase drugs places himself "at risk," and—at least as a practical matter—the culpability of the defendants is reduced. It is no longer a "solid" case.

CONCLUSION

One essential concern of a critical approach to criminal justice processing is the assumption that the legal system does not apply the law impartially. Social class, sex, race, and lifestyle are factors often taken into account in the application of the law. But the implicit (never explicit, of course) use of such attributes in the charging process is not—or at least not only—a measure of outright prosecutorial bias. More often, it emerges as the pragmatism of a prosecutor intent on maximizing convictions and using organizational resources efficiently. Convictions are maximized when only solid cases are brought to trial. A "solid" case must be not only legally sufficient, but also based upon a credible complainant or victim. A victim must be credible not only in the eyes of the prosecutor, but also to the judge and jury. Thus an essential element of the charging decision is the determination of perceived victim credibility.

Credibility is not, however, only a matter of the personal characteristics of the victim. It also pertains to the situation, and to the congruence between situation and individual. Moreover, what emerges most clearly from the cases which I have described, and from my study, is the stereotypical quality of all such attributions. Prosecutors assume that judges and juries—particularly the latter—will find certain *kinds* of victim claims credible and acceptable, others not. It matters less that a victim with a prior record *may* have been robbed and beaten than that a jury may be dubious about such a claim, or merely unsympathetic to the victim. Prosecutors may rely on such stereotypes because of their own ideologies, but may also be influenced in accepting them by bureaucratic self-interest. A high batting average for convictions is a dominant organization goal in many prosecutors' offices. Doubts are resolved against the victim except in cases involving glamorous legal issues or particularly notorious crimes. The results may be that victims' quest for justice is often determined more by stereotypes than by the actual harm rendered against them by their assailants.

REFERENCES

DILL, FORREST (1980) "Reasons for Felony Dismissals." Presented at the Annual Meeting of the Law and Society Association, Madison, Wisconsin (June 6).

GOFFMAN, ERVING (1963) *Stigma: Notes on the Management of Spoiled Identity.* Englewood Cliffs, N.J.: Prentice-Hall.

MATHER, LYNN (1979) *Plea Bargaining or Trial?* Lexington, Mass.: D. C. Heath.

MYERS, MARTHA A. and JOHN HAGAN (1979) "Private and Public Trouble: Prosecutors and the Allocation of Court Resources," 26: *Social Problems,* 439.

SWIGERT, VICTORIA LYNN and RONALD A. FARRELL (1976) *Murder, Inequality, and the Law.* Lexington, Mass.: D. C. Heath.

ARTICLE TEN

Adapting to Plea Bargaining: Prosecutors

MILTON HEUMANN

Plea bargaining has been openly discussed only since the late 1960s. Before then, it was a widespread practice that was one of the secrets of criminal justice officials. In this analysis of the way new prosecutors adapt to plea bargaining, Milton Heumann shows how negotiated justice serves the needs of all participants in the process.

The new prosecutor shares many of the general expectations that his counterpart for the defense brings to the court. He expects factually and legally disputable issues, and the preliminary hearings and trials associated with these. If his expectations differ at all from the naive "Perry Mason" orientation, it is only to the extent that he anticipates greater success than the hapless Hamilton Burger of Perry Mason fame.

The new prosecutor's views about plea bargaining parallel those of the defense attorney. He views plea bargaining as an expedient employed in crowded urban courts by harried and/or poorly motivated prosecutors. He views the trial as "what the system is really about" and plea bargaining

Editor's note: This study is based on data from Connecticut, where, until a reorganization of the court system in July 1978, prosecution was conducted by state's attorneys in the supreme court and by prosecutors in the circuit court. Readers should understand that the powers of each office are essentially the same; only the workplace is different.

as a necessary evil dictated by case volume. The following exchange with a newly appointed prosecutor is illustrative.

> **Q:** Let's say they removed the effects of case pressure, provided you with more manpower. You wouldn't have that many cases. . . .
> **A:** Then everybody should go to trial.
> **Q:** Everybody should go to trial?
> **A:** Yeah.
> **Q:** Why?
> **A:** Because supposedly if they're guilty they'll be found guilty. If they're not guilty they'll be found not guilty. That's the fairest way . . . judged by a group of your peers, supposedly.
> **Q:** So you think that plea bargaining is a necessary evil?
> **A:** Yeah.
> **Q:** Would justice be better served if all cases went to trial?
> **A:** That's the way it's supposed to be set up. Sure. Why wouldn't it?
> **Q:** Would prosecutors be more satisfied?
> **A:** Probably.
> **Q:** If cases went to trial?
> **A:** Sure.
> **Q:** Why?
> **A:** Because they could talk in front of twelve people and act like a lawyer. Right. Play the role.

It should be emphasized that these expectations and preferences of the new prosecutor are founded on the minimal law school preparation. . . . The newcomers simply do not know very much about the criminal justice system.

Unlike defense attorneys, however, the new prosecutor is likely to receive some form of structured assistance when he begins his job. The chief prosecutor or chief state's attorney may provide this aid, if the prosecutor's office is staffed by a number of prosecutors or state's attorneys—that is, if the newcomer is not the only assistant prosecutor—it is more common for the chief prosecutor to assign to one or more of his experienced assistants the responsibility for helping the newcomer adjust. Since the newcomer's actions reflect on the office as a whole, it is not surprising that this effort is made.

The assistance the newcomer receives can be described as a form of structured observation. For roughly two weeks, he accompanies an experienced prosecutor to court and to plea-bargaining sessions and observes him in action. The proximity of the veteran prosecutor—and his designation as the newcomer's mentor—facilitates communication between the two. The experienced prosecutor can readily explain or justify his actions, and the newcomer can ask any and all relevant questions. Certainly, this is a more structured form of assistance than defense attorneys receive.

However, new prosecutors still feel confused and overwhelmed during this initial period. Notwithstanding the assistance they receive, they are disoriented by the multitude of tasks performed by the prosecutor and by the environment in which he operates. This is particularly true in the circuit court, where the seemingly endless shuffling of files, the parade of defendants before the court and around the courtroom, the hurried, early-morning plea-bargaining sessions all come as a surprise to the new prosecutor.

Q: What were your initial impressions of the court during this "orientation period?"

A: The first time I came down here was a Monday morning at the arraignments. Let's face it, the majority of people here, you don't expect courts to be as crowded as they are. You don't expect thirty to thirty-five people to come out of the cell block who have been arrested over the weekend. It was . . . you sit in court the first few days, you didn't realize the court was run like this. All you see, you see Perry Mason on TV, or pictures of the Supreme Court, or you see six judges up there in a spotless courtroom, everyone well dressed, well manicured, and you come to court and find people coming in their everyday clothes, coming up drunk, some are high on drugs, it's . . . it's an experience to say the least.

Q: Could you describe your first days when you came down here? What are your recollections? Anything strike you as strange?

A: Just the volume of business and all the stuff the prosecutor had to do. For the first week or two, I went to court with guys who had been here. Just sat there and watched. What struck me was the amount of things he [the prosecutor] has to do in the courtroom. The prosecutor runs the courtroom. Although the judge is theoretically in charge, we're standing there plea bargaining and calling the cases at the same time and chewing gum and telling people to quiet down and setting bonds, and that's what amazed me. I never thought I would learn all the terms. What bothered me also was the paperwork. Not the Supreme Court decisions, not the *mens rea* or any of this other stuff, but the amount of junk that's in those files that you have to know. We never heard about this crap in law school.

As suggested in the second excerpt, the new prosecutor is also surprised by the relative insignificance of the judge. He observes that the prosecutor assumes—through plea bargaining—responsibility for the disposition of many cases. Contrary to his expectations of being an adversary in a dispute moderated by the judge, he finds that often the prosecutor performs the judge's function.

It is precisely this responsibility for resolving disputes that is most vexing to the new superior court state's attorney. Unlike his circuit court counterpart, he does not generally find hurried conferences, crowded courts, and so on. But he observes that, as in the circuit court, the state's attorney negotiates cases, and in the superior court far more serious issues and periods of incarceration are involved in these negotiations. For the novice state's attorney, the notion that he will in short order be responsible for resolving these disputes is particularly disturbing.

Q: What were your initial impressions of your job here [as a state's attorney]?

A: Well, I was frightened of the increased responsibility. I knew the stakes were high here. . . . I didn't really know what to expect, and I would say it took me a good deal of time to adapt here.

Q: Adapt in which way?

A: To the higher responsibilities. Here you're dealing with felonies, serious felonies all the way up to homicides, and I had never been involved in that particular type of situation. . . . I didn't believe that I was prepared to handle the type of job that I'd been hired to do. I looked around me and I saw the serious charges, the types of cases, and the experienced defense counsel on the one hand and the inexperience on my part on the other, and I was, well. . . .

Q: Did you study up on your own?

A: No more than. . . . Before I came over here I had done some research and made a few notes, et cetera, about the procedures. I think I was prepared from the book end of things to take the job, but, again, it was the practical aspects that you're not taught in law school and that you can only learn from experience that I didn't have, and that's what I was apprehensive about.

These first weeks in the court, then, serve to familiarize the newcomer with the general patterns of case resolution. He is not immediately thrust into the court but is able to spend some time simply observing the way matters are handled. The result, though, is to increase his anxiety. The confusion of the circuit court and the responsibilities of a state's attorney in the superior court were not anticipated. The newcomer expects to be able to prepare cases leisurely and to rely on the skills learned in law school. Yet he finds that his colleagues seem to have neither the time nor the inclination to operate in this fashion. As the informal period of orientation draws to a close, the newcomer has a better perspective on the way the system operates, but still is on very uneasy footing about how to proceed when the responsibility for the case is his alone. In short, he is somewhat disoriented by his orientation.

THE PROSECUTOR ON HIS OWN: INITIAL FIRMNESS AND RESISTANCE TO PLEA BARGAINING

Within a few weeks after starting his job, the prosecutor and the state's attorney are expected to handle cases on their own. Experienced personnel are still available for advice, and the newcomer is told that he can turn to them with his problems. But the cases are now the newcomer's, and, with one exception, he is under no obligation to ask anyone for anything.

The new prosecutor is confronted by a stream of defense attorneys asking for a particular plea bargain in a case. If the prosecutor agrees, his decision is irreversible. It would be a violation of all the unwritten folkways of the criminal court for either a defense attorney or a prosecutor to break his word. On the other hand, if the prosecutor does not plea bargain, offers nothing in exchange for a plea, he at least does not commit himself to an outcome that may eventually prove to be a poor decision on his part. However, a refusal to plea bargain also places him "out of step" with his colleagues and with the general expectation of experienced defense attorneys.

Like the new attorney, the new prosecutor is in no hurry to dispose of the case. He is (1) inclined toward an adversary resolution of the case through formal hearings and trial, (2) disinclined to plea bargain in general, and (3) unsure about what constitutes an appropriate plea bargain for a particular case. Yet he is faced with demands by defense attorneys to resolve the case through plea bargaining. The new defense attorney has the luxury of postponing his decision for any given case. He can seek the advice of others before committing himself to a particular plea bargain in a particular case. For the new prosecutor, this is more difficult, since he is immediately faced with the demands of a number of attorneys in a number of different cases.

When the new prosecutor begins to handle his own cases, then, he lacks confidence about how to proceed in his dealings with defense attorneys. He often masks his insecurity in this period with an outward air of firmness. He is convinced that he must appear confident and tough, lest experienced attorneys think they can take advantage of him.

Q: What happened during your first few days of handling cases on your own?

A: Well, as a prosecutor, first of all, people try to cater to you because they want you to do favors for them. If you let a lawyer run all over you, you are dead. I had criminal the first day, on a Monday, and I'm in there [in the room where cases are negotiated], and a guy comes in, and I was talking to some lawyer on his file, and he's just standing there. Then I was talking to a second guy, and he was about fourth or fifth. So he looked at me and says: "When the hell you going to get to me?" So I says: "You wait your fucking turn. I'll get to you when I'm ready. If you don't like it, get out." It's sad that you have to swear at people, but it's the only language they understand—especially lawyers. Lawyers are the most obstinate, arrogant, belligerent bastards you will ever meet. Believe me. They come into this court—first of all—and we are really the asshole of the judicial system [circuit court], and they come in here and don't really have any respect for you. They'll come in here and be nice to you, because they feel you'll give them a *nolle.* That's all. Lawyers do not respect this court. I don't know if I can blame them or not blame them. You can come in here and see the facilities here; you see how things are handled; you see how it's like a zoo pushing people in and out. . . . When they do come here, lawyers have two approaches. One, they try to soft-soap and kiss your ass if you give them a *nolle.* Two, they'll come in here and try to ride roughshod over you and try to push you to a corner. Like that lawyer that first day. I had to swear at him and show him I wasn't going to take shit, and that's that. The problem of dealing with lawyers is that you can't let them bullshit you. So, when I first started out I tried to be. . . . It's like the new kid on the block. He comes to a new neighborhood, and you've got to prove yourself. If you're a patsy, you're going to live with that as long as you're in court. If you let a couple of lawyers run over you, word

> will get around to go to ______, he's a pushover. Before you know it, they're running all over you. So you have to draw a line so they will respect you.
>
> At first I was very tough because I didn't know what I was doing. In other words, you have to be very wary. These guys, some of them, have been practicing in this court for forty years. And they'll take you to the cleaners. You have to be pretty damn careful.

The new prosecutor couples this outward show of firmness toward attorneys with a fairly rigid plea-bargaining posture. His reluctance to offer incentives to the defendant for a plea or to reward the defendant who chooses to plead is, at this point in the prosecutor's career, as much a function of his lack of confidence as it is a reflection of his antipathy toward plea bargaining. During this very early stage he is simply afraid to make concessions. Experienced court personnel are well aware that new prosecutors adopt this rigid stance.

> **Q:** Have you noticed any differences between new prosecutors and prosecutors that have been around awhile?
>
> **A:** Oh, yes. First of all, a new prosecutor is more likely to be less flexible in changing charges. He's afraid. He's cautious. He doesn't know his business. He doesn't know the liars. He can't tell when he's lying or exaggerating. He doesn't know all the ramifications. He doesn't know how tough it is sometimes to prove the case to juries. He hasn't got the experience, so that more likely than not he will be less flexible. He is also more easily fooled. [Circuit court judge]
>
> I can only answer that question in a general way. It does seem to me that the old workhorses [experienced prosecutors] are more flexible than the young stallions. [Superior court judge]

> **Q:** You were saying about the kids, the new prosecutors, the new state's attorneys. Are they kind of more hard-assed?
>
> **A:** They tend to be more nervous. They tend to have a less well defined idea of what they can do and what they can't do without being criticized. So, to the extent that they are more nervous, they tend to be more hard-assed. [Private criminal attorney]
>
> **Q:** What about new prosecutors? Do they differ significantly from prosecutors who have been around awhile?
>
> **A:** Initially a new prosecutor is going to be reluctant to *nolle*, reluctant to give too good a deal because he is scared. He is afraid of being taken advantage of. And if you are talking about the circuit court, they've got the problem that they can't even talk it over with anybody. They've got a hundred fifty cases or whatever, and they make an offer or don't make an offer, that's it. Maybe at the end of the day they may get a chance to talk it over and say: "Gee, did I do the right thing?" The defense attorney, when the offer is made, has the opportunity to talk to somebody plus his client before making a decision. So I think it takes the prosecutor a longer time to come around and work under the system. [Legal aid attorney]

It is not difficult to understand why the new prosecutor is reluctant to plea bargain and why he appears rigid to court veterans. Set aside for the moment the prosecutor's personal preference for an adversary resolution and consider only the nature of the demands being made on him. Experienced attorneys want charges dropped, sentence recommendations, and *nolles.* They approach him with the standard argument about the wonderful personal traits of the defendant, the minor nature of the crime, the futility of incarceration, and so on. When the new prosecutor picks up the file, he finds that the defendant probably has an extensive prior criminal record and, often, that he has committed a crime that does not sound minor at all. Under the statute for the crime involved, it is likely that the defendant faces a substantial period of incarceration, yet in almost all circuit court cases and in many superior court cases, the attorneys are talking about a no-time disposition. What to the new prosecutor frequently seems like a serious matter is treated as a relatively inconsequential offense by defense attorneys. And, because the newcomer views the matter as serious, his resolve to remain firm—or, conversely, his insecurity about reducing charges—is reinforced.

Illustrations of this propensity for the new prosecutor or state's attorney to be "outraged" by the facts of the case, and to be disinclined to offer "sweet" deals, are plentiful. The following comments by two circuit court prosecutors and a superior court state's attorney, respectively, illustrate the extent to which the newcomer's appraisal of a case differed from that of the defense attorney and from that of his own colleagues.

Q: You used to go to ______ [chief prosecutor] for help on early cases. Were his recommendations out of line with what you thought should be done with the case?

A: Let's say a guy came in with a serious crime . . . a crime that I thought was serious at one time, anyway. Take fighting on ______ Avenue [a depressed area of Arborville]. He got twenty-five stitches in the head and is charged with aggravated assault. One guy got twenty-five stitches, the other fifteen. And the attorneys would want me to reduce it. I'd go and talk to ______ [chief prosecutor]. He'd say: "They both are drunk, they both got head wounds. Let them plead to breach of peace, and the judge will give them a money fine." Things like that I didn't feel right about doing, since, to me, right out of law school, middle class, you figure twenty-five stitches in the head, Jesus Christ.

Q: How did you learn what a case was worth?

A: What do you mean, what it's worth?

Q: In terms of plea bargaining. What the going rate. . . .

A: From the prosecutors and defense attorneys who would look at me dumbfounded when I would tell them that I would not reduce this charge. And then they would go running to my boss and he'd say, "Well, it's up to him." Some would even go running to the judge, screaming. One guy claimed surprise when I intended to go to trial for assault in second, which is a Class D felony. Two counts of that and two misdemeanor counts. It was set for jury trial. His witnesses were there. His experience in this court, he said, having handled two or three hundred cases, was that none has ever gone to trial. So he claimed surprise the day of trial. He just couldn't believe it.

Q: Were you in any way out of step with the way things were done here when you first began handling cases on your own?

A: In one respect I was. I evaluated a case by what I felt a proper recommendation should be, and my recommendations were almost always in terms of longer time. I found that the other guys in the office were breaking things down more than I expected. As a citizen, I couldn't be too complacent about an old lady getting knocked down, stuff like that. I thought more time should be recommended. I might think five to ten, six to twelve, while the other guys felt that three to seven was enough

Implicit in these remarks are the seeds of an explanation for a prosecutor's gradually becoming more willing to plea bargain. One can hypothesize that as his experience with handling cases increases, he will feel less outraged by the crime, and thus will be more willing to work out a negotiated settlement. One assistant state's attorney likened his change in attitude to that of a nurse in an emergency room.

It's like nurses in emergency rooms. You get so used to armed robbery that you treat it as routine, not as morally upsetting. In the emergency room, the biggest emergency is treated as routine. And it's happening to me. The nature of the offense doesn't cause the reaction in me that it would cause in the average citizen. Maybe this is a good thing; maybe it isn't.

Though there is merit in this argument—prosecutors do become accustomed to crime—it is hardly a sufficient explanation of prosecutorial adaptation to plea bargaining. Other factors, often far more subtle, must be considered if we are to understand how and why the novice prosecutor becomes a seasoned plea bargainer.

LEARNING ABOUT PLEA BARGAINING

In the preceding sections I have portrayed the new prosecutor as being predisposed toward an adversary resolution of a case, uncertain about his responsibilities, rigid in his relations with defense attorneys, reluctant to drop charges and to plea bargain in cases that he considers serious, and anxious to try out the skills he learned in law school. This characterization of the newcomer contrasts sharply with that of the veteran prosecutor. [The veteran prosecutor takes] an active role in plea bargaining—urging, cajoling, and threatening the defense attorney to share in the benefits of a negotiated disposition. How is the veteran prosecutor to be reconciled with the new prosecutor . . . ?

The answer lies in what the prosecutor learns and is taught about plea bargaining. His education, like the defense attorney's, is not structured and systematic. Instead, he works his way through cases, testing the adversary and plea-bargaining approaches. He learns piecemeal the costs and benefits of these approaches, and only over a period of time does he develop an appreciation for the relative benefits of a negotiated disposition.

Rather than proceed with a sequential discussion of the newcomer's experience, I think it more profitable at this point to distill from his experiences those central concerns that best explain his adaptation to the plea-bargaining system. Some of the "flavor" of the adaptation process is sacrificed by proceeding in this fashion, but in terms of clarity of presentation, I think it is a justifiable. Thus, I will discuss separately the considerations that move the prosecutor in the plea-bargaining direction, and later tie these together into an overall perspective on prosecutorial adaptation.

THE DEFENDANT'S FACTUAL AND LEGAL GUILT

Prosecutors and state's attorneys learn that their roles primarily entail the processing of factually guilty defendants. Contrary to their expectations that problems of establishing factual guilt would be central to their job, they find that in most cases the evidence in the file is sufficient to conclude (and prove) that the defendant is factually guilty. For those cases where there is a substantial question as to factual guilt, the prosecutor has the power—and is inclined to exercise it—to *nolle* or dismiss the case. If he himself does not believe the defendant to be factually guilty, it is part of his formal responsibilities to filter the case out. But of the cases that remain after the initial screening, the prosecutor believes the majority of defendants to be factually guilty.

Furthermore, he finds that defense attorneys only infrequently contest the prosecutor's own conclusion that the defendant is guilty. In their initial approach to the prosecutor they may raise the possibility that the defendant is factually innocent, but in most subsequent discussions their advances focus on disposition and not on the problem of factual guilt. Thus, from the prosecutor's own reading of the file (after screening) and from the comments of his "adversary," he learns that he begins with the upper hand; more often than not, the factual guilt of the defendant is not really disputable.

Q: Are most of the defendants who come to this court guilty?

A: Yeah, or else we wouldn't have charged them. You know, that's something that people don't understand. Basically the people that are brought here are believed very definitely to be guilty or we wouldn't go on with the prosecution. We would *nolle* the case, and, you know, that is something, when people say, "Well, do you really believe. . . ." Yeah. I do. I really do, and if I didn't and we can clear them, then we *nolle* it, there's no question about it.

But most cases are good, solid cases, and in most of them the defendant is guilty. We have them cold-cocked. And they plead guilty because they are guilty . . . a guy might have been caught in a package store with bottles. Now, he wasn't there to warm his hands. The defendant may try some excuse, but they are guilty and they know they are guilty. And we'll give them a break when they plead guilty. I don't think we should throw away the key on the guy just because we got him cold-cocked. We've got good cases, we give them what we think the case is worth from out point of view, allowing the defendant's mitigating circumstances to enter.

Q: The fact that you're willing to offer a pretty good bargain in negotiations might lead a person to plead guilty even if he had a chance to beat it at trial. But if he was found guilty at the trial he might not get the same result?

A: That's possible. I mean, only the accused person knows whether or not he's committed the crime, and. . . . It's an amazing thing, where, on any number of occasions, you will sit down to negotiate with an accused's attorney . . . and you know [he will say]: "No, no, he's not guilty, he wants his trial." But then if he develops a weakness in the case, or points out a weakness to you, and then you come back and say: "Well, we'll take a suspended sentence and probation," suddenly he says, "Yes, I'm guilty." So it leads you to conclude that, well, all these people who are proclaiming innocence are really not innocent. They're just looking for the right disposition. Now, from my point of view, the ideal situation might be if the person is not guilty, that he pleads not guilty, and we'll give him his trial and let the jury decide. But most people who are in court don't want a trial. I'm not the person who seeks them out and says, "I will drop this charge" or "I will reduce this charge, I will reduce the amount of time you have to do." They come to us, so, you know, the conclusion I think is there that any reasonable person could draw, that these people are guilty, that they are just looking for the best disposition possible. Very few people ask for a speedy trial.

In addition to learning of the factual culpability of most defendants, the prosecutor also learns that defendants would be hard-pressed to raise legal challenges to the state's case. As was discussed earlier, most cases are simply barren of any contestable legal issue, and nothing in the prosecutor's file or the defense attorney's arguments leads the prosecutor to conclude otherwise.

The new prosecutor or state's attorney, then, learns that in most cases the problem of establishing the defendant's factual and legal guilt is nonexistent. Typically, he begins with a very solid case, and, contrary to his expectations, he finds that few issues are in need of resolution at an adversary hearing or trial. The defendant's guilt is not generally problematic;

it is conceded by the defense attorney. What remains problematic is the sentence the defendant will recieve.

DISTINGUISHING AMONG THE GUILTY DEFENDANTS

Formally, the prosecutor has some powers that bear directly on sentence. He has the option to reduce or eliminate charges leveled against the defendant; the responsibility for the indictment is his, and his alone. Thus, if he *nolles* some of the charges against the defendant, he can reduce the maximum exposure the defendant faces or ensure that the defendant is sentenced only on a misdemeanor (if he *nolles* a felony), and so forth. Beyond these actions on charges, the formal powers of the prosecutor cease. The judge is responsible for sentencing. He is supposed to decide the conditions of probation, the length of incarceration, and so on. Notwithstanding this formal dichotomy of responsibility, prosecutors find that defense attorneys approach them about both charge and sentence reduction.

Since charge reduction bears on sentence reduction, it is only a small step for defense attorneys to inquire specifically about sentence; and, because there is often an interdependence between charge and sentence, prosecutors are compelled at least to listen to the attorney's arguments. Thus, the prosecutor finds attorneys parading before him asking for charge and sentence reduction, and, in a sense, he is obligated to hear them out.

It is one thing to say that prosecutors and state's attorneys must listen to defense attorneys' requests about disposition and another to say that they must cooperate with these attorneys. As already indicated, new prosecutors feel acutely uneasy about charge and sentence reduction. They have neither the confidence nor the inclination to usurp what they view as primarily the judge's responsibility. Furthermore, one would think that their resolve not to become involved in this area would be strengthened by their learning that most defendants are factually and legally guilty. Why should they discuss dispositions in cases in which they "hold all the cards?"

This query presupposes that prosecutors continue to conceive of themselves as adversaries, whose exclusive task is to establish the defendant's guilt or innocence. But what happens is that as prosecutors gain greater experience handling cases, they gradually develop certain standards for evaluating cases, standards that bear not just on the defendant's guilt or innocence, but, more importantly, on the disposition of the defendant's case. These standards better explain prosecutorial behavior in negotiating dispositions than does the simple notion of establishing guilt or innocence.

Specifically prosecutors come to distinguish between serious and nonserious cases, and between cases in which they are looking for time and cases in which they are not looking for time. These standards or distinctions evolve after the prosecutor has processed a substantial number of factually and legally guilty defendants. They provide a means of sorting the raw material—the guilty defendants. Indeed, one can argue that the adversary component of the prosecutor's job is shifted from establishing guilt or innocence to determining the seriousness of the defendant's guilt and whether he should receive time. The guilt of the defendant is assumed, but the problem of disposition remains to be informally argued.

Prosecutors and state's attorneys draw sharp distinctions between serious and nonserious cases. In both instances, they assume the defendant guilty, but they are looking for different types of dispositions, dependent upon their classification of the case. If it is a nonserious matter, they are amenable to defense requests for a small fine in the circuit court, some short, suspended sentence, or some brief period of probation; similarly, in a nonserious superior court matter the state's attorney is willing to work out a combination suspended sentence and probation. The central concern with these nonserious cases is to dispose of them quickly. If the defense attorney requests some sort of no-time disposition that is dependent upon either a prosecutorial reduction of charges or a sentence recommendation, the prosecutor and state's attorney are likely to agree. They have no incentive to refuse the attorney's request, since the attorney's desire comports with what they are "looking for." The case is simply not worth the effort to press for greater penalty.

On the other hand, if the case is serious, the prosecutor and state's attorney are likely to be looking for time. The serious case cannot be quickly disposed of by a no-time alternative. These are cases in which we would expect more involved and lengthy plea-bargaining negotiations.

Whether the case is viewed as serious or nonserious depends on factors other than the formal charges the defendant faces. For example, these nonformal considerations might include the degree of harm done the victim, the amount of violence employed by the defendant, the defendant's prior record, the characteristics of the victim and defendant, the defendant's motive; all are somewhat independent of formal charge, and yet all weigh heavily in the prosecutor's judgment of the seriousness of the case. Defendants facing the same formal charges, then, may find that prosecutors sort their cases into different categories. Two defendants charged with robbery with violence may find that in one instance the state's attorney is willing to reduce the charge and recommend probation, while in the second case he is looking for a substantial period of incarceration. In the former case, the defendant may have simply brushed against the victim (still technically robbery with violence), whereas in the second, he may have dealt the victim a severe blow. Or possibly, the first defendant was a junkie supporting his habit, whereas the second was operating on the profit motive. These are, of course, imperfect illustrations, but the point is that the determination as to whether a case is serious or not serious only partially reflects the charges against the defendant. Often the determination is based on a standard that develops with experience in the court, and operates, for the most part, independently of formal statutory penalties.

The following excerpts convey a sense of the serious/nonserious dichotomy and also support the argument that charge does not necessarily indicate seriousness.

Q: How did you learn what cases were worth?

A: You mean sentences.

Q: Yeah.

A: Well, that's a hit-or-miss kind of an experience. You take a first offender; any first offender in a nonviolent crime certainly is not going to jail for a nonviolent crime. And a second offender, well, it depends again on the type of crime, and maybe there should be some supervision, some probation. And a third time, you say, well now this is a guy who maybe you should treat a little more strictly. Now, a violent crime, I would treat differently. How did I learn to? I learned because there were a few other guys around with experience, and I got experience, and they had good judgments, workable approaches, and you pick it up like that. In other words, you watch others, you talk to others, you handle a lot of cases yourself.

Q: Does anybody, the public, put pressure on you to be tougher?

A: Not really.

Q: Wouldn't these sentences be pretty difficult for the public to understand?

A: Yeah, somewhat. . . . Sure, we are pretty easy on a lot of these cases except that. . . . We are tough on mugging and crimes by violence. Say an old lady is grabbed by a kid and knocked to the ground and her pocketbook taken as she is waiting for the bus. We'd be as tough as anybody on that one, whether you call it a breach of peace or a robbery. We'd be very tough. And in this case there would be a good likelihood of the first offender going to jail, whatever the charge we give him. The name of the charge isn't important. We'd have the facts regardless.

Q: So you think you have changed? You give away more than you used to?

A: I don't give away more. I think that I have reached the point where. . . . When I started I was trying to be too fair, if you want to say that, you know, to see that justice was done, and I was severe. But, you know, like ______ [head prosecutor] says, you need to look for justice tempered with mercy, you know, substantial justice, and that's what I do now. When I was new, a guy cut [knifed] someone he had to go to jail. But now I look for substantial justice—if two guys have been drinking and one guy got cut, I'm not giving anything away, but a fine, that's enough there.

Q: But you are easier now? I mean, you could look for time?

A: Look, if I get a guy that I feel belongs in jail, I try to sentence bargain and get him in jail. We had this one guy, ______. He was charged with breach of peace. We knew he had been selling drugs but we couldn't prove anything. He hits this girl in ______'s parking lot [large department store], and tried to take her purse. She screams and he runs. This was a real son-of-a-bitch, been pimping for his own wife. On breach of peace I wanted the full year, and eventually got nine months. Cases like that I won't give an inch on. And the lawyer first wanted him to plead to suspended sentence and a money fine. I said this guy is a goddamned animal. Anybody who lets his wife screw and then gets proceeds from it, and deals in drugs . . . well, if you can catch the bastard on it, he belongs behind bars.

. . .

The second standard used by prosecutors and state's attorneys in processing factually and legally guilty defendants is the time/no-time distinction. There is an obvious relationship between the serious/nonserious standard and this one: in the serious case time is generally the goal; whereas in the nonserious case, a no-time disposition is satisfactory to the prosecutor. But this simple relationship does not always hold, and it is important for us to consider the exceptions.

In some serious cases, the prosecutor or state's attorney may not be looking for time. Generally, these are cases in which the prosecutor has a problem establishing either the factual or legal guilt of the defendant, and thus is willing to settle for a plea to the charge and offer a recommendation of a suspended sentence. The logic is simple: the prosecutor feels the defendant is guilty of the offense but fears that if he insists on time, the defense attorney will go to trial and uncover the factual or legal defects of the state's case. Thus, the prosecutor "sweetens the deal" to extract a guilty plea and to decrease the likelihood that the attorney will gamble on complete vindication.

Of the prosecutors I interviewed, a handful expressed disenchantment with plea bargaining. They felt that their associates were being too lenient, giving away too much in return for the defendant's plea. They argued that the prosecutor's office should stay firm and go to trial if necessary in order to obtain higher sentences. They were personally inclined to act this way: they "didn't like plea bargaining." But when pushed a bit, it became clear that their antipathy to plea bargaining was not without its exceptions. In the serious case with factual or legal defects they felt very strongly that plea bargaining was appropriate. The sentiments of such an "opponent" to plea bargaining are presented below.

Q: So you are saying that you only like some kinds of plea bargaining?

A: I like to negotiate cases where I have a problem with the case. I know the guy is guilty, but I have some legal problem, or unavailability of a witness that the defendant doesn't know about that will make it difficult for us to put the case on. I would have trouble with the case. Then it is in my interest to bargain; even in serious cases with these problems, it is in the best interests of the state to get the guy to plead, even if it's to a felony with suspended sentence.

Q: If there was no plea bargaining, then the state wold lose out?

A: Yes, in cases like these. These would be cases that without plea bargaining we would have trouble convicting the defendant. But this has

> nothing to do with the defendant's guilt or innocence. Yet we might have to let him go. It is just to plea bargain in cases like this. It is fair to get the plea from the defendant, since he is guilty. Now, there is another situation; whereas in the first situation, I have no philosophical problems with plea bargaining. We may have a weak case factually. Maybe the case depends on one witness, and I have talked to the witness and realized how the witness would appear in court. Maybe the witness would be a flop when he testifies. If I feel the defendant is guilty, but the witness is really bad, then I know that we won't win the case at trial, that we won't win a big concession in plea bargaining. So I will evaluate the case, and I will be predisposed to talking about a more lenient disposition.

. . .

The other unexpected cross between the standards—nonserious case/looking for time—occurs in several types of situations. First, there is the case in which the defendant has a long history of nonserious offenses, and it is felt that a short period of incarceration will "teach him a lesson," or at least indicate that there are limits beyond which prosecutors cannot be pushed. Second, there is the situation where the prosecutor holds the defense attorney in disdain and is determined to teach the attorney a lesson. Thus, though the defendant's offense is nonserious, the prosecutor would generally be amenable to a no-time disposition, the prosecutor chooses to hold firm. It is precisely in those borderline cases that the prosecutor can be most successful in exercising sanctions against the uncooperative defense attorney. The formal penalties associated with the charges against the defendant give him ample sentencing range, and by refusing to agree to a no-time disposition, the costs to the defense attorney become great. The attorney is not able to meet his client's demands for no time, and yet he must be leery about trial, given the even greater exposure the defendant faces. These borderline decisions by prosecutors, then, are fertile grounds for exploring sanctions against defense attorneys. It is here that we can expect the cooperative defense attorney to benefit most, and the recalcitrant defense attorney to suffer the most. Relatedly, one can also expect prosecutors to be looking for time in nonserious offenses in which the defendant or his counsel insists on raising motions and going to trial. These adversary activities may be just enough to tip the prosecutor into looking for time.

In addition to its relationship to the serious/nonserious standard, the time/no-time standard bears on prosecutorial plea-bargaining behavior in another way. As prosecutors gain experience in the plea-bargaining system, they tend to stress "certainty of time" rather than "amount of time." This is to say that they become less concerned about extracting maximum penalties from defendants and more concerned with ensuring that in cases in which they are looking for time, the defendant actually receives some time. Obviously, there are limits to the prosecutor's largesse—in a serious case 30 days will not be considered sufficient time. But prosecutors are willing to consider periods of incarceration substantially shorter than the maximum sentence allowable for a particular crime. In return, though, prosecutors want a guarantee of sorts that the defendant will receive time. They want to decrease the likelihood that the defendant, by some means or other, will obtain a suspended sentence. Thus, they will "take" a fixed amount of time if the defendant agrees not to try to "pitch" for a lower sentence, or if the defendant pleads to a charge in which all participants know some time will be meted out by the judge. In the latter instance, the attorney may be free to "pitch," but court personnel know his effort is more a charade for the defendant than a realistic effort to obtain a no-time disposition. The following excerpts illustrate prosecutorial willingness to trade off years of time for certainty of time.

> I don't believe in giving away things. In fact _____ [a public defender] approached me; there's this kid _____, he has two robberies, one first degree, one second, and three minor cases. Now, this kid, I made out an affidavit myself for tampering with a witness. This kid is just n.g. _____ came to me and said, "We'll plead out, two to five." He'll go to state's prison. I agreed to that—both these offenses are bindovers. These kids belong in jail. I'd rather take two to five here than bind them over to superior court and take a chance on what will happen there. At least my two to five will be a year and three-quarters in state's prison. The thing is, if I want to get a guy in jail for a year, I'll plea bargain with him, and I'll take six months if I can get it, because the guy belongs in jail, and if I can get him to jail for six months why should I fool around with that case, and maybe get a year if I am lucky? If I can put a guy away for six months I might be cheated out of six months, but at least the guy is doing six months in jail.
>
> What is a proper time? It never bothers me if we could have gotten seven years and instead we got five. In this case, there was no violence; minor stuff was stolen. We got time out of him. That is the important thing.
>
> **A:** It makes no difference to me really if a man does five to ten or four to eight. The important thing is he's off the street, not a menace to society for a period of time, and the year or two less is not going to make that great a difference. If If you do get time, I think it's . . . you know, many prosecutors I know feel this way. They have achieved confinement, that's what they're here for.
>
> **Q:** Let's take another example. Yesterday an attorney walked in here when I was present on that gambling case. He asked you if it could be settled without time?
>
> **A:** And I said no. That ended the discussion.
>
> **Q:** What will he do now?
>
> **A:** He'll file certain motions that he really doesn't have to file. All the facts of our case were spelled out; he knows as much about our cases as he'll ever know. So his motions will just delay things. There'll come a point, though, when he'll have to face trial; and he'll come in to speak with us, and ask if we still have the same position. We'll have the same position. We'll still be looking for one to three. His record goes back to 1923, he's served two or three terms for narcotics, and he's been fined five times for

gambling. So we'd be looking for one to three and a fine. Even though he's in his sixties, he's been a criminal all his life, since 1923. . . .

Q: But if the attorney pushes and says, "Now look. He's an old guy. He's sixty-two years old, how about six months?"

A: I might be inclined to accept it because, again, confinement would be involved. I think our ends would be met. It would show his compadres that there's no longer any immunity for gambling, that there is confinement involved. So the end result would be achieved.

Justice Holmes, who is supposed to be the big sage in American jurisprudence, said it isn't the extent of the punishment but the certainty of it. This is my basic philosophy. If the guy faces twelve years in state's prison, I'm satisfied if on a plea of guilty he'll go to state's prison for two or three years.

The experienced prosecutor, then, looks beyond the defendant's guilt when evaluating a case. He learns—from a reading of the file and from the defense attorney's entreaties—that most defendants are factually and legally guilty and that he generally holds the upper hand. As he gains experience in processing these cases, he gradually begins to draw distinctions within this pool of guilty defendants. Some of the cases appear not to be serious, and the prosecutor becomes willing to go along with the defense attorney's request for no-time dispositions. The cases simply do not warrant a firmer prosecutorial posture. In serious cases, when he feels time is in order, he often finds defense attorneys in agreement on the need for some incarceration.

In a sense, the prosecutor redefines his professional goals. He learns that the statutes fail to distinguish adequately among guilty defendants, that they "sweep too broadly," and give short shrift to the specific facts of the offense, to the defendant's prior record, to the degree of contributory culpability of the victim, and so on. Possessing more information about the defendant than the judge does, the prosecutor—probably unconsciously—comes to believe that it is his professional responsibility to develop standards that distinguish among defendants and lead to "equitable" dispositions. Over time, the prosecutor comes to feel that if he does not develop these standards, if he does not make these professional judgments, no one else will.

The prosecutor seems almost to drift into plea bargaining. When he begins his job he observes that his colleagues plea bargain routinely and quickly finds that defense attorneys expect him to do the same. Independent of any rewards, sanctions, or pressures, he learns the strengths of his cases, and learns to distinguish the serious from the nonserious ones. After an initial period of reluctance to plea bargain at all (he is fearful of being taken advantage of by defense attorneys), the prosecutor finds that he is engaged almost unwittingly in daily decisions concerning the disposition of cases. His obligation to consider alternative charges paves the way for the defense attorney's advances; it is only a small jump to move to sentence discussions. And as he plea bargains more and more cases, the serious/nonserious and time/no-time standards begin to hold sway in his judgments. He feels confident about the disposition he is looking for, and if a satisfactory plea bargain in line with his goals can be negotiated, he comes to feel that there is little point to following a more formal adversary process. . . .

CASE PRESSURE AND POTENTIAL BACKLOG

Though they may do so during the first few weeks, the newcomer's peers and superiors do not generally pressure him to move cases because of volume. Instead, he is thrust in the fray largely on his own and is allowed to work out his own style of case disposition. Contrary to the "conspiratorial perspective" of the adaptation process, he is not coerced to cooperate in processing "onerously large caseloads."

The newcomer's plea-bargaining behavior is conditioned by his reactions to particular cases he handles or learns about and not by caseload problems of the office. The chief prosecutor within the jurisdiction may worry about his court's volume and the speed with which cases are disposed, but he does not generally interfere with his assistant's decision about how to proceed in a case. The newcomer is left to learn about plea bargaining on his own, and for the reason already discussed, he learns and is taught the value of negotiating many of his cases. The absence of a direct relationship between prosecutor plea bargaining and case pressure is suggested in the following remarks.

Q: Is it case pressure that leads you to negotiate?

A: I don't believe it's the case pressure at all. In every court, whether there are five cases or one hundred cases, we should try to settle it. It's good for both sides. If I were a public defender I'd try to settle all the cases for my guilty clients. By negotiating you are bound to do better. Now take this case. [He reviewed the facts of a case in which an elderly man was charged with raping a 7-year-old girl. The defendant claimed he could not remember what happened, that he was drunk, and that, though the girl might have been in the bed with him, he did not think he raped her.] I think I gave the defense attorney a fair deal. The relatives say she was raped, but the doctor couldn't conclusively establish that. I offered him a plea to a lesser charge, one dealing with advances toward minors, but excluding the sex act. If he takes it, he'll be able to walk away with time served [the defendant had not posted bail and had spent several months in jail]. It's the defendant's option though. He can go through trial if he wants, but if he makes that choice, the kid and her relatives will have to be dragged through the agonies of trial also. Then I would be disposed to look for a higher sentence for the defendant. So I think my offer is fair, and the offer has nothing to do with the volume of this court. It's the way I think the case—all things considered—should be resolved.

Q: You say the docket wasn't as crowded in 1966, and yet there was plea bargaining. If I had begun this interview by saying why is there plea bargaining here. . . .

A: I couldn't use the reason there's plea bargaining because there are a lot of cases. That's not so; that's not so at all. If we had only ten cases down for tomorrow and an attorney walked in and wanted to discuss a case with me, I'd sit down and discuss it with him. In effect, that's plea bargaining. Whether it's for the charge or for an agreed recommendation or reduction of the charge or what have you, it's still plea bargaining. It's part of the process that has been going on for quite a long time.

Q: And you say it's not because of the crowded docket, but if I gave you a list of reasons for why there was plea bargaining and asked you to pick the most important. . . .

A: I never really thought about the. . . . You talk about the necessity for plea bargaining, and you say, well, it's necessary, and one of the reasons is because we have a crowded docket, but even if we didn't we still would plea bargain.

Q: Why?

A: Well, it has been working throughout the years, and the way I look at it, it's beneficial to the defendant, it's beneficial to the court, and not just in saving time but in avoiding police officers coming to court, witnesses being subpoenaed in, and usually things can be discussed between prosecutors and defense counsel which won't be said in the open court and on the record. There are many times that the defense counsel will speak confidentially with the prosecutor about his client or about the facts or about the complainant or a number of things. So I don't know if I can justify plea bargaining other than by speaking of the necessity of plea bargaining. If there were only ten cases down for one day, it still would be something that would be done.

Maybe in places like New York they plea bargain because of case pressure. I don't know. But here it is different. We dispose of cases on the basis of what is fair to both sides. You can get a fair settlement by plea bargaining. If you don't try to settle a case quickly, it gets stale. In New York the volume probably is so bad that it becomes a matter of "getting rid of cases." In Connecticut, we have some pretty big dockets in some cities, but in other areas—here, for example—we don't have that kind of pressure. Sure, I feel some pressure, but you can't say that we negotiate our cases out to clear the docket. And you probably can't say that even about the big cities in Connecticut either.

Prosecutors, then, do not view their propensity to plea bargain as a direct outcome of case pressure. Instead, they speak of "mutually satisfactory outcomes," "fair dispositions," "reducing police overcharging," and so on. We need not here evaluate their claims in detail; what is important is that collectively their arguments militate against according case pressure the "top billing" it so often receives in the literature.

Another way to conceptualize the relationship between case pressure and plea bargaining is to introduce the notion of a "potential backlog." Some prosecutors maintain that if fewer cases were plea bargained, or if plea bargaining were eliminated, a backlog of cases to be disposed of would quickly clog their calendars. A potential backlog, then, lurks as a possibility in every jurisdiction. Even in a low-volume jurisdiction, one complex trial could back up cases for weeks, or even months. If all those delayed cases also had to be tried, the prosecutor feels he would face two not-so-enviable options. He could become further backlogged by trying as many of them as was feasible, or he could reduce his backlog by outright dismissal of cases. The following comments are typical of the potential backlog argument.

> **Q:** Some people have suggested that plea bargaining not be allowed in the court. All cases would go to trial before a judge or jury and. . . .
>
> **A:** Something like that would double, triple, and quadruple the backlog. Reduce that 90 percent of people pleading guilty, and even if you were to try a bare minimum of those cases, you quadruple your backlog. It's feasible.
>
> Well, right now we don't have a backlog. But if we were to try even 10 percent of our cases, take them to a jury, we'd be so backed up that we couldn't even move. We'd be very much in the position of. . . . Some traffic director in New York once said that there will come a time that there will be one car too many coming into New York and nobody will be able to move. Well, we can get ourselves into that kind of situation if we are going to go ahead and refuse to plea bargain even in the serious cases.

Though a potential backlog is an ever-present possibility, it should be stressed that most prosecutors develop this argument more as a prediction as to the outcome of a rule decreasing or eliminating plea bargaining than as an explanation for why they engage in plea bargaining. If plea bargaining were eliminated, a backlog would develop; but awareness of this outcome does not explain why they plea bargain.

Furthermore, prosecutors tend to view the very notion of eliminating plea bargaining as a fake issue, a straw-man proposition. It is simply inconceivable to them that plea bargaining could or would be eliminated. They maintain that no court system could try all of its cases, even if huge increases in personnel levels were made; trials consume more time than any realistic increase in personnel levels could manage. They were willing to speculate on the outcome of a rule proscribing plea bargaining, but the argument based on court backlog that they evoked was not a salient consideration in understanding their day-in, day-out plea-bargaining behavior.

It is, of course, impossible to refute with complete certainty an argument that prosecutors plea bargain because failure to do so would cause a backlog of unmanageable proportions to develop. However, the interviews indicate other more compelling ways to conceptualize prosecutorial adaptation to plea bargaining, and these do not depend on a potential backlog that always can be conjured up. Though the backlog may loom as a consequence of a failure to plea bargain, it—like its case-pressure cousin—is neither a necessary nor sufficient explanatory vehicle for understanding the core aspects of prosecutorial plea-bargaining behavior.

A PERSPECTIVE ON PROSECUTORIAL ADAPTATION

Perhaps the most important outcome of the prosecutor's adaptation is that he evidences a major shift in his own presumption about how to proceed with a case. As a newcomer, he feels it to be his responsibility to establish the defendant's guilt at trial, and he sees no need to justify a decision to go to trial. However, as he processes more and more cases, as he drifts into plea bargaining, and as he is taught the risks associated with trials, his own assumption about how to proceed with a case changes. He approaches every case with plea bargaining in mind, that is, he presumes that the case will be plea bargained. If it is a "nonserious" matter, he expects it to be quickly resolved; if it is "serious" he generally expects to negotiate time as part of the disposition. In both instances, he anticipates that the case will eventually be resolved by a negotiated disposition and not by a trial. When a plea bargain does not materialize, and the case goes to trial, the prosecutor feels compelled to justify his failure to reach an accord. He no longer is content to simply assert that it is the role of the prosecutor to establish the defendant's guilt at trial. This adversary component of the prosecutor's role has been replaced by a self-imposed burden to justify why he chose to go to trial, particularly if a certain conviction—and, for serious cases, a period of incarceration—could have been obtained by means of a negotiated disposition.

Relatedly, the prosecutor grows accustomed to the power he exercises in these plea-bargaining negotiations. As a newcomer, he argued that his job was to be an advocate for the state and that it was the judge's responsibility to sentence defendants. But, having in fact "sentenced" most of the defendants whose files he plea bargained, the distinction between prosecutor and judge becomes blurred in his own mind. Though he did not set out to usurp judicial prerogatives—indeed, he resisted efforts to engage him in the plea-bargaining process—he gradually comes to expect tht he will exercise sentencing powers. There is no fixed point in time when he makes a calculated choice to become adjudicator as well as adversary. In a sense, it simply "happens"; the more cases he resolves (either by charge reduction or sentence recommendations), the greater the likelihood that he will lose sight of the distinction between the roles of judge and prosecutor.

PART FOUR

DEFENSE ATTORNEYS

Criminal lawyers have traditionally been caught between divergent conceptions of their position. On the one hand, defense attorneys are viewed as "Perry Masons," involved in a constant searching and creative questioning of official decisions at all stages of the justice process. On the other hand, they are seen as somehow "soiled" by their clients, engaged in shady practices to free clients who have committed crimes from the rightful demands of the law. Although Perry Mason remains a hero, the public retains the more tarnished image.

The public's assumption probably accurately reflects the lifestyles of many lawyers engaged in criminal practice in large urban areas. In the vicinity of many metropolitan courthouses, one can find the offices of those who are called the "Fifth Streeters" in the District of Columbia and the "Clinton Street Bar" in Detroit. These terms refer to attorneys who prowl criminal courts in search of clients who can pay a modest fee. Some have referral arrangements with police officers, bondsmen, and other minor officials. Rather than prepare cases for disposition through the adversary process, these lawyers negotiate guilty pleas and try to convince their clients that they received exceptional treatment. Such lawyers are not true professionals; they act as fixers for a fee. They exist in a relatively closed system where there are great pressures to process large numbers of cases for small fees, and they are dependent on the cooperation of judicial officials. This small group of practitioners is usually less well educated, works harder, and in a more precarious financial situation than peers in corporate practice.

A number of nationally known attorneys, such as Melvin Belli, F. Lee Bailey, and Edward Bennett Williams, have built reputations by adhering to the Perry Mason model, but these counselors are few and expensive. They usually take only dramatic, widely publicized cases; they are rarely found at the county courthouse. Between the polar types of a Melvin Belli and a "Fifth Streeter" are many general practitioners who sometimes take criminal cases but have little experience in trial work and do not have well-developed relationships with actors in the criminal justice system. Lacking inside knowledge, they may find that a client would be better served if a courtroom regular took the case.

With increased specialization and institutionalization of the bar, individuals engaged in the practice of criminal law seem to have been assigned a lower status, both by other lawyers and by the community at large. In addition, the unpleasant aspects of criminal law practice are not offset by monetary inducements. Criminal cases, as well as those concerned with matrimonial problems, tend to involve lawyers in emotional situations. Most services they render involve preparing defendants and their relatives for the possible outcome. The lawyer must share the client's troubles. Even exposure to "guilty knowledge" may be a psychological burden. Criminal lawyers are also called on to interact continuously with a lower class of clients and with police officials and minor political appointees. They may have to visit such depressing places as the local jail at all hours of the day or night. After winning a case, they may be unable to collect their fee. As Blumberg notes in Article 11, the financial aspect is the key variable, influencing most other aspects of criminal practice. The vast majority of criminal defendants are poor and are judged guilty.

DEFENSE OF INDIGENTS

Most criminal defendants come to court without lawyers of their own. Because the U.S. Supreme Court has ruled that a defendant may not be sent to prison unless he or she has been represented by counsel, the court usually appoints a public defender or private attorney in cases of indigency. One study by the National Legal Aid and Defender Association estimated that 65 percent of felony defendants are too poor to pay a private attorney and that in urban areas the percentage is higher. In large cities, such as New York and Chicago, up to 90 percent of criminal defendants fall into this category.

In the United States there are three basic ways of providing indigent defendants with counsel: (1) through assigned counsel, in which the attorney is appointed by the court to represent a particular defendant; (2) through the contract system, under which the government has an arrangement with an individual law firm or private attorney to handle cases on a fixed-price basis; and (3) through a defender system, in which a salaried public attorney is counsel for indigents. Although the defender system is growing rapidly, 1,833 counties (60 percent) still use the assigned counsel system, and 6 percent contract for defender services. The public defender system is the dominant form in forty-three of the fifty most populous counties, however, and such programs serve 68 percent of the U.S. population.

DEFENSE COUNSEL IN THE EXCHANGE PROCESS

In a judicial system where bargaining within an administrative context is a primary decision-making method, it is not surprising that defense attorneys find it essential to have close personal ties with the police, prosecutor, and other court officials. Their own professional survival and the opportunity to serve clients' needs may depend on establishing and maintaining relations with these actors. At each point in the criminal process, from the first contact with the accused until the final disposition of the case, the defense attorney is dependent on decisions made by other judicial actors. Even such seemingly minor activities as visiting the defendant in jail, learning from the prosecutor what the case against the defendant is, and setting bail can be made difficult by the officials involved unless there is cooperation from the defense attorney. Concern with preserving these relationships within the criminal justice system may have greater weight for defense attorneys than any short-term interest in particular clients.

Counsel is not completely at the mercy of judicial actors. At any phase, the defense has the ability to invoke the adversary model, with its formal rules and public battles. The potential for an expensive, time-consuming, and disputatious trial can be used by the effective counsel as a bargaining tool with the police, prosecutor, and judge. A well-known tactic of defense attorneys, certain to raise the ante in the bargaining process, is to ask for a trial and to proceed as if they meant it. However, because judicial personnel must interact on a continuing basis, they try to make sure that personal relationships are cordial. The introduction of adversary tactics is disruptive, so potential animosities are tempered for the benefit of the participants. The defendant passes through the system; the others involved in the case must meet again.

SUGGESTIONS FOR FURTHER READING

BAILEY, F. LEE. *The Defense Never Rests.* New York: Stein & Day, 1971. One of the best-known criminal defense specialists in the United States describes his work, featuring some of the famous cases he has won.

CASPER, JONATHAN D. *American Criminal Justice: The Defendant's Perspective.* Englewood Cliffs, N.J.: Prentice-Hall, 1972. Views of the criminal justice system from the vantage point of persons who have been arrested, tried, and incarcerated.

LEWIS, ANTHONY. *Gideon's Trumpet.* New York: Vintage, 1964. A vivid account of the case of Clarence Gideon and the opinion of the U.S. Supreme Court requiring appointment of counsel for indigents in criminal prosecutions.

WICE, PAUL. *Criminal Lawyers: An Endangered Species.* Beverly Hills, Calif.: Sage Publications, 1978. Of 400,000 lawyers in the United States, only about 15,000 accept criminal cases on more than an occasional basis. Some 4,000 of these are public defenders. Wice's national study of the private criminal bar found that the quality of these attorneys varied from city to city, with legal, institutional, and political factors accounting for much of the variation.

WISHMAN, SEYMOUR. *Confessions of a Criminal Lawyer.* New York: Times Books, 1981. As the title indicates, the author describes his life as a criminal lawyer and raises questions about the ethics of some tactics he used to secure acquittals.

ARTICLE ELEVEN

The Practice of Law as a Confidence Game: Organization Co-optation of a Profession

ABRAHAM S. BLUMBERG

Central to the adversary system is the defense attorney, who will engage the prosecution in a "fight" to ensure that the defendant's rights are protected and that the case is presented to the judge and jury in the best possible light. What happens when the professional environment of the criminal lawyer moderates the adversarial stance? Bargain justice occurs when it is believed to be in the best interests of both the prosecutor and the defense attorney to avoid the courtroom confrontation. Abraham Blumberg argues that the defense attorney acts as a double agent, to get the defendant to plead guilty.

A recurring theme in the growing dialogue between sociology and law has been the great need for a joint effort of the two disciplines to illuminate urgent social and legal issues. Having uttered fervent public pronouncements in this vein, however, the respective practitioners often go their separate ways. Academic spokesmen for the legal profession are somewhat critical of sociologists of law because of what they perceive as the sociologist's preoccupation with the application of theory and methodology to the examination of legal phenomena, without regard to the solution of legal problems. Further, it is felt that "contemporary writing in the sociology of law . . . betrays the existence of painfully unsophisticated notions about the day-to-day operations of courts, legislatures, and law

Source: From *Law and Society Review* 1 (June 1967): 15–39. By permission of the author and publisher.

offices."[1] Regardless of the merit of such criticism, scant attention—apart from explorations of the legal profession itself—has been given to the sociological examination of legal institutions, or their supporting ideological assumptions. Thus, for example, very little sociological effort is expended to ascertain the validity and viability of important court decisions, which may rest on wholly erroneous assumptions about the contextual realities of social structure. A particular decision may rest upon a legally impeccable rationale; at the same time it may be rendered nugatory or self-defeating by contingencies imposed by aspects of social reality of which the lawmakers are themselves unaware.

Within this context, I wish to question the impact of three recent landmark decisions of the United States Supreme Court, each hailed as destined to effect profound changes in the future of criminal law administration and enforcement in America. The first of these, *Gideon v. Wainwright*, 372 U.S. 335 (1963), required states and localities henceforth to furnish counsel in the case of indigent persons charged with a felony.[2] The *Gideon* ruling left several major issues unsettled, among them the vital question: What is the precise point in time at which a suspect is entitled to counsel?[3] The answer came relatively quickly in *Escobedo v. Illinois*, 378 U.S. 478 (1964), which has aroused a storm of controversy. Danny Escobedo confessed to the murder of his brother-in-law after the police had refused to permit retained counsel to see him, although his lawyer was present in the station house and asked to confer with his client. In a 5 to 4 decision, the court asserted that counsel must be permitted when the process of police investigative effort shifts from merely investigatory to that of accusatory: "when its focus is on the accused and its purpose is to elicit a confession—our adversary system begins to operate, and, under the circumstances here, the accused must be permitted to consult with his lawyer."

As a consequence, Escobedo's confession was rendered inadmissible. The decision triggered a national debate among police, district attorneys, judges, lawyers, and other law-enforcement officials, which continues unabated, as to the value and propriety of confessions in criminal cases.[4] On June 13, 1966, the Supreme Court in a 5 to 4 decision underscored the principle enunciated in *Escobedo* in the case of *Miranda v. Arizona*.[5] Police interrogation of any suspect in custody, without his consent, unless a defense attorney is present, is prohibited by the self-incrimination provision of the Fifth Amendment. Regardless of the relative merit of the various shades of opinion about the role of counsel in criminal cases, the issues generated thereby will be in part resolved as additional cases move toward decision in the Supreme Court in the near future. They are of peripheral interest and not of immediate concern in this paper. However, the *Gideon*, *Escobedo*, and *Miranda* cases pose interesting general questions. In all three decisions, the Supreme Court reiterates the traditional legal conception of a defense lawyer based on the ideological perception of a criminal case as an *adversary, combative* proceeding, in which counsel for the defense assiduously musters all the admittedly limited resources at his command to *defend* the accused.[6] The fundamental question remains to be answered: Does the Supreme Court's conception of the role of counsel in a criminal case square with social reality?

The task of this paper is to furnish some preliminary evidence toward the illumination of that question. Little empirical understanding of the function of defense counsel exists; only some ideologically oriented generalizations and commitments. This paper is based upon observations made by the writer during many years of legal practice in the criminal courts of a large metropolitan area. No claim is made as to its methodological rigor, although it does reflect a conscious and sustained effort for participant observation.

COURT STRUCTURE DEFINES ROLE OF DEFENSE LAWYER

The overwhelming majority of convictions in criminal cases (usually over 90 percent) are not the product of a combative, trial-by-jury process at all, but instead merely involve the sentencing of the individual after a negotiated, bargained-for plea of guilty has been entered.[7] Although more recently the overzealous role of police and prosecutors in producing pretrial confessions and admissions has achieved a good deal of notoriety, scant attention has been paid to the organizational structure and personnel of the criminal court itself. Indeed, the extremely high conviction rate produced without the features of an adversary trial in our courts would tend to suggest that the "trial" becomes a perfunctory reiteration and validation of the pretrial interrogation and investigation.[8]

The institutional setting of the court defines a role for the defense counsel in a criminal case radically different from the one traditionally depicted.[9] Sociologists and others have focused their attention on the deprivations and social disabilities of such variables as race, ethnicity, and social class as being the source of an accused person's defeat in a criminal court. Largely overlooked is the variable of the court organization itself, which possesses a thrust, purpose, and direction of its own. It is grounded in pragmatic values, bureaucratic priorities, and administrative instruments. These exalt maximum production and the particularistic career designs of organizational incumbents, whose occupational and career commitments tend to generate a set of priorities. These priorities exert a higher claim than the stated ideological goals of "due process of law," and are often inconsistent with them.

Organizational goals and discipline impose a set of demands and conditions of practice on the respective professions in the criminal court to which they respond by abandoning their ideological and professional commitments to the accused client, in the service of these higher claims of the court organization. All court personnel, including the accused's own lawyer, tend to be co-opted to become agent-mediators[10] who help the accused redefine his situation and restructure his perceptions concomitant with a plea of guilty.

Of all the occupational roles in the court, the only private individual who is officially recognized as having a special status and concomitant obligations is the lawyer. His legal status is that of "an officer of the court" and he is held to a standard of ethical performance and duty to his client as well as to the court. This obligation is thought to be far higher than that expected of ordinary individuals occupying the various occupational statuses in the court community. However, lawyers, whether privately retained or of the legal-aid, public defender variety, have close and continuing relations with the prosecuting office and the court itself through discreet relations with the judges via their law secretaries or "confidential" assistants. Indeed, lines of communication, influence, and contact with those offices, as well as with the Office of the Clerk of the Court, the Probation Division, and the press, are essential to present and prospective requirements of criminal law practice. Similarly, the subtle involvement of the press and other mass media in the court's organizational network is not readily discernible to the casual observer. Accused persons come and go in the court system schema, but the structure and its occupational incumbents remain to carry on their respective career, occupational, and organizational enterprises. The individual stridencies, tensions, and conflicts a given accused person's case may present to all the participants are overcome, because the formal and informal relations of all the groups in the court setting require it. The probability of continued future relations and interaction must be preserved at all costs.

This is particularly true of the "lawyer regulars"—that is, those defense lawyers, who by virtue of their continuous appearances in behalf of defendants, tend to represent the bulk of a criminal court's nonindigent case workload, and those lawyers who are not "regulars," who appear almost casually in behalf of an occasional client. Some of the lawyer "regulars" are highly visible as one moves about the major urban centers of the nation; their offices line the back streets of the courthouses, at times sharing space with bondsmen. Their political "visibility" in terms of local clubhouse ties, reaching into the judge's chambers and the prosecutor's office, is also deemed essential to successful practitioners. Previous research has indicated that the "lawyer regulars" make no effort to conceal their dependence upon police, bondsmen, and jail personnel. Nor do they conceal the necessity for maintaining intimate relations with all levels of personnel in the court setting as a means of obtaining, maintaining, and building their practice. These informal relations are the *sine qua non* not only of retaining a practice but also in the negotiation of pleas and sentences.[11]

The client, then, is a secondary figure in the court system as in certain other bureaucratic settings.[12] He becomes a means to other ends of the organization's incumbents. He may present doubts, contingencies, and pressures which challenge existing informal arrangements or disrupt them; but these tend to be resolved in favor of the continuance of the organization and its relations as before. There is a greater community of interest among all the principal organizational structures and their incumbents than exists elsewhere in other settings. The accused's lawyer has far greater professional, economic, intellectual, and other ties to the various elements of the court system than he does to his own client. In short, the court is a closed community.

This is more than just the case of the usual "secrets" of bureaucracy which are fanatically defended from an outside view. Even all elements of the press are zealously determined to report on that which will not offend the board of judges, the prosecutor, and probation, legal-aid, or other officials, in return for privileges and courtesies granted in the past and to be granted in the future. Rather than any view of the matter in terms of some variation of a "conspiracy" hypothesis, the simple explanation is one of an ongoing system handling delicate tensions, managing the trauma produced by law enforcement and administration, and requiring almost pathological distrust of "outsiders" bordering on group paranoia.

The hostile attitude toward "outsiders" is in large measure engendered by a defensiveness itself produced by the inherent deficiencies of assembly-line justice, so characteristic of our major criminal courts. Intolerably large caseloads of defendants, which must be disposed of in an organizational context of limited resources and personnel, potentially subject the participants in the court community to harsh scrutiny from appellate courts and other public and private sources of condemnation. As a consequence, an almost irreconcilable conflict is posed in terms of intense pressures to process large numbers of cases, on the one hand, and the stringent ideological and legal requirements of "due process of law," on the other hand. A rather tenuous resolution of the dilemma has emerged in the shape of a large variety of bureaucratically ordained and controlled "work crimes," shortcuts, deviations, and outright rule violations adopted as court practice in order to meet production norms. Fearfully anticipating criticism on ethical as well as legal grounds, all the significant participants in the court's social structure are bound into an organized system of complicity. This consists of a work arrangement in which the patterned, covert, informal breaches and evasions of "due process" are institutionalized but are, nevertheless, denied to exist.

These institutionalized evasions will be found to occur to some degree in all criminal courts. Their nature, scope, and complexity are largely determined by the size of the court and the character of the community in which it is located—for example, whether it is a large, urban institution or a relatively small rural county court. In addition, idiosyncratic, local conditions may contribute to a unique flavor in the character and quality of the criminal law's administration in a particular community. However, in most instances a variety of stratagems are employed—some subtle, some crude, ineffectively disposing of what are often too-large caseloads. A wide variety of coercive devices are employed against an accused client, couched in a depersonalized, instrumental, bureaucratic version of due process of law, and which are in reality a perfunctory obeisance to the ideology of due process. These include some very explicit pressures which are exerted in some measure by all court personnel, including judges, to plead guilty and avoid trial. In many instances the sanction of a potentially harsh sentence is utilized as the visible alternative to pleading guilty, in the case of recalcitrants. Probation and psychiatric reports are "tailored" to organizational needs, or are at least responsive to the court organization's requirements for the refurbishment of a defendant's social biography, consonant with his new status. A resourceful judge can, through his subtle domination of the proceedings, impose his will on the final outcome of a trial. Stenographers and clerks, in their function as record keepers, are on occasion pressed into service in support of a judicial need to "rewrite" the record of a courtroom event. Bail practices are usually employed for purposes other than simply assuring a defendant's presence on the date of a hearing in connection with his case. Too often, the discretionary power as to bail is part of the arsenal of weapons available to collapse the resistance of an accused person. The foregoing is a most cursory examination of some of the more prominent "shortcuts" available to any court organization. There are numerous other procedural strategies constituting due process deviations, which tend to become the work-style artifacts of a court's personnel. Thus, only court "regulars" who are "bound in" are really accepted; others are treated routinely and in almost a coldly correct manner.

The defense attorneys, therefore, whether of the legal-aid, public defender variety or privately retained, although operating in terms of pressures specific to their respective role and organizational obligations, ultimately are concerned with strategies which tend to lead to a plea. It is the rational, impersonal elements involving economies of time, labor, expense, and a superior commitment of the defense counsel to these rationalistic values of maximum production[13] of court organization that prevail in his relationship with a client. The lawyer "regulars" are frequently former staff members of the prosecutor's office and utilize the prestige, know-how, and contacts of their former affiliation as part of their stock-in-trade. Close and continuing relations between the lawyer "regular" and his former colleagues in the prosecutor's office generally overshadow the relationship between the regular and his client. The continuing colleagueship of supposedly adversary counsel rests on real professional and organizational needs of a *quid pro quo,* which goes beyond the limits of an accommodation or *modus vivendi* one might ordinarily expect under the circumstances of an otherwise seemingly adversary relationship. Indeed, the adversary features which are manifest are for the most part muted and exist even in their attenuated form largely for external consumption.

The principals, lawyer and assistant district attorney, rely upon one another's cooperation for their continued professional existence, and so the bargaining between them tends usually to be "reasonable" rather than fierce.

FEE COLLECTION AND FIXING

The real key to understanding the role of defense counsel in a criminal case is to be found in the area of the fixing of the fee to be charged and its collection. The problem of fixing and collecting the fee tends to influence to a significant degree the criminal court process itself, and not just the relationship of the lawyer and his client. In essence, a lawyer-client "confidence game" is played. A true confidence game is unlike the case of the emperor's new clothes wherein that monarch's nakedness was a result of inordinate gullibility and credulity. In a genuine confidence game, the perpetrator manipulates the basic dishonesty of his partner, the victim or mark, toward his own (the confidence operator's) ends. Thus, "the victim of a con scheme must have some larceny in his heart."[14]

Legal service lends itself particularly well to confidence games. Usually, a plumber will be able to demonstrate empirically that he has performed a service by clearing up the stuffed drain, repairing the leaky faucet or pipe—and therefore merits his fee. He has rendered, when summoned, a visible, tangible boon for his client in return for the requested fee. A physician, who has not performed some visible surgery or otherwise engaged in some readily discernible procedure in connection with a patient, may be deemed by the patient to have "done nothing" for him. As a consequence, medical practitioners may simply prescribe or administer by injection a placebo to overcome a patient's potential reluctance or dissatisfaction in paying a requested fee, "for nothing."

In the practice of law there is a special problem in this regard, no matter what the level of the practitioner or his place in the hierarchy of prestige. Much legal work is intangible either because it is simply a few words of advice, some preventive action, a telephone call, negotiation of some kind, a form filled out and filed, a hurried conference with another attorney or an official of a government agency, a letter or opinion written, or a countless variety of seemingly innocuous and even prosaic procedures and actions. These are the basic activities, apart from any possible court appearance, of almost all lawyers, at all levels of practice. Much of the activity is not in the nature of the exercise of the traditional, precise professional skills of the attorney such as library research and oral argument in connection with appellate briefs, court motions, trial work, drafting of opinions, memoranda, contracts, and other complex documents and agreements. Instead, much legal activity, whether it is at the lowest or highest "white shoe" law firm levels, is of the brokerage, agent, sales representative, lobbyist type of activity, in which the lawyer acts for someone else in pursuing the latter's interests and designs. The service is intangible.[15]

The large-scale law firm may not speak as openly of their "contacts," their "fixing" abilities, as does the lower-level lawyer. They trade instead upon a facade of thick carpeting, walnut paneling, genteel low pressure, and superficialities of traditional legal professionalism. There are occasions when even the large firm is on the defensive in connection with the fees they charge because the services rendered or results obtained do not appear to merit the fee asked.[16] Therefore, there is a recurrent problem in the legal profession in fixing the amount of fee and in justifying the basis for the requested fee.

Although the fee at times amounts to what the traffic and the conscience of the lawyer will bear, one further observation must be made with regard to the size of the fee and its collection. The defendant in a criminal case and the material gain he may have acquired during the course of his illicit activities are soon parted. Not infrequently the ill-gotten fruits of the various modes of larceny are sequestered by a defense lawyer in payment of his fee. Inexorably, the amount of the fee is a function of the dollar value of the crime committed and is frequently set with meticulous precision at a sum which bears an uncanny relationship to that of the net proceeds of the particular offense involved. On occasion, defendants have been known to commit additional offenses while at liberty on bail, in order to secure the requisite funds with which to meet their obligations for payment of legal fees. Defense lawyers condition even the most obtuse clients to recognize that there is a firm interconnection between fee payment and the zealous exercise of professional expertise, secret knowledge, and organizational "connections" in their behalf. Lawyers, therefore, seek to keep their clients in a proper state of tension, and to arouse in them the precise edge of anxiety which is calculated to encourage prompt fee payment. Consequently, the client attitude in the relationship between defense counsel and an accused is in many instances a precarious admixture of hostility, mistrust, dependence, and sycophancy. By keeping his client's anxieties aroused to the proper pitch, and establishing a seemingly causal relationship between a requested fee and the accused's ultimate extrication from his onerous difficulties, the lawyer will have established the necessary preliminary groundwork to assure a minimum of haggling over the fee and its eventual payment.

In varying degrees, as a consequence, all law practice involves a manipulation of the client and a stage management of the lawyer-client relationship so that at least an *appearance* of help and service will be forthcoming. This is accomplished in a variety of ways, often exercised in combination with each other. At the outset, the lawyer-professional employs with suitable variation a measure of sales puff which may range from an air of unbounding self-confidence, adequacy, and dominion over events, to that of complete arrogance. This will be supplemented by the affectation of a studied, faultless mode of personal attire. In the larger firms, the furnishings and office trappings will serve as the backdrop to help in impression management and client intimidation. In all firms, solo or large-scale, an access to secret knowledge and to the seats of power and influences is inferred, or presumed to a varying degree as the basic vendable commodity of the practitioners.

The lack of visible end product offers a special complication in the course of the professional life of the criminal court lawyer with respect to his fee and in his relations with his client. The plain fact is that an accused in a criminal case always "loses" even when he has been exonerated by an acquittal, discharge, or dismissal of his case. The hostility of an accused which follows as a consequence of his arrest, incarceration, possible loss of job, expense, and other traumas connected with his case is directed, by means of displacement, toward his lawyer. It is in this sense that it may be said that a criminal lawyer never really "wins" a case. The really satisfied client is rare, since in the very nature of the situation even an accused's vindication leaves him with some degree of dissatisfaction and hostility. It is this state of affairs that makes for a lawyer-client relationship in the criminal court which tends to be a somewhat exaggerated version of the usual lawyer-client confidence game.

At the outset, because there are great risks of nonpayment of the fee, due to the impecuniousness of his clients, and the fact that a man who is sentenced to jail may be a singularly unappreciative client, the criminal lawyer collects his fee *in advance.* Often, because the lawyer and the accused both have questionable designs of their own upon each other, the confidence game can be played. The criminal lawyer must serve three major functions, or stated another way, he must solve three problems. First, he must arrange for his fee; second, he must prepare and then, if necessary, "cool out" his client in case of defeat[17] (a highly likely contingency); third, he must satisfy the court organization that he has performed adequately in the process of negotiating the plea, so as to preclude the possibility of any sort of embarrassing incident which may serve to invite "outside" scrutiny.

In assuring the attainment of one of his primary objectives, his fee, the criminal lawyer will very often enter into negotiations with the accused's kin, including collateral relatives. In many instances, the accused himself is unable to pay any sort of fee or anything more than a token fee. It then becomes important to involve as many of the accused's kin as possible in the situation. This is especially so if the attorney hopes to collect a significant part of a proposed substantial fee. It is not uncommon for several relatives to contribute toward the fee. The larger the group, the greater the possibility that the lawyer will collect a sizeable fee by getting contributions from each.

A fee for a felony case which ultimately results in a plea, rather than a trial, may ordinarily range anywhere from $550 to $1,500. Should the case go to trial, the fee will be proportionately larger, depending upon the length of the trial. But the larger the fee the lawyer wishes to exact, the more impressive his performance must be, in terms of his stage-managed image as personage of great influence and power in the court organization. Court personnel are keenly aware of the extent to which a lawyer's stock-in-trade involves the precarious stage management of an image which goes beyond the usual professional flamboyance, and for this reason alone the lawyer is "bound in" to the authority system of the court's organizational discipline. Therefore, to some extent, court personnel will aid the lawyer in the creation and maintenance of that impression. There is a tacit commitment to the lawyer by the court organization, apart from formal etiquette, to aid him in this. Such augmentation of the lawyer's stage-managed image as this affords is the partial basis for the *quid pro quo* which exists between the lawyer and the court organization. It tends to serve as the continuing basis for the higher loyalty of the lawyer to the organization; his relationship with his client, in contrast, is transient, ephemeral, and often superficial.

DEFENSE LAWYER AS DOUBLE AGENT

The lawyer has often been accused of stirring up unnecessary litigation, especially in the field of negligence. He is said to acquire a vested interest in a cause of action or claim which was initially his client's. The strong incentive of possible fee motivates the lawyer to promote litigation which would otherwise never have developed. However, the criminal lawyer develops a vested interest of an entirely different nature in his client's case: to limit its scope and duration rather than do battle. Only in this way can a case be "profitable." Thus, he enlists the aid of relatives not only to assure payment of his fee, but he will also rely on these persons to help him in his agent-mediator role of convincing the accused to plead guilty, and ultimately to help in "cooling out" the accused if necessary.

It is at this point that an accused-defendant may experience his first sense of "betrayal." While he had perhaps perceived the police and prosecutor to be adversaries, or possibly even the judge, the accused is wholly unprepared for his counsel's role performance as an agent-mediator. In the same vein, it is even less likely to occur to an accused that members of his own family or other kin may become agents, albeit at the behest and urging of other agents or mediators, acting on the principle that they are in reality helping an accused negotiate the best possible plea arrangement under the circumstances. Usually, it will be the lawyer who will activate next of kin in this role, his ostensible motive being to arrange for his fee. But soon latent and unstated motives will assert themselves with entreaties by counsel to the accused's next of kin to appeal to the accused to "help himself" by pleading. *Gemeinschaft* sentiments are to this extent exploited by a defense lawyer (or even at times by a district attorney) to achieve specific secular ends, that is, of concluding a particular matter with all possible dispatch.

The fee is often collected in stages, each installment usually payable prior to a necessary court appearance required during the course of an accused's career journey. At each stage, in his interviews and communications with the accused, or in addition, with members of his family, if they are helping with the fee payment, the lawyer employs an air of professional confidence and "inside-dopesterism" in order to assuage anxieties on all sides. He makes the necessary bland assurances, and in effect manipulates his client, who is usually willing to do and say the things, true or not, which will help his attorney extricate him. Since the dimensions of what he is essentially selling, organizational influence and expertise, are not technically and precisely measurable, the lawyer can make extravagant claims of influence and secret knowledge with impunity. Thus, lawyers frequently claim to have inside knowledge in connection with information in the hands of the district attorney, police, or probation officials or to have access to these functionaries. Factually, they often do, and need only to exaggerate the nature of their relationships with them to obtain the desired effective impression upon the client. But, as in the genuine confidence game, the victim who has participated is loath to do anything which will upset the lesser plea which his lawyer has "conned" him into accepting.[18]

In effect, in his role as double agent, the criminal lawyer performs an extremely vital and delicate mission for the court organization and the accused. Both principals are anxious to terminate the litigation with a minimum of expense and damage to each other. There is no other personage or role incumbent in the total court structure more strategically located, who by training and in terms of his own requirements, is more ideally suited to do so than the lawyer. In recognition of this, judges will cooperate with attorneys in many important ways. For example, they will adjourn the case of an accused in jail awaiting plea or sentence if the attorney requests such action. While explicitly this may be done for some innocuous and seemingly valid reason, the tacit purpose is that pressure is being applied by the attorney for the collection of his fee, which he knows will probably not be forthcoming if the case is concluded. Judges are aware of this tactic on the part of lawyers, who, by requesting an adjournment, keep an accused incarcerated awhile longer as a not too subtle method of dunning a client for payment. However, the judges will go along with this, on the ground that important ends are being served. Often, the only end served is to protect a lawyer's fee.

The judge will help an accused's lawyer in still another way. He will lend the official aura of his office and courtroom so that a lawyer can stage-manage an impression of an "all-out" performance for the accused in justification of his fee. The judge and other court personnel will serve as a backdrop for a scene charged with dramatic fire, in which the accused's lawyer makes a stirring appeal in his behalf. With a show of restrained passion, the lawyer will intone the virtues of the accused and recite the social deprivations which have reduced him to his present stage. The speech varies somewhat, depending on whether the accused has been convicted after trial or has pleaded guilty. In the main, however, the incongruity, superficiality, and ritualistic character of the total performance is underscored by a visibly impassive, almost bored reaction on the part of the judge and other members of the court retinue.

Afterward, there is a hearty exchange of pleasantries between the lawyer and district attorney, wholly out of context in terms of the supposed adversary nature of the preceding events. The fiery passion in defense of his client is gone, and the lawyers for both sides resume their offstage relations, chatting amiably and perhaps including the judge in their restrained banter. No other aspect of their visible conduct so effectively serves to put even a casual observer on notice that these individuals have claims upon each other. These seemingly innocuous actions are indicative of continuing organizational and informal relations, which, in their intricacy and depth, range far beyond any priorities or claims a particular defendant may have.[19]

Criminal law practice is a unique form of private law practice since it really only appears to be private practice.[20] Actually it is bureaucratic practice, because of the legal practitioner's enmeshment in the authority, discipline, and perspectives of the court organization. Private practice, supposedly, in a professional sense, involves the maintenance of an organized, disciplined body of knowledge and learning; the individual practitioners are imbued with a spirit of autonomy and service, the earning of a livelihood being incidental. In the sense that the lawyer in the criminal court serves as a double agent, serving higher organizational rather than professional ends, he may be deemed to be engaged in bureaucratic rather than private practice. To some extent the lawyer-client "confidence game," in addition to its other functions, serves to conceal this fact.

THE CLIENT'S PERCEPTION

The "cop-out" ceremony, in which the court process culminates, is not only invaluable for redefining the accused's perspectives of himself, but also in reiterating publicly in a formally structured ritual the accused person's guilt for the benefit of significant "others" who are observing. The accused not only is made to assert publicly his guilt of a specific crime, but also a complete recital of its details. He is further made to indicate that he is entering his plea of guilt freely, willingly, and voluntarily, and that he is not doing so because of any promises or in consideration of any commitments that may have been made to him by anyone.

This last is intended as a blanket statement to shield the participants from any possible charges of "coercion" or undue influence that may have been exerted in violation of due process requirements. Its function is to preclude any later review by an appellate court on these grounds, and also to obviate any second thoughts an accused may develop in connection with his plea.

However, for the accused, the conception of self as a guilty person is in large measure a temporary role adaptation. His career socialization as an accused, if it is successful, eventuates in his acceptance and redefinition of himself as a guilty person.[21] However, the transformation is ephemeral, in that he will, in private, quickly reassert his innocence. Of importance is that he accept his defeat, publicly proclaim it, and find some measure of pacification in it.[22] Almost immediately after his plea, a defendant will generally be interviewed by a representative of the probation division in connection with a presentence report which is to be prepared. The very first question to be asked of him by the probation officer is: "Are you guilty of the crime to which you pleaded?" This is by way of double affirmation of the defendant's guilt. Should the defendant now begin to make bold assertions of his innocence, despite his plea of guilty, he will be asked to withdraw his plea and stand trial on the original charges. Such a threatened possibility is, in most instances, sufficient to cause an accused to let the plea stand and to request the probation officer to overlook his exclamations of innocence. Table 1 is a breakdown of the categorized

Table 1 Defendant responses as to guilt or innocence after pleading guilty (Years: 1962, 1963, 1964; $N = 724$)

Nature of response		*Number of defendants*
Innocent (manipulated)	"The lawyer, judge, police, or D.A. 'conned me'"	86
Innocent (pragmatic)	"Wanted to get it over with" "You can't beat the system" "They have you over a barrel when you have a record"	147
Innocent (advice of counsel)	"Followed my lawyer's advice"	92
Innocent (defiant)	"Framed"—Betrayed by "complainant," "police," "squealers," "lawyer," "friends," "wife," "girlfriend"	33
Innocent (adverse social data)	Blames probation officer or psychiatrist for "bad report," in cases where there was prepleading investigation	15
Guilty	"But I should have gotten a better deal" Blames lawyer, D.A., police, judge	74
Guilty	Won't say anything further	21
Fatalistic (doesn't press his "innocence," won't admit "guilt")	"I did it for convenience" "My lawyer told me it was only thing I could do" "I did it because it was the best way out"	248
No response		8
Total		724

responses of a random sample of male defendants in Metropolitan Court[23] during 1962, 1963, and 1964 in connection with their statements during presentence probation interviews following their plea of guilty.

It would be well to observe at the outset that of the 724 defendants who pleaded guilty before trial, only 43 (5.94 percent) of the total group had confessed prior to their indictment. Thus, the ultimate judicial process was predicated upon evidence independent of any confession of the accused.[24]

As the data indicate, only a relatively small number (95) out of the total number of defendants actually will even admit their guilt following the cop-out ceremony. However, even though they have affirmed their guilt, many of these defendants felt that they should have been able to negotiate a more favorable plea. The largest aggregate of defendants (373) were those who reasserted their "innocence" following their public profession of guilt during the cop-out ceremony. These defendants employed differential degrees of fervor, solemnity, and credibility, ranging from really mild, wavering assertions of innocence which were embroidered with a variety of stock explanations and rationalizations, to those of an adamant, "framed" nature. Thus, the "innocent" group, for the most part, were largely concerned with underscoring for their probation interviewer their essential "goodness" and "worthiness," despite their formal plea of guilty. Assertion of innocence at the postplea stage resurrects a more respectable and acceptable self-concept for the accused defendant who has pleaded guilty. A recital of the structural exigencies which precipitated his plea of guilt serves to embellish a newly proferred claim of innocence, which many defendants mistakenly feel will stand them in good stead at the time of sentence, or ultimately with probation or parole authorities.

Relatively few (33) maintained their innocence in terms of having been "framed" by some person or agent-mediator, although a larger number (86) indicated that they had been manipulated or conned by an agent-mediator to plead guilty, but as indicated, their assertions of innocence were relatively mild.

A rather substantial group (147) preferred to stress the pragmatic aspects of their plea of guilty. They would only perfunctorily assert their innocence and would in general refer to some adverse aspect of their situation which they believed tended to negatively affect their bargaining leverage, including in some instances a prior criminal record.

One group of defendants (92), while maintaining their innocence, simply employed some variation of a theme of following "the advice of counsel" as a covering response to explain their guilty plea in the light of their new affirmation of innocence.

The largest single group of defendants (248) were basically fatalistic. They often verbalized weak suggestions of their innocence in rather halting terms, wholly without conviction. By the same token, they would not admit guilt readily and were generally evasive as to guilt or innocence, preferring to stress aspects of their stoic submission in their decision to plead. This sizeable group of defendants appeared to perceive the total court process as being caught up in a monstrous organizational apparatus, in which the defendant's role expectancies were not clearly defined. Reluctant to offend anyone in authority, fearful that clear-cut statements on their part as to their guilt or innocence would be negatively construed, they adopted a stance of passivity, resignation, and acceptance. Interestingly, they would in most instances invoke their lawyer as being the one who crystallized the available alternatives for them and who was therefore the critical element in their decision-making process.

In order to determine which agent-mediator was most influential in altering the accused's perspectives as to his decision to plead or go to trial (regardless of the proposed basis of the plea), the same sample of defendants were asked to indicate the person who first suggested to them that they plead guilty. They were also asked to indicate which of the persons or officials who made such a suggestion was most influential in affecting their final decision to plead.

Table 2 indicates the breakdown of the responses to the two questions.

It is popularly assumed that the police, through forced confessions, and the district attorney, employing still other pressures, are most instrumental in the inducement of an accused to plead guilty.[25] As Table 2 indicates, it is actually the defendant's own counsel who is most effective in this role. Further, this phenomenon tends to reinforce the extremely rational nature of criminal law administration, for an organization could not rely upon the sort of idiosyncratic measures employed by the police to induce confessions and maintain its efficiency, high production, and overall rational-legal character. The defense counsel becomes the ideal agent-mediator since, as "officer of the court" and confidant of the accused and his kin, he lives astride both worlds and can serve the ends of the two as well as his own.[26]

Table 2 Role of agent-mediators in defendant's guilty plea

Person or official	*First suggested plea of guilty*	*Influenced the accused most in his final decision to plead*
Judge	4	26
District attorney	67	116
Defense counsel	407	411
Probation officer	14	3
Psychiatrist	8	1
Wife	34	120
Friends and kin	21	14
Police	14	4
Fellow inmates	119	14
Others	28	5
No response	8	10
Total	724	724

While an accused's wife, for example, may be influential in making him more amenable to a plea, her agent-mediator role has, nevertheless, usually been sparked and initiated by defense counsel. Further, although a number of first suggestions of a plea came from an accused's fellow jail inmates, he tended to rely largely on his counsel as an ultimate source of influence in his final decision. The defense counsel being a crucial figure in the total organizational scheme for constituting a new set of perspectives for the accused, the same sample of defendants was asked to indicate at which stage of their contact with counsel the suggestion of a plea was made. There are three basic kinds of defense counsel available in Metropolitan Court: legal-aid, privately retained counsel, and counsel assigned by the court (but may eventually be privately retained by the accused).

The overwhelming majority of accused persons, regardless of type of counsel, related a specific incident which indicated an urging or suggestion, either during the course of the first or second contact, that they plead guilty to a lesser charge if this could be arranged. Of all the agent-mediators, it is the lawyer who is most effective in manipulating an accused's perspectives, notwithstanding pressures that may have been previously applied by police, district attorney, judge, or any of the agent-mediators that may have been activated by them. Legal-aid and assigned counsel would apparently be more likely to suggest a possible plea at the point of initial interview as response to pressures of time. In the case of the assigned counsel, the strong possibility that there is no fee involved may be an added impetus to such a suggestion at the first contact.

In addition, there is some further evidence in Table 3 of the perfunctory, ministerial character of the system in Metropolitan Court and similar criminal courts. There is little real effort to individualize, and the lawyer's role as agent-mediator may be seen as unique in that he is in effect a double agent. Although, as "officer of the court" he mediates between the court organization and the defendant, his roles with respect to each are rent by conflicts of interest. Too often these must be resolved in favor of

Table 3 Stage (contact) at which each type of counsel suggests that defendant plead guilty ($N = 724$)

	Privately retained		*Legal-aid*		*Assigned*		*Total*	
Contact	*N*	%	*N*	%	*N*	%	*N*	%
First	66	35	237	49	28	60	331	46
Second	83	44	142	29	8	17	233	32
Third	29	15	63	13	4	9	96	13
Fourth or more	12	6	31	7	5	11	48	7
No response	0	0	14	3	2	4	16	2
Total	190	100	487	101[a]	47	101[a]	724	100

[a]Rounded percentage.

the organization which provides him with the means for his professional existence. Consequently, in order to reduce the strains and conflicts imposed in what is ultimately an overdemanding role obligation for him, the lawyer engages in the lawyer-client "confidence game" so as to structure more favorably an otherwise onerous role system.[27]

CONCLUSION

Recent decisions of the Supreme Court, in the area of criminal law administration and defendants' rights fail to take into account three crucial aspects of social structure which may tend to render the more libertarian rules as nugatory. The decisions overlook (1) the nature of courts as formal organization, (2) the relationship that the lawyer "regular" *actually* has with the court organization, and (3) the character of the lawyer-client relationship in the criminal court (the routine relationships, not those unusual ones that are described in "heroic" terms in novels, movies, and television).

Courts, like many other modern large-scale organizations, possess a monstrous appetite for the co-optation of entire professional groups as well as individuals.[28] Almost all those who come within the ambit of organization authority find that their definitions, perceptions, and values have been refurbished, largely in terms favorable to the particular organization and its goals. As a result, recent Supreme Court decisions may have a long-range effect which is radically different from that intended or anticipated. The more libertarian rules will tend to produce the rather ironic end result of augmenting the *existing* organizational arrangements, enriching court organizations with more personnel and elaborate structure, which in turn will maximize organizational goals of "efficiency" and production. Thus, many defendants will find that courts will possess an even more sophisticated apparatus for processing them toward a guilty plea!

NOTES

1. H. W. Jones, "A View from the Bridge," *Law and Society:* Supplement to Summer 1965 issue of *Social Problems*, p. 42. See G. Geis, "Sociology, Criminology, and Criminal Law," *Social Problems* 7 (1959): 40–47; N. S. Timasheff, "Growth and Scope of Sociology of Law," in *Modern Sociological Theory in Continuity and Change*, H. Becker and A. Boskoff, eds. (1957), pp. 424–449, for further evaluation of the strained relations between sociology and law.

2. This decision represented the climax of a line of cases which had begun to chip away at the notion that the Sixth Amendment of the Constitution (right to assistance of counsel) applied only to the federal government and could not be held to run against the states through the Fourteenth Amendment. An exhaustive historical analysis of the Fourteenth Amendment and the Bill of Rights will be found in C. Fairman, "Does the Fourteenth Amendment Incorporate the Bill of Rights? The Original Understanding," *Stanford Law Review* 2 (1949): 5–139. Since the *Gideon* decision there is already evidence that its effect

will ultimately extend to indigent persons charged with misdemeanors—and perhaps ultimately even traffic cases and other minor offenses. For a popular account of this important development in connection with the right to assistance of counsel, see A. Lewis, *Gideon's Trumpet* (1964). For a scholarly historical analysis of the right to counsel, see W. M. Beaney, *The Right to Counsel in American Courts* (1955). For a more recent and comprehensive review and discussion of the right to counsel and its development, see Note, "Counsel at Interrogation," *Yale Law Journal* 73 (1964): 1000–1057.

With the passage of the Criminal Justice Act of 1964, indigent accused persons in the federal courts will be defended by federally paid legal counsel. For a general discussion of the nature and extent of public and private legal aid in the United States prior to the *Gideon* case, see E. A. Brownell, *Legal Aid in the United States* (1961); see also R. B. von Mehren et al., *Equal Justice for the Accused* (1959).

3. In the case of federal defendants the issue is clear. In *Mallory v. United States*, 354 U.S. 449 (1957), the Supreme Court unequivocally indicated that a person under federal arrest must be taken "without any unnecessary delay" before a U.S. commissioner where he will receive information as to his rights to remain silent and to assistance of counsel which will be furnished, in the event he is indigent, under the Criminal Justice Act of 1964. For a most interesting and richly documented work in connection with the general area of the Bill of Rights, see C. R. Sowle, *Police Power and Individual Freedom* (1962).

4. See *N.Y. Times*, Nov. 20, 1965, p. 1, for Justice Nathan R. Sobel's statement to the effect that based on his study of 1,000 indictments in Brooklyn, N.Y., from February to April 1965, fewer than 10 percent involved confessions. Sobel's detailed analysis will be found in six articles which appeared in the *New York Law Journal*, beginning November 15, 1965, through November 21, 1965, titled "The Exclusionary Rules in the Law of Confessions: A Legal Perspective—A Practical Perspective." Most law-enforcement officials believe that the majority of convictions in criminal cases are based upon confessions obtained by police. For example, the late District Attorney of New York County (a jurisdiction which has the largest volume of cases in the United States), Frank S. Hogan, reported that confessions are crucial and indicated "if a suspect is entitled to have a lawyer during preliminary questioning . . . any lawyer worth his fee will tell him to keep his mouth shut" (*N.Y. Times*, Dec. 2, 1965, p. 1). Concise discussions of the issue are to be found in D. Robinson, Jr., "Massiah, Escobedo and Rationales for the Exclusion of Confession," *Journal of Criminal Law, Criminology and Police Science* 56 (1965): 412–431; D. C. Dowling, "Escobedo and Beyond: The Need for a Fourteenth Amendment Code of Criminal Procedure," *Journal of Criminal Law, Criminology and Police Science* 56 (1965): 143–157.

5. *Miranda v. Arizona*, 384 U.S. 436 (1966).

6. Even under optimal circumstances a criminal case is very much a one-sided affair, the parties to the "contest" being decidedly unequal in strength and resources. See A. S. Goldstein, "The State and the Accused: Balance of Advantage in Criminal Procedure," *Yale Law Journal* 69 (1960): 1149–1199.

7. F. J. Davis et al., *Society and the Law: New Meanings for an Old Profession* (1962), p. 301; L. Orfield, *Criminal Procedure from Arrest to Appeal* (1947), p. 297. D. J. Newman, "Pleading Guilty for Considerations: A Study of Bargain Justice," *Journal of Criminal Law, Criminology and Police Science* 46 (1954): 780–790. Newman's data covered only one year, 1954, in a midwestern community. However, it is in general confirmed by my own data drawn from a far more populous area, and from what is one of the major criminal courts in the country, for a period of fifteen years from 1950 to 1964 inclusive. The English experience tends also to confirm American data; see N. Walker, *Crime and Punishment in Britain: An Analysis of the Penal System* (1965). See also D. J. Newman, *Conviction: The Determination of Guilt or Innocence Without Trial* (1966), for a comprehensive legalistic study of the guilty plea sponsored by the American Bar Foundation. The criminal court as a social system and "bargaining" and its functions in the criminal court's organizational structure, are examined in my book, *The Criminal Court: A Sociological Perspective* (Chicago: Quadrangle Books, 1967).

8. G. Feifer, *Justice in Moscow* (1965). The Soviet trial has been termed "an appeal from the pretrial investigation," and Feifer notes that the Soviet "trial" is simply a recapitulation of the data collected by the pretrial investigator. The notions of a trial being a "tabula rasa" and presumptions of innocence are wholly alien to Soviet notions of justice: "The closer the investigation resembles the finished scripts, the better" (p. 86).

9. For a concise statement of the constitutional and economic aspects of the right to legal assistance, see M. G. Paulsen, *Equal Justice for the Poor Man* (1964); for a brief traditional description of the legal profession, see P. A. Freund, "The Legal Profession," *Daedulus* (1963), pp. 689–700.

10. I use the concept in the general sense that Erving Goffman employed it in his *Asylums: Essays on the Social Situation of Mental Patients and Other Inmates* (1961).

11. A. L. Wood, "Informal Relations in the Practice of Criminal Law," *American Journal of Sociology* 62 (1956): 48–55; J. E. Carlin, *Lawyers on Their Own* (1962), pp. 105–109; R. Goldfarb, *Ransom—A Critique of the American Bail System* (1965), pp. 114–115. . . . Data as to recruitment to the legal profession, and variables involved in the type of practice engaged in will be found in J. Ladinsky, "Careers of Lawyers, Law Practice, and Legal Institutions," *American Sociological Review* 28 (1963): 47–54. See also S. Warkov and J. Zelan, *Lawyers in the Making* (1965).

12. There is a real question to be raised as to whether in certain organizational settings a complete reversal of the bureaucratic ideal has not occurred. That is, it would seem that in some instances the organization appears to exist to serve the needs of its various occupational incumbents, rather than its clients. A. Etzioni, *Modern Organizations* (1964), pp. 94–104.

13. Three . . . items reported in the *New York Times* tend to underscore this point as it has manifested itself in one of the major criminal courts. In one instance the Bronx County Bar Association condemned "mass assembly-line justice," which "was rushing defendants into pleas of guilty and into convictions, in violation of their legal rights." *N.Y. Times*, March 10, 1965, p. 51. Another item, appearing somewhat later that year, reports a judge criticizing his own court system (the New York Criminal Court), that "pressure to set statistical records in disposing of cases had hurt the administration of justice." *N.Y. Times*, Nov. 4, 1965, p. 49. A third and most unusual recent public discussion in the press was a statement by a leading New York appellate judge decrying "instant justice" which is employed to reduce court calendar congestion ". . . converting our courthouses into counting houses . . . , as in most big cities where the volume of business tends to overpower court facilities." *N.Y. Times*, Feb. 5, 1966, p. 58.

14. R. L. Gasser, "The Confidence Game," *Federal Problems* 27 (1963): 47.

15. C. W. Mills, *White Collar* (1951), pp. 121–129; J. E. Carlin, note 11, above.

16. E. O. Smigel, *The Wall Street Lawyer* (1964), p. 309.

17. Talcott Parsons indicates that the social role and function of the lawyer can be therapeutic, helping his client psychologically in giving him necessary emotional support at critical times. The lawyer is also said to be acting as an agent of social control in the counseling of his client and in the influencing of his course of conduct. See T. Parsons, *Essays in Sociological Theory* (1954), p. 384 et seq.; E. Goffman, "On Cooling the Mark Out: Some Aspects of Adaptation to Failure," in *Human Behavior and Social Processes*, A. Rose, ed. (1962), pp. 482–505. Goffman's "cooling out" analysis is especially relevant in the lawyer–accused client relationship.

18. The question has never been raised as to whether "bargain justice," "copping a plea," or justice by negotiation is a constitutional process. Although it has become the most central aspect of the process of criminal law administration, it has received virtually no close scrutiny by the appellate courts. As a consequence, it is relatively free of legal control and supervision. But, apart from any questions of the legality of bargaining, in terms of the pressures and devices that are employed which tend to violate due process of law, there remain ethical and practical questions. The system of bargain-counter justice is like the proverbial iceberg—much of its danger is concealed in secret negotiations and its least

alarming feature, the final plea, is the one presented to public view. See A. S. Trebach, *The Rationing of Justice* (1964), pp. 74–94; Note, "Guilty Plea Bargaining: Compromises by Prosecutors to Secure Guilty Pleas," *University of Pennsylvania Law Review* 112 (1964): 865–895.

19. For a conventional summary statement of some of the inevitable conflicting loyalties encountered in the practice of law, see E. E. Cheatham, *Cases and Materials on the Legal Profession* (2d ed., 1955), pp. 70–79.

20. Some lawyers at either end of the continuum of law practice appear to have grave doubts as to whether it is indeed a profession at all. J. E. Carlin, op. cit., supra note 11, at 192; E. O. Smigel, supra note 16, at 304–305. Increasingly, it is perceived as a business with widespread evasion of the Canons of Ethics, duplicity and chicanery being practiced in an effort to get and keep business. The poet Carl Sandburg epitomized this notion in the following vignette: "Have you a criminal lawyer in this burg?" "We think so but we haven't been able to prove it on him." C. Sandburg, *The People, Yes* (1936), p. 154.

Thus, while there is a considerable amount of dishonesty present in law practice involving fee splitting, thefts from clients, influence peddling, fixing, questionable use of favors and gifts to obtain business or influence others, this sort of activity is most often attributed to the "solo," private lawyer. See A. L. Wood, "Professional Ethics Among Criminal Lawyers," *Social Problems* (1959), pp. 70–83. However, to some degree, large-scale "downtown" elite firms also engage in these dubious activities. The difference is that the latter firms enjoy a good deal of immunity from these harsh charges because of their institutional and organizational advantages, in terms of near monopoly over more desirable types of practice, as well as exerting great influence in the political, economic, and professional realms of power.

21. This does not mean that most of those who plead guilty are innocent of any crime. Indeed, in many instances those who have been able to negotiate a lesser plea have done so willingly and even eagerly. The system of justice-by-negotiation, without trial, probably tends to better serve the interests and requirements of guilty persons, who are thereby presented with formal alternatives of "half a loaf," in terms of, at worst, possibilities of a lesser plea and a concomitant shorter sentence as compensation for their acquiescence and participation. Having observed the prescriptive etiquette in compliance with the defendant's role expectancies in this setting, he is rewarded. An innocent person, on the other hand, is confronted with the same set of role prescriptions, structures, and legal alternatives, and in any event, for him this mode of justice is often an ineluctable bind.

22. "Any communicative network between persons whereby the public identity of an actor is transformed into something looked on as lower in the local scheme of social types will be called a 'status degradation ceremony.' " H. Garfinkel, "Conditions of Successful Degradation Ceremonies," *American Journal of Sociology* 61 (1956): 420–424. But contrary to the conception of the "cop out" as a "status degradation ceremony" is the fact that it is in reality a charade, during the course of which an accused must project an appropriate and acceptable amount of guilt, penitence, and remorse. Having adequately feigned the role of the "guilty person," his hearers will engage in the fantasy that he is contrite, and thereby merits a lesser plea. It is one of the essential functions of the criminal lawyer that he coach and direct his accused client in that role performance. Thus, what is actually involved is not a "degradation" process at all, but instead a highly structured system of exchange cloaked in the rituals of legalism and public professions of guilt and repentance.

23. The name is of course fictitious. However, the actual court which served as the universe from which the data were drawn is one of the largest criminal courts in the United States, dealing with felonies only. Female defendants in the years 1950 through 1964 constituted from 7 to 10 percent of the totals for each year.

24. My own data in this connection would appear to support Sobel's conclusion (see note 4 above) and appears to be at variance with the prevalent view, which stresses the importance of confessions in law enforcement and prosecution. All the persons in my sample were originally charged with felonies ranging from homicide to forgery; in most instances the original felony charges were reduced to misdemeanors by way of a negotiated lesser plea.

The vast range of crime categories which are available facilitates the patterned court process of plea reduction to a lesser offense, which is also usually a socially less opprobrious crime. For an illustration of this feature of the bargaining process in a court utilizing a public defender office, see D. Sudnow, "Normal Crimes: Sociological Features of the Penal Code in a Public Defender Office," *Social Problems* 12 (1964): 255–276.

25. Failures, shortcomings, and oppressive features of our system of criminal justice have been attributed to a variety of sources, including "lawless" police, overzealous district attorneys, "hanging" juries, corruption and political connivance, incompetent judges, inadequacy or lack of counsel, and poverty or other social disabilities of the defendant. See A. Barth, *Law Enforcement Versus the Law* (1963), for a journalist's account embodying this point of view; J. H. Skolnick, *Justice Without Trial: Law Enforcement in Democratic Society* (1966), for a sociologist's study of the role of the police in criminal law administration. For a somewhat more detailed, albeit legalistic and somewhat technical discussion of American police procedures, see W. R. LaFave, *Arrest: The Decision to Take a Suspect into Custody* (1965).

26. Aspects of the lawyer's ambivalences with regard to the expectancies of the various groups who have claims upon him are discussed in H. J. O'Gorman, "The Ambivalence of Lawyers," paper presented at the Eastern Sociological Association meetings, April 10, 1965.

27. W. J. Goode, "A Theory of Role Strain," *American Sociological Review* 25 (1960): 483–496. J. D. Snoek, "Role Strain in Diversified Role Sets," *American Journal of Sociology* 71 (1966): 363–372.

28. Some of the resources which have been an integral part of our courts—for example, psychiatry, social work, and probation—were originally intended as part of an ameliorative, therapeutic effort to individualize offenders. However, there is some evidence that a quite different result obtains than the one originally intended. The ameliorative instruments have been co-opted by the court in order to more "efficiently" deal with a court's caseload, often to the legal disadvantage of an accused person. See F. A. Allen, *The Borderland of Criminal Justice* (1964); T. S. Szasz, *Liberty and Psychiatry* (1963), and also Szasz's most recent, *Psychiatric Justice* (1965); L. Diana, "The Rights of Juvenile Delinquents: An Appraisal of Juvenile Court Procedures," *Journal of Criminal Law, Criminology and Police Science* 47 (1957): 561–569.

ARTICLE TWELVE

Client Games: Defense Attorney Perspectives on Their Relations with Criminal Clients

ROY B. FLEMMING

Is the attorney-client relationship different when the services are being paid for by the public rather than by the individual defendant? The 155 defense attorneys from nine felony trial courts interviewed in this study by Roy Flemming assert that public clients are more skeptical and less willing to accept their professional authority than are private clients, and that they need to take extra steps to gain the cooperation of public clients. The problem of "client control" is addressed.

Lawyer-client relations substantially define the reality of law in society. It is through these interactions and encounters that the legal system takes on form and substance for both parties. What clients learn of the reality of their rights, the operation of courts, and the inner workings of the law, and whether they feel they are treated fairly or justly, are all colored by their experiences with attorneys. By the same token, the satisfactions and disappointments, financial rewards, and social returns of lawyering strongly reflect the kinds of clients attorneys represent. Moreover, as professionals, lawyers presumably have considerable latitude in choosing how to relate to clients, raising concerns over their accountability to clients and equal treatment of them.

The social preconditions for traditional lawyer-client relationships that putatively foster accountability are often missing in the practice of crim-

Source: American Bar Foundation Research Journal (Spring 1986): 253–277. By permission of the publisher.

inal law, however. Criminal clients express deep misgivings about attorneys assigned to them by courts, reactions to a policy reform not anticipated at the time of its adoption. While attention to the client's or defendant's perspective on attorneys has not languished for this reason, the attorney's view of clients has been neglected. And yet a fuller understanding of this relationship obviously demands an exploration of the attorney's side. This study takes this tack and looks at how attorneys feel they are seen by their clients and the implications of client reactions for how they practice criminal law. In this sense it adds another dimension toward a more complete view of the professional behavior of criminal attorneys, a dimension that stresses the difference between public and private clients in affecting the accountability or, at least, responsiveness of attorneys to their clients.

Skepticism about the accountability of criminal defense attorneys is not a new concern. Some twenty years ago Blumberg described the private practice of criminal law as a "confidence game."[1] The intangible quality of the attorney's work, the concern over fees, and the need to prepare clients for guilty pleas or trial convictions while satisfying the interests of the court system all came together as ingredients in this game. A few years later, however, it became clear that clients distrust their public defenders and court-appointed attorneys and hold them in low esteem. Casper neatly captured their views and caught the tone of subsequent studies with the title of his seminal article "Did You Have a Lawyer When You Went to Court? No, I Had a Public Defender."[2] A rather substantial body of research agrees that in contrast with their attitudes toward privately retained attorneys, criminal defendants see publicly paid and assigned counsel as part of the "system"—overly eager to plead them guilty, disinclined to give them much time, and little concerned about their welfare.[3]

Doubts about a lawyer's professional skills and fears of not being faithfully represented raise questions about the attorney's role as described in Blumberg's "confidence game." For what kind of game is it if clients do not trust their attorneys? And how do lawyers cope with this problem? Without the aura of professional legitimacy, do they dominate their clients to the degree found in civil cases? And how do they gain control of them?[4] When faced with these problems, plus the social, racial, and economic differences that usually separate them from criminal defendants, how can they function as "translators" of their needs as they apparently do in civil matters, where the social gap between lawyer and client is often narrower?[5]

This study offers answers to these questions. Specifically, it reports how attorneys feel they are viewed by their clients, how they try to develop working relationships with them, and what roles they think are most useful in dealing with criminal clients. Interviews with 155 defense attorneys provide the data for this study, and excerpts are presented to establish their concerns and views. The study concludes by placing the defense attorneys' relations with criminal clients in a perspective that extends and revises Blumberg's notion of a "confidence game" between attorneys and their clients to show how attorney accountability arises in a situation characterized by mistrust.

The interviews were conducted as part of a larger research project on felony justice in nine medium-sized counties located in three states.[6] The attorneys, almost all of whom were white males, were "regulars": they generally handled substantial portions of the local circuit court felony caseload in the period centering around 1980–1981 as public defenders, assigned counsel, or private attorneys. Because of their pivotal positions in the courts, sizeable caseloads, and usually long tenure in the jurisdictions, they were well-versed, knowledgeable informants. The interviews were semi-structured, recorded, and covered a variety of topics; this study draws on those segments dealing with their encounters with clients.

Overall, 29 full-time public defenders, 34 part-time defenders, 44 court-appointed or -assigned attorneys, and 48 private attorneys were interviewed. The value of including the latter three groups of attorneys is that they had experience with both public and private clients. Table 1 indicates the number of attorneys interviewed, their practice type, and the proportion of the sampled felony cases they handled in each court. This table also shows the proportions of the sampled cases in the nine courts in which defendants were assigned to an attorney by the court or through a public defender's office. As these proportions indicate, public clients often constitute a large proportion of the local felony caseloads in the courts.

PROBLEMATICAL AUTHORITY AND PUBLIC CLIENTS

Attorneys with public clients labor in the shadow of the "public defender" stereotype. Whether they actually work as public defenders makes no difference; their clients give them little respect and distrust them. A sampling of the attorneys' comments illustrates their problem.[7]

> The standard joke around this country is "Do you want a public defender or a real attorney?" (1303)

> Well, I think the general impression is "I don't have the money to hire a real attorney, so I have you." We get a lot of that. (3303)

> A lot of times they don't respect you as an attorney because you accepted this court appointment, and that creates a problem. (6437)

> It's very tough being an appointed defense attorney. I think a lot of the clients . . . really don't trust you. (5419)

> They think because you're free, you're no good. (2306)

> Because you're part of the system, your indigent client doesn't trust you. (6451)

Public clients have doubts about the status of their lawyers, are skeptical about their skills as advocates, and are worried about whose side the

Table 1 Characteristics of interviewed attorneys and trial court caseloads

	Illinois			Michigan			Pennsylvania		
Type of Lawyer	*DuPage*	*Peoria*	*St. Clair*	*Oakland*	*Kalamazoo*	*Saginaw*	*Montgomery*	*Dauphin*	*Erie*
Public defender									
Full-time	6	—	6	—	—	—	2	10	5
Part-time	2	6	3	—	—	—	15	—	8
Court-appointed or private attorney	14	8	10	19	12	13	4	6	6
Total	22	14	19	19	12	13	21	16	19
Proportion of cases handled by interviewed attorneys	36.1%	66.6%	55.7%	18.6%	74.3%	26.8%	24.5%	59.1%	47.6%
Proportion of all sampled cases with public clients	41.6%	70.0%	51.6%	56.2%	79.0%	73.1%	26.5%	47.0%	43.8%
Number of sampled felony cases	649	930	996	900	681	650	673	1,063	588

lawyers are on. These attitudes complicate the attorneys' work. They cannot assume their clients respect them professionally, and they do not presume that they have their trust or confidence. Thus, perhaps even before procedural or substantive issues can be thrashed out, attorneys need to establish relationships with public clients that will quiet their qualms. Attorneys with private clients run into these problems less often.

> Private clients accept that you are going to do a good job or you know what you're doing. Public defender clients have no idea where you come from; no idea of your background, no idea of whether you've ever done another criminal case in your life. (2303)

> A guy that comes in here and pays $5,000 in cash wants to believe you're good, I guess. He handles you with a lot of respect and is less likely to call you every day with some bullshit question. He's more likely to treat you as you want to be treated as an attorney, that you're representing him as best as you can, and you have his interests in mind always. (6437)

A third attorney explained why he refused to take any further public defender cases after a client questioned his professional judgment:

> Well, I like to be my own man, and I was assigned to represent this black man who was caught stone cold in a robbery. I filed a habeas corpus petition, and I took it over to him to show him.
>
> He said, "Not good enough, man." It was fine. It was enough to get me where I wanted to go. It was fine. So I said, "Well, why don't you do this? Why don't you go to law school and learn? And then take my petition and stick it up your ass." I quit. That was the end of it.
>
> I certainly believe you should take your client's interest to heart and do the best job you possibly can, but I'm not going to have some idiot tell me that my paperwork is wrong when it's not. (9427)

Client disrespect dismays and irritates attorneys; it sours associations with clients and makes the job less pleasant. A public defender (1303) complained, "It's frustrating to have to constantly sell yourself" to clients. Moreover, the etiquette of normal client-professional relations seems weaker to public attorneys who find that their clients or family and friends freely criticize them and treat them cavalierly. When asked what makes their work unsatisfying, attorneys often point to their public clients.

> Sometimes we aren't treated the best by our clients. . . . I had someone this morning whose father was yelling about how bad the public defender was right when I was appointed. That wasn't exactly thrilling. (1302)

> I think my dissatisfaction with being a public defender is that the people don't appreciate you. They figure they have a right to an attorney, and you can't really say, "Hey, look. Take a hike. Just get out of here. I don't want to talk to you anymore." There really is a lot of personal abuse, a lot of stuff that gets on my nerves. (3310)

> They tend to feel that since they're getting a lawyer for free that they sometimes can be abusive if that's their personality. (2306)

Mistrust compounds these problems. According to an attorney (6451) who represented both kinds of clients, public clients see him as part of the courthouse machinery: "They just figure that if the prosecutor is part of the system, the judge is part of the system; then, as an attorney, you're part of the system too." Another also said his public clients think he would work more diligently if he were retained. Allaying their suspicions took time and patience: "In three-quarters of the cases, there is an immediate skepticism where they say, 'Well, I suppose if I were paying, you wouldn't hesitate to go dig these witnesses up.' Overcoming their skepticism is a very slow process" (4410). Such anxieties, a public defender (3310) stated, "just put that much more pressure on you when you can't get along with the person." They also stymie communication between attorneys and their clients.

> I had one guy who told me, "I don't like public defenders. All they do is plea bargain. They don't protect your interests." And it was obvious to me that no matter what I said to this guy, he wasn't gonna listen to me. And he was stuck with me, and I was stuck with him. (9307)

> One guy wouldn't even talk to me when I went into the jail. He wouldn't tell me his name or his birth date. "Because you're the public defender, I'm not talking to you." So, we do have problems with that. (3303)

Distrust undermines the chances for cooperation. "Because they think you're part of the system, you end up doing all the worrying, you end up doing all the scrambling around, and your client could really care less," an attorney (6451) quoted earlier concluded. Another (2303) said a "prime frustration" in representing public clients was the feeling that "basically you're out there by yourself because you don't have a client along with you." Finally, trust matters because disgruntled clients can make trouble for attorneys later on. The prospects of facing grievances or appeals loom too large for an attorney to shrug off a client's distrust.

> Doing so much appointed work, you've got to really cover your rear end. These guys, if they're gonna turn on anybody when nothing else is left, they're gonna turn on you. (5519)

> I have to watch myself more with a public defender case because I can't kick the guy out. And if I am nasty to him, he'll complain and make my life miserable later. So I swallow my pride a lot more with a public defender case. (9324)

Attorneys see client disrespect and mistrust as inherent to indigent defense systems. Few mentioned that racial or class differences impede empathy or communication. Still, one attorney (2303) confided, "I don't really identify with my clients. I'm not from that level of society." Three others also commented on this problem.

> I'm an attorney, live in a nice neighborhood. I'm white. I don't know whether the black defendant in particular trusts me as much as he would a black lawyer. (5406)

> In a lot of ways our clientele is our worst enemy. . . . We get quite a few poverty cases in here. Guys come in, they're on welfare. You sit down and work with them. You say, "You're going to trial. I want you dressed like you're going to church." Because I've had guys come in for trial dressed in T-shirts. I say, "Hey, are you crazy?" It's really difficult for me to comprehend. (9304)

> It seems that most attorneys, a lot of them, are dealing with appointed cases. . . . The defendants maybe are repulsive people. They may not even like these guys, but they're representing them. And it's difficult for them. (6437)

Attorneys' perceptions of public clients do not rest on vague, unsubstantiated notions that the grass is greener on the private side of the legal fence; many handled both kinds of clients, and their perceptions corresponded with those of attorneys who had never practiced privately. Attorneys' experience of day-to-day defense work, then, divides sharply according to this public-private dimension and may be underlined by racial or class differences. Attorneys find publicly assigned clients to be more skeptical, less deferential, and less trusting. These perceived qualities are more than mere irritations or inconveniences for attorneys, however, because when they perceive an absence of client respect and trust, they feel that their professional authority is weakened. Consequently, as long as clients question or reject this authority, "client control" remains problematical.

CLIENT CONTROL: GAINING THE CLIENT'S RESPECT AND TRUST

The attorney's craft rests on knowing how to persuade clients who have the most to lose from tactical miscues or strategic errors to listen to them. When considering the stakes involved, an attorney (1310) admitted, "I suppose it's natural to feel like you want to be in control of your own destiny." Nonetheless, attorneys try to disabuse clients of this desire as well as of other misconceptions of their role. As one attorney (4412) put it, "I'm not gonna let any guy [client] tell me how to try my case. . . . So I think client control is a key." In addition, they drive home to them that they are neither novices in the courthouse nor naive about criminal defendants.

> A lot of these defendants are very street-wise, and they will try to manipulate the system and their lawyer. And they look at the lawyer as someone who is going to get them off, as opposed to protect their rights. And that's a problem. You have got to establish yourself from the outset with them, so that they don't take advantage of you. (3401)

> The problem most often is that they want to control their own case. . . . They have a hard time because most are incarcerated on felony cases, and

> they get a lot of jailhouse talk. I think the biggest problem is that they think they know all the answers. (1310)

> I've been through the system ten damn years, and I know the ins and outs. . . . And this schmuck doesn't know from nothing. He wants to run some bullshit by you. He didn't do it. Well, maybe he didn't. But in my experience there's damn few of them like that. When a dude just says, "I didn't do it," white or black, because they're too smart to admit to anything, you got problems. (4415)

> If you're slipshod from the beginning, he's not gonna trust you, he's not gonna do what you say. You've gotta develop trust as soon as possible, get control of the client as much as you can. It's still their decision to make, but they gotta trust you. And once they trust you then they'll work with you, and they'll tell you the truth. (8301)

Client control requires respect and trust for the lawyer. Without respect from the client, the attorney's advice or suggestions may be ignored. Without the client's trust, the attorney may not be believed; in turn, attorneys are not always sure if they can trust their clients. Once attorneys secure their clients' confidence, they can exercise their judgment and satisfy a desire for professional autonomy.

Spending time with clients, attorneys claim, can help win their confidence. Yet time, a limited resource, also carries opportunity costs. Time spent with clients favorably influences their reactions to attorneys, but its effects on case outcomes are questionable.[8] Moreover, client demands are not always reasonable and, because attorneys have no way of knowing in advance which ones deserve attention, time spent with clients may be wasted. Attorneys grow weary of listening to clients if what they say has little bearing on their case; moreover, indigent clients are often detained, which means visiting the jail—an unpleasant chore. Finally, because actions usually speak louder than words, the exchange value of time when purchasing a client's confidence is weak compared with what is gained when the client actually sees the attorney at work in the courtroom.

> The most common complaint of prisoners is that they don't see their attorney enough. The problem frankly is that a lot of the things they want to tell us are irrelevant. It depends on the client. But a lot of times they want to tell you things that are totally irrelevant to your presentation of the case. (1310)

> I don't know how it works in other public defender's offices, but you won't find people here running out to the jail to calm a guy down because he might have a question. More times than not you'll just say, "Ah, shit, let him stew." The only time you see your client is either at arraignment or just before trial. Most of the time you have, maybe, one or two visits of no more than 15 or 20 minutes with your client. And they have to be wondering, "What the fuck is that guy doing?" (9321)

> There are cases where the stigma [of being an assigned attorney] is really strong and where they [the clients] think they're gonna get railroaded. I literally go out of my way to do things. I'll go out there and see them at the jail once a week if that's what it takes. And to be honest with you, I found that it's not all that successful. I think, if they distrust you, you can be out there every week, and, until they see you do something, you can sit there and talk with them every night for three months and it makes no difference to them. (4210)

"Being honest" also can settle client misgivings because, according to one attorney (4417), "The biggest problem with court-appointed counsel is the credibility factor. . . . So you go out to the jail, and you try to be up front and candid with him right off the bat." By extending candor, attorneys hope to purchase their clients' trust, honesty, and cooperation. This overture counters their suspicions that they will not be dealt with squarely. Moreover, by telling them what they think of their stories, what their chances look like, and how the case will be handled in court, attorneys flourish their insider's knowledge, which bolsters efforts to win the clients' respect as well. During these encounters, attorneys who are skilled at impression management take the opportunity to portray themselves as competent, concerned, and not easily fooled or buffaloed. As one attorney (5423) pointed out:

> You can waste a lot of time with criminal defendants unless they have enough confidence in you to skip all the baloney right from the beginning. I think that one of the ways to develop that kind of confidence is to present yourself in a manner so that they think that this time their court-appointed attorney may really know what he or she is doing.

Once again, however, client reactions reflect whether or not the lawyer is privately retained; attorneys believe that deference and honesty are inherent in relations with private clients but not with public ones. Still, regardless of the type of client, attorneys first feel them out so that they can adopt the right manner to elicit the respect, cooperation, and frankness they need.

Respondent: When I'm retained, there is a certain rapport immediately. That means the person paid me for my experience and my judgment. When I'm appointed to a case, generally there is no rapport whatsoever. So in an appointed case, the first thing I have to do is establish that rapport and convince my client (1) I'm being truthful with him, and (2) I'm a good lawyer.

Interviewer: How do you do it?

Respondent: Well, sometimes you don't. It's difficult. A valuable way of doing it is by going to the jail to see your client ahead of time. But that's not always easily done, since you've got a law practice, and time and economics don't allow you to go to the jail and sit down with your client. . . .

I find it absolutely invaluable to be honest. I will not tell my client a fib. These people are far more intelligent than we generally give them credit for. Plus, they have a disbelief in what you're telling them; so if you're honest, you at least don't have anything to worry about. They check out everything you tell them. So you'd better tell them the truth.

And later on when I have to say to him, "Now, look. You make the decision, but here are your alternatives, and you know I've never lied to you." He at least will say, "Well, I don't like Mr. Smith, and I don't like what he's telling me, but the guy's always been honest with me." (5431)

Respondent: It's difficult to establish yourself with the client.

Interviewer: So how do you do that?

Respondent: Well, I think what you do is wait and see what the client is like. You look at the case before you go over and see him. Then you just start to feel the client out. Find out what his thoughts are. Review what his prior record is. And feel him out. If he's the kind of person who, because you're an attorney, is gonna listen to you right off the bat, then you have no problem. You can sit there and say, "Okay. Now this is what I think we should do." Boom, boom, boom.

But if you sit down and the guy starts throwing all kinds of things at you right away, then you just have to sit back and, again, it's hard to give a concrete method of procedure, but you have to determine whether or not this guy is being uncooperative, or is he just concerned with his case? . . If he's just being plain uncooperative, well, then you've got another problem. Then you have to maybe speak a little louder, you know. Speak with a little bit more authority.

Interviewer: In well-modulated, middle-class tones, or what?

Respondent: I've been able to modify my vocabulary to the point where I can usually get the point across no matter who I'm speaking to. I know how to talk to them so that they know I'm not just some clown out of law school who doesn't know anything about what's going on. (9317)

"Client control" too bluntly describes the complex, often-subtle relationships attorneys try to arrange to gain their clients' confidence. Once it is established, they feel they are less likely to be surprised by a sudden balkiness or by unexpected revelations of something the client concealed from them. Again, this task is harder in public cases than in private ones, and it affects the manner in which attorneys approach clients when making decisions about the dispositions and handling of their cases.

STYLES OF CLIENT CONTROL: ADVISING AND RECOMMENDING

If attorneys prepare the ground well enough by giving clients time, frank assessments of their situations, and the impression they can be trusted, and if the clients respond by listening and offering to cooperate, the attorneys' authority takes root in the nascent relationship. This social exchange nurtures and, in effect, legitimates their status with public clients, while with private clients, professional legitimacy generally accompanies the retainer or fee. In either instance, legitimation forms the basis for client control and allows attorneys to moderate their clients' demands and adjust their expectations to courthouse realities. The styles they use, however, range from a soft "advising" approach to a more forceful "recommending" posture,[9] with finer gradations in between. Advising can consist of simply listing the options facing clients and leaving the decision in their hands, or it can mean providing much blunter appraisals that, even without explicit recommendations, make the attorneys' preferences clear. Similarly, recommendations can be made in ways that give clients room to disagree or that present little more than a "take it or leave it" proposition.

A public defender described a situation that approximates the latter extreme of the recommending approach. With the plea conditions set beforehand, the lawyer relies on four factors to convince the client to take the plea offer: a lenient sentence (11½ to 23 months in the local jail), the favorable reactions and support of his client's detained colleagues, the client's doubts about the fairness of the court, and the odds against getting a better sentence.

> Most times I've struck a deal before I even talk to my client. You know pretty well what the hell went on without talking to your guy. I think I've run across three people who I believe to be innocent since I've been here, and that's five years.
>
> If I get a good deal, then I'll go over to the guy, and I'll say, "Look, here's the way it is. That's the best I could get from the D.A. I think you ought to take it." And then I go over the case, you know, what the strong points are, what the weak points are, etc., etc. . . . And then I say, "11½ to 23." The guy says, "No, man, I'm not going to do any time. I want to go to court." You know, "I'm gonna take this up to the Supreme Court."
>
> So, you say, "Fine, are you prepared to spend 10 months in jail asserting your rights?" They aren't completely stupid, you know. They come around. I'll say, "Okay, I'll see you tomorrow. Talk to your guys in the joint because they know what's good and what isn't."
>
> I never really pressure them per se, but I guess you could say that I use some influence upon them. Most of our people are black, and I think they realize they just really aren't going to get that great a shake out here. Either with the jury or with the judge. And most of our guys have street sense. They know what the hell is going on. (9321)

In contrast with this attorney, who exerts "some influence" and orchestrates his client's decision, other adopt a softer, more indirect "advising" style for reasons of effectiveness and professional ethics. As one of these lawyers explained,

> I find that if they are actively involved at all points in the proceedings, they'll give you more help, you'll find out things about the case that you wouldn't have known. And it isn't so much that when they get into court that they're gonna balk at what happened or say "I didn't expect this to happen," it's just keeping them involved at all times is vitally important to your own role as a defense attorney. Also, I don't think it's ethically proper for an attorney to make decisions for his client, especially in a criminal defense situation. (5404)

Attorneys generally prefer this lawyer's advising approach when representing public clients. An emphatic stance and urgent recommendations strain fragile relationships with wary clients and raise the possibility of problems farther down the road. As two lawyers quoted earlier mentioned, attorneys must "cover" their "rear end" and perhaps "swallow" their pride to avoid having public clients "turn on" them. Another attorney underscored the need for caution and the importance of letting public clients make the key decisions in their cases:

> Certainly I'm not gonna twist an arm. If anything, I'm very, very cautious with these guys. I was warned about that when I first took it over. Be very specific that any decision is their decision. Because a lot of times they'll plead, they'll go through it, they'll get sentenced. And they'll immediately say, "My attorney forced me into it." So you try to be very cautious. It puts the burden on them. (4411)

Some attorneys learn the hard way about advising public clients: they discover that even though recommending a course of action may seem more professional, clients may react strongly against what they see as overbearing attitudes. A headstrong style can provoke a client's anger, reawaken suspicions, and undermine an attorney's tentative authority. In private cases, where clients are more accepting of professional authority, attorneys feel freer to recommend what their clients should do, and they push more vigorously those dispositions they see as in their clients' interests. Being privately retained also means that if significant or unresolvable differences arise, clients can go elsewhere for an attorney. The odds, however, of clients switching attorneys after paying nonrefundable fees or retainers undoubtedly are slim, and perhaps these "sunk costs" add to the clients' willingness to listen to and follow their attorneys' recommendations. Nevertheless, for attorneys, the ability of their clients to go elsewhere for service (however chimerical it may be for private clients) represents a psychological escape hatch their public clients do not have at all. As a public defender concluded, the "psychology of representation" in private cases was "totally different" from that of private cases.

> The longer you're [in the public defender's office], the more you get into the psychology of representation. It's totally different than private representation. In private you always have the threat of, "Look, if you don't want to follow my advice, go down the road." Here you don't have that luxury. . . . I think we've learned to deal with the type of client that we're dealing with. But, you know, if we're not dealing with a client who is willing to listen to us, we're not like the private bar. If the guy says, "I want you to file an X, Y, Z motion," you're gonna have to file it. (9318)

> When I started, I found myself getting upset with my clients because they wouldn't settle, and I was just determined I was going to eliminate that. Now I don't force them to do anything. And I find if you put that burden on them and don't give them any reason to get pissed off at you, then they have to start thinking about this thing and making their own decisions. A lot of them turn pretty reasonable the morning of the trial. And, you know, I don't have that many problems with my clients anymore. (2203)

> It used to be I would argue with a client on why he should take the plea. Now, somewhat to his disadvantage, I have said, "Screw him." I just thought, "Why get in an argument with this guy and really lean on him because I know he's gonna be convicted?". . .
>
> I'm not gonna fight with him and tell him he's gonna plead. Because over and over again you see cases in which the defendant is appealing. And one of the grounds is—"I told the lawyer I wasn't guilty, but all he ever wanted to talk about was how I should plead guilty to this charge." That's on appointed.
>
> Now in private cases, I will lean on him. That is the difference that comes out in a private case. If he doesn't like the advice, it's sure easy enough to hire somebody else. But on an appointed case it doesn't work that way. (5406)

> If you walk in and say, "Mr. Jones, I want you to handle my case," then I will talk to you about the facts, I will consider all the alternatives. I will see what it's gonna take in time and money, and I will quote you a fee. And I will decide ahead of time whether or not I'm gonna be able to call the shots with you and if you're gonna listen to me. . . . On an indigent case, I'm assigned by the court. I'm out of the blue, he doesn't trust me, he's not paying me, there's no rapport between us. I may have to try that case, even though it's absolutely deadly. (5431)

As a matter of style, if not substance, attorneys who "advise" public clients seek to impress on them that they sit in the driver's seat, that they are the arbiters of strategy in their cases. Two purposes lie behind this approach. First, advising invites client participation, or at least a *feeling* of participation that counteracts client apprehensions about being railroaded by an attorney. Second, by placing the burden for decisions on their clients' shoulders, attorneys hope to extract a measure of personal commitment to their decisions that will facilitate the handling of cases and forestall later complaints about their performance.

It is not easy to measure the effects of these two styles on case outcomes. Indeed, it may be preferable to view the quality or nature of relationships between attorneys and clients as dependent on "procedural" rather than "substantive" justice. Both Casper and Tyler, for example, offer evidence that perceptions of fairness—and not just the outcomes of their cases—matter greatly to defendants in appraising their treatment in court.[10] The larger study from which this study derived its data did not have information regarding the nature of attorney-client relations and client reactions to their attorneys on a case-by-case basis. Nonetheless, a useful purpose can be served by looking at three selected facets of how public and private cases were handled by attorneys in each of the nine courts. Table 2 compares the proportions of preliminary hearings held, mean or average number of due process–related motions (for example, suppression of statements or exclusion of evidence) filed per case, and the proportion of trials in public and private cases.

In general, the data suggest that public and private clients were treated rather similarly by attorneys in these courts. With respect to preliminary examinations, statistically significant differences existed between the two types of cases in four of the nine courts. But after taking into account the severity of trial court charges lodged against defendants and their prior criminal records, the type of attorney mattered only in DuPage, where public defenders requested preliminary hearings more often than private attorneys, and in Oakland and Kalamazoo, where the pattern reversed itself and attorneys in private cases held these examinations more frequently than when they were appointed by the courts.[11]

A mixed pattern also exists for the mean number of motions. In five of the courts, no statistically significant differences emerged. However, in two (DuPage and Kalamazoo) private attorneys filed more motions than did attorneys with public clients; in two others (St. Clair and Montgomery), motion activity in public cases exceeded that in private cases after controlling for charge and record. In Erie, these control variables erased an apparent difference between types of attorneys. This also happened in the comparison of Erie's trial rates, so that no significant differences were found in eight of the nine trial courts. Only in Dauphin were public defenders significantly more likely to go to trial than were private attorneys.

To the extent overall patterns can be found in this table, Kalamazoo is one court where public cases apparently were handled differently from private ones: In public cases preliminary hearings were less frequent, fewer motions were filed, and while not statistically significant, trial rates were lower than in private cases. However, St. Clair and Erie displayed reverse images of Kalamazoo, with higher, but statistically insignificant, preliminary hearing and trial rates in public cases along with significantly greater motion activity. For the remaining six courts, no consistent patterns emerged.

This short analysis is not definitive. Yet, when viewed in light of systematic, comparative analyses of the impact of defense attorneys on other measures of case outcomes such as sentencing, the evidence indicates

Table 2 Preliminary hearings, motions, and trials by type of attorney

	Illinois			*Michigan*			*Pennsylvania*		
	DuPage	*Peoria*	*St. Clair*	*Oakland*	*Kalamazoo*	*Saginaw*	*Montgomery*	*Dauphin*	*Erie*
				Preliminary hearings held					
Public cases	90.4%	34.1%	98.0%	58.3%	34.6%	73.1%[a]	95.4%	71.0%	68.6%
Private cases	85.3%	41.8%	96.5%	69.8%[b]	48.1%[b]	64.3%	95.4%	70.2%	66.5%
Attorney effect	−.09[a]	.05	−.04	.13[c]	.13[c]	−.08	.00	.01	.03
				Mean no. of motions per case					
Public cases	0.64	0.77	2.36[c]	0.43	0.20	0.46	1.16[c]	0.15	0.65[c]
Private cases	1.08[c]	0.69	1.56	0.43	0.52[c]	0.41	0.63	0.16	0.36
Attorney effect	.22[c]	−.04	−.23[c]	−.01	.19[c]	.00	−.09[a]	.02	−.07
				Bench or jury trials					
Public cases	4.1%	5.4%	9.7%	4.1%	5.0%	4.4%	5.1%	8.6%[b]	8.5%[b]
Private cases	4.1%	4.1%	7.3%	4.5%	7.5%	7.1%	5.2%	4.0%	4.2%
Attorney effect	.02	−.02	−.03	.02	.06	.05	.04	−.09[b]	−.02

Note: Attorney effect is the standardized regression coefficient for the dummy variable "type of attorney," where 0 = public defender or assigned counsel and 1 = privately retained attorney, in a multiple regression equation using severity of the trial charge and criminal record of the defendant as control variables.

[a]$p < .05$ [b]$p < .01$ [c]$p < .001$

that public clients do not fare more poorly in court than their peers who retain private counsel.[12] Although the sampling of attorney complaints about public clients clearly shows that their dealings with these clients are often contentious and at times disagreeable, with few notable exceptions in the nine counties, public clients are not treated in significantly different ways than are private clients. In this sense, attorney-client relations may be best viewed as part of procedural justice, in which style, approach, rapport, attitudes, and perception define "fairness." Thus, in games between attorneys and clients, clients perceive fairness if they trust their attorneys and believe they have a say or voice in the handling of their cases.

CLIENT GAMES: CONCLUDING THOUGHTS, A PARADOX, AND POLICY QUESTIONS

This exploration of attorney-client relations in criminal cases relied on the comments of "regular" attorneys. The picture that emerges reflects their particular angle of vision and exposes only certain aspects of lawyer relationships with criminal clients.[13] For example, in their eyes, public clients were skeptical and uncooperative, but by the same token, some frankly admitted they did not give these clients much of their time. Thus, they stressed the resistance of public clients while downplaying their own actions or inactions that may have played a part in their clients' negative responses.[14]

Most also felt their difficulties with public clients were institutionally rooted in the fact that indigent defense systems rarely allow criminal defendants to choose their lawyers. This fact, when combined with the commonly held precept that "you get what you pay for," suggests that the public client's lack of trust and respect is neither peculiar to certain programs nor characteristic of particular kinds of clients. Instead, these responses are intrinsic to an involuntary relationship in which the client holds no readily available, easily employed, and culturally sanctioned lever to assure professional accountability.

The attorneys quoted in this study worked in a wide variety of settings. The indigent defense systems differed considerably from each other, for instance. Only Dauphin County had a traditional, full-time public defender office in which the attorneys could not practice privately on the side; Peoria used a part-time public defender staff; and the others had mixes of full-time and part-time defenders with different rules regarding private practices. As for the Michigan counties, Oakland and Saginaw used assigned-counsel programs of different designs, but Kalamazoo had a contract-attorney system that closely resembled Peoria's program. These systems also followed varying operating practices; some, for example, had horizontal or "zone" representation, in which clients had different attorneys at each stage of the disposition process; others provided vertical representation, in which clients had the same attorney from beginning to end. Finally, without going into further detail, plea negotiation policies and customs as well as sentencing practices varied widely across these nine courts.[15]

The point here is that attorneys' comments about their relations with public and private clients revealed the same basic themes despite the many dissimilarities of policy and politics in the courts in which they worked. Casper found the same thing to be true for Baltimore, Detroit, and Phoenix, where relationships between client views and type of attorney held across the three different cities.[16]

A few attorneys felt that race and class affected their relations with public clients. According to the case data for the nine counties, 43.6 percent of the public clients were black, whereas the proportion of private clients who were black was 26.8 percent. It is also worth mentioning that public clients were more likely to have prior criminal records (59.0 percent) than were private clients (38.6 percent). Finally, 35.3 percent of the public clients were detained prior to trial, while only 10.7 percent of the private clients were in jail, a reflection of their different economic statuses as well as their criminal histories.

According to Casper, a prior criminal record, but not a defendant's race, has a consistent, eroding effect on defendants' views of public attorneys.[17] Incarceration also diminishes their trust. With the data available for this study, it is not possible to compare the effect of these factors on client behavior with the effect of the institutional factors that most attorneys offered as explanations for client behavior. Undoubtedly these factors combine and possibly interact with one another to exacerbate attorneys' problems with public clients. Although sorting out their relative impacts remains an unresolved problem, the literature provides little evidence that differences between public and private clients can totally replace the fundamental institutional reasons for client mistrust and lack of confidence.

Attorneys in this study say they generally "advised" their public clients, while they "recommended" what their private clients should do. Casper, however, found that most criminal defendants felt public defenders told them what to do instead of offering advice, giving information, or making suggestions. Defendants with private attorneys, in contrast, did not think their lawyers "muscled" them even when they insisted on something. Casper suggests these different views rested on more than just the attorney's behavior:

> The nature of the transaction between attorney and client provides a context for *interpreting* the behavior of the attorney. In part because the defendant (or his family) was paying the attorney, the whole tone of the relationship was altered. For example, insistence upon a particular course of action by a street [private] lawyer (e.g., pleading guilty, commitment for observation to a hospital) is interpreted differently by his client. Similar "advice" from a public defender might well be interpreted as giving orders, as telling the

client what to do rather than discussing it with him. With a street lawyer insistent advice is only the lawyer's "proper" role and the exercise of the expertise that he is supposed to possess.[18]

Defense attorneys work in a social setting where expectations and interpretations of their behavior count as much as what they actually do. Their role, then, is symbolic as well as substantive because they need the respect and trust of clients before they enter the courtroom or do anything on a case. When combined with its intangible qualities, this inherently political side of lawyering produces, as Blumberg argued, a "confidence game" with clients. But it is a confidence game in the literal sense, since attorneys must win the confidence of clients who do not initially recognize or accept their professional authority before they can gain their cooperation. Client control, therefore, is a confidence game in which cooperation between lawyers and mistrustful clients is at stake.

Clients refuse to cooperate in various ways. Some have mild consequences for attorneys, others do not. For instance, attorneys said that public clients were discourteous or that they refused to talk to them, which made their work unpleasant and more arduous. An attorney lamented earlier that some clients were so alienated that "You don't have a client along with you," while another complained that attorneys "end up doing all the worrying" and "doing all the scrambling around" because "your client could really care less." Clients may also spurn advice or balk at suggestions, which not only increases the lawyers' work but threatens their reputation for client control within the courthouse community.

Deception, dishonesty, and a lack of candor are equally serious problems. Clients, especially public ones, were described as "street-wise," often manipulative, sometimes "too smart to admit anything," less than candid "at least 50 percent of the time," and reluctant to talk openly with their lawyer, according to one attorney (5425) whose remarks echoed those made by others.[19] The attorneys' difficulty is that evasion and deception can affect tactical and strategic decisions.[20] Mather describes a case in which a public defender went to trial at the request of a client who claimed she had no prior record. Expecting a sentence of no more than probation if she were found guilty, the defender went through a five-day jury trial that ended in a conviction. To his surprise the defendant's presentence report revealed that she had a five-year history of similar crimes. She was sentenced to the state prison. The public defender said his client "fooled everyone."[21]

By the same token public clients hold serious reservations as to how vigorously attorneys will represent client interests if it means sacrificing their own longer-term interests within the court system—and the attorneys know the clients are thinking this. As one attorney (3310) put it, "You know, the scuttlebutt goes around in jail, 'Hey, the public defenders, they get along well with the state's attorney. They're gonna send you down the river.' " And, as another (5406) explained, "If you say to an indigent client, 'I think you should plead,' and he doesn't want to plead, he'll say, 'See, that proves it. They appointed him to lean on me.' "

By substantial margins, defendants interviewed by Casper and others think public attorneys are less likely to fight hard for them and are more concerned about wrapping up their cases quickly than in getting justice; defendants also doubt whether public attorneys will be honest with them. Overwhelmingly, they believe private attorneys work for their clients, but that public attorneys do not.[22] Indeed, concern that defense attorneys are co-opted by the court system has been a staple of contemporary research on defense attorneys. As "repeat players" with "one-shotter" clients, defense attorneys presumably rely on cooperative relations within the courthouse that would be jeopardized by aggressive advocacy.[23] More generally, Carlin suggested some time ago that "clients are expendable" whenever their lawyers do not depend on them for their fees or future business.[24]

Attorneys acknowledge how they are perceived. Thus, in their relations with clients, they are enmeshed in perceptions and expectations running along the lines of "If he thinks I am thinking of selling him out, he will not trust me even though I am not thinking of that, and if he knew this, he would go along with what I say." Attorneys fear their clients will not cooperate because they think they will be deceived. They fear deceit by clients just as much. Attorneys consequently fret over what kind of game their clients may be playing and whether they will find out soon enough to know if they should try to change their minds or take other precautions. As their comments amply suggested, however, attorneys make important distinctions between public and private clients.

Attorneys claim that because private clients pick them and pay them a fee, these clients respect and trust them, believe they are good, have faith in what they are doing, and are willing to accept a "certain rapport" so that matters can be discussed frankly. One attorney (5406) summed it up by saying, "There is a difference, I think, in the relationship—as far as openness and working together for the same goal—between being an appointed attorney and a retained attorney." Attorneys perceive private clients as generally more cooperative. Even if they encounter fee problems later on or discover a private client is less candid than they thought at first, they nevertheless see private clients as generally more trusting than public clients, largely because of the nature of their contractually based relationship. Private clients choose their attorneys, pay them a fee and, however remote the chance, can replace them. Similarly, attorneys can nip problems in the bud by declining to accept cases.[25] As a private attorney (9427) said, "I blow them out of here" if potential clients refused to heed his directions. In public cases, where this option is usually missing for both parties, a lawyer (3310) described the relationship as a "shotgun wedding."

The ambivalence in attorney-client relationships is cleared away in private criminal cases because the retainer or fee reflects the attorneys' assessment of cases and how they should be handled. Consequently, clients have both an idea and a commitment from their attorneys about their intentions; at the same time, attorneys assume that the fees signal the clients' good faith. Neither expects deception by the other. In public cases, clients have no immediate leverage at hand to assure themselves that their attorneys will serve their interests and, indeed, see them as having long-term commitments to the courts, not to them. Attorneys sense this mistrust and wonder if their clients will cooperate with them. With no easy way of ascertaining, measuring, or purchasing each other's commitment, proclamations of honesty and dependability may be viewed as trying to pull the wool over one another's eyes. From the attorneys' perspective, public clients often act as if they need to avoid being taken advantage of by their attorneys or try to exert misguided efforts to take control of their cases. Their immediate problem focuses on changing these perceptions. Their task with private clients is much easier; the attorneys only have to keep their clients' confidence while making sure that they are not gulled by the appearance of client comity.

Because private clients come to attorneys in an apparently cooperative frame of mind, the attorneys' goal in this client game boils down to simply keeping their trust.[26] Because attorneys first must win the confidence of public clients, the game changes and is more involved. "You've really got to earn their trust," an attorney (5419) declared, but "sometimes you do, sometimes you don't." In attorneys' eyes, clients are the chief losers if they refuse to cooperate; but they also know from personal experience what clients suspect they might do to them under the guise of representing them before the court. Consequently, they face the critical, interrelated problems of not only gaining their confidence but dispelling thoughts that they will desert them.

In this situation, where each side is skeptical of the other's intentions but mutual cooperation is required, attorneys can take the first step by "being honest" and by trying to assure clients that mutual trust is necessary. As an attorney (9307) warned, "If you get to a point where the two of you really can't talk with each other, you're both losing." In addition to being honest, visiting with clients and engaging in courtroom activities are "moves" in this confidence game. These moves give clients a chance to assess their attorneys' preferences and commitments. In turn, through these moves, attorneys try to rid themselves of the public defender stereotype so their clients can see that "this time their court attorney may really know what he or she is doing," as another lawyer quoted earlier said. This helps to counteract the effects of self-confirming labels that impede cooperation. The advising style also reinforces these moves, since it encourages clients to feel they have a say in the handling of their cases.

The decision to cooperate depends lastly on its rewards and costs. If clients believe that confiding in their lawyers will not penalize them, they will be more likely to cooperate. Sentencing weighs heavily in this equation. Client concerns and uncertainties over this issue offer attorneys another opening to persuade them to cooperate, since they are the ones with knowledge of what is likely to occur and the ability to do something about it. The attorney's chore is lightened especially if the client is faced with a lenient sentence on the one hand and the specter of more severe punishment for going to trial on the other. For the nine courts taken as a whole, nearly two-thirds (65.8 percent) of the 4,100 sampled cases that ended in guilty pleas received probation.[27] Defendants who went to trial and were convicted, however, fared worse—even after controlling for relevant sentencing variables.[28] First offenders less often received probation after a jury trial, and repeat offenders were sentenced more severely than comparable defendants who pled guilty.[29]

The mere threat of trial penalties probably eases the attorney's efforts. The prospect of more severe punishment, for whatever reason, usually chills a client's desire to go to trial rather than to plead guilty. Similarly, the price for deceiving an attorney may be a stiffer sentence if the client miscalculates and the deception is uncovered, as in the case Mather described.[30] The upshot is that if attorneys succeed in convincing their public clients to trust them and persuade them to listen to them, they successfully convert the public client confidence game into something more like the cooperative game attorneys perceive to exist with private clients.

A paradox may exist in this confidence game between suspicious public clients and wary attorneys who are involuntarily joined in an association from which they generally cannot exit until the case is over. Rosenthal distinguished between "traditional" and "participatory" models of lawyer-client relations. In the traditional model, "the client who is passive, follows instructions, and trusts the professional without criticism, with few questions or requests, is preferable, and will do better than the difficult client who is critical and questioning."[31] Conversely, the participatory model stresses an active, skeptical client who shares the responsibility for making choices with an attorney who must be patient and earn the client's cooperation. Many criminal attorneys who handle public cases may prefer the traditional model, particularly younger or less experienced ones who are insecure about their professional status and react to questioning clients as though their self-esteem and pride were threatened; but with practice, others learn to adopt more participatory styles because of the suspiciousness of their public clients. The need to win their confidence means attorneys must persuade their clients that they can be trusted or else they may fail to gain control of them.

The paradox here is twofold. First, the mistrust public clients hold for their attorneys may force them to bow more to their clients' wishes than one might expect from folk wisdom or from arguments like Carlin's about "client expendability." Because of their clients' qualms, attorneys may find the advisory role more palatable, with the result that clients participate more actively in the progress of their cases. By including clients in decisions and restraining their own urge to make them alone, attorneys hope to prove that they are not trying to stampede their clients into decisions contrary to their interests. The second aspect involves the involuntary nature of their relationship. The public client's reluctance to recognize an attorney's professional authority denies the lawyer a major resource in gaining the client's compliance and acquiescence, yet the attorney cannot refuse to handle the case as easily as one who is privately retained. The lawyer's overtures and advice also can be shunned, which threatens his or her reputation for "client control," and unless matters between them get totally out of hand, little can be done but to try again. This involuntary relationship means the client gains a measure of power in dealings with the attorney, a certain equalization of positions buttressed further by the client's ability to file grievances or appeal cases. Together these add yet other incentives to adopt the participatory mode—advising public clients about their options and letting them bear the responsibility for making decisions. The paradox, then, is that those things which irritate attorneys about public clients foster what many observers consider a more appropriate professional role, though clients evidently do not see it this way. They still prefer fee arrangements with private lawyers where, ironically, according to the lawyers in this study, more traditional lawyer-client relationships prevail because they have their clients' confidence.

The institutional basis of client estrangement from court-appointed counsel and public defenders calls into question the design of indigent defense policies. In all nine courts, felony defendants deemed to be indigent and eligible for publicly paid counsel had no say in the selection of their attorneys. In one court (Oakland), the judges appointed specific lawyers to handle these cases; in seven of the others (the Illinois and Pennsylvania courts plus Kalamazoo), the public defenders or contract attorneys allocated the cases among themselves, while in the ninth (Saginaw), a court official chose counsel to represent indigent defendants. In each instance, criminal defendants were expected to live with the lawyer assigned to them.

In the eyes of criminal clients, professional accountability hinges on a market conception and fee-for-service definition of lawyer responsibility. They place little faith in the notion that ethical concerns and feelings of professional obligation by themselves are sufficient guarantees that a lawyer picked seemingly "out of the hat" will adequately represent their interests. Postconviction proceedings offer them something of a retributive stick, but by that time they already have paid a price for what they feel was mistakenly listening to their lawyers; moreover, the prevalence of guilty pleas removes many grounds for appeal and grievances. Stuck with their attorneys, and their attorneys stuck with them, they are caught up in a confidence game in which competing interests and the need for accommodation are resolved in ways that are not as self-evidently effective as choosing and paying a lawyer to represent them.

Given the finding of this and other studies that public clients fare no worse but are treated no better than private clients, the policy implications of client mistrust and disrespect reported by attorneys depend on

(1) whether an equivalence of outcomes and attorney behavior is a satisfactory standard for evaluating attorney performance and (2) what weight is given to "procedural justice" in designing indigent defense policies. Comparisons of how attorneys treat public and private clients are necessary but limited indicators of substantive fairness because, while feasible, they also leave the criteria of accountability undefined. Equivalence in and by itself necessarily adopts the outcome of either private or public cases as a benchmark to gauge the other, without stating explicitly whether this benchmark might itself be too high or too low; indeed, it is likely that both are inadequate and that some other criterion is required.

Without alternative evaluation standards, and in the absence of readily apparent, substantive differences in the treatment of publicly and privately represented criminal defendants, changes in the provision of indigent defense counsel may seem unwarranted. Public client mistrust and the problems attendant on the assignment of attorneys may be viewed as the inevitable but nonetheless harmless consequence of an otherwise beneficient policy that, thus, can be safely ignored. A concern for procedural justice, however, suggests that the perceptions, reactions, and feelings of clients regarding policy and institutional arrangements ought to matter as much as substantive effects in prompting reform or change.

From this perspective, it can be asked whether indigent defense systems might be designed to allow criminal defendants to select their own attorneys. If organized along the lines of a voucher system, attorney fees and costs would still be paid publicly, but defendants could, if they wished, select an attorney from among those who wanted to represent indigent criminal clients. Indigent defendants with the freedom to choose might express fewer apprehensions about their attorneys. The disappearance, or at least amelioration, of these fears as public policy is brought into line with client conceptions may, however, weaken the apparent paradox that client mistrust fosters attorney accountability and client participation in public cases.

NOTES

1. Abraham Blumberg, "The Practice of Law as a Confidence Game: Organizational Cooptation of a Profession," 1 *Law and Society Review* 15 (1967).

2. Jonathan D. Casper, "Did You Have a Lawyer When You Went to Court? No, I Had a Public Defender," 1 *Yale Review of Law and Social Action* 4 (1971).

3. Jonathan D. Casper *American Criminal Justice: The Defendant's Perspective* (Englewood Cliffs, N.J.: Prentice-Hall, 1972); idem, *Criminal Courts: The Defendant's Perspective* (Washington, D.C.: U. S. Government Printing Office, 1979); Glen Wilkerson, "Public Defenders as Their Clients See Them," *American Journal of Criminal Law* 141 (1972); Antoinette N. Hetzler and Charles H. Kanter, "Informality and the Court: A Study of the Behavior of Court Officials in the Processing of Defendants," in Sawyer P. Sylvester, Jr., and Edward Sagarin, eds., *Politics and Crime* (New York: Praeger, 1974); F. Arcuri, "Lawyers, Judges, and Plea Bargaining," 4 *International Journal of Criminology and Penology* 177 (1976); Burton M. Atkins and E. W. Boyle, "Prisoner's Satisfaction with Defense Counsel," 12 *Criminal Law*

Bulletin 427 (1976); Geoffrey P. Alpert and Donald A. Hicks, "Prisoners' Attitudes Toward Components of the Legal System," 14 *Criminology* 461 (1977); Stewart O'Brien, Steven Pheterson, Michael Wright, and Carl Hosticka, "The Criminal Lawyer: The Defendant's Perspective," 5 *American Journal of Criminal Law* 283 (1977); Geoffrey P. Alpert and C. Ronald Hutt, "Defending the Accused: Counsel Effectiveness and Strategies," in William F. McDonald, ed., *The Defense Counsel* (Beverly Hills, Calif.: Sage Publications, 1983).

4. Carl Hosticka, "We Don't Care About What Happened, We Only Care About What Is Going to Happen," 26 *Social Problems* 599 (1979); Douglas E. Rosenthal, *Lawyer and Client: Who's in Charge?* (New York: Russell Sage Foundation, 1974).

5. Maureen Cain, "The General Practice Lawyer and the Client," *International Journal of Society and Law* 331 (1979).

6. The counties were chosen on the basis of social, economic, and political criteria that produced diverse triplets of counties within each state while forming roughly comparable triplets of matched counties across states. There were three suburban "ring" counties that were primarily middle class and Republican, three "autonomous" counties, and three declining industrial, Democratic counties. More detailed information on the methods and scope of the larger project can be found in Peter F. Nardulli, Roy B. Flemming, and James Eisenstein, *The Tenor of Justice: Criminal Courts and the Guilty Plea Process* (Champaign: University of Illinois Press, forthcoming).

7. The numbers shown in parentheses after each interview excerpt are codes assigned to assure anonymity to each attorney.

8. Casper, *Criminal Courts,* p. 83.

9. This distinction parallels the two meanings of "representation" identified by Skolnick: in one, an attorney accepts a client's view of how the case should be handled and provides counsel as to how to implement the strategy; in the other, the attorney takes the responsibility for both strategy and tactics. Jerome Skolnick, "Social Control in the Adversary System," 11 *J. Conflict Resolution* 52, 65 (1967).

10. Jonathan D. Casper, "Having Their Day in Court: Defendant Evaluations of the Fairness of Their Treatment," 12 *Law and Society Review* 237 (1978); Tom R. Tyler, "The Role of Perceived Injustice in Defendants' Evaluations of Their Courtroom Experience," 18 *Law and Society Review* 51 (1984).

11. For a more detailed examination of the preliminary hearing decision in these nine courts, see Roy B. Flemming, "Elements of the Defense Attorney's Craft: An Adaptive Expectations Model of the Preliminary Hearing Decision," 8 *Law and Policy* 33 (1986).

12. R. Hermann, E. Single, and J. Boston, *Counsel for the Poor: Criminal Defense in Urban America* (Lexington, Mass.: Lexington Books, 1977). An analysis of "regular" defense attorneys, their "styles," and their negligible impact on case outcomes and sentencing in these nine courts can be found in Peter F. Nardulli, "Insider's Justice: Defense Attorneys and the Handling of Felony Cases" (paper presented at the annual meeting of the Law and Society Association, San Diego, California, June 6–9, 1985).

13. For a discussion of the problems in more direct observation of lawyer-client interaction, see Brenda Danet, Kenneth B. Hoffman, and Nicole C. Kermish, "Obstacles in the Study of Lawyer-Client Interaction: The Biography of a Failure," 14 *Law and Society Review* 905 (1980); Douglas E. Rosenthal, "Comment on 'Obstacles to the Study of Lawyer-Client Interaction: The Biography of a Failure,'" 14 *Law and Society Review* 923 (1980); Stewart Macaulay, "Law and Behavioral Sciences: Is There Any There There?" 6 *Law and Policy* 149 (1984). These problems may not be insurmountable, however; for example, see Hosticka (note 4) and Cain (note 5).

14. Casper found that privately retained lawyers spent dramatically different, more extensive periods with their clients; 47 percent of 132 defendants with private lawyers said they saw their attorneys for more than three hours. In contrast, 59 percent of the 463 defendants with public attorneys reported that their attorneys spent a half hour or less with them. Casper, *Criminal Courts* (note 3), p. 35.

15. See Nardulli et al. (note 6), for further descriptions of the nine courts.

16. Casper, *Criminal Courts,* p. 12.
17. Ibid., pp. 22–23.
18. Casper, *American Criminal Justice* (note 3), pp. 117–118 (emphasis in original).
19. In autobiographies of their work and careers, defense attorneys frequently bemoan their clients' lack of veracity. For example, Moldovsky states, "I know that clients lie to me . . . I just don't know which ones are the liars" (Joel Moldovsky and Rose DeWolf, *The Best Defense* [New York: Macmillan Publishing Co., 1975], p. 76). Wishman also recalls, "It didn't take me long to realize that nearly every client had lied to me" (Seymour Wishman, *Confessions of a Criminal Lawyer* [New York: Times Books, 1981], p. 84). Finally, Kunen describes the awkward situation a new client created for him when he asked, "Do you believe me?" "I didn't want to say I didn't believe him, because then it would seem I wasn't on his side. But I didn't want to say I did believe him, because then he'd think I was a fool" (James S. Kunen, *How Can You Defend Those People? The Making of a Criminal Lawyer* [New York: Random House, 1983], p. 187).
20. Alan M. Dershowitz, *The Best Defense* (New York: Vintage Books, 1983), recounts his shock at discovering his client was a stool pigeon for the prosecution: "After all, when I agreed to become his lawyer I had taken his case to defend a *landsman,* a fellow Boro Parker, a kid from the old neighborhood—not a stool pigeon. How could I ever trust Seigel again? For months he had tricked me and my colleagues into believing that he was a murder suspect, when all the while he was working for the other side, probably reporting every detail of our strategy right back to the prosecutor" (p. 21).
21. Lynn Mather, "The Outsider in the Courtroom: An Alternative Role for Defense," in Herbert Jacob, ed., *The Potential for Reform of Criminal Justice* (Beverly Hills, Calif.: Sage Publications, 1974), p. 283.
22. Casper, *Criminal Court,* p. 16.
23. Marc Galanter, "Why the 'Haves' Come Out Ahead: Speculations on the Limits of Change," 9 *Law and Society Review* 95 (1974).
24. Jerome E. Carlin, *Lawyers on Their Own* (New Brunswick, N.J.: Rutgers University Press, 1962), pp. 161–162.
25. In an early study, Arthur Lewis Wood, *Criminal Lawyer* (New Haven, Conn.: College and University Press, 1967), p. 101, found that of ninety-three criminal lawyers, all of whom were private practitioners, twenty-one said they refused to accept clients who would not follow their advice.
26. This means that attorneys who are successful in this respect can play the kind of "confidence game" Blumberg describes. Blumberg (above, note 1).
27. See Nardulli et al. (note 6) for an analysis of the guilty plea process in the nine courts.
28. See ibid., regarding trial penalties in these courts. For other analyses, see Thomas M. Uhlman and N. Darlene Walker, "He Takes Some of My Time: I Take Some of His: An Analysis of Sentencing Patterns in Jury Cases," 14 *Law and Society Review* 323 (1980); David Brereton and Jonathan D. Casper, "Does It Pay to Plead Guilty? Differential Sentencing and the Functioning of Criminal Courts," 16 *Law and Society Review* 45 (1981–1982).
29. While sentences are important components of the client's decision, grievances and appeals are part of the attorney's choice and concerns. Between 1973 and 1983, criminal appeals more than doubled in Michigan and rose by 80 percent in Illinois (U.S. Department of Justice, Bureau of Justice Statistics, *The Growth of Appeals: 1973–1983 Trends* [Feb. 1985]). However, all appeals do not center on the attorney's performance, and success rates for defendants are not high. Thomas Y. Davies, "Affirmed: A Study of Criminal Appeals and Decision-Making Norms in a California Court of Appeals," 1982 *American Bar Foundation Research Journal* 543.
30. See text accompanying note 21.
31. Rosenthal (note 4), p. 13.

ARTICLE THIRTEEN

The Outsider in the Courtroom: An Alternative Role for Defense

LYNN M. MATHER

Although guilty pleas are offered in up to 90 percent of criminal cases, there are defendants who plead not guilty and go to trial. What factors encourage this decision, and who are the "maverick" attorneys that do not abide by the cooperative norms of the system? Lynn Mather explores this section of the bar and offers answers to these questions.

Perhaps because the cooperative role of defense has been so frequently described in the literature, it is time to consider an alternative role—that is, the more traditional adversary role—which does appear, albeit infrequently, in the criminal court. This article, then, will describe: first, the situations in which even the most cooperative attorneys choose a full-fledged adversary trial; second, those defense attorneys who prefer not to plea bargain and are more oriented to trial dispositions; and finally, defendants who, after all, are not socialized into the court bureaucracy and its norms of cooperation, and who may reject the plea bargains recommended by their counsel. The decision-making process for defense which results in either a guilty plea or a trial is the focus of this study. Notwithstanding the frequency of guilty pleas, some criminal cases do go to trial. And thus, investigation into the factors determining the method of disposition may clarify the differences between a cooperative role and an adversary role for defense.

Source: Reprinted from Lynn Mather, "The Outsider in the Courtroom: An Alternative Role for Defense," pp. 263–289, in Herbert Jacob, ed., *The Potential for Reform of Criminal Justice.*

SETTING AND METHOD

The data presented here come from a study of a felony court: the Central District of the Los Angeles Superior Court. The Los Angeles Superior Court is divided into eight districts, the largest being the Central District, located in downtown Los Angeles. In 1970, over 12,000 felony defendants had their cases heard in the Central District. The majority of defendants were black or Mexican-American. Roughly 70 percent of the defendants were represented by attorneys in the Public Defender's Office.

After a preliminary hearing in the municipal courts, defendants were arraigned in the master calendar department of the Superior Court. Almost all the defendants pled not guilty at this arraignment, and the presiding judge assigned each a date and a courtroom for trial. There were twenty-six trial departments. Associated with each one was a judge, two or three deputy district attorneys (hereafter, DAs), a clerk, reporter, and bailiff. Also, several deputy public defenders (hereafter, PDs) usually had settings for cases in the same courtroom. Thus, each courtroom took on its own character with the daily interaction of a small group of people. Defense and prosecuting attorneys did not tend to socialize with each other outside of court, however. For example, at the noon recess, the attorneys generally went to their respective offices (DA or PD) to meet colleagues for lunch. Attorneys shared a great deal of information and folk wisdom this way on the actions of other attorneys and on the behavior of judges in other trial departments.

Research for this study began in July 1970 with almost daily observation in court, listening to and talking with attorneys, judges, and court staff. In each trial department, I would observe the court proceedings (and frequently the discussions in hallways and in judges' chambers), and then question participants on particular dispositions that had occurred. Later, in interviews, I asked attorneys and judges about more general patterns and strategies involved in settling cases. Fieldwork continued through June 1971, with a total of five months of observation in court, interviews with numerous participants, analysis of case files, and the collection of some statistical data.

GENERAL PATTERN OF CASE DISPOSITION

For most defendants, about two months elapsed between arraignment in the master calendar department and the date set for trial. During that period, pretrial motions would be heard (for example, motions to quash the information or to suppress evidence). These motions occurred in an estimated 20 percent of the cases and were generally independent of any plea negotiations. If successful, the case would be dismissed; if not, the defense attorney would discuss with his client the alternatives for disposition. The frequency of different methods of disposition in 1970 is summarized below (Bureau of Criminal Statistics 1970:12):

47.6%	Guilty plea
32.3%	Trial by "submission on the transcript"
8.0%	Court trial
3.6%	Jury trial
8.5%	Dismissal (following a pretrial motion or "in the interests of justice")
100.0%	(31,571 defendants in Los Angeles County)

Only the full court or jury trial can really be considered adversary proceedings. Trial by "submission on the transcript" (SOT) frequently operates as a slow plea of guilty. The SOT proceeding, while authorized for all of California, rarely occurs outside of Los Angeles. By this method of disposition, the defendant submits the transcript of his preliminary hearing (with additional evidence or argument if desired) to the trial judge for final adjudication. Some SOT trials are used in place of a dismissal, as it is known to all parties beforehand that the judge will find the defendant not guilty. In other cases, SOT is a semi-adversary proceeding where the defendant concedes certain points but wishes to contest others, thus argument is focused only on the issues in conflict. But in general, SOT substitutes for a plea of guilty and often involves the same kinds of bargains as to charge and sentence as in a guilty plea. For example, the defendant may be found guilty of a lesser offense, or of only one of several offenses charged against him. Or, the judge may commit himself, formally or informally, on what the sentence is likely to be. . . .

There are various possible sentences for convicted defendants. If a defendant is sent to state prison, then the actual length of his prison term is determined by the Adult Authority, within a range set by law. But most of the other options are set entirely by the trial judge. For defendants convicted in 1970, the distribution of sentences was as follows (Bureau of Criminal Statistics, 1970:5):

6%	State prison
70%	Probation (about one-third of these also with jail time)
15%	County jail
9%	Other commitments (fine, California Youth Authority, California Rehabilitation Center and Department of Mental Hygiene)
100%	(25,642 convicted defendants in Los Angeles County)

Much of the information for the sentencing decision comes from the "probation report," a presentence investigation prepared by an officer of the probation department. The report includes a summary of the defendant's record, background, and the circumstances of the offense, along with a recommendation on the advisability of probation. Most judges tended to follow these recommendations and, to the extent that they did not, it was generally the judges (often as a result of a plea bargain) who were more lenient than the probation officers. . . .

PUBLIC DEFENDERS

The Norm

There was a consensus among most PDs as to which cases "ought" to be tried and which "ought" to be settled without trial. This view was based upon predictions of case outcomes, in terms of the chances of acquittal and the probable sentence if convicted. In making these predictions, PDs investigated their client's version of what happened, the arrest report made by police, the transcript of the preliminary hearing, testimony of possible witnesses, any physical evidence, and other pertinent information. There was a staff of investigators for attorneys in the public defender's office to help check out evidence and interview witnesses, and the PDs themselves had one day a week with no cases assigned to allow them time for investigation in the field. The PDs then evaluated all of the strengths and weaknesses in each case against perceived judge and jury behavior on the issue of reasonable doubt. PDs referred to cases with a very high chance of conviction as "dead bang" cases—that is, cases with very strong evidence against the defendant and no credible or consistent explanation by the defendant for innocence. "Reasonable doubt" cases, on the other hand, were those with limited or conflicting evidence and some plausible defense. They were essentially of two kinds. In one type of "reasonable doubt" case, the doubt centered on the degree of the defendant's involvement in the crime or on the gravity of the offense; defense attorneys considered these cases to be "overfiled," and while there was a chance of acquittal on the original charge, there was a high likelihood of conviction on a lesser offense. In the other type of "reasonable doubt" case, the doubt arose from insufficient evidence either to clearly connect the defendant with the crime or to prove that any crime had been committed; in these cases, there was a good chance of complete acquittal.

Few cases in court were perceived as this latter type of "reasonable doubt" case (with a good chance of complete acquittal). The majority were "dead bang" or overfiled "reasonable doubt" cases. As one PD commented:

> The fact is that the doctrine of reasonable doubt is not useful anymore. In most cases, there's hardly any doubt at all. In fact, most of the cases we win at trial are because of sloppy prosecution.

And another PD explained:

> Most of the cases we get are pretty hopeless—really not much chance of acquittal. But often the defendant realizes that too. The important thing to

> understand is that a "win" for the defense does not necessarily mean that the defendant walks home free. Instead a "win" to a burglary accused may mean petty theft with six months suspended. Or a "win" to a defendant with a long prior record may mean a year in county jail—which is the maximum time for a misdemeanor but could be a terrific break for that particular defendant.

Thus, not only did PDs evaluate cases for the legal sufficiency of the evidence, but they also evaluated cases according to the sentencing alternatives. In view of current patterns of sentencing, PDs considered the alleged offense as well as their client's background and prior record in order to determine how "serious"the case was.

A "serious" case was one with a high probability of a harsh sentence, such as state prison. Either a bad criminal record for a defendant or a severe offense identified a case as "serious." To determine whether a case was "serious" or "light," PDs considered all of the criteria used in sentencing, such as the defendant's background (age, family, employment, and so on) and the circumstances of the offense. "Light" cases were those with no real possibility of a state prison sentence, and a good chance of a sentence of probation and a misdemeanor level of conviction.

The most important features of a case for constructing a disposition strategy were the strength of the prosecution's case and the seriousness of the case, in terms of the likely sentence on conviction. The terms presented above, "dead bang" versus "reasonable doubt" and "serious" versus "light" cases, are described each as dichotomous categories, but clearly strength and seriousness are continua and some cases fall in between the extremes. Nevertheless, these categories were used by the PDs as they talked about their cases, and they are useful analytical devices for explaining the processes of case disposition. Figure 1 illustrates how the categories of strength and seriousness interacted to produce trial or nontrial dispositions.

In "light" cases which were either "dead bang" or with "reasonable doubt" of the degree of the defendant's involvement in the crime, generally a nontrial disposition was chosen—either a guilty plea or SOT. There was little explicit bargaining accompanying most of these dispositions, as specific outcomes were fairly well known and predictable. That is, it was known that the DA would get some type of conviction (whether on the original charge or on a lesser charge), and since the cases were "light," the defendant would get a lenient sentence. Further, both parties knew the kinds of charge reductions and dismissals routinely permitted according to DA office policies. If the judge hearing the case would not "chamberize" (indicate to defense counsel in chambers what the likely sentence would be), then the PD (with the approval of the DA) could have the case transferred to a "short-cause" court. There were two short-cause courts among the twenty-six trial departments; they were designed to handle only guilty pleas or SOT trials which would last less than an hour. Judges

		Seriousness of case (prediction of severity of sentence)		
		"Light" case	*"Serious" case*	
			If good offer from DA	If bad offer from DA
Strength of prosecution's case (prediction of conviction or acquittal)	*"Dead bang" case*	Negotiated disposition (implicit bargaining)	Negotiated disposition (explicit bargaining)	Trial
	"Reasonable doubt" case — Chance of conviction on lesser charge	Negotiated disposition (implicit bargaining)	Negotiated disposition (explicit bargaining—easier to obtain good offer here than above)	Trial
	"Reasonable doubt" case — Chance of complete acquittal	Indeterminate	Negotiated disposition (explicit bargaining)	Indeterminate

Figure 1 Recommendations by defense attorneys on method of disposition as a function of strength of prosecution's case, seriousness of case, and defense attorney's perception of DA's offer

who would chamberize and who were known to be lenient sentencers were generally assigned to the short-cause departments, thus facilitating nontrial dispositions. Typical "light, dead bang" cases would include bookmaking, forgery and bad check cases, and possession of marijuana or pills. A typical "light" case which was seen as overfiled might be a minor burglary (which would be reduced to petty theft) or auto theft (which would be reduced to joyriding).

In "light" cases which were weak because there was reasonable doubt that the defendant was guilty of *any* offense, PDs would seek a complete acquittal, either by explicit bargaining or by trial. Depending upon his perception of the DA handling the case, the PD might try to persuade the DA to dismiss the charge or to talk with the judge to arrange an SOT trial for not guilty. But many DAs were not perceived as very receptive to such a suggestion for acquittal, and so the PD would go directly for adversary trial disposition. He would choose between court and jury trial depending on the type of case and the judge in the court where the case was set. There were few or no sentencing risks involved in a trial disposition on a "light" case, as the sentence even after trial would probably be quite lenient. An example of this type of case would be a defendant with little or no record charged with possession of marijuana, auto theft, or drunk driving, who had a credible explanation in his defense.

"Serious" cases presented more problems for constructing a defense strategy because both DAs and judges hesitated to exercise discretion in cases involving grave offenses or defendants with bad records. In cases of this type where there was a good chance of conviction on the original charge ("dead bang") or on a lesser charge, PDs would bargain for leniency and try to settle the case by guilty plea or SOT. After explicit bargaining, the PDs would recommend a negotiated disposition or a trial disposition depending upon their perception of the final offer. In the overfiled "reasonable doubt" cases, the PDs were frequently successful in their bargaining because they could point to the weak points in the prosecution's case. In the "dead bang" cases the bargaining was more difficult; here, any mitigating factors in the offense or in the defendant's background were emphasized to show that this was "not really a state prison case." But where a favorable bargain could not be obtained, the case would be settled by trial since "the defendant's got nothing to lose—he'd go to the joint anyway." One judge commented:

> If the defendant did what he did and he's going to prison for it anyway—particularly if it's a heinous offense—then he's not going to get any consideration from me or the probation department. In that case, his lawyer will tell him that he can't do anything for him, so he might as well go to trial, and take his chances on an acquittal.

Typical cases which are likely to go to trial because "there is no room for negotiation" included (the judge continued):

> Armed robbery—that gets five to life. Forcible rape. First-degree burglary with maybe some injuries involved. Murder cases. Some child molestation cases.

In "serious" cases where there was "reasonable doubt" that the defendant was guilty of any offense, the disposition choice was difficult. Here the sentencing risks were high but the possible gain, complete acquittal, was considerable. The sentencing risks were high since, if the defendant was convicted as charged, the judge might be statutorily restricted from granting a misdemeanor sentence or probation (because of the gravity of the offense or the defendant's prior record). In a bargained disposition to a lesser charge (or if the DA agreed to offer no evidence on any prior felony convictions), then the judge would be able (and was perceived to be more willing) to use his discretion for a lenient sentence. The PD's perception of the value of a DA's offer in cases of this type depended not only on considerations of sentence and charge, but also on whether he believed his client was in fact guilty of the offense. If the defendant admitted his guilt to his attorney, then the PD would probably recommend a negotiated disposition because of the high sentencing risks of trial. But what if the defendant solidly maintained his innocence, in addition to having a chance of acquittal based on the evidence? Then any offer of a lenient sentence was bad, and yet the sentencing risks of trial were high, and a negotiated dismissal or SOT for not guilty was nearly impossible to obtain because of the seriousness of the case. The PD's final recommendation on disposition method was indeterminate because it depended so heavily on the attorney-client interaction and specific characteristics of the case. Frequently the PDs would recommend trial in spite of the risks, but they were also likely to leave the decision more to their clients with no recommendation. Interestingly, very few cases in this category (of "serious" with a chance of complete acquittal) were observed. Perhaps because they did present the most serious questions on the propriety of plea bargaining, there was a tendency for attorneys to redefine cases of this type—that is, to describe them as "dead bang" instead of "reasonable doubt"— or to minimize the seriousness of the case. Or, perhaps earlier pretrial screening had diverted these cases so that they didn't reach the trial stage.

These patterns of case disposition correspond roughly to the ways in which most PDs routinely recommended trial or nontrial disposition. Certainly PDs varied in their judgments and their predictions, so that one attorney might evaluate his client's chances differently than another would have. Or, what is a "good" bargain to one PD might not be to his colleague. But in general there was a consensus on how to evaluate cases and choose the best method for disposition. Most PDs then strongly encouraged their clients to accept the recommended disposition method. However, a significant subgroup of PDs (described in the next section on "The Mavericks") felt that they should do "just what their client wants to do" rather than "what's best for their client." Obviously *all* PDs tried to do both in theory, but the reality of disposition choice forced them to lean to one role or another. Thus, most PDs would urge a negotiated disposition if it appeared to be in their client's best interest. Three different PDs expressed this view as follows (italics added in each comment):

> There's too much risk involved to take [some of] these cases to trial. It makes whores out of us. *We'd like to do jury trials. But that's not what's best for our clients.*

> I try to tell them [clients] what all the possibilities are, the different alternatives for disposition. I try to avoid telling clients what to do. I don't overrule them. . . . *Well, sometimes I go down on them a little harder. You've got to for their own good.*

> Yeah, I'll twist arms. They [some other PDs] kid that it's because I'm lazy. The others in the office, they'll say "Fuck him. Give him his jury trial if he wants it." But I won't do that. I think *it's in my clients' interests for me to get them the best deal that I can. . . . That's what I'm here for.* I've had some nasty, arrogant people that I've defended. "Society" hasn't been helped by what I've done. But I figure that's not my problem. *My job is to do what I can for my client. If you've got a bad case and it's a loser, then it's not worth the risks of trial. You've gotta come down hard on a client sometimes.*

The Mavericks

Skolnick (1967:65) distinguished between two normative meanings of the notion that an attorney "represents" a client: first, "that he accepts his client's view of the strategy of the case" and offers advice on how to implement that strategy; and second, "that the attorney is responsible both for strategy and tactics." Skolnick found that defense attorneys typically accepted the latter definition. As indicated above, most PDs in this study also accepted that view of the proper role of defense attorney. However, between four and seven PDs (out of the fifty in felony trials) were designated by their fellow PDs and by DAs as being "mavericks." These PDs were generally more trial-minded and more willing to accept their client's view on the strategy for case disposition.

For example, one PD described a rape case for trial that he had had transferred from department 64 to department 107, since department 64 was too congested to handle a jury trial. This was an unusual move, because Judge O'Neill (in department 64) was considered to be the best judge (from defense point of view) on issues of reasonable doubt. When asked why he didn't waive jury and have a court trial before Judge O'Neill, the PD replied:

> I would have. And O'Neill is probably the only judge that I would have waived jury before, judging by what the other PDs say about him. But my client wouldn't waive jury. . . . You see, the defendants don't understand the finesse of court-shopping, or the risks there are with different judges, etc. They just get some bullheaded notion and stick to it.

I then asked the PD, "Don't you try to explain the situation to them and talk them into what you think is best for them?" He answered:

> No. *And I'm kind of a maverick that way.* Among the people in our office, I'm certainly different. I can't talk to these clients—it's frustrating and you never really do get through to them. So if they want their jury trial, then okay, I'll give it to them. I prefer to deal with the people of the court—*I'd rather talk and argue my case with reasonable people in court, instead of arguing with my clients.* Particularly with a state prison case. . . . Remember in talking to me that I'm a maverick. I take probably more cases to jury trials than any of the other deputies. Well, except maybe for George Birch, Ted Peterson, and Mark Rothenberg. They do a lot of jury trials too. . . .
>
> My position is, *"I don't insist that a defendant do anything other than what he wants to do."* It's just like if a patient goes to a doctor and the doctor thinks maybe he should operate, but the patient doesn't want him to. Then the doctor should not operate. If the patient were to die from that operation, it should be the result of the patient's choice, not the doctor's. It's the same thing with lawyers. The client must ultimately be the one to consent to a disposition or to trial. *With many cases, I cannot say with absolute certainty that it would go one way or the other.* And since I cannot, I don't want to try to convince my client that one way is definitely preferable. I don't want a guy in state prison thinking that he was copped out by his attorney. [Emphasis added.]

Most of the other PDs could not say "with absolute certainty" what the outcome of a case would be at trial. But they were more willing than the "mavericks" to play the game of predicting the costs and benefits of trial and to impress upon their clients the importance of those predictions. The "maverick" PDs also settled cases through bargaining, but handled a much larger proportion of their cases at full trial than did their colleagues. It did not appear that the bargains arranged by "maverick" PDs were any better or worse than deals arranged by others. Several of the "mavericks" were among the more senior members of the PD's office. This meant they often were assigned tougher, more "serious" cases than their junior colleagues, and hence bargains were harder to obtain. For example, one DA described plea discussions in his court between two PDs, Bill Hirsch and Mark Rothenberg, and the other DA:

> Rothenberg makes such a big deal out of everything. He's so different from Bill. Bill comes in and sits down with Herb (the other DA) and in ten minutes, they're all disposed of—all four cases. Rothenberg had just *one* case this morning and he's still yelling about it. *Although Bill does get the more dealable cases. He doesn't have as much seniority as Rothenberg.* [Emphasis added.]

The only real sanction against the "mavericks" is that their clients may be hurt on sentencing because of the risks taken at trial. In one case, the defendant was charged with grand theft auto and receiving stolen property. The offenses were considered very minor, but the defendant (age twenty-six, in custody, Mexican-American) had a record which included, among other charges, two misdemeanor convictions for burglary, one for forgery, and a prior felony conviction for robbery (for which he did two years in prison). Riley, a "maverick" PD, took the case to jury trial and the defendant was convicted of grand theft auto, the more serious of the two counts. The main defense raised was the defendant's denial of knowledge that the car was stolen, but his prior convictions were brought out on cross-examination to somewhat discredit his testimony. After the trial, the DA complained:

> Riley is incompetent. He doesn't know how to evaluate a case realistically. . . . And his client will suffer.

I asked the DA, "Will he be sentenced more severely?" The DA answered:

> Sure, he probably will. He got on the stand and perjured himself by making up that story. So the judge isn't going to think much of him. . . . Riley's so bad. We offered to let him plead to receiving stolen property as a misdemeanor . . . and to strike the prior. He'd probably be out of custody by now. Well, not exactly. He'd have to wait the three weeks for the probation report. And then he'd get time served [which was four months] or maybe ten days more. But now he'll be sentenced on GTA [grand theft auto] with a prior. He's going to face a lot more.

But actually in the above case it is difficult to say if the defendant really was hurt by having an attorney who was "not realistic." The probation report included a statement from the defendant's parole officer which said that the defendant's behavior on parole was "marginal to fair," and that he would probably be returned to prison on *any* new conviction as a violation of parole. In this light, the PD's behavior was more "realistic" and the DA's offer was not so attractive. The problem is that, especially with "serious" cases, one cannot ever say for certain "what the punishment would have been if. . . ." Outcomes are shaped by predictions and interactions of many participants, some of whom may not be directly involved in the case at hand (such as the parole officer in this case). What does emerge, however, is that the "mavericks," in comparison to the other PDs, seemed to care much less about sentence predictions, preferring to concentrate on argument over the facts and their legal implications. One of the maverick PDs said, at the end of his interview:

> I can't get emotional about these guys [clients]. They're nuts. They've got to be to do the things they do. *It doesn't matter really what you do for them. They keep coming back.* There are only a very few that you can really help.

When asked "Doesn't that depress you? How can you keep going?" The PD replied:

> I enjoy my work. It's fun. We've got a great office here with a good competitive spirit.

And thus, the "mavericks" defined themselves more as "real lawyers" engaged in the adversary process, instead of being client advocates in the business of sentencing.

COMPARISON OF PRIVATE ATTORNEYS WITH PUBLIC DEFENDERS

Several studies have found that private defense attorneys settle fewer of their cases by guilty plea than do public defenders (see, for example, Silverstein 1965; Sudnow 1965; Oaks and Lehman 1968). This finding has variously been explained by differences in the quality and motivation of the attorneys and by differences in the characteristics of their clients. Skolnick (1967), on the other hand, found that most private attorneys were just as likely to bargain for guilty pleas as the public defenders, and further, that five of the six leading private defenders in the county he studied reported that they settled a greater percentage of their cases by pleas of guilty than did the public defenders. Skolnick also warned of the impossibility of making any systematic comparison between the private attorney and the public defender because of the fact that clients are *assigned* to the public defender, rather than personally selected by him. This leads to the problem of "client-control," which "is experienced by all defense attorneys, but is exaggerated in relations between the public defender and his client" (Skolnick 1967: 65). . . .

There was a group of private attorneys who handled a high volume of criminal cases and who were regularly seen in the Central District of the Superior Court. And then there were the "nonregulars"—attorneys who handled primarily civil cases, or a general practice, or who were just beginning their law practice. Informal relationships and mutual trust were important to working out case dispositions, and so, as one DA put it,

> The best thing for a defense attorney is that he mix well with the criminal law community. He shouldn't be a lone wolf or a shyster. He should be able to walk into the DA's office or the city attorney's office and he'd have some friends there. He should be able to walk into courtrooms and the clerks would know him by first name. He's got to be willing to become a part of the community he's working in. Then he can do a lot for his client.

A comment heard several times was, "The best private attorneys are the ex-DAs and ex-PDs." Naturally, those were the attorneys who had been part of that crucial "criminal law community," as well as having had extensive experience with criminal law.

In general, the regular private defense attorneys used the same factors as the PDs to recommend the best method for case disposition. Thus, trial or nontrial disposition depended upon predictions of case outcomes, according to the strength of the prosecution's case and the seriousness of the case (see Figure 1). One very old, experienced private attorney described these two factors used in settling cases:

> Let me put it to you this way: What is our job as a criminal lawyer in most instances? Number one is . . . no kidding, we know the man's done it, or we feel he's done it, he may deny it, but the question is: *Can they prove it?* The next thing is: *Can we mitigate it?* Of course you can always find something good to say about the guy—to mitigate it. Those are the two things that are important, and that's what you do. [Emphasis added.]

But while these same factors were relevant to determining case disposition for private attorneys, the frequency of cases settled by full trial was estimated by prosecuting and defense attorneys to be *less* for private attorneys than for PDs. Court participants suggested two reasons for this: financial considerations for private attorneys and the problem of client-control for PDs.

Many private attorneys set the same fee for handling a case, whether it was settled by trial or by guilty plea or SOT. So, because of the time involved with a trial, especially a jury trial, there was a financial incentive for private attorneys to settle cases by nontrial means. The following comments illustrate this view:

PD: Private attorneys have much fewer trials than the PDs, because they must wait for Witness Green.

DA: PDs take many more cases to jury trial than do private attorneys, because they're the only ones who can afford to. A private attorney can usually only lose money because of the time involved.

Said one private attorney who had been practicing criminal law for four years (the first two years in association with a high-volume criminal attorney):

> The problem is private attorneys can't afford to go to trial too much really. Like I set two fees—one for [nontrial] disposition and the other for trial. And I tell my client the risks of trial. But most attorneys won't do that. Like the other guy I used to work with. He'd ask a flat fee. . . . That wasn't right.

Some attorneys did set separate fees according to the method of disposition, and then cases might be settled by trial for clients who could afford the high fee. But it should be noted that most of the private attorney clients in this downtown court could not afford these trial fees. One probation officer (with fourteen years experience) noted that PDs took more cases to trial than private attorneys, then added:

> When some of these private attorneys do go to trial, it's just for the money they'll get. They know their client doesn't have a chance.

Hence, while private attorneys (as did the PDs) examined the strength and seriousness of a case to determine the best method for disposition, the final choice of the private attorneys was usually determined, in addition, by financial considerations.

Defense and prosecuting attorneys suggested a second reason for the greater frequency of trial dispositions by PDs than by private attorneys. This reason was expressed by one DA as follows:

> When a man pays money to hire an attorney, he's more likely to listen to his advice. After all, this is what he's paying for. While the PD's clients won't even listen to them sometimes. So if the private attorney thinks a [nontrial] disposition would be better, he can talk to his client like a Dutch uncle. He can do a little arm twisting. But the PDs can't do that. They have to do what the defendant wants even if they don't think it's in his best interest.

As noted earlier, the PDs may "twist arms," but only to a point. Some cases went to trial as a result of disagreement between a PD and his client. But a private attorney had sanctions available to make his client accept his advice on case disposition; he could threaten to withdraw from the case, or he could set an extremely high fee for trial disposition. Note that most private attorneys (like most PDs) believed that their role as defense attorney meant that *they* should suggest the proper strategy for settling a case, rather than implementing the strategy suggested by their client. A private attorney described this aspect of the lawyer-client relationship using an analogy to the doctor-patient relationship. Interestingly, this is the same analogy used by a "maverick" PD quoted earlier, but with an opposite conclusion:

> I think this way. . . . If I go to my doctor, first of all I go to him because I have faith in him. If he tells me to take the blue pill, I guess I'll take that blue pill. It might kill me, but I'm gonna take that blue pill. . . . So when a client starts telling you what to do, he's a dummy. The poor PDs, they get most of these wise guys—it never dawns on them that if they were so smart, maybe they wouldn't have to have a PD. Not that there's anything wrong with the PD. . . . I'll say on record, the PD office does a good job.

While most of the regular criminal attorneys settled a very high percentage of their cases without trial, some of them, like the "maverick" PDs, were more trial-minded. These few lawyers were characterized as either respected, capable trial lawyers or incompetent obstructions. It was not clear whether these more trial-oriented lawyers were sanctioned in any way by DAs or judges, because of the large number of different courtrooms involved and the infrequency with which I encountered them. In addition, there were the "nonregular" attorneys who appeared only occasionally in court and were inexperienced with criminal law, often coming from primarily civil law practices. One DA described "the nonregulars—some just bumble around. Often they cooperate and we help them out. Some you trust and others you don't." Unfortunately, again because of the size of the court system studied, these attorneys cannot be systematically described with respect to their attitudes and behavior on choosing disposition methods.

Finally, some defendants were represented by private attorneys who were appointed and paid on an hourly basis by the court. These court appointments were authorized by Section 987a of the Penal Code for indigent defendants who, for one reason or other, could not be represented by the PD. Usually this occurred in multidefendant cases, where there was a conflict of interest if the PD were to represent both defendants in the case. In 1966, approximately 2 percent of the defendants in the county were represented by court-appointed attorneys (Smith and Wendell 1968). The figure has increased slightly since then, and it would be somewhat higher for the Central District since there were more indigent defendants there than in the county as a whole. One PD characterized these 987a attorneys as follows:

> 987a attorneys run the gamut completely from new guys just starting out in practice to ex-PDs or DAs with a great deal of expertise who are just starting to build a criminal practice of their own. Court appointments don't pay as well as fees for most private attorneys with big practices. So it's often for guys just starting out. The balance are known to the judge and he chooses them. . . . You don't see the most common criminal lawyers seeking 987a appointments. . . . They have a big criminal practice already. So they wouldn't need the 987a work—unless they're right there in court and do it as a favor to the judge.

While some attorneys saw no particular difference in the choice of disposition method by court-appointed attorneys, a few indicated that these attorneys were more likely to take cases to trial. For example, one DA commented:

> Some 987a attorneys will take cases to trial because they are getting paid by the court for their time. But the cases don't warrant a trial. Some attorneys don't do this, but others do. Even where their client wants to plead, they'll go to trial. Or, where it is a case that clearly should be disposed of, they'll go to trial for the money.

However, court-appointed attorneys who blatantly took cases to trial just "for the money" could risk not being appointed in the future. The presiding judge who made the appointments had a list of attorneys eligible for 987a work, and he said that he crossed off the names of people he knew to be "incompetent, dishonest, or just bad attorneys. . . ."

CONCLUSION

The cooperative role for defense was clearly the dominant one in the court studied. While financial incentives helped to dictate this role for private defense attorneys, for them and certainly for most of the public defenders this role was seen to be in the best interests of their clients. And most defendants tended to accept, at least formally, their attorney's view on the best strategy for case disposition. But the cooperative role did not prescribe plea bargaining for every case. Adversary trial proceedings were chosen in principally two situations. A DA summarized these situations as follows:

> Cases for full trial . . . let's see. . . . The weaker a case is from our standpoint, the more likely it will be tried. There the defendant thinks he can walk away from it. Rather than take a disposition, he'll try to beat it altogether. Another kind of case that's often tried is the really hopeless case. There we have an overwhelmingly strong case and it's a bad, very serious case where the defendant has a long record. So he'll go to state prison anyway. He's got nothing to lose by trying it.

In terms of the framework presented earlier, these cases which called for full trial were the "reasonable doubt" cases with a chance of complete acquittal, and the "serious, dead bang" case where a lenient sentence bargain could not be obtained. According to this prevailing defense role, the most effective way a defense attorney could represent his client was to seek an acquittal where there was a predictable chance of it, but where there was not (and these were most of the cases), then the attorney should seek the disposition which minimizes the sentence for his client. Further, this defense role prescribed that the attorney should represent his client by doing what was best for him, rather than simply implementing what the client wanted.

But there were also "outsiders" in the courtroom; defense attorneys and defendants who followed more closely the traditional adversary role. The "maverick" public defenders, their few counterparts among private attorneys, and some of the court-appointed attorneys (who had financial incentives to go to trial) represented clients by settling cases more the way their clients wanted, which frequently called for full trial. The negative consequences of this adversarial posture occurred primarily with sentencing, particularly for "serious" cases which were taken to trial. But these attorneys accepted the consequences because, within the adversary tradition, "effectiveness" was evaluated according to how well the attorney argued on behalf of his client's innocence, not according to how well he argued his client's potential for rehabilitation. "Winning" a case for the adversary role meant working vigorously for an acquittal; "winning" a case for the cooperative role meant obtaining the most lenient sentence for clients who were factually guilty.

Finally, some defendants were "outsiders" because they were more interested in fighting for an acquittal than they were interested in minimizing their penal "time," regardless of how good their chances looked for an acquittal. Defendants who were more experienced with probation officers and parole boards may have distrusted how those authorities would exercise their discretion after the plea-bargaining process was over. And there was some evidence to indicate that black defendants were more likely to choose this adversarial role.

While the cooperative defense posture may secure more lenient treatment for offenders, the adversary posture may secure a higher proportion of acquittals but with harsher treatment for those convicted. With increasing emphasis on the importance of defense counsel in criminal proceedings it is necessary to consider by what criteria the quality of defense representation should be evaluated. Any attempt to prescribe these criteria leads ultimately to questions about the function of the criminal courts. For if defense counsel are necessary to protect the rights of accused persons in court, it must be made clear what the tasks of the court are.

Traditionally the primary task of the criminal court was to ascertain facts in dispute and to determine their legal significance, thus deciding the guilt or innocence of accused persons. Theoretical models of the criminal process, such as Packer's (1968) Crime Control model (which views the process as an assembly line) or the Due Process model (which depicts an obstacle course), essentially end their concern with defendants at the point of conviction or acquittal. But these models are not adequate to explain the dynamics of what actually is occurring in court, nor are they useful to guide defense attorneys who sincerely want to improve the quality of representation for criminal defendants. For in the vast majority of cases the conflict between the accused and the state is not over the question of guilt or innocence, but it is over the question of what punishment will be imposed on them.

The question of punishment has assumed much larger proportions with the emphasis upon individual rehabilitation as a guide to sentencing. Courts are not only supposed to "sort" defendants into categories of convicted and acquitted, but they are also charged with "sorting" convicted offenders according to their prospects for rehabilitation. Thus one convicted burglar goes to state prison, another to county jail, and a third walks home free on probation. And this decision is expressly made according to individual personal characteristics of offenders, characteristics which are irrelevant to the decision on guilt or innocence. The dilemma for the defense attorney is how can he best defend his client when both of these sorting processes occur simultaneously, as they may in the decision on whether to plead guilty or go to trial. And the dilemma is intensified by the fact that frequently defendants, as part of the general public, are unaware of dimensions of the sentencing decision and its interactions with the issue of guilt or innocence.

In order to improve the quality of defense representation, we must decide what that job means, and that calls for a thorough reevaluation of the functions of criminal courts. The public, not the individual interactions within the court community, ought to decide what should be done with the task of sentencing. As Wilson (1973: 9) has written:

> Indeed there has been very little serious public discussion of what we even mean by a "good" or a "bad" sentence. And only by deciding that question can we begin to think seriously about what other reforms are necessary in the criminal courts.

REFERENCES

ALSCHULER, A. (1968) "The prosecutor's role in plea bargaining." *University of Chicago Law Review* 36:50.

BLUMBERG, A. S. (1967a) *Criminal Justice.* Chicago: Quadrangle.

———(1967b) "The practice of law as a confidence game: organizational co-optation of a profession." *Law and Society Review* 1:15.

BUREAU OF CRIMINAL STATISTICS (1969) *Crime and Delinquency in California.* Sacramento: State of California, Department of Justice, Division of Law Enforcement.

———(1970) *Felony Defendants Disposed of in California Courts: Reference Tables.* Sacramento: State of California, Department of Justice, Division of Law Enforcement.

COLE, G. (1970) "The decision to prosecute." *Law and Society Review* 7:331.

FEELEY, M. M. (1973) "Two models of the criminal justice system: an organizational perspective." *Law and Society Review* 7:407.

GREENWOOD, P. W., et al. (1973) *Prosecution of Adult Felony Defendants in Los Angeles County: A Policy Perspective.* Santa Monica, Calif.: Rand Corporation.

HUITT, R. K. (1961) "The outsider in the Senate: an alternative role." *American Political Science Review* 55:566.

MATHER, L. M. (1972) "To Plead Guilty or Go to Trial?" Paper presented at the Annual Meeting of the American Political Science Association, Washington, D.C.

MILESKI, M. (1971) "Courtroom encounters: an observation study of a lower criminal court." *Law and Society Review* 5:473.

NEWMAN, D. J. (1956) "Pleading guilty for considerations: a study of bargain justice." *Journal of Criminal Law, Criminology and Police Science* 46:780.

———(1966) *Conviction: The Determination of Guilt or Innocence Without Trial.* Boston: Little, Brown.

OAKS, D. H., and W. LEHMAN (1968) *A Criminal Justice System and the Indigent.* Chicago: University of Chicago Press.

PACKER, H. (1968) *The Limits of the Criminal Sanction.* Stanford, Calif.: Stanford University Press.

SILVERSTEIN, L. (1965) *Defense of the Poor in Criminal Cases in American State Courts.* Chicago: American Bar Foundation.

SKOLNICK, J. (1967) "Social control in the adversary system." *Journal of Conflict Resolution* 11:51.

SMITH, G. W., and M. A. WENDELL (1968) "Public defenders and private attorneys: a comparison of cases." *The Legal Aid Briefcase* 27:95.

SUDNOW, D. (1965) "Normal crimes: sociological features of the Penal Code in a Public Defender Office." *Social Problems* 12:255.

WAHLKE, J. C., H. EULAU, W. BUCHANAN, and L. C. FERGUSON (1962) *The Legislative System: Explorations in Legislative Behavior.* New York: John Wiley.

WILSON, J. Q. (1973) "If every criminal *knew* he would be punished if caught. . . ." *New York Times Magazine* 9 (January 28).

PART FIVE

COURTS

Conditions in the lower criminal courts are shocking to observers. Most city courtrooms have little of the quiet dignity one expects to see when decisions concerning individual freedom and justice are being made. The scene is usually one of noise and confusion as attorneys, police, and prosecutors mill around conversing with one another and making bargains to keep the assembly line of the criminal justice process in operation. One might see a judge accepting guilty pleas and imposing sentences at a rapid pace, going through the litany of procedure like a bored priest. It is not surprising that visitors are shocked and that first offenders are confused by what they see.

The courts, like other parts of the justice system, function under conditions of mass production, congestion, and limited resources. Even in the courts, the interests of the organization and of the principal actors often take precedence over the claims of justice. The mass production of judicial decisions is accomplished because the street-level bureaucrats in the system work on the basis of three assumptions. The first is that only people for whom there is a high probability of guilt will be brought before the courts; doubtful cases will be filtered out of the system by the police and the prosecution. Second, the vast majority of defendants will plead guilty. In Los Angeles, Superior Court Judge Nutter estimated that an increase of only 5 percent in not-guilty pleas in the arraignment and master calendar courts "would result in a flooding of the trial courts and a breakdown of the entire system." Third, those charged with minor offenses will be processed en masse. This usually means that all the defendants charged with a particular offense will be herded before the bench, that the citation will be read by the clerk, and that sentences will be summarily pronounced by the judge.

It is tempting to believe that adding more judges and constructing new facilities will relieve courtroom overload, but other factors contribute to the situation—for example, poor management, the rise in the amount of crime, and the presence of lawyers. Some argue that the procedural requirements laid down by the U.S. Supreme Court have lengthened the processing time, yet observers point out that defendants are typically informed en masse of their rights by a droning bailiff. In addition, most defendants actually waive their right to a trial, and many do not even want the services of an attorney.

The problem of court congestion has become widely recognized during the past decade. Observers both inside and outside of government have deplored the fact that defendants in criminal cases often wait in jail for months before they come to trial. More important conditions in the criminal courts are the filtering effect, the administrative determination of guilt, and the exchange relationships that characterize the system. As long as the system is able to function in accordance with the needs of the players, the additional judges and courtrooms demanded by reformers will not bring about a shift to due process values.

JUDGING

Of the many actors in the criminal justice process, judges are perceived as having the greatest amount of leverage and influence. Decisions made by the police, defense attorneys, and prosecutors are greatly affected by the rulings and sentencing practices of judges. Although we tend to think of judges primarily in connection with trials, their work is much more varied; they are a continuous presence throughout the range of activities leading to disposition of a case. Signing warrants, fixing bail, arraigning defendants, accepting guilty pleas, scheduling cases—all are portions of the judge's work outside the formal trial.

More than any other actor in the system, the judge is expected to embody justice, making sure that due process rights are respected and that the defendant is treated fairly. The judge is expected to act inside and outside the courthouse according to well-defined role prescriptions that are designed to prevent involvement in activities that could bring the judicial office into disrepute. Yet the pressures of today's justice system often relegate the ideals associated with the judge's position to secondary status. The need for speedy disposition of cases takes priority.

In most cities the criminal court judge occupies the lowest rank in the judicial hierarchy. Neither lawyers nor laypersons accord judges the prestige that is part of the mystique usually surrounding the bench. Perhaps their status is tarnished by the defendants with whom they have to deal. Studies have shown that criminal judges tend to come from backgrounds that have lower socioeconomic characteristics than those of civil judges. Often, the jurist has assumed the bench directly from a criminal law practice before the same court and has come to the position through influence in party politics. Yet the lower-court judge is able to exercise discretion in the disposition of summary offenses without the constant supervision of higher courts. This is especially noticeable in courts of first instance, where sentencing is carried out in a hurried manner, usually without any record of the session being kept.

Popular election of judges occurs in more than half the states, with thirteen states using the partisan approach. This method has probably received the most criticism because of the belief that judgeships go only to those who have earned their robes through duty to a political party. Yet this criticism is not universal. The reformist American Judicature Society claims that political parties usually provide competent candidates and that the worst judges emerge from nonpartisan elections where the voter is not guided by the party emblem.

In many states, judgeships furnish much of the fuel for party engines. Because of the honorific and material rewards of the position, political parties can secure the energy and money of attorneys who view a judgeship as the capstone of a legal career. In addition, a certain amount of courthouse patronage may adhere to the position. Clerks, bailiffs, and secretaries—all positions that may be filled with active party workers—are appointed by the judge. Because of the hegemony of the Democratic party in such cities as New York and Chicago, selections for judicial posts are solely in the hands of political leaders. There usually are many interested candidates, and it is often charged that money is a prime factor in selecting one. In some cities a contribution to the party equal to two years' salary is the going price. More common are such approaches as making contributions to fund-raising benefits or "loans" to the party.

The nature of the road to a judgeship greatly determines the type of person who will handle the gavel and wear the robes. The political and social milieu encourages the advancement of individuals with certain attitudes and leaves others by the wayside. These factors, in turn, influence the decisions made from the bench. In most communities, the selection of judges is of minor interest to the general public. Good persons must be recruited to the bench, but the definition of *good* remains in dispute.

DECISION MAKING

What factors influence the making of decisions by prosecutors, defense attorneys, and judges during the adjudication process? Although the traditional picture of the courtroom emphasizes the adversarial posture, in reality interactions among the major actors take place within the normative context of the local legal culture. Established informal rules and practices arise within particular settings, and "the way things are done" differs from place to place. Differences between legal cultures can often explain why court processes and decisions vary even though the formal rules of criminal procedure are similar throughout the United States.

Adjudication takes place in the local legal setting, but decisions are also influenced by the fact that courtroom participants are organized as work groups. From this perspective, the reciprocal relationships of the judge, prosecutor, and defense attorney, along with those of the support cast (clerk, reporter, and bailiff), are necessary to complete the group's basic task—the disposition of cases.

Although sharing norms and goals, each member of the courtroom group occupies a specialized position and is expected to fit into the socially accepted definition of that status. Because each member has specific rights and duties, there is no exchange of roles. When the career of a lawyer takes him or her from the public defender's office to the prosecutor's office, or ultimately to the bench, he or she lives out each status as a different role in the courtroom group. Because actors are expected to conform to the role prescriptions for the positions they occupy in the group, there can be a high degree of stability in the interpersonal relations among group members. This stability allows members of the courtroom work group to become proficient at the routines associated with their roles and allows the group to develop reliable expectations about the actions of its members. In this way, the business of the courtroom proceeds in a regularized, informal manner. Members rely on many "understandings" that are never recorded but ease much of the work of the court.

In addition to these interrelationships there are ties that bind each actor to a "sponsoring organization"—units that provide the staff and the resources for the court. Thus, although the judges are the formal leaders of their own work groups, they have their own organizations that assign members to various courtrooms and enact policies that each is expected to follow. Likewise, the individual prosecutor has links to the office of the prosecuting attorney, and the defense attorney is associated with either the public defender's office or the private bar. Because of the influence of the sponsoring organizations, courtroom participants are expected to adhere to the norms and policies of these "outside" groups when they are on the courtroom stage. Judges must keep in mind the reaction of their associates to particular sentences; prosecutors may feel peer pressure to reduce charges only under specific circumstances; and public defenders may believe they are expected to ensure that a certain number of cases are processed each day. These constraints from outside the workshop influence the activities in the courtroom and may even serve to bolster the shared norms of the work group, with the effect that cohesion is increased—that is, the secrets of the proceedings must be shielded from the view of the audience.

To a significant degree, the same prosecutors, judges, and defense attorneys find themselves in contact face to face, handling similar cases month after month, with only the defendant changed. Accused persons pass through the system while the court personnel remain, carrying on their careers and organizational enterprises. Individual cases may cause tensions, but these are generally overcome because of the larger need to preserve relationships so that work-group interaction may continue in the future. The officers of the court have more in common, both in cultural values and in goals, than any one of them shares with the defendant. The major actors have been socialized by law school to the norms of the legal profession, values that have been learned "on the job" by the supporting cast. They share the technical language of the law and can use it to distinguish their roles from those of others. All share a social status with corresponding cultural values that may be different from those of the predominantly lower-class defendants being processed.

The arrangement of the actors on the courtroom stage further illustrates the close relationship of the group. Although the judge's bench is usually elevated, symbolizing authority, it faces the lawyer's table. Persons in the audience, and sometimes even the defendant, are unable to observe all the verbal and nonverbal exchanges. In some courts the attorneys for both sides sit at either end of a long table—the furniture does not define them as adversaries. Throughout the proceedings, lawyers from both sides periodically engage in muffled conversations with the judge, out of the hearing of defendant and spectators. When the judge calls the principals into the judicial chamber for private discussion, the defendant remains in the courtroom. In most settings the role of the accused is defined physically: isolated, sitting either in the "dock" or in a chair behind defense counsel. To observers, defendants are silent onlookers, persons unable to negotiate their own fate.

JURY

Although only 8 percent of criminal cases are disposed of through jury trial, the benefit of "trial by jury" is one of the most ingrained features of the American ideology. Like the exposed tip of an iceberg, the jury exerts a greater influence than the case volume might suggest. As we have noted, the potential call for a jury trial weighs in decisions to prosecute, plea bargaining, and the sentencing behavior of judges. The jury thus affects not only the formal resolution of controversies, but also the informal disposition of cases that never get to trial.

Although every member of the community should have an equal chance to be chosen for jury duty, selection methods stipulate various qualifications that exclude citizens with certain characteristics. For example, in most states jurors must be registered voters. In addition, particular occupational categories, such as doctors, lawyers, teachers, and police officers, are excluded because their professional services are needed or because of their connection to the court. Even if chosen for jury duty, a citizen may be dropped during the process of *voir dire* ("to speak the truth"). This questioning of potential jurors is designed to ensure a fair trial by excluding those who may be biased toward the issues of a specific case. If it appears that a person will be unable to be fair, he or she may be challenged for *cause* by one of the attorneys. If the judge agrees, the person will be excused from service. When an attorney is unable to give a reason that a potential juror should not sit, a *peremptory challenge* may be issued. This is often done when an attorney has a hunch that the person will be unsympathetic. The number of peremptory challenges available to defense and prosecution is limited by law, but challenges for cause depend only upon the ruling of the judge.

The value of the jury system has long been debated. Jerome Frank noted in the 1930s that "jury-made law" was a prime example of capricious and arbitrary decision making. From time to time, public interest has been aroused by this controversy. When juries in highly publicized trials reach verdicts that are in accord with community sentiment, great praise is heaped on the system; when the outcome is unpopular, the public raises questions about the value of this method of fact finding. It must be kept in mind that juries are a factor in only a small number of the decisions in the administration of criminal justice. Our due process ideals may have obscured this fact.

THE SENTENCING WILDERNESS

Among judges in Western nations, only U.S. judges have the power to decide absolutely the minimum period of time a convicted offender must remain in prison. In other countries the power belongs to a panel of judges, or a panel of judges and laypersons, and the panel's decision is often subject to review. In Europe becoming a judge is a distinct career objective, and special training is required for the post. Judges in the United States are chosen from the bar, and there is nothing in the law curriculum or their experience as lawyers that prepares them to assume the extensive power they receive when they don the robes. Further, they may be trained in the rules of evidence and courtroom procedure but know nothing about correctional theories.

In the administrative context of the criminal courts, judges often do not have time to consider all the crucial elements of the offense and the special characteristics of the offender before imposing a sentence. Especially when the violation is minor, there is a tendency for judges to routinize decision making, announcing sentences to fit certain categories of crimes without paying much attention to the particular offender. Individuals convicted of minor offenses, and therefore possibly the most likely to be reformed, are frequently sentenced immediately after being found guilty or when they enter a guilty plea. If counsel requests a presentence report before imposition of sentence, the necessary delay may require that the defendant remain in jail—a price many are unwilling to pay.

Individual differences in the sentencing tendencies of judges have fascinated social scientists. These disparities can be attributed to a number of factors: the conflicting goals of criminal justice; the differing backgrounds and social values of judges; administrative pressures on judges; and the influence of community values on the system. Each of these factors influences a judge's exercise of discretion in sentencing offenders. In addition, a judge's perception of these factors can be dependent on his or her own attitudes toward the law, toward a particular crime, or toward a type of offender.

Who receives unfavorable treatment as a result of sentencing decisions? At first we might suspect that out-groups (such as minorities, the poor, substance abusers, and mental patients) would receive the longest prison terms, pay the highest fines, and be placed on probation the fewest times. Although some investigations have sustained these assumptions, the evidence is not totally conclusive. In most states the racial composition of the prisons shows a higher percentage of blacks to whites than in the general population. Is this a result of biased attitudes on the part of judges, police officers, and prosecutors? Are poor people more liable to commit violations that elicit a greater response from society? Are enforcement resources distributed in such a way that certain groups are subject to closer scrutiny than other groups? These are but a few of the questions that must be answered if we are to correct present inequities in the criminal justice system and find our way out of the "sentencing wilderness."

SUGGESTIONS FOR FURTHER READING

BALBUS, ISAAC D. *The Dialectics of Legal Repression.* New York: Russell Sage Foundation, 1973. An analysis of the response of the criminal courts in Chicago, Detroit, and Los Angeles to the black ghetto riots of the 1960s.

EISENSTEIN, JAMES, and HERBERT JACOB. *Felony Justice.* Boston: Little, Brown, 1977. An analysis of the processing of felony cases in Baltimore, Chicago, and Detroit. Develops the concept of the courtroom work group.

FEELEY, MALCOLM. *The Process Is the Punishment.* New York: Russell Sage Foundation, 1979. An analysis of a misdemeanor court and the finding that it is not the sentence handed out by the judge, but rather the costs, both monetary and emotional, associated with the pretrial process, that constitute the real punishment.

FRANKEL, MARVIN E. *Criminal Sentences: Law Without Order.* New York: Hill & Wang, 1972. What factors should a judge consider when imposing sanctions? Judge Frankel explores the "sentencing wilderness" and finds that there are a few standards to guide this important decision. This results in a disparity among the sentences given to offenders.

GAYLIN, WILLARD. *The Killing of Bonnie Garland.* New York: Simon & Schuster, 1982. This account of the murder of a Yale student and the conviction of her lover raises disturbing questions about the goals of the criminal sanction by viewing the process and the punishment from the perspectives of Christianity, law, and psychiatry.

KALVEN, HARRY, JR., and HANS ZEISEL. *The American Jury.* Boston: Little, Brown, 1966. A major study of the jury, with emphasis on decision making.

NEUBAUER, DAVID W. *America's Courts and the Criminal Justice System.* North Scituate, Mass.: Duxbury Press, 1979. A test describing the criminal courts and the participants in the administration of justice within the work-group framework.

RYAN, JOHN PAUL, ALLAN ASHMAN, BRUCE D. SALES, and SANDRA SHANE-DU BOW. *American Trial Judges.* New York: Free Press, 1980. The results of a national survey of trial judges, describing their work patterns, recruitment, attitudes, and performance.

ARTICLE FOURTEEN

Discretion, Exchange, and Social Control: Bail Bondsmen in Criminal Courts

FORREST DILL

Bail bondsmen are private entrepreneurs who perform many important functions within the criminal justice system. As Forrest Dill shows, bondsmen supply the money that allows defendants to be free awaiting trial and shepherd them through the procedural maze. Throughout the system, they engage in exchange relationships with officials so that both their tasks are eased.

BUSINESS IMPERATIVES AND ILLEGITIMATE PRACTICES IN BAIL BONDING

The bail system is at once an important legal procedure and a lucrative business enterprise. By allowing commercial intermediaries to post bail for the release of arrested persons prior to trial, the state has created a business operation within the criminal courts. The bondsman's role cannot be easily catalogued. Freed and Wald (1964: 30) assigned the institution of bail "a hybrid status, somewhere between a free enterprise and a public utility." Bail bondsmen are private businessmen who render a service to individuals in return for remuneration at levels fixed by the state. In one sense, then, bondsmen are government subcontractors. But their work injects them into direct participation in the business of criminal courts, where their actions can and do affect the outcomes of criminal cases.

Source: Law and Society Review 9 (1975): 644–674. Notes omitted. Reprinted by permission of the author and the publisher.

Their behavior must be examined from two different and somewhat conflicting perspectives, the first emphasizing business concerns and the second stressing legal responsibilities.

The Business Setting

Bail may be looked upon as a specialized insurance system. It is designed to reconcile the conflicting interests between defendants, who desire to be at liberty before trial, and the state, which insists that defendants be present for court proceedings. Bail bondsmen are the visible commercial operatives of this system. In principle, these conflicting interests will be held in balance by the operation of a set of positive and negative incentives. There must be, on the one hand, sufficient financial gain to induce bondsmen to invest in defendants to relieve pressures on custodial facilities. Bondsmen, then, are legally permitted to collect nonrefundable premiums or interest charges (usually 10 percent of the amount of bail) from defendants for whom they post bail. Bondsmen regain the bail amounts posted when they have satisfied their promises that defendants will appear in court as required. On the other hand, the state needs to protect itself against the inconvenience and public outrage likely to arise when bailed defendants fail to appear for trial. Thus, the law requires that amounts pledged as security for defendants released on bail will be forfeited to the state in the event of nonappearance.

At one time, bondsmen were marginal, independent entrepreneurs operating with scant resources (Beeley 1927). Today, major insurance companies stand behind the individual bondsmen who operate the bail-bonding business. A dozen companies are said (Sutherland and Cressey 1970: 404) to control nearly all the corporate bail bonds written in this country. The policies of these companies affect the administration of criminal law. Bail bondsmen are located at the bottom of this business described by Goldfarb (1965: 95–96) as:

> a straight line beginning with the large national insurance companies and running down through the regional subadministrators and eventually to local agents (the bondsmen) who camp around the local courthouses and actually hustle the business. . . . There is little real business interplay between these three levels. The business functions begin at the top; and the responsibilities and risks increase on the way down, while inversely the profit risks also increase on the way down. The insurance company on top sets the public image of a respectable business and within the working scheme of its bail setup takes no risk with its agents. The agents go about their business in their own fashion, and for this privilege agree to retain only a small percentage of the profit.

This surety-company dominance of the bail bond business is found in most states and in all large metropolitan areas—wherever criminal court activity is sizeable enough to attract and support corporate investment.

A key feature of the business is the low degree of risk for the surety companies. To protect themselves against loss, companies which sell bail bonds require bondsmen to deposit with the companies reserve funds, built up through assessments on fees or premiums bondsmen collect from customers. For each corporate bond used, the bondsman must contribute 10 percent of the premium he collects from the customer to reserve funds. In addition, the surety company levies a 20 percent charge on each premium the bondsman collects for posting a corporate bond. This leaves the bondsman with a gross profit of 70 percent of each premium collected on a corporate surety bond. In theory, the amount of bonds that the bondsman can write is determined by the amount in his reserve fund. Any forfeitures declared against bonds he has written are paid with the reserve fund. If forfeitures exceed the total amount of reserves, the company may take the remaining amount from future premiums the bondsman receives.

The sale of bail bonds is thus an immensely profitable, low-risk arena of enterprise within the insurance industry. Individual bondsmen supply nearly all the labor necessary for corporate profit from the sale of bail bonds and are sometimes said to work for the companies. Bondsmen in fact are not employees of these companies; they are independent businessmen who, by serving as agents of the surety companies, obtain financial backing necessary to satisfy solvency standards set by the state. Bondsmen are not salaried; rather, they receive their earnings on something nearer to a sales-commission basis. They pay their own business expenses, set their own hours, and work out their own local arrangements for conducting their affairs. For example, a bondsman who has developed a large business may employ additional persons on various terms—hourly wages, salaries, or commissions. Moreover, instead of using corporate bonds, they may post their own assets (for example, treasury bonds or cash) as bail and reap a higher rate of profit. In this respect, their business arrangement is quite different from that of other insurance salesmen.

Surety companies have little direct control over the activities of individual bondsmen despite—or possibly because of—the pattern of corporate authority. Corporate policy may make itself felt in a very general way by placing broad limits on the amount of bonds that particular bondsmen may write at any period of time. Where bondsmen represent several surety companies, corporate influence is weakened. The ability of surety companies to insure themselves against loss reduces their need to exercise continuous supervision and control over bondsmen.

Competition for Business

Within the local court system, the bondsman's interactions with defendants, attorneys, and law-enforcement and court officials are permeated by a multitude of legal and illegal commercial possibilities. For this reason the bondsman's business affairs are subject to comprehensive legal regulation, and his work therefore has some unusual restraints. He must maintain detailed accounts of all his transactions and submit them to state insurance commission officials as matters of public record. He may not legally enter into any special agreements with government officials about when or on what terms he is to supply his services. Moreover, he is forbidden to offer as incentives to potential clients or as advantages to actual customers any extra services such as legal advice, attorney referral information, or assistance with court cases. Finally, he may bargain with potential clients over fees, but must sell his services at rates set by the state.

The bondsman's primary occupational difficulties stem from the fact that legal restrictions compel him to meet business imperatives without the use of many standard business techniques. Like many small businessmen, the bondsman operates in an environment offering neither steady demand for his services nor reliable means for guarding against incursions by competitors. In other business settings such conditions foster highly competitive modes of behavior. Legal regulations drastically narrow the initiative the bondsman can legitimately exercise, theoretically closing off all but a few forms of competition as illegal practices. Beyond rendering "prompt, courteous service twenty-four hours a day," the only legitimate business technique that the bondsman can use is advertising. In practice, however, only marginal returns are expected from this source.

The principal competitive devices employed by bondsman are illegal. Reciprocal referrals are a common business arrangement among bondsmen and criminal lawyers. All the bondsmen I talked to have client-sharing agreements with lawyers and assume that the practice is universal. Many bondsmen seek to develop illegal ways of gaining access to potential clients and transforming them into paying customers. They also attempt to cultivate informal exchange relationships with police, judges, and other officials for the information, protection, and administrative influence—in short, the business advantages—that such relationships can provide.

Bondsmen devote considerable effort to developing and expanding illegitimate sources of business within the legal system. One means of illegal recruitment of customers is the "jailhouse lawyer." Typically this role is filled by a person who spends a great deal of time in jail on minor charges like intoxication, begging, or loitering. His job is to steer defendants from inside the jail to a particular bondsman on the outside. These services may come quite cheaply, and the relationship is likely to be very casual. The arrangement is not capable of much formalization owing to the irregular habits of the destitute alcoholics available as personnel; for the same reason it is not very productive for bondsmen. Only a few customers are likely to be recruited in this way and they tend to be first offenders facing minor charges. Experienced defendants are more likely to know bondsmen from past encounters with the law or by reputation, and defendants arrested on serious charges are likely to make contact with bondsmen through other channels, usually lawyers.

Practicing attorneys offer a much more important opportunity through which the bondsman recruits business. The bondsman can count on criminal lawyers for a certain proportion of his clientele, since even attorneys not wishing to deal with bondsmen must occasionally enlist their services for defendants. Attorneys may legitimately refer cases to bondsmen, but reciprocal client-referral agreements between lawyers and bondsmen are forbidden. When questioned during field observations, some bondsmen expressed apprehension about this subject and offered insistent denials that any such arrangements existed. In several instances, the subject of bondsman-attorney arrangements had not even arisen in conversation before bondsmen began making unsolicited denials. The phenomenon is so widespread and so much a part of bail bonding and criminal law practice, however, that it is impossible to conceal for long.

The following event occurred after one week of steady observation with a bondsman in Mountain City. The case was instructive because the relationship between the bondsman and the attorney was still being defined at the time of the meeting.

> Late one morning, Walt told me that he would be meeting a young lawyer named Dave Redding for lunch. Walt explained that he had sent some cases to this attorney in the past. Opening his desk drawer to show me the business cards of several attorneys, he said, "It's against the law to refer attorneys, so I usually show the people these cards and allow them to choose which lawyer they want."
>
> When Redding arrived, Walt suggested that I join them for lunch, but qualified his invitation by saying to Redding, "If you have any private business to talk over, then we of course won't consider this." Redding's immediate reply was: "What do you mean, private business? We have nothing to hide. Our contacts are well regulated by the state insurance commission. Sure he can come along."
>
> On the way to the restaurant, Walt asked: "Well, Dave, what's the purpose of today's meeting, and what can I do for you?" Redding responded: "Oh, there's no special purpose. I just wanted to thank you for the business. This is a courtesy lunch, a social visit, if you will."
>
> After lunch, the two kidded each other about the $200 fee that Redding had collected from Martinez, a young Mexican-American whom Walt had bailed out two weeks earlier on charges of narcotics possession and suspicion of burglary. They also discussed another case involving a defendant's hit-and-run accident. Walt had referred this case to Redding, who had taken it without hesitation. Now some question had arisen about the defendant's ability or willingness to pay Redding's fee. Walt assured him that the defendant had money and counseled Redding to "work on him."
>
> Then Redding said, "I certainly appreciate the business you've sent me. I'm trying to build up a practice and this helps a great deal. I knew this

wasn't a get-rich-quick business, but I had no idea it would be this hard." Walt assured him that the future held great promise for a fine young attorney like himself, and then added: "Sure, I'll send you some more cases. And let me ask that in return you refer your cases to me. Now if you ever have anybody who needs to get out and you know he's a good risk, just call me and tell me that he's good as gold and I'll take him right out without collateral. Understand?"

As this case illustrates, the bondsman may have vital knowledge of the defendant's financial situation. First-time defendants in particular may unwittingly reveal financial information to the bondsman during "routine" questioning. Such defendants frequently do not understand the nature of the bondsman's role and may see him as yet another official whose powers must be respected. Inexperienced defendants are more vulnerable to the attorney-referral arrangement. Bondsmen in some other cities are said to exploit defendants by requiring them to take their cases to certain attorneys as a condition of posting bail for their release (Goldfarb 1965: 114). No evidence of this practice could be found in Westville or Mountain City, where the bondsman-attorney referral system may have been working in favor of defendants. One lawyer speculated that attorneys needed to exercise caution with cases referred from bondsmen. "They have to give these clients a fair deal," he said, "or the defendants might resent the attorney and mess up the system. It's too risky for the attorney working with a bondsman not to give good representation."

Collusion with jail personnel may be another valuable means of customer recruitment for the bondsman. During the period of field observation, it became apparent to me that certain jail police in Mountain City were assisting certain bondsmen in getting customers. The simplest and most reliable method was one that required only a moment's effort by an individual jail staff member. "All he has to do," an attorney explained, "is find out if the defendant has a bondsman lined up. If not, he points to a particular bondsman's number in the telephone directory and pushes a dime into the guy's hand." Even this simple arrangement can result in unexpected complications, as the following account reveals:

I was present with Walt in his office when he received a call from a woman requesting that bail be posted for one of her employees. The defendant had been arrested the night before for driving on a suspended license. Walt told the woman that he would call the jail to determine the amount of bail and then call her back. Bail had been set at $296, making the premium charge $39.60—ten percent of the amount of bail plus an additional $10 charge which bondsmen are allowed to collect on all bails under $500. Walt called the woman back advising her that she would need to submit the premium as well as her signature to a deed promising to pay the full amount of bail if the defendant failed to appear in court. The woman said that she would send another of her employees with the money to Walt's office.

When the second employee arrived, Walt and I went to jail across the street "to get the body." At the jail another bondsman was waiting to post bail for the defendant Walt had come to get. Walt immediately sensed what was happening and informed one of the jailors that he wanted to talk to the defendant. A jail policeman stepped forward and said, "No, Alvarez wants to go with the other guy." There was some discussion, and eventually it was decided that the defendant would determine which bondsman would "get the bail."

Alvarez (a black) was brought out, and he turned to the other bondsman (also a black). The two spoke briefly in hushed tones. Then Walt (not black) approached Alvarez and said, "Mrs. McGee called me to help you. Your friend Smith is over in my office right now waiting for you." Alvarez turned to the other bondsman, shrugged apologetically, and said, "I guess I'll have to go with him," indicating Walt. As we rode down in the elevator, the other bondsman mumbled that he had also received a telephone call. Walt remained silent. Alvarez said, "Well, that's the way it goes."

After Alvarez and Smith left, I asked Walt how the other bondsman had become involved. Walt speculated that someone in the jail had persuaded Alvarez to call the other bondsman. Smith, Alvarez's co-worker, knew nothing about the other bondsman. I asked whether one of the jail police we had just seen had been responsible for the other bondsman's appearance. Walt replied, "Well, you saw the way he wanted Alvarez to be taken out by the other guy, didn't you?"

The same bondsman related an incident illustrating another variation of this method:

A man entered Walt's office and presented a slip of paper on which had been written the name of the defendant, the charge in exact penal code section terminology, the date of the next court appearance, and the amount of bail. The man was a supervisor in a public utility company where the defendant, a woman, was employed. The slip of paper, Walt was convinced, was prima facie evidence that one of the police had recommended a bondsman. Apparently the man had come to the wrong address.

Walt gladly cooperated with the man, however, and immediately went to the jail to take the woman out. When one of the jailors asked about the slip of paper, Walt "played dumb," saying that he never got any slips of paper from the jail. With great reluctance, the jailor released the defendant to Walt, who patiently explained several times that the woman's supervisor was waiting over in his office. "That guy was pretty unhappy, because he'd lost some sure money in the mixup."

Other methods requiring collective efforts by jail police may sometimes be employed. These are more complicated and carry greater risks of discovery and failure. A Westville bondsman recounted an experience of his at the Mountain City jail:

I got a call from the relative of a guy who had been put in jail over there. It was a pretty good bail, so I decided to drive over and take him out myself.

> When I got there I found a police hold on him. Now that hold wasn't on him when I left Westville only a half an hour before, so whoever put it on him should have still been around. But I couldn't find anybody who knew anything about it. They passed the buck and I went from one office to another trying to find out whose hold it was. Nobody knew, and finally they said they were going to let him go. Next thing I knew another bondsman came walking out with the defendant. Then they told me that they had taken the hold off him, but actually they were keeping him for this other bondsman.

In general, collective agreements among jail officials appear necessary to protect the system of collusion. Since this system functions as a means of restricting competition, its value depends on excluding some bondsmen so that business can be channeled to other bondsmen. But competition among bondsmen may result in some degree of participation in the system by nearly all local bondsmen.

There was no evidence to indicate the existence of collusion between jail police and bondsmen in Westville at the time of my study. With a smaller population, a more professionally disciplined police force, and a different political complexion, Westville presented relatively poor opportunities for collusive relations to develop between police and bondsmen. All of my informants claimed that defendants selected bondsmen on their own from inside the jail. If the Westville police were collaborating with particular bondsmen, the arrangement was either very well concealed or quite minor in scale.

In some cities, bondsmen reportedly refuse to extend services to defendants accused of minor offenses which require "nominal"—that is, low—bail, because they view the modest premiums in such cases as not worth the trouble and risk of posting bond (Freed and Wald 1964: 33). It seems likely that this practice would be found only where bail bonding had fallen under monopoly control by a small number of bondsmen. By assuring privileged bondsmen a guaranteed share of the profits, monopoly conditions would make it possible for bondsmen to neglect defendants in minor cases.

Aside from some petty collusion in Mountain City bail practices, bail bonding in the two cities seemed to offer relatively undisturbed market conditions. For most bondsmen operating there, defendants in minor cases appeared to constitute the bulk of business and the most reliable source of income. Such cases were especially attractive because the bondsman could post his own assets and thereby avoid the costs of using corporate surety bonds. Although minor cases yield small premiums, they may be attractive to bondsmen as business opportunities precisely because of the low bail amounts on which the premiums are based. Also, by permitting bondsmen to charge defendants an extra $10 for posting bail in amounts less than $500—as done in the state where this research was carried out—the legal system increases the attractiveness of such cases.

PROFIT MAXIMIZATION AND CASE MANAGEMENT BY BONDSMEN

Shortly after bondsmen enter the criminal justice process, some defendants are granted pretrial liberty and others are ordered held in detention to await further action in their cases. The timing of these events has created the impression that bondsmen are "purveyors of freedom" who play a key role in determining whether defendants will obtain release before trial (Wice 1974). This view greatly exaggerates the influence that bondsmen have in such determinations, however.

Although bail procedures in different parts of the country are far from uniform (Silverstein 1966), it is clear that bail administration everywhere belongs primarily to law-enforcement and court officials. The most critical decisions—the bail amounts set in particular cases—are entirely controlled by local criminal justice officials, with prosecuting attorneys taking the dominant role. Bondsmen do not participate at all in these decisions for cases making up the largest volume of criminal court business. This is because of the widespread use of the bail schedule, a form approved by local judges listing uniform bail amounts for the most common misdemeanor violations (for example, disorderly conduct, petty theft, simple assault, and certain vehicle offenses). It is true that bondsmen can and sometimes do refuse to post bail for defendants in such cases, but decisions as to the amounts required in particular cases are determined more or less automatically as a matter of clerical routine, usually by stationhouse police.

For cases involving charges of serious misdemeanor and felony offenses, bail setting typically takes place in court at the time of arraignment. This process involves negotiation between the judge, prosecutor, and defense attorney; the prosecutor's recommendations usually determine the final decision (Suffet 1966). The bondsman plays no formal part in this process either. In many cases of this kind, the defendant or his attorney may contact a bondsman before the bail hearing, and the bondsman may supply informal advice to the judge or the prosecutor concerning his willingness to post bail for the defendant. This may help the defendant by inducing the judge to set bail at a level which the defendant can afford. It can hardly work to the defendant's disadvantage.

Unlike the standardized bail amounts required in the most common misdemeanor cases, amounts set in cases involving serious offenses often vary a good deal, even when the charges are identical. Defendants who are unable to secure release at amounts initially set may request that bail be lowered. The frequency of bail reduction probably provides a rough measure of the extent of excessive bail in various jurisdictions, although in general bail reduction does not occur with much frequency in most places (Silverstein 1966: 634–637). Both the bail schedule and the bail hearing lead to decisions that discriminate against sizeable proportions of the defendant population (Foote 1954, 1958; Ares and Sturz 1962; Silverstein 1966). But it is mistaken to attribute these discriminatory results to bail bondsmen, given the economics of the situation in general and the bondsmen's inclinations to seek profits in particular.

The Bondsman's Interest in Court Efficiency

If bondsmen play only a minor role in determining defendants' chances for release, the same cannot be said of their role in handling defendants who are released on bail. Bondsmen actively employ a number of different techniques of case management. These practices are aimed at protecting investments and maximizing profits, but they also have positive functions for the court system. Nominally, bondsmen are private businessmen situated outside the criminal courts. Examination of their routine activities, however, indicates that they serve as agents of the court system responding to many of the problems that concern those who occupy official positions within it.

The strategies bondsmen use in managing cases reveal many generic similarities to the practices of lawyers, probation officers, and other agent-mediators within the court system (Blumberg 1970). An important first step is often to establish a good relationship with the defendant. The bondsman usually extends a cordial, businesslike manner to each customer, seeking to convey a willingness to separate the defendant's specific dereliction from his or her general moral character. He therefore treats in a routine or "professional" way matters that his customers may regard as emergencies, but his mode of dealing with particular customers may vary depending on his perception of situational demands. A bondsman explained, "Each one of these people is different, and you've gotta handle them in different ways." Thus when the customer is a first-time defendant charged with a relatively minor offense, the bondsman's strategy may be to play down the seriousness of the defendant's plight by reciting such homilies as "We get cases like this every day. Don't worry, it'll come out all right." In other minor cases, where the customer is an experienced defendant and perhaps an old customer behind in payments for previous bail bond services, the bondsman may act in a slightly patronizing and officious manner, counseling the defendant to "be a good boy, don't get into any more trouble, and bring that money in next Friday." In cases involving more serious charges, the bondsman may deal calmly and quietly with the customer, emphasizing his neutrality by carefully avoiding any mention of the alleged offense.

Another and more important element of case management involves giving various forms of legal assistance and advice. Bondsmen always remind their customers of future court dates and instruct them about how to find the room in the court building where their cases will be heard, what time to show up, and what to expect during the proceeding. An indirect form of advice is sometimes employed if the defendant has already retained an attorney or has a particular attorney in mind. In this situation, the bondsman may issue a reassuring comment to the defendant, as, for example, "Oh, I know Bart will give you all the help he can. He's a fine lawyer." In another instance, I observed a bondsman attempting vigorously to persuade a defendant whom he had just bailed out to call an attorney whose name the defendant had mentioned as we walked from the jail to the bondsman's nearby office. The defendant was allowed to leave the office only after promising that he would go directly to look up the attorney. Bondsmen may also refer unrepresented defendants to attorneys. Here, the practice of recommending attorneys appears in a different light, for it has the same purpose as is intended by congratulating the legally sophisticated defendant on his choice of attorney. Both of these techniques serve to increase the customer's feeling of personal competence and to reinforce his self-definition as a "defendant"—a person who is going through the court process and who will accept its judgment. The chances of panic and flight are thereby reduced.

In other cases, the bondsman gives direct legal advice. The following observed instances, both involving the same bondsman, suggest typical possibilities. In the first case, the bondsman counseled against retaining an attorney:

> At about one o'clock one afternoon, one of Al's customers came into his office. The man had been arrested for drunk driving many weeks before. His court date was for two o'clock that day. Al told him that he had two alternatives: either he could demand a jury trial and hope that the complaint would be withdrawn, or he could plead guilty and ask the judge for probation and some time "to put a few beans aside and pay the fine."
>
> Al explained: "If you ask for a jury trial, you'll need a lawyer and that can run into money. It might easily run you $250, and then you have no guarantee that you'll be acquitted. Of course, if you get a jury trial and an attorney, you will have a better judge. But with no priors the fine's only $296, so you might as well plead guilty, ask the judge for probation, and then get the money together over a period of time."
>
> The customer contemplated Al's advice, then gave a resigned shrug and said, "Well, I guess I'll plead guilty. See you later."

The second case also involved a motor vehicle code violation:

> Shortly after lunch on another afternoon, a young man who had been charged with littering and possessing open containers of beer in his car stopped by to see Al about his case. He was apprehensive about the outcome because the girl who had been arrested with him had already "copped out as charged." He asked: "What will happen if I change my earlier plea to guilty?"
>
> Al answered: "It won't make any difference. They got the girl and all they want are guilty pleas. The judge will fine you $25, and that will be the end of it."
>
> Al was correct. Later that afternoon the client returned and jubilantly told Al, "It's all over. I got out for $29."

Two features of these incidents deserve attention. First, each involved a minor offense. The bondsman's ability to offer sound legal advice depends on the degree to which court processing of the kind of case involved is routinized and therefore predictable. His legal expertise thus seems to be confined to traffic violations, public order offenses such as drunkenness and disturbing the peace, and minor property crimes. For the bondsman this may be a happy coincidence, since the typically small penalties facing defendants in such cases may take much of the risk out of the prospect of confronting the court without legal representation.

Second, the examples suggest that bondsmen share the interests of court officials in guilty pleas. More generally, both groups are interested in efficiency. The bondsman's liability for each bond he posts does not end until the defendant's case is cleared from the court docket. Every new customer represents a case that will remain open and a bond that will remain "out" for an indeterminate but roughly predictable amount of time. For example, after posting bail for a woman charged with welfare fraud, a Westville bondsman explained why this had been a good business decision: "She'll plead guilty and be put on probation. The case will be over in about two and a half months." The strength of the bondsman's business position depends on the volume of cases he handles: the amount of bonds in use is inversely related to the amount of new bonds that he can post. Therefore, his interests lie in efficient, routinized court procedures and compliant defendants. Anything that lengthens the duration of criminal cases—disorderly judicial administration, militant defense attorneys, nonappearance by defendants, new and unfamiliar legal procedures—weakens the bondsman's position.

The Quasi-Bureaucratic Role of the Bondsman

An important consideration for understanding the bondsman's activities is that cooperation from defendants may be contingent on the administrative practices of courts. Some defendants may fail to make required court appearances because they get lost in the system. For example, they may have separate appearances scheduled in two different court departments at exactly the same time, or they may be uninformed or confused about the court dates. In other cases, defendants may be unable to comply with required court appearances because of employment obligations or family emergencies.

Such problems are less likely to arise for defendants who have private legal representation. One of the key functions performed by attorneys in the criminal process is to direct the passage of cases through the procedural and bureaucratic mazes of the court system (Blumberg 1967). For unrepresented defendants, however, the bondsman may perform the crucial institutional task of helping to negotiate court routines. In order to protect his investment, the bondsman may find it not merely desirable but necessary to guide defendants through the court process. By providing legal advice to his customers, arranging more convenient court dates for them, and negotiating their passage through the court process, the bondsman increases his chances of collecting fees and reduces the amount of time that his assets are encumbered. At the same time, these methods of case management promote orderly and efficient court administration. They also implicate bondsmen in the unauthorized practice of law.

Efforts by bondsmen to organize the actions of individual customers in relation to the actions of court officials deepen the involvement of bondsmen in the criminal justice process. Not only do these efforts require frequent visits to courtrooms, but they may also require informal assistance from court personnel. The experienced bondsman knows each of the bailiffs, court clerks, and accounting office members on a first-name basis and how much and what kinds of assistance each is willing to provide. The bondsman typically takes advantage of mutualized exchange opportunities at Christmas and New Year's to reciprocate favors received through court "connections." If it is consistent with his personal style, he may seek to improve his relations with court clerks, bailiffs, and other court participants by "buttering them up" through flattery and other forms of interpersonal artifice. He may also supplement his day-to-day dealing with officials by occasionally dispensing gifts (such as free passes to professional sports events) and supplying drinks at nearby bars in after-hours gatherings.

One measure of the degree of cooperativeness of court officials is whether they will comply with the bondsman's request to bring a case forward on a particular day's court calendar. This small but nonetheless significant service, which can be easily rendered by the court clerk, is a favor that the bondsman may seek in order to keep track of his cases or to accelerate release of a new customer for whom bail has just been posted. Without this assistance, the bondsman cannot "move" cases in court. Where such influence is available, however, the bondsman can sometimes negotiate convenient court dates, coordinate multiple appearances, and forestall issuance of bench warrants.

A more important form of assistance that the bondsman may wish to arrange is for certain of his customers to be released on recognizance—that is, without being required to make financial bail. If a defendant is returned to jail because of new difficulties with the law before he has paid his debt to the bondsman, the bondsman's fee may be jeopardized. When this happens, the bondsman may face two unsatisfactory options: either lose the balance of the money owed by the defendant or assume a greater risk by posting another bail bond in hopes of collecting the fees owed on the original bond. If a judge or prosecutor can be persuaded to grant release without requirement of financial bail on the new charges, however, the need for deciding between the two options is eliminated.

By now it has become evident that the court clerk is a figure of major importance to the bondsman. In high-volume urban courts, there are many persons with this designation—one, in fact, for every separate court "part" or "department" to which each of the judges of a given court district is assigned. The administrative position of the court clerk makes him an object of continuous attention from other participants seeking information about or access to the court calendar. The resources he holds may be an important means for the bondsman's efforts to protect his investments. One bondsman stated:

> The court clerk is probably one of the most important people I have to deal with. He moves cases, he can get information to the judge, and he has control over various calendar matters. When he's not willing to help you out, he can make life very difficult. He know's he's important, and he acts like it.

Observations confirmed the value of cooperation from the court clerk for case management strategies employed by bondsmen. Two examples are given below:

> A bondsman and a court clerk were chatting amiably during a recess in one of the Westville courtrooms. They kidded each other for a short time, each complaining about the "easy life" of the other. Then the court clerk asked the bondsman: "Hey, what about O'Hanlon? Isn't he your case? He didn't show this morning and I've got a bench warrant on him sitting on my desk right now. You'd better get in touch with Sheldon [an attorney] and have him call the judge for a continuance right away or that warrant is gonna be on its way."
>
> On another occasion, a Westville bondsman was summoned to a nearby city by a prospective customer. After obtaining a verbal promise from the defendant's brother that the premium would be paid, the bondsman went to that city to post bail. When we arrived there at mid-morning, the bondsman's first contact was with the court clerk:
>
> **Al:** You've got Mallen scheduled to come up this afternoon, don't you?
>
> (The clerk checked his records and nodded affirmatively.)
>
> **Al:** Look, this guy was picked up last night on plain drunk and he's still got a george heat on. I don't think he's fit to appear in anybody's court. He's still so stiff I swear I could smell it over the phone.
> **Clerk:** Hmmm.
> **Al:** I'm going over to the jail and take him out. How's about putting the guy on for tomorrow? He's gotta get himself cleaned up.
>
> (After momentary hesitation, the clerk agreed.)
>
> **Clerk:** Okay, I'll set him up for nine tomorrow.
>
> As we walked to the jail, the bondsman told me that he had done a favor for the defendant. The postponement would give the defendant an extra day to sober up and would enable him to appear in court freshly shaved and wearing clean clothes. "Makes a much better impression on the judge if the guy looks decent." A short time later the defendant appeared at the jail booking desk. A middle-aged man, he had spent the night and most of the

morning in jail. He was now completely sober, and although he presented a shabby appearance there seemed little doubt that he could have stood trial that afternoon. After posting bail, Al counseled the man: "Go home and get some rest, and then come back tomorrow morning at nine and put on your best manners. I don't think you've got anything to worry about. Judge Gardner is one of the best in the country."

In later conversation, the bondsman said that he regarded the man as "an alcoholic obviously beyond the point of being helped." He revealed that the reason for arranging postponement of the man's case was to increase the likelihood that the man would make his court appearance. "I've seen hundreds of cases like this guy—just simple drunks. In that condition, they're likely to wander off somewhere and fall asleep for a whole day. This way the guy doesn't have to worry about it. He can go home, sack out, and his chances of being able to make a court appearance in the morning are much better than if he has to hang around the court building for a couple of long, dry hours until his case is called."

Court "connections" are primarily useful to the bondsman for managing minor cases. One bondsman reported that a high proportion of his clientele consisted of persons arrested for traffic warrant violations. When asked about the business consequences of this fact, he replied:

> Great! [Laughter] What I mean by great is that these cases make up a lot of the bread and butter in this business. But they're much more work than the big cases. Felony cases can't be moved around in the courts, but chickenshit cases can. With traffic cases, you sometimes find yourself doing a lot of extra work in getting postponements and that kind of thing. You know, like when a guy is afraid he'll lose his job if he has to appear in court on a working day without permission from his boss.

This parallels the situation described above in which dispensation of legal advice appears to be confined to relatively trivial, although statistically frequent, criminal matters. Thus, minor cases provide a more reliable basis of income, higher returns on investments, and greater opportunity to exercise influence in the process of criminal justice.

BAIL ADMINISTRATION AND CONTROL OF ARRESTEES

Bail administration does not come to an abrupt end with the release of some defendants and the detention of others. On the contrary, it extends throughout the entire period between arrest and disposition. Official actions in this process have been described in several empirical studies (Foote 1954, 1958). This section shows how the bondsman's decisions to post bail are linked to considerations of subsequent decisions by court officials. Through collaborative exercise of their respective discretionary powers, bondsmen and court officials exchange outcomes which strengthen legal control over arrested persons in the period before disposition.

Decisions to Post Bail

Compared with its importance for official decisions, the factor of offense appears to play a very minor role in the bondsman's assessment of defendants as possible customers. More serious crimes involve high bails, of course, and bondsmen have greater reason to be concerned over the possibility that defendants in these cases will "skip." At the same time, higher bails mean higher premiums. Some bondsmen believe that drug addicts and certain kinds of violent offenders tend to be less reliable than other criminals, and in such cases the bondsman may exercise special care in deciding to post bail. In general, however, bondsmen do not make categorical judgments about defendants based upon the offenses with which they are charged.

Similarly, bondsmen are not concerned about the possibility that released defendants might be rearrested on new charges while at liberty. Bondsmen believe, just as do criminal justice officials, that chances of rearrest may be quite high among certain classes of defendants, especially those accused of minor offenses like prostitution and shoplifting. Indeed, bondsmen share the view of many law-enforcement and court officials that for some defendants release on bail and return to "the streets" signals a period of intensified criminal activity in order to earn money to pay fees owed to bondsmen and attorneys. But bondsmen cannot afford to base their decisions on the probability of recidivism by released defendants. One bondsman revealed the tough-minded outlook required by his business:

> I don't care what any bondsmen's association says on this score. We don't care and we can't care about protecting society. We have means and methods of making these people pay, so we take the risks and the gambles. That's what we're in business for. There is almost nobody I won't take out, including people I'm certain will repeat their crimes.

The most important question is whether the defendant is likely to pay the premium for his bail. Ideally, full payment of the premium is demanded before the bondsman agrees to post bail. Depending on his assessment of the defendant's background, character, and financial capacity, however, the bondsman may decide to post bail on credit—that is, to allow the defendant to pay the premium in installments. The financial qualifications of family members and friends may become an important consideration at this point. Surety companies seem to discourage installment agreements, but bondsmen generally operate on the assumption that it is better to extend credit broadly, accepting the risks of nonpayment and partial payment that this method implies. Therefore, bondsmen usually have collection problems.

Bondsmen sometimes appear to make attempts at estimating the probability of defaults or "skips" by prospective customers before posting bonds, but not primarily because they entertain any special concern for the efficiency or integrity of court operations. The dominant question is rather the defendant's reliability as a paying customer. One bondsman said that he regarded the family life of defendants as being particularly important in this respect. "If a man is happily married and loves his kids, he's not going to leave town." Another bondsman attempted to sum up the problem by stating, "The good people are gonna cooperate and the bad people are gonna run." Later, however, he qualified this by explaining that he, like other bondsmen, looks into each defendant's criminal record, employment history, residence, and family situation before deciding to post bail. A third bondsman commented, "Good actors have roots in the community."

Having determined that a defendant has the ability to pay the premium, however, the bondsman is extremely likely to accept the defendant as a customer. He may refuse to post bail on a defendant who already owes him a considerable amount of money for past services. Similarly, he will probably refuse to extend credit to a defendant whom he knows—either from his own past experience or occasionally on the advice of another bondsman—to be a "wise guy" or a "bad actor," that is, a person likely to withhold payments or to go into hiding. Hesitancy on the bondsman's part is also likely when police records indicate outstanding warrants, for in such cases the defendant may be rearrested and returned to custody before the bondsman has collected his fee. The police follow the business dealings of bondsmen with special interest and can sometimes use this knowledge to advantage when they wish to prevent particular defendants from gaining release.

Indemnification Agreements

Of course, if he chooses to do so, the bondsman can insure himself against all losses from forfeited bonds by requiring each customer to complete a collateral agreement. To accomplish this, the defendant signs a collateral form or persuades another person to act as a guarantor. This step would eliminate all uncertainty in client selection, since such an agreement guarantees complete indemnification of the surety for any losses he may incur. But bondsmen usually do not require indemnification contracts from their customers, for most criminal defendants are extremely poor and are unable to find guarantors to co-sign indemnification agreements on bail bonds posted for defendants. Although the guarantor may not fully understand the legal significance of his role, he generally recognizes that he is being asked to pledge an amount of money or perhaps his property for the defendant's good conduct. The guarantor must place great trust in the defendant, which for most defendants narrows the field of potential guarantors to a small circle of persons.

It is difficult to determine the frequency with which bondsmen post bail unaccompanied by collateral agreements. No official figures are collected to indicate how often this happens, but some reasonable estimates can be made. During field interviews, bondsmen stated that they received "hard" collateral—indemnification contracts backed up by specific assets such as bank accounts or property deeds—in five to ten percent of their cases. These are probably cases involving more serious offenses and thus higher bail amounts. Estimates of the frequency of "hard" collateral were all within this range (see National Conference on Bail and Criminal Justice 1965: 234). Similarly, another study of bail practices (Hoskins 1968: 1141) concluded that "complete indemnification is seldom achieved" by bail bondsmen. However, in a fairly large proportion of cases, written promises of indemnification are obtained.

In these cases, the bondsman accepts from defendants or guarantors the pledge of such possessions as automobiles, jewelry, or household furnishings and appliances as collateral. Estimates by bondsmen of the frequency of such agreements ranged from forty to sixty percent. The realizable market value of these items is often considerably less than the personal value they have for the guarantors who offer them. Thus it appears that most of the indemnification agreements obtained by bondsmen have relatively little value as collateral.

This impression is strengthened by bondsmen's reports concerning the difficulties of enforcing collateral agreements. "Unless you hold the collateral in your hand, it isn't worth anything," stated one bondsman. In five years of writing bail bonds, this informant claimed, three guarantors had reimbursed him for forfeited bonds without protesting. Another bondsmen said that he had received voluntary compensation from a co-signer only once in fifteen years. Legal remedies are available to the bondsman, and when enforcement of collateral agreements becomes necessary the bondsman can turn to these. In many states, for example, co-signers are legally liable to pay costs incurred by bondsmen in attempting to recapture fugitive defendants up to the limit of the outstanding bond. Given the inevitable costs and uncertainties of litigation, however, bondsmen are more likely to resort to informal means of enforcing indemnification agreements with defendants and co-signers. The overriding purpose of indemnification agreements appears to be their presumed "psychological" value for protecting investments by underlining the obligations of defendants and co-signers to the bondsman.

In practice, therefore, whether to post bail on a defendant without obtaining collateral is the most important decision facing the bondsman. Because most defendants are unable to provide adequate collateral, the bondsman confronts this decision often. It is in exercising discretion not to impose "hard" collateral conditions on defendants and guarantors that the bondsman runs his largest risks and stands to make his highest profits. The bondsman must summon all of his business acumen and skill in "human relations" to make this decision. It is here that the bondsman's greatest impact on the justice system occurs, and it is here also that cooperative relations with court officials become most important.

Nonenforcement of Bail Forfeitures

The key factor in this aspect of bail bonding is the discretionary power of judges to exonerate outstanding bonds and to set aside bail forfeitures. When a bailed defendant fails to appear in court, the bondsman may have to forfeit the bail he has posted if he is unable to produce the defendant within the legal "grace" period (six months in the state where this study was done). Whether forfeiture is actually imposed is decided by the judge who presides in the case. Remission procedures, which permit this decision to be made, set out the conditions under which judges may authorize the return of forfeited bonds to sureties.

The law gives judges wide latitude in these procedures, creating the suspicion that such decisions may sometimes reflect judicial improprieties. The opportunity for official misconduct would, of course, be present even if judges were not directly involved in approving requests for exoneration of forfeited bonds. But from another standpoint, the existence of these procedures is fortunate, for without them officials would be compelled to carry out a policy of strict and uniform enforcement of forfeited bail bonds. This would probably lead to a considerable increase in the number of persons unable to gain release on bail. Bondsmen ordinarily obtain complete indemnification on only a small percentage of all defendants for whom they post bonds, and insistence of bondsmen on full collateral would be a very likely adjustment to a policy of strict enforcement. Many defendants would thus fail to qualify for the services of bondsmen due to inability to raise collateral. This might be compounded by another effect of a policy of strict enforcement of bail forfeitures: such a policy quickly drives noncorporate sources of bail, including friends and relatives of defendants, out of the system (see Foote 1954: 1060–1066).

Virtually every study of bail administration ever conducted has found that a large proportion of forfeitures are set aside by judges. This generous use of judicial discretion stems from one or more of several possible sources. As already suggested, one possibility is that forfeitures are routinely set aside because judges recognize the dependence of the court on the willingness of bondsmen to post bail for defendants who cannot provide full collateral. That bondsmen accept many defendants as customers without securing legally enforceable indemnification agreements not only increases the overall profitability of writing bail bonds, but it also enables large numbers of defendants to obtain release who would otherwise face pretrial detention, thereby preventing intolerable pressures on detention facilities. The stake of the criminal justice system in the willingness of bail bondsmen to depart from norms of conservative business practice is considerable.

A second reason that judges so often exercise their power to remit bail forfeitures in favor of bondsmen is that they sometimes need reciprocity from bondsmen to prevent defendants from obtaining release. When court officials desire that a particular defendant not be released, they may pass the word on to local bondsmen (National Conference on Bail and Criminal Justice 1966: 118). I learned of no such instance during my study, but it is fairly common knowledge that bondsmen in various cities were subject to severe pressures against writing bonds for persons arrested during civil rights protests during the last decade (Goldfarb 1965: 84–85). Because bondsmen need the court's cooperation for a variety of reasons, they are unlikely to offend court officials by posting bail in such instances. In this way, judges can prevent release without actually denying bail or setting bail in an amount that the legally competent defendant might challenge as "excessive." The effective discretion exercised by court officials is therefore augmented by informal relationships with bondsmen.

These relationships also help explain why it is that bondsmen ordinarily make no efforts to supervise defendants for whom they post bail. Bondsmen require only those defendants who owe money to make regular reports, and then the purpose is not to remind the defendant that his behavior is under scrutiny but to enable the bondsman to collect his fee. Even when a defendant fails to make a required court appearance the bondsman is likely to make only minimal efforts to locate the defendant—for example, by placing a few telephone calls to persons whom the defendant has named as references or by sending a telegram to an address given by the defendant. Only once during field observations did I learn of a case in which a bondsman was actively attempting to locate a defendant for reasons other than payment.

Despite the extensive protection afforded, bail bondsmen cannot place complete reliance on court officials to return all forfeited bonds. In some instances, particularly when large bail amounts are at stake, bondsmen may need to attempt to locate fugitive defendants. Bondsmen have extraordinary powers of arrest and extradition over bailed defendants who have fled. No criminal justice official possesses the degree of legal authority over citizens that the bondsman holds and occasionally wields over his customers. Under powers vested in him by law, the bondsman can compel a defendant for whom he has posted bail to return with him to court at the point of a gun. The bondsman does not need to obtain a warrant for this purpose, and the defendant legally cannot offer resistance. The frequency with which bondsmen exercise their powers to retrieve fugitive defendants is not readily ascertainable and officials hold divergent views. Some law-enforcement officials claim that the most important service the bondsman renders to the state is in retrieving defendants who have absconded (Hoskins 1968: 1144; National Conference on Bail and Criminal Justice 1965: 237). But others assert that bondsmen rarely make special efforts to locate defaulting defendants for whom they have assumed bail obligations and that fugitive defendants are returned only when they later commit crimes for which they are rearrested (U.S. Senate 1964: 131). Of course, both of these views may be correct.

Even when bondsmen make use of their powers to capture and return fugitive defendants to court, they rarely engage directly in efforts to locate defendants. During field observations, several Westville bondsmen mentioned a legendary case in which one of their colleagues had spent considerable time and money "chasing a $14,000 skip all over the country" without result. But the more common practice involves indirect search operations whereby the bondsman seeks to purchase information about the location of a fugitive defendant for whom he is financially responsible. A Westville bondsman described one possibility:

> I have a case right now of a $1,100 skip. The guy is down in Valley City somewhere, I know that much. I've got a pimp down there working on it for me. There's no way anybody could find out that this pimp works for me, because he's cool and I'm cool. He's going to ask around to see if he can locate this guy. Then I'll go down there with another guy and we'll bring him back to Westville. It'll cost me about $150 to catch the guy, so I'll just about break even on this one. [The bondsman had already collected the $110 premium.]

Other bondsmen indicated that they contract with specialists—either professional detectives ("skip tracers") or underworld figures—to locate defaulting defendants. Such persons receive a certain proportion of the bail amount for information leading to successful capture of the defendant.

The bondsman's legal powers of arrest and extradition, like his discretion in posting bail, may occasionally be put to the advantage of criminal justice officials. Bondsmen "own" defendants for whom they post bail. Therefore, law-enforcement officials can informally borrow the bondsman's legal authority to avoid having to comply with expensive and cumbersome procedures necessary for interstate extradition of fugitive defendants. Under this arrangement, defendants who have been arrested in another state are turned over to bondsmen for return to face original charges in the state where they jumped bail. It is not known how widespread this practice is, but the use of bail bondsmen to circumvent formal extradition procedures is thought to be quite common in some states (see U.S. Senate 1966: 23–24; *Yale Law Journal*, 1964).

SUMMARY AND DISCUSSION OF FINDINGS

The presence of bail bondsmen in American criminal courts rests upon the right of bail to which all persons accused of noncapital crimes are said to be entitled. The basis of this familiar legal concept is embedded in a tersely ambiguous clause of the United States Constitution. Most state constitutions, and particularly those adopted after ratification of the U.S. Constitution, contain similar provisions. But the Eighth Amendment clause in question simply states that "excessive bail shall not be required of defendants" in criminal cases. It says nothing about bail bondsmen, the surety companies which stand behind them, forfeitures of bail, and so on. These and other details of bail administration are spelled out in statutes and case law at both the federal and state levels (see Foote 1965; Paulsen 1966).

The bail system has come in for much criticism in the past decade and a half, mostly directed at the excessive reliance placed on money as a means of securing the presence of defendants for hearings and—on the rare occasions when they are held—trials. The problem, however, is not only that the bail system makes release before trial hinge on the defendant's financial situation. It is also that American law refuses to entrust officials with formal power to detain citizens who are only accused of crime.

Two comparative law scholars (Mueller and Le Poole-Griffiths 1969: 23–24) highlight the problem in the following way:

> Continental law has faced this issue with great candor. Pretrial detention, despite the probable guilt of the defendant, is always an exceptional measure and can be imposed only when . . . extremely high standards for issuance of a warrant can be met. But when, thus, the guilt of the perpetrator is highly probable, when the offense is major, when there is danger that he will flee, tamper with the evidence and repeat his offense, why then bother with an insurance contract insuring the defendant's next appearance? To release a suspect under those circumstances would be more than a gambler's folly, or the premium should have to be so high that nobody could meet it. Realizing this, continental law rarely insists on preliminary detention when we do, and, while nearly all codes have provisions on bail, there is rarely any occasion to apply them. When the risk of release is worth taking, release is ordered. Any other system is nonutilitarian and would only discriminate against the poor, a reason which led Sweden to abandon this institution.

In contrast, American law forbids criminal court officials from detaining a defendant who may appear dangerous or likely to flee if released. Our procedures, by defining pretrial release decisions as questions of judicial and prosecutorial responsibility, are also unique in the extent to which they aim at excluding the police from such decisions (Goldfarb 1965: 213). American law's institutionalized suspicion of official discretion is apparent in the case of bail. Admittedly, the bail system fails to guarantee pretrial freedom to every defendant claiming it as a right. But even if such claims often go unrecognized, it is clear that officials are not absolutely free to ignore them.

Bail bondsmen serve several functions in the criminal court system. First, they facilitate pretrial release of large numbers of arrested persons. Of course, the defendant must pay for this "service." However, in deciding whether to post bail for a defendant's release, the only question in which the bondsman has any real interest is whether the defendant will pay the fee for what is in effect a loan of money. This means that monetary considerations override other concerns, such as the offense with which the defendant is charged, the likelihood of guilt, the probability of rearrest, or even the risk of flight.

Bondsmen can afford to ignore these matters because of their intimate knowledge of court operations and the personalized relationships they cultivate with court officials. In large part, their work consists of drawing upon these resources to manage cases and protect investments. This is related to a second function performed by bondsmen, which is to help move defendants through the courts. Because their earnings depend directly upon the number of customers they handle, bondsmen gear their activities toward promoting rapid disposition of cases.

Third, bondsmen aid officials in dealing selectively with difficult cases. In one such arrangement, for example, the bondsman acts upon his legitimate business prerogatives by refusing to bond a certain defendant for pretrial release, thereby tacitly carrying out official wishes. In another, the bondsman exercises his legal power of interstate extradition in order to help officials avoid the problems and expense of securing the return for prosecution of a fugitive defendant who has been apprehended in another state. Both of these arrangements work on the same principle. They require bondsmen to carry out informal and extralegal directives issued by court officials. In turn, officials cooperate with bondsmen because of the organizational benefits that bondsmen confer on the legal system. Official reciprocity takes several forms, the most important of which is judicial nonenforcement of forfeited bail bonds.

The bail system, then, links the personal interests of bondsmen with the organizational requirements of criminal court operations. This linkage is accomplished by means of discretionary exchanges of outcomes which augment the effective authority of law-enforcement and judicial personnel and which also take much of the risk out of bondsmen's business transactions. This system of interlocking obligations strengthens official control over arrested persons at the same time that it increases the profitability of selling bail bonds.

CONCLUSION

The last twenty years of appellate court rulings on criminal procedure have had profound effects on local court operations. For example, one articulate judge, viewing the scene from an intermediate appellate court, maintains that the cumulative impact on criminal courts has been literally devastating.

The mood of alarm expressed by contemporary observers of American criminal courts can be more readily understood by recalling that at no time since the beginning of this century has anything but the roughest kind of justice been available for the majority of the cases in these courts.

As the appellate judiciary over the last two decades has attempted to raise the standards of treatment accorded criminal defendants by local criminal justice officials, the resulting improvements have been slight by comparison with expectations for change which have been generated by these decisions.

In addition to the tensions generated by the politics of local justice, criminal courts now face a qualitatively different set of problems arising from the fact that their activities have been drawn into the politics of constitutional law.

In this vastly changed situation, the practical achievements of criminal court administration seem always to be lagging farther behind the evolving constitutional criteria of fair treatment. One should not imagine that this growing divergence has gone unrecognized by criminal justice officials or that it has caused them only minor inconveniences. In fact, as gaps between written law and official practice have widened, the exact role that trial courts are to play in the criminal justice system has become increasingly unclear.

Ambiguity is reflected in many ways. For instance, one innovation which has received great acclaim from judges and prosecutors in recent years is the idea that some individuals accused of crime can usefully be channeled away from the coercive context of court proceedings and toward the beneficent environment of informal "treatment" (Vorenberg and Vorenberg 1973). In point of fact, every program based on the concept of "diversion" uses "the threat or possibility of conviction of a criminal offense to encourage an accused to do something," and the agreement thus obtained "may not be entirely voluntary, as the accused often agrees to participate in a diversion program only because he fears formal criminal prosecution" (National Advisory Commission 1973: 27). There can be little doubt that the growing appeal of this concept among local criminal justice officials has an intimate and paradoxical connection with developments in constitutional law over the past two decades (Balch 1974).

At the same time, a controversy has arisen over the question of whether and to what extent it falls to criminal courts to supervise the police in order to assure their compliance with changed procedural requirements (Milner 1971). For it can be argued that the changes in police practices which have been mandated by appellate decisions over the last two decades are so sweeping, and the lack of any alternative enforcement mechanism so patent, as to presuppose a substantially new function for local-level judicial officials. Many of these decisions, indeed, seem aimed precisely at extending the political doctrine of separation of powers, and the companion doctrine of judicial supremacy, to the administration of local criminal justice. The core assumption in nearly all of them has been that criminal courts must counterbalance the activities of police agencies in order to prevent mistreatment of citizens accused of crime. In this view, it becomes the responsibility of trial courts to monitor the actions of law-enforcement officials and, using the remedy of dismissal as a sanction, check any tendencies toward official lawlessness (LaFave and Remington 1965).

The period between arrest and disposition has special importance in American criminal law, for it is during this period that defendants are supposed to begin taking advantage of the procedural protections to which appellate courts hold them entitled (Karlen 1967: 135–166). In practice, however, relatively few defendants get any opportunity to do so. In most cases the period after arrest involves perfunctory official acknowledgment of the defendant's rights, followed by out-of-court negotiations aimed at rapid disposition. In lower criminal courts, the defendant's first appearance tends to be his only appearance (Mileski 1971). The disposition process is somewhat less abbreviated in higher-level trial courts, but the same tendency toward truncated procedure can be observed there (Blumberg 1970).

The conception of the criminal court as a supervisor of police activities and the essentially hierarchical model of the criminal justice system implied in this conception have been criticized before (Bittner 1970: 22–30; Feeley 1973). The present article casts further doubt on these assumptions. It focuses on the stage of the criminal justice process that begins when law-enforcement functions give way, in principle at least, to judicial functions. The findings indicate that the business of court administration virtually merges with the enterprise of law enforcement at this period and strengthen the argument that the criminal court actually serves as an agency of law enforcement (Skolnick 1969: 236–243). Thanks to the growing interest in criminal courts among social scientists, we now have some idea of why this merger takes place and how it affects the treatment of defendants. We are also coming to realize that the problems of criminal courts are both causes and effects of the chronic crisis in American criminal justice.

REFERENCES

ARES, CHARLES, and HERBERT STURZ (1962) "Bail and the Indigent Accused." 8 *Crime and Delinquency* 12.

BALCH, ROBERT W. (1974) "Deferred Prosecution: The Juvenilization of the Criminal Justice System." 38 *Federal Probation* 46.

BEELEY, ARTHUR L. (1927) *The Bail System in Chicago.* Chicago: University of Chicago Press (reissued 1966).

BITTNER, EGON (1970) *The Functions of the Police in Modern Society.* Washington, D.C.: U.S. Government Printing Office.

BLUMBERG, ABRAHAM S. (1967) "The Practice of Law as a Confidence Game." 1 *Law and Society Review* 15.

——— (1970) *Criminal Justice.* Chicago: Quadrangle Books.

CHAMBLISS, WILLIAM J. (1971) "Vice, Corruption, Bureaucracy, and Power." *Wisconsin Law Review* 1150.

COX, ARCHIBALD (1968) *The Warren Court.* Cambridge, Mass.: Harvard University Press.

DOWNIE, LEONARD (1971) *Justice Denied.* Baltimore: Penguin Books.

FEELEY, MALCOLM M. (1973) "Two Models of the Criminal Justice System: An Organizational Perspective." 7 *Law and Society Review* 407.

FLEMING, MACKLIN (1974) *The Price of Perfect Justice.* New York: Basic Books.

FOOTE, CALEB (1954) "Compelling Appearance in Court: Administration of Bail in Philadelphia." 102 *University of Pennsylvania Law Review* 1031.

——— (1958) "A Study of the Administration of Bail in New York City." 106 *University of Pennsylvania Law Review* 693.

——— (1965) "The Coming Constitutional Crisis in Bail." 113 *University of Pennsylvania Law Review* 959.

FREED, DANIEL J., and PATRICIA M. WALD (1964) *Bail in the United States: 1964.* Washington, D.C.: National Conference on Bail and Criminal Justice.

FRIEDMAN, LAWRENCE M. (1973) *A History of American Law.* New York: Simon & Schuster.

GOLDFARB, RONALD (1965) *Ransom: A Critique of the American Bail System.* New York: Harper & Row.

HOSKINS, JOHN (1968) "Tinkering with the California Bail System." 56 *California Law Review* 1134.

INGRAHAM, BARTON L. (1974) "The Impact of Argersinger—One Year Later." 8 *Law and Society Review* 615.

JACKSON, DONALD DALE (1975) *Judges.* New York: Atheneum.

JAMES, HOWARD (1971) *Crisis in the Courts.* New York: David McKay.

KARLEN, DELMAR (1967) *Anglo-American Criminal Justice.* New York: Oxford University Press.

LAFAVE, WAYNE R., and FRANK J. REMINGTON (1965) "Controlling the Police: The Judge's Role in Making and Reviewing Law Enforcement Decisions." 63 *Michigan Law Review* 987.

LEFSTEIN, N., et al. (1969) "In Search of Juvenile Justice." 5 *Law and Society Review* 491.

LEMERT, EDWIN M. (1970) *Social Action and Legal Change.* Chicago: Aldine.

LEVIN, MARTIN (1972) "Urban Politics and Judicial Behavior." 1 *Journal of Legal Studies* 193.

LEVY, LEONARD W. (1974) *Against the Law.* New York: Harper & Row.

MATHER, LYNN M. (1973) "Some Determinants of the Method of Case Disposition: Decision-Making by Public Defenders in Los Angeles." 8 *Law and Society Review* 187.

MILESKI, MAUREEN (1971) "Courtroom Encounters: An Observation Study of a Lower Criminal Court." 5 *Law and Society Review* 473.

MILNER, NEAL A. (1971) *The Court and Local Law Enforcement.* Beverly Hills, Calif.: Sage Publications.

MOLEY, RAYMOND (1930) *Our Criminal Courts.* New York: Minton, Balch & Co.

MUELLER, GERHARD O. W., and FRE LE POOLE-GRIFFTHS (1969) *Comparative Criminal Procedure.* New York: New York University Press.

NATIONAL ADVISORY COMMISSION (1973) *National Advisory Commission on Criminal Justice Standards and Goals Report on Courts.* Washington, D.C.: U.S. Government Printing Office.

NATIONAL CONFERENCE ON BAIL AND CRIMINAL JUSTICE (1965) *Proceedings and Interim Report.* Washington, D.C.

——— (1966) *Bail and Summons: 1965.* Washington, D.C.

OHLIN, LLOYD E., ed. (1973) *Prisoners in America.* Englewood Cliffs, N.J.: Prentice-Hall.

PAULSEN, MONRAD (1966) "Pre-Trial Release in the United States." 66 *Columbia Law Review* 109.

POUND, ROSCOE (1945) *Criminal Justice in America.* Cambridge, Mass.: Harvard University Press.

PRESIDENT'S COMMISSION (1967) *The President's Commission on Law Enforcement and Administration of Justice Task Force Report: Courts.* Washington, D.C.: U.S. Government Printing Office.

ROTHMAN, DAVID (1972) "Of Prisons, Asylums, and Other Decaying Institutions." 26 *The Public Interest* 3.
SCHUBERT, GLENDON (1970) *The Constitutional Polity.* Boston: Boston University Press.
SILVERSTEIN, LEE (1966) "Bail in the State Courts—A Field Study and Report." 50 *Minnesota Law Review* 621.
SKOLNICK, JEROME H. (1967) "Social Control in the Adversary System." 11 *Journal of Conflict Resolution* 52.
——— (1969) *The Politics of Protest.* Washington, D.C.: U.S. Government Printing Office.
SUFFET, FREDERICK (1966) "Bail Setting: A Study of Courtroom Interaction." 12 *Crime and Delinquency* 318.
SUTHERLAND, EDWIN H., and DONALD R. CRESSEY (1970) *Principles of Criminology.* Philadelphia: J. B. Lippincott Company.
U.S. SENATE (1964) Hearings, Bills to Improve Federal Bail Procedures. 88th Cong., 2nd Sess.
——— (1966) Hearings, A Proposal to Modify Existing Procedures Governing the Interstate Rendition of Fugitive Bailees. 89th Cong., 2nd Sess.
VIRTUE, MAXINE BOORD (1962) *Survey of Metropolitan Courts.* Ann Arbor: University of Michigan Press.
VORENBERG, ELIZABETH W., and JAMES VORENBERG (1973) "Early Diversion from the Criminal Justice System." In Lloyd E. Ohlin, ed., *Prisoners in America.* Englewood Cliffs, N.J.: Prentice-Hall.
WASBY, STEPHEN L. (1970) *The Impact of the United States Supreme Court: Some Perspectives.* Homewood, Ill.: Dorsey Press.
WICE, PAUL (1974) "Purveyors of Freedom: The Professional Bondsmen." 11 *Society* 34.
WICE, PAUL, and RITA JAMES SIMON (1970) "Pretrial Release: A Survey of Alternative Practices." 34 *Federal Probation* 60.
WOOD, ARTHUR L. (1967) *Criminal Lawyer.* New Haven: College and University Press.
YALE LAW JOURNAL (1961) "Bail: An Ancient Practice Reexamined." 70 *Yale Law Journal* 966.
——— (1964) "Bailbondsmen and the Fugitive Accused—The Need for Formal Removal Procedures." 73 *Yale Law Journal* 1098.

ARTICLE FIFTEEN

Adjudication and Sentencing in a Misdemeanor Court: The Outcome Is the Punishment

JOHN PAUL RYAN

In a study of the New Haven lower court, Malcolm Feeley concluded that the "process is the punishment" because, although sentences were light, the additional costs borne by the people who were arrested and prosecuted were significant. John Paul Ryan's study of the Columbus (Ohio) Municipal Court showed that criminal sanctions imposed upon convicted defendants were much more severe. Ryan attributes these differences to the contrasting local political cultures, whose influence upon the courts is mediated by police department orientations, relationships between the police and prosecutors, and methods of judicial assignment.

A . . . published work on misdemeanor courts concludes that the major punishment of defendants occurs during the processing of their cases (Feeley 1979). Feeley contends that the pretrial costs associated with arrests on misdemeanor charges typically outweigh any punishments imposed after conviction. The need to make bail, hire an attorney, be present at court appearances, and even help prepare one's defense drain the economic and psychological resources of many defendants, whether they are ultimately adjudicated guilty or innocent. By contrast, the punishments meted out to defendants upon conviction appear insubstantial. Few are incarcerated, and fines rarely exceed $50.

These findings and arguments have a distinct appeal. They provide a new and creative interpretation to case processing in the lower criminal

Source: Law and Society Review 15 (1980–1981): 79–108. Reprinted by permission of the authors and the publisher.

courts, one at variance with our understanding of felony courts. Yet as Feeley himself acknowledges, his work is a case study. His data are drawn exclusively from the New Haven (Connecticut) Court of Common Pleas. What about other misdemeanor courts? Is it reasonable to believe that most lower courts are like New Haven's? Studies of criminal justice and political culture might suggest otherwise. Levin's (1977) study of the felony courts of Pittsburgh and Minneapolis indicates substantial differences in sentencing severity, attributable in part to the political culture or values of the two communities. Levin found that sentences were typically less severe in the highly partisan, ethnically diverse, working-class city (Pittsburgh) than in the reform-minded, socially homogeneous city (Minneapolis). Eisenstein and Jacob (1977) found sentencing practices in Baltimore to be much more harsh than in either Detroit or Chicago, and they attributed the greater harshness to a heritage of conservatism and racism in that southern border city. Likewise, the working environments of courts differ. Church and colleagues (1978) found that the pace at which cases are processed differs markedly from one large city to another, in part because of intangible factors which they termed "local legal culture." And Ryan and colleagues (1980) found that various administrative procedures, relationships among courtroom work group members, and judicial perceptions are sensitive to the partisan climate of the local political environment. In short, the character of a community—its history, politics, and lifestyle—affects what takes place in its courts, both in terms of process and outcomes.

If the relationships between political culture and trial courts are viewed at all seriously (see Kritzer 1979), one must question not only the generalizability of Feeley's data but also his primary argument. More data from different communities would help to show whether the process actually constitutes a substantial punishment in the lower courts. These data should speak to the processing of cases and defendants, because it can be expected that some courts minimize pretrial costs by expediting cases, liberalizing indigency requirements for counsel, and utilizing cash bonds infrequently. Perhaps even more important, additional data should be collected on case outcomes, for likewise it can be expected that lower courts vary in the severity of sanctions imposed upon convicted defendants.

Data relating to process and outcomes in the Franklin County, Ohio, Municipal Court (Columbus) are reported below. This inquiry, like Feeley's, is a case study, but one that serves as a counterpoint. The findings suggest that New Haven may be among the least punitive lower courts in the nation. The Columbus court is sufficiently more severe in its sanctions—and less demanding in its process costs—that the outcome is the primary punishment. Throughout the article, comparative reference is made with an eye toward dramatizing the very real differences between the two courts. In the conclusion, some explanation as to why the courts differ is provided. As background for that analysis, an overview of the two cities and their courts follows.

COLUMBUS AND NEW HAVEN: CONTRASTING LOCAL POLITICAL CULTURES

Columbus is a medium-sized American city, more populous and more sprawling than New Haven. Over half a million people live in the city of Columbus, a figure sharply on the rise in the 1960s and early 1970s, compared with a steadily declining population in New Haven of only 125,000. The citizenry of Columbus is better educated, more affluent, and of different ethnic origins that that of New Haven. Feeley (1979: 37–38) aptly characterizes New Haven as a town "beset with the standard ills of many old urban areas—shrinking population, declining tax base, deteriorating housing, smog, poor schools, encroaching superhighways, and an increasing underemployed minority population." In a comparative vein, Feeley goes on to say:

> It [New Haven] represents neither the worst nor the best of American urban centers. It does not convey the sense of hopelessness and decay that observers report in such urban centers as Newark or Gary, nor . . . the same sense of optimism as do new and more culturally homogeneous and prosperous cities as Des Moines or Minneapolis . . . [or, one might add, Columbus].

These differences in the physical and cultural characteristics of the two cities predictably presage differences of political culture. New Haven is predominantly Democratic in partisanship; Columbus is heavily Republican—an "urban Republican stronghold" (Barone et al. 1980: 694). Differences in partisan orientation are evident in presidential votes, mayoralty elections, and congressional representation. Columbus has not had a Democratic mayor in the last decade; New Haven has not had a Republican mayor in two decades. Two conservative Republicans represent portions of Columbus and its surrounding suburbs in Washington; one liberal Democrat represents New Haven. The political affiliation of judges, too, parallels community orientations, though judges are formally appointed on a statewide basis in Connecticut and elected locally in Ohio. Feeley (1979: 63) reported four Democratic and three Republican judges in the New Haven lower court. At the time of the study in Columbus, twelve Republican judges sat with a lone Democratic judge in that municipal court. Equally important, the significance of partisanship in the delivery of public services is much greater in New Haven than in the "good government" atmosphere of Columbus.

The political structure of the two communities also differs. Though both claim mayor-council forms of government, the similarity ends there. New Haven has been described as having a pluralistic leadership structure (Dahl 1961; Feeley 1979: 37). More impressionistically, Columbus has been described as relatively monolithic, dominated economically by big banks and insurance companies and ideologically by the Wolfe family and their newspaper (Barone et al. 1980: 694–695), and lacking New Haven's "vigorous group of residents involved in actively trying to cope with problems" (Feeley 1979: 38).

The courts also look quite different in their personnel, operations, and informal relationships. These differences are often traceable to the local political culture. Feeley (1979: 53–61) reports a substantial patronage system surrounding the New Haven courthouse, even after reforms intended to alleviate political influence in the courts were enacted. For example, judgeships are viewed as rewards for faithful party service. Prosecutors and public defenders are likely to be drawn from families active in the local political organizations. Lower-level personnel (deputies, clerks, and so on) are likely to come from the ranks of "ward leaders and vote mobilizers." Columbus, by contrast, reflects little political influence of this kind in its courts. Judgeships come either from association with the governor or a popular local campaign, possibly aided by bar endorsement. Prosecutors and public defenders need not have political sponsors. Lower-level court personnel are recruited through an elaborate system of checks and balances designed to remove partisan politics and judicial whim.

The orientation of the police department and its relations with the prosecutor's office are also quite distinctive in the two communities. Feeley (1979: 45–47) describes the New Haven police department as oriented to dispute resolution or, in Wilson's (1968) terminology, "order maintenance." Accordingly, it is not surprising that the police appear to play a small role in the development of prosecution cases, having little communication with the prosecutor and rarely appearing as witnesses in court. Prosecutors seem dominant vis-à-vis the police in the New Haven court, albeit both share dispute-processing views of the role of the lower court. In Columbus, the police department is much better characterized as "law-enforcement" oriented, accounting for the importance which police officers attach to successful prosecution of minor cases. Officers regularly appear as witnesses in brief trials and are ready to appear on other occasions when a plea is entered. Indeed, when police officers "hang around" the Columbus court waiting for their cases to be called, they often sit in other courtrooms watching outcomes (with occasional astonishment at the perceived leniency of some judges). In short, by custom the police in Columbus have been an important, perhaps dominant, force in the lower court, much to the chagrin of the local defense bar.

Finally, there are differences of court structure, rooted in political history, that affect relationships among courtroom actors, notably between judges and others. Connecticut, unlike Ohio, does statewide assignment of judges (Feeley 1979; Ryan et al. 1980), which in practice means that lower-court judges are frequently rotated. Feeley (1979: 67) argues that one important consequence of rotation is the gravitation of judicial responsibility toward prosecutors and others permanently assigned to one court. Judges in New Haven have been heard to ask prosecutors about the "going rate" for particular offenses, suggesting a desire to adhere to work-group norms. In Columbus, the judges—who are elected or appointed to that municipal court—are much more individualistic and autonomous in their approach to sentencing.

New Haven, in sum, is a criminal court system that reflects the "particularistic values of ethnic, religious, political, and family associations" in its rendering of "swift, substantive justice" (Feeley 1979: 61). Columbus, by contrast, is a system that reflects the universalistic values of professional competence and technical efficiency in its rendering of swift but formal justice through the mechanisms of an adversary system as applied to a misdemeanor court.

METHODS OF DATA COLLECTION

Data were collected on 2,764 cases in the Franklin County (Columbus) Municipal Court. These represent the universe of cases scheduled for a "pretrial" during March, April, and May of 1978. Sampling from pretrials was necessitated by the court's assignment and scheduling systems: only cases which are *not* disposed of at arraignment can be scheduled for a pretrial hearing.[1] Nevertheless, cases scheduled for a pretrial are not an unrepresentative sample of all cases. Pretrials are routinely scheduled for nearly *all* cases which proceed beyond arraignment,[2] including a wide variety of criminal and traffic cases.

All available information was collected for each of these cases, including type and seriousness of offense, number of charges, type of defense counsel, judge at pretrial and disposition,[3] mode of disposition, and sentence or sanctions imposed. Because of the court's effective computerized system, there were virtually no missing data on these items. Additionally, prior record information was collected from prosecutor files for OMVI (drunk driving) cases.

Formal, semi-structured interviews were conducted with the supervisor of the municipal unit of the prosecutor's office (hereafter, Prosecutor), two assistant prosecutors, and an administrative assistant. Also interviewed were the Supervisor of the municipal unit of the public defender's office (hereafter, Defender), supervisors in the Probation Department and the Pre-Trial Release Program, and six of the thirteen municipal court judges. These interviews focused variably upon modes of case disposition, judicial styles in plea bargaining and sentencing, the treatment of OMVI cases, the operations of arraignment court, and the role of the pretrial stage. In addition, ten of the thirteen municipal court judges were observed, typically for several hours at a time, usually in pretrial sessions[4] but also at arraignments, in trials, and in the entry of guilty pleas. The observations focused upon judicial behaviors such as sentencing philosophy, involvement in plea negotiations, and relationships with prosecuting and defense attorneys.

THE COLUMBUS COURT'S CASELOAD: AN OVERVIEW

The Franklin County (Columbus) Municipal Court has jurisdiction over a variety of matters, including small claims, civil cases up to $10,000, and preliminary hearings in felony cases. As Table 1 indicates, the court's misdemeanor caseload is composed of almost equal proportions of traffic and criminal cases. Operating a motor vehicle under the influence of alcohol (OMVI) is the most frequent type of case, and it accounts for nearly two-thirds of all traffic cases. Other traffic cases include reckless operation of a motor vehicle (ROMV), driving without a valid license or with a suspended license, hit-and-run, speeding, and lesser violations. The dominance of OMVI cases is not unique to Columbus. Although arrests for drunk driving are more frequent in Columbus than elsewhere in Ohio (Ohio Courts 1978), other municipal courts also report a large percentage of drunk driving cases (see Neubauer 1974).

Assault is the most frequent type of criminal case, followed by theft and passing bad checks. Other criminal cases include trespass, carrying a concealed weapon, obstructing justice, disorderly conduct, soliciting, drug use, public indecency, housing code violations, fleeing from a police officer, and resisting arrest. The Columbus court's criminal caseload is presumably lightened by the operation of a night prosecutor program which screens all citizen-initiated complaints and diverts interpersonal disputes and bad-check cases, in substantial numbers, from the court (see Palmer 1975).

The majority (58 percent) of cases involve a single charge against a defendant, but a substantial proportion (42 percent) involve more than

Table 1 Distribution of the court's misdemeanor caseload

	Percent	*Number*
Traffic		
OMVI	30.2	834
Other traffic	17.8	492
Criminal		
Assault	17.1	472
Theft	10.8	300
Bad checks	7.1	196
Other criminal	17.0	470
	100.0	2,764

Note: Limited to cases scheduled for a pretrial

one charge (typically two or three). Multiple-charge cases most often occur with the OMVI offense, where another more visible violation brings the intoxication of the driver to the attention of the police officer. Only 23 percent of OMVI cases involve a single charge; other violations, especially driving on the wrong side of the road, out of control, across lanes, or speeding, are likely to accompany a charge of drunk driving. Similarly, certain other traffic offenses, such as driving without a valid license, are likely to involve multiple charges, as a result of more visible traffic violations. By contrast, most criminal cases involve only a single charge against a defendant.

Modes of Case Disposition

The court utilizes a number of ways to dispose of cases that proceed beyond arraignment. These include guilty plea to the original charge, guilty plea to a reduced charge, court trial, jury trial, bond forfeiture, dismissal, and—in multiple-charge cases—combinations of these. In addition, some defendants fail to appear, and these "no shows" are treated, for statistical purposes, as case terminations.

Almost half of the sample of cases in Columbus were disposed through a guilty plea, similar to the percentage in New Haven (Feeley 1979: 127). The majority of these represent pleas to *reduced* charges, indicating a form of charge bargaining. Case type is the most important factor in determining whether a reduction of charges will occur (see Table 2). In OMVI cases in particular, a charge reduction is common. This reflects some uneasiness in imposing the required incarceration where a defendant is convicted of drunk driving.[5]

Three other factors, not readily available in case files, were cited by the prosecutor as influencing his decision to reduce charges: prior record of the defendant, strength of the evidence, and actions of the defendant vis-à-vis the arresting officer. Where the arresting police officer takes offense at the actions or attitude of the suspect, a charge reduction will not usually occur. This reflects the police dominance of the lower court described earlier. Only recently have public defenders fostered the idea that the prosecutor, not the police, should run the courtroom. The public defender's office still feels that prosecutors defer "too much" to police officers. Strength of evidence, on the other hand, may be the kind of nebulous factor which operates more in the minds of prosecutors than in their actual behavior. Individual prosecutors, in this and other misdemeanor courts, rarely have the time or inclination to gauge evidentiary matters precisely.

Prosecutors and defense counsel are the primary actors in the forging of guilty pleas, particularly in charge bargaining. But what about the role of the trial judge? Trial judges in misdemeanor courts do not always restrict

Table 2 Distribution of case disposition modes, by case type

	All cases	*OMVI*	*Other traffic*	*Assault*	*Theft*	*Bad checks*	*Other criminal*
Conviction at trial	1.9%	2.2%	2.3%	1.9%	1.3%	1.0%	1.5%
Guilty plea—original charge	17.3	19.5	35.0	5.1	7.3	9.2	17.1
Guilty plea—reduced charge	28.0	64.1	18.1	4.7	27.0	1.0	11.2
Bond forfeiture	6.3	.7	6.4	3.2	13.7	18.9	9.0
Dismissal	34.0	4.7	26.1	75.9	36.7	43.4	45.0
Acquittal at trial	1.0	.4	.8	3.0	.3	0	1.1
No show	11.5	8.4	11.3	6.2	13.7	26.5	15.1
	100.0%	100.0%	100.0%	100.0%	100.0%	100.0%	100.0%
N =	(2,715)	(807)	(486)	(469)	(300)	(196)	(457)

Note: Disposition for multiple-charge cases has been coded as follows. Dismissals have been disregarded in the presence of guilty pleas or bond forfeitures. Where there were guilty pleas to original and reduced charges, the disposition was treated as a guilty plea to a reduced charge. These coding decisions flow from discussions of multiple-charge cases in the text.

their role to ratifying bargains struck by other parties (Ryan and Alfini 1979). Observations in Columbus suggest that at least a few judges do actively engage in sentence bargaining from the bench. For example, Judge H,[6] who has the reputation for making sentence commitments in advance as his normal practice, remarked to defense counsel in one case that was observed: "If the defendant wants to plead, I'll put on a fine and wrap it up today" (assault case). Judge D also encouraged guilty pleas, through a mixture of occasional sentence leniency and frequent gratuitous comments to defendants about the "break" they were getting. Furthermore, Judge D sometimes intimated that he would find a defendant guilty were the case to go to trial ("you gotta keep your eyes open" to a defendant charged with jay walking, or "a driver has a responsibility, even under icy road conditions" to a defendant ticketed in an auto accident).

Determining exactly how much negotiating actually precedes the guilty pleas entered in this court is not simple. Charge bargaining may involve little more than the application of standard discounts, unless there are unusual circumstances. Sentence bargaining occurs in some guilty pleas, but its frequency varies from judge to judge. Nevertheless, the amount of bargaining accompanying guilty pleas in Columbus is almost certainly higher than, say, in Neubauer's Prairie City or even Feeley's New Haven. Unlike Prairie City in 1970 or New Haven more recently, many more cases in Columbus involve defendants represented by counsel. Defense attorney presence seems to lead inexorably toward increased bargaining in the guilty pleas entered in misdemeanor cases (see Alfini and Doan 1977: 431; Neubauer 1974: 209).

Trials are very infrequent in Columbus, but they are by no means the extinct species which Feeley reports in New Haven (1979: 127). In the sample of 2,764 cases, 32 (1.1 percent) were resolved by jury trial and 46 (1.6 percent) by court trial.[7] One gained the distinct impression from interviews and observations that trials are welcomed by many judges and attorneys, as an occasional relief from the monotony of calendar calls. Judge G remarked, "I enjoy trials when I get two good lawyers." The defender noted of Judge G, "He gives you a good trial." Not surprisingly, then, trials proceeded in a thorough and unharried manner.

Comparatively serious cases are more likely to go to a *jury* trial. For example, OMVI cases account for 30 percent of the sample of cases but 41 percent of all jury trials, and assault cases represent 17 percent of the sample of cases but 34 percent of all jury trials. By contrast, less serious cases more frequently go to a *court* trial. For court trials, OMVI cases are significantly underrepresented, whereas other traffic cases comprise a substantial share.

Conviction at trial is likely, but far from certain. Defendants fared better at jury trials, where the conviction rate was 56.3 percent (18 of 32 cases). In court trials, the conviction rate was 71.7 percent (33 of 46 cases).

Likelihood of conviction varies by case type. Combining jury and court trials, the conviction rate was 5.5:1 in OMVI cases, 4:1 in theft cases, 3:1 in other traffic cases, 3:2 in other criminal cases, and a mere 2:3 in assault cases. The individual judge also makes some difference. Consider that two of the court's most active plea-bargaining judges, D and H, did not acquit a single defendant in the seven court trials which they heard. Their "inducements" to defendants to plead guilty, then, were reinforced by a reluctance to find for a defendant in a court trial.

Bond forfeitures are not convictions in a legal sense. In the words of one prosecutor, they represent a "hybrid between conviction and dismissal . . . a sentencing alternative occasionally used to dispose of cases expeditiously."[8] In Columbus, cases are sometimes disposed by bond forfeiture upon agreement of both sides. There may be evidentiary problems for the prosecutor, or uncertainty by the defense as to the outcome of a trial or plea negotiations. The court receives some money, and the defendant escapes the stigma of conviction. Bond forfeitures occur most often in minor cases.

Dismissals are a frequent occurrence in Columbus. One-third of the cases in the sample were dismissed (*nolle prosequi*). According to both the prosecutor and the defender, the most frequent cause of dismissal is the failure of the complaining witness to prosecute. These perceptions are supported by data collected and analyzed in the prosecutor's office. An examination of dismissals in January 1979 revealed the lack of a prosecuting witness to be the most frequently noted reason. Most often it was a civilian witness, but occasionally it was the failure of a police witness to appear.[9]

Other reasons cited for dismissals were "at the request of the prosecutor," correction of code violations, and restitution. Some prosecutor requests for dismissal probably do result from lack of preparation (as one person in the prosecutor's office charged),[10] but primarily it is a screening decision. Because police-filed complaints are not screened before the pretrial session, this court appearance offers the first opportunity to weed out weak cases. Given the power of the police in municipal court, it may be easier for prosecutors to request dismissals in the "full view," and occasional scrutiny, of the judge rather than in the "secrecy" of an aggressive screening unit in the prosecutor's office.

The role of the judge in the decision to dismiss appears to be little more than ratification of attorney requests. According to the prosecutor, judges play a significant role only "very occasionally." The defender cited the instance of prosecutorial objection to a defense motion for dismissal as the only occasion for judicial scrutiny. In interviews, judges themselves typically indicated a minimal role in the decision to dismiss. In the words of Judge G, "prosecutors should know." Thus, just as prosecutors defer to police in the charging decision, judges defer to the prosecutor in the screening decision at the pretrial.[11]

Cases with more than one charge may be disposed in more than one way. For example, one charge may be dismissed if there is a guilty plea to a second charge. This is, in fact, the most common pattern of multiple disposition in Columbus. It is also common in New Haven, where Feeley refers to this apparent give-and-take as "splitting the difference" (1979: 134). There may, however, be less bargaining in these dispositions than Feeley implies. It is hard to believe that many defendants feel a sense of victory when they are convicted on one charge rather than two. This must especially be the feeling among defendants who face conviction in drunk driving cases, the very defendants most likely to receive a "splitting the difference" disposition.

Defendants in Columbus who fail to appear for a pretrial session in the courtroom are not as lucky as some of the "no-shows" in New Haven. It is one thing not to appear at arraignment in a petty case; these cases in Columbus typically result in a bond forfeiture and termination. Failure to appear at a pretrial invariably results in the issuing of a bench warrant by the judge, often with a substantial bond.[12] No precise data are available on the percentage of these defendants who return to court for disposition, but court participants think the figure is quite high. For the sample period, 12 percent of all defendants scheduled to appear at a pretrial session failed to appear.

Table 2 illustrates that the variation in disposition across types of cases is enormous. At one extreme, most assault cases (76 percent) are dismissed. This is partly because the civilian complainant often has a change of mind regarding prosecution, but partly reflects the poor conviction ratio (only 2:3) of assault cases actually tried. At the other extreme, OMVI cases are rarely dismissed (only 5 percent). The charge is a serious one and is typically accompanied by other traffic violations. Furthermore, acquittal at trial in OMVI cases is rare (1 in 5.5). Between these two extremes, variations are modest.

A MULTIVARIATE ANALYSIS OF CASE DISPOSITION

We have a limited range of variables with which to explain case disposition. Some of these variables are characteristics of the case (or what Feeley calls "legal factors"); others bear upon individual courtroom actors; one reflects the court's processing of a case. No information about the characteristics of defendants—for example, race or age—was available.

A stepwise regression model was used to analyze data, in order to facilitate the disentanglement of joint effects among these variables. Type of case was operationalized as a series of dummy variables; also included were seriousness of charge (Ohio has five classifications of misdemeanor offenses ranging from six months incarceration to a $100 fine), the number of charges, the number of court appearances, the type of defense counsel, and the identity of the disposition judge. For the distribution of these variables, refer to Table A-1 [at the end of this article].

Case disposition, a categorical variable, has been collapsed into two categories: adjudicated guilty or not guilty. Included in the "guilty" category are pleas to original or reduced charges, convictions at trial, and bond forfeitures. Included in the "not guilty" category are dismissals and acquittals at trial. (No-shows have been excluded from the analysis.) Treating bond forfeitures as guilty dispositions stretches the legal meaning of the disposition, but not their functional meaning. In Columbus, bond forfeitures are little more than a variant of the guilty plea.[13] Based upon this dichotomy, 61 percent of defendants were found guilty, and the remaining 39 percent were found not guilty.[14]

Table 3 illustrates that most of the explanatory variables entered in the regression equation are predictive of case disposition. The two most important variables are assault and OMVI cases. Assault cases are very likely to be dismissed, whereas OMVI cases are very likely *not* to be dismissed. Other case and structural characteristics are of some predictive value. By contrast, the identity of courtroom actors bears little upon disposition. The judge appears to make no difference once other factors are controlled. Presence of counsel also makes no difference. Type of counsel shows a very small effect: public defender cases are slightly more likely to result in not-guilty dispositions, when other factors are controlled, than are private counsel cases.

Table 3 A multivariate model of case disposition: stepwise regression[a]

	Beta weights[b]
Assault case	.31
OMVI case	−.24
Number of charges	−.16
Number of court appearances[c]	−.13
Seriousness of case[d]	−.09
Public defender counsel	.05
$R_2 = .60$	
$R = 36\%$	
$(N = 2{,}279)$	

[a]Case disposition is coded: not guilty (high), guilty (low).
[b]Each of the beta weights is statistically significant at .05; in no instance does the standard error approach beta.
[c]Number of court appearances is dichotomized, based upon the nonlinear relationship present in bivariate analysis: one appearance versus two or more appearances.
[d]Seriousness of case is dichotomized, based upon a curvilinear relationship present in bivariate analysis: most and least serious coded high; in-between coded low.

The six variables listed in Table 3 account for fully 36 percent of the variation in case dispositions ($R = .60$). This is a large amount when one considers the nature of the variables available in the court files and, correspondingly, other variables which are surely important but not available. The identity of the prosecutor, for example, may be important, especially in a court like Columbus where "prosecutor shopping" has been facilitated by the office's horizontal assignment system.

These findings parallel Feeley (1979) in some respects and contrast in other ways. The most important discrepancy occurs in the impact of counsel, where Feeley found that unrepresented defendants fare significantly less well (see also Katz 1968). One explanation may be the different proportions of unrepresented defendants in New Haven and Columbus. The large number of defendants without counsel in New Haven suggests a reluctance to implement fully the spirit of *Argersinger v. Hamlin* (1972). Columbus is not such a court. Most defendants have counsel (or access to counsel at arraignment), but those without fare equally well in case disposition. Limited courtroom observations support these interpretations. Indeed, in arraignment court, one judge consistently encouraged unrepresented defendants to consult with the public defender available in the courtroom before entering any plea.

FORMS OF SENTENCE OR SANCTION

Misdemeanor courts inflict upon their convicted defendants a wider variety of less-severe sanctions than do felony courts. The Columbus misdemeanor court is no exception. Fines, bond forfeitures, terms in the county jail or municipal workhouse, suspensions of a driver's license, attendance at programs for alcoholics and drunk drivers, and probation are among the primary sanctions available and employed by the court. Sometimes convicted defendants receive only one form of sentence, but quite often they face several sanctions.

Fines are routinely imposed upon convicted defendants in Columbus. Some judges frequently hand out stiff fines, then suspend a portion of the fine. The practice may be designed to enhance a judge's popularity, as a skeptical Judge G remarked, declaring that "a heavy fine makes the police happy . . . suspending part of it makes the defense happy." Alternatively, the suspension may help to "keep in line" a defendant placed on probation, as Judge E noted. Both of these judges occasionally suspend portions of fines. The motives of judges who frequently suspend large portions of stiff fines, like Judges C and M, are not always clear.[15]

Figure 1 displays the net fines imposed, once suspensions are taken into account. Only 13 percent of defendants in Columbus escape a fine entirely. Of the remainder, fines range from a mere $5 to $1,750. The mean

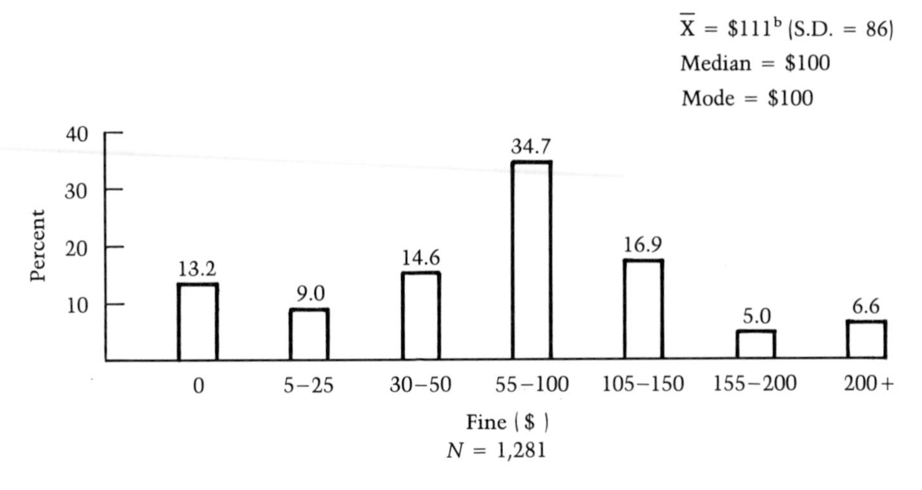

[a]Cumulates fines imposed upon a defendant convicted on more than one charge.
[b]Statistics are based on a distribution excluding defendants not fined (0).

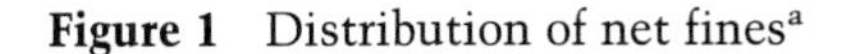

Figure 1 Distribution of net fines[a]

fine is $111, and the median and mode are both $100. Not unexpectedly, OMVI cases draw the heaviest fines ($\overline{X}$) = 128).

These fines represent a significant amount of money to most defendants, even in our presently inflated economy. This is particularly true for indigent defendants represented by the public defender's office. The severity of fines in Columbus is all the more striking when compared with New Haven (see Table 4). The two courts differ substantially in the amount of the fines they impose. In Columbus, nearly three-fourths of the net fines exceeded $50, whereas only a handful of fines (4 percent) in New Haven were greater than $50. Furthermore, in Columbus 87 percent of all convicted defendants paid some fine, compared with only 45 percent in New Haven (Feeley 1979: 138).

Several caveats should be applied to this comparison. The New Haven data were collected for three months in 1974, compared with three months in 1978 in Columbus. Nevertheless, according to Judge G, a veteran on

Table 4 Comparison of fines in the Columbus and New Haven lower courts

	Columbus	*New Haven*
$50 or less	27.2%	96.0%
More than $50	72.8	4.0
N	(1,112)[a]	(377)[a]

[a]For comparative purposes, only convicted defendants receiving some fine have been included.

the court, "fines are less today than ten years ago," a diminution which he attributed to the "more lenient judges now on the bench." Also, the range of cases heard in the New Haven court is different from Columbus. No traffic cases are heard in New Haven, and these cases in Columbus (notably OMVI) draw consistently the heavier fines. Still, the New Haven court had felony cases (about 20 percent of the docket), indicating that in some respects the Columbus court hears more petty cases. Thus, neither the different range of cases nor the different time periods studied appear to account for the variation in fines between the two courts.

Bond forfeitures are tantamount to fines, particularly in view of *when* the bond amount is set. The decision is made at the time of case disposition, and the defendant agrees to pay the fine. The modal amount of bond forfeitures is $50, and the mean is only slightly higher ($\overline{X} = 57$). Again, in comparison with New Haven (where Feeley reports most bond forfeitures to be between $5 and $25), the sanction is greater in Columbus.[16]

Jail terms are announced to a majority (52 percent) of convicted defendants. However, one-third of these terms are entirely suspended, and many others are suspended in part. The use of suspended sentences for *jail terms* is much more widespread among the court's judges; nine judges suspend, in part or whole, more than half of their jail terms. Figure 2 reveals that 35 percent of convicted defendants serve some jail time, most often in the city workhouse. About half of these defendants serve three or four days; most of the others serve either thirty days or a longer sentence. Defendants convicted in OMVI cases are most likely to be incarcerated (44 percent), but typically serve a short sentence (three or four days).

Comparisons with New Haven again are striking. Only 4.9 percent of convicted defendants in New Haven served a jail term (Feeley 1979: 138), whereas almost *six times* as many defendants received a jail term in Columbus. Some mitigating factors should be considered in this comparison. Many defendants who do serve time in Columbus do not have their lives totally disrupted (for example, by loss of job). It is common for shorter sentences, and even some longer sentences, to be served on weekends, a phenomenon growing in popularity elsewhere (see Parisi, 1980). Also, drunk driving cases contribute a moderately disproportionate number of jail terms in the Columbus court. Nevertheless, it appears that across a similar range of criminal cases (for example, assault, theft) a defendant in Columbus stands a much higher likelihood of incarceration, if convicted.

In traffic cases the court acts as an administrative entity in monitoring the driver's licenses of individual citizens. In sprawling and decentralized Columbus, the license is a valuable—often necessary—commodity. For a variety of offenses, the court is authorized, or even required, to suspend licenses. The Columbus lower court uses its authority selectively, but not infrequently. Fully one-third (36 percent) of defendants convicted in OMVI or other traffic cases have their license suspended for a period of time. The standard suspension is thirty days, but in a few instances the term

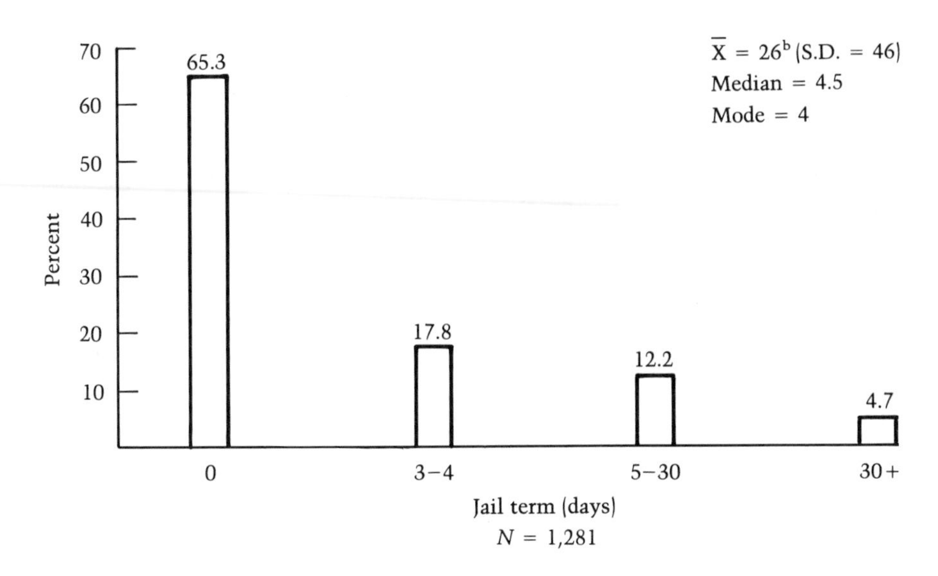

[a]Cumulates jail terms imposed upon a defendant convicted on more than one charge.
[b]Statistics are based on a distribution excluding defendants not incarcerated (0).

Figure 2 Distribution of net jail terms[a]

may be for sixty or ninety days, or even one year. Defendants convicted in OMVI cases are much more likely to have their license suspended than those convicted of other traffic offenses.

The Columbus court also frequently requires attendance at drunk driver schools and alcohol-control programs upon conviction in traffic cases. At the least, this constrains defendants in time and transportation, no matter how "therapeutic" the program may be. Fully one-third of defendants convicted in OMVI cases are required to attend one or another local program as part of their sentence.

Probation is extensively used as a sanction in this court. A supervising officer in the probation department reported that more than 2,000 defendants convicted on misdemeanor charges are currently on probation, and he noted that probation is more frequently used now than ever before. The bulk of the department's caseload stems from theft, bad check, and alcohol-related cases—areas where recidivism is high. Judges themselves vary in how often they use probation, some imposing it frequently, others selectively ("taking into account our caseload problems"), and one judge not at all. We have no further data on the use of probation, because the case files do not contain such information.

Finally, more than one type of sanction is often imposed. In criminal cases, about one defendant in five is incarcerated and fined. In traffic cases, fully half of all defendants face multiple sanctions involving some combination of fines, incarceration, suspension of the driver's license, and attendance at drunk driver programs. Furthermore, the use of multiple sanctions is seemingly not considered in determining the severity of each sanction. For example, leniency in fines is generally *not* granted to defendants who are sentenced to serve time in jail. Indeed, defendants who are sentenced to serve jail time are fined *more* heavily ($121 on average) than those not incarcerated ($83 on average), differences mostly attributable to traffic cases. Similarly, defendants do not typically attend a drunk driver's program in lieu of a (heavier) fine; it is usually in addition to the fine. The heaviest fines in OMVI and other traffic cases are levied against defendants who are incarcerated, lose their license for a period of time, and must attend an alcohol-control program.

In sum, the Columbus misdemeanor court views the variety of sanctions available in a relatively punitive, rather than ameliorative, light. Instead of choosing which one sanction to employ against convicted defendants, this court often chooses *how much* of several sanctions. In this regard, the court is quite different from New Haven, where fines are used much less frequently and where combinations of probation and suspended sentence often serve as punishment. No wonder, perhaps, that Feeley viewed the process to be the primary punishment. In Columbus, the outcome is the punishment.

A Multivariate Analysis of Sanctions

No single measure of sanction severity could adequately represent the variations described above. Thus, the correlates of two sanctions—fines and incarceration—are examined separately. All of the predictor variables earlier utilized were included here, as were two additional variables relevant for sentencing decisions: prior record and case disposition mode.

Defendant's prior record has been viewed by courtroom participants to be of the utmost importance in sentencing decisions. Previous research has cautiously, if not convincingly, demonstrated its predictive value (see Farrell and Swigert 1978; Gibson 1978; Rhodes 1978; but also, Eisenstein and Jacob 1977). In Columbus, prosecutors usually possess this information about a defendant. Based upon observations and interviews, prior record influences both plea-bargaining practices and the sentencing decision of the judge.[17]

It has long been suspected that a defendant's pursuit of the right to trial—particularly a jury trial—triggers a penalty upon conviction. Evidence was marshaled by early studies (see, for example, American Friends Service Committee 1971), but recent studies utilizing more sophisticated statistical techniques have reached varying conclusions (see Eisenstein and Jacob 1977; Rhodes 1978; Nardulli 1978; Uhlman and Walker 1979). Nevertheless, even Eisenstein and Jacob, who find no statistical effect, assert that the *perception* of a penalty for going to trial is still widely held by "court officials and defendants alike," one that is "instrumental in promoting a steady flow of guilty pleas" (1977: 271).

The regression equation for fines yielded a weak explanatory model. Only 14 percent of the variation was explained by the predictor variables (R = .38); the most important of these was whether the case was OMVI or not (beta = .30). Analysis of variations in fines by different types of cases proved more fruitful. Table 5 presents these data.

In OMVI cases, several variables are about equally important in explaining a small amount of variation (11 percent). Judge G, who has the reputation of being the toughest sentencer on the court,[18] contributes to the likelihood of receiving a heavier fine. So do multiple charges, being convicted upon a trial, and having a relevant prior record. In traffic cases, a similarly small amount of variation is explained (10 percent). The key variable is the number of charges; in traffic cases other than OMVI, the amount of the fine rises dramatically as the number of charges increases. In theft cases, a much larger proportion (41 percent) of variation is explained. Three of the four predictor variables are individual judges. Again, being in the courtroom of Judge G contributes to the likelihood of a more severe fine; so does conviction upon trial.

Two points bear further comment. First, the contrast in predictors between OMVI and theft cases highlights the degree to which the court has routinized the handling of drunk driving cases. Judicial sentencing philosophies are muted; variation across judges in fines levied is small. Only the court's tough sentencer, Judge G, is far from the court's norm. This routinization is facilitated by the comparative frequency of OMVI cases and by the unquestioned seriousness with which all courtroom actors view this type of case. In the words of Judge E, a self-characterized middle-of-the-road sentencer, "Judges are swayed by the community in which they live . . . people don't want to see rapists, thieves or *drunk drivers* go

Table 5 A multivariate model of severity of fines by type of case: stepwise regression[a]

OMVI		*Traffic*		*Theft*	
	Beta[b]		Beta[b]		Beta[b]
Judge G	.17	Number of charges	.27	Judge M	.36
Number of charges	.15	Judge J	−.12	Judge G	.32
Disposition mode[c]	.13			Judge J	−.25
Prior record	.12			Disposition mode[c]	.23
R = .33		R = .32		R = .64	
R^2 = 11%		R^2 = 10%		R^2 = 41%	
(N = 313)		(N = 269)		(N = 107)	

[a]Equations for the other three case types did not reach standard levels of statistical significance.
[b]Each of the beta weights is statistically significant at .05; in no instance does the standard error approach beta.
[c]Disposition mode: guilty at trial coded high; guilty upon plea coded low.

free" (emphasis added). Petty theft or larceny, on the other hand, may present value conflicts for judges sympathetic to poor people, accounting for the wide variation in sanction severity among the court's judges.

The second point to be emphasized is the effect on fines resulting from conviction at trial. Although not significant in the ordinary range of traffic cases where most trials are highly abbreviated, going to trial in OMVI or theft cases is a different matter. In these cases, there is a distinguishable penalty attached to pursuing full constitutional rights. Or in the words of several Columbus courtroom actors, "Rent is charged for the use of the courtroom."

Analysis of incarceration directs attention to two questions: (1) should the defendant serve any time in jail? and (2) if so, how much time? Accordingly, separate regressions were performed for the use of the sanction and for its severity where used. In the former instance, the dependent variable is a dichotomy wherein 65 percent of defendants were not incarcerated and 35 percent were incarcerated. In the latter case, the dependent variable is interval, ranging from three days to one year. Table 6 presents the results of both regressions.

The decision to incarcerate is poorly explained by the model (only 11 percent of the variance). Six variables are statistically significant predictors, but the effect of each is small. The most important of these is OMVI; such cases are the most likely to result in incarceration. Four of the six predictor variables for incarceration also appeared in the model for case fine severity. Thus, many of the same forces at work in one kind of sentencing decision are at work in another.

The severity of incarceration is somewhat better explained (19 percent of the variance). Again, OMVI is the most important variable, but in a negative direction. Most drunk driving cases receive very short sentences,

Table 6 A multivariate model of the use and severity of incarceration: stepwise regression

	Use of incarceration	*Severity of incarceration*
	Beta[a]	Beta[a]
OMVI case	.19	−.37
Disposition mode[b]	.12	.11
Judge M	.11	ns
Judge G	.10	.28
Number of charges	.10	.13
Judge A	−.07	ns
	R = .33	R = .44
	R^2 = 11%	R^2 = 19%
	(N = 1,271)	(N = 439)

[a]Each of the beta weights is statistically significant at .05; in no instance does the standard error approach beta.
[b]Disposition mode: guilty at trial coded high; guilty upon plea coded low.

usually the three days mandated by statute as the minimum. The court's reputed tough sentencer lives up to that reputation. As most defendants seem acutely aware, being in the courtroom of Judge G will result in a much longer sentence.

Attempts to improve explanation of incarceration by analyzing within types of cases were generally unsuccessful, probably because of skewed distributions and small numbers. In OMVI cases, however, a substantial 26 percent of the variance in the use of incarceration was explained (R = .51). The most important predictor was the type of plea, whether to the original or reduced charge (beta = .36). This is to be expected, since conviction on the original charge in OMVI cases requires some type of confinement. Prior record also showed a significant effect (beta = .16), suggesting the importance of tapping this difficult-to-collect variable.

SUMMARY AND CONCLUSIONS

The Columbus lower court yields a quite different picture from that of New Haven. Outcomes are costly to convicted defendants. Fines are substantial, incarceration is not infrequent, and in traffic cases one's license is in jeopardy. In many cases, more than one type of sanction is imposed. Furthermore, courtroom actors including defendants behave as if the outcome is important. Defendants hope to avoid Judge G. Seemingly minor cases appear on the pretrial docket, indicative of a decision not to plead guilty at first appearance. Defense counsel stall at pretrial hoping for a more sympathetic prosecutor or bargain on the day of trial. Prosecutors operate under strict guidelines for charge reduction in OMVI cases. The outcome *is* important to defendants and courtroom actors alike.

By contrast, the process of having one's case adjudicated is not very costly in Columbus. Indigency requirements are liberally interpreted by the public defender's office and by judges in arraignment court. Few defendants await the outcome of their case in custody. Many receive personal recognizance release or supervised release without bond; others pay a 10 percent appearance bond directly to the court (90 percent of which is returned upon appearance). Finally, the court requires few appearances of its defendants. Cases are not routinely continued. In all, the median elapsed time from initial arraignment to disposition is approximately thirty days. Process costs may seem high to unconvicted defendants, but for convicted defendants the outcome is unmistakably the more important punishment.

Why outcomes are more punishing in Columbus than in New Haven cannot be answered definitively. But differences in the political culture and structure of the two communities, described earlier, clearly play a key role. The political culture of Columbus breeds a climate of severity. This is manifested in the institutional domination of the police in the lower court, in the Columbus police department's orientation to law enforcement rather than order maintenance, and in the community's expectations that traffic laws will be enforced. Moreover, judges in Columbus may be more responsive to community expectations of full enforcement and meaningful sanctions[19] because they are elected locally and attached permanently to Columbus, unlike the rotating judges who serve the New Haven lower court. More precise linkages of the nexus between political culture and lower-court outcomes must necessarily await comparative research.

The data from Columbus suggest several additional themes. First, the type of case structures the substance of the decision-making process (see also Feeley 1979: xv). Throughout the analysis, this is the most significant predictor of whether defendants are found guilty or go free, and which defendants go to jail if convicted. In particular, assault and drunk driving cases are handled in highly distinctive ways. This apparent "pigeonholing" of cases in lower courts contrasts, at least in degree, with felony courts.

Secondly, the adjudication and sentence decisions are often indistinct. In this respect the Columbus lower court is like many felony courts where the determination of guilt and negotiations over sentence run together. In Columbus, the two decision stages merge in the use of bond forfeitures where money is appropriated without any formal decision on guilt or innocence. The two stages also merge in plea bargaining in multiple-charge cases, where a decision to dismiss one charge occurs in exchange for submission of a guilty plea on other charges. And the two stages merge in the overlapping uses of prior record. Decisions to dismiss or to dispose of cases by way of bond forfeiture are often made in light of a defendant's prior record, a piece of data ordinarily, and legally, reserved for the sentence decision alone.

Finally, the perceptions of courtroom work group members conform quite closely to the realities of case disposition in Columbus. For example, attorneys perceive that "rent is charged for the courtroom" (in trials), and the case data indicate a clear penalty for going to trial in more serious cases. Prior record is perceived by attorneys and judges to be significant in bargaining and sentencing, and likewise the case data indicate (in drunk driving cases) that a relevant prior conviction reduces the likelihood of severe fine and a jail term. Furthermore, personalities are perceived accurately. Everyone agrees that Judge G is a much tougher sentencer than any other judge on the court; Judge G himself says he is "likely to give the maximum," and the case data unmistakably paint Judge G as the dispenser of the heaviest fines and the longest jail terms. Such convergences of perception and behavior indicate the *rationality* of the court, a theme insufficiently highlighted either in misdemeanor or felony courts. Courtroom actors may have an excellent sense of how their own court operates, even if their world view is limited (Heumann 1977) or they are unable to articulate theories of criminal courts.

Table A–1 Frequency distribution of selected case characteristics[a]

	Percent	*Number*
Seriousness of offense		
M1	82.4	2,273
M2	3.7	103
M3	3.5	97
M4	6.4	173
MM (minor misdemeanor)	4.0	111
Number of charges		
1	57.6	1,586
2	28.3	780
3	10.3	284
4	2.5	70
5	.8	22
6 or more	.5	13
Type of defense counsel		
Private	59.6	1,626
Public defender	32.2	880
Pro se	8.2	225
Number of court appearances		
1 (disposed at arraignment)	—[b]	—[b]
2 (disposed at pretrial)	59.7	1,577
3	30.4	801
4	8.0	211
5	1.6	43
6	.3	7
Prior record[c]		
None	62.8	206
1 conviction	23.5	77
2 or more convictions	13.7	45

[a]For the distribution of case type, refer to Table 1; for disposition mode, refer to Table 2.
[b]Cases disposed at arraignment, due to their unavailability, were not included in this study.
[c]Refer to note 17 for operationalization of prior record; includes only OMVI cases.

NOTES

1. The percentage of cases disposed at arraignment is not available.
2. Cases in which there is no jury demand can be scheduled directly for a court trial, without the scheduling of a pretrial. These constitute a small percentage of all cases, perhaps 100 in the three-month sampling period.
3. Although there is a central scheduling office, the court operates under an individual case assignment system (after arraignment), in which the same judge hears a case from the pretrial through final disposition. The individual assignment system is mandated by Ohio Rules of Superintendence promulgated for the lower trial courts in 1974 by the state supreme court. (Ohio Sup R.4).
4. Pretrial hearings in this court are always conducted in the courtroom, in full view and hearing of all. Chambers are rarely used for plea-negotiation discussions.
5. Conviction of drunk driving carries a statutory minimum incarceration of three days. Judges may substitute for the jail term a confinement of a similar period in a drunk driving program. For a theory of penalty mitigation in OMVI cases, see Ross 1976.

6. All judges will be referenced by alphabetic letters selected at random in order to preserve anonymity. Though such a promise was not required to conduct observations, it was needed to gain access to case data.

7. But see note 2 above.

8. Bond forfeiture is also used to dispose of petty cases (for example, disorderly conduct) where the defendant fails to appear at arraignment, after having made bond with the court. Feeley (1979: 138) found that 16.6 percent of his sample was disposed in this way.

9. To alleviate this problem, a Police Liaison Program was recently instituted, whereby a small number of police officers are assigned on a regular basis to the courtroom for pretrial sessions.

10. Until 1980, prosecutors were assigned cases on a master calendar principle, from one to two weeks in advance of a court date. Thus, the prosecutor assigned for the pretrial was not necessarily the prosecutor on the day scheduled for trial, in the event it was not resolved at the pretrial.

11. Interestingly, though most dismissals did occur at the pretrial session, a significant percentage of all dismissals (22 percent) occurred on the scheduled trial date.

12. The median amount is $300, with a few bonds set as high as $1,000 or even $2,500.

13. In Columbus, "no contest" pleas are counted as guilty pleas for the purpose of statistical record keeping. Some judges like to encourage defendants to plead "no contest" if that will facilitate a disposition, notably Judge D.

14. The use of a dichotomous dependent variable in multiple regression analysis is less than ideal (see Goodman 1972). Nevertheless, the distribution of case disposition is insufficiently skewed to warrant such statistical transformations as Goodman's log linear technique.

15. Judge C suspended some portion of a fine in 69 percent of his cases; the amount suspended averaged $150. Judge M suspended part of a fine in 63 percent of his cases, on the average for $135. Together, these two judges accounted for 56 percent of all cases in which a fine was suspended in whole or in part.

16. It is more difficult to compare accurately bond forfeitures in the two courts, since Columbus also utilizes bond forfeitures in cases where defendants do not skip.

17. Due to difficulties in finding (in the prosecutor's basement) prior record information, collection efforts were restricted to OMVI cases. For these cases, prior record was operationalized as *relevant prior convictions,* defining "relevant" as OMVI, ROMV (reckless; the charge to which most OMVI cases are reduced), physical control (of an automobile), and intoxication. These were the types of cases cited by members of the prosecutor's and public defender's offices as bearing upon a sentence decision in OMVI cases.

18. According to the Defender, defendants initially ask two questions: (1) can I get a personal recognizance bond and (2) is Judge G assigned to the case? In the interview with Judge G, he confirmed his tough sentencing philosophy ("I'm likely to give them the maximum"), noting that his association with crimes has primarily been with the *victims* of crimes (through his stint as a prosecutor).

19. It seems clear that judges in Columbus perceive the community to be basically conservative and expecting of tough sentences. A major newspaper article about this study appeared in the *Columbus Dispatch* on June 22, 1980, in which the municipal court was characterized as "tough" and "efficient." The administrative judge was quoted in the article as being delighted that "somebody thinks that we're doing a good job." The author of the newspaper article inferred from my comparisons that, because Columbus was tougher, it was a better court.

REFERENCES

ALFINI, JAMES J., and RACHEL DOAN (1977) "A New Perspective on Misdemeanor Justice." 60 *Judicature* 425.

AMERICAN FRIENDS SERVICE COMMITTEE (1971) *Struggle for Justice: A Report on Crime and Punishment in America.* New York: Hill & Wang.

BARONE, MICHAEL, GRANT UJIFUSA, and DOUGLAS MATTHEWS (1980) *Almanac of American Politics.* New York: E. P. Dutton.

CHURCH, THOMAS W., JR., ALAN CARLSON, JO-LYNNE LEE, and THERESA TAN (1978) *Justice Delayed: The Pace of Litigation in Urban Trial Courts.* Williamsburg, Va.: National Center for State Courts.

DAHL, ROBERT (1961) *Who Governs? Democracy and Power in an American City.* New Haven: Yale University Press.

EISENSTEIN, JAMES, and HERBERT JACOB (1977) *Felony Justice: An Organizational Analysis of Criminal Courts.* Boston: Little, Brown.

FARRELL, RONALD A., and VICTORIA LYNN SWIGERT (1978) "Prior Offense Record as a Self-Fulfilling Prophecy." 12 *Law and Society Review* 437.

FEELEY, MALCOLM M. (1979) *The Process Is the Punishment: Handling Cases in a Lower Criminal Court.* New York: Russell Sage Foundation.

GIBSON, JAMES L. (1978) "Race as a Determinant of Criminal Sentences: A Methodological Critique and a Case Study." 12 *Law and Society Review* 455.

GOODMAN, LEO A. (1972) "A Modified Multiple Regression Approach to the Analysis of Dichotomous Variables." 37 *American Sociological Review* 28.

HEUMANN, MILTON (1977) *Plea Bargaining: The Experiences of Prosecutors, Judges, and Defense Attorneys.* Chicago: University of Chicago Press.

KATZ, LEWIS R. (1968) "Municipal Courts—Another Urban Ill." 20 *Case Western Reserve Law Review* 87.

KRITZER, HERBERT M. (1979) "Political Cultures, Trial Courts, and Criminal Cases." In Peter F. Nardulli, ed., *The Study of Criminal Courts: Political Perspectives.* Cambridge, Mass.: Ballinger.

LEVIN, MARTIN (1977) *Urban Politics and the Criminal Courts.* Chicago: University of Chicago Press.

NARDULLI, PETER F. (1978) *The Courtroom Elite: An Organizational Perspective on Criminal Justice.* Cambridge, Mass.: Ballinger.

NEUBAUER, DAVID W. (1974) *Criminal Justice in Middle America.* Morristown, N.J.: General Learning Press.

OHIO COURTS (1978) Columbus: Supreme Court, Office of the Administrative Director.

PALMER, JOHN W. (1975) "The Night Prosecutor." 59 *Judicature* 22.

PARISI, NICOLETTE (1980) "Part-Time Imprisonment: The Legal and Practical Issues of Periodic Confinement." 63 *Judicature* 385.

RHODES, WILLIAM M. (1978) *Plea Bargaining: Who Gains, Who Loses?* Washington, D.C.: Institute for Law and Social Research.

ROSS, H. LAURENCE (1976) "The Neutralization of Severe Penalties: Some Traffic Law Studies." 10 *Law and Society Review* 403.

RYAN, JOHN PAUL, and JAMES J. ALFINI (1979) "Trial Judges' Participation in Plea Bargaining: An Empirical Perspective." 13 *Law and Society Review* 479.

RYAN, JOHN PAUL, ALLAN ASHMAN, BRUCE D. SALES, and SANDRA SHANE-DU BOW (1980) *American Trial Judges: Their Work Styles and Performance.* New York: Free Press.

UHLMAN, THOMAS M., and N. DARLENE WALKER (1979) "A Plea Is No Bargain: The Impact of Case Disposition on Sentencing." 60 *Social Science Quarterly* 218.

WILSON, JAMES Q. (1968) *Varieties of Police Behavior.* Cambridge, Mass.: Harvard University Press.

ARTICLE SIXTEEN

Urban Politics and Policy Outcomes: The Criminal Courts

MARTIN A. LEVIN

Martin A. Levin compares the sentencing behavior of judges in two cities to determine the impact of a traditional partisan system and that of a system subscribing to the nonpartisan, reform ethos. Social background, recruitment, and political culture all seem to exert an influence on the judges' treatment of defendants.

In recent years students of urban government have analyzed the ways in which conflict is managed in various cities. Some large cities (of over 300,000 in population) have a "traditional" political system with (typically) a formally partisan city government, with, to a varying degree, strong parties that (1) rely on material rewards rather than issues to attract members, (2) have a generally working-class orientation toward politics, (3) emphasize conferring material benefits upon individuals, (4) identify with local areas of the city, rather than the city "as a whole," and (5) centralize influence. Other large cities have a "good government" or reform political system with (typically) a formally nonpartisan city government and weak parties which (1) rely on nonmaterial rewards (primarily issues or personalities), (2) have a generally middle-class orientation toward politics, (3) emphasize maximizing such values as efficiency, honesty,

Source: First published in the first edition of *Criminal Justice: Law and Politics,* by George F. Cole. Copyright © 1972 by Wadsworth Publishing Company, Inc. Reprinted by permission. Some footnotes omitted; others renumbered.

impartiality, professionalism, and an identification with the city "as a whole," and (4) decentralize influence.

In short, these studies sought to answer the question "Who governs?" However, even more recently students of urban government have attempted to raise and answer a second and probably more important question: "What difference does it make who governs?" What difference does it make to *average citizens* whether they live in a city with a "traditional" political system or a "good government" political system? It is very likely, as James Q. Wilson has argued, that the struggle for power in a city has little direct effect on the life of average citizens, but that the services provided by the government once in power (such as the administration of criminal justice, education, and welfare) are very likely to affect them directly and significantly. Moreover, it is possible that the policies followed in providing these services are closely related to, and indeed perhaps the product of, the city's political system. Thus these policies can be viewed as the outputs of the city's political system, and the political processes of the city can be viewed as the inputs.

This paper attempts to ascertain what consequences different political systems have for the sentencing decisions of the criminal court judges in Minneapolis and Pittsburgh and thus for the individuals that come into the courts. It also attempts to discover what happens when the selection of judges is taken "out of politics."

JUDICIAL AND POLITICAL REFORM, EVALUATION, AND THE APPROACH OF THIS STUDY

For many years attorneys, their professional associations, many (but by no means all) judges, and reform-minded laypersons have advocated taking the selection process of judges out of politics. The proposals for this vary, but are typically variations of the "Missouri Plan" or the "merit selection plan" in which the governor appoints the judges from a list of nominees selected by a nonpartisan nominating commission composed of lawyers and laypersons (and in some instances judges). Another selection method which is also designed to remove judges from politics, but which reformers feel is less ideal, is the selection of judges in truly nonpartisan elections. The advocates of reform argue that judges are experts and should be selected by fellow experts in a nonpolitical manner and that expert, nonpolitical selection procedures will produce higher-quality, more efficient, more independent, and, therefore, more impartial and just judges. None of the reform advocates support their assertions with systematic evidence indicating that taking the selection of judges out of politics does in fact produce such judges, or indeed that it has any consequences for judicial behavior. Opponents of taking the selection of judges "out of politics" premise their argument on democratic values, but also fail to support their assertions with evidence that a political selection procedure would help attain such values.

To empirically evaluate the consequences of differing political systems and differing judicial selection systems, comparative research was undertaken on the criminal courts and political systems of Pittsburgh and Minneapolis. These cities represent two more or less opposed types of political systems (the "traditional" and the "good government," respectively) and both types of judicial selection systems (the political and the reform, respectively).

Pittsburgh has a formally partisan and highly centralized city government. In 1966, when this research was begun, the Democratic party organization was strong, hierarchical, disciplined, highly cohesive, and attracted workers with material incentives. It has dominated city politics since the early 1930s and has been influential in state and national politics. Public and party offices are filled by party professionals whose career patterns are hierarchical and regularized. They patiently "wait in line" because of the party's need to maintain ethnic and religious balance, even on a judicial ticket. There is a high degree of centralization of influence, and the citizens tend to accept pro-union and liberal social welfare policies. There is wide acceptance of partisanship and party activity in almost every sphere of Pittsburgh local government. Indeed, there has been little public enthusiasm for efforts to take the selection of judges out of politics, and parties view positions on the courts and their related agencies as primary sources of rewards for their workers.

There are nineteen judges on the Pittsburgh (Allegheny County) common pleas court (the trial court for both criminal and civil jurisdictions), and they are elected on a partisan basis for ten-year terms. Party designation appears on the ballot. In practice the political parties, especially the Democratic party, dominate primaries and the general elections for judicial positions in Pittsburgh, and the local bar association usually plays a very limited role.

When a court vacancy occurs, the governor appoints a successor who must stand for reelection at the next general election. Ten of the nineteen incumbent judges in 1965 initially reached the bench in this manner. These interim appointments have also been controlled by the local parties.[1] The Pittsburgh judges' career patterns also reflect the dominance of the parties and the limited role of the bar association in judicial selection. Almost all of the judges held a government position such as city solicitor, assistant prosecutor, city council member, state legislator, or even congressional representative, prior to coming to the bench (all are partisan offices and are controlled by the parties). They were also active members of the party organization.

Minneapolis has a formally nonpartisan and structurally fragmented city government. The Democratic-Farmer-Labor (DFL) party and the Republican party play a significant but limited role in city politics. They are both formally (because of nonpartisan elections) and informally (because of the wide acceptance of nonpartisanship) limited. The parties are moderately weak, loosely organized, highly democratic and undisciplined. They attract workers through nonmaterial incentives. Thus the parties do not overcome the formal decentralization of authority in the city. Individuals, including "amateur" politicians, with the ability and willingness to work, but with little seniority in the party, can and do rise rapidly in the party and in city government. The citizens tend to be disposed toward conservative policies for city government. Nonpartisanship in city politics is accepted by the people, and even by many party workers and some party leaders. Indeed, the electorate has had a strong negative response to candidates or incumbents who violate, or seem to violate, this ideal. This is especially true of the courts and their related agencies, and thus party leaders and workers tend not to regard them as a source of party rewards.

There are sixteen judges on the Minneapolis (Hennepin County) district court (the trial court for both criminal and civil jurisdictions), and they are formally elected for six-year terms on a nonpartisan basis. In practice the political parties have almost no role in the selection of judges in Minneapolis, while the local bar association generally plays a major role. Prior to a judicial election, the Minneapolis Bar Association polls its members and publicizes the results. The "winner" of the poll (or the second or third highest candidate) almost always wins the election. The governor makes appointments to interim vacancies, and fourteen of the sixteen incumbent judges in 1965 initially reached the bench in this manner. When vacancies occur the Minneapolis Bar Association conducts a poll, and the Minnesota governors have closely adhered to the bar's preferences. The two DFL governors who have served in the last ten years have been significant exceptions to this pattern, but they were strongly criticized for this (even by some of their own party members) and had to work carefully around the bar association. Moreover, during the administrations of these DFL governors, the party played almost no role in judicial selections because the governor's decisions were, at the most, influenced by "political" rather than "party" considerations (for example, the appointees' relationships to these governors were personal rather than organizational).

The Minneapolis judges' career patterns also reflect the minor role of the parties and the major role of the bar association in judicial selection. Prior to coming to the bench, fourteen of the eighteen Minneapolis judges in this study had been exclusively or predominantly in private legal practice (usually business-oriented, and often corporate, practices). Those who held public positions before coming to the bench did not hold elective positions (with one exception) and were generally not active in either party.

This paper focuses on the criminal division of the courts in these two cities, in part because judges typically have a very high degree of discretion in criminal-sentencing decisions. Criminal statutes in Pennsylvania and Minnesota, as in most states, allow judges the choice of incarcerating a convicted defendant or of granting probation, in most felony cases. If they choose the former, the statutes also allow them, within prescribed limits, to fix the term of imprisonment. The high degree of discretion in sentencing decisions presents an opportunity to study judicial behavior that is shaped by the fewest external variables, such as the actual degree of the defendant's guilt and the quality of police investigation and prosecution. In contrast, conviction rates are not simply the product of the judges' discretion and are greatly affected by these three factors.

To understand typical judicial behavior patterns in each city, sentencing decisions were compared statistically for the nine most common felony offenses. To understand the judges' attitudes, decision-making processes, and courtroom behavior, interviews were conducted with all but one of the judges in both cities, and courtroom trial proceedings were observed over a period of several months in 1966. The judges' interview statements were crossvalidated on the basis of their actual sentencing decisions, observation of their courtroom behavior, and interviews with more than twenty criminal court participants in each city.

THE JUDGES' SENTENCING DECISIONS

There are significant differences in the sentencing decisions of the judges in each city. On the whole, the decisions are more lenient in Pittsburgh than in Minneapolis. White and black defendants receive both a greater percentage of probation and a shorter length of incarceration in Pittsburgh. This pattern persists when the defendant's previous record, plea, and age are also controlled, and it is rather consistent among all nine of the offenses compared. Table 1 indicates this pattern in summary terms. For probation, when the sentencing decisions are controlled for type of prior record and race, there is a sufficient number of cases to compare the nine offenses in each city for twenty-five categories. In twenty-two categories there is a greater percentage of probation in Pittsburgh, in two categories there is a greater percentage of probation in Minneapolis, and in one there is no significant difference between the cities. For incarceration, when type of prior record and race are controlled, there is a sufficient number of cases to compare the nine offenses for sixteen categories. In thirteen categories there is a shorter length of incarceration in Pittsburgh, in two categories there is a shorter length of incarceration in Minneapolis, and in one there is no significant difference between the cities. Throughout every aspect of the data the pattern runs almost entirely in one direction—greater leniency in Pittsburgh—and there are only some marginal variations in the degree of this greater leniency.

Table 1 Percentage of probation in Pittsburgh and Minneapolis

	Pittsburgh	*(Percent "acquitted plus costs")*[a]	*Minneapolis*	*Ratio*[b]
WHITES, NO PRIOR RECORD				
Burglary	58.4	7.9	56.0	1.04
	(60)	(6)	(275)	
Grand larceny	87.5	24.2	62.7	1.40
	(32)	(15)	(188)	
Aggravated assault	87.5	28.5	37.5	2.33
	(8)	(4)	(24)	
Aggravated robbery	0.0	0.0	5.9	NR
	(8)		(68)	
Indecent assault	50.0	36.9	50.0	1.0
	(6)	(7)	(70)	
Aggravated forgery	50.0	9.1	55.6	−1.11
	(8)	(1)	(117)	
Nonsufficient funds	81.8	23.8	67.3	1.22
	(11)	(5)	(101)	
BLACKS, NO PRIOR RECORD				
Burglary	47.5	3.8	38.2	1.24
	(40)	(2)	(34)	
Grand larceny	68.0	7.5	45.4	1.50
	(25)	(3)	(22)	
Aggravated assault	60.0	27.2	28.0	2.14
	(10)	(6)	(25)	
Aggravated robbery	25.0	10.0	12.0	2.08
	(8)	(1)	(25)	
Possession of narcotics	50.0	0	33.3	1.5
	(6)		(15)	
WHITES, PRIOR RECORD				
Burglary	59.4	6.8	22.0	2.7
	(227)	(21)	(159)	
Grand larceny	62.1	8.4	34.8	1.78
	(103)	(12)	(69)	
Aggravated assault	47.4	21.4	15.4	3.08
	(19)	(6)	(13)	
Aggravated robbery	26.1	3.6	2.8	9.32
	(23)	(1)	(36)	
Simple robbery	33.3	24.3	27.8	1.20
	(21)	(9)	(18)	
Indecent assault	72.4	16.9	28.6	2.53
	(47)	(13)	(28)	
Aggravated forgery	54.6	0	25.5	2.14
	(11)		(106)	
Nonsufficient funds	56.2	20.9	35.7	1.57
	(16)	(5)	(70)	
Possession of narcotics	77.8	7.7	55.6	1.40
	(9)	(1)	(9)	
BLACKS, PRIOR RECORD				
Burglary	32.6	3.7	28.6	1.14
	(291)	(14)	(28)	

(continued)

Table 1 Percentage of probation in Pittsburgh and Minneapolis *(continued)*

	Pittsburgh	*(Percent "acquitted plus costs")*[a]	*Minneapolis*	*Ratio*[b]
Grand larceny	38.2 (115)	5.8 (9)	15.8 (19)	2.42
Aggravated robbery	8.3 (36)	4.4 (2)	0 (10)	NR
Aggravated forgery	50.0 (16)	5.6 (1)	28.6 (7)	1.75
Possession of narcotics	48.0 (25)	2.6 (1)	12.5 (8)	3.84

[a]This verdict is used in Pittsburgh but not in Minneapolis. Therefore, in comparing the sentencing decisions between cities, the percentage of defendants who receive this verdict is treated as an added increment of freedom resulting from the judges' discretion, which is comparable to an increment of probation. (By contrast, the proportion of defendants acquitted outright [that is, without being ordered to pay court costs] is an increment of freedom, but it is not comparable to an increment of probation because it is not the product of the judge's discretionary decision. His decision whether to convict or acquit is the product of many factors over which he has only minor control, such as the facts of the case as presented in the trial, and the quality of the police investigation and prosecution.) However, in making these comparisons the percentage of defendants who are "acquitted plus costs" and the percentage who receive probation are reported separately because their sum is not the precise percentage of the total number of defendants who receive freedom as the result of the judge's discretionary decision. Their sum would slightly overstate the size of this total group because each percentage has a different base point. (The percentage of defendants who are "acquitted plus costs" is a proportion of the *total* number of *defendants,* whereas the percentage of defendants who receive probation is a proportion of the total number of *convicted* defendants.)
[b]The ratio is calculated by dividing the greater percentage of probation in the two cities by the lesser percentage of probation in the cities. When the percentage of probation is greater in Pittsburgh, the ratio is a positive number; when it is greater in Minneapolis, the ratio is a negative number. When the percentage of probation is zero in the one city, it is impossible to calculate the ratio, and the term "NR" (signifying no ratio) is used.

From: Martin A. Levin, *Urban Politics and the Criminal Courts* (Chicago: University of Chicago Press, 1977), pp. 271–272. By permission of the University of Chicago Press, © the University of Chicago and by permission of the author. This table is a substitute for the tables appearing in Martin A. Levin, "Urban Politics and Policy Outcomes: The Criminal Courts," in George F. Cole, ed., *Criminal Justice: Law and Politics,* 1st ed. (North Scituate, Mass.: Duxbury Press, 1976).

Although both white and black defendants receive more lenient sentences in Pittsburgh, in both cities whites receive a greater percentage of probation than blacks in most categories, and in Minneapolis whites receive a shorter length of incarceration than blacks in most categories. In Pittsburgh blacks receive a shorter length of incarceration than whites in almost all offenses. On the whole, sentencing decisions are more favorable for blacks in Pittsburgh than in Minneapolis, both in absolute terms and relative to whites.

In the comparison of sentencing decisions by type of plea, the Minneapolis judges penalize defendants who plead not guilty by giving them more severe sentences more frequently than do the Pittsburgh judges. On the whole, in Pittsburgh, decisions for such defendants are only slightly more severe than those for defendants who plead guilty; in Minneapolis they are much more severe.

There is also much more consistency in the length of the terms of incarceration in Minneapolis than in Pittsburgh. In Minneapolis, white and black defendants with the same type of prior record received the identical or nearly identical median term of incarceration in five of the seven offenses in which there is a sufficient number of cases for comparison. By contrast, there is almost none of this consistency in Pittsburgh. White and black defendants with the same type of prior record receive a nearly identical median term of incarceration in two of the nine offenses in which there are sufficient cases.

THE JUDGES' VIEWS AND DECISION-MAKING PROCESSES

The Minneapolis judges typically tend to be more oriented toward "society" and its needs and protection than toward the defendant. They are also more oriented toward the goals of their professional peers. Their decision making is legalistic and universalistic. The Pittsburgh judges typically are oriented toward the defendant, and they tend to lack orientation toward punishment or deterrence. Their decision making is nonlegalistic in that it tends to be particularistic, pragmatic, and based on policy considerations.

There are also significant differences in the judges' courtroom behavior prior to sentencing. Most nonjury trials in Pittsburgh are informal (for example, witnesses stand at the front bar) and abbreviated, and most of the judges prefer this arrangement. Most of the Pittsburgh judges also prefer informal procedures for obtaining information concerning defendants (the defense attorney's trial presentation, individuals intervening with the judge outside of court, the court staff's knowledge about the defendant) rather than the presentence investigations of the probation department. Trials in Minneapolis are formal, deliberate, and unabbreviated, and all of the judges prefer this arrangement. They also use presentence investigations in almost every case, and most of them dislike utilizing any informal sources of information concerning the defendant. In both cities plea bargaining is infrequent.[2]

The Minneapolis and Pittsburgh judges' views, decision-making processes, and sentencing behavior very closely approximate two general models of decision making. The Minneapolis judges' views and behavior approximate a judicial decision-making model, and the Pittsburgh judges' approximate an administrative decision-making model. The judicial model has the following characteristics: (1) Decisions are made on the basis of the "best" evidence as defined under the laws of evidence. (2) Decisions are made on the basis of complete evidence as developed by the adversary system. (3) Judges feel that they must maintain an image of detached objectivity, because it is as important to appear just as to be just. (4) A judge's decisions have a dichotomous specificity (yes-no), and they must assign legal wrong to one of the two parties. (5) Judges deduce their decision by a formal line of reasoning from legal principles that exist independent of policy considerations. (6) Judges evaluate their success by the degree to which their decisions have followed these procedures and by their satisfaction of abstract notions of justice and law. They generally have greater concern for procedure than for substantive issues, and thus are more concerned with satisfying "the law" as an abstract doctrine than arriving at "just" settlements of individual cases. (7) Judges base their decisions on what they feel is best in objective terms—their criteria usually come from "the law"—rather than what might be considered best from the perspective of the individual's self-interest, and they reach their decisions regardless of considerations of person.

The administrative model of decision making has the following characteristics: (1) Decisions are made on the basis of the kind of evidence on which reasonable people customarily make day-to-day decisions. (2) Decisions are made on the basis of sufficient evidence gathered by the administrator's own investigation, and the length and depth of the investigation is determined by the resources available. (3) Administrators feel that they must seek intimate contact with the real world to be able to administer effectively. They feel that this is more important than maintaining an image of detached objectivity (that is, appearing just). (4) Administrators may adopt dichotomous (yes-no) or intermediate decisions (for example, compromise decisions or delayed enforcement of a decision). (5) Administrators deduce their decisions by pragmatic methods from the policy goals incorporated in the programs they administer. They have greater concern for arriving at "just" settlements based on the particular merits of individual cases than for adherence to abstract notions of justice and the law. They seek to give their clients what they feel they "deserve," and they base their decisions in large part on the needs of their individual clients. (In some instances administrators may perceive that one of their client needs is exemption from the treatment involved in their program.) (6) Administrators have greater concern for substantive issues than for procedure, and thus they evaluate their success by the way the programs they administer "fit" real-world demands and supports. Thirteen of the seventeen Minneapolis judges seem to have little empathy for the defendants whom they describe as "coming from low intelligence groups," "crummy people," "congenital criminals," "not learning from their mistakes," or "not able to consider the consequences before they act." They tend to be resigned to the "criminality" of most defendants and often seem inclined to "give up" on them.[3] The Minneapolis judges' tendency to penalize with more severe sentences defendants who plead not guilty seems to be an indication of their greater concern for the needs of society than for the defendants.[4]

Thirteen of the seventeen judges are also oriented toward their professional peers (for example, correction authorities and law enforcement officials) and their goals. Thus though in general they want to exercise discretion, they are willing to sacrifice some of it to achieve both greater consistency in their own sentencing and the goals of some of these peers (for example, "professional expertise" and "better law enforcement"). In almost all instances in recent years, the effect of pursuing these goals has been more severe sentences.[5]

In short, these judges tend to be enlightened in terms of professional doctrine rather than benevolent toward the defendant. Indeed, many Minneapolis judges explain that one reason they dislike and discourage informal sources of information about the defendant (which tend to convey personal and mitigating information) and prefer the probation department's formal presentence investigations (which tend to be professional and objective) is that they "don't want to become emotionally involved in individual cases."

Twelve of the seventeen Minneapolis judges believe in the effectiveness of institutional rehabilitation and penal deterrence, and thus are not reluctant to punish defendants by incarcerating them. For example, Judge Rasmussen told an interviewer, "I know I am considered a tough judge here, but that doesn't bother me because punishment works. You won't sit on a hot stove if you have been burned." Few of these judges are critical of the quality of prisons, but several complain about "the failure rate of the people we put on probation." Many of the judges spoke of the therapeutic effect of the "shock" of incarceration.[6]

The decision-making of thirteen of the seventeen Minneapolis judges is legalistic and universalistic, and this seems to reinforce the effect of their greater orientation toward society. They feel little "closeness" to the defendant and thus, instead of acting as a buffer between them and the law, they act as if they *are* the law. The nature of the offense dominates these judges' considerations ("the offense itself is an indication of the man and his motives"), especially when the offense is a crime against person.[7] Thus, for example, though sentences in all offenses are more severe in Minneapolis than in Pittsburgh, this differential is much greater for armed robbery than for crimes against property. Moreover, ten of the seventeen Minneapolis judges even consider most crimes against property as "serious crimes."[8]

Universal criteria dominate these judges' decision making. They rarely regard individual characteristics (age, whether only property is involved in the crime, a black defendant's environment, a favorable family or employment situation, or addiction to alcohol or narcotics) as legitimate bases for making exceptions. They tend to follow a doctrine of equity rather formalistically: their consideration of individual and personal characteristics tends to be limited to highly unusual situations. Judge Slovack described such a situation:

> There are only a few situations in which I will give a fellow extra consideration. I had one in here on burglary and his attorney made a very emotional plea about the fellow's wife going blind and that he had to raise some money to help her. So I gave him probation.

In short their legalistic decision making is based on attributes of behavior rather than attributes of person. It tends to be based on the legal view of the act with little consideration of the context of the act—especially the personal context—or distinctions that might be made on this basis.

Many of these Minneapolis judges seem to be aware of nonlegalistic factors that they might consider, but they do not seem to feel that they are proper or relevant. For example, they feel that the stability of lower-income families is the proper concern of public agencies other than the criminal court.

Sixteen of the eighteen Pittsburgh judges seem to be oriented toward the defendant. Their view of most defendants is benevolent, and they describe their decision making as usually "giving the benefit of the doubt" to the defendant, "taking a chance on the defendant," or "err[ing] in the direction of being too soft." They feel that these "chances" are worth taking despite getting "taken in sometimes" because "some are rehabilitated." They explicitly seek to "help" them especially by "emphasiz[ing] probation and parole." Moreover, they tend to feel that they have a "closeness" and "kinship with the people that come into criminal court," that they are "more human" than the judges of the past, and that they have a "greater empathy and awareness of the [defendant's] problems" and "more insight into the different types of people" that come before them. Several judges explain this empathy and closeness as part of a general attachment to the "underdog," others explain it as a product of experience in their previous careers in political parties and government,[9] and some say it stems from their own minority ethnic and lower-income backgrounds.[10]

The Pittsburgh judges' sentencing decisions for defendants who plead not guilty seem to be a manifestation of their greater orientation toward the defendant and his needs than toward "society."[11] The Pittsburgh judges' preference for using informal sources for information concerning the defendant—individual's intervention with the judge, the defense attorney's trial presentation, and the court staff—also seems to be a manifestation of this orientation.[12]

The Pittsburgh judges' closeness to and empathy with the defendant cause them to stand apart from the law and to act as a buffer between it and the people upon whom it is enforced. Most of them act as if they view the law primarily as a constraint within which they have to operate to achieve substantive justice for the defendant. Sixteen of the eighteen Pittsburgh judges tend to eschew a literal application of the law and prefer to exercise their discretion. They are critical of the law's inflexibilities, and they resist standardization of any of their sentencing decisions (even in offenses such as drunken driving and gambling).[13]

Most of the Pittsburgh judges tend to base their decisions on policy considerations rather than legalistic ones—especially policy considerations derived from criteria of "realism," "practicality," and pragmatism. Specifically, fourteen of the eighteen judges do not seem to be oriented toward institutional rehabilitation, punishment, or deterrence in their sentencing decisions because of their pragmatic and "realistic" attitudes concerning deterrence and the actual quality and effectiveness of prisons. For example, they feel that prisons today usually are ineffective in achieving rehabilitation or even deterrence because of their low quality ("not much is done for [defendants] in jail," "it's not helpful," the jails do "more damage" and defendants leave "worse off"). Moreover, they feel that this policy consideration is relevant to their decision making.

The judges' views on the gravity of offenses also seem to be based on "realistic" criteria. Twelve of the eighteen judges often tend to view criminal behavior as a manifestation of a dispute between two private parties rather than a conflict between an individual and society. Thus they often act as if they view this behavior less as a criminal act than as a civil act or a tort. From this perspective many acts appear less serious to the judges, especially when there is a special relationship between the defendant and the victim.[14] Similarly, thirteen of the eighteen Pittsburgh judges believe that many crimes against property that do not involve violence are "minor," involve "only money," and are "less serious than [harm to] a human being."

Thirteen of the eighteen judges feel that they should consider "realistic" and "practical" factors such as "how the defendants live," the heterogeneity of the city's population, and particularly the "mill town" character of the population in ascertaining the standards of proper conduct. Thus they often seem to base their sentencing decisions on extralegal standards—the standards of the group in which the offense occurred (for example, youths, blacks, lower-income persons, homosexuals, sex offenders and their "victims"). For example, several of the judges feel that many blacks often deserve "breaks" because of their "different code of morality." These judges seem to act as if they feel that in the context of a city with a heterogeneous population whose standards and values usually differ from those of the law, the frequent use of these extralegal standards is both more realistic and equitable than the "rule of law" (that is, the assumption that there is a single standard of conduct—the standard prescribed by law—to which all individuals are subjected). The use of these extralegal standards tends to reduce the gravity of these acts in their view because, according to these standards, these acts seem less inappropriate and less repugnant. Also, most of the Pittsburgh judges justify their use of informal courtroom procedures which can potentially endanger a defendant's rights to due process, such as the verdict "acquitted plus costs"—

on grounds that they introduce "compromise" and "practical considerations" into the law.

In addition to most of the judges' emphasis on policy, their decision making is nonlegalistic in that it tends to be particularistic. Sixteen of the eighteen judges base their sentencing decisions on a very wide range of individualistic and personal characteristics. The major criterion in their sentencing is the *individual defendant* rather than the *offense* which the defendant committed. Moreover, they feel that "everything counts"; it is the "whole system" and the "complete picture" that must be considered. They describe their decision making as "intuitive," "impressionistic," "unscientific," and "without rules of thumb." Thus their decision making seems to focus beyond individualistic differences in behavior. In addition they make distinctions on the basis of differences in the defendants' personal attributes and characteristics (for example, the "type of person" he is and his relationship with his family); they attempt to establish an "idea of the 'person'" distinct from his conduct.

In part, they seem to base their sentencing decisions on the general criteria of the defendant's offense and the "type of person" he is, but they tend to act as if no general norm covers all individuals that fit one of these criteria. Within these general criteria they make numerous fine distinctions based on very diffuse and particularistic considerations (for example, "how the defendant conducted himself" during the commission of the offense, how "cooperative" he was when arrested, or the culpability and background of the victim, such as the degree of actual consent or female provocation and the past "purity" of a victim in a rape case).[15]

Thus these judges' decision making is characterized by numerous exceptions, which tend to be made in the direction of lenient decisions. Sixteen of the eighteen judges describe their decision making as being exceptional and expedient. They speak of seeking a basis for making an exception, giving defendants "breaks," and "helping" them. For example, Judge Guggliemi explained,

> If I can find a way—if the evidence ameliorates in some way—I'll give (the defendant) a "break." I suppose that it's unfair, but I try to help as many as I can. . . . I'm not constrained in sentencing by viewing defendants in set categories; I'm just trying to help them out.

The bases of these exceptions are not distinctions defined by the law as being relevant; they are distinctions based on the policy considerations which the judges feel are relevant to their decision making. These judges seem to consider one of the following characteristics as bases for making exceptions and giving "breaks": the absence of a prior record, youthfulness, the commission of "only" a crime against property, the defendant's "nonprofessional criminal" status, the environmental background of a black defendant, or the defendant's "favorable" employment or family situation.

THE EXPLANATION OF THE JUDGES' VIEWS AND BEHAVIOR

The behavior of the Pittsburgh and Minneapolis judges appears to be the indirect product of the cities' political systems. These systems influence judicial selection, leading to differential patterns of socialization and recruitment that in turn influence the judges' views and decision-making processes. The pre-judicial careers of most of the Pittsburgh judges in political parties and government and their minority ethnic and lower-income backgrounds[16] seem to contribute to the development of the characteristic which many successful, local professional politicians possess—the ability to empathize and to grasp the motives of others by entering imaginatively into their feelings.

This pre-judicial experience (reinforced by the lack of highly legalistic experience) seems to have contributed to the nonlegalistic, particularistic character of the judges' decision making, their focus on police considerations, and their use of pragmatic criteria. In this experience in party- and policy-oriented government positions general rules usually seem to have been subordinated to achieve more immediate ends (for example, those of a constituent). In the milieu of the party organization, personal relationships were emphasized (especially with their constituents), and the judges seem to have focused on particular and tangible entities. Their successes in this milieu depended largely on their ability to operate within personal relationships. It depended on *whom* they knew, rather than what they knew. Abstractions such as "the good of society as a whole" seem to have been of little concern to them.

Thus their client relationships were usually characterized by expedient, exceptional, benevolent, and affirmative decisions which were the antithesis of legalistic behavior. Their decisions focused on interpersonal relationships and involved a great deal of discretion with little attention given to general rules. Indeed, a primary task of local party workers is to view a situation in personal terms, to dispense favors, and to make exceptions rather than to apply legal rules. It is usually their job to say "yes," particularly to an individual who has a problem or who is in trouble. The Pittsburgh judges seem to have brought many of these patterns to the bench with them.

The predominantly legalistic pre-judicial careers of most of the Minneapolis judges and their predominantly middle-class northern-European-Protestant backgrounds seem to have contributed to the development of their greater orientation toward "society" than toward the defendant. In their careers few had contact with individuals from lower-income backgrounds. Their experience in predominantly business-oriented private practice typically involved major societal institutions such as the "law," corporations, and commercial transactions.

This pre-judicial experience (reinforced by their lack of party policy-oriented experiences) seems to have contributed to the legalistic and universalistic character of their decision making and their eschewal of policy considerations. In this milieu, rules are generally emphasized, especially legalistic ones; these rules were used to maintain and protect these societal institutions. Learning to "get around" involved skill in operating in a context of rules. Their success seems to have depended more on their objective achievements and skills than on personal relationships. Furthermore, the predominantly middle-class background of these judges may in itself have contributed directly to the development of their universalistic decision making and their emphasis on the importance of laws.

Both the judges' social backgrounds and pre-judicial career experiences seem to have influenced their decision making. However, in both cities the decision making of the judges with cross-cutting backgrounds and experiences in effect serves as a control, and it seems to indicate that pre-judicial career experiences have been the more important influence. The decision making of the few Pittsburgh judges with middle-class Protestant backgrounds who also had careers in party and government positions tends to be oriented toward the defendant, particularistic, and based on policy considerations. Unfortunately all of the Pittsburgh judges with minority ethnic and lower-class backgrounds also had party and government careers, and thus this conclusion cannot be tested with both variables independently controlled, but it can be in Minneapolis. The decision making of the few Minneapolis judges with middle-class northern-European-Protestant backgrounds who had less legalistic careers tend to be less oriented toward "society" and less legalistic and universalistic than that of most of the other Minneapolis judges.

The covariation of the dominant socialization and recruitment patterns of the judges in each city and their decision-making process suggests a causal linkage as the best available explanation. This is especially suggested by the deviant socialization and recruitment patterns which in effect serve as controls; in each city, interview and sentencing data indicate that the decision making of the judges whose socialization and recruitment patterns deviate from the dominant pattern also tends to deviate significantly from that of most of the city's judges. In Pittsburgh the few judges with little party or policy experience tend to be less oriented toward the defendant, less particularistic, less pragmatic, and less policy-oriented than most of the other Pittsburgh judges. In Minneapolis the few judges with less legal experience and more political experience than most of their colleagues tend to be less oriented toward society and their professional peers, less legalistic, and less universalistic than most of the other Minneapolis judges.

We have seen how the judges' views and decision-making processes, influenced by their socialization and recruitment patterns, structure sentencing decisions. The Pittsburgh judges' predominant orientation toward the defendant, their tendency to "empathize" with many of the defendants, to act as a buffer between the law and the people upon whom it is enforced, seem to make leniency "natural." Their tendency to base decisions on "realistic" policy considerations (the defendant's background, the effect of the crime, the standards of proper conduct of the group in which the offense occurred) reduces the gravity of many of the defendant's acts in the judges' minds. Their emphasis on individualistic and personal characteristics leads them to view many defendants as "exceptional" and thus deserving of a "break."

In contrast, the various elements of the Minneapolis judges' views and decision-making processes seem to cumulatively contribute to severe sentencing decisions. Their predominant orientation toward "society," which leads them to emphasize its protection, their view of both crimes against person and crimes against property as very serious, and their tendency to be critical of defendants who plead not guilty seem to shape their severe sentencing decisions. This is reinforced by their low degree of empathy for most defendants and their belief in the effectiveness of institutional rehabilitation and penal deterrence. Mitigating exceptions are infrequent because judges' formalistic decision making rarely allows for consideration of personal characteristics, and because of their belief in the standards of conduct prescribed by law. The judges' orientation toward the goals of their professional peers (such as maximum indeterminate terms of incarceration and uniform severe sentencing for prostitution) contribute to severe decisions, as does their reliance on formal sources of information concerning defendants, which, unlike informal sources, provide them with both mitigating and aggravating information.

The covariation in both cities of the judges' views and decision-making processes and the ultimate substance of these decisions suggests this linkage, but it does not demonstrate it. Nevertheless, the evidence presented in this section and above seems to suggest this linkage as the best available explanation. Also, there are several additional pieces of evidence that seem to further suggest the existence of linkage between the cities' political and judicial selection systems, the judges' socialization and recruitment patterns, the judges' views and decision-making processes, and finally their sentencing decisions. Some of this evidence in effect allows us to partially test this conclusion by controlling for other possible explanatory variables. First, in each city there is a dominant pattern in the judges' attitudes and decision-making processes which seems to represent a "system." This seems to indicate that the judges' attitudes and decisions are the product of structural factors, such as the influence of the cities' political system on judicial selection and judicial socialization and recruitment, rather than simply the product of the individual personal characteristics of the eighteen judges in each city.

Second, the characteristics and the sentencing decisions of the Pittsburgh "visiting" judges seem to further suggest the existence of linkage between a city's political and judicial selection system, socialization and recruitment, and judicial decisions. In addition to the three Pittsburgh judges regularly assigned to the criminal bench on a rotating basis, three or four "visiting" judges from rural counties in western Pennsylvania usually hear criminal cases in Pittsburgh. These are the same type of cases heard by the Pittsburgh judges and are tried by the same group of prosecutors and defense lawyers. Therefore the "visiting" judges' sentencing decisions in effect can serve as a limited control to test the validity of the suggested linkage between political systems and sentencing decisions.

The political systems of the rural areas from which the visiting judges come are very different from Pittsburgh's. The visiting judges' social backgrounds and pre-judicial careers are also different. Conservative and business-oriented Republican party organizations dominate these areas. A high proportion of both the population and political leadership in these areas is Protestant and of northern European background. In comparison with the Pittsburgh judges, a smaller proportion of the "visiting" judges had pre-judicial experience in public positions and a smaller proportion were active in a political party. Most were predominantly in private legal practice, and they were selected more *by* the Republican party than *from* the party. The visiting judges' sentencing decisions are less lenient than those of the Pittsburgh judges. There is no direct evidence that these different political systems and different social backgrounds and career experiences are the primary factors accounting for the visiting judges' different sentencing decisions, but it is the explanation most often offered by attorneys and other participants in the Pittsburgh courts and by the Pittsburgh judges themselves.[17]

Third, an additional piece of evidence of the linkage suggested here is the findings of studies of the way a city's political system affects such services as police, education, welfare, and urban renewal. These studies indicate that while there is usually little day-to-day political direction of these services, many of the policies of those administering the services reflect the values of the city's political system. Often this seems to be a result of the selection by the political system of the top administrators of these services. For example, the mayor or city council's criteria and goals in selecting a police chief (the "most professional" person, an "outsider," an "insider" who gets along with the people in the department, or a person "close to the party") are likely to affect the subsequent policies that the chief pursues. This also seems to be true of the school board's or mayor's choice of a school superintendent. Similarly, the influence of the Pittsburgh and Minneapolis political systems on judicial behavior has been indirect and through their effect on judicial selection. Indeed, the specific outcomes of their effect probably have been largely unintended. As already stated, Pittsburgh citizens tend to accept pro-union and liberal, social welfare policies, but Minneapolitans do not. However, no elements of either city's political system have consciously sought to develop the judicial decision making that exists in each city. For example, the Pittsburgh political parties have not sought to develop a criminal court bench which follows informal procedures and particularistic and pragmatic decision making producing lenient sentencing decisions. They view these positions on common pleas court primarily as sources of rewards for leading party members. Only secondarily do they hope that the judges will decide the rare policy-related civil cases favorably for the party or city administration. Similarly, neither the Minneapolis parties (which play almost no role in judicial selection) nor the bar association have sought to develop a criminal court bench which follows formal procedures and formalistic decision making producing severe sentencing decisions. The bar association is primarily concerned with keeping judicial selection out of partisan politics and within its own control, and with the selection of lawyers with the preferred party affiliation and social, career, and bar association backgrounds.

Fourth, several similarities in the political systems of Pittsburgh and Minneapolis and their judges' behavior are indirectly and tentatively suggestive of the linkage between the two factors. The formal trial procedures and formal sources of information concerning the defendant which the Minneapolis judges use are generally advocated by professional and reform judicial organizations. By contrast, the informal trial procedures and informal sources of information concerning the defendant which the Pittsburgh judges use are generally criticized by professional and reform judicial organizations. Patterns somewhat similar to these forms of judicial behavior seem to exist in each city's political system. Minneapolis' political system is characterized by procedures advocated by professional and reform organizations in city government (nonpartisan elections, widespread popular participation in governmental and party decision making, frequent referenda and grass roots party-nomination procedures, merit recruitment and appointments, and an emphasis on procedures as important ends in themselves). In contrast, Pittsburgh's political system is characterized by procedures that are generally criticized by most of these professional and reform organizations (partisan elections, hierarchical control of government and party decision making, and party recruitment and appointments).

Some alternative explanations also should be noted. Recent studies have indicated the importance of political factors in judicial decision making. However, political influence does not seem to shape the behavior of the Pittsburgh and Minneapolis judges in criminal court. Almost all common felony defendants have no influence because they are literally on the bottom rung of society. Typically they are young lower-income males, often from a minority group. In other cases in which defendants do have political influence, these judges' decisions may be shaped by it (though it seems less likely to occur in Minneapolis). For example, organized labor is quite influential in Pittsburgh, and almost all of the judges are reluctant to preside over a case involving a union (especially strike injunction requests) because they are wary of taking the "wrong" position.

Studies have also suggested that judges' social backgrounds significantly shape their decisions. Thus it is possible that the Pittsburgh judges are lenient primarily because of their predominant minority ethnic backgrounds and the Minneapolis judges are more severe primarily because of their northern-European-Protestant backgrounds. However, two other explanations regarding the effect of the judges' ethnicity on their sentencing decisions are suggested by some control data and by data on the ethnicity of the courts and the cities as a whole and seem more persuasive. First, as the data above—and especially the controls provided by the deviant instances—seem to suggest, both the judges' pre-judicial career experiences and their social background seem to have influenced their decision making, but in both cities the former seems to have been the more important influence. Second, any relationship between the judges' background characteristics and their decision making seems to be indirect. The crucial intervening variable seems to be the city's political system and its influence on judicial selection, recruitment, and socialization. Judges with these social and career backgrounds are recruited by the city's political and judicial selection systems. The ethnic composition of the bench in each city can serve as a partial test of the intervening impact of these political and judicial selection systems on judicial decision making. This composition is more reflective of the influence of particular groups in the city's political system than it is of the precise ethnic composition of the city's population.[18]

EVALUATING THE COURTS AND SOME POLICY IMPLICATIONS

This analysis of the Pittsburgh and Minneapolis judges' decision making in criminal court indicates some of the consequences of these cities' political systems and methods of judicial selection. However, to more fully understand these consequences, some evaluation of these judges' decisions in themselves is necessary. To what degree and in what manner does each pattern of decisions (more lenient in Pittsburgh and more severe in Minneapolis) affect the defendants in crime in the community, all other factors being equal? Which type of sentencing has the greatest tendency to rehabilitate the defendant; which is most likely to reduce recidivism and deter future criminals?

My analysis elsewhere of the factors affecting recidivism indicated that both nonexperimental and experimental studies found that offenders who have received probation generally have significantly lower rates of recidivism than those who have been incarcerated.[19] They also found that of those incarcerated, the offenders who have received a shorter term of incarceration generally have a somewhat lower recidivism rate than those who receive longer terms. With a few exceptions, these differences persist when one controls for factors such as type of offense, type of community, the offender's age, race, and number of previous convictions. However, for those with certain characteristics there are some significant variations in the overall recidivism rates when type of treatment is controlled (for example, for all those who receive probation the recidivism rates are highest for the youngest and for those with the greatest prior record).

On this basis one might conclude that the Pittsburgh judges' decisions on the whole tend to contribute more effectively to reduced recidivism because they grant probation more frequently. However, their frequent grants of probation for individuals with a high probability of recidivating (for example, those with a prior record and blacks) probably does not effectively contribute to reduced recidivism. By contrast, the Minneapolis judges' decisions for these specific individuals may contribute to reduced recidivism more effectively. Moreover, there are other goals of the criminal court in addition to reduced recidivism, and there is considerable tension among them.

Thus recidivism data do not present a complete means of evaluating criminal courts. Ultimately the Pittsburgh and Minneapolis criminal court judges also must be evaluated directly in terms of their behavior—lenient decisions and informal procedures in Pittsburgh and more severe decisions and formal procedures in Minneapolis. It is possible to make a persuasive case for the Minneapolis criminal court in terms of the goals of equality and the "rule of law," all other things being equal. In actual policy situations, however, "all other things" are rarely equal. Realistic policy choices are never made in an ideal context, but in a real, and therefore imperfect, context. Most big-city criminal courts, including those in this study, operate in a context of a heterogeneous population which includes a large proportion of lower-class and minority-group individuals.

In this context, it is possible to make a persuasive case for the Pittsburgh criminal court whose judges often tend to base their decisions on the standards of conduct of the group in which the offense occurred. Indeed, the assumptions of the "rule of law" (that all men are equal or similar) seldom square with the realities of our urban context. Nevertheless, despite the benevolence of intention, criminal court decisions based on these extralegal standards may tend to have serious unintended consequences. John Dollard suggests this with respect to criminal justice in the South. He concludes that among the institutional features of southern life that sustain the high level of aggression among poor blacks is the double standard of justice—viewing "black crime" as less serious than "white crime."

This tension between the style of criminal court which may be preferable in an ideal context and that which may be necessary because of the actual context and the difficulties inherent in the latter style seems to be a product of a more general tension in the larger cities of our society and in our theory of democracy. According to the "rule of law" and democratic theory, we ought to ignore class differences, but urban realities are such that it is difficult. "Two cultures" exist in our large cities—a large lower-class as well as the dominant middle-class culture—but our theory of democracy assumes that we will be a society with one culture. It assumes that we will be able and willing to live together under a single set of rules or standards. The idea that two sets of rules may be necessary—one for the middle class and the other for the lower class—cannot be reconciled to our theory.

This tension indicates that any evaluation or policy prescription concerning the criminal courts in our large cities must consider the existence of these "two cultures." The Minneapolis judges tend to adhere to the "rule of law," but they fail to consider these "two cultures." On the other hand, the Pittsburgh judges, in part, often tend to base their decisions on the existence of these "two cultures," but they usually fail to adhere to the "rule of law." These shortcomings in both courts are thus largely a function of these "two cultures"—a factor *external* to these court systems. Any prescription for remedying these inadequacies should be primarily directed at this external factor and more basic cause. As long as these "two cultures" exist, there will be a tension in our theory of democracy, and the criminal courts will have to ignore either the "rule of law" or the realities of urban life.

NOTES

1. The only names that Democratic governors have considered for a judicial appointment are those which came from the Pittsburgh organization. Some Republican governors have requested, and sometimes followed, the Pittsburgh Bar Association's recommendations, but its influence has been limited even during Republican state administrations (including reform-oriented administrations). Its recommendations have first been cleared (and sometimes modified) by the Pittsburgh Republican organization, and then often they were ultimately blocked by the Democratic organization which has successfully opposed interim Republican judicial appointments at the next election several times since 1950.

2. Informal discussions between the judge and attorneys occur in Minneapolis, but they are infrequent in Pittsburgh. Moreover, in both cities these discussions concern the defendant's sentence and are dominated by the judge rather than the prosecutors.

3. For example, Judge White explained his severe sentences for aggravated forgery: "I feel that once a fellow is a 'paper hanger' (that is, a check forger), he'll always be one. So the best thing is to get him off the street." In a comparison of the frequency with which the other Minneapolis judges grant probation for aggravated forgery, Judge White ranks last with 11.1 percent (11). All the judges' names in this study are pseudonyms which were chosen to reflect the actual ethnic and religious backgrounds of the judges.

4. Twelve of the seventeen judges feel that trials should not be used by the "guilty" to escape a conviction. Thus if a defendant pleads not guilty and is then convicted, they are critical of him because "he has put the state through the expense of a trial." They then feel that his plea indicated "a wrong attitude" or that he "wasn't repentant" and that he "deserves less consideration" in sentencing. Minneapolis defense attorneys are aware of the judges' attitudes and behavior concerning pleas of not guilty, and thus they usually discourage their clients from pleading not guilty. Only 14.4 percent of the defendants in this study's sample plead not guilty in Minneapolis, but 71.1 percent of the Pittsburgh sample plead not guilty.

5. For example, in the early 1960s the Minnesota Department of Correction requested that those defendants incarcerated by the Minneapolis judges receive uniform terms to achieve greater consistency and thus make prisoners more manageable. They specifically requested that all the incarcerated defendants receive maximum indeterminate terms because this would achieve consistency and would also give them the discretion to determine the prisoner's exact term. They argued that prison and parole officials were in the best position to make these determinations because they could observe the prisoner closely and because of their professional expertise. Within a few years many of the Minneapolis judges began to comply with these requests to a great extent because they agreed with the Correction Department's view—they felt that sentences ought to be consistent, and they respected the professional expertise of the correction authorities.

6. For example, Judge Jensen said, "Many times those young fellows need the jolt that comes when the jail door closes behind them. So I give them probation coupled with six to twelve months in the workhouse."

7. Judge Edwards' view seems to be typical: "If the crime involves violence—like robbery or rape—then the defendant is a danger to society, and I won't place him on probation. For example, in a rape case I have no sympathy for the defendant because I have two daughters and I know the feeling I would have if they were attacked."

8. For example, Judge Swanson said, "In auto theft you always get such crummy people. It's not that they just drive the car around and abandon it—they do it as a steady practice. . . . Burglary is serious; it's just an awful experience to have someone in your house. I know people that have been burglarized, and it's terrible. Forgery is awful because if you can't trust another person's money (that is, check) then business couldn't be carried on. I probably feel this way because my (pre-judicial) office practice dealt with banking, real estate, trust, and corporate work."

9. For example, Judge Bloom told an interviewer, "A judge should feel a kinship with the people that come into criminal court. Through my thirty years of active political work I worked with Negroes and other poor persons, and I developed a kinship with them and an awareness of their problems."

10. Judge Guggliemi explained: "I was brought up in a semi-industrial neighborhood, and my father worked in the mills. I was a solicitor for the township, so I got to know people with problems more intimately. I learned that it's really tough for some people just to get along in this world. . . . You also see this inability to cope with life in the people in (criminal) court, particularly the minorities."

11. They penalize defendants who plead not guilty much less frequently than do the Minneapolis judges, and, on the whole, their decisions for such defendants are only slightly more severe than those for defendants who plead guilty. (In Pittsburgh, unlike Minneapolis, most defendants are not reluctant to plead not guilty. In the Pittsburgh sample, 71.1 percent pleaded not guilty, but only 14.4 percent pleaded not guilty in Minneapolis.) Also, eleven of the eighteen Pittsburgh judges state that they usually do not penalize defendants who plead not guilty. Most of the judges seem to view not-guilty pleas in terms of "fairness to the defendant" rather than "the expense to the state."

12. These informal sources focus almost exclusively on mitigating information. By contrast, the formal presentence report is made by a "third party," the probation officer, whose professional ethos stresses objectivity and it includes both mitigating *and* aggravating information. The informal sources—with the partial exception of the court staff—do not attempt to be objective.

13. Judge Bloom told an interviewer, "I don't feel bound to follow suggestions for uniform sentencing. An individual judge should not be obligated by another judge's system. For example, some send a sodomy case to jail, but I don't. If the legislature had wanted us to sentence all the same, it would have said so; it wanted the sentence determined by each individual judge. I was elected to exercise my discretion."

14. Some of these "special" relationships include prior acquaintance and sometimes strong ties (for example, as a relative, friend, or lover), the victim's physical or sexual prov-

ocation (for example, in assault or rape cases), monetary provocation (for example, in forged check or theft cases), or the "victim's" desire for revenge.

15. In crimes against person the nature of the offense tends to become the dominant criterion for the decisions of fourteen of the eighteen judges and thus tends to operate as a general standard. However, these judges significantly qualify the generality of this standard by making several distinctions—most of which are diffuse—among various types of crimes against person (for example, the degree of viciousness involved in the violence, the degree of aggressiveness, the degree of passion, whether a weapon was involved, the degree of provocation involved or whether the act caused an injury). For example, a comparison of the Pittsburgh and Minneapolis judges' sentencing decisions for armed robbery indicates that the Pittsburgh judges frequently qualify this general standard and the Minneapolis judges almost always adhere to it.

16. Four of the Pittsburgh judges are Jewish (two of whom were foreign-born), seven are Catholic (one of whom was foreign-born, three have Irish backgrounds, two Italian, one Polish, one Hungarian), one is black, and six are white Protestants. Eleven of the judges have working-class backgrounds and seven have middle-class backgrounds.

17. For example, most Pittsburgh judges contrasted the standards upon which they and the "visiting" judges base their decisions: " 'Visiting' judges have a different view because they come from smaller towns with homogeneous populations: ours [Pittsburgh's] is very heterogeneous; . . . it's a mill town." The view of a black defense attorney is also typical: " 'Visiting' judges come from the smaller rural counties . . . , and it affects their evaluations. They think that if a man is guilty, then he's guilty. Our [local] judges have different backgrounds, and they are more kindhearted; they make social judgments."

18. For example, in Pittsburgh a much higher proportion of the bench is Jewish (four of the eighteen judges) and Irish (three of the eighteen) than is the city's population. (Approximately 4 percent of the city's population is Jewish and 10 percent is Irish.) There are more Protestants than Catholics in Minneapolis, but the proportion of Catholics on the bench in Minneapolis (two of the eighteen judges) is much lower than that of the city's population (approximately 37 percent of the population).

19. M. A. Levin, "Policy Evaluation and Recidivism," *Law and Society Review,* August 1971. This analysis is based on studies of over twenty-two different court and prison jurisdictions, including several studies of recidivism in California's thirteen largest counties.

ARTICLE SEVENTEEN

The Effect of Race on Sentencing: A Reexamination of an Unsettled Question

CASSIA SPOHN/JOHN GRUHL/SUSAN WELCH

Questions about racial bias in the sentencing process have been a major concern for decades, but past studies on this issue have had methodological problems. Cassia Spohn, John Gruhl, and Susan Welch attempted to overcome these problems by using a large number of cases, a large number of offenses, and other research controls. They show that race does not have a direct effect on sentence severity, but that blacks are more likely than whites to be sent to prison.

Observers have noted that black criminal defendants tend to receive more severe sentences than white defendants do. For years social scientists have examined this disparity (Sellin 1928) and have put forth three explanations to account for it. Some researchers have suggested that it is due to racial discrimination. Others have emphasized wealth discrimination resulting from poor defendants' inability to obtain a private attorney or pretrial release. As the effect of wealth discrimination on black defendants is likely to be greater than on white defendants, since blacks are more likely to be poor, it amounts to indirect racial discrimination. Still others have suggested that this disparity is due to the effect of legal factors, such as the seriousness of the charge or prior criminal record. Since blacks are more likely to have a serious charge or prior criminal record, they are also likely to receive a more severe sentence.

Source: Law and Society Review 16 (1981-1982): 71–88 (footnotes deleted). By permission of the authors and publisher.

Early studies often concluded that this disparity in sentencing was due to racial discrimination (see studies cited in Hagan 1974). But in his review of these studies, Hagan found that most employed inadequate controls or improper statistical techniques and were thus methodologically unsound. The evidence of racial discrimination in capital cases in the South could be supported, but little else could.

More recent sentencing studies by social scientists sometimes concluded that the continued disparity in sentencing is due to racial discrimination (Pope 1975; Levin 1977; Uhlman 1977; Sutton 1978a; Unnever et al. 1980) or wealth discrimination (Lizotte 1978), but these studies more often concluded that the disparity is due to the effect of legal factors (Baab and Furgeson 1967; Engle 1971; Cook 1973; Burke and Turk 1975; Chiricos and Waldo 1975; Tiffany et al. 1975; Clarke and Koch 1976; Eisenstein and Jacob 1977; Lotz and Hewitt 1977; Gibson 1978; Sutton 1978b). These recent studies generally corrected the obvious methodological defects of the earlier research. Nevertheless, many of them had less-obvious defects which cast some doubt on their findings. These defects include:

1. Use of a relatively small number of cases (Clarke and Koch 1976; Bernstein et al. 1977; Unnever et al. 1980). Presumably to avoid this problem, some researchers lumped numerous federal or state jurisdictions together (Tiffany et al. 1975; Sutton 1978a, 1978b; Pope 1975). Given different regional perspectives toward racial matters, this approach risks obscuring discrimination which may exist in some jurisdictions but not in others. Some studies included both men and women defendants but did not provide adequate controls for gender (Unnever et al. 1980). Given the potential for different treatment of men and women, this approach too risks distorting the amount of racial discrimination which may exist.

2. Use of a relatively small number of offenses (Cook 1973; Tiffany et al. 1975; Clarke and Koch 1976). No particular offenses are so "typical" that just one or two or three or four of them can be analyzed to ascertain the existence of a pattern of discrimination. Certainly draft evasion (Cook 1973) is not necessarily generalizable to other crimes, and neither are auto theft, bank robbery, and forgery (Tiffany et al. 1975).

3. Use of inadequate controls for relevant "legal" and "extralegal" variables. Some researchers failed to control adequately for the seriousness of the charge when they collapsed disparate offenses into broad categories (Baab and Furgeson 1967; Burke and Turk 1975; Pope 1975; Gibson 1978). Collapsing offenses into categories of "violent crimes," "theft crimes," or "vice crimes" (Burke and Turk 1975) does not adequately control for the seriousness of the charge. Collapsing offenses into categories based upon some statutory classification, when the result is a single category encompassing driving while intoxicated, auto theft, rape, and murder (Baab and Furgeson 1967), also does not adequately control for the seriousness of the charge. Some researchers failed to control for prior criminal record (Uhlman 1977), and some failed to control for such extralegal variables as

type of attorney or pretrial bail status (Pope 1975; Levin 1977; Gibson 1978).

4. Use of one sentence decision rather than two. The sentence is actually a product of two decisions—the decision whether to incarcerate and the decision on length of sentence. These are separate decisions based upon different criteria; the seriousness of the prior criminal record may be the best predictor of the decision to incarcerate, while the seriousness of the charge may be the best predictor of length of sentence (Sutton 1978a). Consequently, it is necessary to analyze the two decisions separately in order to avoid masking discrimination which may exist (Nagel 1969). Very few recent studies have done this (but see Eisenstein and Jacob 1977; Levin 1977; Sutton 1978a; 1978b).

5. Use of an inadequate measure of sentence severity. Most researchers employed a scale to measure severity. Some of these scales do not distinguish sufficiently between degrees of severity (Bernstein et al. 1977; Lotz and Hewitt 1977; Lizotte 1978). The range is quite wide, but certainly a scale which has three categories of fines, one category of probation, and just one category of incarceration (Bernstein et al. 1977) does not make fine enough distinctions between degrees of severity.

6. Use of inadequate statistical techniques. Some researchers did not use adequate multivariate analysis or tests of significance (Greenwood et al. 1973; Chiricos and Waldo 1975; Clarke and Koch 1976; Levin 1977). Failure to control for other factors influencing sentence may allow spurious relationships between race and sentence to be interpreted as valid ones.

The findings of prior studies, even recent ones, are contradictory and often inconclusive because of the methodological problems we have noted. The findings of these studies are not necessarily invalid, but additional research on this unsettled question is needed.

THE STUDY

Our study of the relationship between race and sentencing replicates and elaborates upon the research conducted by Uhlman (1977), who concluded that there seemed to be evidence of racial discrimination in "Metro City." His study was one of the most sophisticated yet done in its use of an appropriate scale to measure sentence severity and in its use of path analysis. However, it had two serious defects. One, which Uhlman himself pointed out, was its failure to control for prior criminal record; this information was not available to him. Another, in our judgment, was its failure to divide sentencing into two decisions and analyze them separately.

We examine the sentences imposed on 2,366 black (N = 1,939) and white (N = 427) defendants in Metro City. Although we analyze data from the same city studied by Uhlman, we expect that our findings, unlike his, will show no direct relationship between race and sentencing once we control for the seriousness of the charge and prior criminal record. Accordingly, we hypothesize that we will find no direct racial discrimination either in the decision to impose a more or less severe sentence or in the decision to incarcerate.

The Data

The data for this project were drawn from a file of nearly 50,000 felony cases heard between 1968 and 1979 in Metro City, a city in the Northeast which is one of the largest cities in the United States. The initial data file consisted of a stratified random sample of all felony cases disposed of during this time period. From this sample we selected those cases where the "maximum charge" was one of the fourteen most common offenses appearing in the sample: murder, manslaughter, rape, robbery, assault, minor assault, burglary, auto theft, embezzlement, receiving stolen property, forgery, sex offenses other than rape, drug possession, and driving while intoxicated. We then eliminated cases where all charges were dismissed.

Our master data file included information on the race and sex of the defendant; the charges against the defendant; and, for each charge, the type of plea entered, whether or not the defendant was convicted, and, when the defendant was convicted, the sentence imposed. Information on the amount of bail set and whether or not the defendant made bail also was included in this data file. Data on the prior criminal record of the defendant and on the type of attorney representing the defendant were not included in the master data file, but instead were contained in a separate file. Due to the difficulty and expense of adding this information to the master file for all defendants, we randomly selected over 4,000 defendants for whom to code this information. After eliminating defendants who were not convicted, and thus not sentenced, and defendants for whom there was missing data on one or more variables, we had a base of about 2,700 cases. To eliminate one possible source of variation, we then dropped all cases with female defendants. This left us with 2,366 cases.

The Variables

Two dependent variables measuring sentence severity were used in the analysis. The first measures sentence severity on a 93-point scale which ranges from a suspended sentence at one end to life imprisonment at the other. The second measures sentence severity by focusing on the decision to incarcerate or not; this decision is measured by a dichotomous prison/no prison variable. This variable reflects the important distinction between sanctions involving suspended sentences, fines, or probation, on the one hand, and those involving prison terms, on the other hand.

Eight independent variables were employed: the defendant's race, charge, prior criminal record, type of attorney, type of plea, evidence of charge reduction, bail amount, and pretrial bail status. The prior criminal record variable was chosen from thirteen separate measures of prior record for each defendant. The measure of prior record selected—the number of times the defendant had been sentenced to prison for more than one year—was the one that had the strongest relationship with the sentence given for the current charge, controlling for type of crime. The dependent and independent variables and their codes are summarized in Table 1.

Table 1 Independent and dependent variables included in the study

Variable	*Description*	*Code*
Defendant race	Whether the defendant was black or white; persons of other racial groups were eliminated from the analysis	1 = black 0 = white
Charge	Fourteen felonies were included (see text)	Dummy variables were used to measure the charges
Prior criminal record	Number of times the defendant had been sentenced to prison for more than one year	A number ranging from 0 to 9
Type of attorney	Representation by either a private attorney or a public defender	1 = private attorney 0 = public defender
Type of plea	Plea of guilty or not guilty	1 = guilty plea 0 = not guilty plea
Evidence of charge reduction	Sentencing on either the most serious charge or a lesser charge	1 = sentencing on lesser charge 0 = sentencing on most serious charge
Bail amount	Amount of bail requirement in dollars	Dollar amount
Pretrial bail status	Released or detained prior to trial	1 = pretrial release 0 = pretrial detention
Sentence severity	Severity of the sentence imposed on the defendant	Measured by a 93-point scale
Prison/no prison	Whether or not the defendant was sentenced to prison	1 = sentenced to prison 0 = not sentenced to prison

The Analysis

Our analysis includes correlation, regression, and path analysis. Path analysis, based on multiple regression, allows one to examine both the direct and indirect effects of an independent variable on a dependent variable. Thus, for example, we can analyze not only the direct effects of race on sentence controlling for other factors, as we could with multiple regression, but also the indirect effects of race on sentence resulting from the effect of race on other factors related to sentencing (see Asher 1976 for a good discussion of path analysis). In this path analysis, the impact of our group of dummy variables measuring type of charge was handled through the block variable approach suggested by Heise (1972).

Because of precautions taken in the design and execution of this study, we believe we have been able to avoid the most troublesome methodological problems of previous studies. Our study includes a large number of cases and a large number of offenses. It controls for relevant legal and extralegal variables. It examines two sentence decisions—the decision to impose a more or less severe sentence and the decision to incarcerate or not. It uses a 93-point scale to distinguish between more- or less-severe sentences, and it employs path analysis.

FINDINGS

Data from Metro City reveal consistent differences between black and white male defendants on both the dependent and the independent variables utilized in this study. Table 2, which presents the zero-order correlations between the variables, shows an absolute disparity in the sentences imposed on black and white defendants. Black males receive harsher sentences than white males; more specifically, they are more likely than whites to receive prison terms. These black and white defendants also differ in terms of legal factors (prior criminal record and charge) and extralegal factors (type of attorney, charge reduction, bail amount, pretrial status). Blacks have more serious criminal records and are charged with more serious crimes. They also are more likely than whites to be represented by a public defender, to engage in plea bargaining, to have high bail set, and to be detained prior to trial.

These findings are in accord with previous reseach. They also indicate the plausibility of the earlier noted explanations of racial disparities in sentencing. Blacks may receive harsher sentences than whites (1) because of racial discrimination within the criminal justice system, (2) because of wealth discrimination, or indirect racial discrimination, resulting from their inability to obtain a private attorney or pretrial release, or (3) because they are charged with more serious crimes and have more serious criminal records.

Table 2 Matrix of intercorrelations

	Sentence severity	*Prison/no prison*	*Race*	*Prior record*	*Charge*	*Type of attorney*	*Type of plea*	*Charge reduction*	*Bail amount*	*Pretrial status*
Sentence severity	—									
Prison/no prison	.79[a]	—								
Race	.09	.14	—							
Prior record	.07	.14	.12	—						
Charge	.58	.54	.17	−.25	—					
Type of attorney	.20	.13	−.12	−.06	.31	—				
Type of plea	−.09	−.12	.00	−.01	.20	−.02	—			
Charge reduction	−.12	−.14	−.06	.01	.72	−.03	.01	—		
Bail amount	.23	.22	.04	.08	.27	.08	.00	.06	—	
Pretrial status	−.22	−.32	−.17	−.25	.31	.12	.03	.05	−.18	—

[a]All correlations are Pearson's *r* except with charge variable, whose correlations are multiple *R*.
Coding: See Table 1.

Race and Sentence Severity

We expected to find no direct relationship between race and sentence severity, as measured by the 93-point sentence scale, once we controlled for the charge against the defendant and the defendant's prior criminal record. The data presented in Table 3 and in Figure 1 confirm this hypothesis.

As shown in Table 3, the bivariate relationship between race and sentence severity (Pearson's $r = .092$) is statistically significant. Controlling the seriousness of the charge against the defendant reduces the correlation substantially (beta = 45), but the relationship between the two variables is still significant. Adding a control for the seriousness of the defendant's prior criminal record, however, further reduces the correlation (beta = .017) to the point where the relationship between race and sentence severity no longer is significant.

These findings illustrate the importance of the legal factors, including prior criminal record, in explaining sentence severity. Merely controlling for the seriousness of the charge against the defendant, without taking into account the seriousness of the defendant's prior criminal record, might lead one to conclude, incorrectly, that racial disparities in sentencing are due to racial discrimination. Instead, it appears that these disparities can be attributed to racial differences in the seriousness of the charges against the defendants and to racial differences in the seriousness of the defendants' prior criminal records.

Our hypothesis was tested further using path analysis. We defined and operationalized a causal model that would allow us to explore the direct and indirect influences of race on sentence severity. We began with a fully defined model, one in which all of the relevant paths linking race to sentence were identified and all of the correlations were calculated. We then eliminated paths which were not significant ($p \leq .01$). The reduced model is presented in Figure 1.

The data presented in Figure 1 substantiate the lack of direct racial discrimination in determining sentence severity in Metro City. After removing the effects of the six other independent variables, no direct path

Table 3 Relationship of race to sentence severity with various controls[a]

	Sentence
No controls	.092*
Control for charge	.025*
Controls for charge and prior record	.017
Controls for charge, prior record, and extralegal factors[b]	.009

[a]The measure of the bivariate relationship between race and sentence is Pearson's r. All of the other measures are betas.
[b]The extralegal factors include type of attorney, type of plea, charge reduction, pretrial bail status, and bail amount.
*$s \leq .05$

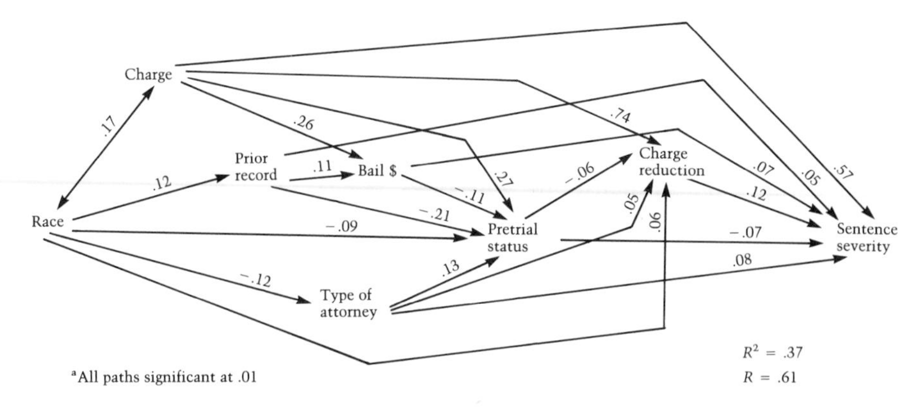

Figure 1 The impact of race and other variables on sentence severity[a]

remains between race and sentence. Judges in Metro City apparently do not take the defendant's race into consideration when determining sentence severity.

From this alone, however, we cannot conclude that race has *no* effect on sentence severity. As Figure 1 clearly reveals, there are a number of significant indirect relationships between these variables. The most important compound paths, measured by the percentage of the total variance in sentence severity explained by the path, are those from race to the legal factors to sentence. After controlling for all other factors included in the model, we still find that blacks' harsher sentences can be attributed, first and foremost, to the fact that they are charged with more serious crimes and have more serious prior criminal records. But Figure 1 also reveals that race affects sentence length in other, less explicable, ways. There are a number of indirect paths from race to extralegal factors to sentence. Although these paths clearly are less important than those involving the legal factors, they nonetheless are statistically significant. While space limitations prohibit analyzing each of these paths, the nature of the relationships can be illustrated by examining the two most significant of them:

- Black males are less likely than white males to be released prior to trial and thus receive harsher sentences than whites.
- Black males are less likely than white males to be represented by private attorneys, who are more likely than public defenders to get their clients released prior to trial. Because they are less likely than whites to be released, blacks receive harsher sentences.

These findings are a futher indication of indirect racial discrimination in Metro City. A defendant's socioeconomic status influences, at least to a moderate degree, the sanction imposed. Defendants who cannot obtain a private attorney or pretrial release receive slightly harsher sentences than those who can.

To put our findings thus far in perspective, we again emphasize that race has no direct effect on sentence severity in Metro City. Rather, black males receive harsher sentences than white males primarily because of legal factors but secondarily because of extralegal factors.

Race and the Decision to Incarcerate

In addition to exploring the relative severity of sentences imposed on black and white male defendants, we also examined the frequency with which defendants of each race were sentenced to prison. For most defendants this is probably the critical decision. As Uhlman (1977: 22) has noted, "Qualitatively, there is almost an incalculable jump between non-prison sanctions . . . and a jail term."

In accord with our first hypothesis, we expected to find no direct relationship between race and the decision to incarcerate once we controlled for the seriousness of the crime and prior record. But as shown in Table 4 and Figure 2, this hypothesis was not confirmed. A statistically significant relationship between race and incarceration remains after controlling for both legal and extralegal factors. After entering all controls in the regression equation, the *b*-value is .048, indicating that black males are incarcerated about 5 percent more often than white males. Twenty-nine percent of convicted blacks, but only 24 percent of convicted whites, were sent to prison. Thus, black defendants are 20 percent more likely than white defendants to be incarcerated.

That judges do discriminate against black males in deciding whether or not to sentence defendants to prison is confirmed further by the causal model presented in Figure 2. We should point out, however, that the direct path from race to incarceration is not as predictive as the indirect path from race to charge to incarceration. The correlation of the indirect path, obtained by multiplying the individual coefficients that comprise the path

Table 4 Relationship of race to incarceration with various controls[a]

	Prison/no prison
No controls	.144*
Control for charge	.074*
Controls for charge and prior record	.061*
Controls for charge, prior record, and extralegal factors	.042[b]

[a]The measure of the bivariate relationship between race and incarceration is Pearson's *r*. All of the other measures are betas.
[b]The *b* here is .048 (S.E. = .020), which means that blacks are incarcerated about 5 percent more than whites.
*s ≤ .05

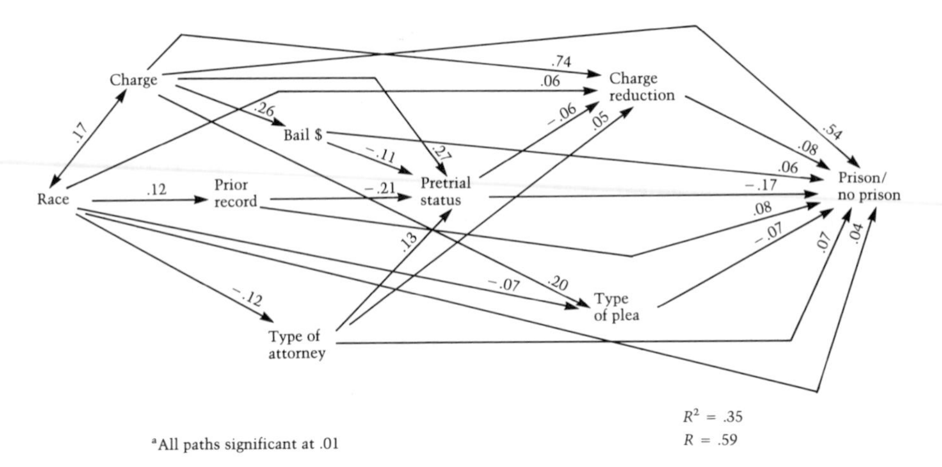

Figure 2 The impact of race and other variables on the decision to incarcerate[a]

(Asher 1976), is .09, while the correlation of the direct path is only .04. Thus, black males receive prison sentences more often than white males because they are charged with more serious crimes *and* because they are black.

Since both dependent variables are based on the same sentence severity scale, it might seem inconsistent that the first hypothesis was confirmed but the second hypothesis was not. The data presented in Table 5, however, reconcile this seeming inconsistency.

We divided all defendants into two groups—those not sentenced to prison and those sentenced to prison—and, controlling for the legal and extralegal factors, compared the severity of sentences imposed on defendants of each race within each group. We found that within each group blacks received *lighter* sentences than whites and that the differences between the races were statistically significant in the "not incarcerated" group.

Table 5 Comparison of the effect of race on sentence severity among defendants not incarcerated and incarcerated[a]

	Not incarcerated	*Incarcerated*
Pearson's *r*	−.10	.07
Beta	−.05	− .02
b	−.82	−1.31
S.E.	.41	2.18
F	4.08*	0.36
N	1,767	599

[a]All of the legal and extralegal factors were controlled for in calculation of the beta, *b*, and standard error.
*s ≤ .05

Thus, while black males *are* more likely than white males to receive prison terms, those who do are, as a group, given lighter sentences than their white counterparts. We interpreted this to mean that in "borderline cases"—cases where the judge could either decide to impose a lengthy (eight to nine years) probation sentence or a short (one to two years) prison sentence—the judge selected the probation option for whites more than blacks, the prison option for blacks more than whites. Consequently, more whites than blacks are found at the upper end of the "not incarcerated" category, while more blacks than whites are found at the lower end of the "incarcerated" category. Our findings, therefore, are not inconsistent. The way in which black and white male defendants were distributed along the 93-point sentence scale, and the comparison of defendants across the entire continuum, tended to mask important differences.

CONCLUSION

We expected to find no direct relationship between race and sentence severity once we controlled for the seriousness of the charge and prior criminal record. Accordingly, we hypothesized that we would find no direct racial discrimination either in the decision to impose a more or less severe sentence, or in the decision to incarcerate.

Our first hypothesis was confirmed. Black males did receive harsher sentences than white males, but this disparity was due primarily to the fact that blacks were charged with more serious offenses and had more serious prior criminal records. We found no statistical evidence of direct racial discrimination in determining sentence severity. We did, however, find some evidence of wealth discrimination. Defendants who could not obtain a private attorney or pretrial release received harsher sentences than those who could. Since blacks are more likely than whites to be poor, this type of discrimination affects blacks more than whites. It can, therefore, be seen as a possible source of indirect racial discrimination.

Our second hypothesis was not confirmed. Even after controlling for both legal and extralegal factors, black males still were sentenced to prison 5 percent more often than white males, resulting in a 20 percent higher rate. Race by itself accounted for 4 percent of the variation in this sentencing decision. Thus, judges in Metro City apparently do discriminate against black males in deciding between incarceration and lengthy probation. White males are more likely to receive probation, black males a short prison term. This is consistent with the findings of Nagel (1969), Pope (1975), Levin (1977), and Unnever and colleagues (1980), all of whom concluded that blacks were less likely than whites to receive probation. These earlier findings, then, hold up even when given a more rigorous test.

One might question whether a 5 percent difference between blacks and whites in the rate of incarceration is substantively significant. As we noted earlier, however, this 5 percent difference means that blacks are 20 percent more likely than whites to be incarcerated. We have been so sensitized to racial discrimination that the absence of a glaring disparity may seem trivial (see Hagan 1974). But as Nagel (1977: 189) has pointed out, the relationship between race and sentence severity should not be treated "as if it were just another statistical relationship like the relation between the religion of voters and whether they vote Democratic or Republican." Even though race accounts for "only" 4 percent of the variation in our study in the decision to incarcerate, the tremendous difference between being confined and being free makes it a difference which is both "substantial and disturbing" (Nagel 1977: 194). Our study examined only the most visible aspect of the criminal justice process. It says nothing about the well-documented and pervasive discrimination elsewhere in the process—the police officer's decision to arrest, the prosecutor's decision to charge, the judge's or jury's decision to convict, and the parole board's decision to grant parole (see Black 1974).

We think that our findings are an advance over previous work on race and sentencing. The large number of cases and offenses, controls for relevant legal and extralegal factors, the division of the sentencing decision, and the use of multivariate analysis have contributed to somewhat more refined conclusions about the influence of race on sentencing. But our study also has its limitations. It only examined sentences imposed on male offenders in one large city in the Northeast. And there is other evidence that the patterns found here might not apply to females (Spohn et al. 1981; see also Kruttschnitt 1980). In short, our findings support, but certainly do not prove, the existence of racial discrimination in sentencing.

REFERENCES

ARNOLD, WILLIAM R. (1971) "Race and Ethnicity Relative to Other Factors in Juvenile Court Dispostions." 77 *American Journal of Sociology* 211.

ASHER, HERBERT B. (1976) *Causal Modeling*. Sage University Paper Series on Quantitative Applications in the Social Sciences, No. 07-003. Beverly Hills, Calif.: Sage Publications.

BAAB, GEORGE WILLIAM, and WILLIAM ROYAL FURGESON, JR. (1967) "Texas Sentencing Practices: A Statistical Study." 45 *Texas Law Review* 471.

BERNSTEIN, ILENE NAGEL, WILLIAM R. KELLY, and PATRICIA A. DOYLE (1977) "Societal Reaction to Deviants: The Case of Criminal Defendants." 42 *American Sociological Review* 743.

BLACK, CHARLES L. (1974) *Capital Punishment: The Inevitability of Caprice and Mistake*. New Haven: Yale University Press.

BURKE, PETER J., and AUSTIN T. TURK (1975) "Factors Affecting Postarrest Decisions: A Model for Analysis." 22 *Social Problems* 313.

CHIRICOS, THEODORE G., and GORDON P. WALDO (1975) "Socioeconomic Status and Criminal Sentencing: An Empirical Assessment of a Conflict Propostion." 40 *American Sociological Review* 753.

CLARKE, STEVENS H., and GARY G. KOCH (1976) "The Influence of Income and Other Factors on Whether Criminal Defendants Go to Prison." 11 *Law* and *Society Review* 57.

COHEN, LAWRENCE E., and JAMES R. KLUEGEL (1978) "Determinants of Juvenile Court Dispositions." 43 *American Sociological Review* 162.

COOK, BEVERLY B. (1973) "Sentencing Behavior of Federal Judges: Draft Cases—1972." 42 *University of Cincinnati Law Review* 597.

EISENSTEIN, JAMES, and HERBERT JACOB (1977) *Felony Justice: An Organizational Analysis of Criminal Courts*. Boston: Little, Brown.

ENGLE, CHARLES DONALD (1971) *Criminal Justice in the City: A Study of Sentence Severity and Variation in the Philadelphia Criminal Court System*. Ph.D. dissertation, Temple University.

FARRELL, RONALD A., and VICTORIA LYNN SWIGERT (1978) "Prior Offense Record as a Self-Fulfilling Prophecy." 12 *Law and Society Review* 437.

GIBSON, JAMES L. (1978) "Race as a Determinant of Criminal Sentences: A Methodological Critique and a Case Study." 12 *Law and Society Review* 455.

GREENWOOD, PETER C., SORREL WILDHORN, EUGENE C. POGGIO, MICHAEL J. STRUMWASSER, and PETER DELEON (1973) *Prosecution of Adult Felony Defendants in Los Angeles County: A Policy Perspective*. Santa Monica: Rand Corporation.

GRUHL, JOHN, CASSIA SPOHN, and SUSAN WELCH (1981) "Women as Policy Makers: The Case of Trial Judges." 25 *American Journal of Political Science* 308.

HAGAN, JOHN (1974) "Extra-Legal Attributes and Criminal Sentencing: An Assessment of a Sociological Viewpoint." 8 *Law and Society Review* 357.

HAGAN, JOHN, and ILENE N. BERNSTEIN (1979) "Conflict in Context: The Sanctioning of Draft Resisters, 1963–76." 27 *Social Problems* 109.

HEISE, DAVID R. (1972) "Employing Nominal Variables, Induced Variables, and Block Variables in Path Analysis." 1 *Sociological Methods and Research* 147.

KRUTSCHNITT, CANDACE (1980) "Social Status and Sentences of Female Offenders." 15 *Law* and *Society Review* 247.

LEVIN, MARTIN A. (1977) *Urban Politics and Criminal Courts*. Chicago: University of Chicago Press.

LIZOTTE, ALAN J. (1978) "Extra-Legal Factors in Chicago's Criminal Courts: Testing the Conflict Model of Criminal Justice." 25 *Social Problems* 564.

LOTZ, ROY, and JOHN D. HEWITT (1977) "The Influence of Legally Irrelevant Factors on Felony Sentencing." 47 *Sociological Inquiry* 39.

NAGEL, STUART S. (1964) *The Legal Process from a Behavioral Perspective*. Homewood, Ill.: Dorsey Press.

NAGEL, STUART S., and MARIAN NEEF (1977) *The Legal Process: Modeling the System*. Beverly Hills, Calif.: Sage Publications.

POPE, CARL E. (1975) *Sentencing of California Felony Offenders*. Washington, D.C.: United States Department of Justice, Law Enforcement Assistance Administration, Criminal Justice Research Center.

SCARPITTI, FRANK, and RICHARD STEPHENSON (1971) "Juvenile Court Dispositions: Factors in the Decision Making Process." 17 *Crime and Delinquency* 142.

SELLIN, THORSTEN (1928) "The Negro Criminal: A Statistical Note." 140 *Annals of the American Academy of Political and Social Science* 52.

SPOHN, CASSIA, SUSAN WELCH, and JOHN GRUHL (1981) "Women Defendants in Court: The Interaction Between Sex and Race in Convicting and Sentencing." Unpublished paper.

SUTTON, L. PAUL (1978a) *Federal Sentencing Patterns: A Study of Geographical Variations*. Albany, N.Y.: Criminal Justice Research Center.

——— (1978b) *Variations in Federal Criminal Sentences: A Statistical Assessment at the National Level*. Albany, N.Y.: Criminal Justice Research Center.

SWIGERT, VICTORIA LYNN, and RONALD A. FARRELL (1977) "Normal Homicides and the Law." 42 *American Sociological Review* 16.

TERRY, ROBERT (1967) "Discrimination in the Handling of Juvenile Offenders by Social-Control Agencies." 4 *Journal of Research in Crime and Delinquency* 218.

THOMAS, CHARLES W., and ROBIN J. CAGE (1977) "The Effect of Social Characteristics on Juvenile Court Dispositions." 18 *Sociological Quarterly* 237.

THORNBERRY, TERENCE P. (1973) "Race, Socioeconomic Status, and Sentencing in the Juvenile Justice System." 64 *Journal of Criminal Law, Criminology, and Police Science* 90.

TIFFANY, LAWRENCE P., YAKOV AVICHAI, and GEOFFREY W. PETERS (1975) "A Statistical Analysis of Sentencing in Federal Courts: Defendants Convicted After Trial, 1967–1968." 4 *Journal of Legal Studies* 369.

UHLMAN, THOMAS M. (1977) "The Impact of Defendant Race in Trial Court Sentencing Decisions." In John A. Gardiner, ed., *Public Law and Public Policy*. New York, Praeger.

UNNEVER, JAMES D., CHARLES E. FRAZIER, and JOHN C. HENRETTA (1980) "Race Differences in Criminal Sentencing." 21 *Sociological Quarterly* 197.

WELLFORD, CHARLES (1975) "Labelling Theory and Criminology: An Assessment." 22 *Social Problems* 332.

PART SIX

CORRECTIONS

Few citizens of the United States realize that their country gave the world the modern prison system, and still fewer know that our prison system came about in response to concern for humanitarian treatment of criminals. During the first decades of the nineteenth century, the creation of penitentiaries in Pennsylvania and New York attracted the attention not only of legislators in other states but also of observers from Europe. In 1831, France sent Alexis de Tocqueville and Gustave Auguste de Beaumont, England sent William Crawford, and Prussia dispatched Nicholas Julius. And even travelers from abroad who had no special interest in penology made it a point to include a penitentiary in their itineraries, just as they would want to see a Southern plantation, a textile mill in Lowell, or a frontier town. The U.S. penitentiary had become world famous by the middle of the nineteenth century.

During the colonial and early postrevolutionary years, Americans used physical punishment, a legacy from Europe, as the main criminal sanction. Together with the fine and the stocks, flogging was a primary means of controlling deviancy and maintaining public safety. For more serious crimes, the gallows was used frequently. In New York criminals were regularly sentenced to death, with about 20 percent of all offenses being capital ones, including picking pockets, burglary, robbery, and horse stealing. Especially for recidivists, hanging was the preferred sanction in the early days of the republic. Jails throughout the country served only the limited purpose of holding people awaiting trial or unable to pay their debts.

With the spread of the humanistic ideas of the Enlightenment during the latter part of the eighteenth century, the concept of criminal punishment was revised. Part of the impetus came from the postrevolutionary patriotic fervor that blamed recidivism and criminal behavior on the English laws. To a greater degree, however, the new correctional philosophy coincided with the ideals of the Declaration of Independence, stressing an optimistic view of human nature and a belief in its perfectibility. The conviction followed that social progress and advancement were possible through reforms carried out according to the dictates of "pure reason." Further, emphasis shifted from the assumption that deviance was inherent in human nature to a belief that crime was a result of forces operating in the environment.

THE INVENTION OF THE PENITENTIARY

Reform of the penal structure became the goal of a number of humanist groups, the oldest of which was the Philadelphia Society for Alleviating the Miseries of Public Prisons, formed in 1787. Under the leadership of Dr. Benjamin Rush, a signer of the Declaration of Independence, this group, which included a large number of Quakers, urged that capital and corporal punishment be replaced with incarceration. The Quakers believed that criminals could best be reformed if they were placed in solitary confinement so that, in the isolation of their cells, they could consider their deviant acts, repent, and make changes in themselves. The word "penitentiary" comes from the Quaker idea that criminals needed an opportunity for penitence and repentance.

Through a series of legislative acts, Pennsylvania made provision in 1790 for the solitary confinement of "hardened and atrocious offenders" in the existing three-story Walnut Street Jail in Philadelphia. Pressed by the reformers, the legislature also decided to build additional institutions: Western Penitentiary on the outskirts of Pittsburgh, and Eastern Penitentiary near Philadelphia. Eastern's opening in 1829 marked the culmination of forty-two years of reform activity by the Philadelphia Society. The first prisoners were assigned to a cell twelve by eight by ten feet, with an individual exercise yard some eighteen feet long. In the cell was a fold-up steel bedstead, a simple toilet, a wooden stool, a workbench, and eating utensils. Light came through an eight-inch window in the ceiling. Solitary labor, Bible reading, and reflection were the keys to the moral regeneration that was to occur within the prison walls. Although the cell was larger than most currently in use today, it was the only world the prisoner would see for the duration of the sentence. The only other human voice heard would be that of a clergyman who would visit on Sundays. Nothing was to distract the penitent from the path to reformation.

Eastern Penitentiary provided an example for reform efforts in other states. In 1823 the "Auburn System" of New York evolved as a rival to Pennsylvania's system. The Auburn System did not question the use of incarceration, only the regimen to which the prisoners were exposed. Rather than the complete isolation espoused by the Philadelphians, New York's reformers urged that criminals be kept in individual cells at night but be together in workshops during the day. The inmates were forbidden to talk with one another or even to exchange glances while on the job or at meals. In a sense, Auburn reflected the spirit of the industrial revolution: inmates were to have the benefits of both labor and meditation. They were to live under tight control, on a spartan diet, according to an undeviating routine.

During this period of reform, advocates of the Pennsylvania and Auburn plans debated on the public platforms and in the periodicals of the nation. Although the approaches seem very similar in retrospect, an extraordinary amount of intellectual and emotional energy was spent on the argument. Often the two have been contrasted by noting that the Quaker method sought to produce honest people, whereas that of New York intended to mold obedient citizens. Advocates of both the congregate and solitary systems agreed that the prisoner must be isolated from society and placed in a disciplined routine. They believed that deviance was a result of corruptions pervading the community and that institutions such as the family and the church were not providing the counterbalance. Convicts were not inherently depraved but rather were the victims of a society that had not protected them from vice. Only removing these temptations and substituting a steady and regular regimen could make the offenders useful citizens.

By the middle of the nineteenth century, reformers had become disillusioned with the results of the penitentiary movement. They believed that deterrence and the reclamation of prisoners had not been achieved in either the Auburn or Pennsylvania systems. A new approach, advocated by Zebulon Brockway, took effect in Elmira, New York, in 1877. According to Brockway, the key to rehabilitation was education; he persuaded the legislature to provide for indeterminate sentences and the release of inmates on parole when there was evidence that they had been reformed. At Elmira attempts were made to create a school-like atmosphere, with courses in both academic and moral subjects. Inmates who performed well were placed in separate categories so that they could progress to a point where they were ineligible for parole.

By 1900 the reformatory movement had spread throughout the nation, yet by World War I it was already in decline. In most institutions the architecture, the demeanor of the guards, and the emphasis upon discipline differed little from the custodial orientation of the past. Too often, education and rehabilitation took a back seat to the punitive ideology. Even Brockway admitted it was difficult to distinguish between inmates whose attitudes had changed and inmates who only superficially conformed to prison rules. As before, "being a good prisoner" became the way to win parole in most of these institutions.

Although the declaration of principles adopted by the National Prison Association in 1870 declared that "reformation, not vindictive suffering, should be the purpose of penal treatment," the fortress prison emphasizing custody and discipline remained the dominant type of institution for most of the twentieth century. Until the end of World War II, the "big house" dominated the penological landscape. These walled prisons, holding an average of 2,500 men, with large cell blocks containing stacks of one- or two-man cells in three or more tiers, could be found in most states by the 1920s. The "big house" was the image that most Americans conjured up when they thought of prison.

Beginning in the 1940s some states began to implement the rehabilitative philosophy first advocated in 1870. Emphasis was shifted to the treatment of criminals, offenders whose social, intellectual, or biological deficiencies had caused them to engage in illegal activity. Using a model analogous to the medical concept of disease, rehabilitation theorists blamed such conditions as poverty, unstable family relations, and limited mental capacity for producing maladjusted individuals who were unable to live by society's rules. Vocational and educational training, individual counseling and psychotherapy, honor farms, group therapy, work-release programs, chemotherapy, behavior modification—all were incorporated into the modern penal system. California became the standard-bearer for this movement; by 1960 correctional rehabilitation had become the preeminent theme in penology. But the failure of these new techniques to stem crime, changes in the characteristics of the prison population, and misuse of the discretion required by the treatment model prompted another cycle of correctional reform. By 1980 rehabilitation as a goal had been discredited.

It is important to emphasize that each of the reform movements was the work of well-intentioned people who had pushed for change in the name of humanity. Unfortunately, the reformers' ideals were never achieved, and the changes that were made often produced unsatisfactory results. The assumptions underlying one correctional period proved to be unfounded in the next period. In the 1970s the reform movement appeared to be so fruitless that many penologists threw up their hands in despair. By the end of the decade new records for size of the prison population in the United States were being set, and correctional officials became concerned primarily with making custody in overcrowded institutions as humane as possible.

THE MODERN PRISON: LEGACY OF THE PAST

For someone schooled in criminal justice history, entering one of today's U.S. penitentiaries is like entering a time machine. Elements of each of the major penology reforms may be seen within the walls of today's prisons. Conforming to the early notion that the prison should be located away from the community, most correctional facilities are still in rural areas, far from the urban homes of the inmates' families. The architecture of the typical prison is like that of a fortress. Prison industries, founded on the principles of Auburn, remain an important activity. Treatment programs are available, including vocational education, group therapy, and counseling, with participation rewarded. Although the lexicon of modern penology stresses corrections, "a prison remains a prison whatever it's called." The overriding emphasis of most prisons still appears to be on the time-honored goal of custody and punishment.

PRISON ORGANIZATION

Prison is different from almost any other institution or organization in modern society. More than its physical features set it apart; it is a place where a group of free people devote themselves to managing a group of captives. Prisoners do not commit themselves voluntarily, as do hospital patients, for instance. Prisoners are brought forcibly through the gates and prevented from leaving by guards, walls, and fences. Prisoners are required to live according to the dictates of their keepers, and their movements are greatly restricted.

Over and above these features of the prison, three important organizational characteristics dictate the administrative structure, and these factors influence the nature of prison society. First, the prison, like the mental hospital and monastery, is a closed institution. Whatever the inmates do or do not do begins and ends in the prison; every minute behind bars must be lived according to the rules of the institution, as enforced by the staff. Second, the administrative structure of the prison is organized down to the lowest level. However, unlike the factory or the military, where there are separate groups of supervisors and workers, the lowest-status prison employee—the guard—is both a supervisor and a worker. Guards are seen as workers by the warden but as supervisors by the inmates. Guards must face the problem that their efficiency is being judged by the warden, on the basis of their ability to manage the prisoners. Because this can be achieved only if there is some degree of cooperation from the inmates, the guard must often ease up on enforcement of some rules in order to secure compliance with other rules. Third, the prison exists to carry out a number of functions related to the keeping (custody), the using (working), and the serving (treatment) of the inmates. Employees are divided into groups to perform these functions, but since the goals are often at cross-purposes, the administration of the correctional institution is often filled with conflict and ambiguities.

A view widely held by the public is that prisons are operated in an authoritarian manner. In such a society of captives, guards are taught to give orders and inmates to take orders. Forcing people to follow commands is, however, basically an inefficient way to make them carry out tasks. In addition, the threatened use of physical force by correctional officers has many limitations. As a result, prisons can be said to conform to an authoritarian model of control only in a formal sense. In reality, the prison society, like society at large, operates through an informal network of social and exchange relationships among the administrators, guards, prisoner leaders, and general population of captives. Changes in the leadership of the institution, attempts to shift from custodial to treatment goals, and pressures to "tighten up" discipline have all been cited as forces that can create instability in the system.

Prison Culture

In an institutional setting, the social distance between staff and inmates works to enhance the prison subculture. Powerful inmates may dominate others through a system of friendships, mutual obligations, intimidation, deception, and violence. The norms of the subculture may reflect the belief that prisoners should have as little as possible to do with the guards. "Do your own time," "Play it cool," "Mind your own business" are slogans that express this aloofness from and indifference to the interests of the staff and of other inmates.

Subculture leaders tend to be persons with extensive prison experience who have been tested through their relationships with other inmates—they are neither "pushed around" by their peers nor distrusted as "stool pigeons." Because they can be trusted by the staff, they serve as the essential middlepersons in communication between the inmates and the authorities. Because of their ability to acquire "inside information" and their access to decision makers, the inmate leaders are in a position to command deference from other prisoners. In many institutions, this aspect of the subculture is used as a means for the staff to maintain control.

Given the conflicting purposes and the complex set of role relationships, it is amazing that prisons do not degenerate into a chaotic "mess of social relations that have no order and make no sense." Although the U.S. prison may not conform to the enunciated goals of treatment and rehabilitation, and the formal organization of the staff with respect to the inmates may have little resemblance to the ongoing reality of their informal relations, order *is* kept and a routine is followed.

Violence

The following might be an ideal recipe for violence. Confine in cramped quarters a thousand men, some of whom have a history of engaging in violent interpersonal acts; restrict their movement and behavior; allow no contact with women; guard them by using other men; and keep them in this condition for indefinite periods of time. Although collective violence like the riots at Attica, Rahway, and Santa Fe has become well known to the public, little has been said about the interpersonal violence that exists in U.S. prisons. Each year more than a hundred inmates die and countless others are injured through suicides, homicides, and assaults. Still others live in a state of constant uneasiness, always on the lookout for persons who might subject them to homosexual demands, steal their few possessions, and in general increase the pangs of imprisonment.

Too often, explanations of prison violence merely recite the deprivations and injustices of life in penal institutions. Mention is usually made of the rules enforced by brutal guards, the loss of freedom, and the boredom. Incarceration is undoubtedly a harsh and painful experience, but it need not be intensified by physical assault or death at the hands of fellow inmates. Prisons must be made safe places. Because the state puts offenders there, it has a responsibility for preventing violence and maintaining order.

PRISONERS' RIGHTS

Until the 1960s the courts generally took the position that the internal administration of prisons or the conditions within the prisons did not fall within the courts' purview. A hands-off policy existed, on the ground that such concerns belonged to the executive branch of government, not the judicial branch. With the civil rights movement and the expansion of due process rights by the Warren Court, prisoner groups and their supporters pushed to secure inmate rights. Prisoners mounted cases that reached the U.S. Supreme Court, arguing that their rights under the First Amendment (freedom of speech, assembly, petition, and religion), the Fourth Amendment (forbidding unreasonable searches), and the Eighth Amendment (forbidding cruel and unusual punishment) had been violated. Many of these actions were brought under the provisions of Section 1983 of the United States Code, which have been interpreted to allow prisoners to sue public officials in the federal courts over the conditions of their confinement.

The prisoners' rights movement has been responsible for some changes in corrections during the past decade, changes that resulted from court orders to bring prison conditions up to constitutional standards. Religious practices have been protected, legal assistance has been provided, and due process requirements have been upheld. Federal judges in a number of states have ordered renovation of existing facilities and construction of new facilities. To ensure implementation of their orders, judges have taken over administration of some correctional institutions through the appointment of special masters. The judicial intervention has generally led to increased correctional budgets, reformulation of policies, and creation of new organizational structures. The impact of the prisoners' rights movement on the behavior of correctional officials has not yet been measured, but the evidence suggests that court decisions have had a broad effect. Because prisoners and their supporters have been asserting their rights, wardens and their subordinates may be holding back from traditional disciplinary actions that might result in judicial intervention.

COMMUNITY CORRECTIONS

During the social and political turmoil of the late 1960s there was a change of direction with regard to the way offenders should be handled. Referred to as "community corrections," this shift in policy emphasized the reintegration of the offender into society. Although probation and parole had long been parts of the criminal justice system, the new direction has supplemented these efforts. The community corrections movement attracted the attention of penological groups and was broadly supported in the 1967 report of the President's Commission on Law Enforcement and Administration of Justice. The commission stated that crime results from disorganization in the community and the inability of some persons to receive and to be sustained by the stable influences and resources that are necessary for living as productive members of society.

The goal of community corrections is reintegration of offenders into society by building ties between them and the community: restoring family links, obtaining employment and education, and securing a sense of place and pride in daily life. This model of corrections focuses attention both on the offender and on the community, for it not only assumes that the offender must change but also recognizes that factors within the community that might encourage criminal behavior (unemployment, for example) must change as well.

Three trends in the new penology reflect the emphasis of community corrections: (1) smaller institutions, located near urban areas, (2) special programs designed to create links between the offender and the community, and (3) increased use of probation and parole. All these features of community corrections spring from the concept that offenders should be given opportunities to succeed in lawful activities and to reduce their contact with the criminal world.

The community corrections movement appeals to people who believe that most prison terms in the United States are too long and that institutionalization does not lead to the eventual successful reintegration of the offender into the community. In this view, incarcerating some types of offenders not only puts the punishment out of proportion to the crime but also exposes "first-timers" to the prison "crime factory" and reduces the chances for successful reintegration upon release. If the objective is to avoid the negative impact of separation from the community, of the severing of family ties, and of the prison culture, then probation may be more beneficial to many offenders. Because most probationers do well with minimal supervision, some penologists suggest that many offenders who are now incarcerated might also succeed under intensive community supervision.

A change in crime-control policies has taken place over the past decade. Community corrections is no longer a rising star in penology. Deserved punishment and incapacitation are now seen as dominant purposes of the criminal sanction, so the idea of allowing offenders who have committed serious crimes to remain in the community is not popular. The number of people on probation remains high, and some of the programs developed under the community corrections aegis still function, but the concept of community corrections is no longer a motivating factor for reform of the criminal justice system.

RELEASE FROM INCARCERATION

Parole is the conditional release of adult prisoners from incarceration, but not from the legal custody of the state. Not the product of any single reformer or movement, parole evolved in the United States during the nineteenth century under a variety of influences. Among these were the work of Zebulon Brockway at Elmira, the earlier British practice of allowing prisoners to become indentured servants in its colonies, and the Australian system, begun in the 1840s, whereby a "ticket-of-leave" was given convicts who had earned credits for satisfactory performance while incarcerated. By 1900 some system of parole existed in twenty states; by 1922, in forty-four states, the federal system, and Hawaii. At first the approach was used primarily for young and first offenders, who were released with little supervision. Gradually, eligibility for parole was broadened and supervision by professional agents was added. After World War II, parole was incorporated into every state correctional system. With the movement away from rehabilitation and toward definite sentencing, the discretionary power of parole boards to release convicts has been restricted or abandoned in twenty-nine states, the District of Columbia, and the federal system.

With the passage of determinate-sentencing laws and parole guidelines in some jurisdictions during the past decade, it is necessary to distinguish mandatory release from discretionary release. Where parole boards have been restricted or abandoned, felons reenter the community through mandatory release mechanisms that allow correctional authorities little leeway to consider whether the offender is ready for community supervision. Release is mandated at the end of a certain period of time, as stipulated by the sentencing judge, minus good time and other reductions. Discretionary release prevails where the parole board has extensive authority to consider the prisoner's behavior, participation in a treatment program, and readiness for a return to the community.

A major criticism of release by parole boards is that it shifts responsibility for many of the primary decisions of criminal justice from the judge, who holds legal procedures to be foremost, to an administrative board, where discretion rules. In states using discretionary release, parole decisions are made in secret hearings, with only the board members, the inmate, and correctional officers present. Usually, no published criteria are used to guide the decisions, and prisoners are given no reason for the denial or granting of their release. The question remains whether even good people should be trusted with such uncontrolled discretionary power.

Community Supervision

The concept of parole involves more than just release. It is assumed that the offender will go back into the community only under the supervision of a trained agent, who will assist in the adjustment and may continue some of the therapeutic endeavors begun in prison. Parole officers are asked to play two different roles: "cop" and social worker. As "cops" they are given the power to restrict many aspects of parolees' lives, to enforce conditions of release, and to initiate revocation proceedings if there are violations. As social workers they are responsible for helping parolees find jobs and restore ties with their families. The parole officer must develop the kind of relationship that will make the parolee feel comfortable about confiding his or her frustrations and concerns. This is a relationship that is difficult to maintain, because the parolee recognizes the parole officer's ability to send him or her back to prison.

Impact of Release Mechanisms

Parole and the indeterminate sentence have recently drawn close legislative scrutiny. The impetus came from a curious coalition of correctional officials, former inmates, and academic penologists, who argued that rehabilitation as the primary goal was unrealistic, that parole supervision was oppressive, and that the decision to release was often made on the basis of inappropriate criteria. These pressures brought about a number of changes: flat sentences with no parole; assistance for rather than supervision of released offenders; and (where parole was retained) more carefully structured procedures for decisions in parole matters. Record numbers of offenders are being held in overcrowded jails and prisons. The new sentencing and release systems seem to have contributed to this population increase. Citizens and legislatures are demanding stiffer sentences but are unwilling to appropriate the money to build new facilities. In some states emergency release procedures have been enacted so that offenders can be placed in the community under supervision when correctional facilities become excessively crowded. These conditions may lead to new ways of applying the concept of parole.

THE FUTURE OF CORRECTIONS

Methods for dealing with criminal offenders have come a long way since the reform activities of Philadelphia's Quakers, yet there is still uncertainty about what methods should be used. The 1971 riot by the inmates of Attica, and the police response to it, forced penologists in the United States to reexamine the correctional system and its underlying assumptions. With the rate of recidivism remaining about constant, there is increasing doubt about the value of the rehabilitative model. Crime continues to be a major national concern, and questions have been raised about the deterrent effect of correctional methods.

Reformers considering alternative correctional policies claim that the goal of rehabilitation has dominated the thinking of penologists during the past half century to the exclusion of other goals for criminal sanctions. Although some offenders do have social and psychological deficiencies that may be the basis for their criminal behavior, it is also recognized that this type may be only a small part of the offender population. Implementing a correctional policy based solely on rehabilitation neglects the goals of deterrence, incapacitation, and retributive justice that are also important elements in the prevention and control of crime. With the inmate population now at a record high and the average term of incarceration increasing, the pressures on the corrections system are intense. This has led to much soul-searching among penologists and officials. It is clear that changes in correctional policy will have an important impact on the actions of the police and courts, but there have been other periods of reform in corrections when new approaches created high hopes that were eventually dashed. The pendulum has swung back and forth before. Are we now seeing merely another swing?

SUGGESTIONS FOR FURTHER READING

BRALY, MALCOLM. *On the Yard.* Boston: Little, Brown, 1967. Written by a former prisoner, this novel describes a maximum-security institution in the 1950s. An excellent "big house" novel.

CLEAR, TODD R., and GEORGE F. COLE. *American Corrections.* Monterey, Calif.: Brooks/Cole, 1986. A comprehensive look at the corrections enterprise.

FOUCAULT, MICHEL. *Discipline and Punish.* Translated by Alan Sheriden. New York: Pantheon Books, 1977. An analysis of the philosophical and historical changes that took place in Europe during the seventeen and eighteenth centuries, as criminal behavior was viewed as resulting from the person rather than from the body.

FREEDMAN, ESTELLE B. *Their Sisters' Keepers.* Ann Arbor: University of Michigan Press, 1981. The role of female reformers in the creation of prisons for female offenders.

GOLDFARB, RONALD, and LINDA R. SINGER. *After Conviction.* New York: Simon & Schuster, 1973. An exploration of the entire postconviction process from sentencing to release. The authors find much that is wrong with the system and point to some recommendations for change.

IRWIN, JOHN. *Prisons in Turmoil.* Boston: Little, Brown, 1980. A view of the contemporary prison, with comparisons to the "big house" and the correctional institution. Irwin shows the extent to which factors of race and gang membership have fragmented prison society.

JACOBS, JAMES B. *Stateville.* Chicago: University of Chicago Press, 1977. A Study of Stateville Penitentiary, with emphasis upon the organization of the institution. One of the few sociological studies to look at the role of the guard.

LOMBARDO, LUCIEN X. *Guards Imprisoned.* New York: Elsevier, 1981. One of the few full-length treatments of the life of correctional officers. Describes the role complexity of the position in that the guard is both a "people worker" and a "bureaucrat."

ROTHMAN, DAVID J. *The Discovery of the Asylum: Social Order and Disorder in the New Republic.* Boston: Little, Brown, 1971. A history of the invention of the penitentiary. Rothman shows the links among the ideology of the 1830s, assumptions concerning corrections, and the design of institutions.

SHEEHAN, SUSAN. *A Prison and a Prisoner.* Boston: Houghton Mifflin, 1978. A fascinating description of life in Green Haven Prison and the way one prisoner "makes it" through "swagging," "hustling," and "doing time." An excellent discussion of the inmate economy.

STANLEY, DAVID. *Prisoners Among Us.* Washington, D.C.: Brookings Institution, 1976. An analysis of the parole system. The title indicates the theme of the book: on the average, two-thirds of convicted felons are living in the community on parole.

ARTICLE EIGHTEEN

The Society of Captives: The Defects of Total Power

GRESHAM M. SYKES

In theory, prisons are organized in an authoritarian manner. In such a "society of captives," one might assume that guards have only to give orders and inmates will follow them. Because the guards have a monopoly on the legal means of enforcing rules, many people believe that there should be no question about how the prison is run. In reality, however, the relationship between the guards and the prisoners is based on a more fragile foundation. As this article shows, there are limitations on the ability of correctional officers to use total power.

"For the needs of mass administration today," said Max Weber, "bureaucratic administration is completely indispensable. The choice is between bureaucracy and dilettantism in the field of administration."[1] To the officials of the New Jersey State Prison the choice is clear, as it is clear to the custodians of all maximum security prisons in the United States today. They are organized into a bureaucratic administrative staff—characterized by limited and specific rules, well-defined areas of competence and responsibility, impersonal standards of performance and promotion, and so on—which is similar in many respects to that of any modern, large-

Source: Selection from Gresham M. Sykes, *The Society of Captives: A Study of a Maximum Security Prison* (copyright © 1958 by Princeton University Press; Princeton Paperback, 1971), pp. 40–first 2 paragraphs p. 53. Reprinted by permission of Princeton University Press. Portions of this article concerning the corruption of the guards' authority are to be found in Gresham M. Sykes, *Crime and Society* (New York: Random House, 1956). Reprinted by permission of Random House, Inc.

scale enterprise; and it is this staff which must see to the effective execution of the prison's routine procedures.

Of the approximately 300 employees of the New Jersey State Prison, more than two-thirds are directly concerned with the supervision and control of the inmate population. These form the so-called custodian force which is broken into three eight-hour shifts, each shift being arranged in a typical pyramid of authority. The day shift, however—on duty from 6:20 A.M. to 2:20 P.M.—is by far the largest. As in many organizations, the rhythm of life in the prison quickens with daybreak and trails off in the afternoon, and the period of greatest acvitity requires the largest number of administrative personnel.

In the bottom ranks are the wing guards, the tower guards, the guards assigned to the shops, and those with a miscellany of duties such as the guardianship of the receiving gate or the garage. Immediately above these men are a number of sergeants and lieutenants, and these in turn are responsible to the warden and his assistants.

The most striking fact about this bureaucracy of custodians is its unparalleled position of power—in formal terms, at least—vis-à-vis the body of men which it rules and from which it is supposed to extract compliance. The officials, after all, possess a monopoly on the legitimate means of coercion (or, as one prisoner has phrased it succinctly, "They have the guns and we don't"); and the officials can call on the armed might of the police and the National Guard in case of an overwhelming emergency. The twenty-four-hour surveillance of the custodians represents the ultimate watchfulness, and presumably noncompliance on the part of the inmates need not go long unchecked. The rulers of this society of captives nominally hold in their hands the sole right of granting rewards and inflicting punishments and it would seem that no prisoner could afford to ignore their demands for conformity. Centers of opposition in the inmate population—in the form of men recognized as leaders by fellow prisoners—can be neutralized through the use of solitary confinement or exile to other state institutions. The custodians have the right not only to issue and administer the orders and regulations which are to guide the life of the prisoner, but also the right to detail, try, and punish any individual accused of disobedience—a merging of legislative, executive, and judicial functions which has long been regarded as the earmark of complete domination. The officials of the prison, in short, appear to be the possessors of almost infinite power within their realm; and, at least on the surface, the bureaucratic staff should experience no great difficulty in converting their rules and regulations—their blueprint for behavior—into a reality.

It is true, of course, that the power position of the custodial bureaucracy is not truly infinite. The objectives which the officials pursue are not completely of their own choosing and the means which they can use to achieve their objectives are far from limitless. The custodians are not total despots, able to exercise power at whim, and thus they lack the essential mark of infinite power, the unchallenged right of being capricious in their rule. It is this last which distinguishes terror from government, infinite power from almost infinite power, and the distinction is an important one. Neither by right nor by intention are the officials of the New Jersey State Prison free from a system of norms and laws which curb their actions. But within these limitations the bureaucracy of the prison is organized around a grant of power which is without an equal in American society; and if the rulers of any social system could secure compliance with their rules and regulations—however sullen or unwilling—it might be expected that the officials of the maximum security prison would be able to do so.

When we examine the New Jersey State Prison, however, we find that this expectation is not borne out in actuality. Indeed, the glaring conclusion is that despite the guns and the surveillance, the searches and the precautions of the custodians, the actual behavior of the inmate population differs markedly from that which is called for by official commands and decrees. Violence, fraud, theft, aberrant sexual behavior—all are commonplace occurrences in the daily round of institutional existence in spite of the fact that the maximum security prison is conceived of by society as the ultimate weapon for the control of the criminal and his deviant actions. Far from being omnipotent rulers who have crushed all signs of rebellion against their regime, the custodians are engaged in a continuous struggle to maintain order—and it is a struggle in which the custodians frequently fail. Offenses committed by one inmate against another occur often, as do offenses committed by inmates against the officials and their rules. And the number of undetected offenses is, by universal agreement of both officials and inmates, far larger than the number of offenses which are discovered.

Some hint of the custodial bureaucracy's skirmishes with the population of prisoners is provided by the records of the disciplinary court which has the task of adjudicating charges brought by guards against their captives for offenses taking place within the walls. The following is a typical listing for a one-week period:

Charge	*Disposition*
1. Insolence and swearing while being interrogated	1. Continue in segregation
2. Threatening an inmate	2. Drop from job
3. Attempting to smuggle roll of tape into institution	3. 1 day in segregation with restricted diet
4. Possession of contraband	4. 30 days loss of privileges
5. Possession of pair of dice	5. 2 days in segregation with restricted diet
6. Insolence	6. Reprimand

7. Out of place	7. Drop from job. Refer to classification committee for reclassification
8. Possession of home-made knife, metal, and emery paper	8. 5 days in segregation with restricted diet
9. Suspicion of gambling or receiving bets	9. Drop from job and change Wing assignment
10. Out of place	10. 15 days loss of privileges
11. Possession of contraband	11. Reprimand
12. Creating disturbance in Wing	12. Continue in segregation
13. Swearing at an officer	13. Reprimand
14. Out of place	14. 15 days loss of privileges
15. Out of place	15. 15 days loss of privileges

Even more revealing, however, than this brief and somewhat enigmatic record are the so-called charge slips in which the guard is supposed to write out the derelictions of the prisoner in some detail. In the New Jersey State Prison, charge slips form an administrative residue of past conflicts between captors and captives and the following accounts are a fair sample:

> This inmate threatened an officer's life. When I informed this inmate he was to stay in to see the Chief Deputy on his charge he told me if he did not go to the yard I would get a shiv in my back. Signed: Officer A ______
>
> Inmate X cursing an officer. In mess hall inmate refused to put excess bread back on tray. Then he threw the tray on the floor. In the Center, inmate cursed both Officer Y and myself. Signed: Officer B ______
>
> This inmate has been condemning everyone about him for going to work. The Center gave orders for him to go to work this A.M. which he refused to do. While searching his cell I found drawings of picks and locks.
> Signed: Officer C ______
>
> Fighting. As this inmate came to 1 Wing entrance to go to yard this A.M. he struck inmate G in the face. Signed: Officer D ______
>
> Having fermented beverage in his cell. Found while inmate was in yard.
> Signed: Officer E ______
>
> Attempting to instigate wing disturbance. When I asked him why he discarded [*sic*] my order to quiet down he said he was going to talk any time he wanted to and ______ me and do whatever I wanted in regards to it.
> Signed: Officer F ______
>
> Possession of home-made shiv sharpened to razor edge on his person and possession of 2 more shivs in cell. When inmate was sent to 4 Wing officer H found 3" steel blade in pocket. I ordered Officer M to search his cell and he found 2 more shivs in process of being sharpened. Signed: Officer G ______
>
> Insolence. Inmate objected to my looking at papers he was carrying in pockets while going to the yard. He snatched them violently from my hand and gave me some very abusive talk. This man told me to ______ myself,

and raised his hands as if to strike me. I grabbed him by the shirt and took him to the Center. Signed: Officer H _____

Assault with knife on inmate K. During Idle Men's mess at approximately 11:10 A.M. this man assaulted Inmate K with a home-made knife. Inmate K was receiving his rations at the counter when Inmate B rushed up to him and plunged a knife in his chest, arm, and back. I grappled with him and with the assistance of Officers S and V, we disarmed the inmate and took him to the Center. Inmate K was immediately taken to the hospital.
Signed: Officer I _____

Sodomy. Found inmate W in cell with no clothing on and inmate Z on top of him with no clothing. Inmate W told me he was going to lie like a _____ _____ _____ to get out of it. Signed: Officer J _____

Attempted escape on night of 4/15/53. This inmate along with inmates L and T succeeded in getting on roof of 6 Wing and having home-made bombs in their possession. Signed: Officer K _____

Fighting and possession of home-made shiv. Struck first blow to Inmate P. He struck blow with a roll of black rubber rolled up in his fist. He then produced a knife made out of wire tied to a toothbrush.
Signed: Officer L _____

Refusing medication prescribed by Doctor W. Said "What do you think I am, a damn fool, taking that _____ for a headache, give it to the doctor."
Signed: Officer M _____

Inmate loitering on tier. There is a clique of several men who lock on top tier, who ignore rule of returning directly to their cells and attempt to hang out on the tier in a group. Signed: Officer N _____

It is hardly surprising that when the guards at the New Jersey State Prison were asked what topics should be of first importance in a proposed in-service training program, 98 percent picked "what to do in event of trouble." The critical issue for the moment, however, is that the dominant position of the custodial staff is more fiction than reality, if we think of domination as something more than the outward forms and symbols of power. If power is viewed as the probability that orders and regulations will be obeyed by a given group of individuals, as Max Weber has suggested, the New Jersey State Prison is perhaps more notable for the doubtfulness of obedience than its certainty. The weekly records of the disciplinary court and charge slips provide an admittedly poor index of offenses or acts of noncompliance committed within the walls, for these form only a small, visible segment of an iceberg whose greatest bulk lies beneath the surface of official recognition. The public is periodically made aware of the officials' battle to enforce their regime within the prison, commonly in the form of allegations in the newspapers concerning homosexuality, illegal use of drugs, assaults, and so on. But the ebb and flow of public attention given to these matters does not match the constancy of these problems for the prison officials who are all too well aware that

"Incidents"—the very thing they try to minimize—are not isolated or rare events but are instead a commonplace. The number of "incidents" in the New Jersey State Prison is probably no greater than that to be found in most maximum security institutions in the United States and may, indeed, be smaller, although it is difficult to make comparisons. In any event, it seems clear that the custodians are bound to their captives in a relationship of conflict rather than compelled acquiescence, despite the custodians' theoretical supremacy, and we now need to see why this should be so.

In our examination of the forces which undermine the power position of the New Jersey State Prison's custodial bureaucracy, the most important fact is, perhaps, that the power of the custodians is not based on authority.

Now power based on authority is actually a complex social relationship in which an individual or a group of individuals is recognized as possessing a right to issue commands or regulations and those who receive these commands or regulations feel compelled to obey by a sense of duty. In its pure form, then, or as an ideal type, power based on authority has two essential elements: a rightful or legitimate effort to exercise control on the one hand and an inner, moral compulsion to obey, by those who are to be controlled, on the other. In reality, of course, the recognition of the legitimacy of efforts to exercise control may be qualified or partial and the sense of duty, as a motive for compliance, may be mixed with motives of fear or self-interest. But it is possible for theoretical purposes to think of power based on authority in its pure form and to use this as a baseline in describing the empirical case.

It is the second element of authority—the sense of duty as a motive for compliance—which supplies the secret strength of most social organizations. Orders and rules can be issued with the expectation that they will be obeyed without the necessity of demonstrating in each case that compliance will advance the subordinate's interests. Obedience or conformity springs from an internalized morality which transcends the personal feelings of the individual; the fact that an order or a rule is an order or a rule becomes the basis for modifying one's behavior, rather than a rational calculation of the advantages which might be gained.

In the prison, however, it is precisely this sense of duty which is lacking in the general inmate population. The regime of the custodians is expressed as a mass of commands and regulations passing down a hierarchy of power. In general, these efforts at control are regarded as legitimate by individuals in the hierarchy, and individuals tend to respond because they feel they "should," down to the level of the guard in the cellblock, the industrial shop, or the recreation yard. But now these commands and regulations must jump a gap which separates the captors from the captives. And it is at this point that a sense of duty tends to disappear, and with it goes that easily won obedience which many organizations take for granted in the naïveté of their unrecognized strength. In the prison, power must be based on something other than internalized morality, and the custodians find themselves confronting men who must be forced, bribed, or cajoled into compliance. This is not to say that inmates feel that the efforts of prison officials to exercise control are wrongful or illegitimate; in general, prisoners do not feel that the prison officials have usurped positions of power which are not rightfully theirs, nor do prisoners feel that the orders and regulations which descend upon them from above represent an illegal extension of their rulers' grant of government. Rather, the noteworthy fact about the social system of the New Jersey State Prison is that the bond between recognition of the legitimacy of control and the sense of duty has been torn apart. In these terms the social system of the prison is very similar to a *Gebietsverband,* a territorial group living under a regime imposed by a ruling few. Like a province which has been conquered by force of arms, the community of prisoners has come to accept the validity of the regime constructed by their rulers but the subjugation is not complete. Whether he sees himself as caught by his own stupidity, the workings of chance, his inability to "fix" the case, or the superior skill of the police, the criminal in prison seldom denies the legitimacy of confinement.[2] At the same time, the recognition of the legitimacy of society's surrogates and their body of rules is not accompanied by an internalized obligation to obey and the prisoner thus accepts the fact of his captivity at one level and rejects it at another. If for no other reason, then, the custodial institution is valuable for a theory of human behavior because it makes us realize that men need not be motivated to conform to a regime which they define as rightful. It is in this apparent contradiction that we can see the first flaw in the custodial bureaucracy's assumed supremacy.

•

Since the officials of prison possess a monopoly on the means of coercion, as we have pointed out earlier, it might be thought that the inmate population could simply be forced into conformity and that the lack of an inner moral compulsion to obey on the part of the inmates could be ignored. Yet the combination of a bureaucratic staff—that most modern, rational form of mobilizing effort to exercise control—and the use of physical violence—that most ancient device to channel man's conduct—must strike us as an anomaly and with good reason. The use of force is actually grossly inefficient as a means for securing obedience, particularly when those who are to be controlled are called on to perform a task of any complexity. A blow with a club may check an immediate revolt, it is true, but it cannot assure effective performance on a punch-press. A "come along," a straightjacket or a pair of handcuffs, may serve to curb one rebellious prisoner in a crisis, but they will be of little aid in moving more than 1,200 inmates through the mess hall in a routine and orderly fashion. Furthermore, the custodians are well aware that violence once unleashed is not easily brought to heel and it is this awareness that lies behind the standing order that no guard should ever strike an inmate with his hand—he should always use a night stick. This rule is not an open invitation to brutality but an attempt to set a high threshold on the use of force in order to eliminate the casual cuffing which might explode into extensive and violent retaliation. Similarly, guards are under orders to throw their night sticks over the wall if they are on duty in the recreation yard when a riot develops. A guard without weapons, it is argued, is safer than a guard who tries to hold on to his symbol of office, for a mass of rebellious inmates may find a single night stick a goad rather than a restraint and the guard may find himself beaten to death with his own means of compelling order.

In short, the ability of the officials to physically coerce their captives into the paths of compliance is something of an illusion as far as the day-to-day activities of the prison are concerned and may be of doubtful value in moments of crisis. Intrinsically inefficient as a method of making men carry out a complex task, diminished in effectiveness by the realities of the guard-inmate ratio,[3] and always accompanied by the danger of touching off further violence, the use of physical force by the custodians has many limitations as a basis on which to found the routine operation of the prison. Coercive tactics may have some utility in checking blatant disobedience—if only a few men disobey. But if the great mass of criminals in prison are to be brought into the habit of conformity, it must be on other grounds. Unable to count on a sense of duty to motivate their captives to obey and unable to depend on the direct and immediate use of violence to ensure a step-by-step submission to the rules, the custodians must fall back on a system of rewards and punishments.

Now if men are to be controlled by the use of rewards and punishments—by promises and threats—at least one point is patent: The rewards and punishments dangled in front of the individual must indeed be rewards and punishments from the point of view of the individual who is to be controlled. It is precisely on this point, however, that the custodians' system of rewards and punishments founders. In our discussion of the problems encountered in securing conscientious performance at work, we suggested that both the penalties and the incentives available to the officials were inadequate. This is also largely true, at a more general level, with regard to rewards and punishments for securing compliance with the wishes of the custodians in all areas of prison life.

In the first place, the punishments which the officials can inflict—for theft, assaults, escape attempts, gambling, insolence, homosexuality, and all the other deviations from the pattern of behavior called for by the regime of the custodians—do not represent a profound difference from the prisoner's usual status. It may be that when men are chronically deprived of liberty, material goods and services, recreational opportunities, and so on, the few pleasures that are granted take on a new importance and the threat of their withdrawal is a more powerful motive for conformity than those of us in the free community can realize. To be locked up in the solitary confinement wing, that prison within a prison; to move from the monotonous, often badly prepared meals in the mess hall to a diet of bread and water; to be dropped from a dull, unsatisfying job and forced to remain in idleness—all, perhaps, may mean the difference between an existence which can be borne, painful though it may be, and one which cannot. But the officials of the New Jersey State Prison are dangerously close to the point where the stock of legitimate punishments has been exhausted and it would appear that for many prisoners the few punishments which are left have lost their potency. To this we must couple the important fact that such punishments as the custodians can inflict may lead to an increased prestige for the punished inmate in the eyes of his fellow prisoners. He may become a hero, a martyr, a man who has confronted his captors and dared them to do their worst. In the dialectics of the inmate population, punishments and rewards have, then, been reversed and the control measures of the officials may support disobedience rather than decrease it.

In the second place, the system of rewards and punishments in the prison is defective because the reward side of the picture has been largely stripped away. Mail and visiting privileges, recreational privileges, the supply of personal possessions—all are given to the inmate at the time of his arrival in one fixed sum. Even the so-called good time—the portion of the prisoner's sentence deducted for good behavior—is automatically subtracted from the prisoner's sentence when he begins his period of imprisonment. Thus the officials have placed themselves in the peculiar position of granting the prisoner all available benefits or rewards at the time of his entrance into the system. The prisoner, then, finds himself unable to win any significant gains by means of compliance, for there are no gains left to be won.

From the viewpoint of the officials, of course, the privileges of the prison social system are regarded as rewards, as something to be achieved. That is to say, the custodians hold that recreation, access to the inmate store, good time, or visits from individuals in the free community are conditional upon conformity or good behavior. But the evidence suggests that from the viewpoint of the inmates the variety of benefits granted by the custodians is not defined as something to be earned but as an inalienable right—as the just due of the inmate which should not turn on the question of obedience or disobedience within the walls. After all, the inmate population claims these benefits have belonged to the prisoner from the time when he first came to the institution.

In short, the New Jersey State Prison makes an initial grant of all its rewards and then threatens to withdraw them if the prisoner does not conform. It does not start the prisoner from scratch and promise to grant its available rewards one by one as the prisoner proves himself through continued submission to the institutional regulations. As a result a subtle alchemy is set in motion whereby the inmates cease to see the rewards of the system as rewards, that is, as benefits contingent upon performance; instead, rewards are apt to be defined as obligations. Whatever justification might be offered for such a policy, it would appear to have a number of drawbacks as a method of motivating prisoners to fall into the posture of obedience. In effect, rewards and punishments of the officials have been collapsed into one and the prisoner moves in a world where there is no hope of progress but only the possibility of further punishments. Since the prisoner is already suffering from most of the punishments permitted by society, the threat of imposing those few remaining is all too likely to be a gesture of futility.

•

Unable to depend on that inner moral compulsion or sense of duty which eases the problem of control in most social organizations, acutely aware that brute force is inadequate, and lacking an effective system of legitimate rewards and punishments which might induce prisoners to conform to institutional regulations on the grounds of self-interest, the custodians of the New Jersey State Prison are considerably weakened in their attempts to impose their regime on their captive population. The result, in fact, is, as we have already indicated, a good deal of deviant behavior or noncompliance in a social system where the rulers at first glance seem to possess almost infinite power.

Yet systems of power may be defective for reasons other than the fact that those who are ruled do not feel the need to obey the orders and regulations descending on them from above. Systems of power may also fail because those who are supposed to rule are unwilling to do so. The unissued order, the deliberately ignored disobedience, the duty left unperformed—these are cracks in the monolith just as surely as are acts of defiance in the subject population. The "corruption" of the rulers may be far less dramatic than the insurrection of the ruled, for power unexercised is seldom as visible as power which is challenged, but the system of power still falters.

Now the official in the lowest ranks of the custodial bureaucracy—the guard in the cellblock, the industrial shop, or the recreation yard—is the pivotal figure on which the custodial bureaucracy turns. It is he who must supervise and control the inmate population in concrete and detailed terms. It is he who must see to the translation of the custodial regime from blueprint to reality and engage in the specific battles for conformity. Counting prisoners, periodically reporting to the center of communications, signing passes, checking groups of inmates as they come and go, searching for contraband or signs of attempts to escape—these make up the minutiae of his eight-hour shift. In addition, he is supposed to be alert for violations of the prison rules which fall outside his routine sphere of surveillance. Not only must he detect and report deviant behavior after it occurs; he must curb deviant behavior before it arises as well as when he is called on to prevent a minor quarrel among prisoners from flaring into a more dangerous situation. And he must make sure that the inmates in his charge perform their assigned tasks with a reasonable degree of efficiency.

The expected role of the guard, then, is a complicated compound of policeman and foreman, of cadi [judge], counselor, and boss all rolled into one. But as the guard goes about his duties, piling one day on top of another (and the guard too, in a certain sense, is serving time in confinement), we find that the system of power in the prison is defective not only because the means of motivating the inmates to conform are largely lacking but also because the guard is frequently reluctant to enforce the full range of the institution's regulations. The guard frequently fails to report infractions of the rules which have occurred before his eyes. The guard often transmits forbidden information to inmates, such as plans for searching particular cells in a surprise raid for contraband. The guard often neglects elementary security requirements and on numerous occasions he will be found joining his prisoners in outspoken criticisms of the warden and his assistants. In short, the guard frequently shows evidence of having been "corrupted" by the captive criminals over whom he stands in theoretical dominance. This failure within the ranks of the rulers is seldom to be attributed to outright bribery—bribery, indeed, is usually unnecessary, for far more effective influences are at work to bridge the gap supposedly separating captors and captives.

In the first place, the guard is in close and intimate association with his prisoners throughout the course of the working day. He can remain aloof only with great difficulty, for he possesses few of those devices which normally serve to maintain social distance between the rulers and the ruled. He cannot withdraw physically in symbolic affirmation of his superior position; he has no intermediaries to bear the brunt of resentment springing from orders which are disliked; and he cannot fall back on a dignity adhering to his office—he is a *hack* or a *screw* in the eyes of those he controls and an unwelcome display of officiousness evokes that great destroyer of unquestioned power, the ribald humor of the dispossessed.

There are many pressures in American culture to "be nice," to be a "good Joe," and the guard in the maximum security prison is not immune. The guard is constantly exposed to a sort of moral blackmail in which the first sign of condemnations, estrangement, or rigid adherence to the rules is countered by the inmates with the threat of ridicule or hostility. And in this complex interplay, the guard does not always start from a position of determined opposition to "being friendly." He holds an intermediate post in a bureaucratic structure between top prison officials—his captains, lieutenants, and sergeants—and the prisoners in his charge. Like many such figures, the guard is caught in a conflict of loyalties. He often has reason to resent the actions of his superior officers—the reprimands, the lack of ready appreciation, the incomprehensible order—and in the inmates he finds willing sympathizers. They, too, claim to suffer from the unreasonable irritants of power. Furthermore, the guard in many cases is marked by a basic ambivalence toward the criminals under his supervision and control. It is true that the inmates of the prison have been condemned by society through the agency of the courts, but some of these prisoners must be viewed as a success in terms of a worldly system of values which accords high prestige to wealth and influence even though they may have been won by devious means; and the poorly paid guard may be gratified to associate with a famous racketeer. Moreover, this ambivalence in the guard's attitudes toward the criminals nominally under his thumb may be based on something more than a sub rosa respect for the notorious. There may also be a discrepancy between the judgments of society and the guard's own opinions as far as the "criminality" of the prisoner is concerned. It is difficult to define the man convicted of deserting his wife, gambling, or embezzlement as a desperate criminal to be suppressed at all costs, and the crimes of even the most serious offenders lose their significance with the passage of time. In the eyes of the custodian, the inmate tends to become a man in prison rather than a criminal in prison, and the relationship between captor and captive is subtly transformed in the process.

In the second place, the guard's position as a strict enforcer of the rules is undermined by the fact that he finds it almost impossible to avoid the claims of reciprocity. To a large extent the guard is dependent on inmates for the satisfactory performance of his duties; and like many individuals in positions of power, the guard is evaluated in terms of the conduct of the men he controls. A troublesome, noisy, dirty cellblock reflects on the guard's ability to "handle" prisoners and this ability forms an important component of the merit rating which is used as the basis for pay raises and promotions. As we have pointed out above, a guard cannot rely on the direct application of force to achieve compliance nor can he easily depend on threats of punishment. And if the guard does insist on constantly using the last few negative sanctions available to the institution—if the guard turns in charge slip after charge slip for every violation of the rules which he encounters—he becomes burdensome to the top officials of the prison bureaucratic staff who realize only too well that their apparent dominance rests on some degree of cooperation. A system of power which can enforce its rules only by bringing its formal machinery of accusation, trial, and punishment into play at every turn will soon be lost in a haze of pettifogging detail.

The guard, then, is under pressure to achieve a smoothly running tour of duty not with the stick but with the carrot, but here again his legitimate stock is limited. Facing demands from above that he achieve compliance and stalemated from below, he finds that one of the most meaningful rewards he can offer is to ignore certain offenses or make sure that he never places himself in a position where he will discover them. Thus the guard—backed by all the power of the state, close to armed men who will run to his aid, and aware that any prisoner who disobeys him can be punished if he presses charges against him—often discovers that his best path of action is to make "deals" or "trades" with the captives in his power. In effect, the guard buys compliance or obedience in certain areas at the cost of tolerating disobedience elsewhere.

Aside from winning compliance "where it counts" in the course of the normal day, the guard has another favor to be secured from the inmates which makes him willing to forgo strict enforcement of all prison regulations. Many custodial institutions have experienced a riot in which the tables are turned momentarily and the captives hold sway over their quondam captors; and the rebellions of 1952 loom large in the memories of the officials of the New Jersey State Prison. The guard knows that he may some day be a hostage and that his life may turn on a settling of old accounts. A fund of goodwill becomes a valuable form of insurance and this fund is almost sure to be lacking if he has continually played the part of a martinet. In the folklore of the prison, there are enough tales about strict guards who have had the misfortune of being captured and savagely beaten during a riot to raise doubts about the wisdom of demanding complete conformity.

In the third place, the theoretical dominance of the guard is undermined in actuality by the innocuous encroachment of the prisoner on the guard's duties. Making out reports, checking cells at the periodic count, locking and unlocking doors—in short, all the minor chores which the guard is called on to perform—may gradually be transferred into the hands of inmates whom the guard has come to trust. The cellblock runner, formally assigned the tasks of delivering mail, housekeeping duties, and so on, is of particular importance in this respect. Inmates in this position function in a manner analogous to that of the company clerk in the armed forces and like such figures they may wield power and influence far beyond the nominal definition of their role. For reasons of indifference, laziness, or naïveté, the guard may find that much of the power which he is supposed to exercise has slipped from his grasp.

Now power, like a person's virtue, once lost is hard to regain. The measures to rectify an established pattern of abdication need to be much more severe than those required to stop the first steps in the transfer of control from the guard to his prisoner. A guard assigned to a cellblock in which a large portion of power has been shifted in the past from the officials to the inmates is faced with the weight of precedent; it requires a good deal of moral courage on his part to withstand the aggressive tactics of prisoners who fiercely defend the patterns of corruption established by custom. And if the guard himself has allowed his control to be subverted, he may find that any attempts to undo his error are checked by a threat from the inmate to send a *snitch-kite*—an anonymous note—to the guard's superior officers explaining his past derelictions in detail. This simple form of blackmail may be quite sufficient to maintain the relationships established by friendship, reciprocity, or encroachment.

It is apparent, then, that the power of the custodians is defective, not simply in the sense that the ruled are rebellious, but also in the sense that the rulers are reluctant. We must attach a new meaning to Lord Acton's aphorism that power tends to corrupt and absolute power corrupts absolutely. The custodians of the New Jersey State Prison, far from being converted into brutal tyrants, are under strong pressure to compromise with their captives, for it is a paradox that they can ensure their dominance only by allowing it to be corrupted. Only by tolerating violations of "minor" rules and regulations can the guard secure compliance in the "major" areas of the custodial regime. Ill-equipped to maintain the social distance which in theory separates the world of the officials and the world of the inmates, their suspicions eroded by long familiarity, the custodians are led into a *modus vivendi* with their captives which bears little resemblance to the stereotypical picture of guards and their prisoners.

•

The fact that the officials of the prison experience serious difficulties in imposing their regime on the society of prisoners is sometimes attributed to inadequacies of the custodial staff's personnel. These inadequacies, it is claimed, are in turn due to the fact that more than 50 percent of the guards are temporary employees who have not passed a Civil Service examination. In 1952, for example, a month and a half before the disturbances which dramatically underlined some of the problems of the officials, the deputy commissioner of the Department of Institutions and Agencies made the following points in a report concerning the temporary officers of the New Jersey State Prison's custodian force:

1. Because they are not interested in the prison service as a career, the temporary officers tend to have a high turnover as they are quick to resign to accept more remunerative employment.
2. Because they are inexperienced, they are not able to foresee or forestall disciplinary infractions, the on-coming symptoms of which the more experienced officer would detect and take appropriate preventive measures against.
3. Because they are not trained as the regular officers, they do not have the self-confidence that comes with the physical training and defensive measures which are part of the regular officers' pre-service training and, therefore, it is not uncommon for them to be somewhat timid and inclined to permit the prisoner to take advantage of them.
4. Because many of them are beyond the age limit or cannot meet the physical requirements for regular employment as established by Civil Service, they cannot look forward to a permanent career and are therefore less interested in the welfare of the institution than their brother officers.
5. Finally, because of the short period of employment, they do not recognize the individual prisoners who are most likely to incite trouble or commit serious infractions, and they are at a disadvantage in dealing with the large groups which congregate in the cellblocks, the mess hall, the auditorium, and the yard.

The fact that the job of the guard is often depressing, dangerous, and possesses relatively low prestige adds further difficulties. There is also little doubt that the high turnover rate carries numerous evils in its train, as the comments of the deputy commissioner have indicated. Yet even if higher salaries could counterbalance the many dissatisfying features of the guard's job—to a point where the custodial force consisted of men with long service rather than a group of transients—there remains a question of whether or not the problems of administration in the New Jersey State Prison would be eased to a significant extent. This, of course, is heresy from the viewpoint of those who trace the failure of social organizations to the personal failings of the individuals who man social organizational structure. Perhaps, indeed, there is some comfort in the idea that if the budget of the prison were larger, if higher salaries could be paid to entice "better" personnel within the walls, if guards could be persuaded to remain for longer periods, then the many difficulties of the prison bureaucracy would disappear. From this point of view, the problems of the custodial institution are rooted in the niggardliness of the free community and the consequent inadequacies of the institution's personnel rather than flaws in the social system of the prison itself. But to suppose that higher salaries are an answer to the plight of the custodian is to suppose, first, that there are men who by reason of their particular skills and personal characteristics are better qualified to serve as guards if they could be recruited; and second, that experience and training within the institution itself will better prepare the guard for his role, if greater financial rewards could convince him to make a career of his prison employment. Both of these suppositions, however, are open to some doubt. There are few jobs in the free community which are comparable to that of the guard in the maximum security prison and which, presumably, could equip the guard-to-be with the needed skills. If the job requirements of the guard's position are not technical skills, but turn on matters of character such as courage, honesty, and so on, there is no assurance that men with these traits will flock to the prison if the salary of the guard is increased. And while higher salaries may decrease the turnover rate—thus making an in-service training program feasible and providing a custodial force with greater experience—it is not certain if such a change can lead to marked improvement. A brief period of schooling can familiarize the new guard with the routines of the institution, but to prepare the guard for the realities of his assigned role with lectures and discussions is quite another matter. And it seems entirely possible that prolonged experience in the prison may enmesh the guard deeper and deeper in patterns of compromise and misplaced trust rather than sharpening his drive toward a rigorous enforcement of institutional regulations.

We are not arguing, of course, that the quality of the personnel in the prison is irrelevant to the successful performance of the bureaucracy's task, nor are we arguing that it would be impossible to improve the quality of the personnel by increasing salaries. We are arguing, however, that the problems of the custodians far transcend the size of the guard's paycheck or the length of his employment and that better personnel is at best a palliative rather than a final cure. It is true, of course, that it is difficult to unravel the characteristics of a social organization from the characteristics of the individuals who are its members, but there seems to be little reason to believe that a different crop of guards in the New Jersey State Prison would exhibit an outstanding increase in efficiency in trying to impose the regime of the custodians on the population of prisoners. *The lack of a sense of duty among those who are held captive, the obvious fallacies of coercion, the pathetic collection of rewards and punishments to induce compliance, the strong pressures toward the corruption of the guard in the form of friendship, reciprocity, and the transfer of duties into the hands of trusted inmates—all are structural defects in the prison's system of power rather than individual inadequacies.*

The question of whether these defects are inevitable in the custodial institution—or in any system of total power—must be deferred. For the moment it is enough to point out that in the New Jersey State Prison the custodians are unable or unwilling to prevent their captives from committing numerous violations of the rules which make up the theoretical blueprint for behavior and this failure is not a temporary, personal aberration but a built-in feature of the prison social system. It is only by understanding this fact that we can understand the world of the prisoners, since so many significant aspects of inmate behavior—such as coercion of fellow prisoners, fraud, gambling, homosexuality, sharing stolen supplies, and so on—are in clear contravention to institutional regulations. It is the nature of this world which must now claim our attention.

NOTES

1. Max Weber, *The Theory of Social and Economic Organization,* Talcott Parsons (New York: Oxford University Press, 1947), p. 337.
2. This statement requires two qualifications. First, a number of inmates steadfastly maintain that they are innocent of the crime with which they are charged. It is the illegitimacy of their particular case, however, rather than the illegitimacy of confinement in general, which moves them to protest. Second, some of the more sophisticated prisoners argue that the conditions of imprisonment are wrong, although perhaps not illegitimate or illegal, on the grounds that reformation should be the major aim of imprisonment and the officials are not working hard enough in this direction.
3. Since each shift is reduced in size by vacations, regular days off, sickness, and so on, even the day shift—the largest of the three—can usually muster no more than ninety guards to confront the population of more than 1,200 prisoners. The fact that they are so heavily outnumbered is not lost on the officials.

ARTICLE NINETEEN

The Prison Experience: The Convict World

JOHN IRWIN

What is it like to be incarcerated? Because the population of a prison is made up of felons, one might expect that chaos would prevail if it were not for the discipline imposed by the authorities. John Irwin, a former convict who is now a sociologist, describes how offenders adapt to the world of the prison. He finds that a complete social organization exists on the "inside," with norms, role relationships, and leadership patterns functioning within the parameters of the formal organization set by correctional officials. Some scholars have argued that prisons are really microcosms of society: with some exceptions, they reflect the conflicts and tensions of the larger world.

Many studies of prison behavior have approached the task of explaining the convict social organization by posing the hypothetical question: How do convicts adapt to prison? It was felt that this was a relevant question because the prison is a situation of deprivation and degradation, and, therefore, presents extraordinary adaptive problems. Two adaptive styles were recognized: (1) an individual style—withdrawal and/or isolation—and (2) a collective style—participation in a convict social system which, through its solidarity, regulation of activities, distribution of goods and prestige, and apparent opposition to the world of the administration, helps the individual withstand the "pains of imprisonment."

I would like to suggest that these studies have overlooked important alternate styles. First let us return to the question that theoretically every

Source: From John Irwin, *The Felon,* © 1970, pp. 67–85. Reprinted by permission of Prentice-Hall, Inc., Englewood Cliffs, New Jersey.

convict must ask himself: How shall I do my time? or, What shall I do in prison? First, we assume by this question that the convict is able to cope with this situation. This is not always true; some fail to cope with prison and commit suicide or sink into psychosis. Those who do cope can be divided into those who identify with and therefore adapt to a broader world than that of the prison, and those who orient themselves primarily to the prison world. This difference in orientation is often quite subtle but always important. In some instances it is the basis for forming very important choices, choices which may have important consequences for the felon's long-term career. For example, Piri Thomas, a convict, was forced to make up his mind whether to participate in a riot or refrain:

> I stood there watching and weighing, trying to decide whether or not I was a con first and an outsider second. I had been doing time inside yet living every mental minute I could outside; now I had to choose one or the other. I stood there in the middle of the yard. Cons passed me by, some going west to join the boppers, others going east to neutral ground. The call of rep tore within me, while the feeling of being a punk washed over me like a yellow banner. I had to make a decision. *I am a con. These damn cons are my people. . . . What do you mean, your people? Your people are outside the cells, home, in the streets. No! That ain't so. . . . Look at them go toward the west wall. Why in hell am I taking so long in making up my mind? Man, there goes Papo and Zu-Zu, and Mick the Boxer; even Ruben is there.*[1]

This identification also influences the criteria for assigning and earning prestige—criteria relative to things in the outside world or things which tend to exist only in the prison world, such as status in a prison social system or success with prison homosexuals. Furthermore, it will influence the long-term strategies he forms and attempts to follow during his prison sentence.

It is useful to further divide those who maintain their basic orientation to the outside into (1) those who for the most part wish to maintain their life patterns and their identities—even if they intend to refrain from most law-breaking activities—and (2) those who desire to make significant changes in life patterns and identities and see prison as a chance to do this.

The mode of adaptation of those convicts who tend to make a world out of prison will be called "jailing." To "jail" is to cut yourself off from the outside world and to attempt to construct a life within prison. The adaptation of those who still keep their commitment to the outside life and see prison as a suspension of that life but who do not want to make any significant changes in their life patterns will be called "doing time." One "does time" by trying to maximize his comfort and luxuries and minimize his discomfort and conflict and to get out as soon as possible. The adaptation made by those who, looking to their future life on the outside, try to effect changes in their life patterns and identities will be called "gleaning."[2] In "gleaning," one sets out to "better himself" or "improve himself" and takes advantage of the resources that exist in prison to do this.

Not all convicts can be classified neatly by these three adaptive styles. Some vacillate from one to another, and others appear to be following two or three of them simultaneously. Still others, for instance the noncopers mentioned above, cannot be characterized by any of the three. However, many prison careers fit very closely into one of these patterns, and the great majority can be classified roughly by one of the styles.

DOING TIME

> When you go in, now your trial is over, you got your time and everything and now you head for the joint. They furnish your clothing, your toothbrush, your toothpaste, they give you a package of tobacco, they put you up in the morning to get breakfast. In other words, everything is furnished. Now you stay in there two years, five years, ten years, whatever you stay in there, what difference does it make? After a year or so you've been . . . after six months, you've become accustomed to the general routine. Everything is furnished. If you get a stomachache, you go to the doctor; if you can't see out of your cheaters, you go the optician. It don't cost you nothing.[3]

As the above statement by a thief indicates, many convicts conceive of the prison experience as a temporary break in their outside career, one which they take in their stride. They come to prison and "do their time." They attempt to pass through this experience with the least amount of suffering and the greatest amount of comfort. They (1) avoid trouble, (2) find activities which occupy their time, (3) secure a few luxuries, (4) with the exception of a few complete isolates, form friendships with small groups of other convicts, and (5) do what they think is necessary to get out as soon as possible.[4]

To avoid trouble the convict adheres to the convict code—especially the maxims of "do your own time" and "don't snitch," and stays away from "lowriders"—those convicts engaged in hijacking and violent disputes. In some prisons which have a high incidence of violence—knifings, assaults, and murders—this can appear to be very difficult even to the convicts themselves. One convict reported his first impression of Soledad:

> The first day I got to Soledad I was walking from the fish tank to the mess hall and this guy comes running down the hall past me, yelling, with a knife sticking out of his back. Man, I was petrified. I thought, what the fuck kind of place is this. [Interview, Soledad Prison, June 1966.]

Piri Thomas decided to avoid trouble for a while, but commented on the difficulty in doing this:

> The decision to cool myself made the next two years the hardest I had done because it meant being a smoothie and staying out of trouble, which in prison is difficult, for any of a thousand cons might start trouble with you

> for any real or fancied reason, and if you didn't face up to the trouble, you ran the risk of being branded as having no heart. And heart was all I had left.[5]

However, except for rare, "abnormal" incidents, convicts tend not to bother others who are "doing their own number." One convict made the following comments on avoiding trouble in prison:

> If a new guy comes here and just settles down and minds his business, nobody'll fuck with him, unless he runs into some nut. Everyone sees a guy is trying to do his own time and they leave him alone. Those guys that get messed over are usually asking for it. If you stay away from the lowriders and the punks and don't get into debt or snitch on somebody you won't have no trouble here. [Interview, San Quentin, July 1966.]

To occupy their time, "time-doers" work, read, work on hobbies, play cards, chess, and dominoes, engage in sports, go to movies, watch television, participate in some group activities, such as drama groups, gavel clubs, and slot car clubs, and while away hours "tripping" with friends. They seek extra luxuries through their job. Certain jobs in prison, such as jobs in the kitchen, in the officers' and guards' dining room, in the boiler room, the officers' and guards' barber shop, and the firehouse, offer various extra luxuries—extra things to eat, a radio, privacy, additional shows, and more freedom. Or time-doers purchase luxuries legally or illegally available in the prison market. If they have money on the books, if they have a job which pays a small salary, or if they earn money at a hobby, they can draw up to $20 a month which may be spent for foodstuffs, coffee, cocoa, stationery, toiletries, tobacco, and cigarettes. Or using cigarettes as currency, they may purchase food from the kitchen, drugs, books, cell furnishings, clothes, hotplates, stingers, and other contraband items. If they do not have legal access to funds, they may "scuffle": sell some commodity which they produce—such as belt buckles or other handicraft items—or some commodity which is accessible to them through their job—such as food items from the kitchen. "Scuffling," however, necessitates becoming enmeshed in the convict social system and increases the chances of "trouble," such as conflicts over unpaid debts, hijacking by others, and "beefs"—disciplinary actions for rule infractions. Getting into trouble is contrary to the basic tenets of "doing time," so time-doers usually avoid scuffling.

The friendships formed by time-doers vary from casual acquaintanceships with persons who accidentally cell nearby or work together, to close friendship groups who "go all the way" for each other—share material goods, defend each other against others, and maintain silence about each other's activities. These varying friendship patterns are related closely to their criminal identities.

Finally, time-doers try to get out as soon as possible. First they do this by staying out of trouble, "cleaning up their hands." They avoid activities and persons that would put them in danger of receiving disciplinary actions, or "beefs." And in recent years, with the increasing emphasis on treatment, they "program." To program is to follow, at least tokenly, a treatment plan which has been outlined by the treatment staff, recommended by the board, or devised by the convict himself. It is generally believed that to be released on parole as early as possible one must "get a program." A program involves attending school, vocational training, group counseling, church, Alcoholics Anonymous, or any other special program that is introduced under the treatment policy of the prison.

All convicts are more apt to choose "doing time," but some approach this style in a slightly different manner. For instance, doing time is characteristic of the thief in prison. He shapes this mode of adaptation and establishes it as a major mode of adaptation in prison. The convict code, which is fashioned from the criminal code, is the foundation for this style. The thief has learned how to do his time long before he comes to prison. Prison, he learns when he takes on the dimensions of the criminal subculture, is part of criminal life, a calculated risk, and when it comes he is ready for it.

> Long before the thief has come to prison, his subculture has defined proper prison conduct as behavior rationally calculated to "do time" in the easiest possible way. This means that he wants a prison life containing the best possible combination of a maximum amount of leisure time and maximum number of privileges. Accordingly, the privileges sought by the thief are different from the privileges sought by the man oriented to prison itself. The thief wants things that will make prison life a little easier—extra food, a maximum amount of recreation time, a good radio, a little peace.[6]

The thief knows how to avoid trouble; he keeps away from "dingbats," "lowriders," "hoosiers," "square johns," and "stool pigeons" and obeys the convict code. He also knows not to buck the authorities; he keeps his record clean and does what is necessary to get out—even programs.

He occasionally forms friendships with other criminals, such as dope fiends, heads, and possibly disorganized criminals, but less often with square johns. Formerly he confined his friendship to other thieves with whom he formed very tight-knit groups. For example, Jack Black, a thief in the last century, describes his assimilation into the "Johnson family" in prison:

> Shorty was one of the patricians of the prison, a "box man," doing time for bank burglary. "I'll put you in with the right people, kid. You're folks yourself or you wouldn't have been with Smiler."
>
> I had no friends in the place. But the fact that I had been with Smiler, that I had kept my mouth shut, and that Shorty had come forward to help me, gave me a certain fixed status in the prison that nothing could shake but some act of my own. I was naturally pleased to find myself taken up by the "best people," as Shorty and his friends called themselves, and accepted as one of them.

> Shorty now took me into the prison where we found the head trusty who was one of the "best people" himself, a thoroughgoing bum from the road. [The term "bum" is not used here in any cheap or disparaging sense. In those days it meant any kind of traveling thief. It has long since fallen into disuse. The yegg of today was the bum of twenty years ago.]
>
> "This party," said Shorty, "is one of the 'Johnson' family." (The bums called themselves "Johnsons" probably because they were so numerous.) "He's good people and I want to get him fixed up for a cell with the right folks."[7]

Clemmer described two *primary* groups out of the fourteen groups he located, and both of these were groups of thieves.[8]

Presently in California prisons, thieves' numbers have diminished. This and the general loosening of the convict solidarity have tended to drive the thief into the background of prison life. He generally confines his friendships to one or two others, usually other thieves or criminals who are "all right"; otherwise he withdraws from participation with others. He often feels out of place amid the changes that have come about. One thief looking back upon fifteen years in California prisons states:

> As far as I'm concerned their main purpose has been in taking the convict code away from him. But what they fail to do when they strip him from these rules is replace it with something. They turn these guys into a bunch of snivelers and they write letters on each other and they don't have any rules to live by. [Interview, Folsom Prison, July 1966.]

Another thief interviewed also indicated his dislocation in the present prison social world:

> The new kinds in prison are wild. They have no respect for rules or other persons. I just want to get out of here and give it all up. I can't take coming back to prison again, not with the kind of convicts they are getting now. [Interview, Soledad Prison, June 1966.]

Like the majority of convicts, the dope fiend and the head usually just "do time." When they do, they don't vary greatly from the thief, except that they tend to associate with other dope fiends or heads, although they too will associate with other criminals. They tend to form very close bonds with one, two, or three other dope fiends or heads and maintain a casual friendship with a large circle of dope fiends, heads, and other criminals. Like the thief, the dope fiend and the head tend not to establish ties with squares.

The hustler in doing time differs from the other criminals in that he does not show a propensity to form very tight-knit groups. Hustling values, which emphasize manipulation and invidiousness, seem to prevent this. The hustler maintains a very large group of casual friends. Though this group does not show strong bonds of loyalty and mutual aid, they share many activities such as cards, sports, dominoes, and "jiving"—casual talk.

Square johns do their time quite differently from the criminals. The square john finds life in prison repugnant and tries to isolate himself as much as possible from the convict world. He does not believe in the convict code, but he usually learns to display a token commitment to it for his own safety. A square john indicated his forced obedience to the convict code:

> Several times I saw things going on that I didn't like. One time a couple of guys were working over another guy and I wanted to step in, but I couldn't. Had to just keep moving as if I didn't see it. [Interview, Soledad Prison, June 1966.]

He usually keeps busy with some job assignment, a hobby, cards, chess, or various forms of group programs, such as drama groups. He forms friendships with one or two other squares and avoids the criminals. But even with other squares there is resistance to forming *close* ties. Square johns are very often sensitive about their "problems," and they are apt to feel repugnance toward themselves and other persons with problems. Besides, the square usually wants to be accepted by conventional people and not by other "stigmatized" outcasts like himself. So, many square johns do their time isolated from other inmates. Malcolm Braly in his novel *On the Yard* has captured the ideal-typical square john in prison:

> Watson had finally spoken. Formerly a mild-mannered and mother-smothered high school teacher, he had killed his two small sons, attempted to kill his wife, cut his own throat, then poisoned himself, all because his wife had refused a reconciliation with the remark, "John, the truth is you bore me."
>
> Watson stood with culture, the Republic, and motherhood, and at least once each meeting he made a point of reaffirming his position before launching into his chronic criticism of the manner in which his own case had been, was, and would be handled. ". . . And I've been confined almost two years now, and I see no point in further imprisonment, further therapy, no point whatsoever since there's absolutely no possibility I'll do the same thing again. . . . "
>
> "That's right," Red said softly. "He's run out of kids."
>
> And Zeke whispered, "I just wish he'd taken the poison *before* he cut his throat."
>
> Watson ignored the whispering, if he heard it at all, and went on, clearly speaking only to Erlenmeyer. "Surely, Doctor, as a college man yourself you must realize that the opportunities for a meaningful cultural exchange are sorely limited in an institution of this nature. Of course, I attend the General Semantics Club and I'm taking the course Oral McKeon is giving in Oriental religions, but these are such tiny oases in this desert of sweatsuits and domino games, and I can't understand why everyone is just thrown together without reference to their backgrounds, or the nature of their offense. Thieves, dope addicts, even sex maniacs—"
>
> Zeke threw his hands up in mock alarm. "Where'd you see a sex maniac?"
>
> "I don't think it cause for facetiousness," Watson said coldly. "Just yesterday I found occasion to step into the toilet off the big yard and one of the sweepers was standing there masturbating into the urinal."
>
> "That's horrible," Zeke said. "What'd you do?"

"I left, of course."

"Naturally. It violates the basic ideals of Scouting."[9]

The lower-class man, though he doesn't share the square john's repugnance toward criminals or the convict code, usually does not wish to associate closely with thieves, dope fiends, heads, and disorganized criminals. In his life outside he has encountered and avoided these persons for many years and usually keeps on avoiding them inside. He usually seeks a job to occupy himself. His actual stay in prison is typically very short, since he is either released very early and/or is classified at minimum custody and sent to a forestry camp or one of the minimum-custody institutions, where he has increased freedom and privileges.

JAILING

Some convicts who do not retain or who never acquired any commitment to outside social worlds tend to make a world out of prison.[10] These are the men who

> seek positions of power, influence, and sources of information, whether these men are called "shots," "politicians," "merchants," "hoods," "toughs," "gorillas," or something else. A job as secretary to the captain or warden, for example, gives an aspiring prisoner information and consequent power, and enables him to influence the assignment or regulation of other inmates. In the same way, a job which allows the incumbent to participate in a racket, such as clerk in the kitchen storeroom where he can steal and sell food, is highly desirable to a man oriented to the convict subculture. With a steady income of cigarettes, ordinarily the prisoner's medium of exchange, he may assert a great deal of influence and purchase those things which are symbols of status among persons oriented to the convict subculture. Even if there is not a well-developed medium of exchange, he can barter goods acquired in his position for equally desirable goods possessed by other convicts. These include information and such things as specially starched, pressed, and tailored prison clothing, fancy belts, belt buckles or billfolds, special shoes, or any other type of dress which will set him apart and will indicate that he has both the influence to get the goods and the influence necessary to keep them and display them despite prison rules which outlaw doing so. In California, special items of clothing, and clothing that is neatly laundered, are called "bonaroos" (a corruption of *bonnet rouge,* by means of which French prison trustees were once distinguished from the common run of prisoners), and to a lesser degree even the persons who wear such clothing are called "bonaroos."[11]

Just as doing time is the characteristic style of the thief, so "jailing" is the characteristic style of the state-raised youth. This identity terminates on the first or second prison term, or certainly by the time the youth reaches thirty. The state-raised youth must assume a new identity, and the one he most often chooses, the one which his experience has prepared him for, is that of the "convict." The prison world is the only world with which he is familiar. He was raised in a world where "punks" and "queens" have replaced women, "bonaroos" are the only fashionable clothing, and cigarettes are money. This is a world where disputes are settled with a pipe or a knife, and the individual must form tight cliques for protection. His senses are attuned to iron doors banging, locks turning, shakedowns, and long lines of blue-clad convicts. He knows how to survive, in fact prosper, in this world, how to get a cell change and a good work assignment, how to score for nutmeg, cough syrup, or other narcotics. More important, he knows hundreds of youths like himself who grew up in the youth prisons and are now in the adult prisons. For example, Claude Brown describes a friend who fell into the patterns of jailing:

> "Yeah, Sonny. The time I did in Woodburn, the times I did on the Rock, that was college, man. Believe me, it was college. I did four years in Woodburn. And I guess I've done a total of about two years on the Rock in about the last six years. Every time I went there, I learned a little more. When I go to jail now, Sonny, I live, man. I'm right at home. That's the good part about it. If you look at it, Sonny, a cat like me is just cut out to be in jail.
>
> "It could never hurt me, 'cause I never had what the good folks call a home and all that kind of shit to begin with. So when I went to jail, the first time I went away, when I went to Warwick, I made my own home. It was all right. Shit, I learned how to live. Now when I go back to the joint, anywhere I go, I know some people. If I go to any of the jails in New York, or if I go to a slam in Jersey, even, I still run into a lot of cats I know. It's almost like a family."
>
> I said, "Yeah, Reno, it's good that a cat can be so happy in jail. I guess all it takes to be happy in anything is knowin' how to walk with your lot, whatever it is, in life."[12]

The state-raised youth often assumes a role in the prison social system, the system of roles, values, and norms described by Schrag, Sykes, and others. This does not mean that he immediately rises to power in the prison system. Some of the convicts have occupied their positions for many years and cannot tolerate the threat of every new bunch of reform-school graduates. The state-raised youth who has just graduated to adult prison must start at the bottom; but he knows the routine, and in a year or so he occupies a key position himself. One reason he can readily rise is that in youth prison he very often develops skills, such as clerical and maintenance skills, that are valuable to the prison administration.

Many state-raised youth, however, do not tolerate the slow ascent in the prison social system and become "lowriders." They form small cliques and rob cells, hijack other convicts, carry on feuds with other cliques, and engage in various rackets. Though these outlaws are feared and hated by all other convicts, their orientation is to the convict world, and they are definitely part of the convict social system.

Dope fiends and hustlers slip into jailing more often than thieves, due mainly to the congruities between their old activities and some of the patterns of jailing. For instance, a central activity of jailing is "wheeling and dealing," the major economic activity of prison. All prison resources—dope, food, books, money, sexual favors, bonaroos, cell changes, jobs, dental and hospital care, hot plates, stingers, cell furnishings, rings, and buckles—are always available for purchase with cigarettes. It is possible to live in varying degrees of luxury, and luxury has a double reward in prison as it does in the outside society: first, there is the reward of consumption itself, and second there is the reward of increased prestige in the prison social system because of the display of opulence.

This prison lifestyle requires more cigarettes than can be obtained legally; consequently, one wheels and deals. There are three main forms of wheeling and dealing for cigarettes: (1) gambling (cards, dice, and betting on sporting events); (2) selling some commodity or service which is usually made possible by a particular job assignment; and (3) lending cigarettes for interest—two for three. These activities have a familiar ring to both the hustler and the dope fiend, who have hustled money or dope on the outside. They very often become intricately involved in the prison economic life and in this way necessarily involved in the prison social system. The hustler does this because he feels at home in this routine, because he wants to keep in practice, or because he must present a good front—even in prison. To present a good front one must be a success at wheeling and dealing.

The dope fiend, in addition to having an affinity for wheeling and dealing, may become involved in the prison economic life in securing drugs. There are a variety of drugs available for purchase with cigarettes or money (and money can be purchased with cigarettes). Drugs are expensive, however, and to purchase them with any regularity one either has money smuggled in from the outside or he wheels and deals. And to wheel and deal one must maintain connections for securing drugs, for earning money, and for protection. This enmeshes the individual in the system of prison roles, values, and norms. Though he maintains a basic commitment to his drug subculture which supersedes his commitment to the prison culture, and though he tends to form close ties only with other dope fiends, through his wheeling and dealing for drugs he becomes an intricate part of the prison social system.

The head jails more often than the thief. One reason for this is that the head, especially the "weed head," tends to worship luxuries and comforts and is fastidious in his dress. Obtaining small luxuries, comforts, and "bonaroo" clothing usually necessitates enmeshing himself in the "convict" system. Furthermore, the head is often vulnerable to the dynamics of narrow, cliquish, and invidious social systems, such as the "convict" system, because many of the outside head social systems are of this type.

The thief, or any identity for that matter, *may* slowly lose his orientation to the outside community, take on the convict categories, and thereby fall into jailing. This occurs when the individual has spent a great deal of time in prison and/or returned to the outside community and discovered that he no longer fits in the outside world. It is difficult to maintain a real commitment to a social world without firsthand experience with it for long periods of time.

The square john and the lower-class man find the activities of the "convicts" petty, repugnant, or dangerous, and virtually never jail.

GLEANING

With the rapidly growing educational, vocational training, and treatment opportunities, and with the erosion of convict solidarity, an increasing number of convicts choose to radically change their lifestyles and follow a sometimes carefully devised plan to "better themselves," "improve their mind," or "find themselves" while in prison.[13] One convict describes his motives and plans for changing his lifestyle:

> I got tired of losing. I had been losing all my life. I decided that I wanted to win for a while. So I got on a different kick. I knew that I had to learn something so I went to school, got my high school diploma. I cut myself off from my old YA buddies and started hanging around with some intelligent guys who minded their own business. We read a lot, a couple of us paint. We play a little bridge and talk a lot of time about what we are going to do when we get out. [Interview, Soledad Prison, June 1966.]

Gleaning may start on a small scale, perhaps as an attempt to overcome educational or intellectual inferiorities. For instance, Malcolm X, feeling inadequate in talking to certain convicts, starts to read:

> It had really begun back in the Charlestown Prison, when Bimbi first made me feel envy of his stock of knowledge. Bimbi had always taken charge of any conversation he was in, and I had tried to emulate him. But every book I picked up had few sentences which didn't contain anywhere from one to nearly all of the words that might as well have been in Chinese. When I just skipped those words, of course, I really ended up with little idea of what the book said. So I have come to the Norfolk Prison Colony still going through only book-reading motions. Pretty soon, I would quit even these motions, unless I had received the motivation that I did.[14]

The initial, perfunctory steps into gleaning often spring the trap. Gleaning activities have an intrinsic attraction and often instill motivation which was originally lacking. Malcolm X reports how once he began to read, the world of knowledge opened up to him:

> No university would ask any student to devour literature as I did when this new world opened to me, of being able to read and *understand.*[15]

In trying to "improve himself," "improve his mind," or "find himself," the convict gleans from every source available in prison. The chief source is books: he reads philosophy, history, art, science, and fiction. Often after getting started he devours a sizeable portion of world literature. Malcolm X describes his voracious reading habits:

> I read more in my room than in the library itself. An inmate who was known to read a lot could check out more than the permitted maximum number of books. I preferred reading in the total isolation of my own room.
>
> When I had progressed to really serious reading, every night at about 10 P.M. I would be outraged with the "lights out." It always seemed to catch me right in the middle of something engrossing.
>
> Fortunately, right outside my door was a corridor light that cast a glow into my room. The glow was enough to read by, once my eyes adjusted to it. So when "lights out" came, I would sit on the floor where I could continue reading in that glow.[16]

Besides this informal education, he often pursues formal education. The convict may complete grammar school and high school in the prison educational facilities. He may enroll in college courses through the University of California (which will be paid for by the Department of Corrections), or through other correspondence schools (which he must pay for himself). More recently, he may take courses in various prison college programs.

He learns trades through the vocational training programs or prison job assignments. Sometimes he augments these by studying trade books, correspondence courses, or journals. He studies painting, writing, music, acting, and other creative arts. There are some facilities for these pursuits sponsored by the prison administration, but these are limited. This type of gleaning is done mostly through correspondence, through reading, or through individual efforts in the cell.

He tries to improve himself in other ways. He works on his social skills and his physical appearance—has his tattoos removed, has surgery on physical defects, has dental work done, and builds up his body "pushing iron."

He shys away from former friends or persons with his criminal identity who are not gleaners and forms new associations with other gleaners. These are usually gleaners who have chosen a similar style of gleaning, and with whom he shares many interests and activities, but they may also be those who are generally trying to improve themselves, although they are doing so in different ways.

Gleaning is a style more characteristic of the hustler, the dope fiend, and the state-raised youth than of the thief. When the former glean, though they tend to associate less with their deviant friends who are doing time or jailing, they are not out of the influence of these groups, or free from the influence of their old subculture values. The style of gleaning they choose and the future life for which they prepare themselves must be acceptable to the old reference group and somewhat congruent with their deviant values. The life they prepare for should be prestigious in the eyes of their old associates. It must be "doing good" and cannot be "a slave's life."

The state-raised youth who gleans probably has the greatest difficulty cutting himself off from his former group because the state-raised values emphasize loyalty to one's buddies:

> I don't spend much time with my old YA [Youth Authority] partners and when I do we don't get along. They want me to do something that I won't do or they start getting on my back about my plans. One time they were riding me pretty bad and I had to pull them up. [Interview, Soledad Prison, June 1966.]

He also has the greatest difficulty in making any realistic plans for the future. He has limited experience with the outside, and his models of "making it" usually come from the mass media—magazines, books, movies, and television.

The dope fiend and the head, when they glean, tend to avoid practical fields and choose styles which promise glamor, excitement, or color. Most conventional paths with which they are familiar seem especially dull and repugnant. In exploring ways of making it they must find some way to avoid the humdrum life which they rejected long ago. Many turn to legitimate deviant identities such as "intellectual outsiders," "bohemians," or "mystics." Often they study one of the creative arts, the social sciences, or philosophy with no particular career in mind.

The hustler, who values skills of articulation and maintained a good "front" in his deviant life, often prepares for a field where these skills will serve him, such as preaching or political activism.

The square john and the lower-class man, since they seldom seek to radically change their identity, do not glean in the true sense, but they do often seek to improve themselves. The square john usually does this by attacking his problem. He is satisfied with his reference world—the conventional society—but he recognizes that to return to it successfully he must cope with that flaw in his makeup which led to his incarceration. There are three common ways he attacks this problem: (1) he joins self-help groups such as Alcoholics Anonymous, (2) he seeks the help of experts (psychiatrists, psychologists, or sociologists) and attends the therapy programs, or (3) he turns to religion.

The lower-class man is usually an older person who does not desire or deem it possible to carve out a radically new style of life. He may, however, see the prison experience as a chance to improve himself by increasing his education and his vocational skills.

The thief tends to be older and his commitment to his identity is usually strong, so it is not likely that he will explore other lifestyles or identities. This does not mean that he is committed for all time to a life of crime. Certain alternate conclusions to a criminal career are included in the definitions of a proper thief's life. For instance, a thief may retire when he becomes older, has served a great deal of time, or has made a "nice score." When he retires he may work at some well-paying trade or run a small business, and in prison he may prepare himself for either of these acceptable conclusions to a criminal career.

THE DISORGANIZED CRIMINAL

In the preceding discussion of prison adaptive modes, the "disorganized criminal" was purposely omitted. It is felt that his prison adaptation must be considered separately from the other identities.

The disorganized criminal is human putty in the prison social world. He may be shaped to fit any category. He has weaker commitments to values or conceptions of self that would prevent him from organizing any course of action in prison. He is the most responsive to prison programs, to differential association, and to other forces which are out of his control. He may become part of the prison social system, do his time, or glean. If they will tolerate him, he may associate with thieves, dope fiends, convicts, squares, heads, or other disorganized criminals. To some extent these associations are formed in a random fashion. He befriends persons with whom he works, cells next to, and encounters regularly through the prison routine. He tends not to seek out particular categories, as is the case with the other identities. He does not feel any restraints in initiating associations, however, as do the square john and the lower-class man.

The friendships he forms are very important to any changes that occur in this person. Since he tends to have a cleaner slate in terms of identity, he is more susceptible to differential association. He often takes on the identity and the prison adaptive mode of the group with which he comes into contact. If he does acquire a new identity, however, such as one of the deviant identities that exist in prison, his commitment to it is still tentative at most. The deviant identities, except for that of the convict, exist in the context of an exterior world, and the more subtle cues, the responses, the meanings which are essential parts of this world cannot be experienced in prison. It is doubtful, therefore, that any durable commitment could be acquired in prison. In the meantime, he may be shaken from this identity, and he may continue to vacillate from social world to social world, or to wander bewildered in a maze of conflicting world views as he has done in the past.

RACE AND ETHNICITY

Another variable which is becoming increasingly important in the formation of cleavages and identity changes in the convict world is that of race and ethnicity. For quite some time in California prisons, hostility and distance between three segments of the populations—whites, Negroes, and Mexicans—have increased. For several years the Negroes have assumed a more militant and ethnocentric posture, and recently the Mexicans—already ethnocentric and aggressive—have followed with a more organized, militant stance. Correspondingly, there is a growing trend among these two segments to establish, reestablish, or enhance racial-ethnic pride and identity. Many "blacks" and "Chicanos" are supplanting their criminal identity with a racial-ethnic one. This movement started with the blacks.[17] A black California convict gives his recently acquired views toward whites:

> All these years, man, I been stealing and coming to the joint. I never stopped to think why I was doing it. I thought that all I wanted was money and stuff. Ya know, man, now I can see why I thought the way I did. I been getting fucked all my life and never realized it. The white man has been telling me that I should want his stuff. But he didn't give me no way to get it. Now I ain't going for his shit anymore. I'm a black man. I'm going to get out of here and see what I can do for my people. I'm going to do what I have to do to get those white motherfuckers off my people's back. [Interview, San Quentin, March 1968.]

Chicanos in prison have maintained considerable insulation from both whites and blacks—especially blacks—toward whom they have harbored considerable hostility. They possess a strong ethnic-racial identity which underpins their more specialized felonious one—which has usually been that of a dope fiend or lower-class man. This subcultural identity and actual group unity in prison has been based on their Mexican culture—especially two important dimensions of Mexican culture. The first is their strong commitment to the concept of "machismo"—which is roughly translated manhood. . . . The second is their use of Spanish and Calo (Spanish slang), which has separated them from other segments. Besides these two traits there are many other ethnic subcultural characteristics which promote unity among Chicanos. For instance, they tend to be stoic and intolerant of "snitches" and "snivelers" and feel that Anglos and blacks are more often snitches and snivelers. Furthermore, they respect friendship to the extreme, in fact to the extreme of killing or dying for friendship.

Until recently this has meant that Chicanos constituted the most cohesive segment in California prisons. In prison, where they intermingle with whites and Negroes, they have felt considerable distance from these segments and have maintained their identification with Mexican culture. However, there have been and still are some divisions in this broad category. For instance, various neighborhood cliques of Chicanos often carry on violent disputes with each other which last for years. Furthermore, Los Angeles or California cliques wage disputes with El Paso or Texas cliques. Many stabbings and killings have resulted from confrontations between different Chicano groups. Nevertheless, underpinning these different group affiliations and the various criminal identities there has been a strong identification with Mexican culture.

Recently the Chicanos, following the footsteps of the Negroes in prison and the footsteps of certain militant Mexican-American groups outside (for example, MAPA and the Delano strikers), have started organizing cultural-activist groups in prison (such as Empleo) and shaping a new identity built upon their Mexican ancestry and their position of disadvantage in the white society. As they move in this direction, they are cultivating some friendship with the Negroes, toward whom they now feel more affinity.

This racial-ethnic militance and identification will more than likely become increasingly important in the prison social world. There is already some indication that the identity of the black national and that of the Chicano is becoming superordinate to the criminal identities of many Negroes and Mexican-Americans, or at least is having an impact on their criminal identities.

> A dude don't necessarily have to become a Muslim or a Black National now to get with Black Power. He may still be laying to get out there and do some pimping or shoot some dope. But he knows he's a brother and when the shit is down we can count on him. And maybe he is going to carry himself a little differently, you know, like now you see more and more dudes—oh, they're still pimps, but they got naturals now. [Interview, San Quentin, April 1968.]

The reassertion or discovery of the racial-ethnic identity is sometimes related to gleaning in prison. Frequently, the leaders of blacks or Chicanos, for example, Malcolm X and Eldridge Cleaver, have arrived at their subcultural activism and militant stance through gleaning. Often, becoming identified with this movement will precipitate a gleaning course. However, this is not necessarily the case. These two phenomena are not completely overlapping among the negro and Chicano.

The nationalistic movement is beginning to have a general impact on the total prison world—especially at San Quentin. The blacks and Chicanos, as they focus on the whites as their oppressors, seem to be excluding white prisoners from this category and are, in fact, developing some sympathy for them as a minority group which itself is being oppressed by the white establishment and the white police. As an indication of this recent change, one convict comments on the present food-serving practices of Muslim convicts:

> It used to be that whenever a Muslim was serving something (and this was a lot of the time, man, because there's a lot of those dudes in the kitchen), well, you know, you wouldn't expect to get much of a serving. Now, the cats just pile it on to whites and blacks. Like he is giving all the state's stuff away to show his contempt. So I think it is getting better between the suedes and us. [Interview, San Quentin, April 1968.]

THE CONVICT IDENTITY

Over and beyond the particular criminal identity or the racial-ethnic identity he acquires or maintains in prison, and over and beyond the changes in his direction which are produced by his prison strategy, to some degree the felon acquires the perspective of the "convict."

There are several gradations and levels of this perspective and attendant identity. First is the taken-for-granted perspective, which he acquires in spite of any conscious efforts to avoid it. This perspective is acquired simply by being in prison and engaging in prison routines for months or years. Even square johns who consciously attempt to pass through the prison experience without acquiring any of the beliefs and values of the criminals do to some extent acquire certain meanings, certain taken-for-granted interpretations and responses which will shape, influence, or distort reality for them after release. . . .

Beyond the taken-for-granted perspective which all convicts acquire, most convicts are influenced by a pervasive but rather uncohesive convict "code." To some extent most of them, especially those who identify with a criminal system, are consciously committed to the major dictum of this code—"do your own time." As was pointed out earlier, the basic meaning of this precept is the obligation to tolerate the behavior of others unless it is directly affecting your physical self or your possessions. If another's behavior surpasses these limits, then the problem must be solved by the person himself; that is, *not* by calling for help from the officials.

> The convict code isn't any different than stuff we all learned as kids. You know, nobody likes a stool pigeon. Well, here in the joint you got all kinds of guys living jammed together, two to a cell. You got nuts walking the yard, you got every kind of dingbat in the world here. Well, we got to have some rules among ourselves. The rule is "do your own number." In other words, keep off your neighbors' toes. Like if a guy next to me is making brew in his cell, well, this is none of my business. I got no business running to the man and telling him that Joe Blow is making brew in his cell. Unless Joe Blow is fucking over me, then I can't say nothing. And when he is fucking over me, then I got to stop him myself. If I can't, then I deserve to get fucked over. [Interview, San Quentin, May 1968.]

Commitment to the convict code or the identity of the convict is to a high degree a lifetime commitment to do your own time—that is, to live and let live, and when you feel that someone is not letting you live, to either take it, leave, or stop him yourself, but never call for help from official agencies of control.

At another level, the convict perspective consists of a more cohesive and sophisticated value and belief system. This is the perspective of the elite of the convict world—the "regular." A "regular" (or, as he has been variously called, "people," "folks," "solid," a "right guy," or "all right") possesses many of the traits of the thief's culture. He can be counted on when needed by other regulars. He is also not a "hoosier"—that is, he has some finesse, is capable, is levelheaded, has "guts" and "timing." The following description of a simple bungled transaction exemplifies this trait:

> Man, you should have seen the hoosier when the play came down. I thought that that motherfucker was all right. He surprised me. He had the stuff and was about to hand it to me when a sergeant and another bull came through the door from the outside. Well, there wasn't nothing to worry about. Is all he had to do was go on like there was nothin' unusual and hand me the stuff and they would have never suspected nothing. But he got so fucking nervous and started fumbling around. You know, he handed me the sack and then pulled it back until they got hip that some play was taking place. Well, you know what happened. The play was ranked and we both ended up in the slammer. [Field notes, San Quentin, February 1968.]

The final level of the perspective of the convict is that of the "old con." This is a degree of identification reached after serving a great deal of time, so much time that all outside-based identities have dissipated and the only meaningful world is that of the prison. The old con has become totally immersed in the prison world. This identification is often the result of years of jailing, but it can result from merely serving too much time. It was mentioned previously that even thieves after spending many years may fall into jailing, even though time-doing is their usual pattern. After serving a very long sentence or several long sentences with no extended period between, any criminal will tend to take on the identity of the "old con."

The old con tends to carve out a narrow but orderly existence in prison. He has learned to secure many luxuries and learned to be satisfied with the prison forms of pleasure—for example, homosexual activities, cards, dominoes, handball, hobbies, and reading. He usually obtains jobs which afford him considerable privileges and leisure time. He often knows many of the prison administrators—the warden, the associate wardens, the captain, and the lieutenants, whom he has known since they were officers and lesser officials.

Often he becomes less active in the prison social world. He retires and becomes relatively docile or apathetic. At times he grows petty and treacherous. There is some feeling that old cons can't be trusted because their "head has become soft" or they have "lost their guts" and are potential "stool pigeons."

The convict identity is very important to the future career of the felon. In the first instance, the acquiring of the taken-for-granted perspective will at least obstruct the releasee's attempts to reorient himself on the outside. More important, the other levels of the identity, if they have been acquired, will continue to influence choices for years afterward. The convict perspective, though it may become submerged after extended outside experiences, will remain operative in its latency state and will often obtrude into civilian life contexts.

The identity of the old con—the perspective, the values and beliefs, and other personality attributes which are acquired after the years of doing time, such as advanced age, adjustment to prison routines, and complete loss of skills required to carry on the normal activities of civilians—will usually make living on the outside impossible. The old con is very often suited for nothing except dereliction on the outside or death in prison.

NOTES

1. Piri Thomas, *Down These Mean Streets* (New York: Alfred A. Knopf, 1967), p. 281. Reprinted by permission.

2. "Gleaning" is one term which is not natural to the prison social world, and the category itself is not explicitly defined. Convicts have recognized and labeled subparts of it, such as "intellectuals," "programmers," and "dudes on a self-improvement kick," but not the broader category which I have labeled gleaners. However, whenever I have described this category to convicts, they immediately recognized it and the term becomes meaningful to them. I chose the term gleaning because it emphasizes one very important dimension of this style of adaptation, the tendency to pick through the prison world (which is mostly chaff) in search of the means of self-improvement.

3. David W. Mauer, *Whiz Mob* (Princeton: Princeton University Press, 1964), p. 196.

4. Erving Goffman has described this mode of adaptation, which he calls "playing it cool." *Asylums* (Garden City, N.Y.: Doubleday, 1961), pp. 64–65.

5. Thomas, *Down These Mean Streets,* p. 280.

6. John Irwin and Donald Cressey, "Thieves, Convicts, and the Inmate Culture," *Social Problems,* Fall 1962, p. 150. Reprinted by permission of the Society for the Study of Social Problems and of the authors.

7. Black, *You Can't Win,* pp. 104–105.

8. Donald Clemmer, *The Prison Community* (New York: Holt, Rinehart & Winston, 1966), pp. 123, 127.

9. Malcolm Braly, *On the Yard* (Boston: Little, Brown, 1967), pp. 106–107.

10. Fifteen percent of the 116 ex-prisoners were classified as "jailers."

11. Irwin and Cressey, "Thieves, Convicts, and the Inmate Culture," p. 149.

12. Claude Brown, *Manchild in the Promised Land* (New York: Macmillan, 1965), p. 412. Reprinted by permission.

13. In the sample of 116 ex-prisoners, the records indicated that 19 percent had followed a gleaning course in prison.

14. Malcolm X and Alex Haley, *The Autobiography of Malcolm X* (New York: Grove Press, 1966), p. 171. Reprinted by permission of Hutchison as U.K. and Commonwealth publisher.

15. Ibid., p. 173.

16. Ibid., pp. 173–174.

17. This movement was foretold by Malcolm X (ibid., p. 183).

ARTICLE TWENTY

Judicial Reform and Prisoner Control: The Impact of *Ruiz v. Estelle* on a Texas Penitentiary

JAMES W. MARQUART/BEN M. CROUCH

During the past two decades, federal courts have become increasingly involved in upholding the rights of prisoners in state correctional facilities. Judicial decisions ordering administrators to implement procedures and standards that meet constitutional requirements have often had widespread and unintended consequences.

In the 1960s a "due process revolution" occurred in which the judiciary addressed and attempted to remedy aspects of many of this society's institutional ills. Almost since the start of this revolution jails and prisons have been an important focus of judicial attention. In general, the courts have expanded the constitutional rights of prisoners at the expense of the so-called "hands-off" doctrine (Calhoun 1978; Jacobs 1980). That is, the courts have rejected the traditional view that prisoners were socially "dead" and managed at the discretion of the prison staff. Courts for the past fifteen years have responded sympathetically to prisoners' grievances and have issued as well as administered many rulings forcing prison organizations to modify or cease numerous institutional policies and procedures. To illustrate, as of December 1983 thirty state prison systems were operating under court order or consent decrees designed to alleviate prison overcrowding (U.S. Department of Justice 1984). This change in court posture has made possible the fuller integration of the penitentiary within

Source: Law and Society Review 19 (1985): 557–586. By permission of the authors and publisher.

the central institutional and value systems of the society (Shils 1975: 93; Jacobs 1977).

Despite the proliferation of "prisoner rights" cases, there exists relatively little empirical research on the impact of judicially mandated reforms on prison structures and operations. The sociology of confinement literature typically describes court-ordered reforms as part of or ancillary to changes wrought by shifts in prison administration (Carroll 1974; Jacobs 1977; Colvin 1982), goals (Carroll 1974; Stastny and Tyrauner 1982), or inmate populations (Irwin 1980; Crouch 1980). When researchers have directly examined court-ordered reforms (for example, Kimball and Newman 1968; *UCLA Law Review* 1973; Champagne and Haas 1976; Turner 1979), their analyses have been narrowly focused and do not assess the long-term effects of intervention on the prison community. Because systematic empirical research is lacking, we have only some general ideas about what happens in prisons when courts intervene and alter an established order. Jacobs (1980) summarizes those general ideas and notes that court-ordered reforms often lead to a demoralized staff, a new generation of prison administrators, a bureaucratic prison organization, a redistribution of power within the prison, and a politicized and often factionalized inmate society.

The most general observation made about the consequences of judicial intervention has been that prisons have become increasingly bureaucratized (Jacobs 1977; Turner 1979). Authority in prisons is no longer unrestricted but based instead on formal procedures and policies. The days of the autonomous "big house" warden are history. Bureaucratization has also affected prisoner control. The harsh disciplinary measures of the past have been replaced with a legalistic due process model, similar, in some respects, to hearing procedures in nonprison settings. We do not know, however, how the bureaucratization of prisons and prisoner control that judicial intervention has engendered has affected day-to-day life within the prison community. We need to know what transpires within prisons after court-ordered reforms have been implemented by the administrators. In particular, we need to know more about the consequences of court-ordered reforms for prison control systems and for relationships among the parties—inmates, guards, and administrators—on whom control ultimately depends.

This paper is a case study and institutional analysis that examines the impact of legal intervention on a Texas penitentiary—the Eastham Unit. This study, unlike many legal impact studies, is not primarily concerned with the "gap" question—whether or not compliance has been achieved. Rather, it analyzes the institutional implications of a judicial remedy that has been implemented in good faith. The case in question is *Ruiz v. Estelle* (1980), a massive class action suit against the Texas Department of Corrections (TDC) in which a federal district judge ordered TDC to make wholesale organizational changes (for example, in health care, overcrowding, inmate housing). Our focus is on a central feature of *Ruiz* which ordered TDC and Eastham to abandon certain official and unofficial methods of prisoner control. Our objective is to analyze the prisoner control structure at Eastham prior to this case, the specific changes that were ordered, and how these changes affected the prison community. In the last section, we contrast several organizational elements of the old order with the emerging bureaucratic-legal order and discuss the implications of this shift in structure and philosophy for daily control. In effect, this analysis examines a penitentiary before, during, and after the implementation of a legal reform.

THE SETTING AND METHOD OF STUDY

The research site was the Eastham Unit of the Texas penal system. Eastham is a large maximum security institution located on 14,000 acres of farmland, which housed, in 1981, nearly 3,000 inmates (47 percent black, 36 percent white, 17 percent Hispanic). Inmates assigned to this prison were classified by the Texas Department of Corrections as recidivists over the age of twenty-five, all of whom had been in prison (excluding juvenile institutions) three or more times. Eastham has a reputation for tight disciplinary control and so receives a large number of inmate troublemakers from other TDC prisons. Structurally, the prison has eighteen inside cell blocks (or tanks) and twelve dormitories which branch out from a single central hall—a telephone pole design. The Hall is the main thoroughfare of the prison and is almost one-quarter of a mile long, measuring sixteen feet wide by twelve feet high.

The data for this paper were collected in two phases through participant observation, interviews with guards and inmates, searching documents and inmate records, and informal conversations resulting from the participant observation. In phase one, the first author entered the penitentiary as a guard and collected dissertation data on social control and order for nineteen months (June 1981 through January 1983). He worked throughout the institution (for example, in cell blocks, shops, dormitories) and observed firsthand how the guards cultivated "rats" and meted out official and unofficial punishments. In addition, he cultivated twenty key informants among the guards and inmate elites, with whom he discussed control and order as a daily phenomenon. The first author's close relationship with these informants and their "expert" knowledge about prison life and prisoner control were essential to the research (see Jacobs 1974b; Marquart 1984). Most important, his presence allowed observation and documentation of the control structure before, during, and for a short period after the reform measures were implemented.

In the second phase of research, the authors returned to Eastham and collected data from late September 1984 until January 3, 1985. Data collection procedures involved intensive observation and open-ended structured interviews (tape-recorded) with a cross-section of thirty officers and sixty inmates. The inmate interviews addressed such issues as race relations, gang behavior, violence, relations with guards, and prison rackets. The officer interviews focused on such topics as morale, violence, gang behavior, unionism, and relations with inmates. While formal and taped interviews were conducted, the researchers also obtained valuable insights from daily observations of and informal conversations with guards on and off duty throughout the prison as well as from inmates at work, recreation, meals, and in their cells. Furthermore, we closely interacted with seventeen key informants—ten inmates and seven officers—who provided a constant source of support and information. Available official documents (for example, memos, inmate records, solitary confinement log books) were used to substantiate and corroborate the interview and observational data.

THE CHANGE AGENT: *RUIZ v. ESTELLE*

In December 1980 Judge William W. Justice (Eastern District of Texas) delivered a sweeping decree against the Texas Department of Corrections in *Ruiz v. Estelle*. That decree, a year in the writing following a trial of many months, was the culmination of a suit originally filed with the court in 1972. The order recited numerous constitutional violations, focusing on several issues. First, TDC was deemed overcrowded. Prison officials were ordered to cease quadruple and triple celling.[1] To deal with the overcrowding problems, TDC erected tents, expanded furloughs, and in May 1982 even ceased accepting new prisoners for approximately ten days. Moreover, a "safety valve" population control plan passed by the legislature in 1983 and a liberalized "good time" policy have been used to expand parole releases. Nevertheless, overcrowding continues. A second issue was TDC's security practices. The judge ordered the prison administrators to sharply reduce and restrict the use of force by prison personnel. He also demanded the removal and reassignment of special inmates known as "building tenders" since the evidence clearly indicated that these inmates were controlling other inmates. To further increase security, the decree called for TDC to hire more guards and to develop a much more extensive inmate classification plan. Third, the judge found health care practices, procedures, and personnel in need of drastic upgrading. A fourth shortcoming involved inmate disciplinary practices. Problems included vague rules (for example, "agitation," "laziness"), the arbitrary use of administrative segregation, and a failure to maintain proper disciplinary hearing records. Fifth, the court found many problems with fire and safety standards in TDC. Finally, TDC was found to have unconstitutionally denied inmates access to courts, counsel, and public officials.

To implement this sweeping decree, Judge Justice appointed Vincent Nathan to serve as special master. Because TDC encompassed twenty-three units in 1981 (it now has twenty-seven), a group of monitors was hired to visit the prisons regularly and gauge compliance. The nature and extent of noncompliance with each aspect of the decree are contained in a series of lengthy monitors' reports and have served as the basis for ongoing negotiation and policy changes by the prison system.

Since our concern in this paper is with the official and unofficial means of prisoner control that were ruled unconstitutional by the court, we limit our analysis to those parts of the court order (for example, removal of building tenders and changes in security practices and personnel) relevant to that concern. To appreciate the effects of the order, we must first understand how Eastham was organized and how it operated prior to the court's intervention.

PRISONER CONTROL UNDER THE OLD OLDER

The control of older, hard-core criminals presents special problems in any prison. At Eastham, the staff maintained tight discipline and control through a complex system of official rewards and punishments administered by an elite group of prison officers. Basically, this control system rewarded those inmates who had good prison records with such privileges as good time, furloughs, dormitory living instead of a cell, and jobs other than field work. On the other hand, the staff severely punished those inmates who challenged the staff's definition of the situation. The most unusual and important element in controlling the prisoners in the old order centered on the staff's open and formal reliance upon a select group of elite inmates to extend their authority and maintain discipline. It was this latter system of prisoner control, called the "building tender (BT) system,"[2] that the court ordered TDC to abolish.

The Building Tender/Turnkey System

The staff employed a strategy of co-opting the dominant or elite inmates with special privileges (for example, separate bathing and recreational periods, better laundered uniforms, open cells, clubs or knives, "friends" for cell partners, craft cards) in return for aid in controlling the ordinary inmates in the living areas, especially the cell blocks. The use of select inmates to control other inmates is ubiquitous and has been documented in such various prison settings as the Soviet Union (Solzhenitsyn 1974; 1975), India (Adam, n.d.), Australia (Shaw 1966), and French Guiana (Charriere 1970), as well as in Nazi concentration camps (Bettelheim 1943; Kogon 1958) and the management of slaves (Blassingame 1979). The most notable as well as notorious use of pro-staff-oriented inmates (convict guards) has occurred in the Mississippi, Arkansas, and Lousiana prison systems (see McWhorter 1981; Murton and Hyams 1969; Mouledous 1962). In these prisons, selected inmates were issued pistols and carbines to guard the other inmates. However, these elite inmates, unlike the inmate agents at Eastham, were housed in separate living quarters.

Structure and Work Role The BT system at Eastham involved three levels of inmates. At the top of the hierarchy were the "head" building tenders. In 1981, each of the eighteen blocks had one building tender who was assigned by the staff as the "head" BT and was responsible for all inmate behavior in "his" particular block. Indeed, "ownership" of a block by a head BT was well recognized: inmates and officers alike referred informally but meaningfully to, for example, "Jackson's tank" or "Brown's tank." Essentially, the head BT was the block's representative to the ranking officers. For example, if a knife or any other form of contraband was detected in "his" living area, it was the head BT's official job to inform the staff of the weapon's whereabouts and who had made it, as well as to tell the staff about the knife-maker's character. In addition, these BTs would help the staff search the suspected inmate's cell to ferret out the weapon. Because of their position, prestige, and role, head BTs were the most powerful inmates in the prisoner society. They acted as overseers and frequently mediated and settled disputes and altercations among the ordinary inmates. This role frequently called for the threat of or use of force. They stood outside ordinary prisoner interaction but by virtue of their position and presence kept all other inmates under constant surveillance.

At the second level of the system were the rank-and-file building tenders. In every cell block or dormitory, there were generally between three and five inmates assigned as building tenders, for a total of nearly 150 BTs within the institution. These inmates "worked the tank," and their official role was to maintain control in the living areas by tabulating the daily counts, delivering messages to other inmates for the staff, getting the other inmates up for work, cleaning, and reporting any serious misbehavior by inmates to the head BT who, in turn, told the staff. Another important duty of the BTs was the socialization of new inmates into the system. When new inmates arrived at a living area, BTs informed them of the "rules," which meant "keep the noise down, go to work when you are supposed to, mind your own business, and tell us [the BTs] when you have a problem." In addition to these tasks, the BTs broke up fights, gave orders to other inmates, and protected the officers in charge of the cell blocks from attacks by the inmates.

The BTs also unofficially meted out discipline to erring inmates. For example, if an inmate had to be told several times to be quiet in the dayroom (the living area's television and recreation room), stole another inmate's property, or threatened another inmate, he was apt to receive some form of physical punishment. If this initial encounter did not correct the problem, the BTs, with tacit staff approval, would severely beat the inmate (sometimes with homemade clubs) and have him moved to another cell block. This process, called "whipping him off the tank" or "counseling," was not uncommon, and some inmates were moved frequently throughout the prison. Although the BTs were "on call" twenty-four hours a day, the head BT assigned the other BTs to shifts (morning, evening, and night) to provide the manpower needed to manage the block. The living areas were their turf, and the staff basically left the management of these areas in their hands.

The third level of the building tender system consisted of inmates referred to as runners, strikers, or hitmen. Runners were not assigned to work in the blocks by the staff; rather, these inmates were selected by the BTs for their loyalty and willingness to act as informants. They also worked at regular jobs throughout the prison. Runners performed the janitorial work of the block, sweeping and dispensing supplies to the cells. They also served as conduits of information for the BTs since they had more contact with the ordinary inmates than BTs and picked up important information. More important, runners served as the physical backups for the BTs. If a fight or brawl broke out, the runners assisted the BTs in quelling the disturbance. As a reward for their services, runners enjoyed more mobility and privileges within the block than the other inmates (but less than the BTs). The BT crew in each tank recruited their runners, and selection was based primarily on the inmate's ability to work and willingness to inform. Moreover, many runners were friends of or known by the BTs in the free world; some runners were also the homosexual partners of their BT bosses. Some tanks had three or four runners, while others had seven, eight, or even nine. The numbers of runners totaled somewhere in the vicinity of 175 to 200 inmates.

The final aspect of the building tender system consisted of inmates referred to as turnkeys, who numbered seventeen in 1981. As mentioned earlier, the prison contained a large corridor known as the Hall. Within the Hall were seven large metal barred doors, or riot barricades. Turnkeys worked in six-hour shifts, carrying on long leather straps the keys that locked and unlocked the barricades. They shut and locked these doors during fights or disturbances to prevent them from escalating or moving throughout the Hall. In addition to operating the barricades, turnkeys routinely broke up fights, assisted the BTs, and protected the prison guards from the ordinary inmates. These doorkeepers also passed along information to the BTs about anything they heard while "working a gate." More important, turnkeys assisted the cell block guards by locking and unlocking the cell block doors, relaying messages, counting, and keeping the Hall free of inmate traffic. In fact, the block guards and turnkeys worked elbow to elbow and assisted one another so much that only their respective uniforms separated them. When off duty, the turnkeys, who lived in the blocks, assisted the BTs in the everyday management of the block. In terms of power and privileges, turnkeys were on the same level as the regular BTs.

The building tender system functioned officially as an information network. Structurally, the staff was at the perimeter of the inmate society, but the building tender system helped the staff penetrate, divide, and control the ordinary inmates. BTs and turnkeys in turn had snitches working for them, not only in the living areas but throughout the entire institution. Thus, the staff secured information that enabled them to exert enormous power over the inmate's daily activities. As mentioned earlier, the BTs and turnkeys were handsomely rewarded for their behavior and enjoyed power and status far exceeding that of ordinary inmates and lower ranking guards. Unofficially, these inmates maintained order in the blocks through fear, and they physically punished inmates who broke the rules.

Selection of BTs and Turnkeys These inmate "managers" of the living areas performed a dangerous job for the staff. Vastly outnumbered, BTs and turnkeys ruled with little opposition from the ordinary inmates. In reality, most of the ordinary inmates justifiably feared their "overseers" because of their status and physical prowess. The BTs and turnkeys were selected through an official appointment procedure to perform a "formal" job within the living areas. The selection procedure began with the staff at Eastham (and the other TDC prisons), who recommended certain inmates as BTs/turnkeys to the Classification Committee (a panel of four TDC officials, all with prison security backgrounds). This committee then reviewed each inmate's record and made the final selections. Recommendations to the Classification Committee from the staff were not always honored, and fewer than half of those recommended were selected for BT/turnkey jobs. One supervisor who was an active participant in the recruitment process at Eastham expressed his preference, which was typical:

> I've got a personal bias. I happen to like murderers and armed robbers. They have a great deal of esteem in the inmate social system, so it's not likely that they'll have as much problem as some other inmate because of their esteem, and they tend to be a more aggressive and a more dynamic kind of individual. A lot of inmates steer clear of them and avoid problems just because of the reputation they have and their aggressiveness. They tend to be aggressive, you know, not passive.

The majority of the individuals selected for BT and turnkey positions were the physically and mentally superior inmates who appeared to be natural leaders. Generally, BTs and turnkeys were more violent and criminally sophisticated than the regular inmates. For example, of the eighteen head BTs at Eastham, eight were in prison for armed robbery, five for murder (one was an enforcer and contract-style killer), one for attempted murder, one for rape, one for drug trafficking, and two for burglary. Their average age was thirty-nine and their average prison sentence was thirty-two years. Of the seventeen turnkeys, there were three murderers, three armed robbers, six burglars, two drug traffickers, one rapist, one car thief, and one person in for aggravated assault. Their average age was thirty-one and their average sentence was twenty-two years. In contrast, the average TDC inmate in 1981 had a twenty-one-year sentence, with a modal age category between twenty-two and twenty-seven. These data clearly show that the BTs and turnkeys were older than most inmates and more likely to be violent recidivists. This is consistent with the patterns noted by others who have described inmate leaders (for example, Clemmer 1940; Schrag 1954).

Race Most of the regular BTs/turnkeys came from the black and white inmate populations. Only a handful of Hispanic inmates were ever recruited for these positions. The staff distrusted most Hispanic inmates, perceiving them as dangerous, clannish, and above all "sneaky." Hispanic inmates, primarily for cultural reasons, were tight-lipped and generally avoided any voluntary interaction with the staff or other inmates. They feared being labeled as pro-staff because physical reprisals from other Hispanics for snitching were common inside as well as outside the prison world. Moreover, Hispanic inmates were generally not as imposing physically as inmates of other races.

Although black and white inmates both served as BTs, power was not equally distributed between the races. The predominantly rural, white, ranking guards kept the "real" power in the hands of the white BTs. That is, of the eighteen head BTs, there were fourteen whites, three blacks, and one Hispanic. The ranking staff members were prejudiced and "trusted" the white BTs more than members of the other two races. In short, with the help of the staff, a "white con" power structure similar to a caste system dominated the inmate society in the same way the "old con" power structure ruled Stateville (Joliet, Illinois) in the 1930s through the 1950s (see Jacobs 1977).

The Staff and Unofficial Control

The staff at Eastham did not leave control of the prison totally in the hands of their inmate agents. In addition, the guards actively enforced "unofficial" order through intimidation and the routine use of physical force. Rules were quickly and severely enforced, providing inmates with clear-cut information about where they stood, what they could and could not do, and who was boss (see McCleery 1960). The unification or symbiotic relationships of these two groups—that is, guards as inside outsiders and inmate agents as elite outside insiders—precluded revolt at practically every level.

Intimidation Inmates who challenged a guard's authority (for example, by insubordination, cursing at him, or "giving him a hard time") were yelled at by guards or supervisors (sergeants, lieutenants, and captains). Racial epithets, name-calling, derogation, threats of force, and other scare tactics were common. These methods, though physically harmless, ridiculed, frightened, or destroyed the "face" of the offending inmate. The following remarks by one ranking officer are an example. "You stupid nigger, if you ever lie to me or to any other officer about what you're doing, I'll knock your teeth in." On another occasion, a supervisor made this typical threat: "Say, big boy, you're some kind of motherfucker, aren't you? I oughta just go ahead and whip your ass here and now."

Verbal remarks such as these were routine. In some cases, inmates were threatened with extreme physical force (for example, "You'll leave here [the prison] in an ambulance") or even death ("Nobody cares if a convict dies in here; we'll beat you to death"). Such threats of physical force were scare tactics meant to deter inmates from future transgressions.

Physical Force Coercive force is an important means of controlling people in any situation or setting. At Eastham, the unofficial use of physical force was a common method of prisoner control. Inmates were roughed up daily as a matter of course. Within a two-month period, the first author *observed* over thirty separate instances of guards using physical force against inmates. Key informants told the researcher that this number of instances was not surprising. Indeed, as Marquart (1985) notes, fighting inmates was an important value in the guard subculture. Guards who demonstrated their willingness to fight inmates who challenged their authority were often rewarded by their supervisors with promotions, improved duty assignments, and prestigious labels such as "having nuts" or being a "good" officer. The willingness to use force was a rite of passage for new officers, and those who failed this test were relegated to unpleasant jobs such as cell block and gun tower duty. Those who refused to fight were rarely promoted, and many of these "deviant" officers eventually quit or transferred to other TDC prisons.

Generally, the physical force employed by ranking officers was of two kinds. First, some inmates received "tune-ups" or "attitude adjustments." These inmates were usually slapped across the face or head, kicked in the buttocks, or even punched in the stomach. The intent of a "tune-up" was to terrorize the inmate without doing physical damage. More serious, but still a "tune-up," was the "ass whipping" in which the guards employed their fists, boots, blackjacks, riot batons, or aluminum flashlights. These were meant to hurt the inmate without causing severe physical damage. Like simple "tune-ups," "ass whippings" were a common and almost daily form of unofficial control. Both were "hidden" in that they were conducted in private settings free from inmate witnesses.

The second form of force was beatings. Beatings occurred infrequently and were reserved for inmates who violated certain "sacred" rules by, for instance, attacking an officer verbally or physically, inflicting physical harm on other inmates, destroying prison property, or attempting to lead work strikes, to escape, or to foment rebellion against the rules or officers. Inmates who broke these rules were defined as "resisting" the system and were severely injured—often suffering concussions, loss of consciousness, cuts, and broken bones. Although beatings were rare, many were conducted in front of other inmates (always in the name of "self-defense") and served to make examples of those inmates who dared to break important norms.

The threat and use of force were an everyday reality under the old order, and the guards routinely used force to subdue "unruly" inmates (see *Ninth Monitor's Report* 1983). Although rewards and privileges served as important official means of control, the prison order was ultimately maintained through the "unofficial" use of fear and terror. The staff ruled the penitentiary with an iron hand and defined most situations for the inmates. Those inmates who presented a serious challenge (for example, threatening or attacking officers, fomenting work strikes) to the system were harassed, placed in solitary confinement, and sometimes beaten into submission. To the outsider, it might seem that this control structure would create enormous tension and foster mass revolt, but, as we have seen, the small number of guards did not face the inmates alone. The BTs and turnkeys with whom the guards shared power served as a first line of control and functioned as a buffer group between the staff and ordinary inmates.

This type of prisoner control can be referred to as internal because of the important official role given to insiders. It was proactive in nature since the elite inmates knew when trouble was likely to arise and could move to forestall it. BTs and turnkeys functioned as the communication link between the officials and ordinary inmates. The BTs dealt with most of the inmate problems within the living areas and thereby insulated the staff from the multitude of petty squabbles arising in the course of prison life. Riots and mob action were obviated by this relentless BT surveillance and control. Problem situations were passed upward to the guards. In this old order, the staff, BTs, and turnkeys maintained an alliance that ensured social order, peace, the status quo, and stability. But the institutional arrangement that made for such a "well-working" prison fostered an atomistic inmate community fraught with fear and paranoia.

EASTHAM IN TRANSITION

Although there were some efforts to ease overcrowding and to reform prison operations such as medical services, the dominant posture of TDC in 1981 and most of 1982, at all levels, was to resist the court order both through legal action and by noncompliance. Prison officials rejected the intrusion of the court as a matter of principle and particularly feared the consequences of relinquishing such traditional control measures as the

BT system. Initially, TDC fought the BT issue. However, additional court hearings in February 1982 made public numerous examples of BT/turnkey perversion and brutality.[3] In late May 1982, attorneys for the state signed a consent decree agreeing to dismantle the decades-old inmate-guard system by January 1, 1983.

Compliance

To comply with the decree, the staff in September 1982 reassigned the majority of the BTs to ordinary jobs (for example, laundry, gym, showers) and stripped them of all their former power, status, and duties. Even BTs reassigned as orderlies or janitors in the living areas were not permitted to perform any of their old BT duties. Court-appointed investigators, called monitors, oversaw the selection of orderlies and kept close tabs on their behavior. These outside agents periodically visited Eastham and asked their own inmate informants to make written statements about any orderly misbehavior. Consequently, several inmate orderlies lost their jobs for fighting with and giving orders to the ordinary inmates; they were replaced by less quarrelsome ordinary inmates.

To reduce the chances of violence against the former BTs, the staff moved many of them into several blocks and dormitories for mutual protection. While some former BTs were indeed fearful, most did not fear retaliation. As one former BT stated:

> Man, I've been doing this [prison] for a long time and I know how to survive. I know how to do it. I'm not going to stab nobody, I'm going to cut his fucking head off. I'm doing seventy years and it doesn't make a bit of difference and I'm not going to put up with any of that shit.

These inmates all spoke of their willingness to use force, even deadly force, in the event of attacks from the ordinary inmates. The ordinary inmates were well aware of the BTs' reputations and propensity for violence. They did not seek revenge. In short, the ordinary inmates were glad to be "free" from the BT system and stayed away from the BTs, whom they still feared. As a general rule, when an inmate exemplifies his courage and willingness to fight and stand up for his rights under adverse conditions, he is left alone. Turnkeys were formally removed from their jobs and reassigned elsewhere during the last week of December 1982. These inmates were moved in with their BT counterparts and did not experience any retaliation from the ordinary inmates.

In addition to removing the BTs and turnkeys, TDC was ordered to hire more officers to replace the former inmate-guards. Eastham received 141 new recruits during November and December 1982. The guard force was almost doubled. Guards were assigned to the barricades and had to learn from the former turnkeys how to operate them (for example, how to lock and unlock the doors, what to do when fights broke out). More important, a guard was assigned to every block and dormitory. For the first time in Eastham's history (since 1917), guards had assignments within the living areas. Also for the first time, the guards maintained the security counts.[4]

Compliance with the court order also required the TDC to quit using physical force as an unofficial means of punishment and social control. At Eastham, in early 1983, ranking guards were instructed to "keep their hands in their pockets" and refrain from "tuning up" inmates. In fact, guards were told that anyone using unnecessary force—more force than was needed to subdue an unruly inmate—would be fired. The staff at first believed this rule would be "overlooked" and that the TDC administration would continue to support a guard's use of force against an inmate. But in this they were disappointed. In March 1983, a ranking guard was fired and two others were placed on six months' probation for beating up an inmate. Another incident in April 1983 led to the demotions and transfers of three other ranking guards. These incidents were investigated by TDC's Internal Affairs, which was organized in November 1982 to investigate and monitor all inmate complaints about guards' use of force. The termination and demotions had their intended effect, for they spelled the end of the guards' unofficial use of force (see *Houston Chronicle*, January 28, 1984). This series of events sent a message to the guards and inmates at Eastham (as well as throughout the TDC) that noncompliance with the court order would be dealt with harshly.

In sum, within six months the staff (aided by the BTs) changed the prisoner control system by abolishing the decades-old building tender/turnkey system without incident. Although the guards initially attempted to resist complying with the decree's restrictions on the use of force, a firing and several demotions broke their will to resist. These changes in response to the reform effort were substantial, and they set in motion a series of further changes that fundamentally altered the guard and inmate societies.

THE NEW ORDER

Once the BTs/turnkeys were removed from their jobs and the guards finally quit using unofficial force, the highly ordered prison social structure began to show signs of strain. The balance of power and hierarchical structure within the prisoner society were leveled, and the traditional rules governing inmate behavior, especially in the living areas, were discarded. That is, the ordinary inmates no longer had to act according to the BTs' rules or fear physical reprisals from BTs. The guards' use of physical force as a means of punishment was abolished, and a new system of prisoner discipline/control was established that emphasized due process, fairness, and prisoners' rights. The implementation of these reforms resulted in three major changes within the prison community.

Changes in Interpersonal Relations Between the Guards and Inmates

The initial and most obvious impact of the *Ruiz* ruling has been on the relations between the keepers and the kept. Formerly, inmates were controlled through relentless surveillance and by a totalitarian system that created a docile and passive ordinary inmate population. In all interactions and encounters, the guards and their agents defined the situation for the ordinary inmates. The penitentiary's social structure was in effect a caste system, whereby those in the lowest stratum (the ordinary inmates) were dictated to, exploited, and kept in submission.

Now, however, with the abolition of the BT/turnkey system and the disappearance of "tune-ups" and "beatings," a new relationship between keepers and kept has emerged. It is characterized by ambiguity, belligerence, confrontation, enmity, and the prisoners' overt resentment of the staff's authority (see, for example, Carroll 1974). Inmates today no longer accept "things as they are." They argue with the guards and constantly challenge their authority. Moreover, the guards now find themselves in the position of having to explain and justify the rules to the inmates. The guards no longer totally define situations for the inmates.

Disciplinary reports show the contrast between the new (1983 and 1984) and old (1981 and 1982) orders.[5] We see from Table 1 that reported inmate threats toward and attacks on the guards increased by 500 percent and more over two years. The data do not precisely mirror behavior since some challenges to authority that would have been dealt with by unofficial coercion under the old order had to be reported or ignored under the new one. Nevertheless, it is clear from these data, as well as from interviews and observations, that the behavior of inmates toward the staff became

Table 1 Selected disciplinary cases resulting in solitary confinement: direct challenges to authority from 1981 to 1984[a]

	1981	*1982*	*1983*	*1984*
Striking an officer	4 (1.3)	21 (6.5)	38 (12.0)	129 (49.4)
Attempting to strike an officer	7 (2.3)	9 (2.7)	18 (5.7)	21 (8.0)
Threatening an officer	4 (1.3)	5 (1.5)	38 (12.0)	109 (41.8)
Refusing or failing to obey an order	90 (30.6)	65 (20.1)	72 (22.8)	213 (81.7)
Use of indecent/vulgar language (cursing an officer)	11 (3.7)	14 (4.3)	89 (28.2)	94 (36.0)
Total	116	114	255	566
Population levels	2,938	3,224	3,150	2,607

[a]Numbers in parentheses indicate the rate per 1,000 inmates. The population figures are based on the average monthly population at Eastham.

increasingly hostile and confrontational. Simple orders to inmates (for example, "tuck your shirt in," "get a haircut," "turn your radio down") were often followed by protracted arguments, noncompliance, and such blistering verbal attacks from inmates as "Fuck all you whores, you can't tell me what to do anymore," "Get a haircut yourself, bitch," "Quit harassing me, you old country punk," or "Get your bitchy ass out of my face. This is my radio not yours." Not surprisingly, the number of cases for using indecent and vulgar language also steadily rose from 1981 to 1984. Indeed, the experience of verbal abuse became so commonplace that many officers overlooked this rule violation. On one occasion, for example, one author observed an officer ask an inmate why he was leaving his living area. The inmate walked past the officer and gruffly responded, "I'm going to work, so what the hell are you fucking with me for? If you got any other questions, call the kitchen." The officer turned around and walked away.

There are several reasons for this drastic change in interpersonal relations between guards and prisoners. First, there are simply more guards, which translates into more targets for assaults, verbal abuse, and disciplinary reports. Second, the guards are restricted from physically punishing "agitators," so fear of immediate physical reprisals by the guards has been eliminated. Third, the guards no longer have their inmate-agents to protect them from physical and verbal abuse or challenges to their authority by the ordinary inmates. By and large, the inmates feared the BTs more than the security staff. Purging the BT system eliminated this buffer group between the guards and ordinary inmates. Today the guards are "alone" in dealing with the prisoners, and the inmates no longer fear physical retaliation from the officials.

In addition to, and perhaps as important as, these changes in the control structure, the social distance between the guards and prisoners has diminished. The "inmates-as-nonpersons" who once inhabited our prisons have become citizens with civil rights (see Jacobs 1980). In the past, inmates at Eastham, subjected to derogation and physical force and ignored by extramural society, saw little to gain from challenging the system. Recent court reforms, however, have introduced the rule of law into the disciplinary process. Inmates now have many due-process privileges. They can present documentary evidence, call witnesses, secure representation or counsel, and even cross-examine the reporting guard. They are in an adversarial position vis à vis their guards, which at least in some procedural senses entails a kind of equality. Moreover, the inmates' moral status has been improved because the guards can no longer flagrantly abuse them without fear of retaliation—verbal, physical, and/or legal. Although the guards ultimately control the prison, they must now negotiate, compromise, or overlook many difficulties with inmates within the everyday control system (see for example, Sykes 1958; Thomas 1984).

Reorganization Within the Inmate Society

The second major change concerns a restructuring of the inmate social system. The purging of the BT/turnkey system and the elimination of the old caste system created a power vacuum. The demise of the old informal or unofficial rules, controls, and status differentials led to uncertainty and ambiguity. In such situations, as Jacobs (1977) and Irwin (1980) suggest, realignments of power in prison often mean the heightened possibility of violence.

The Rise of Inmate-Inmate Violence Prior to *Ruiz* and the compliance that followed, inmate-inmate violence at Eastham was relatively low, considering the types of inmates incarcerated there and the average daily inmate population. Table 2 illustrates the trends in inmate-inmate violence at Eastham. The data in this table clearly document a rise in serious violence between inmates. The most remarkable point here is that the incidence of violence increased while the prison population decreased by over 300 inmates.

Prison overcrowding raises constitutional problems, but it is extremely difficult for a judge to decide when population levels constitute cruel and unusual punishment barred by due process or the Eighth Amendment. To make this decision, judges attempt to link population levels with various major forms of institutional violence (that is, assaults, homicides, suicides). Cox and colleagues (1984) maintain that high degrees of overcrowding (especially in large institutions) have a variety of negative psychological and physical side effects, including higher death and disciplinary infraction rates. However, Ekland-Olson (1985: 32) tested the overcrowding-tension-violence model and concluded, among other things, that "there is no supportable evidence that institutional size or spatial density is related to natural death, homicide, suicide, or psychiatric commitment

Table 2 Selected inmate-inmate offenses resulting in solitary confinement: weapons offenses 1981–1984

	1981	*1982*	*1983*	*1984*
Fighting with a weapon	25	31	46	31
	(8.5)	(9.6)	(14.6)	(11.8)
Striking an inmate with a weapon	21	25	40	57
	(7.1)	(7.7)	(12.6)	(21.8)
Possession of a weapon	40	25	59	134
	(13.6)	(7.7)	(18.7)	(51.4)
Homicide	0	1	0	3
	(0)	(.3)	(0)	(1.1)
Total	86	82	145	225
Population levels	2,938	3,224	3,150	2,607

rates in prison. . . . There is evidence to support the idea that crowding is not uniformly related to all forms of prison violence." While the Eastham data do not allow us to choose between these views, they are consistent with Ekland-Olson's position and suggest that there is no simple relationship between crowding and violence. They also suggest that the social organization of a prison is a more important predictor of violence than crowding per se.

When the BTs were in power, one of their unofficial roles was to settle disputes, disagreements, and petty squabbles among the inmates in the living areas. Inmates came to the BTs not only for counsel but to avoid discussing a problem with the guards. The disputes often involved feuding cell partners, love affairs, petty stealing, or unpaid debts. The BTs usually looked into the matter and made a decision, thereby playing an arbitrator role. Sometimes the quarrelers were allowed to "fight it out" under the supervision of the BTs and without the staff's knowledge. Inmates rarely took these matters into their own hands by attacking another inmate in a living or work area. To do so would invite a serious and usually injurious confrontation with the BTs. Fistfights were the primary means for settling personal disputes or grudges. Weapons were rarely used because the BTs' information network was so extensive that it was difficult for an inmate to keep a weapon for any length of time. Furthermore, any inmate who attacked another inmate with a weapon was usually severely beaten by the BTs and/or the guard staff. Although the BTs ruled through fear and terror, their presence helped restrain serious violence among the inmates.

To avoid the labels of punk, rat, or being weak, inmates involved in personal disputes shy away from telling guards about their problems. With the BTs gone, this leaves the inmates on their "own" to settle their differences. The inmates' sense of justice—a revenge and machismo-oriented system with characteristics of blood feuds—is given full sway (see Ekland-Olson 1985). The system means that inmates are virtually "cornered" and forced to use serious violence as a problem-solving mechanism. Physical threats, sexual come-ons, stealing, and unpaid debts are perceived as similarly disrespectful and as threats to one's "manhood." For example, not paying a gambling debt is a form of disrespect, and in a maximum security prison being "disrespectful" can lead to physical confrontations. Not *collecting* a gambling debt or *submitting* in the face of threats is also seen as weak or unmanly behavior. Inmates who are labeled weak are often preyed upon by inmates anxious to maintain or establish their reputations as "strong."

Fistfights, the "traditional" dispute-settling mechanism in the old order, are no longer an effective means of settling a problem. One inmate, whose response was typical, described the transition from fistfights to serious violence:

> Used to, you could fight on the tank [block] or in the field. You know, they'd [BTs and/or staff] let you settle it right then and there. After a fight, they'd

> make you shake hands. Yeah, grown men shaking hands after a fight. But it was over, you didn't have to worry about the dude creeping [sneak attack] on you. Now, oh man, there's more knifings and less fistfights. If somebody has trouble, they're gonna try to stick the other guy. Whoever beats the other to the draw wins. See, their attitude has changed. They don't believe in fistfights anymore, it's kidstuff to them. If you got a problem with a dude today, you better stick him. It wasn't like that when I was here in the sixties and seventies.

To the inmates, using a weapon proves more effective because if a "tormentor" is seriously wounded he will be transferred to another prison hospital and, when recovered, to another Texas prison. Furthermore, an inmate who uses serious violence for self-protection obtains a reputation for being "crazy" or dangerous, which reduces the possibility of other personal disputes.

To many inmates, killing or seriously wounding a tormentor in response to a threat is justifiable behavior. At Eastham, violent self-help has become a social necessity as well as a method of revenge. Rather than lose face in the eyes of one's peers and risk being labeled weak, which is an open invitation to further victimization, many inmates see assaultive behavior as a legitimate way to protect their "manhood" and self-respect. This is a dangerous situation for all, and especially for genuinely "weak" inmates who feel trapped and may use extreme violence as a last resort.

The Emergence of Inmate Gangs As personal violence escalated, inmate gangs developed, partly as a response to the violence but chiefly to fill the void left by the BTs. Prior to 1982, only one inmate gang, the Texas Syndicate, or TS, existed at Eastham. This group, which evolved in California prisons (see Davidson 1974), consisted of Hispanic inmates primarily from San Antonio and El Paso. It was estimated to have had about fifty full-fledged members and is reputed to have carried out "hits" or contracts on other prisoners at other TDC prisons.

Since 1983 a number of cliques or gangs have appeared at Eastham. Several white groups (Aryan Brotherhood or AB, Aryan Nations or AN, Texas Mafia or TM) and several black groups (Mandingo Warriors, Interaction Organization, Seeds of Idi Amin) have gained a foothold within the inmate society. All of these groups have a leadership structure and recruitment procedures, such as "kill to get in and die to get out" for the AB. Like the TS, these are system-wide organizations. Top-ranking guards at Eastham estimate the number of prisoners who are members at between 8 and 10 percent of the prison population. Of the various groups, the TS and AB are the largest and best organized groups at Eastham.

The presence of the gangs was not really felt or perceived as a security problem until late 1984. Prior to this time, the staff had identified and kept tabs on the gang leaders as well as on recruiting trends. The staff also uncovered several "hits," but violence did not erupt. Then, in November 1984, two ABs stabbed two other ABs; one victim was the AB leader. Early December saw four TS members stab another TS in a cell block. Shortly thereafter, several members of the Texas Mafia murdered another TM in an administrative segregation block, a high security area housing inmates with violent prison records, known gang leaders, and many gang members. In the final incident a TS leader at Eastham murdered a fellow TS member, in the same segregation block as the previous murder, on January 1, 1985. Thus, gang-related violence has emerged at the prison, but within the gangs themselves. In short, the gangs are locked in internal power struggles.

The rise of inmate-inmate violence has created a "crisis" in self-protection. Some inmates have sought safety in gangs, as we have seen. The staff is perceived—with justification—as unable to maintain control. Interviews with inmates reveal that gang membership offers identity, a sense of belonging, and a support system for the member. Revenge is also a powerful drawing card (see Jacobs 1974a). Gang members know that if they are threatened, assaulted, or stolen from, they will have assistance in retaliating against the offender. On the other hand, nonmembers who fear for their personal safety feel they must rely on themselves. These inmates have felt it increasingly important to obtain weapons (see Table 2). In short, violence has almost become an expectation, both as a threat and as a means of survival.

Reactions of the Guards

The reforms have upset the very foundations of the guard subculture and work role. Their work world is no longer smooth, well ordered, predictable, or rewarding. Loyalty to superiors, especially the warden, the job, and/or organization—once the hallmark of the guard staff at Eastham—is quickly fading. The officers are disgruntled and embittered over the reform measures that have "turned the place over to the convicts."

Fear of the Inmates Part of the *Ruiz* ruling ordered TDC to hire hundreds of guards to replace the BTs. Eastham received 150 new guards between November 1982 and January 1983. For the first time guards were assigned to work in the living areas. It was hoped this increase in uniformed personnel would increase order and control within the institution. Contrary to expectations, the increase in inexperienced personnel and the closer guard-inmate relationships resulted in more violence and less prisoner control. As indicated earlier, assaults on the staff skyrocketed between 1981 (4) and 1984 (129). In addition, one officer was taken hostage and three guards were stabbed by inmates at Eastham in 1984.

Fear of the inmates is greatest among the rank-and-file guards, most of whom are assigned to cell block duty and have close contact with the inmates. These personnel bear the brunt of the verbal abuse, assaults, and intimidation that have increased since the new system was implemented. The new guards are hesitant to enforce order, and this is evidenced in the officers' less authoritative posture toward the inmates. One guard put it this way: "Look, these guys [prisoners] are crazy, you know, fools, so you gotta back off and let them do their thing now. It's too dangerous around here to enforce all these rules." Previously, guards were not subjected to verbal abuse, threats, and derogation. Compliance was effected through fear and physical force. Today, the guards cannot physically punish "troublemakers" and must informally bargain with the inmates for control. Many officers have stated that they try to enforce the rules but to no avail, since their supervisors overlook most petty rule violations to avoid clogging the prison's disciplinary court docket.[6]

The traditional authoritarian guarding style at Eastham has been replaced with a tolerant, permissive, or "let's get along" pattern of interaction. Furthermore, the guards, especially new officers,[7] fear retaliation from inmates and officials to the point of not enforcing the rules at all. The attitude currently prevailing among the guards is summed up by the following guard's statement: "I don't give a damn about what they do, as long as they leave me alone. I'm here to do my eight hours and collect a pay check, and that's it."

"We've Lost Control" The rise in inmate-inmate violence, the emergence of violent gangs, the loss of traditional control methods, the combative nature of guard-inmate interactions, the derogation of guards, and the influx of inexperienced guards have contributed to a "crisis in control" for the guards (Alpert et al. 1985). Many of the guards, especially the veterans, perceive the changes wrought in the wake of *Ruiz* as unjustified and undermining their authority. They feel they can no longer maintain control and order within the penitentiary. This is not because they have not tried the new disciplinary system. Indeed, as we see in Table 3, the total number of solitary confinement cases has skyrocketed since 1981.

These data reveal that the rate of serious disciplinary infractions (violence and challenges to guards' authority) rapidly increased after the reforms in 1983 despite a decrease in the inmate population. The rapid increase in rule violations has demoralized the guard staff to the point of frustration and resignation. Interviews with guards and inmates revealed that most inmates are no longer afraid of being "written up," losing good time, and spending time in solitary confinement.[8]

Table 3 Inmates sentenced to solitary confinement from 1981 to 1984

	1981	*1982*	*1983*	*1984*
All offenses	487 (165.7)	404 (175.3)	889 (282.2)	1,182 (453.0)
Population levels	2,938	3,224	3,150	2,607

The traditional means of dealing with "unruly" prisoners have been abolished and replaced with more official, due process methods. Standards and guidelines for the guards' use of force have been implemented. Whenever a guard uses force to control an inmate for whatever reason (for example, breaking up fights, taking an inmate into custody), the officer must submit a written report detailing all phases of the incident. When a use of force involves a scuffle, all parties are brought to the prison's hospital to photograph any injuries or abrasions. Forced cell moves are also videotaped. Documentation and accountability are musts for the guard force today. Furthermore, whenever physical force is used against inmates, Internal Affairs investigates the incident. Their investigation of a guard taken hostage on October 15, 1984, involved interviews with thirty-eight prison officials and twenty-one inmates. Twenty-four polygraph tests were also administered (*Houston Chronicle*, February 14, 1984). This investigation revealed that unnecessary force was used to quell the disturbance. Eleven guards and two wardens were reprimanded, and two guards were demoted and transferred to other prisons. Thus, the disciplinary process itself frustrates the line officers—so much so that they often "look the other way" or simply fail to "see" most inmate rule violations. Moreover, the implementation of the new disciplinary process has strained the once cohesive relations between the guards and their superior officers. Not only do the latter sometimes fail to back up the guards' disciplinary initiatives because of the pressures of crowded dockets, but they may also initiate investigations that result in guards being sanctioned.

SOME CONCLUSIONS ON COURT REFORMS AND PRISONER CONTROL

The *Ruiz* ruling sounded the death knell for the old prison order in Texas. Legal maneuverings and a new prison administration have given increasing substance to the new order that *Ruiz* initiated. Table 4 summarizes the distinctions between the old, or inmate-dependent, order and the new, bureaucratic-legal order. We have included only those elements of each order that are directly relevant to prisoner control.

We do not mean by our headings to suggest that prior to the court ruling Eastham was not bureaucratically organized. Indeed, all of the trappings (for example, rules, records, accountability) were present. Under the old order, however, those trappings rarely penetrated the daily operations of the prison. Eastham officials enjoyed considerable autonomy from the central prison administration. Guards, particularly those in the mid-ranks, exercised much discretion in their dealings with inmates. The inmate-dependent order openly recognized the importance of informal relations between officers and inmates and the manipulation by staff of a sub rosa reward system. The old regime fostered particularistic relations (the "major's

Table 4 A summary depiction of Eastham before and after *Ruiz*

	Inmate-dependent order *Pre-*Ruiz *era*	*Bureaucratic-legal order* *Post-*Ruiz *era*
Decision-making power	Decentralized. Warden establishes many policies and procedures at the prison. Prison administrators enjoy a high degree of autonomy.	Centralized. Warden carries out directives established in central TDC office. Less unit flexibility; prison officials allowed little autonomy.
Staff/inmate relations	Based on paternalism, coercion, dominance, and fear. The majority of the inmates are viewed and treated as nonpersons. Guards define the situation for the inmates.	Based on combative relations wherein guards have less discretion and inmates challenge the staff's authority. Guards fear the inmates.
Prisoner control apparatus	Internal-proactive control system based on information. Guards penetrate the inmate society through a system of surrogate guards. Organized violence, riots, mob action, and general dissent are obviated. Punishment is swift, severe, certain, and often corporal. Control is an end in itself.	External-reactive control system in which the guard staff operates on the perimeter of the inmate society. Loss of information prevents staff from penetrating inmate society; thus they must contain violence. Punishment is based on hearings and due process considerations. Control mechanisms are means-oriented.
Inmate society	Fractured and atomistic due to the presence of BTs—official snitches.	Racially oriented with the emergence of violent cliques and gangs.

boy," BTs, and other institutionalized snitches), which were important to control and kept the inmate community fractured and atomistic. The elite inmates were a reliable source of information about inmate activities that could threaten order. Finally, the control mechanisms consistent with this regime were ends-oriented. That is, order and the dominance of staff over the inmates were maintained by pragmatic means selected over time to achieve these ends. Where force and other sanctions were used by BTs and guards, they were employed immediately following a transgression. This strategy engendered fear among both the offenders and those who observed the punishment.

The transition toward a bureaucratic-legal order at Eastham permits much less autonomy. To increase central office control over TDC's many prisons, the new TDC administration (under Raymond Procunier) established, in 1984, regional directors to supervise more closely the wardens of individual units. As elsewhere, new policies to carry out court-ordered reforms have also reduced the discretion of all unit officials (Glazer 1978).

Written directives regarding disciplinary or supervisory procedures emphasize legal standards more than the traditional, cultural values that once defined prison objectives. The precedence of legal standards is especially evident in the "use of force" policy. Each time some physical means of control is used, a "use of force" report (a series of statements and photographs) must be completed and filed with the central office. Whenever a physical confrontation is anticipated (for example, forced cell moves), the action is videotaped. The watchword is documentation. The bureaucratic-legal order also discourages informal relations between officers and inmates. Yet fewer staff-inmate links limit organizational intelligence and thus the ability to anticipate trouble. Officers regularly complain, "We don't know what's going on back there [in the tanks]." At the same time, prison relations are universalistic; all inmates are to be treated alike, and unless they are officially found to have violated some prison rule, they are due equal benefits and freedom regardless of demeanor or attitude. Last, control mechanisms are more means-oriented. The focus is as much on how the control is effected as it is on whether or to what extent it is effective. The legality of the means appears to many staff members to take precedence over the deterrent effect of the control effort. One consequence of this focus is a disciplinary procedure that effectively distances the punishment from the offense in both time and place. Thus, the staff's authority rests not on threat of force or other informal means of domination but on explicit rules.

Although court intervention has made Eastham's operations more consistent with constitutional requirements of fairness and due process, the fact remains that life for the inmates and guards at Eastham is far less orderly than it was before. Authority has eroded, and the cell blocks and halls are clearly more dangerous. Our observations and the data presented in Tables 1 through 3 suggest that the push toward the bureaucratic-legal order, at least in the first few years after the decree, lessened control to the point that many are increasingly at risk behind the walls.

The court-prompted reforms have created for prison officials a dilemma analogous to that experienced by police (Skolnick 1966). Guards, like police, must balance two fundamental values: order and rule by law. Clearly, order can be maintained in a totalitarian, lawless manner. In a democratic society, order must be maintained under rules of law. Having been mandated to maintain control by constitutional means, Eastham prison officials face a problem that pervades our criminal justice system today. Specifically, as Jacobs and Zimmer (1983: 158) note: "[T]he great challenge for corrections is to develop an administrative style that can maintain control in the context of the legal and humane reforms of the last decade."

Officials at Eastham certainly feel this challenge. They feel pressure to comply with the court and the central office directives designed to operationalize that compliance. Yet the unanticipated consequences of today's reforms have jeopardized the staff's ability to maintain and enforce order.

While prisoners in many institutions now have enhanced civil rights and are protected by many of the same constitutional safeguards as people in the free society, they live in a lawless society at the mercy of aggressive inmates and cliques. The dilemma apparently facing society and prison administrators revolves around the issues of rights versus control. Should prisons be managed through an authoritarian structure based on strict regimentation, fear, few civil rights, and controlled exploitation, in which inmates and guards are relatively safe? Or should prisons be managed within a bureaucratic–due process structure espousing fairness, humane treatment, and civil rights, in which inmate and guard safety is problematic—and where uncontrolled exploitation is likely? One would like to believe that civil rights and personal safety goals within prison settings are not incompatible, but we may ultimately have to confront the fact that to some extent they are. At the very least, the experience at Eastham suggests that reforms, especially in maximum security prisons, should be: (1) phased in gradually rather than established by rigid timetables, (2) implemented with a fundamental appreciation of the entire network of relationships and behaviors involved, and (3) undertaken with a healthy sensitivity to the unanticipated negative consequences that have often surrounded attempts to "do good" (Glazer 1978; Rothman 1980).

NOTES

1. The order also called for an end to double celling, but this element was later vacated by the Fifth Circuit Court of Appeals.
2. For a more detailed analysis of the BT system, see Marquart and Crouch (1984).
3. The news media extensively covered these hearings, and press releases provided grisly examples of BT/turnkey brutality and perversions (see the numerous *Houston Post* and *Houston Chronicle* articles between February 16, 1982, and July 1, 1982).
4. The former BTs had to show the guards how to keep the living area counts. Thus, the staff adopted a system of counting that the BTs had developed.
5. The data presented in the three tables reflect only disciplinary infractions resulting in solitary confinement. We recognize the limitations here and know our data are quite conservative. The TDC's recordkeeping on all disciplinary cases (minor and major) was nonsystematic, and we had to rely on Eastham's disciplinary log books. However, our interviews and observations are consistent with the rise in violent and other behavior reflected in the tables.
6. This is like the situation in many large cities, where police and prosecutors have relationships of accommodation with minor criminals. Some crimes must be prosecuted, whatever the cost to the system. Other crimes are not worth the trouble, so agents of justice ignore them or find ways to handle them simply.
7. Interviews with ranking guards indicated that the rise of inmate-guard and inmate-inmate violence has contributed to the turnover of new guards. Of the 246 guards assigned inside the building, 125, or 51 percent, have less than one year of experience, and these numbers include ranking guards.
8. A guard's threat to seek solitary confinement has also become less intimidating since *Ruiz* because of the due process protections imposed and limitations on the good time that can be forfeited. Also, the guard who seeks solitary confinement for an inmate knows he is triggering a hearing in which his own actions may be questioned. The increase in solitary confinement cases should be read in light of these disincentives.

REFERENCES

ADAM, H. L. (n.d.) *Oriental Crime.* Clifford's Inn, London: T. Werner Laurie.

ALPERT, G., B. M. CROUCH, and C. R. HUFF (1985). "Prison Reform by Judicial Decree: The Unintended Consequences of *Ruiz v. Estelle.*" *Justice System Journal* 291.

BETTELHEIM, BRUNO (1943) "Individual and Mass Behavior in Extreme Situations." 38 *Journal of Abnormal and Social Psychology* 417.

BLASSINGAME, JOHN W. (1979) *The Slave Community.* New York: Oxford University Press.

CALHOUN, EMILY (1978) "The Supreme Court and the Institutional Rights of Prisoners: A Reappraisal." 4 *Hastings Constitutional Law Quarterly* 219.

CARROLL, LEO (1974) *Hacks, Blacks, and Cons.* Lexington, Mass.: Lexington Books.

CHAMPAGNE, ANTHONY, and K. C. HAAS (1976) "Impact of *Johnson v. Avery* on Prison Administration." 43 *Tennessee Law Review* 275.

CHARRIERE, HENRI (1970) *Papillon.* New York: Basic Books.

CLEMMER, DONALD C. (1940) *The Prison Community.* Boston: Christopher Publishing House.

COLVIN, MARK (1982) "The 1980 New Mexico Prison Riot." 29 *Social Problems* 449.

COX, V. C., P. B. PAULUS, and G. McCAIN (1984) "Prison Crowding Research: The Relevance for Prison Housing Standards and a General Approach Regarding Crowding Phenomena." 39 *American Psychologist* 1148.

CROUCH, BEN M. (1980) "The Guard in a Changing Prison World." In B. M. Crouch, ed., *The Keepers: Prison Guards and Contemporary Corrections.* Springfield, Ill.: C. H. Thomas.

DAVIDSON, R. T. (1974) *Chicano Prisoners: Key to San Quentin.* New York: Holt, Rinehart & Winston.

EKLAND-OLSON, SHELDON (1985) "Judicial Decisions and the Social Order of Prison Violence: Evidence from the Post-*Ruiz* Years in Texas." Unpublished manuscript.

GLAZER, NATHAN (1978) "Should Judges Administer Social Services?" 50 *Public Interest* 64.

IRWIN, JOHN (1980) *Prisons in Turmoil.* Boston: Little, Brown.

JACOBS, JAMES B. (1974a) "Street Gangs, Behind Bars." 21 *Social Problems* 395.

——— (1974b) "Participant Observations in Prison." 3 *Urban Life and Culture* 221.

——— (1977) *Stateville: The Penitentiary in Mass Society.* Chicago: University of Chicago Press.

——— (1980) "The Prisoners' Rights Movement and Its Impact, 1960–1980." 2 *Crime and Justice: An Annual Review of Research* 429.

JACOBS, JAMES B., and L. ZIMMER (1983) "Collective Bargaining and Labor Unrest." In J. Jacobs. ed., *New Perspectives in Prisons and Imprisonment.* Ithaca, N.Y.: Cornell University Press.

KIMBALL, EDWARD L., and DONALD J. NEWMAN (1968) "Judicial Intervention in Correctional Decisions: Threat and Response." 14 *Crime and Delinquency* 1.

KOGON, E. (1958) *The Theory and Practice of Hell.* New York: Berkley Publishing.

MARQUART, JAMES W. (1984) "Outsiders as Insiders: Participant Observation in the Role of a Prison Guard." Unpublished manuscript.

——— (1985) "Prison Guards and the Use of Physical Coercion as a Mechanism of Prisoner Control." Unpublished manuscript.

MARQUART, JAMES W., and BEN M. CROUCH (1984) "Co-opting the Kept: Using Inmates for Social Control in a Southern Prison." 1 *Justice Quarterly* 491.

McCLEERY, RICHARD H. (1960) "Communication Patterns as Bases of Systems of Authority and Power." In R. A. Cloward et al., *Theoretical Studies in Social Organization of the Prison.* New York: Social Science Research Council.

McWHORTER, WILLIAM L. (1981) *Inmate Society: Legs, Halfpants, and Gunmen: A Study of Inmate Guards.* Saratoga, Calif.: Century Twenty-One Publishing.

MOULEDOUS, J. C. (1962) "Sociological Perspectives on a Prison Social System." Master's thesis, Department of Sociology, Louisiana State University.

MURTON, TOM, and JOE HYAMS (1969) *Accomplices to the Crime: The Arkansas Prison Scandal.* New York: Grove Press.

NINTH MONITOR'S REPORT OF FACTUAL OBSERVATIONS TO THE SPECIAL MASTER (1983).

ROTHMAN, DAVID (1980) *Conscience and Convenience.* Boston: Little, Brown.

SCHRAG, CLARENCE (1954) "Leadership Among Prison Inmates." 19 *American Sociological Review* 37.

SHAW, ALAN G. L. (1966) *Convicts and the Colonies.* London: Faber & Faber.

SHILS, EDWARD A. (1975) *Center and Periphery: Essays in Macrosociology.* Chicago: University of Chicago Press.

SKOLNICK, JEROME H. (1966) *Justice Without Trial.* New York: John Wiley.

SOLZHENITSYN, ALEKSANDR I. (1974) *The Gulag Archipelago.* New York: Harper & Row.

——— (1975) *The Gulag Archipelago II.* New York: Harper & Row.

STASTNY, CHARLES, and GABRIELLE TYRAUNER (1982) *Who Rules the Joint?* Lexington, Mass.: Lexington Books.

SYKES, GRESHAM M. (1958) *The Society of Captives.* Princeton: Princeton University Press.

THOMAS, J. (1984) "Some Aspects of Negotiated Order, Loose Coupling, and Mesostructure in Maximum Security Prisons." 4 *Symbolic Interaction* 213.

TURNER, WILLIAM BENNETT (1979) "When Prisoners Sue: A Study of Prisoner Section 1983 Suits in the Federal Courts." 92 *Harvard Law Review* 610.

UCLA LAW REVIEW (1973) Note, "Judicial Intervention in Corrections: The California Experience—An Empirical Study." 20 *UCLA Law Review* 452.

U.S. DEPARTMENT OF JUSTICE (1984) "Prisoners in 1983." *Bureau of Justice Statistics Bulletin.* Washington, D.C.: U.S. Government Printing Office.

ARTICLE TWENTY-ONE

The Dilemma of Parole Decision Making

SUSETTE M. TALARICO

In a majority of states today, most felons leave prison through mandatory release upon expiration of a determinate sentence or guideline—minus good time. In the rest of the states, offenders are returned to society through action of a parole board. What criteria do parole boards use to determine when an offender is ready to leave prison? Susette Talarico describes the actions of one parole board that uses discretion in determining whether a felon should be released.

A black minister active in party politics, a retired corporate executive, and a man who owns a small business sit as a parole board to consider the sentence lengths of Maurice Williams and nineteen other inmates.[1] Williams has been imprisoned for first-degree robbery and is serving his first major sentence—five to ten years. As he enters the hearing room at the maximum security prison in Somers, Connecticut, he appears relaxed and confident, somewhat more sure of himself than most inmates are at parole hearings. His time in prison has been productive: he has earned his high school equivalency diploma; he has received a good report from the director of the narcotics rehabilitation program and a supporting report from the prison psychiatrist; and the commissioner of correction has given him a commendation for self-improvement efforts.

The panel, however, is skeptical of his prison performance and wonders if he is merely a good "con artist" who will do anything to earn early release from the "can." In the course of the fifteen-minute hearing they ponder the Williams case, compromise, and decide to grant an extended parole—that is, parole, but at a date past initial eligibility. One member has already started to study another of the several files stacked before him. It is 9:30 A.M. on a typical hearing day, and there are nineteen more cases to consider before the three citizens can return to their own worlds.

For the inmates, parole hearings are crucial. Parole represents the last resort—the last chance to earn an early release and thereby avoid a major segment of their prison term. The decisions to arrest, prosecute, and sentence are key points in the criminal justice system. As the last point in this system, the parole decision shares the norms and features of the earlier stage of administrative decision making: discretion and low visibility—discretion because the board is asked to make a choice among almost unlimited options and without specified criteria; low visibility because the board functions in a private setting without the presence of defense counsel.

At each point in the criminal justice system, decision makers must weigh the essential dilemma of the criminal law: the contrasting demands of individual freedom and public order. For the parole board the dilemma is especially severe, because society has already judged the offender to be sufficiently threatening to warrant imprisonment. In addition, the board's function is wrapped in the rhetoric of rehabilitation, which hinges release on the premise of successful treatment, a factor not susceptible to empirical criteria.[2] The parole board, then, weighs these elements as the system's final voice and the inmate's last hope.

The parole board bears the brunt of the contesting forces of individual freedom and public order because the responsibility for actual sentence determination has been transferred from the trial court to the board by the prevailing system of indeterminate sentences. Since the rise of the penitentiary in the nineteenth century, parole has coexisted with this type of sentencing structure as a hallmark of the rehabilitative approach to criminal behavior:[3] the convicted felon is given an indefinite prison term with the possibility of early release prior to the expiration of the maximum portion of the sentence. Theoretically the indeterminate sentence might result in commitment for life, since release is based on treatment success. In the United States, however, this system has not been completely implemented because legislatures set the minimum and maximum allowable terms, thus limiting the exercise of discretion.[4]

PAROLE IN CONNECTICUT

The ten members of the Connecticut Board of Parole are appointed by the governor and confirmed by the legislature. The law requires no particular qualifications or skills for board membership and it is commonly asserted that party affiliation and activity are the prevailing requisites. At present the membership ranges from a retired probation supervisor to a tavern keeper, with representation from minorities and women. For their services the members receive $75 for each hearing attended and reimbursement for travel expenses. Meeting in panels of three at the state's four major correctional institutions, the members hear individual cases and make the final determinations on release dates.

For the inmate, his day before the board is fixed by his parole eligibility, a date determined by the expiration of the minimum portion of his sentence, less credits earned for good time. Thus a robber sentenced by a judge to be incarcerated for a minimum of three years to a maximum of six will normally be eligible for parole after two years (twelve months being deducted for good time). This is far from the maximum set by the judge in the courtroom, a difference frequently commented upon in newspaper reports.

In Connecticut the board does in fact release most inmates at this juncture. During the period of this study 67 percent of the offenders were paroled at the first appearance before the board. To observe the process, two months were spent with the board, attending all hearings, discussing cases and problems with members, examining inmate files, and interviewing correctional officials. The unlimited access to these data allowed a comprehensive analysis of the decision process.

The average hearing lasts eighteen minutes—a short time to evaluate criminal history, family background, institutional adjustment, vocational skills, attitudes toward authority, and the offender's insights into his own conduct—the criteria listed by the board as determining release.[5] Eighteen minutes, however, represents a long period compared to the averages in other states. The New York Parole Board, for example, spends between five and twelve minutes per case in hearings, and its members have been criticized for failure to read the inmate's file before the decision.[6] Yet eighteen minutes is not much time for three laymen, well-intentioned though they may be, to weigh justice in the balance.

The statutory provision that specifies release criteria states that an inmate may be paroled when "(1) it appears from all available information . . . that there is reasonable probability that such inmates will live and remain at liberty without violating the law and (2) such release is not incompatible with the welfare of society."[7] This mandate assumes that the Board of Parole will make an assessment of the offender's rehabilitative progress and predict his future behavior as it relates to society's need for protection. Thus decision makers are expected to have the scientific knowledge to make diagnostic judgments, an expectation questioned by many social scientists.[8] Four dimensions illustrate the board's attempt to fulfill its responsibility: (1) assessment of institutional behavior, (2) evaluation of psychological change, (3) equalization of sentence, and (4) pre-

Table 1 Summary of parole decisions, State of Connecticut

Fiscal year	*Number of paroles granted*	*Number of cases continued*	*Number of paroles denied*	*Percent paroled (of total)*	*Percent continued (of total)*	*Percent denied (of total)*	*Total*
1969	945	145	381	64	10	26	1,471
1970	1,043	220	452	61	13	26	1,715
1971	1,285	313	336	66	16	17	1,934
1972	1,191	290	350	65	16	19	1,831
1973	1,151	249	280	69	15	17	1,680
One-half FY 1974 (7/1–12/31)	507	132	85	70	18	12	724
February–March 1975	108	21	51	61	10	29	180

Note: Percentages rounded.

diction of public reaction. These demonstrate the complexity of the decision process and the limitations to the parole board's resolution of the dilemma of individual freedom and public order.

Evaluating Institutional Behavior

Erving Goffman characterizes prisons as total institutions that do not approximate real-world conditions.[9] The rigidity of confinement, the predictability of events, and the regularity of dress, food, and activity make for an unnatural environment. As a result, adjustment may be most successful among the immature, and hostility may be a healthy sign of the assertiveness necessary for survival on the "outside." The board is required to evaluate the inmate's adjustment to the institution, looking at his behavior while confined, and to assess its implications for conduct upon release. Connecticut board members acknowledged that the inmate who makes it in prison, the "good soldier," is not necessarily the best candidate for parole. Some even admitted that such adjustment and passivity often indicated to them that the offender might not be a responsible individual.

Robert Owens was sentenced to a term of from four to nine years for robbery with violence, to be served concurrently with a term for four assault and larceny charges. While incarcerated in the maximum security correctional institution for adult offenders, Owens was a model prisoner. He participated in group therapy and Alcoholics Anonymous, and learned to become an auto mechanic. In his file were generally good reports from the custodial staff. He appeared before the same panel that sat for Williams. During the hearing and executive session that followed, panel attention focused on Owens' criminal record as it contrasted with his behavior while incarcerated. One member claimed, "I don't care how he acted at Somers, we just can't let a guy with this sort of a record out." While Owens waited, the board concluded that he was a poor risk for parole.

Institutional adjustment is a significant issue in parole policy. If the sentencing judge indicates to the felon that good prison performance will earn an early release on parole, there may be an incentive to cooperate within the walls. The board, however, is mainly concerned with post-release behavior. It does not need to be reminded that public attention and criticism will follow if heinous offenses are committed by parolees; consequently, it looks for only good risks. As in the case of Owens, how does the board reconcile incentives to upright behavior behind bars with its task of risk assessment? In explaining the decision to Owens, members emphasized that he had previously been a parole violator, that he had committed a serious and violent offense, and that they believed that back on the streets he would be still prone to disruptive acts. At no time did they mention or acknowledge Owens' praised prison record.

Evaluation of Psychological Change

Related to institutional performance and parole risk is the issue of behavioral change. Theoretically, parole boards are designed to furnish clinical expertise. In fact, the behavioral sciences offer inconclusive evidence on crime causation and most research questions the effectiveness of rehabilitative efforts.[10] How, then, are behavioral changes assessed? How do laypeople evaluate psychological reports? How does an eighteen-minute hearing allow for a valid appraisal of change? One former board member characterized the situation by saying that the decision makers were as much the victims as the inmates. While the former undoubtedly experience some of this frustration, what about the latter, whose release dates are at stake?

Bill Gardner is the only member of his family with a criminal record. At the age of twenty-three he is serving a fifteen-month to five-year sentence for second-degree larceny resulting from a series of house breaks. While the original charges consisted of several counts, including one for second-degree robbery, eight for third-degree robbery, one for fourth-degree larceny, and one for disorderly conduct, he pleaded guilty and was sentenced for the single offense. Gardner has been incarcerated before, twice at the institution for young adults at Cheshire from which he had been paroled on two previous occasions. It was during his second parole from Cheshire that he was convicted for his current offense.

Before the hearing the chairman noted that Gardner had participated in a drug treatment program for several months. From the record before them, however, the members had no way of knowing what participation entails and what the resultant changes might be. "This says he has 'a history of sociopathic tendencies.' Now what does that mean?" one asked. The chairman complained that psychologists are all alike and their reports all equally unclear. The third member points out that Gardner had been confined in a mental hospital at one time, but that the staff there seemed supportive.

During a rather lengthy discussion with the board, Gardner was very talkative about the change in his behavior and reminded the members that this had been recognized by hospital personnel. Two members challenged him directly and questioned the sincerity of his desire to lead a lawful life. When Gardner left the room, they speculated whether in fact an attitude change had taken place and wondered if there were a situation at the hospital that could explain the support given by a woman staff member. In all, they were not impressed by either the man or the psychological appraisal.

In the criteria listed in the board's policy manual, the offender's attitudes and insights into his past conduct, along with clinical reports, are cited as important factors in decision making.[11] How does the board assess such elusive factors? Although the board did parole Gardner, it seemed hesitant and not sure that the behavioral improvement described by him had taken place. Two members participated in the deliberations; the third was silent. When Gardner was told that parole had been granted, no reasons were offered for the decision. It appeared that the board was willing to assume that some degree of attitudinal betterment had come about, but it was unable to spell out the rationale for its choice and the validity of that choice.

Sentence Equalization

Advocates of parole emphasize that the boards are indispensable in the criminal justice system for the equalization of sentence disparities. While such assertions are not based on empirical investigations, the very idea enters into the decisional process and adds to the issue of individual freedom that lies at the heart of the release dilemma.

Nathaniel Parker was arrested on the charge of robbery, pleaded not guilty, and demanded a jury trial. His co-defendant did not exercise these constitutional rights but pleaded guilty with the expectation that his sanction would be comparatively lighter. Parker received a term of from four to eight years, while the man who pleaded guilty received three to five. In the course of Parker's appearance before the parole board, it became evident to the members that although the two had shared responsibility for the offense, Parker had received the harsher treatment. They remarked that it was not the first time that they had been confronted by what seemed to be a miscarriage of justice. "This happens all the time, and I'm ready to parole this man now," said one member. The others mentioned that too often the judges create such disparities on the assumption that the parole board will correct them. The feeling is that this is a responsibility that the judge should not pass on.

Nowhere in the policy guidelines does mention of amelioration of harsh sentences appear, yet the norm of individualized justice is strong. This raises important questions since our law and ideology place sentencing in the hands of the judges, who are deemed to be skilled at dispensing justice. In reality, the actual amount of time incarcerated is determined by the parole board, which uses criteria that may be described at best as vague.

Prediction of Public Reaction

The weighing of contrasting goals of individual freedom and public order often leaves the parole board vulnerable to sporadic yet potentially vehement public reaction. After the Connecticut Board of Parole began to function on a statewide basis in 1968, a convict was released who then abducted one suburban housewife and murdered another. Public reaction was immediate and hostile, with the result that the board, regardless of the infrequency of such outcomes, is fearful that it might again become the target of popular wrath should it make another mistake of that dimension.

This trepidation comes into play when the board confronts an inmate who has committed an especially repugnant or violent offense. Philip Rosadini was one. Incarcerated for a brutal murder in which he and his co-defendants had repeatedly driven an automobile over the body of their victim to ensure that he was indeed dead, Rosadini became an exemplary prisoner. He had successfully functioned on work release, was the leader of the prison Alcoholics Anonymous group, had received extensive psychological counseling, and his folder contained many commendations from the custodial staff. Letters to the board from family members, work associates, and clergymen urged his parole. What most concerned the board was that the crime was related to his history of alcoholism. In addition, the brutality of the offense and the general revulsion occasioned by it at the time weighed heavily.

When the board considered the case in the hearing and the following executive session, the probability of another murder by Rosadini and the inevitable attendant outcries were brought up, even though parole prediction models—actuarial devices used for risk assessment—indicate that offenders with single convictions of manslaughter are good risks not to recidivate.[12] Rosadini admitted that he was an alcoholic and that complete abstinence was the only form of his rehabilitation, but the members were concerned lest his control weaken. They were compelled nonetheless to acknowledge his efforts at self-improvement. The retired executive commented, "If rehabilitation is the name of the game, then how can we deny this guy?" The decision to parole came with some reluctance; denial could not be justified, but there were significant risks.

CONCLUSION

As the parole board considers each inmate's case, it attempts to reconcile the competing aims of individual freedom and public order. Problems in the assessment of institutional behavior and psychological change, in the evaluation of public reaction, and in the attempt to equalize sentence disparities certainly limit the task of reconcilement.

Parole decision making and the general parole process have come under severe scrutiny. Questions are raised about the viability of criteria for decision making, about the influence of parole on recidivism, and about the constitutional rights of incarcerated felons. There are many charges that parole has failed in both theoretical and practical terms. Because parole is based on a single model of corrections, the rehabilitative model, and because that model has been shown to be ineffectively implemented, critics allege that the concept of parole has no validity. Criminologists, prison administrators, and former offenders have been among parole's detractors who call for its abolition. Some have even suggested that parole and indeterminate sentencing be replaced with a system of fixed sentences wherein offenders are incarcerated for a definite term with no prospect of parole. In this vein, researchers such as David Fogel[13] point out that justice, not rehabilitation, is the primary goal of the criminal sanction, that human freedom and public safety can be ensured by just and equitable criminal administration procedures that leave rehabilitation to individual choice and responsibility.

Much of this negativism about parole stems from a recognition of the illusion of rehabilitation as a correctional goal. This dissatisfaction, however, is intensified by the manner in which parole boards have exercised the discretionary power that the criminal law delegates to this the last stop in the justice process. As the cases illustrate, there are very real impediments to rational and equitable decision making. The vagueness of statutory criteria and the absence of scientific measures of rehabilitation indicate that parole boards are faced with an insurmountable task. Witness the board's predicament as it tries to evaluate institutional adjustment and psychological change, and as it attempts to take into account public reaction and fairness in sentencing. The present state of the art suggests that parole boards are seriously constrained in their capacity to resolve the dilemma of individual freedom and public order. Until they are expressly recognized by statute as having functions other than rehabilitation assessment (that is, sentence review), parole boards will continue to serve both offenders' and society's lowest expectations.

NOTES

1. All names are fictitious.
2. In this regard see R. W. Kastenmeir and H. C. Eglit, "Parole Release Decision Makings: Rehabilitation Expertise and the Demise of Mythology," *American University Law Review* 22 (1973): 477.
3. See David Rothman, *The Discovery of the Asylum* (Boston: Little, Brown, 1971), for elaboration.
4. For a survey of sentencing systems and processes see Resource Center on Correctional Law and Legal Service, *Sentencing Computation—Laws and Practice: A Preliminary Survey* (Washington, D.C.: American Bar Association, 1974).
5. See State of Connecticut Board of Parole, *Statement of Organization and Procedures* (Hartford, 1974).
6. See Citizens Inquiry on Parole and Criminal Justice, Inc., *Summary Report on New York Parole* (New York, 1974), pp. 17–18.
7. *Connecticut General Statutes:* Section 54–125.
8. See James A. Inciardi, "Parole Prediction: A Fifty-Year Fantasy," in Edward Sagarin and Donald E. J. MacNamara, eds., *Corrections: Problems of Punishment and Rehabilitation* (New York: Praeger, 1973), and Robert Martinson, "What Works—Questions and Answers About Prison Reform," *Public Interest* 35 (1974): 22.
9. Erving Goffman, *Asylums: Stigma and Notes on the Management of Spoiled Identity* (Englewood Cliffs, N.J.: Prentice-Hall, 1963).

10. Robert Martinson, "The Age of Treatment: Some Implications of the Custody-Treatment Dimension," *Issues in Criminology* 2 (1966): 2; Walter C. Bailey, "An Evaluation of One Hundred Reports," *Journal of Criminal Law, Criminology and Police Science* 57 (1966): 155; and James Robison and Gerald Smith, "The Effectiveness of Correctional Programs," in Benjamin Frank, ed., *Contemporary Corrections* (Reston, Va.: Reston Publishing Company, 1973), p. 119.

11. See note 5, above.

12. For references on prediction models see Vincent O'Leary and Daniel Glaser, "The Assessment of Risk in Parole Decision-Making," in D. J. West, ed., *The Future of Parole* (London: Duckworth, 1972), p. 135; Hermann Manheim and Leslie T. Wilkins, "The Requirements of Prediction," in Norman Johnston et al., eds., *The Sociology of Punishment and Correction* (New York: John Wiley, 1970), p. 772; and L. E. Ohlin and O. D. Duncan, "The Efficiency of Prediction in Criminology," *American Journal of Sociology* 54 (1949): 441.

13. David Fogel, "We Are the Living Proof" (unpublished manuscript, 1975) (Report of National Institute of Law Enforcement and Criminal Justice Grant No. 74-TA-05-0001).

PART SEVEN

POLICY AND REFORM

Crime and the administration of justice have been prominent on the public policy agenda for more than two decades. During this period, Congress has created and abolished the Law Enforcement Assistance Administration (LEAA), two presidential commissions have made extensive suggestions for reform, and billions of dollars have been spent in attempts to reduce crime and improve the justice system. Initially, an air of certainty about the causes of crime and the way to reform criminals characterized official and scholarly statements on the problem. But only during the past few years have the true dimensions of crime and the potential for dealing with it been viewed with a new realism. As James Q. Wilson, a leading exponent of this realistic stance, stated, our efforts to understand and curb the rise in crime have been frustrated by "our optimistic and unrealistic assumptions about human nature." This view is a far cry from the previously prevalent belief that crime, like poverty, could be ended if only there were enough money to apply the techniques of the social and behavioral sciences to the "root causes"—poor housing, unemployment, and racial prejudice.

During the early period of activity by the LEAA, it was apparently assumed that, because the criminal justice system had been given a low public resources priority for such a long time, there was a need for "more of everything." The states were given generous grants to purchase new equipment (especially for the police), to encourage education and training, and to experiment with a variety of programs. Battles over the distribution of federal money seem to have taken on more importance than the development of a systematic and comprehensive approach to the problem to be solved: how to control crime yet maintain due process values. Programs tried out new approaches to crime prevention, court efficiency, and offender rehabilitation in a scattershot manner. The accent was on implementing the experiment; less attention was paid to theoretical foundations, testable hypotheses, or methods of evaluation. Because of the nature of the congressional mandate, the interest groups waiting to stake their claim to portions of the funds, and the philosophy that multiple approaches should be used in order to discover "what works," the LEAA soon was charged with being a captive of political forces and with making no headway in dealing with crime. Congress abolished the LEAA in 1982.

In the past fifteen years, research has provided a glimmer of hope for those who believe that the social sciences have the analytical tools to understand crime and to contribute to formation of public policies to deal with it. This research appears to be more systematic, to be based on empirical findings, and to challenge much of the "conventional wisdom" about crime, criminal behavior, and the administration of justice. There is a new appreciation of the complex dimensions of criminal behavior and of the fact that the law-enforcement function is only one role of the police. The courts are increasingly viewed as organizations composed of small groups, and it is recognized that rehabilitative techniques have had a low success rate. In addition, the dominant approach has been that criminal justice is a system.

Research should be the essential activity on which public policies are built. If government decisions were not influenced by politics, one might be able to show how the findings of social scientists could be directly applied to solving a public problem. However, public decisions are made in the political arena, where negotiation among relevant interest groups and political leaders is the way policy is formed. The solutions discussed by experts usually have little relation to the operational plans that emerge from the policy process. Consequently, efforts at change are often depicted as "too little, too late" or as only skirting the issue, while the real problem remains. Given these limiting circumstances, it appears that bringing about true reform is difficult.

Reform efforts are also doomed unless there is an understanding of the ability of a system to resist change. New policies are often forced on the police or courts, only to be reversed later because the new orientation did not take into account personal and bureaucratic goals. Reformers are often surprised when they return to an organization that has supposedly been changed by a new procedure; they find that nothing has really been altered and that, behind the formal facade, bureaucratic life goes on as usual.

Because criminal justice may be understood as a system made up of a series of interrelated parts—police, prosecution, courts, and corrections—changes in one portion may force adjustments in the others. For example, efforts to end plea bargaining through formal restrictions on the discretion of prosecuting attorneys have often resulted in the negotiations taking place elsewhere, such as at the police station. Likewise, changes in sentencing policies have an impact on the size of the prison population, the work of the parole board, court congestion, plea bargaining, and eventually law enforcement.

Given the political nature of policy formation and the ability of criminal justice organizations to resist change, one might conclude that there are few possibilities for reducing crime and improving the administration of justice. But it would be wrong to adopt this view, which could support maintenance of the status quo on the grounds that nothing can be changed and that things might in fact get worse. There have been important changes in the criminal justice system during the past decade, especially in areas where incentive systems have brought about reform. What is not clear is what impact crime policies have on reduction of illegal behavior and the promotion of justice. Social scientists as well as government planners appear to be more cautious in their approaches to this problem. The result is that incremental changes may prove to be more effective than the grandiose schemes proposed in the past.

SUGGESTIONS FOR FURTHER READING

AMERICAN FRIENDS SERVICE COMMITTEE. *Struggle for Justice.* New York: Hill & Wang, 1971. A thoughtful examination of some of the major criminal justice issues, with recommendations for change.

CULLEN, FRANCIS T., and KAREN E. GILBERT. *Reaffirming Rehabilitation.* Cincinnati: Anderson, 1982. A defense of the rehabilitative goal of corrections and a critique of the justice model.

FEELEY, MALCOLM M. *Court Reform on Trial.* New York: Basic Books, 1983. Examination of programs designed to reform the courts and the problems of bringing about innovations.

GOLDSTEIN, HERMAN. *Policing a Free Society.* Cambridge, Mass.: Ballinger, 1977. An analysis of the role of the police in a democratic society, with special emphasis on the problem of discretion.

VON HIRSCH, ANDREW. *Doing Justice.* New York: Hill & Wang, 1976. The best statement of the philosophy of the "just deserts" model, with recommendations for implementing it.

WALKER, SAMUEL. *Sense and Nonsense About Crime.* Monterey, Calif.: Brooks/Cole, 1985. Conservative and liberal proposals for dealing with the crime problem are critically examined by taking a "What works?" perspective.

ARTICLE TWENTY-TWO

Crime and Public Policy

JAMES Q. WILSON

Many strongly held assumptions of the past are now being questioned. James Q. Wilson argues here that reduction of crime requires consideration of such basic issues as the nature of human beings and the capacity of institutions to change behavior. He sets forth what he calls a reasonable set of policies to deal with the crime problem.

If we are to make the best and sanest use of our laws and liberties, we must first adopt a sober view of man and his institutions that would permit reasonable things to be accomplished, foolish things abandoned, and utopian things forgotten. A sober view of man requires a modest definition of progress. A 20 percent reduction in the number of robberies would still leave us with the highest robbery rate of almost any Western nation but would prevent over 100,000 robberies. A small gain for society, a large one for the would-be victims. But even this gain is unlikely if we do not think clearly about crime and public policy.

The quest for the causes of crime is an intellectually stimulating, though, thus far, rather confusing, endeavor. To the extent we have learned anything at all, we have learned that the factors in our lives and history that most powerfully influence the crime rate—our commitment to liberty, our general prosperity, our childrearing methods, our popular values—are precisely the factors that are hardest or riskiest to change. Those things

Source: James Q. Wilson, *Thinking About Crime,* rev. ed. (New York: Basic Books, 1983), pp. 250–260. Notes omitted.

that can more easily and safely be changed—the behavior of the police, the organization of neighborhoods, the management of the criminal justice system, the sentences imposed by courts—are the things that have only limited influence on the crime rate.

If the things we can measure and manipulate had a large effect on the crime rate, then those effects would by now be evident in our statistical studies and police experiments. If crime were easily deterred by changes in the certainty or severity of sanctions, then our equations would probably have detected such effects in ways that overcome the criticisms now made of such studies. If giving jobs to ex-offenders and school dropouts readily prevented crime, the results of the Manpower Demonstration Research Corporation experiments would not have been so disappointing. If new police patrol techniques made a large and demonstrable difference, those techniques would have been identified.

In a sense, the radical critics of American society are correct: if you wish to make a big difference in crime, you must make fundamental changes in society. But they are right only in that sense, for what they propose to put in place of existing institutions, to the extent that they propose anything at all except angry rhetoric, would probably make us yearn for the good old days when our crime rate was higher but our freedoms were intact. Indeed, some versions of the radical doctrine would leave us yearning for the good old days when not only were our freedoms intact, but our crime rate was lower.

I realize that some people, not at all radical, find it difficult to accept the notion that if we are to think seriously about crime, we ought to think about crime and not about poverty, unemployment, or racism. Such persons should bear two things in mind. The first is that there is no contradiction between taking crime seriously and taking poverty (or other social disadvantages) seriously. There is no need to choose. Quite the contrary; to the extent that our efforts to measure the relationships among crime, wealth, and sanctions can be said to teach any lessons at all, it is that raising the costs of crime while leaving the benefits of noncrime untouched may be as shortsighted as raising the benefits of noncrime while leaving the costs of crime unchanged. Anticrime policies are less likely to succeed if there are no reasonable alternatives to crime; by the same token, employment programs may be less likely to succeed if there are attractive criminal alternatives to working. If legitimate opportunities for work are unavailable, some people may turn to crime, but if criminal opportunities are profitable, some persons will not take the legitimate jobs that exist.

Some persons may believe that if legitimate jobs are made absolutely more attractive than stealing, stealing will decline even without any increase in penalties for it. That may be true, provided there is no practical limit on the amount that can be paid in wages. Since the average "take" from a burglary or mugging is quite small, it would seem easy to make the income from a job exceed the income from crime. But this neglects the advantages of a criminal income: one works at crime at one's convenience, enjoys the esteem of colleagues who think a "straight" job is stupid and skill at stealing is commendable, looks forward to the occasional "big score" that may make further work unnecessary for weeks, and relishes the risk and adventure associated with theft. The money value of all these benefits (that is, what one who is not shocked by crime would want in cash to forgo crime) is hard to estimate but is almost certainly far larger than either public or private employers could offer to unskilled or semi-skilled young workers. The only alternative for society is to so increase the risks of theft that its value is depreciated below what society can afford to pay in legal wages, and then take whatever steps are necessary to ensure that those legal wages are available.

The desire to reduce crime is the worst possible reason for reducing poverty. Most poor persons are not criminals; many either are retired or have regular jobs and lead conventional family lives. The elderly, the working poor, and the willing-to-work poor could benefit greatly from economic conditions and government programs that enhance their incomes without there being the slightest reduction in crime (indeed, if the experience of the 1960s is any guide, there might well be, through no fault of most beneficiaries, an increase in crime). Reducing poverty and breaking up the ghettos are desirable policies in their own right, whatever their effects on crime. It is the duty of government to devise other measures to cope with crime, not only to permit antipoverty programs to succeed without unfair competition from criminal opportunities, but also to ensure that such programs do not inadvertently shift the costs of progress, in terms of higher crime rates, onto innocent parties, not the least of whom are the poor themselves.

One cannot press this economic reasoning too far. Some persons will commit crimes whatever the risks; indeed, for some, the greater the risk the greater the thrill, while others (the alcoholic wife beater, for example) are only dimly aware that there are any risks. But more important than the insensitivity of certain criminals to changes in risks and benefits is the impropriety of casting the crime problem wholly in terms of a utilitarian calculus. The most serious offenses are crimes not simply because society finds them inconvenient, but because it regards them with moral horror. To steal, to rape, to rob, to assault—these acts are destructive of the very possibility of society and affronts to the humanity of their victims. Parents do not instruct their children to be law abiding merely by pointing to the risks of being caught, but by explaining that these acts are wrong whether or not one is caught. I conjecture that those parents who simply warn their offspring about the risks of crime produce a disproportionate number of young persons willing to take those risks.

Even the deterrent capacity of the criminal justice system depends in no small part on its ability to evoke sentiments of shame in the accused. If all it evoked were a sense of being unlucky, crime rates would be even higher. James Fitzjames Stephens makes the point by analogy. To what extent, he asks, would a man be deterred from theft by the knowledge that by committing it he was exposing himself to one chance in fifty of catching a serious but not fatal illness—say, a bad fever? Rather little, we would imagine—indeed, all of us regularly take risks as great or greater than that: when we drive after drinking, when we smoke cigarettes, when we go hunting in the woods. The criminal sanction, Stephens concludes, "operates not only on the fears of criminals. [A] great part of the general detestation of crime . . . arises from the fact that the commission of offenses is associated . . . with the solemn and deliberate infliction of punishment wherever crime is proved."

Much is made today of the fact that the criminal justice system "stigmatizes" those caught up in it, and thus unfairly marks such persons and perhaps even furthers their criminal careers by "labeling" them as criminals. Whether the labeling process operates in this way is as yet unproved, but it would indeed be unfortunate if society treated a convicted offender in such a way that he had no reasonable alternative but to make crime a career. To prevent this, society should ensure that one can "pay one's debt" without suffering permanent loss of civil rights, the continuing and pointless indignity of parole supervision, and the frustration of being unable to find a job. But doing these things is very different from eliminating the "stigma" from crime. To destigmatize crime would be to lift from it the weight of moral judgment and to make crime simply a particular occupation or avocation which society has chosen to reward less (or perhaps more!) than other pursuits. If there is no stigma attached to an activity, then society has no business making it a crime. Indeed, before the invention of the prison in the late eighteenth and early nineteenth centuries, the stigma attached to criminals was the major deterrent to and principal form of protection from criminal activity. The purpose of the criminal justice system is not to expose would-be criminals to a lottery in which they either win or lose, but to expose them in addition and more importantly to the solemn condemnation of the community should they yield to temptation.

If we grant that it is proper to try to improve the criminal justice system without apologizing for the fact that those efforts do not attack the "root causes" of crime, the next thing to remember is that we are seeking, at best, marginal improvements that can only be discovered through patient trial-and-error accompanied by hardheaded and objective evaluations.

There are, we now know, certain things we can change in accordance with our intentions, and certain ones we cannot. We cannot alter the number of juveniles who first experiment with minor crimes. We apparently cannot lower the overall recidivism rate, though within reason we should keep trying. We are not yet certain whether we can increase significantly the police apprehension rate. We may be able to change the teenage unemployment rate, though we have learned by painful trial-and-error that doing this is much more difficult than once supposed. We can probably reduce the time it takes to bring an arrested person to trial, even though we have as yet made few serious efforts to do so. We can certainly reduce any arbitrary exercise of prosecutorial discretion over whom to charge and whom to release, and we can most definitely stop pretending that judges know, any better than the rest of us, how to provide "individualized justice." We can confine a larger proportion of the serious and repeat offenders and fewer of the common drunks and truant children. We know that confining criminals prevents them from harming society, and we have grounds for suspecting that some would-be criminals can be deterred by the confinement of others.

Above all, we can try to learn more about what works and, in the process, abandon our ideological preconceptions about what ought to work. This is advice, not simply or even primarily to government—for governments are run by men and women who are under irresistible pressures to pretend they know more than they do—but to my colleagues: academics, theoreticians, writers, advisers. We may feel ourselves under pressure to pretend we know things, but we are also under a positive obligation to admit what we do not know and to avoid cant and sloganizing.

In the last decade or so, we have learned a great deal, perhaps more than we sometimes admit. But we have learned very little to a moral certainty. Any effort to reduce crime is an effort to alter human behavior at moments when it is least well observed and by methods (deterrence, incapacitation, rehabilitation) whose effect is delayed and uncertain. Under these circumstances, we may never know "what works" to a moral certainty. Why, then, gamble on what we (or at least I) think we know? I offer Pascal's wager. If altering the rewards and penalties of crime affects the rate of crime, and I act on that belief, I reduce crime. If such strategies do not work, and I act on the false belief that they do, I have merely made swifter, more certain, or more severe the penalties that befall a person guilty in any event and to that extent have served justice, though not utility. But if I do not believe in them, and they do in fact work, then I have condemned innocent persons to suffer needlessly and have served neither justice nor utility.

But what, precisely, ought we to do if we act on the belief that we know, though with some uncertainty, how to reduce crime marginally? The purpose of this book is not to offer a detailed set of anticrime policies, it is only to teach people how to think about crime (and especially how to think about the kind of research that is done about crime control). But it would be unfair to the reader to leave him or her to guess what the author believes ought to be done after learning to think this way.

The policy implications of what I have learned are in many ways so obvious that many readers will wonder why it is necessary to struggle through all these facts, regression equations, and experiments to accept them. There are many reasons why it is necessary to find evidence for the obvious, not the least of which is that many people still do not find them obvious, or even reasonable. If you doubt this, attend a city council meeting on the police budget, a legislative debate on the criminal laws, a convention of judges discussing sentencing, or a conference of criminologists.

A reasonable set of policies would, to me, include the following. Neighborhoods threatened with crime or disorder would be encouraged to create self-help organizations of citizens who, working in collaboration with the police, patrol their own communities to detect, though not to apprehend, suspicious persons. Densely settled neighborhoods would make extensive use of foot-patrol officers and would hire off-duty police and, perhaps, private security guards to help maintain order and to prevent disreputable behavior in public places from frightening decent persons off the sidewalks or from encouraging predatory offenders to use the anarchy and anonymity of the streets as an opportunity for serious crime. Drug dealers would be driven off the streets.

The police would organize their patrol units to help maintain order and to identify and, where possible, arrest high-rate offenders. Detectives and patrol officers would make thorough, on-the-spot investigations of recent serious offenses. As much information as possible would be gathered about the records and habits of high-rate offenders, and officers would be given strong incentives to find and arrest them. Even when they are caught committing a relatively minor crime, these career criminals would be the object of intensive follow-up investigations so as to make the strongest possible case against them.

All persons arrested for a serious offense and all high-rate offenders arrested for any offense would be screened by prosecutors who would have immediately accessible the juvenile and adult criminal records of such persons so that a complete picture of their criminal history could be readily assessed. Those who commit very serious offenses and high-rate offenders who have committed any offense would be given priority treatment in terms of prompt follow-up investigations, immediate arraignment, bail recommendations to ensure appearance at trial, and an early trial date so that those who cannot post bail will have their cases disposed of swiftly. One prosecutor would handle each priority case from intake to final disposition. Victims and witnesses would be given special assistance, including counseling on procedures, money aid (where appropriate) to compensate them for their time away from work, and the early return of any stolen property that has been recovered.

Well-staffed prosecutorial and public defender's offices would be prepared for an early trial (or plea bargain) in these priority cases; judges would be loath to grant continuances for convenience of counsel. Sentencing would be shaped, though not rigidly determined, by sentencing guidelines that take into account not only the gravity of the offense and the prior conviction record of the accused, but also the full criminal history, including the juvenile record and the involvement, if any, of the accused with drug abuse. The outer bounds of judicial discretion would be shaped by society's judgment as to what constitutes a just and fair penalty for a given offense; within those bounds, sentencing would be designed to reduce crime by giving longer sentences to high-rate offenders (even when convicted of a less serious offense) and shorter sentences to low-rate offenders (even if the offense in question is somewhat more serious).

Persons convicted of committing minor offenses who have little or no prior record would be dealt with by community-based corrections: in particular, by supervised community service and victim restitution. Probation officers would ensure that these obligations are in fact met; individuals failing to meet them would promptly be given short jail sentences.

Offenders sentenced to some period of incarceration would be carefully screened so that young and old, violent and nonviolent, neurotic and psychotic offenders would be assigned to separate facilities and, within those facilities, to educational and treatment programs appropriate to their personalities and needs. Progress in such programs would have nothing to do, however, with the date on which the offenders are released. Time served would be set by the judge, perhaps with stated discounts for good behavior; rehabilitation, to the extent that it occurs at all, would be a benefit of the programs but not a circumstance determining the length of the sentence. Parole boards might make recommendations to the sentencing judge or to the governor about sentences that ought to be commuted or shortened in the manifest interests of justice, but they would not determine release dates. Parole officers would continue to assist ex-offenders in returning to the community, especially with jobs and limited financial assistance, but there would be no assumption that these services would reduce the recidivism rate or that the parole officer would oversee the behavior of the offender in the community.

Prisons would be of small to moderate size, and in no facility housing violent or high-rate offenders would double-bunking occur. Contraband flowing into or out of the prisons would be strictly controlled. The first objective of the guards would be to protect society by maintaining secure custody; their second (and perhaps equally important) objective would be to protect the inmates from one another. Guards would be sufficiently numerous so that they were not forced to choose between controlling the prison by terror or abdicating control of it to organized groups of inmates.

People will disagree with one or more elements of this sketchy set of proposals; I myself may change my mind about the details as I learn more about what works and think harder about what justice requires. But in broad outline, it strikes me neither as an unreasonable set of ideas nor one likely to be rejected by most citizens. There is no idea on this list that is not now being implemented in at least one jurisdiction, and large numbers of these ideas are being practiced in a few jurisdictions. But in general, and in most places, this package of ideas is resisted in practice just as it may be applauded in theory. The blunt fact is that the criminal justice system in this country does not, for the most part, operate as I have suggested.

Neighborhood and citizen patrols are often resisted by the police who fear a loss of their monopoly of power, by individual officers who fear a loss of their jobs, and by citizens who are quickly bored with volunteer work. Community-involved foot patrol is resisted by many police supervisors who fear loss of control of the beat officers. Assigning officers to neighborhoods on the basis of levels of public disorder and concentrating police investigations on high-rate offenders are resisted by citizens who judge the police entirely on the basis of how swiftly they dispatch a patrol car in response to a telephone call reporting a burglary that might have occurred many hours or even many days earlier.

Supporters of the family court system resist making juvenile criminal records routinely available in adult courts, and many prosecutors who, in fact, could obtain such records often do not because of the expense and bother. Prosecutors have come to embrace the idea of "career criminal" programs, but most of these are limited to adult offenders and even to those adult offenders who have committed very serious crimes, regardless of whether they are in fact high-rate offenders. The offices of prosecutors and public defenders are often so thinly staffed that asking for court continuances is absolutely essential. And even where it is not essential, it is usually convenient. Postponing cases is for prosecutors a way of evening out the workload and for defenders a way of making the evidence turn cold and the witnesses lose interest.

Many probation departments have created victim restitution and community service programs, but they often discover that persons ordered to participate in them ignore the order with impunity, because judges are not inclined (or are too busy) to enforce the order with appropriate sanctions. If a large fraction of all fines levied by judges are not paid in full, is it any wonder that community-based corrections so often result in offenders walking away from them?

Judges are by and large opposed to any substantial restriction on their right to sentence as they see fit, whatever the cost in crime control or fairness. They favor "guidelines," but only those they themselves have developed and that they are free to ignore. Some thoughtful legislators support more restrictive guidelines, but these are often based merely on the gravity of the instant offense and take little account of the crime control possibilities of selectively incapacitating high-rate offenders. And less thoughtful legislators find it much more appealing to call for massively severe sentences without regard to whether they will ever be imposed.

Taxpayers overwhelmingly want the system to crack down on serious and repeat offenders, but they regularly vote down bond issues designed to build the necessary additional prisons and they oppose having new facilities located in their neighborhoods. These taxpayer revolts are aided and abetted by pressure groups that are hostile to incarceration, retaining in the face of all evidence to the contrary a faith in rehabilitation and reserving their feelings of vengeance for "white-collar" criminals (especially those who might have served in conservative administrations).

In short, the entire criminal justice system, from citizen to judge, is governed by perverse incentives. Though many of its members agree on what they wish to achieve, the incentives faced by each member acting individually directs him or her to act in ways inconsistent with what is implied by that agreement.

In evidence of this, consider the following. Police officers want to arrest serious offenders—they are "good collars"—but making such arrests in ways that lead to conviction is difficult. Those convictions that are obtained are usually the result of the efforts of a small minority of all officers. Arrests that stand up in court tend to involve stranger-to-stranger crimes, to occur soon after the crime, and to be accompanied by physical evidence or eyewitness testimony. The officers who look hard for the perpetrators of stranger-to-stranger crimes, who gather physical evidence, and who carefully interview victims and potential witnesses are a small minority of all officers. . . . Brian Forst found, in six police jurisdictions, that about half of all convictions resulted from arrests made by only one-eighth of all officers. Indeed, one-quarter of the officers who made arrests produced zero convictions. Though these differences were in part the result of differences in duty assignments, they persisted after controlling for assignments. For many officers, it is much easier to take reports of crimes, mediate disputes, and turn big cases over to detectives who often take up the trail when it is cold. Despite these differences in behavior, Forst found that the most productive officers tend to get about the same number of commendations and awards as the least productive ones.

Prosecutors also behave in many cases in ways inconsistent with a crime control objective. In the 1960s, many of them took cases to court more or less in the order in which the arrests had been made. Then they began to assign higher priority to grave offenses. While an improvement, this still resulted in resources being concentrated on persons who had committed serious offenses, rather than on high-rate offenders. These are not necessarily the same persons. By the late 1970s, many career criminal programs had become quite sophisticated: they gave highest priority to grave offenses and to offenders with long or serious records. But even now, many jurisdictions limit the selection of cases to persons with serious adult records, ignoring the high predictive value of the juvenile record and the drug-abuse history. Some prosecutors will concentrate their follow-up investigations on persons who have committed serious crimes and neglect the crime control value of investigating suspected high-rate offenders who may have been caught for a nonserious offense.

Judges must manage a crowded docket, dispose of cases quickly, and make decisions under uncertainty. Some are also eager to minimize their chances of being reversed on appeal. These managerial concerns, while quite understandable, often get in the way of trying to use the court hearing as a means of establishing who is and who is not a high-rate offender and of allowing such distinctions, as well as the facts about the gravity of the case, to shape the sentence.

To the extent that the incentives operating in the criminal justice system have perverse and largely unintended effects, it is not clear what can be done about it. The "system" is not, as so many have remarked, in fact a system—that is, a set of consciously coordinated activities. And given the importance we properly attach to having an independent judiciary and to guaranteeing, even at some cost in crime control, the rights of accused by means of the adversarial process, there is no way the various institutions can be made into a true system. The improvements that can be made are all at the margin and require patient effort and an attention to detail. Sometimes a modest leap forward is possible, as when prosecutors began using computers to keep track of their cases and to learn about the characteristics of the defendants, or when legislators began experimenting with various kinds of sentencing guidelines. But mostly, progress requires dull, unrewarding work in the trenches. There is no magic bullet.

Throughout all this, our society has been, with but few exceptions, remarkably forbearing. We have preserved and even extended the most comprehensive array of civil liberties found in any nation on earth despite rising crime rates and (in the 1960s) massive civil disorder. Though proposals are now afoot to modify some of these procedural guarantees—especially those having to do with the exclusionary rule, the opportunity for unlimited appeals, and the right to bail—they constitute, at most, rather modest changes. If adopted, they would still leave our criminal justice system with a stronger set of guarantees than one could find in most other nations, including those, such as Great Britain and Canada, that we acknowledge to be bastions of freedom. We have chosen, as I think we should, to have a wide-ranging bill of rights, but we must be willing to pay the price of that choice. That price includes a willingness both to accept a somewhat higher level of crime and disorder than we might otherwise have and to invest a greater amount of resources in those institutions (the police, the prosecutors, the courts, the prisons) needed to cope with those who violate our law while claiming its protections.

For most of us, the criminal justice system is intended for the other fellow, and since the other fellow is thought to be wicked, we can easily justify to ourselves a pinch-penny attitude toward the system. It is, after all, not designed to help us but to hurt him. If it is unpleasant, congested, and cumbersome, it is probably only what those who are caught up in its toils deserve. What we forget is that the more unpleasant the prisons, the less likely judges will be to send people to them; the more congested the prosecutor's office, the less likely that office will be to sort out, carefully, the serious and high-rate offender from the run-of-the-mill and low-rate offender; the more cumbersome the procedures, the less likely we and our neighbors will be to take the trouble of reporting crimes, making statements, and testifying in court.

Wicked people exist. Nothing avails except to set them apart from innocent people. And many people, neither wicked nor innocent, but watchful, dissembling, and calculating of their chances, ponder our reaction to wickedness as a clue to what they might profitably do. Our actions speak louder than our words. When we profess to believe in deterrence and to value justice, but refuse to spend the energy and money required to produce either, we are sending a clear signal that we think that safe streets, unlike all other great public goods, can be had on the cheap. We thereby trifle with the wicked, make sport of the innocent, and encourage the calculators. Justice suffers, and so do we all.

ARTICLE TWENTY-THREE

Plea Bargaining and the Structure of the Criminal Process

MALCOLM M. FEELEY

Do plea bargaining and other accommodations in the system occur because of heavy caseloads, organizational influences, or limited resources? Malcolm Feeley views the criminal justice system at a higher level of analysis, pointing to historical, structural, and legal factors that he believes are the cause of increased plea bargaining. His thesis is that negotiation has increased in direct proportion to adversariness—precisely the opposite of what people think.

As a society we have high expectations for our courts, and when they are not met, as inevitably they will not be, we are disappointed. No doubt disappointment serves as an important stimulus for change, but it can also lead to exaggeration and misdiagnosis. An exaggerated sense of urgency can easily lead to misunderstanding and superficial analysis, lacking in perspective and context. In the concern with the practice of plea bargaining, something of this distortion has taken place. The result has been, I think, a misunderstanding of both the origins and nature of plea bargaining. This in turn has contributed to an inaccurate analysis of the operations of the courts and a downgrading of the magnitude and significance of changes in the adversary process in recent years. In general many so-called improvements, and indeed some of their seeming shortcomings, can also be seen as signs of strength. Plea bargaining is one such change.[1]

We have been told time and time again within recent years that plea

Source: From *Justice System Journal* 7 (Winter 1982): 338–355. Reprinted by permission.

bargaining has reached epidemic proportions, that reliance on the guilty plea has all but displaced the traditional trial as the means for handling criminal cases. In a widely read book, Abraham Blumberg concludes that the defense attorney has shifted from being a fighter in behalf of his client to a "confidence man," whose primary function is to "manipulate the client and stage manage the case so that help and service at least appear to be rendered" (Blumberg 1967: 111). Blumberg sees in this shift the "twilight of the adversary system" and the emergence of bureaucratic justice, where nominal adversaries—the prosecutor and the defense attorney—are bound together in a common desire to maintain a smooth-functioning system. Organizational maintenance and financial self-interest, he argues, have replaced a concern with justice. Hence the demise of the adversary process and the rise of plea bargaining, a device which can *appear* to operate in the interests of the accused but in fact serves other more salient organizational interests.

Blumberg is not alone in ascribing the demise of the adversary system to the rise of plea bargaining. In what have quickly become classics, University of Colorado law professor Albert Alschuler has examined plea bargaining from the perspectives of the prosecutor, judge, and defense attorney (Alschuler 1968, 1975, 1976, 1979). He concludes that from each of these views the prevailing incentive is one of institutional convenience and organizational maintenance rather than in the interests of the accused and the concern with justice. What disturbs Alschuler most is the threat (implicit or explicit) that the accused who exercises his right to trial and is convicted will be sentenced more severely than one who pleads guilty. That such practices are common few would seriously deny. Systematic studies of a number of courts all indicate that the practice of offering "discounts" for guilty pleas—or conversely penalties for trials—is common, although it is not always explicitly acknowledged by court officials. Even where such penalties do not occur, court officials, defense attorneys, and defendants clearly believe they do and act accordingly (Feeley 1979).

Prosecutors and judges agree with the scholars that plea bargaining has become the primary means of securing conviction, but tend to be less critical of the practice. Some see it as a necessary evil, a practical response to rising crime and limited resources. Others view plea bargaining more positively, arguing that it introduces flexibility into an otherwise rigid system. Despite some dramatic pronouncements and much rhetoric, few practitioners seriously work to abolish the practice of plea bargaining. Indeed, there seems to be a growing belief that plea bargaining is inevitable.

My intention here is neither to defend the institution of plea bargaining nor to challenge its critics. Rather it is to examine its antecedents, origins, practices, and functions in light of the charge that it signifies a decline of the adversary process and the rise of bureaucratic justice. Put bluntly, the charge against plea bargaining is that it is a cooperative practice which has come to replace the combative trial, and as such has reduced the vigor of the adversary process. This charge, if that is what it is, is false. It is a charge unduly fettered by the constraints of organizational theory; it lacks historical perspective and fails to place plea bargaining in broader structural and social context.

My thesis here is that adversariness and negotiation are directly related. Plea bargaining is not a cooperative practice that undermines or compromises the adversary process; rather, the opportunity for adversariness has expanded in direct proportion to, and perhaps as a result of, the growth of plea bargaining. As the requirements of due process have expanded, as resources have become more accessible to both the prosecution and the criminally accused, as the substantive criminal law has developed, and as the availability and role of defense counsel have expanded, the opportunity for both adversariness and negotiations has increased. At first glance, this thesis runs counter to most of the theoretical and practical discussions of the criminal process. But when examined in historical perspective and seen in comparative context, the argument can be sustained.

This thesis does not so much purport to refute the findings of contemporary studies on or critics of plea bargaining as its means to build on them and place the process of plea bargaining in broader perspective and context. By identifying the importance of hitherto unrecognized or underrecognized factors shaping the institution of plea bargaining (and negotiation in the criminal process generally), I hope to broaden and correct the conventional understanding of plea bargaining that has risen in recent years.

ORGANIZATIONAL ANALYSIS AND PLEA BARGAINING

One concern for students of formal organizations is the process by which the formal goals of an organization are displaced as a consequence of pressures to adapt to the larger environment, to serve the personal interests of its members, and to cope with scarce resources. This approach, which by now has become the conventional approach to studying criminal courts, accounts for plea bargaining in terms of goal displacement and adaptation (Nardulli 1979a). The frequent contact between defense attorneys and prosecutors fosters a tendency to replace formal adversarial roles with cooperative relationships. Others emphasize that the pressure to "produce" within the constraints of severely limited resources leads to the replacement of slow and deliberate formal practices with more expeditious forms of decision making. Thus plea bargaining comes to be understood as a consequence of these and related extralegal organizational factors.

This approach is not without considerable merit and insight. It has successfully challenged long-standing myths about the causes and consequences of plea bargaining. For instance, it has revealed dynamics that foster cooperation in a system that many feel should be conflictual (Skolnick 1967). It has challenged heavy caseloads and limited resources as the primary causes for plea bargaining. For instance, Heumann (1975, 1978), Feeley (1975, 1979), Nardulli (1979b), Rosett and Cressey (1976), and the Vera Institute (1981) have marshaled evidence suggesting that heavy caseloads are not necessarily the important causes of plea bargaining so many practitioners assert they are. Other studies anchored in organizational theory examine the incentive structures of the primary participants, and in doing so have shed considerable light on the ways courts operate, and on the functions of plea bargaining (Eisenstein and Jacob 1977; Nardulli 1978; Mather 1979; Utz 1978; Cole 1970). Some of these studies examined the important policy issue about the extent to which a defendant who exercises a right to trial is or is not penalized for exercising this right. Although the results of these investigations are mixed, and indeed different jurisdictions may follow different policies (Miller et al. 1978), these studies have provided useful theoretical insights into the operations of courts and contributed important data for the policy issues about the desirability and nature of plea bargaining. Above all, what these studies have shown is that factors fostering plea bargaining are not confined to a few unskilled lawyers, overworked prosecutors, or uncaring judges, but are part and parcel of the *structure* of the criminal court system itself. Both individual case studies (for example, Nardulli 1978; Mather 1979; Feeley 1979; Utz 1978) and ambitious comparative analyses (Miller et al. 1978) show that plea bargaining must be seen in a larger context, as only one facet of an elaborate structure of negotiation in the criminal courts. These insights go a long way to explain the findings of Church (1976), Heumann and Loftin (1979), Rubenstein and White (1979), and others who have found that when plea bargaining is "abolished" it usually reappears in slightly different forms elsewhere within the court system.

Although these and other related studies have made significant contributions in clarifying the nature and function of plea bargaining and the operations of the criminal courts in general, they have been most successful in debunking myths and cataloging the functions of plea bargaining. *But what the organizational approach does not and cannot easily explain is why the practice of plea bargaining grew up in the first place, and what legal, theoretical, and structural factors (as opposed to organizational functions) gave birth to and help sustain it.* The exigencies of the pressures on organizations with limited resources may help to explain the contemporary practice of plea bargaining in America, but these same factors cannot easily account for its rise in the first place. Nor do they account for the limitations of resources that in turn encourage such practices as plea bargaining. To pursue the full explanation for plea bargaining a historical and comparative perspective, examining practices in light of a host of social, doctrinal, and structural factors is required.

A BROADER FRAMEWORK FOR UNDERSTANDING PLEA BARGAINING

Below I sketch out a broader framework for understanding plea bargaining. This approach identifies the historical origins of plea bargaining in terms of the influence of legal doctrine and the formal legal process. My argument is that plea bargaining has become the standard method for securing convictions for a complex set of reasons that go well beyond limitations of resources. Indeed, I argue that it has been the increase in resources and opportunities that has in fact fostered the rise of plea bargaining. To sustain this thesis, I will first demonstrate the shortcoming of conventional discussions of the origins of plea bargaining by reviewing its history, and then I will turn to comment on five factors that together have fostered the rise and helped sustain the practice of plea bargaining. These factors are:

1. Plea bargaining in relation to the operative assumptions of the criminal process as it developed from a tradition of private prosecution
2. Plea bargaining in relation to changes in the substantive criminal law
3. Plea bargaining in relation to changes in criminal procedure
4. Plea bargaining in relation to the rise of full-time criminal court "professionals," specialists who replaced "amateur" officials who once staffed the court system
5. Plea bargaining in relation to the expansion of the availability of defense attorneys

PLEA BARGAINING IN HISTORICAL PERSPECTIVE

A cursory look at court records reveals that disposition by means of guilty pleas is a phenomenon of the late nineteenth and twentieth centuries. What little readily available evidence there is all points in the same direction. In 1928 Raymond Moley (1928) reported on his survey of dispositional practices of American criminal courts in the early part of this century. In the 1920s in New York City, guilty pleas accounted for 88 percent of all convictions, in Cleveland 86 percent, in Chicago 85 percent, in Des Moines 79 percent, and in Dallas 70 percent. Moley presented additional figures to show that these high rates of guilty pleas were not restricted to large or rapidly growing urban centers, but were found in less populated areas with less crowded courts as well. For instance, guilty pleas accounted for 91 percent of all convictions in rural upstate New York in the 1920s, a figure even higher than that for New York City during the same period (Moley 1928: 163–164). Similarly high figures were presented for other rural and less congested courts. Two recent studies of Connecticut reveal that while trial rates have fluctuated over the past ninety years, they have hovered around 10 percent throughout this period (Feeley 1975; Heumann 1975). These data suggest that plea bargaining—or at least the guilty plea—has a long history that predates the reported dramatic increase in crime and arrests of the past two or three decades.

Was there a time when trials were much more common? In a word, yes. Albert Alschuler reports that in the United States the guilty plea began to replace the trial as the dominant mode of disposition at around the time of the Civil War (Alschuler 1979). My own work with court records in New Haven, Connecticut, New York, and London's Old Bailey reinforces this impression. Analysis of these records is still under way, but the broad trends they reveal are instructive. In London's Central Criminal Court in the 1830s, trials accounted for over 95 percent of all dispositions. This figure steadily declined throughout the nineteenth and into the twentieth century. An even more pronounced pattern of decline is found in the United States. For instance, in Superior Court in New York City in 1846 only 28 percent of dispositions were by confessions; by 1860 this figure had risen to 47 percent; in 1890, it was 61 percent; and by 1919 it was 88 percent. A sample of criminal court records from New Haven, Connecticut, during roughly the same period reveals a similar shift: in 1837, 21 percent of my sample cases were disposed of by guilty pleas; in 1860, the figure was 50 percent; in 1888, it was 73 percent; in 1914, it was 91 percent; in 1934, it was 97 percent. There has been little room for increase since then. Furthermore, another pattern emerged in the late 1800s: the practice of changing initial pleas of not guilty to guilty, which were accompanied by the prosecutor's decision to drop one charge or more in a multiple-charge case. In 1873, this practice accounted for roughly one-half of all guilty pleas; by 1934 two-thirds of all guilty pleas involved switches of this nature, and of those who switched almost half involved pleas to lesser or fewer charges than they had originally faced. The only striking difference in disposition patterns since the 1930s has been the increased tendency to plead guilty to lesser or only some charges, a practice that clearly indicates *plea bargaining.*

What can we make of all this? Certainly these figures support Raymond Moley's 1928 argument, lamenting "our vanishing jury" (1928). And they appear to support the more recent contention that we are witnessing the "twilight of the adversary process" which is being replaced by a cooperative bureaucratic process that relies upon the guilty plea.

But let us penetrate the surface of these data and consider the *substance* of these processes. Once we do, the "decline" thesis loses much of its power. Indeed, it can be stood on its head.

Recall my original thesis. It was not that things have remained relatively constant, but that in fact the adversary process has become more vigorous in recent years and that plea bargaining is in fact an indicator of this vigor. To examine this argument we must go beyond rates of trial and inspect the *process* of court decision making more closely. Two issues concern us here. What were trials like in this earlier era when they were most frequent? And what is entailed in the modern process of pleading guilty?

First the trials. Lawrence Friedman and Robert Percival have sifted through the court files in Florida and California for the period around the turn of the century. While they found that there was an appreciably higher rate of trials at that time than there is today (although trials still constituted a distinct minority of dispositions), they proceeded to inquire into the nature of these trials. Let them describe what they found (Friedman and Percival 1981: 194).

> We have to ask, however, what kind of trial? Trial to most of us conjures up a definite image: a real courtroom battle, with two sides struggling like young stags and the judge acting as umpire, applying fair and honorable rules. Reality was quite different. In many places, the normal case was nasty and short. We examined the minute books of a Florida county from the 1890s. Here "trials" lasted a very short time, half an hour at most. A jury was hurriedly thrown together. Case after case paraded before them. The complaining witness told his story; sometimes another witness or two appeared; the defendant told his story, with or without witnesses; the lawyers (if any) spoke; the judge charged the jury. The jury retired, voted, and returned. Then the court went immediately into the next case on its list.

My own inspection of contemporary accounts on the trial process in London and New Haven, Connecticut, is equally revealing. Transcripts of the trial court proceedings in mid-nineteenth-century London reveal practices that are at odds with our image of the trial. Defendants were *not* represented by counsel; they did not confront hostile witnesses in any meaningful way; they rarely challenged evidence or offered defenses of any kind. Typically when they or occasionally someone in their behalf did take the witness stand they requested mercy or offered only perfunctory excuses or defenses. Similar practices appear to have characterized trials in Connecticut during this same period as well.

Perhaps what is most revealing about their substance is the speed at which these early trials were conducted. The record of proceedings in London reveals that the same judge *and* jury would hear several cases per day with hardly a pause between them. Similarly, the New Haven court register indicates that the same judge and jury might handle several cases in a one- or two-day period; trial, deliberation, and sentencing could all occur within the span of an hour or two. It should be emphasized that these cases usually involved felonies and that substantial sentences were often involved.

Contemporary accounts flesh out still more the nature of the nineteenth-century trial. In all but the occasional celebrated cases, preparation was negligible. For all practical purposes, the courtroom and trial were the location and the event at which evidence and witnesses were gathered and examined *for the first time* by both the prosecutor and (when there was one) the defense attorney. Trials during this period must be understood as events where those centrally involved met for the first (and usually only) time to "muck about" with the available evidence in order to arrive at an immediate judgment.

This brief examination points to an inescapable conclusion: there was no golden era or "high noon" of the adversary process. To speak of the "twilight" of the adversary process is to foster a myth of a nonexistent past. When trials were once extensively relied upon, they were perfunctory affairs that bear but scant resemblance to contemporary trials, which while few and far between are often deliberate and painstaking affairs, at least as compared to what they once were. In a real sense, the very nature of what a trial is has undergone revolutionary changes to such an extent that comparisons across lengthy periods are not even meaningful.

Indeed it is my contention that when it was used with great frequency, the criminal trial was one of the very few devices available to the accused to try to protect his interests. That is, the trial was relied on extensively when criminal justice was administered in a rough way, often by "amateurs." During this time it served to protect the interests of a largely dependent accused. But as other institutions emerged to protect these interests, the significance and frequency of the trial declined. In brief, as the criminal process became more professionalized, as other opportunities for the defense expanded, the need to rely on the trial to protect the interests of the accused declined.

From this historical perspective, the ability to negotiate and bargain must be seen as an extension of or increase in adversariness. The very terms "negotiation" and "bargaining" imply some degree of parity between prosecution and defense, something that was often lacking in an earlier era when trials were more prevalent but an unrepresented defendant was more likely to be at the mercy of the court. While I do not want to argue that the process has shifted from a position of complete dependency to one of full equivalency, I do mean to argue that some movement in this direction has taken place and that this change can go a long way to accounting for the vanishing jury and the rise of plea bargaining. Several components of this thesis are examined below.

1. *Plea bargaining in relation to the operating assumptions and structure of the criminal process.* Criminal law has its roots in the law of torts, private wrongs pursued at the initiative of the aggrieved party. Although crimes are now offenses against the public, the criminal process retains residual practices of this earlier era. For instance, even today in England, the fiction remains that prosecutors are private parties acting in behalf of private complainants.

Even more important is another vestige of private prosecution. In the United States and England, the prosecutor in "public" criminal law has inherited the private complainant's discretion to bring or drop charges. Under both common and statutory law in the United States, the prosecutor's power to *nolle prosequi*, that is, to suspend prosecution, has remained intact and complete. Although there is some move toward judicial supervision of this function, legal controls are generally weak and American judges remain quite passive (Davis 1971; Goldstein 1981). The residue of this practice under the common law goes a long way toward explaining a *structure* that permits, if not encourages, plea bargaining.

The authority and discretion of the prosecutor has fostered a passivity on the part of the judiciary. Historically this has led to heavy reliance on confessions as sufficient to prove guilt. While confessions in capital cases and obtained under coercion have long been prohibited, freely made confessions in lesser cases have long been recognized if not encouraged by law and by the very structure of Anglo-American criminal process. For instance, a bifurcated court structure, which provides limited sentencing authority in lower courts, has long functioned on an inducement for the accused, if given the opportunity, to plead guilty in order to avoid exposure to harsher penalties that could be meted by a higher court (Langbein 1974; Vera Institute 1981; Feeley 1979).

In the United States, we find a long tradition of prosecutorial discretion, judicial passivity, and court structures with overlapping jurisdictions. While these factors alone do not explain plea bargaining, they do foster the practice by creating and legitimizing structures that invite it. It is interesting to note that in Germany, where plea bargaining is largely unknown, prosecutors do not have such discretionary authority and judges are much more active than their Anglo-American counterparts (Langbein 1974, 1979; Langbein and Weinreb 1978). More generally, see Damaska (1973), Weinreb (1977), Goldstein and Marcus (1977).

2. *Plea bargaining in relation to changes in the substantive law.* This century has witnessed a mushrooming of new criminal offenses and redefinitions of old ones. Not long ago criminal laws were brief statements written in broad language.

Today they are long; types of crimes are defined in minute detail and distinguished in several degrees. Plea bargaining can in part be accounted for by this change. Rather than falling under a single broad definition, any given incident of criminal conduct may now easily be defined as illegal in any of several ways or degrees. In short, we have an overdetermined system of law that invites the exercise of discretion and negotiation. Indeed, much of what is characterized as "plea bargaining" involves assessment or reassessment of the facts as they fit under various definitions or categories of offenses (Feeley 1979; Utz 1978). Because many of these fine-lined distinctions involve exposure to sentences of quite different lengths, the incentive to clarify them is obvious and important in a way and to a degree that it was not when there were simpler and more sweeping definitions of criminal offenses.

3. *Plea bargaining in relation to changes in criminal procedure.* Changes in the law of evidence and criminal procedure have paralleled developments in the substantive criminal law. The criminal trial is governed by more carefully constructed rules than its counterpart in the nineteenth century, and the criminally accused are today surrounded by many more procedural protections than they once were when trials were more common. Many of these new or newly enforced provisions come into play at the early stages of the criminal process. Probable cause hearings, bills of particulars, motions to suppress evidence, and the like, all shape the criminal process prior to trial and formal adjudication of guilt or innocence. In many cases, pretrial hearings—or for that matter negotiations in the shadow of the law—can become mini-trials. Whether the early review of the evidence reveals a strong or weak case or whether the testimony of a particular witness or the introduction of a specific piece of evidence will or will not be admitted into the record can make or break a case, and depending on the conclusion reached, charges may be dropped, reduced, or the accused may plead guilty or take his case to trial. So, while we have witnessed the demise of the trial, we have at the same time experienced an increase in pretrial opportunities to review in adversarial context some of the same types of issues that once were *less* carefully considered by the jury at trial.

Similarly the rules for introducing evidence into trial have been refined and tightened since the mid-nineteenth century. While once the jury was expected to weigh the value of a vast amount of evidence, the modern tendency has been to screen out problematic information from the jury (presumably on the theory that it cannot recognize the possible weaknesses in the evidence). The objective has been to improve the trial process, to ensure fairness in decision making. But one consequence is that these refinements have placed increased importance on pretrial decision making and have made the trial more costly, more time-consuming, and perhaps more unpredictable. Although there are many other differences between American and European criminal justice systems, it is perhaps not surprising that on the Continent, where a larger proportion of cases are taken to trial, trial procedure and the rules of evidence are much simpler—as they once were in the United States when, here too, trials were more common. Thus, ironically, as the price for this quest for perfect justice has increased, so too has the incentive to avoid it. Plea bargaining is one such alternative.

4. *Plea bargaining in relation to the rise of full-time professionals.* Reports on the operations of the criminal justice system in the United States and England at the turn of the century and earlier reveal a time when trials were much more frequent than they are today. But they also describe practices that by today's standards are wanting. Frequently courts were staffed with part-time officers; often prosecutors and judges were not trained in the law (as most magistrates in England still are not). Typ-

ically, the accused was not represented by counsel of any sort. Police officers often acting as prosecutors in court were unfamiliar with the rudiments of the law and cared even less (Haller 1970, 1979). Admissibility of evidence was capricious, points of law were treated with casualness.

Historically, the modern trial by jury emerged when the criminal justice system was staffed by untrained amateurs who were charged with the task of trying to cope with the problem of accusing, trying and convicting, or acquitting someone. Presumably the public and collective nature of the proceedings and often the personal knowledge of the judge and jury compensated for the lack of training of officials and the simplicity of the proceedings.

Although trained professionals—judges, prosecutors, defense attorneys—have over the years assumed increasing importance in handling criminal cases in the courts, especially with major felony charges, it is only in a relatively recent past that courtrooms have routinely been staffed by law-trained specialists who devote substantial portions of their time to criminal matters. Universal representation by counsel of those accused of criminal charges and who cannot afford their own attorney has not yet been fully realized.

What we have witnessed in recent years is—in the most basic and obvious sense of the term—the professionalization of the court system. Part-time lay officials have been replaced by full-time officials, and in many instances lay officials have been replaced by law-trained specialists. The demise of the trial and the rise of plea bargaining has paralleled this development, and I am suggesting there is a connection.

Why? The modern trial by jury, as I have suggested, originated at a time when laypeople administered many of the positions in the criminal justice system and at a time when few resources were available and few rules governed pretrial and trial practices. The trial was the major focus and institution in this simplified process. It was usually the first time that the evidence was collectively considered. But as reliance on professionals with staffs has expanded, opportunities for considering issues, other than at trial, have also emerged. Ironically, the expanded use of defense counsel may have sounded the death knell for the trial. A defendant who might have once sat passively through a perfunctory trial without an attorney is now likely to be represented by counsel, who has an opportunity for early review of evidence and who may prefer to bargain under the shadow of the law than go to trial. Similarly, full-time prosecutors with staffs have replaced part-time and untrained police prosecutors, who earlier had replaced private prosecutors. They have the opportunity to scrutinize cases prior to trial in ways that once were largely unavailable. Thus, as trials have decreased, pretrial activities have assumed many of the functions that were once performed at trials themselves. And as professionals have replaced untrained laypeople, some of the benefits provided by trials have declined.

Let me summarize the essence of my argument about the impact of professionalism. The trial declined in the latter part of the nineteenth century (in both England and the United States) at roughly the same time the criminal process was undergoing a transformation from a lay-administered process to one dominated by legally trained, full-time professionals. (It should be noted also that in the United States this transformation took place during the same period that the modern university-associated law school was rapidly expanding, and more generally during a period when the modern professions were gaining in strength and prestige [Larson 1977].) During this same period both pretrial procedures and the rules of evidence expanded in number and complexity. These various rules were designed in large to structure and restrict the power to lay decision makers, but they had the effect of giving greater authority to lawyers who could then exercise their expertise prior to trial. And as resources earmarked for criminal justice expanded, these professional decision makers had increased opportunity and incentive to use the pretrial process. Ironically, if I am correct, if resources for prosecutors and defense attorneys are further increased, one might expect an increase in negotiations and a further decrease in trials—precisely the opposite of what is often assumed!

Still, there is a troublesome problem. If, as I contend, plea bargaining is the result of an expansion of adversariness, why is plea bargaining so often perceived as a sign of decline, decay, or demise of the adversary system? Why do the old days of frequent trials appear to be preferable to the bargained justice of today? Let me suggest two reasons. The first I have already alluded to—the romantic yearning for a nonexistent yesterday. But in fact trials of, say, the nineteenth century were perfunctory affairs, where meaningful defenses were rarely offered and the accused was often dependent on the court.

Second, discontent is inherent and is a by-product of the rise of professionalism in general (Freidson 1970). Even as it fosters valuable talents that serve useful functions, professionalism brings with it a distinctive set of problems. Because of his or her own monopoly on information, training, access, and language, there is the danger that the (professional) agent becomes the master. Professionals foster client dependence, which in turn breeds discontent and suspicion. Furthermore, the technical language of professionals fosters rapid communication among themselves that is not easily understood by their clients, and as such links them together in a way that alienates professionals from clients. This tension is common in all walks of professional life. Patients are suspicious of doctors, homeowners of architects, students of teachers, and the like, but it creates special strains in an adversarial setting.

The evils of plea bargaining are asserted more frequently than they are documented (although undoubtedly a great many of them are real and deplorable), and the explanation, in part, is due to a suspicion and discontent with professionals in general. Ironically much of the discontent with the rapid and seemingly perfunctory decision making in the criminal courts may be an inevitable by-product of the *increased* resources available to the accused rather than any decrease in standards, practices, or capacity.

5. *Plea bargaining and the rise of public defense services.* There is one particular feature of the rise of professionalism that merits special attention. It is the expanded role and availability of defense counsel. Until well into the nineteenth century in England, defense counsel had only a limited role in felony trials. They could help prepare a defense but could not appear at trial (Langbein and Weinreb 1978). Thus throughout much of the period during which the criminal trial emerged in its modern form, counsel for the accused was not allowed to take part. Although the theory on which this exclusion rested was relaxed and eventually rejected in the nineteenth century, the actual impact of these changes was evolutionary, because most criminally accused could not afford counsel. In the United States the first legal-aid societies were formed in the late nineteenth century as services provided by ethnic organizations to help newly arrived immigrants. During the twentieth century, provision of defense counsel for the poor has expanded, first on a volunteer basis, then in many jurisdictions by legislation, and finally as a matter of constitutional right. I think there is a link between the expansion of this resource for the defense and the decline of the trial.

A perusal of accounts of criminal court proceedings when trials were common reveals a process that is difficult for the contemporary observer to recognize: those accused of criminal offenses—misdemeanor or felony alike—were typically rushed through crowded and noisy courts either subjected to a perfunctory trial lasting an hour or two or pressured to plead guilty by overbearing prosecutors whose practices were condoned by judges. All this took place without benefit of counsel. While expansion of the right to counsel has not provided all the benefits many had hoped for, the change has made a substantial difference in the ways criminal courts now operate. Current observers of American courts would be hard-pressed to find many of the practices that were commonplace when trials were more common. Seen from this perspective, the presence of an attorney who is able to *bargain* with the prosecutor constitutes something of a substantial increase in adversariness. The attorney's presence replaces intimidation with negotiation, domination with exchange. The very terms *negotiation* and *bargaining* imply that both the prosecutor and defense possess resources, a relationship that did not hold in a great many criminal cases when trials were more prevalent but the accused was more dependent. Even if defense attorneys do not pursue their tasks as vigorously as we would like, their collective presence and their familiarity with the courthouse all go a long way toward preventing the types of problems of dependence that once were commonplace. In this respect, whatever one thinks about plea bargaining, it is difficult to characterize it as ushering in the "twilight" of the adversary process. On the contrary, it appears to be a step toward a more evenly balanced relationship between the state and the accused, and as such it represents an increase not a decrease in adversariness.

CONCLUSION

My objective in this discussion is to demonstrate that plea bargaining has its roots in a host of often overlooked factors which are part and parcel of generally acknowledged improvements in the modern criminal process. That is, plea bargaining is a product of the very nature and structure of the modern criminal process rather than a result of extralegal factors or organizational pressures that have caused the criminal process to deviate from its true purposes. In elaborating this thesis, I do not mean to give the impression that I think plea bargaining is either inevitable or desirable. Indeed, I think it is neither. But I do want to emphasize that the factors that give rise to plea bargaining are intertwined with a host of factors that are generally regarded as highly desirable. In our quest for perfect justice, we have constructed an elaborate and costly criminal process. When this reality confronts the long-standing discretion granted to prosecutors, plea bargaining emerges. I do not believe that plea bargaining can be eliminated or even substantially reduced over the long run, without either significantly restricting prosecutors' discretion or relaxing the rigorous standards that currently infuse the criminal process. Despite a great deal of opposition to the practice of plea bargaining, I see little support for either type of these fundamental changes. More generally, the policy debate over plea bargaining has all too often taken place in a vacuum, neither placing bargaining in a broad perspective nor seriously contemplating the nature and implications of a criminal process that could handle cases expeditiously in the absence of plea bargaining. Nor, as I suggested at the outset, has plea bargaining been treated as part of a broader process of negotiation that permeates the entire criminal process. This no doubt goes a long way in explaining why so many policies banning plea bargaining have had such short lives.

NOTE

1. By plea bargaining I mean the waiver of the right to trial and the exchange of a guilty plea by the defendant for a promise of more lenient treatment than would be meted out if convicted at trial. Thus, I use the term generically to include several quite different types of bargaining—over the number of counts, the number and types of charges, the length of sentence, and the like. Plea bargaining can also take place at various stages of the pretrial process and involve different officials (for example, judges are more likely to be involved in sentence bargaining than in charge bargaining) which in turn can significantly affect the nature of this process. But whatever the structure, plea bargaining provides inducements to the accused for waiving their rights to trial or conversely provide threats of enhanced sanctions if they do not. It is this common feature that I wish to address here. I should also note

that there are a host of factors other than expeditious dispositions that can motivate prosecutors and defendants to negotiate pleas. In white-collar crime cases, considerations when prosecuting a low-level employee, where the investigation points to high-level corporate involvement, are different from considerations when prosecuting most ordinary street crime. Similarly, negotiating concessions with defendants who provide evidence against others is generally seen differently from negotiating with single defendants in isolated cases. This is not the place for an exhaustive catalog of types of and reasons for plea bargaining. Suffice it to say that this article focuses primarily on bargaining in so-called street crime cases not encumbered by the types of factors just suggested.

Even this relatively simple focus on plea bargaining is difficult to define operationally. Not all bargains are explicit (many jurisdictions have implicit bargaining—going rates for those who plead guilty to certain offenses), nor are all guilty pleas bargained (there are a host of reasons for pleading guilty). Furthermore, not all negotiations involve "bargains" (charges may be reduced because a defense attorney has convinced the prosecutor that the original charges cannot be sustained; many negotiations result in dropping *all* charges—without the quid pro quo normally associated with the term bargaining). While these and other factors mean that any operational definition must necessarily be fuzzy, my discussion here is aimed at the core and less ambiguous cases. It should be noted, however, that scholars have not given adequate attention to the process of dropping *all* charges. This is too bad, since what little evidence there is suggests that in these cases the structure and process of negotiation are not appreciably different from negotiation in those which result in guilty pleas (Feeley 1979; Utz 1978). This suggests that plea bargaining may be more principled than is ordinarily thought. For insightful reflections on the principled nature of negotiation, see Eisenberg (1976) and Utz (1978).

REFERENCES

ALSCHULER, ALBERT W. (1968) "The Prosecutor's Role in Plea Bargaining." 36 *University of Chicago Law Review* 50.

——— (1975) "The Defense Attorney's Role in Plea Bargaining." 84 *Yale Law Journal* 1179.

——— (1976) "The Trial Judge's Role in Plea Bargaining." 76 *Columbia Law Review* 1059.

——— (1979) "Plea Bargaining and Its History." 13 *Law and Society Review* 211.

BLUMBERG, ABRAHAM (1967) *Criminal Justice*. New York: Quadrangle.

CHURCH, THOMAS, JR. (1976) "Plea Bargains, Concessions and the Courts: Analysis of a Quasi-Experiment." 10 *Law and Society Review* 377.

COLE, GEORGE (1970) "The Decision to Prosecute." 4 *Law and Society Review* 331.

DAMASKA, MIRJAN (1973) "Evidentiary Barriers to Conviction and Two Models of Criminal Procedure: A Contemporary Study." 121 *University of Pennsylvania Law Review* 506.

DAVIS, KENNETH CULP (1971) *Discretionary Justice: A Preliminary Inquiry*. Urbana: University of Illinois Press.

DAVIS, WILLIAM, II (1974) "*Nolle Prosequi* in the Sixth Circuit Court: Prosecutor Discretion to Dispense with Charge." Paper on file at the Yale Law Library.

EISENBERG, MELVIN A. (1976) "Private Ordering Through Negotiation: Dispute Settlement and Rule Making." 89 *Harvard Law Review* 376.

EISENSTEIN, JAMES, and HERBERT JACOB (1977) *Felony Justice*. Boston: Little, Brown.

FEELEY, MALCOLM M. (1975) "The Effects of Heavy Caseloads." Paper presented at the annual conference of the American Political Science Association.

——— (1979) *The Process Is the Punishment: Handling Cases in a Lower Criminal Court*. New York: Russell Sage Foundation.

FLEMING, MACKLIN (1974) *The Price of Perfect Justice*. New York: Basic Books.

FRIEDMAN, LAWRENCE (1979) "Plea Bargaining in Historical Perspective." 13 *Law and Society Review* 247.

FRIEDMAN, LAWRENCE M., and ROBERT V. PERCIVAL (1981) *The Roots of Justice: Crime and Punishment in Alameda County, California 1870–1910.* Chapel Hill: University of North Carolina Press.

FRIEDSON, ELIOT (1970) *Professional Dominance.* Chicago: Aldine Publishing Co.

GOLDSTEIN, ABRAHAM S. (1981) *The Passive Judiciary.* Baton Rouge: Louisiana State University Press.

——— and MARTIN MARCUS (1977) "The Myth of Judicial Supervision in Three 'Inquisitorial' Systems: France, Italy and Germany." 87 *Yale Law Journal* 240.

HALLER, MARK (1970) "Urban Crime and Criminal Justice: The Chicago Case." 57 *Journal of American History* 619.

——— (1978) *Plea Bargaining: The Experiences of Prosecutors, Judges, and Defense Attorneys.* Chicago: University of Chicago Press.

——— (1979) "Comment: Urban Courts." 13 *Law and Society Review* 273.

HEUMANN, MILTON (1975) "A Note on Plea Bargaining and Case Pressure." 9 *Law and Society Review* 515.

——— and COLIN LOFTIN (1979) "Mandatory Sentencing and Abolition of Plea Bargaining: The Michigan Felony Firearms Statute." 13 *Law and Society Review* 373.

LANGBEIN, JOHN H. (1974a) "Controlling Prosecutorial Discretion in Germany." 41 *University of Chicago Law Review* 445.

——— (1974b) *Prosecuting Crime in the Renaissance: England, Germany, and France.* Cambridge, Mass.: Harvard University Press.

——— (1978) "The Criminal Trial Before the Lawyers." 45 *University of Chicago Law Review* 263.

——— (1979) "Land Without Plea Bargaining: How the Germans Do It." 78 *Michigan Law Review* 204.

——— and LLOYD WEINREB (1978) "Continental Criminal Procedure: Myth and Reality." 87 *Yale Law Journal* 1549.

LARSON, MAGALI S. (1977) *The Rise of Professionalism: A Sociological Analysis.* Berkeley: University of California Press.

MATHER, LYNN (1979) *Plea Bargaining or Trial.* Lexington, Mass.: Lexington Books.

MILLER, HERBERT S., WILLIAM F. McDONALD, and JAMES A. CRAMER (1978) *Plea Bargaining in the United States.* Washington, D.C.: National Institute of Justice.

MOLEY, RAYMOND (1928) "The Vanishing Trial Jury." 2 *Southern California Law Review* 97.

NARDULLI, PETER (1978) *The Courtroom Elite.* Cambridge, Mass.: Ballinger Publishing Co.

——— (ed.) (1979a) *The Study of Criminal Courts: Political Perspectives.* Cambridge, Mass.: Ballinger Publishing Co.

——— (1979b) "The Caseload Controversy and the Study of Criminal Courts." 70 *Journal of Criminal Law and Criminology* 125.

ROSETT, ARTHUR, and DONALD CRESSEY (1976) *Justice by Consent.* Philadelphia: Lippincott.

RUBENSTEIN, MICHAEL, and TERRESSA WHITE (1979) "Plea Bargaining: The Alaska Experience." 13 *Law and Society Review* 367.

SKOLNICK, JEROME (1967) "Social Control in the Adversary System." 11 *Journal of Conflict Resolution* 52.

UTZ, PAMELA (1978) *Settling the Facts.* Lexington, Mass.: Lexington Books.

VERA INSTITUTE (1981) *Felony Arrests: Their Prosecution and Disposition in New York City.* Rev. ed. New York: Longman.

WEINREB, LLOYD (1977) *Denial of Justice.* New York: Free Press.

ARTICLE TWENTY-FOUR

Sentencing Alternatives: Development, Implementation, Issues, and Evaluation

PHILIP W. HARRIS/ALAN T. HARLAND

Throughout American history, incarceration has been the expected disposition for most felons and serious misdemeants. Philip W. Harris and Alan T. Harland argue that although in recent decades alternatives to incarceration have become part of the sentencing repertoire, they have been applied primarily to offenders who were not likely to have been incarcerated in the first place.

The topic of criminal sentencing has undergone a pronounced shift in status in recent years. In 1972, Judge Marvin Frankel described the imposition of sentence as "probably the most critical point in our system of administering justice," but pointed out the tragic incongruity "that we weave the most elaborate procedures to safeguard the rights of those who stand trial, but then treat as a casual anticlimax the perfunctory process of deciding whether, and for how long, the defendant will be locked away or 'treated.'"[1]

Throughout the 1970s and continuing unabatedly in the 1980s, however, we have seen an explosion of academic, legislative, and professional interest in sentencing issues. Whether prompted by public or professional concerns about inequity, inefficacy, or inefficiency in sentencing practices, the resultant outpouring of scholarly works, research projects, and statutory and administrative reforms has elevated the sentencing func-

Source: Judicature 68 (December 1984/January 1985): 211–219. By permission of the authors.

tion to a position of indisputable prominence in current criminal justice debate.

Predictably, dissatisfaction with existing policies, procedures, and programs has given the quest for "sentencing alternatives" an especially central position. Indeed, the topic has become an almost routine addition to professional conference agendas in recent years, and a number of "national" organizations have been founded to develop and propagate information and expertise about the latest and most promising approaches.[2] At the heart of all this activity may be seen an attempt to supply criminal justice professionals with the very "best" sentencing strategies, responding to their putative demands, and those of the public, for alternatives that "work."

The question of what works, however, leads to a complex set of underlying issues which themselves require separate treatment and which generally fall into categories of effectiveness (will this alternative work under *any* circumstances?) and implementation (can this alternative be installed under *specific* circumstances in such a way that it has a chance of working?). One clear indicator of the complexity of these issues is the widespread tendency among criminal justice professionals to equate the many reforms categorized as sentencing alternatives with the very few that can be said to operate as alternatives to incarceration. Although almost any of the sentencing reforms currently under consideration, such as community service, might be used as alternatives to incarceration, especially to shorter jail terms, they can obviously also be used as alternatives to probation, alternatives to each other, or alternatives to doing nothing at all.

What little empirical evidence we have suggests that most recent reform efforts have not resulted in the use of alternative dispositions for offenders who would previously have been incarcerated. Rather, sanctions such as restitution and community service appear to have been used almost entirely as additional conditions imposed upon offenders who would otherwise have received more traditional probation orders.[3]

What can be concluded from this confusion of aims is that sentencing alternatives intended as alternatives to incarceration but distributed among offenders who would not previously have been incarcerated can be viewed as effective or ineffective depending on the evaluative criteria applied. If we apply the aim of reducing the prison population, the reforms will likely be judged a failure. If, on the other hand, one wishes to see offenders be made more accountable to their victims as opposed to simply serving time or having occasional contact with a probation officer, success in getting *any* offenders to pay restitution may be viewed as a success.

This shift in aims illustrates one of several problems of implementation. Our intent in this article is to underscore the importance of clarifying the aims of recommended reforms, to highlight the need for increased attention to issues of implementation, and to focus attention on the necessary interplay between aims of sentencing alternatives and the implementation process.[4]

THE SEARCH FOR EFFECTIVE ALTERNATIVES

When interest is expressed by decision makers in increasing the range of available sentencing options, their inquiries are frequently framed as concern for finding ones that "work." What is regarded as effectiveness is often couched with considerable skepticism in terms that imply that new sentencing options must be "as good" as prison or "better" than other traditional sanctions, most usually probation. The precise meaning of such evaluative statements is rarely made explicit, however, permitting assumptions that a greater degree of consensus exists about system goals and the nature and priority of problems to be addressed than may actually be the case.

Addressing the question of effectiveness requires the obvious but often slighted step of supplying answers to the implied question "works in terms of what?" or "as good at doing what?" The task is to compare various options along dimensions contained in a statement of desirable outcome. For example, substantive options might be compared in terms of the amount of suffering they inflict upon offenders (retribution), their potential for discouraging others from committing the same offense (general deterrence), or in terms of reducing recidivism (specific deterrence/rehabilitation/incapacitation). Procedural options might be compared in terms of their impact on reducing unwarranted disparity and guaranteeing that similarly situated offenders are handled similarly.

The variety of possible responses reflects the myriad of normative and functional goals which impinge upon policy decisions in the criminal justice system. Public safety, crime control, and retribution are normative expectations against which various sentencing options can be compared. Corresponding functional goals include relative performance with respect to concerns such as costs, efficient case processing, and maintaining power and public image by key decision makers.

When the range of logical and empirical issues expressed in such a comparative exercise is combined with the potentially large number of key actors for whom their salience must first be assessed, the complexity of the innovation task is made clear. Each potential option must be compared on each of the dimensions identified and assessed in terms of its relative advantage with respect to specific goals and the salience of those goals to key policy makers and practitioners.

In the face of such complexity, a common response is to attempt accommodation of a range of aims and interests, thus avoiding debilitating conflict and assuring widespread support for the innovation. Support for California's Determinate Sentencing Law, for instance, arose from an interest among law enforcement personnel in seeing an increase in the prison commitment rate.[5] This aim was achieved, however, as a result of their also supporting reduced sentence lengths, an interest expressed by judges and liberal legislators.

What concerns policy analysts observing these developments is the variety of contradictory evaluation criteria which emerge. Success will be defined by one group in terms of an increase in the number of offenders being committed to prison, while those who supported the innovation out of concern for excessive and disparate sentences are likely to view success in terms of equality in sentencing and an overall reduction in time served. Absent common criteria for assessing success, it is likely that conflict will occur regarding retention of the innovation. Of more fundamental concern, however, is the possibility that the system's capacity to develop and implement future innovations will be curtailed as a consequence of increased conflict and mistrust.

AN IMPLEMENTATION PERSPECTIVE

Current crises in both probation and institutional corrections have greatly stimulated efforts to increase the range of sentencing options, accommodating a wide variety of values and goals expressed by decision makers. Such options have included community service, paying restitution to victims, home-arrest and/or wearing an electrical monitoring device, intensive supervision in the community, and a variety of treatment and educational programs. Ignored entirely, however, has been our ability to implement reforms in intended ways. While it is of critical importance that information regarding procedures and policies which succeed be disseminated, replication is not simply a matter of adoption. Failure to recognize the complexity of the implementation process nearly guarantees failure of the policy, procedure, or program.

Pennsylvania, for example, attempted to replicate Minnesota's highly touted sentencing guidelines and experienced failure largely due to unrecognized political and cultural differences and the absence of a key ingredient in Minnesota's success—a commitment to rationalize the sentencing process.[6] Clearly, innovations are not successful in and of themselves. Environmental conditions largely determine eventual outcome, thus making it as important to design the implementation process with a clear sense of what conditions will facilitate or impede adoption as it is to design an innovation with a specific set of objectives in mind.

From an implementation perspective, it is possible to envisage several possible outcomes of an implementation process: implementation of a policy or program as designed; implementation of a modified version of the original design; implementation of a policy or program that bears little or no resemblance to the original design; or no eventual implementation. Each of these outcomes can be linked to any of the following reform outcomes: success with regard to the original set of goals; failure with regard to the original goals; success regarding a different set of goals (unintended positive consequences); and failure with regard to a different set of goals (unintended negative consequences). The desirable combinations of the above outcomes are implementation outcomes 1 or 2 with reform outcome 1; that is, the implemented reform reflects the original design and its objectives are being achieved.

Past experience has shown that other outcome combinations are dismayingly likely. As Doleschal has pointed out in his disheartening review of a variety of criminal justice reforms, one can easily take the position that reform of any kind is a futile and dysfunctional activity.[7] He notes that pretrial diversion programs have been used by court officials to widen rather than shrink the net of social control. For example, he reports, the San Pablo Adult Diversion Project, designed to reduce both the extent and cost of incarceration, in fact had no impact on the use of incarceration and was more costly than previous processing of offenders.[8] The same has held true in evaluations of restitution projects, community service programs, community correction programs, and probation subsidy programs.[9]

The probability of success, even under the best of circumstances, is small. As Pressman and Wildavsky have noted, each decision point and each requirement for consent slightly decreases the probability of successful implementation.[10] Consistent with this observation, Mathias and Steelman have noted that among options for reducing prison population, sentencing reforms (front-door options) are more difficult to implement than options involving early or graduated release from incarceration (back-door options), mainly due to the larger number of decision makers (police, prosecutors, judges) whose cooperation and support must be enlisted.[11] Great care is therefore needed in assessing the merits of the original designs of sentencing options and in maintaining sufficient control over the implementation process.

COURTS AS ORGANIZATIONS

With regard to court systems, Nimmer has noted that "policies cannot be enforced without cooperation from everyone in the judiciary."[12] While at first glance this conclusion may appear overstated, it points to an observation frequently reported by students of the judicial system that informal accommodations developed and practiced by key decision makers are consistently and tenaciously protected and enforced.[13]

A variety of perspectives on the criminal justice system, including those that stress organizational theory, others that take a more functional view, and recent writings on organizational environments, have in common characterizations of this system as fragmented, diverse in its values and goals, dominated by informal relationships, and politically vulnerable.[14] Within court systems in particular, it has been observed that an absence of hierarchical authority, a need to maintain a smooth flow of cases, and a sense of professional power interact to support a subculture in which informal accommodations and relationships are well defined and compliance is demanded. Given the tenuousness of these arrangements, deviation from status quo is strongly resisted. Indeed, Feeley has suggested that court systems are not only resistant to change but are unlikely to even consider change as an option.[15]

One example of this complex impediment to reform is provided by Grau's analysis of an attempt to introduce a community service restitution program in Austin, Texas.[16] Prosecutors, defense counsel, probation officers, judges, and Austin's bar association all had vested interests in maintaining the status quo and strongly resisted adoption of the new program. Prosecution control of sentencing, a substantial income from fines, established bargaining agreements, and other well-embedded informal accommodations were perceived as threatened by the proposed reform. Furthermore, defense attorneys expressed fear that judges would use this alternative sentence as an *added* penalty. As one might expect, only nominal adoption was achieved.

Within this organizational climate, tolerance of debate regarding normative values is unlikely to be readily forthcoming. The need to protect existing resources, power structures, and case-flow mechanisms in an environment where external political pressures can easily disrupt the status quo suppresses an exchange of views that may further expose internal conflict, undermine the existing system of accommodations and constraints, and provide critics of the system with new ammunition.

PERSPECTIVES ON IMPLEMENTATION

The process of policy and program implementation has become a major focus of attention largely resulting from a recently developed awareness that how one implements a reform may have as much or more to do with its success than its substantive design. While we have yet to see a theory of implementation, several perspectives on the implementation process have been developed which have advanced our understanding and capacity to plan effectively.

Berman, for example, has distinguished programmed implementation from an adaptive process.[17] On the one hand it can be argued that a highly structured process ensures program fidelity, thus increasing the likelihood of achieving program objectives. Alternatively, an adaptive approach begins with a loosely structured policy or procedure and allows the innovation to take shape during the implementation process. While the latter approach may increase the probability of adoption, it also increases the probability that any original objectives will be irrelevant to the final product.

Grau illustrates this dilemma through an analysis of implementation of a community resource brokerage program in the probation department of Tacoma, Washington.[18] This program, which replaces traditional probation caseloads with a program in which teams of specialists manage pooled probationer caseloads, was seen as a valuable innovation in the face of excessively large individual caseloads and decreasing financial resources. An attempt by the probation director to implement the entire model without involving his staff in the decision was met with considerable resentment and resistance, eventually resulting in the director's resignation. His replacement wisely adopted a strategy of full participation in deciding on adoption of this new program, thus slowing down the process considerably. The outcome of the implementation process, however, was a program which varied greatly from the original design: probation officers retained their caseloads, while specialization was limited to developing contacts and information in specific areas which could be shared among their fellow officers.

A more complex typology of perspectives on implementation is provided by Majone and Wildavsky.[19] After discussing versions of the two views addressed in Berman's more recent work, they advocate a perspective termed "evolutionary implementation." This view takes into account the dynamic interaction between a changing environment and evolving policy ideas, leaving room during the implementation process for correcting defects in the original policy. More in keeping with an action research model, this perspective recognizes change as a constant and inevitable process, both for the views and objectives reflected in an innovation and for the system adopting the innovation. Program designs, then, must be responsive to these changes; programs must evolve in order to survive.

A final and very useful view of implementation has been put forward by Elmore and by Fudge and Barrett.[20] Implementation is described by these writers as a process of negotiation. Recognizing that conflict and compromise are inherent to complex organizations and that political intentions are expressed by proposed policies and programs, bargaining becomes a key activity of implementation during which agreements and procedures are negotiated until the program finally takes shape. This view of implementation carries with it a distinct message of acceptance, acceptance of and respect for traditional or institutionalized processes of planned change within complex systems. Crucial to this process, however, is stability of the bargaining structure; changes in roles and personnel require new negotiations, thus adding to the cost and complexity of implementation.

THE "LAW" OF ADAPTATION

It has long been recognized that no policy or program is implemented without experiencing some degree of modification. Any new program will impinge upon protected interests, reactions to which can range from sabotage or neutralization of the change to enthusiastic adoption. While not all of these reactions nor the final shape of the innovation can be predicted, two issues suggest that an attempt to account for this adaptation process is a necessary element of the planning process.

First, it has been suggested that broad participation in planning and implementation enhances the probability of successful adaption of a program. Themes such as ownership over decisions and commitment have been central to the organizational change literature for many years along with substantial empirical support. Recent writings, however, have presented possible disadvantages to extensive participation. Zaltman and Duncan generally, and Grau with regard to probation reform, have shown that extensive program modification may result from efforts to account for the interests of subordinates in an organization.[21] In Grau's report of the community resource brokerage program, for instance, the program as implemented only vaguely resembled the original model. It is thus necessary to balance the perceived need for broad participation against tolerable limits of program redesign.

A further and more crucial issue, however, is that of fidelity. Yin has suggested that if a program has undergone marked redesign during the implementation process, evaluations are likely to be based upon irrelevant objectives.[22] As the program undergoes modification in order to maximize its "fit" within the existing system (that is, in order to minimize its impact on the status quo), the set of objectives manifest in the program actually installed may vary tremendously from those intended by its originators. Evaluation must then include an assessment of those objectives which can realistically be served by the program as well as those expressed by its implementors.

As a step in this evaluation process, recent studies have demonstrated the importance of measuring the extent of implementation. Palumbo, for example, compared thirty-six counties of Oregon in terms of the extent to which new community corrections legislation was being implemented and the relation between extent of implementation and variation in goal achievement.[23] Using a variety of quantitative and qualitative measures, he found wide variation in level of implementation and great success in achieving several policy goals among those counties at higher levels of implementation. For instance, counties which achieved relatively higher degrees of implementation had reduced commitments of felons to prison while commitments of the same category of felons within low integration counties had increased. Fidelity and policy or program impact interact in such a way, then, that failure to account for this interaction can lead to faulty assessments of outcomes.

PHASES OF INNOVATION

One conceptual tool that has facilitated control of the adaptation process as well as implementation planning in general has been the description of implementation as a series of stages or phases, each of which has its own objectives, obstacles and task structures. Zaltman and Duncan, for instance, divide the entire innovation process into two stages, initiation and implementation. The initiation stage is further subdivided to include awareness of a need for change, exploration of alternative solutions, and a decision to adopt a particular solution.

A similar model is used by Mathias and Steelman in their assessment of methods for reducing prison populations: development, enactment, and implementation are each distinguished in the process of change.[24] During the development process, available options are objectively presented and carefully considered, with broad constituent involvement to ensure future understanding and cooperation. Compromise and negotiation are key to this process in order to obtain broad acceptance of the option selected.

Enactment is the selling phase, during which information regarding the selected option is widely disseminated, especially to key decision makers. Influential allies are cultivated and enlisted as supporters, including editorial staff from the media.

Finally, implementation becomes a highly structured process within which lines of communication are established, offender selection criteria are developed, and roles are delineated. It is during implementation that continual performance measures are taken and results of these assessments reported periodically to the public, key officials, and funding sources.

Mathias and Steelman illustrate these stages of the innovation process by analyzing fourteen different reforms in twelve states. For example, development of Delaware's Supervised Custody Program (SCP), a phased reentry program for incarcerated offenders, resulted from dissatisfaction with a poorly administered extended furlough program. A new corrections commissioner, with established credibility at the state level, designed the program with several key staff by means of a brainstorming process. While enactment was greatly facilitated by their being able to present a highly structured program, considerable effort was made by the commissioner to personally lobby community organizations and government leaders. Press conferences, open support from the governor, and editorial support from the press all aided greatly in obtaining enabling legislation and public support.

Implementation involved provision of procedures for selection of inmates for the SCP, an orientation program for inmates, availability of temporary work release centers, criteria for approval of living and working arrangements, and rules for supervision during participation in the program.

One can observe from this process both the need to open many avenues of communication during all three stages and to prepare well for successive stages of the process. In keeping with Zaltman and Duncan's theoretical contributions, it should also be noted that the development process is greatly enhanced by a complex and decentralized decision-making structure, while implementation itself requires a much tighter structure with lines of authority and behavioral expectations clearly established.[25]

Yin has added a further element to the process by distinguishing his "phases" from "stages" of other models and by distinguishing policy from program.[26] Phases can, and typically do, overlap while stages build on each other, each requiring completion prior to moving on to the next. Furthermore, programs are seen as operationalized policies, implemented programs being concrete examples of program design.

In this four-phase model, development and implementation begin with a policy development phase, during which new legislation is passed or a new policy is established. Typically this phase ends with a set of new directives or regulations which must be acted upon. The second phase, then, involves program development, in which projects are assigned to existing units or project awards are made to external contractors. Project design, the third phase, involves articulation of aims, methods, organizational structure, and procedures. Action and outcome are elements of project implementation, the final phase. This is the point in the process where presumptive sentences are issued and monitored (as in the case of Minnesota's Sentencing Guidelines)[27] or where prisoners begin reentry furloughs (as in the case of Connecticut's community reintegration program).[28]

The value of Yin's perspective is that the tasks within each phase follow a pattern of goal-setting and implementation that is repeated in all four phases. Moreover, the phase model helps clarify the process of adaptation as one of increasing clarity, beginning with a clearly articulated but abstract policy and moving toward more differentiated and specific objectives and actions.

While different forms of resistance, different strategies and tactics, and different resources and actors become relevant at each phase, the entire process depends upon a sense of direction spelled out in the first phase. Program development evolves from successful policy development, and selection from among program proposals depends upon a clear sense of what the program should be designed to accomplish.

Even with the benefit of clear objectives, slippage will occur. During each phase of implementation, adaptations will be required that will alter the original policy or program statement. An awareness of this process and monitoring of modifications that take place, however, make possible eventual evaluation relevant to realistic and well-articulated objectives.

CONCLUSION

As Empey once observed, the entire criminal justice process, from arrest to termination of parole, is a correctional process.[29] Viewed from this perspective, it is possible to imagine a system where common objectives can be established for all components of the system. Too often, though, policy and program goals are absent or vaguely stated, thus contributing little to our capacity to achieve normative goals. Implementing new options without the benefit of clearly stated goals can only feed our growing sense of futility. Programs will be implemented only to be criticized for not succeeding to achieve objectives which they were never designed to achieve, others will be neutralized as a result of having been developed and implemented through a process in which conflicting and competing goals were accommodated.

Maintaining a dialogue around normative goals is of value in itself. Its purpose need not be to arrive at consensus; its value lies in focusing attention on the fundamental aims of our system of justice and on our ability to achieve those aims. In fact, as Wright has eloquently argued,[30] goal conflict is likely to be beneficial. Such conflicts present continual challenges to the status quo, and, in particular, serve to sustain minority interests. What is not desirable, however, is a decision-making process in which conflict is avoided, where no dialogue around normative values takes place. Neither the failures of past reforms nor the inevitability of goal conflict can excuse policy makers and reformers from debating and attempting to articulate their goals, from stating explicitly those outcomes deemed desirable.[31]

The difficulty lies in discovering ways to develop the capacity and willingness to openly debate, prioritize, and test both normative and functional goals. Gottfredson and Gottfredson have suggested that we begin by taking a closer look at what we actually do.[32] Empirically derived sentencing guidelines, for example, which reflect a normative decision pattern also, by implication, expose policy. Such goal specificity as is gained through the development and use of guidelines enables decision makers to debate the merits of the policies implied and, consequently, to make rational revisions.

An additional mechanism which has accompanied the implementation of sentencing guidelines and which greatly facilitates policy formation, implementation, and evaluation is the sentencing commission. This approach, although carrying with it a clear element of coercion, has the advantage of championing particular policies from outside the primary decision-making structure as well as maintaining a broad system perspective while monitoring and supporting implementation of reform efforts.[33]

We are beginning to develop a cautious sense of confidence in our ability at least to test our potential for reform. The mutterings of dismayed reformers have begun to be replaced by voices suggesting that we not give up on our reformist ambitions prematurely.[34] In addition, the last decade has witnessed the development of a critical set of skills in the implementation of policies and programs. It is now clear that knowing how to put into action a well-designed program is equally as important as having the skills to design a program that has the potential to achieve its objectives. Both the development and implementation of sentencing options, however, including the vital step of broad and continuous participation in debate over criteria for defining what "works," may be enhanced by a clearer awareness of the organizational and political context in which reform occurs.

NOTES

1. Frankel, *Criminal Sentences: Law Without Order* (New York: Hill & Wang, 1972), p. vii.

2. Examples include the National Institute for Sentencing Alternatives, Ford Hall, Brandeis University, Waltham, Mass. 02154; the National Center on Institutions and Alternatives, 814 N. Saint Asaph Street, Alexandria, Va. 22314; and the Prison Overcrowding Project of the Center for Effective Public Policy, 1701 Arch Street, Suite 100, Philadelphia, Pa. 19103.

3. Blumstein et al., eds., *Research on Sentencing: Summary Report* (Washington, D.C.: U.S. Department of Justice, December 1983), p. 36.

4. A. T. Harland and P. W. Harris, "Developing and Implementing Alternatives to Incarceration: A Problem of Planned Change in Criminal Justice," 1984 *University of Illinois Law Review* 319.

5. J. D. Casper and D. Brereton, "Evaluating Criminal Justice Reforms," 18 *Law and Society Review* 121 (1984).

6. See Martin, "The Politics of Sentencing Reform: Sentencing Guidelines in Minnesota and Pennsylvania," in Blumstein, Cohen, Martin, and Tonry, eds., *Research on Sentencing: The Search for Reform*, vol. 2 (Washington, D.C.: National Academy of Sciences, 1983).

7. Doleschal, "The Dangers of Criminal Justice Reform," *Criminal Just. Abstracts* (1982), p. 134.

8. Ibid.

9. Ibid., p. 135.

10. Pressman and Wildavsky, *Implementation*, 2nd ed. (Berkeley: University of California Press, 1979).

11. Mathias and Steelman, "Controlling Prison Populations: An Assessment of Current Mechanisms" (Unpublished report prepared for the National Council on Crime and Delinquency, 1981.)

12. Nimmer, *The Nature of System Change* (Chicago: American Bar Foundation, 1978).

13. See, for example, Baar, "The Scope and Limits of Court Reform," and Burnstein, "Criminal Case Processing from an Organizational Perspective: Current Research Trends," 5 *Justice System Journal* 258, 274 (1980).

14. Ibid. See also, Feeley, *Court Reform on Trial: Why Simple Solutions Fail* (New York: Basic Books, 1983); and Nimmer, *Nature of System Change*.

15. Feeley, p. 192.

16. Grau, "The Limits of Planned Change in Courts," 6 *Justice System Journal* 84, 99 (1981).

17. Berman, "Thinking About Programmed and Adaptive Implementation: Matching Strategies to Situations," in Ingram and Mann, eds., *Why Policies Fail* (Beverly Hills, Calif.: Sage Publications, 1982).

18. Grau, "Limits of Planned Change."

19. Majone and Wildavsky, "Implementation as Evolution," in Pressman and Wildavsky, *Implementation*.

20. Elmore, "Organizational Models of Social Program Implementation," 26 *Public Policy* 185, 228 (1978); Barrett and Fudge, eds., *Policy and Action: Essays on the Implementation of Policy* (London and New York: Methuen, 1981).

21. Zaltman and Duncan, *Strategies for Planned Change* (New York: John Wiley, 1977): Grau, "Limits of Planned Change."

22. Yin, "Lessons About Federal Implementation" (unpublished mimeo, Cambridge Department of Urban Studies and Planning, M.I.T., 1981).

23. Palumbo, Moody, and Wright, "Measuring Degrees of Successful Implementation: Achieving Policy Versus Statutory Goals," 8 *Evaluation Review* 1, 45 (1984).

24. Mathias and Steelman, "Controlling Prison Populations."

25. For an excellent analysis involving application of this framework, see Galegher and Carroll, "Voluntary Sentencing Guidelines: Prescription for Justice or Patent Medicine?" 7 *Human Behavior* 393, 396 (1983).

26. Yin, "Planning for Implementation" (Draft mimeo, Case Study Institute, Washington, D.C., 1982).

27. Ibid., p. 9.

28. Mathias and Steelman, "Controlling Prison Populations," p. 15.

29. Empey, *Alternatives to Incarceration* (Washington, D.C.: U.S. Government Printing Office, 1967).

30. Wright, "The Desirability of Goal Conflict Within the Criminal Justice System," 9 *Journal of Criminal Justice* 3, 209 (1981).

31. For a discussion of purposeful avoidance of clarifying goals, see Nakamura and Smallwood, *The Policies of Policy Implementation* (New York: St. Martin's Press, 1980).

32. Gottfredson and Gottfredson, "Guidelines for Incarceration Decisions: A Partisan Review" (unpublished paper presented at Symposium on Sentencing Alternatives, Johns Hopkins University, Baltimore, Maryland, April, 1984); see also Galegher and Carroll, *Voluntary Sentencing Guidelines.*

33. For an excellent discussion of the Minnesota Guidelines Commission, see Galegher and Carroll, *Voluntary Sentencing Guidelines.* See also, Knapp, "What Sentencing Reform in Minnesota Has and Has Not Accomplished," 68 *Judicature* 181 (1984).

34. See, for example, Gottfredson, "The Social Scientist and Rehabilitative Crime Policy," 20 *Criminology* 36 (1982).

ARTICLE TWENTY-FIVE

Determinate Sentencing and Prison Crowding in Illinois

JONATHAN D. CASPER

The past decade has been characterized by a doubling of the U.S. prison population and the passing of determinate sentencing legislation in a number of states. Have the new laws contributed to the growth of the prison population? Jonathan Casper examines this question with reference to changes that occurred in Illinois. He finds that the elimination of discretionary release on parole has contributed to crowding. This is one example of the unanticipated consequences of policy change.

The doubling of prison populations within the past decade in Illinois and the nation as a whole is the product of a complex variety of events and processes. One is the brute demographic fact that particularly large birth cohorts—the so-called "baby boom" generations—are now passing through the periods of their lives when they are particularly likely to be sent to prison.[1] Another is the growth of public sentiment favoring increased punitiveness in sentencing. Not only have judges sensed and responded to this sentiment, but state legislatures have passed a variety of mandatory minimum-sentence laws requiring the imposition of prison terms (for example, the "use-a-gun-go-to-prison" statutes passed in so many jurisdictions, or the Class X felony provisions in Illinois). Another development that may have contributed to prison crowding has been the shift to determinate sentencing in several states, including Illinois.

For a variety of reasons, one may plausibly argue that the move to

Source: *University of Illinois Law Review* 1984: 231–252. Reprinted by permission of the publisher.

determinate sentences may have contributed to the growth of prison overcrowding. After a brief discussion of the context surrounding passage of determinate sentence legislation, this article presents arguments and data dealing with the possible connection between determinate sentencing and crowding. The article concludes with a discussion of some alternative policies that deal with the possible connection between determinate sentencing and prison overcrowding.

POLICY MAKING IN CRIMINAL JUSTICE AND THE ADOPTION OF DETERMINATE SENTENCE LAWS

No field of public policy has been more characterized by controversy over goals, symbolic politics, and unintended consequences than the area of criminal justice. At the root of the problem lies basic disagreement and confusion about the very purposes of criminal justice institutions. As Herbert Packer argues, our goals for the criminal justice system are often in conflict and the policies they prescribe for activity by its institutions lack coherence.[2] At one end of the spectrum are the so-called *crime control* values: the sense that the basic purpose of institutions of law enforcement, adjudication, and correction is crime reduction, and the assertion that their processes ought to be structured to produce the maximum amount of crime control. At the other end are the values of *due process:* the belief that the rules governing the behavior of criminal justice institutions ought to focus upon minimizing errors (most particularly the error of apprehending, convicting, or punishing the citizen who is innocent) and upon protecting the privacy and dignity of citizens from excessive intervention in their lives by law enforcement personnel.[3] The result of this tension is both a great deal of disagreement over criminal justice policies (for example, the amount of discretion police should have in gathering evidence against suspects) as well as ambiguous signals to those who work in such institutions as to what constitutes appropriate behavior.

This fundamental tension in values is not the only source of complexity in the criminal justice area. Symbolic politics has played a very prominent role as well.[4] Citizens are justifiably concerned about the possibility of becoming victims of crime. Policy makers have often embraced policies which appear to make the criminal justice system better able to apprehend, convict, and punish defendants but which in reality have little chance of producing such effects. Thus, for example, our policies dealing with sentencing have long had a "bark and bite" quality. The "bark" has been the very high nominal maximum terms imposed by the legislature, while their "bite"—the terms actually served by those sentenced to prison—have been substantially less than the statutorily established maximum terms. Legislators and governors have reaped the political support that emerges from being tough on crime, while neither they nor the society at large has had to face up to the actual costs of sending people to prison for periods approaching the maximum terms.

Another example of such symbolic policy making involves the increased reliance upon mandatory minimum-sentence laws.[5] Legislation requiring imprisonment of all defendants convicted of weapons possession, drug sales, or multiple commission of certain crimes has been touted as providing a means of reducing the crime rate in general. The evidence for such assertions is less than persuasive, because our ability to predict future criminal behavior is imprecise, and our prison capacities are not so large as to accommodate enough offenders to make an appreciable dent in the overall crime rate. Moreover, such policies routinely meet resistance and adaptation on the part of courtroom work-group participants—prosecutors, public defenders, and judges—who believe that these policies are either undesirable on normative grounds or are likely to interfere with the plea negotiation process and the production of large numbers of guilty pleas. The political benefits flowing from such policies, though, emerge not from their actually *producing* crime control effects, but simply from their *passage.* Thus, the incentives for these policies being adopted with great public fanfare remain substantial, quite independent of whether the policies produce the suggested effects. In this manner, innovation in criminal justice policy making often produces substantive benefits to officeholders and aspirants, but largely symbolic rewards to concerned constituents. Both liberals and conservatives have urged a variety of "reforms," but those adopted have typically proved unable to achieve their asserted goals. Moreover, these "reforms" have sometimes produced unintended impacts that may even operate against the putative goals of the policies themselves.

If this account is accurate, one should approach most innovations in the criminal justice area with great care, both prior to adoption and after they are set on their course. Both lack of knowledge of how to achieve purposes and an incentive structure that rewards "reforms" on the basis of their passage rather than their actual implementation suggests that *any* criminal justice reform may fail to achieve its stated purposes and may produce consequences neither intended nor desired by its most ardent supporters. Our brief experience with determinate sentencing, thus far at least, appears to fit such a pattern.

DETERMINATE SENTENCING: A HISTORICAL OVERVIEW

Sentencing policy in the United States has followed a somewhat circular path. Today's exciting new reform has been yesterday's discarded policy and tomorrow's failure. From the development of the prison system in the first half of the nineteenth century until the early decades of the twentieth, most states had determinate sentencing systems. Under these systems, the judge set the term at the time of sentencing, and except for rare cases of executive clemency, the prisoner served out the term and was then released. Although the penitentiary movement began with a reformist/rehabilitationist ideology, sentence structures during the nineteenth century were typically determinate, and during the second half of the nineteenth century the ideology of sentencing had moved toward theories of punishment and just desert. During the waning years of the nineteenth century, however, the development of the disciplines of psychiatry, psychology, and social work as well as the growing realization that criminal behavior appeared related to such social conditions as education, employment, and health, led many to believe that those who committed crimes were appropriately the subject not simply of punishment but of treatment.[6]

As a result of this belief, the so-called "medical model" came to dominate rhetoric and practice in sentencing. This model suggested that those incarcerated in prisons should be treated and cured of the problems that caused them to commit crimes—"rehabilitated" in common parlance. Thus, prisoners should receive psychotherapy, treatment for alcohol or drug abuse, or education and training that would enable them to function effectively in the spheres of "legitimate" activity. This conception of the purpose of prisons carried with it a prescription for a quite new type of sentence structure. Instead of a term imposed at the time of sentencing by the judge, the appropriate decision about length of term should be made later, after the opportunity to see the rate and extent of cure for each individual prisoner.

Thus, the indeterminate sentence systems that came to dominate in both state and federal statutes during the early twentieth century turned much of the control over length of term to an administrative authority, usually called a parole board. Sometimes part of the correctional bureaucracy, sometimes a quasi-independent administrative agency, members of such institutions typically came from correctional backgrounds and were well integrated into the correctional system. Although their manifest function was periodically to review the progress of inmates and to decide when each had made sufficient progress that release was appropriate, their decision making was also influenced by a variety of other factors. Put another way, although the manifest function of parole was individualized sentencing on the basis of rehabilitation, parole served a variety of latent functions as well.[7]

One major function was that of providing a means for control of prison inmates. Since the prisoner's release date was typically not set until shortly before release, and the potential maximum terms under most indeterminate sentence systems were quite long, a prisoner's behavior in the prison context was often an important determinant of the release decision. Behavior of concern to parole authorities included not only effective participation in rehabilitative programs but also good citizenship and rule following within the prison society. Because information about prisoner behavior is basically under the control of the correctional authorities who run the prisons and because of close bureaucratic or personal ties between parole and prison authorities, the parole process became an integral part of social control within the prison setting.

Another latent function of the parole release process is of particular relevance to the current problems of prison overcrowding. The population of a prison at any particular period is a function of two factors: the number of prisoners admitted (by court sentence or parole revocation), and the number released from prison (through parole or the completion of the term of imprisonment). During periods when judges are imposing harsher sentences and prison capacity remains fixed, a potential means to deal with increased crowding lies at the "back end"—letting more prisoners out.[8]

The system of indeterminate sentencing thus vested great discretion in parole authorities, bureaucratic personnel who operated in an environment of low visibility. Not only were these personnel appointed officials whose activities typically were not the subject of great public attention, but also their very work environment—moving from prison to prison, holding hearings behind prison walls without the presence of attorneys or other outsiders—militated against much public attention. In addition to lack of public scrutiny, courts viewed the parole process until very recently as an administrative as opposed to judicial activity. A so-called "hands-off" doctrine precluded appellate review of parole decisions or development of procedural protections such as rules of evidence, confrontation of witnesses, presence of counsel, or the necessity for providing written reasons for decisions.[9] A final feature of indeterminate sentencing and the parole process is worthy of note, for this feature became a primary argument used by its eventual opponents: indeterminate sentencing *embraces* a certain kind of sentence disparity. Defendants who have committed identical crimes and who have similar prior records quite appropriately received, under indeterminate sentencing, substantially different sentences. Because the release decision was intended to be tailored to the rate of cure or rehabilitation, such disparities were not only justifiable but very likely to occur.[10]

During the late 1960s, the indeterminate sentence system was subjected to extensive political and academic criticism coming from both ends of the political spectrum. Many due process liberals were concerned about the low visibility and unconstrained discretion exercised by parole authorities and worried about the possibility for arbitrary decision making, infection by race or class prejudice, and other possible abuses. The uncertainty under which indeterminate sentencing forced prisoners to live—not knowing from year to year when their sentence would be completed—came to be viewed by liberals as producing anxiety, frustration, and contributing to prison violence. Moreover, the basic underpinning of the indeterminate sentence system was a belief that it was tied to rehabilitation. A good deal of anecdotal evidence as well as the "nothing works" school of research called into serious question the assertion that prison rehabilitative programs—at least as currently practiced—had any significant effect upon recidivism rates.[11] The sentence disparities embraced by indeterminate sentencing were troublesome to many, and if these disparities could not be justified in terms of varying rates of rehabilitation, they seemed unfair. Thus, many due process liberals concluded during the early 1970s that the rehabilitationist foundation for sentencing should be rejected, typically in favor of a notion of "just deserts"—an emphasis upon making the punishment fit the crime itself rather than the characteristics of the individual offender.[12] This view led to a renunciation of indeterminate sentence laws in favor of determinate sentencing and its crucial ingredients—term setting by the judge and the elimination of parole.

Conservatives and law-enforcement interests also came to conclude that a move to determinate sentencing was desirable. Their reasons, however, focused upon quite different issues. For law enforcement interests, determinate sentencing came to be seen as a "solution" just as it did for due process liberals; the "problems" it was supposed to solve, though, were quite different. From the law-enforcement perspective, the evidence on recidivism suggested that parole authorities were simply not very good at picking out those who were rehabilitated; rather, parole boards seemed often to release prisoners who continued to pose a danger to society. Moreover, many believed that judges were often reluctant to send "marginal defendants" to prison when the nominal terms were so high.[13] A move to determinate sentencing systems in which such defendants received apparently shorter but certain prison terms, the law-enforcement advocates argued, might induce judges to send higher proportions of such defendants to prison. This higher commitment rate, in turn, might increase the deterrent and incapacitative effects of the criminal law. Finally, if the terms under determinate sentence systems looked or were too short, the possibility for subsequent amendments to raise them were obvious.

Thus, coalitions developed in a number of jurisdictions which brought together political interests that typically fought with one another on criminal justice policies. All agreed that determinate sentences were preferable, although they had quite different expectations about what results these sentences might produce, as well as quite different criteria in mind to evaluate the success or failure of the new innovation. For the purposes of this article, however, two points stand out. First, no extensive discussion of the potential effects of parole abolition on the ability to control prison populations appears to have occurred. Second, the adoption of determinate sentencing came at a time when both demographic factors and a growing concern over crime were militating toward increasing prison commitment rates.

Illinois' determinate-sentence law (DSL)[14] went into effect in early 1978. The statute authorizes the sentencing judge to impose a specific prison term, chosen from a range specified by the legislature for each class of felony.[15] The range is substantially narrower than those available under the indeterminate sentence law (ISL), though wider than those available under some other states' versions of determinate sentencing.[16] In addition to permitting relatively extensive judicial discretion, the good-time rules in Illinois permit prisoners to earn 50 percent off their sentence for good behavior.

Given this set of expectations about the possible effects of adoption of determinate sentencing and the absence of much consideration of its effects upon prison populations, this article next examines evidence relating to the possible contribution of the DSL to the increased prison crowding experienced in Illinois in the years since the statute's passage.

THE ILLINOIS DSL AND PRISON CROWDING

The previous section stressed the widespread, yet often conflicting, expectations about the effects of determinate sentencing entertained by the various interest groups which participated in its adoption. The discussion, however, paid little attention to determinate sentencing's potential effects upon prison populations and crowding. The article's brief review of the history of criminal justice legislation suggested, moreover, that unintended consequences have often occurred. In this section, the focus is upon the potential contribution of the DSL to crowding in Illinois. Because insufficient time has passed for an adequate assessment of the impact of the DSL, this section focuses upon the behavior of the prison system under the old ISL. The argument presented suggests that the available evidence is consistent with the hypothesis that parole release under the ISL was used as a means to deal with prison crowding. To the extent that this hypothesis is correct, elimination of the parole authority produced by determinate sentencing may be one contribution to the current overcrowding in Illinois prisons.

The context in which the Illinois DSL went into effect in 1978 was one full of expectations that the new law might cause increased prison populations. This result was believed likely for a variety of reasons. First, the numerous probation-disqualification provisions associated with the Class X felonies were believed likely to lead judges to send to prison defendants who previously would have received local jail terms.[17] Moreover, the ability of judges under the DSL to specify relatively short terms in "marginal" cases might also lead to an increase in the prison commitment rate. If the average time served under determinate sentencing were longer, moreover, this would cause increased prison populations as well. Finally, the political climate in which the DSL was adopted, as well as a good deal of the rhetoric surrounding it, made the DSL part of a "law and order" movement, stressing punitiveness in sentencing, more frequent resort to prison as a sanction, and a general "get-tough" spirit.[18] As a result, elected judges might take the passage of the DSL as an indication of society's desire for more harshness in sentencing.

Thus, for a variety of reasons, one might have expected that the DSL would be associated with harsher sentencing policies by judges and this might result in larger prison populations. Indeed, the years since the passage of the law have seen very marked increases in the number of men and women held in Illinois prisons. Figure 1[19] presents data on prison populations over roughly the past two decades. Two measures of population are presented: the absolute numbers of men and women in adult prisons, and the rate per 100,000 population of those incarcerated. An examination of these rates during the period since the implementation of the DSL in 1978 indicates extremely large increases. Although there has been some tendency to attribute such increases in the years since the DSL's introduction in several states to the effects of the new sentencing policy,[20] reports of the Illinois Department of Corrections (DOC) have indicated that it may be too early to attribute changes in prison populations to the effects of the DSL.[21]

Examination of the data presented in Figure 1 suggests several other possible conclusions about the impact of the DSL on prison crowding. The first is that there are evidently long-term processes at work that appear to affect prison populations. During the two decades presented, the prison population dropped steadily during the 1960s, reaching a low point in 1972, and then increasing in relatively steady increments. In terms of the rate of incarceration per 100,000, for which more limited data exist, a similar trend may be observed, with a falling rate from 1970 to 1973, and substantial increases in the next decade. Indeed, focusing upon the past decade, the prison population in Illinois (and nationally as well) has doubled. Whatever forces have driven the prison populations up so quickly over the past decade, the evidence available suggests that much more is at work than the DSL alone. Prison populations in Illinois and elsewhere began rising well before the determinate sentence law was on the legislative agenda, and states that have not passed determinate sentence laws have experienced substantial increases. The fact that the law has been in effect only for a few years makes it difficult to distinguish its impact from the broader trend toward increased prison populations in which its introduction is embedded.

The data, however, do counsel caution about attributing recent increases in prison populations in Illinois simply to the adoption of determinate sentencing. Indeed, in a recent study of the California DSL, this author has argued that it may be better to view the DSL as an *effect* of various forces promoting increased harshness in sentencing rather than a *cause* of such developments in the years since its adoption, and perhaps this conclusion may apply to Illinois as well.[22]

What is clear, however, is that prison populations have risen in recent years and that the prison system has been the subject of substantial pressure at that "front-end," that is, at the stage of admissions to prison. Figure 2[23] presents data on prison admissions for the 1961–1982 period. As with populations, a good deal of variation exists over the two decades, but regular and substantial increases in commitments may be observed since 1973. Indeed, the increase in prison commitments between 1973 and 1982 amounts to a whopping 173 percent. Since the introduction of the DSL in 1978, the increases in admissions are also large, amounting to a 51 percent rise in the five years for which data are available.

Two types of admissions are included in these data: new commitments from court (sentences imposed by judges upon convicted defendants) and parole revocations (recommitments to prison of those on parole, either for technical violations or commission of crimes). Commitments from court are beyond the control of prison and parole authorities, for they are decisions by judges; parole revocations are more within prison system control, for alternative dispositions (for example, continuance on parole subsequent to a violation) are possible. During the period for which we have data, the bulk of admissions (averaging 85 percent for the 1961–1982 period) were of the nondiscretionary sort. Thus, during the past decade, as well as during the period since the passage of the DSL, prison authorities have been faced with substantial increases in the numbers of prisoners coming in the "front door," and they can do little to control the flow of such admissions.

Traditionally, a variety of responses to increased prison admissions have been available. One strategy is simply that of absorption. If the prison system has excess capacity in the form of unused beds or facilities, front-end pressure can be handled by utilizing these resources. If there are no empty beds or unused facilities, another method of absorption is to crowd new admissions into existing facilities. A common form of this strategy is double celling, putting two inmates into cells designed or previously used to house single inmates. In this fashion, a prison's "capacity" can be doubled, or halved,[24] simply by changing its rated ability to house prisoners.[25] Another strategy has been that of building new facilities as prison admissions and populations rise. This is a costly and long-term proposition, but one that many jurisdictions are currently considering. Illinois, for example, has built several new prisons during the past decade and is in the process of building several more.[26] A third available strategy for dealing with new admissions is that of releasing prisoners earlier than they might have been in the absence of such front-end pressure. Thus, parole release may be used as a "back-end" response to increased admissions, and the system of indeterminate sentencing provides prison and parole authorities with the ability to pursue such a policy, typically in a low-visibility environment. Sentencing is a public occasion, often reported in local newspapers. Parole release decision making is not public, and is rarely reported.

Thus, under an indeterminate sentence system, one might expect prison and parole authorities to deal with increased admissions by using parole as a mechanism at the back-end. In this view, the DOC and parole authorities would be monitoring inputs and adjusting outputs (parole releases) to stabilize populations. Prison systems may be very good at such tasks, for they pay great attention to keeping track of and counting their inmates and thus are in a position to monitor shifts in flows in or out relatively closely. The relevance of such a policy to the impact of determinate sentencing is clear: the DSL substantially reduces the ability of prison and parole authorities to engage in back-end release policies as a means of dealing with increased admissions.

In conceptualizing the process by which prison authorities in Illinois might historically have utilized parole releases as a safety valve to adapt to increased prison admissions, a distinction similar to the one suggested above between admissions which are beyond the control of the prison system (court commitments) and those that are somewhat within its control (parole revocations) should be made. Under an indeterminate sentencing system, two types of releases occur in any given year: parole releases which are, from the point of view of the prison system, largely discretionary; and releases of prisoners who have reached their maximum terms and must be released, which are, from the perspective of the prison authorities, nondiscretionary. If a prison system uses parole release as a means of controlling population increases, we might expect it to pay attention each year to what is likely to happen to population if parole release is not used at all, as well as to the effects of various release rates upon total population.

To put this into somewhat more concrete terms, consider the following statistics for the year 1975, several years before the DSL went into effect:

Admissions			*Exits*		
Commitments from court	Parole revocations	Total admits	Term expired	Parole releases	Total releases
5,431	601	6,032	1,369	3,307	4,676

On the front-end, or admissions, side, there were a total of 6,032 new admissions during this year. Of these, 5,431 were court ordered and thus were beyond the control of the prison and parole authorities. On the back-end, or release, side, there were 1,369 releases of prisoners whose terms were completed (the nondiscretionary releases in that year). If the prison system did nothing to affect the net inflow and outflow of prisoners and simply relied upon forces beyond its control, the prison population in 1975 would have increased by 4,062 inmates: 5,431 new admissions would have resulted from judicial order and 1,369 inmates would have been released because their terms had expired.

The simple model this article proposes suggests that the prison system in Illinois has behaved historically as though it were paying attention to this uncontrolled net change in population in making its release decisions. A way of testing this model is to see how well we can predict its parole (discretionary) releases in each year by knowing the uncontrolled increment to population occurring in the same year.[27] The model for Illinois release policies during the pre-DSL years, then, suggests that parole releases in each year are a function of the net uncontrolled increment to population in that year occurring as a result of court commitments and term expiration.

The way in which this model fits the data available for 1961–1979[28] can be seen by using a simple regression equation. Using these data, the equation looks as follows:

$$\text{Parole releases} = 1{,}771^{*} + .55^{*}\ (\text{net uncontrolled change})$$
$$R^2 = .50$$
$$^{*}p < .001$$

The results suggest that the model does fit the data, although all of the variation in parole releases cannot be explained by the net uncontrolled change in population. The equation suggests that in a year in which the uncontrolled admissions and releases would produce *no* increase in population, prison and parole authorities typically would parole 1,771 inmates. For each net uncontrolled addition of two inmates in a year, the prison system on average released on additional inmate on parole.

There are numerous reasons why the model might not capture more of the variation in parole release policy. One simplifying assumption of the model is that all prisoners whose terms do not expire *could* be released in response to front-end pressure. This is clearly not an accurate assumption. In any given year, only some of the prisoners whose terms do not expire are "available" for parole release. For example, those who were committed to prison during the previous several years for murder, rape, or armed robbery are very unlikely to receive parole in the current year. Thus, in any given year, the number of prisoners available for possible release on parole is constrained by considerations such as rules for parole eligibility (for example, that an inmate must serve a certain fraction of his or her term before becoming eligible), by political considerations (murderers and robbers released after a short period may be noticed by newspapers or entrepreneurial politicians), and by a sense of equity (prison and parole authorities may not want to make term length depend *too much* upon current crowding conditions, for this may produce excessively disparate terms over time for similar inmates).

As a result, even if the model captures a basic dynamic of the parole release process under the ISL, the model's conceptual simplicity means that it is not likely to explain—statistically or *theoretically—all* of the variation in a very complex process. But the model does appear to capture something about the relationship of releases to admissions and to suggest that the prison system in Illinois under the ISL did indeed behave as though it were monitoring admissions and using parole release as one means of dealing with changes in front-end pressure.

A somewhat better test might involve examining the relationship between parole releases and uncontrolled population increments under conditions of high and low crowding. The prison system might always tend to respond to net additions by using the parole safety valve because of a consistent desire to keep populations generally stable and to avoid increases, but the system might respond more sharply when there was little slack capacity. Thus, one might want to test the model under both conditions of high and low crowding to determine whether the relationship is stronger when there is little slack capacity.[29] Several difficulties prevented the testing of this more complex version of the relationship between admissions and releases. First, defining high and low crowding requires a measure of capacity (crowding might be defined, for example, as the ratio of prison population to prison capacity), and data published by the DOC could only be obtained for the 1970–1982 period. Given the ability to measure crowding at only thirteen points, dividing them into years of high and low crowding produced insufficient data to fashion a reasonable test of whether the model operates differently under conditions of high and low system slack.

An even more difficult problem arises when the available data on prison capacity published by the DOC are considered. Table 1[30] presents DOC data on capacity for the 1970–1982 period. The DOC reports of how many prisoners its facilities can hold show rather marked shifts during the period. Some shifts—for example, the increases between 1979 and 1981—appear to reflect the building and opening of new prison facilities. Other shifts do not reflect such changes in the physical plants of the prison system but rather administrative changes in the definition of how many prisoners their facilities could hold. Thus, the precipitous drop in rated capacity between 1973 and 1974—a reported decrease in capacity of 4,700 beds (a 41 percent decrease)—reflects a change in the *definition* of capacity: the DOC declared that most prison cells that had in recent years held two inmates could now hold only one. The DOC's measures of rated capacity suggest that crowding increased sharply between 1973 and 1974, for the denominator of the crowding ratio has been slashed even though the prison population actually *declined* by 600 in these two years. The rapid rise in rated capacity during the next three years did not reflect increases in beds, but rather reflected a move back toward double celling as prison populations began to grow. The point here is neither to criticize the DOC nor to say that some magic number exists which represents the "real" capacity of prisons. Indeed, as the DOC maintains, capacity is not simply a product of physical facilities, but also of the DOC's ability, given constraints not only of space but of staff and programs, to maintain prison populations in a safe and decent environment.

The peregrinations of rated capacity, however, do reveal some serious difficulties in using the concept of "crowding" as an independent or contextual variable in understanding the process by which admissions may be related to releases. To the extent that capacity is in part an administrative artifact, one must be very careful in using reported capacities as "causes" of other events within the prison system. Their changeability—and sometimes their utility in political or bureaucratic struggles—means that levels of crowding (at least as measured by the ratio of population to rated capacity) may often not be causes but effects of other processes.[31]

Perhaps the *best* evidence for the assertion that parole release did serve the latent function of adjusting at the back-end for front-end pressures on populations comes from the events that occurred in Illinois during the first years of the DSL. As indicated in Figure 2,[32] admissions rose markedly during the years 1978–1982. The number of parole releases "available" to the DOC began to decline as the number of determinately sentenced prisoners rose. As the parole safety valve became less available, the DOC began a program of so-called "forced release" (called by critics "early release"). Using a provision of the DSL which permitted the award of "meritorious" good time, the DOC granted multiple ninety-day increments of meritorious good time to selected inmates and released them before their terms would have expired had they only accrued normal good time credits. Begun in 1980 and declared illegal in 1983,[33] the system of forced release resulted in the early release of 9,000 prisoners.[34] Thus, the substantial growth in populations between 1979 and 1982 occurred even with early release, and the actual populations without this form of quasi-parole presumably would have been substantially higher. The development of a functional equivalent to parole where the DSL made parole releases less available is one more indication that an important latent function of discretionary releases under the ISL was not only selecting those who had been rehabilitated, but also served to deal with problems of prison crowding.

Removal of parole authority, therefore, was an important feature of the DSL. Done in the name of reducing the arbitrary exercise of power (a concern of liberal supporters) or excessive leniency and poor predictions by parole authorities (a view of law-and-order supporters), one of its consequences may have been to contribute to prison crowding. The evidence this article presents suggests that this contribution—in the early years of the DSL, at least—probably came at the back end rather than the front end. By removing parole, the DSL—in Illinois and other states which have adopted similar policies—has restricted use of a means by which the system has traditionally responded to increases at the front end.

Several conclusions appear warranted on the basis of this discussion of the early years of the DSL and its relationship to prison crowding. First, some of the characteristics of criminal justice policy making discussed above can already be seen at work. Discussion of the DSL and its desirability focused upon a variety of consequences that were thought to be likely to flow from its adoption. Crowding was the subject of little discussion. Yet one of the major consequences of adoption of this particular reform may be an unintended one: removing the ability of prison authorities to deal with front-end pressure by back-end releases. Moreover, there is a certain irony in that liberal support for the DSL reform hinged, in part, upon the assertion that this reform might improve the lives of those incarcerated. Because the inmates would no longer be subject to the uncertainties of what the parole board might do and when they might be released, the frustration and anger of inmates would likely subside. If an unintended consequence of this reform has been to contribute to the increased crowding of inmates into prisons, the cure may produce consequences at least arguably as undesirable as the disease.

This argument ought not, to be sure, be pushed too far. The recent prison crowding is the product of a good deal more than determinate sentence reform,[35] and therefore crowding might have occurred even in its absence. Recent reports, though, have suggested that liberal supporters of the DSL have begun to question whether the reform is indeed desirable, given its effects upon sentence length and prison crowding.[36] Developments in the few years since adoption of the DSL suggest, once again, the cyclical nature of policy making in the area of criminal justice and the extent to which unintended consequences plague the process.

PROPOSALS FOR REDUCING PRISON CROWDING UNDER THE DSL

If determinate sentencing indeed may contribute to prison crowding, what alternatives are available? To say that the DSL may have contributed to crowding is far from presenting a compelling case for its abandonment. Several means of dealing with crowding in the context of determinate sentencing are available, though they vary greatly in their approach and political feasibility.

Increasing Prison Capacity

One approach is that of increasing prison capacity to deal both with rising admissions and with the constraints imposed by the DSL on back-end releases. Such a strategy is very costly and time-consuming. The fiscal costs of building and maintaining new prison facilities are enormous, and even modular prisons, which are said to be cheaper and quicker to build, involve substantial capital and operating expenses. In late 1983, the Illinois legislature authorized funds for the further prison construction both of traditional and modular facilities. The difficulties and risks of this strategy involve not only the expense but also the possibility that as the decade comes to a close the demand for prison space may diminish. Such an eventuality might be the product of demographic trends (the passage of the baby-boom birth cohorts beyond their most prison-prone years) and perhaps shifts in public sentiment about appropriate sentencing policy.

Building thus may bring about an excess capacity problem similar to that encountered by the public school system in recent years. Society then may be faced in the 1990s with the choice of what to do with "excess" prison capacity. The "if you build them, you'll fill them" hypothesis suggests that the criminal justice system will continue to utilize the capacity, for its very existence will promote commitment to prison of defendants who otherwise would not be sent there. On the more hopeful side is the possibility that current building might enable the state to close its many old and primitive facilities.[37] Based on past performance in Illinois and elsewhere, however, one ought not be particularly sanguine about the prospects for closing of prison facilities, for the record simply does not indicate that this option has frequently been adopted.

Discretionary Release

Alternatives other than building exist and ought to be explored. One alternative is the reintroduction of some form of discretionary release to be exercised under certain specified circumstances. The Governor's Task Force on Prison Crowding, for example, proposed a form of prison-cap law, similar to that already in use in Iowa and several other states. Under such a plan, when prisons reached a certain level of crowding, 105 percent in the Task Force Recommendation, the DOC would be authorized to declare an emergency, and the Prisoner Review Board would be authorized to release early certain classes of nonviolent prisoners already close to the end of their terms.[38] This proposal met with a "marked lack of enthusiasm" according to the governor, and was shelved.

Although such a system may be politically problematic, the implementation of a discretionary release mechanism remains an attractive alternative. Public officials are hesitant to admit openly that they are releasing inmates "early," regardless of evidence that such releases may detract little from the deterrent, rehabilitative, or incapacitative effects of sentences. Given the increasing concern of conservatives with the fiscal costs of building, though, exploration of the alternative should continue. A system of discretionary release may be one way to maintain the attractive feature of certainty provided by determinate-sentence systems under normal circumstances by providing limited and structured release discretion in periods of high crowding.

Shorter Sentences

A third alternative is also worth considering, though its political feasibility is even more open to question. In the long run, the effects of determinate sentencing upon prison populations depend not only upon the removal of release discretion but also upon the *length* of determinate sentences. If determinate sentences are, on average, longer than those served under an indeterminate sentence system, prison populations will rise even if admissions remain constant. If, however, determinate sentence laws specify that terms should be *short*, many of the advantages of determinancy might be achievable without resort to discretionary release and without contributing to crowding. If prison sentences are imposed more along the lines of European practice, in which prison terms are often meted out in months rather than years, many of the purposes of the criminal law might still be achieved. For many crimes, deterrence may be as well served by short sentences as it is by long terms. If rehabilitation does not work, or if we are not willing to invest sufficiently extensive resources to give it a fair test, then this justification for any imprisonment, much less long periods of confinement, becomes less compelling. Whether a sense of just desert can be fulfilled by a nine- or twelve-month term for a burglar—even if he or she is a recidivist—is a political and moral question worthy of continued serious discussion. The major justification for long terms is that of incapacitation—protecting citizens from violent and dangerous criminals. The evidence regarding the ability to achieve this end by effectively predicting future behavior and selectively incapacitating those who are dangerous is not yet clear.[39] Even if the prediction issue is solved, the length of criminal careers and hence the length of terms required to incapacitate dangerous defendants remains unclear. Thus another avenue for dealing with the relationship of determinate sentencing to prison crowding lies in the area of reducing average term length.

One would have to be more than simply naive to believe that this solution is likely to be considered seriously in the context of current Illinois or national politics. The role of symbolic politics and the apparent irresistibilty of the call for longer terms means that involvement of the legislature in sentencing policy—a phenomenon which determinate sentencing inevitably appears to encourage—will likely produce not shorter but longer terms. This may, from the perspective of "liberal" supporters of the DSL, be the clinching argument that will lead members of this group to abandon the innovation and begin calling for the reintroduction of indeterminancy. For all its disadvantages, indeterminate sentencing does allow the legislature to impose seemingly harsh sentences while administrative authorities muffle the "bite" of the legislatively mandated long nominal terms.

CONCLUSION

Whatever the outcome of the current debate over determinate sentences, the tentative evidence presented in this article suggests that elimination of parole release may contribute to prison crowding. The extent of the increase that has been produced in Illinois and other DSL states over and above the increases that would have been seen in this period without the DSL remains unknown, but past practice with parole suggests that the contribution of determinate sentencing may well be substantial. The future of determinate sentencing remains unclear, in part because of its association with crowding.[40] The experience with the DSL, though, does suggest that the role of unintended consequences and symbolic policy making long characteristic of criminal justice innovation continues to play a significant role.

NOTES

1. A. Blumstein, J. Cohen, and H. Miller, "Demographically Disaggregated Projections of Prison Populations," 8 *Journal of Criminal Justice* 1, 3–4 (1980).

2. H. Packer, *The Limits of the Criminal Sanction* (Stanford, Calif.: Stanford University Press, 1968), pp. 9–16.

3. Ibid.

4. See T. Arnold, *The Symbols of Government* (New York Harcourt, Brace and World, 1935), pp. 128–171; J. Edelman, *The Symbolic Uses of Politics* (Urbana, Ill.: University of Illinois Press, 1964), pp. 22–43.

5. See, generally, Joint Committee on New York Drug Law Evaluation, *The Nation's Toughest Drug Law: Evaluating the New York Experience* (1977); M. Heumann and C. Loftin, "Mandatory Sentencing and the Abolition of Plea Bargaining," 13 *Law and Society Review* 393, 394–395 (1979); Beha, "And Nobody Can Get You Out" (pts. 1–2), 57 *Boston University Law Review* 96, 289 (1977).

6. See D. Rothman, *Conscience and Convenience: The Asylum and Its Alternatives in Progressive America* (Boston: Little, Brown, 1980); D. Rothman, *The Discovery of the Asylum* (Boston: Little, Brown, 1971), pp. xii–xx.

7. See, generally, A. von Hirsh and K. Hanrahan, *The Question of Parole: Retention, Reform, or Abolition* (Cambridge, Mass.: Ballinger, 1979), pp. 2–3; D. Stanley, *Prisoners Among Us* (Washington, D.C.: Brookings Institution, 1976), pp. 1–4, 47–80.

8. See notes 17–18 and 32–34 and accompanying text.

9. *Morrissey v. Brewer*, 408 U.S. 471, 484–489 (1972).

10. Another kind if disparity—intercounty differences based upon differing levels of sentencing harshness imposed in various jurisdictions—was supposed to be meliorated by the parole process. If some jurisdictions tended under indeterminate sentencing to commit defendants to prison for substantially longer maximum terms than others—for example, the common urban/rural difference—parole authorities could use their release discretion to even out such intercounty disparities.

11. See, generally, D. Lipton, R. Martinson, and J. Wilks, *The Effectiveness of Correctional Treatment: A Survey of Treatment Evaluation Studies* (New York: Praeger, 1975).

12. See, for example, American Friends Service Committee, *Struggle for Justice* (New York: Hill and Wang, 1971), pp. 20–47. Twentieth Century Fund, *Fair and Certain Punishment* (New York: McGraw Hill, 1976), pp. 11–34. A. von Hirsh, *Doing Justice: The Choice of Punishments* (New York: Hill & Wang, 1976), pp. 66–76.

13. The term "marginal defendants" refers to those defendants viewed as "on the margin" between a long jail term and a prison term, for example, property offenders with a number of prior convictions but no prior prison commitments.

14. *Ill. Rev. Stat.* ch. 38, §§ 1005–8–1 to –4 (1981).

15. Probation is authorized as an alternative sentence for all crimes except murder, attempted murder, class X felonies, a class 2 or greater felony if the offender had been convicted of a class 2 or greater felony within ten years of the date on which he committed the offense for which he is being sentenced, certain drug-related offenses, and residential burglary. The Illinois statute requires that a term of imprisonment be imposed for these offenses. *Ill. Rev. Stat.* ch. 38, § 1005–5–3(c)(2) (1981).

16. For example, *Cal. Penal Code*, § 1170 (West Supp., 1984). See J. Casper, D. Brereton, and D. Neal, *The Implementation of the California Determinate Sentencing Law* (1982), p. 149. The ranges of the sentences prescribed by the Illinois statues are indicated in the following table.

Class of felony	Range of terms	
	ISL	*DSL*
Class X	(no such class)	6–30 years
Class I	4–no maximum stated	4–15 years
Class II	1–20 years	3–7 years
Class III	1–10 years	2–5 years
Class IV	1–3 years	1–3 years

See *Ill. Rev. Stat.* ch. 38 §§ 1005–8–1 to –4 (1981).

17. See above, note 15.

18. A similar sense surrounded the passage of the DSL in California at about the same time. The preamble of the California Uniform and Determinate Sentence Act of 1976, indeed, renounces the ideal of rehabilitation and states, "The purpose of imprisonment for crimes is punishment." For a discussion of the California law, see S. Messinger and N. Johnson, "California's Determinate Sentencing Statute: History and Issues," in *Determinate Sentencing: Reform or Regression* (1978), pp. 13–58; J. Casper, D. Brereton, and D. Neal, "The California Determinate Sentencing Law," 19 *Criminal Law Bulletin* 405 (1983).

19. **Figure 1** Illinois prison population, 1961–1982

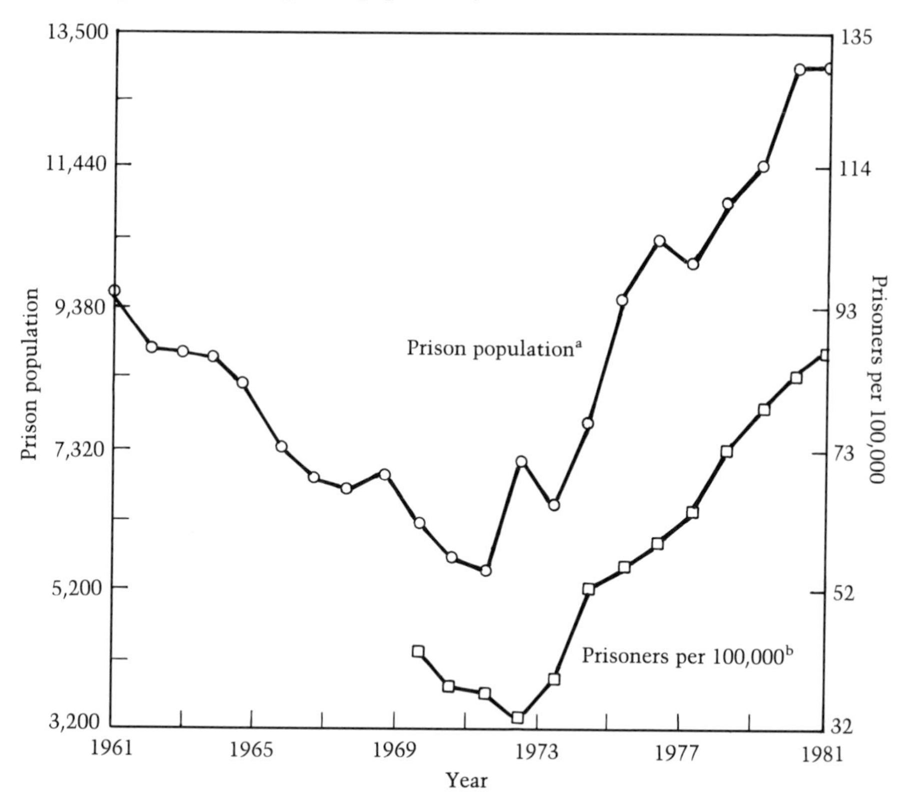

[a]Source: U.S. Department of Justice, National Prisoner Statistics (issued yearly); Illinois Department of Corrections, *Human Resources Data Report* (1983).

[b]Source: III Illinois Department of Corrections, *Human Resources Data Report* (1983).

20. See, for example, *National Institute of Justice, Prisons at Midyear 1983* (1983), p. 3; *National Institute of Justice, Prisoners 1981* (1981): 1.

21. The DOC statistical report for 1982 is cautious: "Though we expect determinate sentencing will, over a period of time, increase the prison population, it is not yet a factor." Illinois Department of Corrections, *Statistical Presentation* (1983).

22. J. Casper, D. Brereton, and D. Neal, above note 16, p. 148; Casper, Brereton, and Neal, above note 18, p. 405.

23. **Figure 2** Prison admissions, 1961–1982

Source: III Illinois Department of Corrections, *Human Resources Data Report* (1983).

24. See text accompanying notes 30–32.

25. For a discussion of the constitutional status of double celling, see *Rhodes v. Chapman.* 452 U.S. 337, 344–350 (1981).

26. New facilities added during the past decade include prisons at Sheridan (opened in 1973), Logan (1977), Graham (1981), Centralia (1981), and Moline (1981). Additional facilities are currently planned or under construction.

27. It is important to stress that this "test" simply asks whether the statistical evidence suggests that release policies are similar to those that would have occurred *if* the prison system were behaving as the model specifies. Another way of "testing" the model would involve interviews with prison and parole authorities to ascertain the extent to which they

perceive that they paid attention to the types of information contained in this model of release policy.

28. 1979 is chosen as the end period because prior to 1980 there were so few determinate sentence cases reaching their maximum terms that the system was still effectively operating under the ISL, even though the law had been in effect for nearly two years at this point. This year also predates the "forced release" program begun in 1980. See notes 32–34 and accompanying text.

29. The relationship between releases and admissions is likely to be very complex, and disentangling the causal forces is, likewise, hard to accomplish. Thus, for example, if the relationship between input and outflow described above *did* prove stronger in years of high crowding then when there was slack capacity, this might suggest a modification of the model but support its basic notion of how parole is used. By the same token, the exact reverse pattern also might support the model: if releases are more strongly related to admissions in years of low crowding than high crowding, one might interpret this result as suggesting that the *reason* for the low crowding was the successful use of parole release, while the weaker relationship under conditions of high crowding might indicate an inability—for some of the reasons suggested above—to use the release mechanism effectively. Thus, testing such a model of the relationship between admissions and releases is difficult even if the data problems discussed below did not exist.

30. **Table 1** Prison population, capacity, and crowding, 1970–1982

Year	*Population*[a]	*Rated capacity*[b]	*Percent full*
1970	6,381	9,978	64.0
1971	5,834	9,862	59.2
1972	5,630	10,880	51.8
1973	7,339	11,440	64.2
1974	6,657	6,719	99.1
1975	7,918	8,049	98.0
1976	9,737	11,075	87.9
1977	10,619	10,895	97.5
1978	10,257	11,320	90.6
1979	11,154	11,395	97.9
1980	11,729	11,959	98.1
1981	13,206	13,245	99.7
1982	13,189	13,245	99.6

[a]Source: U.S. Department of Justice, National Prisoner Statistics (issued yearly): III Illinois Department of Corrections, *Human Resources Data Report* (1983).
[b]Source: 38 Illinois Department of Corrections, *Population and Capacity Report* 175 (1982).

31. This issue is highly relevant to another debate about prison, that over whether "if you build them you'll fill them." Many have maintained that increases in prison capacity themselves *cause* increases in prison populations. See, for example, I Abt Associates, *American Prisons and Jails* 27 (1980). This hypothesis assumes that our political environment has historically been characterized by a virtually infinite demand for increased harshness in sentencing, at least relative to any likely actual prison capacity. As a result of this demand, an increase in available prison space will itself produce changes in sentencing policy (that is, sending people to prison who would not have been sent there if the capacity were not available). In this sense, increases in prison capacity are said to *cause* increases in prison populations. One plausible means to test this hypothesis is to gather data on prison capacity and prison populations over time in order to see whether population changes appear to predate increased capacity or whether, as the hypothesis suggests, capacity changes lead

population. Such a strategy may well run afoul of the fact that capacity changes are often not reflective of physical changes in prison facilities but rather changing bureaucratic definitions. The Abt study avoids this problem by focusing upon the actual *building* of new prison facilities as opposed to reported capacities, but at the cost of making the assumption that in the absence of building no changes occurred. For a critique of this study on several grounds, see A. Blumstein, J. Cohen, and S. Gooding, "The Influence of Capacity on Prison Population," 29 *Crime and Delinquency* 1 (1983).

32. See note 23.

33. The forced release program was challenged in several lawsuits, some of which were instituted by state's attorneys who alleged that the procedures were resulting in the release back into their communities of dangerous prisoners. The Supreme Court of Illinois declared in July 1983 that the system was not authorized by the statute and should be terminated. *Lane v. Slodowski,* 97 Ill. 2d 311, 454 N.E. 2d 322, 73 Ill. Dec. 462 (1983).

34. Illinois House Republican Policy Committee, *Report on Program Population,* July 28, 1983; *Chicago Tribune,* May 17, 1983, p. 1, col. 2.

35. For example, states that have not adopted the determinate sentence reform have also experienced extensive growth in their prison populations.

36. Alvin Bronstein, head of the ACLU's National Prison Project, recently expressed this sentiment: "I think we miscalculated how harshly the public really feels. We were among the so-called liberal reformers who advocated the abolition of parole as a release mechanism and the use of flat or determinate sentencing to eliminate disparity and lead to greater certainty in the minds of the offenders in terms of when they would get out. The problem is that the concept was distorted to mean long and harsh determinate sentencing." "Strict Penalties for Criminals: Pendulum of Feeling Swings," *New York Times,* December 13, 1983, p. 1, cols. 5, 6.

37. More than 70 percent of Illinois inmates are currently housed in facilities that are more than forty years old. House Republican Policy Committee, above, note 34, p. 41.

38. Governor's Task Force on Prison Crowding (Illinois), Recommendations 22-23, September 26, 1983.

39. National Research Council, above, note 31, pp. 64–80.

40. Some of this association with prison overcrowding may be spurious, for apparently no adequate evidence exists at this stage to warrant the conclusion that the DSL in Illinois or in other states has substantially increased commitment rates or term length.